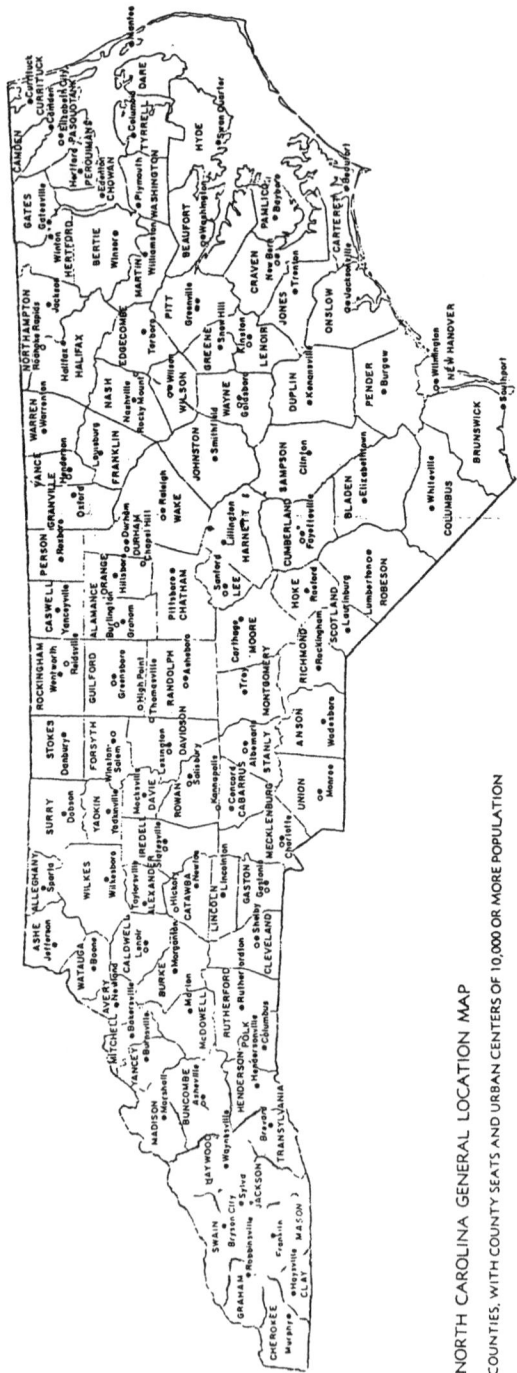

NORTH CAROLINA GENERAL LOCATION MAP

COUNTIES, WITH COUNTY SEATS AND URBAN CENTERS OF 10,000 OR MORE POPULATION

- County seat
- 10,000 or more population

Source: General Statistics

Area 52,712 sq. miles (49,067 land, 3,645 water surface)
Maximum east-west length 503 miles, from 75 degrees 27 minutes to 84 degrees 20 minutes west longitude
Maximum north-south width 185 miles, from 33 degrees 51 minutes to 36 degrees 34 minutes north latitude
Geographical center 10 miles northwest of Sanford in Chatham County
Number of counties 100
Number of urban centers with 10,000 or more population in 1960, 36

SCALE IN MILES
0   20   40   60   80   100

CASWELL COUNTY
NORTH CAROLINA
WILL BOOKS 1777–1814

1784 Tax List
Guardians' Accounts 1794–1819

and

CASWELL COUNTY
NORTH CAROLINA
WILL BOOKS 1814–1843

Guardians' Accounts 1819–1847
1850 & 1860 Census Mortality Schedules
Powers of Attorney from Deed Books 1777–1880

TWO VOLUMES IN ONE

Abstracts by
Katharine Kerr Kendall
Index by
Mary Frances Kerr Donaldson

CLEARFIELD

CASWELL COUNTY NORTH CAROLINA WILL BOOKS 1777-1814

1784 Tax List
Guardians' Accounts
1794-1819

Abstracts
by
Katharine Kerr Kendall
Index by
Mary Frances Kerr Donaldson
1979

CASWELL COUNTY

May 9,
1777 Caswell County, North Carolina, formed from the northern
part of Orange County. Named for Richard Caswell, Governor
of North Carolina from 1776-80 and 1784-87. The 8 districts
within the county were: Caswell, Richmond, Gloucester, St.
David, St. James, Nash, St. Lawrence, and St. Luke.

June 10,
1777 First session of the county governing body, the Court of
Pleas and Quarter Sessions, met at house of Thomas Douglass,
near present day Leasburg, in the "first year of Indepen-
dence" as written by the clerk. John Lea opened the session.
Justices of Peace taking oaths were: James Sanders, John
Payne, Thomas Rice, George Moore, James Scarlet, William
Moore, John Atkinson, Robert Parks, James Rice, William Hub-
bard, George Foote, Jeremiah Poston, John Douglass, Thomas
Harrison, Robert Dickens, Stephen Moore, John Moore,Sr.,
Archibald Murphey, and Jesse Benton, Esquires. William
Moore was elected clerk; David Shelton, sheriff; Archibald
Murphey, register, and John Payne, ranger.

1788 Establishment of town of Leasburg at site of courthouse with
commissioners being: Nicholas Delone, William Lea, Lloyd Vanhook, Thomas Neeley, Gabriel Lea, Samuel Johnston, and John
McFarlin.

1791 Person County formed from the eastern part of Caswell County.
The districts of Nash, St. James, St. Lawrence, and St. Luke
were in Person County.

March 26,
1792 Court met at house of Joseph Smith, a centrally located place,
in the newly surveyed county. In July 1793 it met at ordinary
of Hezekiah Rice. The land of James Ingram was chosen for
the seat of county government. 100 acres was purchased, sold
in blocks to John Buchanon, Jesse Carter, John H. Graves,
Lancelot Johnston, and Atkinson & Johnston. The seat of
government was Caswell Court House from 1792-1833.

1796 The town of Milton established near mouth of Country Line
Creek on land of Asa Thomas.

1831 Court ordered new courthouse and expansion of public square.
The first courthouse completed in 1794 and built by John A.
Wolff was on the public square. Land was given by Azariah,
Elijah, and Barzallai Graves, and Paul A. Haralson to en-
large the public lot and on which to build a courthouse and
jail.

1833 The North Carolina General Assembly enacted act which changed
name of the county seat from Caswell Court House to Yanceyville.
The name compliments the name of James Yancey, planter, legis-
lator, first permanent chairman of the court of Pleas and
Quarter Sessions, and introducer of the act to establish the
first school in Caswell County. A member of the county
governing body from 1808-1829, he led in founding a sound
county government. He was the successful compromiser in se-
curing land for expansion of the public holdings from the
Graves family, thus saving the seat of government from removing
to a more distant site.

1

July
1857 Court ordered "new courthouse shall be built" and old one dis-
      posed of. Appointed to building committee were S. P. Hill,
      C. H. Richmond, John Cobb, N. M. Lewis, and Dr. N. M. Roan.
      (This was third courthouse for Yanceyville.) The War Between
      the States intervened and although the structure was in use,
      the finishing touches were not added until 1868-75. Now in
      "retirement", this magnificent edifice is a monument to the
      glory of Caswell County.

1868 A new state constitution abolished the 4 county districts.
      The townships set up were Stony Creek,. Anderson, Hightowers,
      Locust Hill, Leasburg, Pelham, Dan River, Milton, and
      Yanceyville.

Sept. 10
1921 Dedication of the Confederate Monument in center of public
      square, Yanceyville. Funded by the Caswell County Chapter,
      United Daughters of the Confederacy and by Caswell County,
      the bronze inscription reads: "To the sons of Caswell County
      who served in the War (1861-65) in answer to the call of the
      country. In whatever event they may face our national
      existence may God give us the will to what is right, that
      like our forefathers, we may impress our times with the
      sincerity and steadfastness of our lives."

June
1937 Founding of the first library for Caswell County, the Confed-
      erate Memorial Library, by the Caswell County Chapter, United
      Daughters of the Confederacy. The organizing committee:
      Mrs. H. L. Gwynn, Mrs. H. L. Seagrove, and Mrs. A. Yancey Kerr,
      Chairman.

Katharine Kerr Kendall
2814 Exeter Circle
Raleigh, N.C.27608

Other books by the author:
CASWELL COUNTY,NORTH CAROLINA- Historical Abstracts of Minutes
    of Caswell County. Index by Mary Frances Kerr Donaldson
    1976. 2nd printing 1977
CASWELL COUNTY Land Grants, Tax Lists, apprentice bonds,
    and estate records. 1977. 2nd printing 1978
PERSON COUNTY COMPILATIONS - Land Grants, Tax Lists, Record
    Books Abstracts 1792-1820. 1978

FOREWORD

The Will Books of Caswell County, North Carolina are at the office of the Clerk of Court, Caswell County Courthouse, Yanceyville, North Carolina 27379. The books are actually record books. In addition to wills they contain estate inventories, accounts, sales, and settlements; bills of sale; indentures; letters of attorney; deeds of gifts; and a few reports of county officials.

Extant original wills of Caswell County are at the Department of Archives and History, Raleigh, North Carolina 27611. The file number is CR 020.801.1-7. The 1784 tax list is in a bound volume at the Archives file number CR 020.701.1. It is of especial interest as it includes number of acres of land plus a water course on which the land is located. The book of Guardians' Accounts is at the Archives file number CR 020.510.1. Abstracts are included as the accounts relate to estates and wills.

Will Books A through F covering years 1777 to April 1814 contain 290 wills. One unrecorded will was among the originals. On pages 153-5 is a list of wills included in the abstracts.

ABBREVIATIONS USED IN ABSTRACTS

adm administrator(s)
acct account
adj adjoining
commrs commissioners
d daughter
div division
exec executor(s)
inv inventory
ND no date
test testifier(s)
w. written - date will was written. The probate date of a will is the month and year in which it was proved by the county court.
wit witness(es)
water courses:
  Br Branch
  Cr Creek
  R River

iii

List of the Numbers of the Inhabitants of Caswell County Agreeable to the Different returns from the Several Districts Taken & returned to ... April Court 1786 —

Districts Names.	Names of those who took the Lists	White males from 21 & 60 years	White males from 21 & 60 years	White females from 12 years up	Black slaves from 12 to 30 years	Blacks over & under 12 years
Luck	Taken by Peter Farrar	134	290	336	99	115
Richmond	Taken by John J Farley	215	448	629	222	224
Caswell	Taken by Robert Burton	194	424	566	118	104
Glouster	Taken by William Gooch Jun	183	413	503	79	73
Nash	Taken by Yancey Bailey	132	233	360	168	197
St James's	Taken by Robert Payne	105	225	281	101	81
St Lawrence	Taken by John Chambers	168	365	509	151	153
St Druids	Taken by Waddy Tate	142	350	427	172	150
	Total Amount	1273	2748	3611	1110	1097

Book B page 110

iv

Book A - June 1777 - June 1783

June Court 1777

Page
1&2 missing. Index to Book A lists on page 1 a will for Edward Bumpass. The will is filed at State Archives, Raleigh, N.C.
EDWARD BUMPASS -Will- w. 13 Dec. 1776. Wife Martha; sons and daughters Auguston(?), James, Sarah, Gabriel, Elizabeth, Robert. Exec: friends James Langstone, Gabriel Davey, wife Martha. Wit: William Pratt and John Anderson.
3 ROBERT BARNET (Will unreadable in Book A. Abstracts from original filed at State Archives.) w. 13 Sept. 1776. Wife Sarah; sons Robert, Andrew; daughters Mary Seal, Elizabeth, Jenot; Exec: wife Sarah; Wit: Thos. Douglas, Jean Seaton, John Seton.
4 ROBERT BUMPASS -Will- w. 3 Jan. 1777. Wife Sarah: son John; daughters Lucy Vanhook, Elizabeth Davey, Agnes Pratt, Winefred Kezart, Martha Willson. Exec: friend Gabriel Davey, Sarah and John Bumpass. Wit: William Pratt, James Davey, Agnes Pratt.
6 SAMUEL BUMPASS -Will- w. 9 Sept. 1773. Wife Mary; sons Robert, Nathaniel, John, Samuel; daughters Elizabeth, Nancey, unborn child. Exec: wife Mary and friends William Washington and Gabriel Davey. Wit: Jo McCan, John Oliver, James Debow.
7 ALEXANDER GALASPY -Will- w. 20 Dec. 1775. Wife Ann; son James. Exec: wife and James. Wit:Andrew Haddock, James Glaspy, Benjamin Cragg.
8 JOHN MOORE -Will- w. 20 Sept. 1776. Son Joseph, heir at law; Nancy and Sarah Moore, daughters of Joseph; son John; grandson John, son of John; grandson(not christened but called) Patrick Henry Moore, son of John; daughter Sarah McGehee; grandson John Moore McGehee; daughter Elizabeth Shoemaker and her children; daughter Frances Stewart; grandson John Moore Stewart. Land on Cain Cr. to be sold. Son Joseph Moore,heir at law, and second son John Moore,son in law,Montford McGehee and Archibald Murphey to execute will. Wit: Abm. Rice, Anne Rice, Mary Allen.
11 Inv. estate of Edward Bumpass James Langston, Gabriel Davey.
12 Inv. estate of Robert Barnet by Thomas Douglas and Joseph Dickens. /s/ Sarah Barnet, exec.
14 Inv. estate of Robert Bumpass by Gabriel Davey, & John Bumpass.
15 Sale estate of Joel Nowel. Sales to: Henry Turner, James Nowel, Benjamin Hubbard, Ann Grier,John Richmond,Sen.,Thomas Kimbro,Sen., David Shelton, Thomas Lea,Elisha Powdry, Thomas Rice, Robert Long, Alexander Scott, James Herot, Elizabeth Nowel, Major Lea, John Lea, James Stringer, Bartelot Yancey, John Graves Jun., Thomas Graves.
17 Sale estate of Saml. Bumpass. Sept. 29, 1776.

September Court 1777

20 Sale estate of Edwd. Bumpass by James Langston & Gabriel Davey.
21 Additional sale of Joel Nowel.

December Court 1777

22 JONATHAN DEWEESE -Will- w. 28 Sept. 1774. Wife Rachel; eldest son Elisha; other children: Miriam, Ruth, Hezekiah, Samuel, Isaiah, Jonathan, Matthew, and Cornelius. Exec: wife Rachel; Wit: Timothy Burgess, Hugh Barnet, John Barnet.

1

Book A cont. 1777-1778
Page
23 GEORGE SMITH -Will- w. 2 June 1776. (Of Flat River, Orange Co.)
   Wife Jane; daughter Rebecca; son Francis; 2nd daughter Catharine;
   2nd son George; 3rd son Robert; 3rd d. Ruth. Exec: wife Jane
   and son Francis. Wit: Thomas Rountree and Alexander Robinson.
25 THOMAS KIMBROW -Will- w. 20 Sept. 1777. Wife Elleanah; sons
   John, William, Robert, Thomas; daughters Suckey Nowel, Sarah
   Brown, Mary Bryant, Betty Bruce, Nancy Turner, Frankey Carman;
   son Graves. Sons to receive all part from estate of wife's deceased Father, Thomas Graves. Exec: sons John and William.
   Wit: William Gooch and Jesse Benton.
30 THOMAS HOPPER -Will- w. 12 Oct. 1777. Grandson Benjamin Mackintosh; wife Ann Hopper. estate to be sold and divided among sons
   and daughters. N.B. Son William Hopper. Wit: Robert Middleton,
   Bendick Middleton, Thos. Hopper, Henry Hopper.
31 Inv. estate of Luke Murphey by Thos. Barnett.
32 Sales estate of Richard Clayton. 3 Dec. 1777.
33 Inv. estate of Robert Barnet and appraised by Thomas Douglas and
   Joseph Dixon.
34 Div. estate of Noel Burton to: Robert Burton, Spill Coleman,
   William B. Burton, James Burton, Nancy Burton. By William Moore,
   Thos. Harrison, Dudley Gatewood.

March Court 1778

36 EPHRAIM GOLD -Will- w. 26 July 1777. Wife Rachel; Ephraim Gold,
   son of Daniel; Ephraim Sarjent, son of Stephen Sarjent; William
   Gold, son of Joseph Gold, heir at law. Exec: wife Rachel and
   brother Joseph Gold. Wit: Arch. Murphey, Danl. McFarland, and
   Fred Debo.
38 Inv. estate of Thomas Kimbrow.
39 Inv. estate of Robert Grayham by Eliza Grayham. Valued by Thomas
   Dameron, John Perkyns, and James Miller.
41 Bill of sale from Alexander Coleman to Will Moore for a negro
   named Jack. 4 April 1775. Test: Henry Dixon Jun. and Elijah
   Moore.
42 Bill of sale: Alex. Coleman to Wm. Moore, merchant.
42 Indenture: John Frazer, 5 years old, the son of John Frazer, late
   of Caswell County, apprenticed to Robert McReynolds and his son
   Joseph McReynolds to learn art of a hatter. 21 Jan. 1778. Test:
   John Clixby, John Womack. /s/ John Frazer.
44 John Fraser, soldier in the Tenth Regiment of the Continental Service from North Carolina, binds daughter Anne Frazer to Robert
   McRunnolds and spouse Martha McRunnolds to learn to be a spinster.
   /s/ John Fraser. 21 Jan. 1778.
44 Robert Smith, orphan of 17 last Christmas, apprentice to William
   Glenn. /s/ James Sanders, Chairman of Court of Pleas and Quarter
   Sessions. Wit: A. Tatom.
46 Bill of Sale: Alexander Coleman to Will Moore, a slave named Parice
   now in possession of James Ross. Test: Absolem Tatom.
46 Sale bill : Thomas Stewart to Robert Moore - Land on which Stewart
   lived joining Moore's on Whetstone Branch. 20 Aug. 1777. Wit:
   Edmond Dixon and William Stewart.

June Court 1778

47 Inv. estate of Alexander Moore, by Marian Moore and Robt. Moore,
   administrators.
50 Inv. estate of Antho. Samuel by Anne Samuel, adm. 2 June 1778.
51 Inv. estate of Abner Pryor by Margaret Pryor, adm.

Book A cont. 1778-1779

September Court 1778

Page
52 Patty Hays, 14 years of age, daughter of Jno. Hays, apprentice to
Alexander Hays.
53 Inv. goods and chattles of David Robertson and sale of estate.
/s/ Thos. Robertson.
54 JAMES TERRY -a nuncupative will - 26 March 1779. Samuel Watt
says he heard James Terry say in his last days that the entry
of land he made be transferred to Nathl. Dickerson. Oliver Terry,
son of James, testified to same. (Note by KKK: this document
was inserted in space on page 54 although dated 1779.)
55 SAMUEL STANSBURY -Will- w. 5 Aug. 1778. Wife Mary; Sons Solomon,
Luke, Benjamin, Samuel, Aquilla; daughters: Rachel, Cesinder(or
Lucinder), Elizabeth. Exec: wife and son Solomon. Wit: Jacob
Miles, Sen., John Tolbert, Jesse Tolbert.

December Court 1778

57 ALEXANDER DOBBINS -Will- w. 25 July 1778. Wife Cathrine; sons
John, Hugh; unborn child; brother James Dobbins; daughters Agness
and Elizabeth. Exec: wife Cathrine and brother in law James
Wilson. Wit: Arch. Murphey, Elizabeth Dobbins, Agnes Willson.
59 Inv. goods and chattles of Alexander Dobbins.
61 Sale of estate of Joseph Mabery on 4 Dec. 1778. Buyers: George
Mabery, Nathaniel Williams, William Bethel, Samuel Watt, Daniel
Atkins, Joshua Brown, Mary Mabery, Hezekiah Rice, Thomas Sparks,
William Leigh, John Cook, Isaac Dorris, John Oldham, William Hub-
bard, John Allen, Col. Joseph Williams, Charles Jenkins, Jacob
Williams. By Abner Tatom, D.S.

March Court 1779

62 Samuel Bumpass estate in account with Gabriel Davey. Payments to:
Wm. Hemrick, Moses Bridges, Isaac Vanhook, Doct. Parker, Wm. Wise-
man, Widow Parker, Sarah Bumpas, Thos. Person, Jno. Kemp, Jas.
Wilson, Henry Ford, Wm. Washington, Wm. Tapp, Lawyer Burke, Geo.
Reaves, Thos. Philpot, Robt. Dickens, Wm. Wright, Lawyer Penn,
and David Roberts. Balance of estate 526 lbs. 11 sh. 10 pence.
64 JOHN YATES -Will- w. 1 May 1779. Wife Sarah; sons William, Thos.,
Jno., Jas.; daughter Milly; 3 eldest daughters Joyce, Keziah, and
Elizabeth. 3 eldest sons Wm., Thos., and Jno. to execute will.
Wit: G. Samuel, Edmond Alley, Elizabeth Alley.
65 Inv. estate of Timothy Hatchet by Jno. Atkinson, adm.
66 Inv. personal estate of Andrew Gibson on 29 Sept. 1778. Debts due
from Elias Walock, John Warack, John Stourgen. Taken by Moses
Carson and Thos. Douglas. Return by Mary Gibson, adm.
68 DUNCAN McDONALD (also spelled McDonnel) -Will- w. 8 Oct. 1778.
Wife Elizabeth; grandson David Hemphill to get plantation if
agreeable with John Atkinson, entry taker. David to have negro
Fellow Dick when he reaches age 16. Son-in-law Hugh Hemphill;
daughter Katharine Hemphill and her 2 daughters Mary and Margaret;
daughter Katharine to have book Fisher's Catechism. Daughter-in-
law Margret Wakefield. "I order and devise that nothing of the
flooring of my house where the planks are not laid down be removed".
Exec: Archd. Murphey, John Black. Wit: D. McFarland, George
Black, Robt. Black.
71 JAMES TERRY -Will- w. 31 July 1775. Daughter Sarah; son Oliver
to get land bought of entry of James Tinsley; wife Rebecca;
daughter in law Levina King and her daughter Grace King. Col.
Natl. Terry to make deed for James Murphew. All surviving child-

3

Book A cont. 1779 -1780

Page

ren. Nath. and David Terry to assist with estate sale. Exec: Oliver Terry, Nathaniel Dickerson, and Peter Terry. Wit: Charles Burton, Richd. Boggess, and Lancelot Johnston.

75 Sales estate of Joseph Mabrey on 12 March 1779. Buyers: Wm. Stubblefield, Saml. Bethel, Return by Wm. Stubblefield in right of his wife, adm. of said estate.

June Court 1779

76 EDWARD STRINGER -Will- w. 10 March 1778. Wife Judith; son Simeledge Stringer to get land including cabin in which Robt. Campbell lives; daughter Fanny Southerland, Mary Ann Stringer; grand daughter Sarah Stringer. My children: Jas. William, Cimeledge, Agness Whitlock, Lucia Browning, Tabitha Pead, Sarah Campbell; sons Edmond and Reuben, daughter Frances Vier. Exec: wife. Wit: Jacob Miles, Sen., Jno. Davis, Hezekiah Davis.

78 James Dix of Pittsylvania Co. Va. sale of negro girl, Hanna, to Dudley Gatewood. Wit: Spill Coleman, Ambrose Gatewood.

79 John Irvin of Guilford Co. N.C., power of attorney to Abraham Fulkerson to convey land in Caswell Co. adjoining Abraham Fulkerson, George Black, Duncan McDonnel, Sill Stokes, and Alexander Murphey.

80 Sales estate of James Terry by Peter Terry. exec.

September Court 1779

80 MATHEW JOUETT -Will- w. 9 Sept. 1779. Of St. David's Dist. Wife Sarah; children John, Susannah, Nancy, Mathew, Polly, Thomas, Betsy, Washington. Exec. wife and Thomas Brooks, Absalom Tatom, Richard Moore. Test:Jere Poston, Henry Cobb, Chas. Taylor.

83 JOHN SMITH -Will- w. 5 Aug. 1779. Wife Mary; Duke Whalebone and his wife Elizabeth; daughter Bety Jerrell. Exec: wife. Wit: Thos. Duncan and Thos. Wynn. Mentions William Jerrell.

85 EZEKIEL HARRELSON -Will- w. 6 Aug. 1779. Wife Jane; sons William, Burgess, John; daughter Elizabeth. Exec. wife Jane and her brother John Chambers, Thos. Barnett(Hugh's son). Wit: Thomas Miles, Elizabeth Barnett, Rebekah Chambers.

88 Inv. estate of Samuel Winstead by Ailsey Winstead. Inv. estate of John Smith by Mary Smith, exec.

December Court 1779

89 Bill of sale: Hugh Dobbins to Abraham Fulkerson for 4 negroes. Wit: John J. Farley, Mumford McGee; Bill of sale assigned to John Campbell.

90 Benjamin Carter of Craven County, S. C. - sale of land to David Shelton on Rattlesnake Creek, entered in Lord Granville's office to Benj. Carter. 29 Dec. 1778. Wit: William Lea, Sen. Jurat; Jesse Benton, Charles Trim.

91 Account of estate of Alex. Cochrone with John Cochrone as guardian to orphans and widow's claim.

92 Sales of estate of Samuel Winstead by Ailsey Winstead, adm. /s/ Thos. Neely, D.S.

93 Additional inv. estate of John Smith. Inv. estate Ezekiel Harrelson by Jno. Harrelson and John Chambers.

March Court 1780

94 Sale estate of Joseph Mabery. (Repeat of page 61)
96 Inv. estate of Capt. Mathew Jouett.

4

Book A cont. 1780-

June Court 1780

97 Inv. estate of John Cate by James Benton, adm.
98 Indenture: Judith Gimbo, orphan of 6 years last May, to Frederick Debow.
99 William Garret, son of John Garret, apprentice to William Glenn. Wit: Henry McNeill, Ambrose Arnold, Cornelius Hogarty.
100 Thomas Wyatt, son of Hannah Wyatt, age 9 last May, apprentice to John Low.
101 Thom Day (son of Rachel Day) age 3 years and 10 mos., apprentice to Samuel Winstead.
102 George Day (son of Nan Day) age 4 years, apprentice to Samuel Winstead.

September Court 1780

103 Inv. estate of William Hancock by Susanna Hancock, adm.
103 JACOB ROBINSON, SEN. -Will- w.4 Sept. 1773. Sons James and Samuel; grandson William Kersey, son of John Kersey; daughters Easter, Jemima; sons William, Jacob, John, Thomas, and Alexander; grandson David Kersey. Exec: sons Thomas and Samuel. Wit: James Williams, William Black, Talton East.
104 JESSE JONES -Will- w. 28 Jan. 1780. Sons Drury, Goodrige, Willson; daughter Salley; wife Frances. Exec: wife and son Drury. Wit: Thomas Palmer, Joseph Palmer.

December Court 1780

106 Indenture: Betsy Edwell, child of Winney Edwell, 5 years old, to John Williams, Esq. /s/ John Atkinson, Chairman of the Inferior Court.
107 Joseph Edwell, age 7 , child of Winney, bound to John Williams.
108 Sollomon Seal, orphan, age 15½, apprentice to David Whipple to learn art of silversmith.
109 Children of Winney Edwell, Sarah, Jonathan, Judith, Elisabeth, Joseph, and Robert apprenticed to John Powell.
110 JOHN GUNN -Will- w. 17 Aug. 1780. Sons Jesse, James, Gabriel, and Daniel; daughter Sally; Wife; Exec: wife and son James.
111 ROBERT McFARLAND -Will- w. 6 Oct. 1780. (of Castle Creek) Sons: John, James, William, Walter, Joseph Davis McFarland; daughters: Margaret, Ellen Rogers McFarland; son Robert. John Barnet and daughter Martha Barnet to take care of son Robert; wife Margaret. Exec: wife and son John. Wit: Joseph Johnston, Moses Walker, Buckley Walker.
113 JAMES WILLIAMS -Will- (of State of South Carolina, Ninety Six District, but now in State of North Carolina as a refuge.) w. 12 June 1780. Wife Mary to get part of tract in Ninety Six District. Son Daniel to get land bought of Robert Johnston. Sons Joseph, William; daughters Elizabeth, and Mary; son James to get land bought of John Campoell; son Washington (under age) to get land bought of James Cook. Exec: wife, son Daniel, brother Henry Williams, and Joseph Hays. Wit: William Rice, Jasper Goodman, James Cook.
116 EPHRAIM LOGUE -Will- w. 30 April 1780. Daughter Ellenor, and if she die without issue, land to be divided with Ephraim Thompson and first male heir of brother John Logue, naming him Ephraim Logue; James Linsey son of sister Mary; Saml. Thompson son of sister Margaret. Plantation purchased of James Bracken on Owens Creek to go to wife Mary Logue until her demise and then to go to Alexander Walker's eldest son Ephraim Walker. Exec: Alex. Walker of Guilford Co. and Thomas Thompson of Orange Co.

5

Book A cont. 1780-1781
Page
    Will of Ephraim Logue - Wit: Nathan Rice, John Spencer,
    Nicholas Thorn.
117 John Brown, orphan of 11 years, apprentice to David Whipple to
    learn mastery of silversmith.
119 Sale of part of Thos. Kimbrow estate. Sales to: Jesse Benton,
    Col. Will Moore, Capt. John Graves, Capt. Nat Hart, Will Kimbro,
    Thomas Kimbroe, Robert Kimbroe, Edwd. Nowel, Bazel Graves,
    Robert Cartright, John Kimbroe, Bartlett Yancey, John Bryant.
120 Inv. estate of Jesse Jones by Drury Jones, exec.
121 Inv. estate of John Gunn by exec. Mary Gunn and James Gunn.
    Additional sales of estate of Thos. Kimbro.
122 Inv. estate of Nehemiah Fuller, by Henry Fuller, adm.
123 Sale estate of Nehemiah Fuller. Sales to William Mash, Henry
    Fuller, Elisha Parker, Wm. Breekeen, Elijah Fullar, Peter Fuller,
    Jacob Bull, Thomas Carver, Benj. Long, Charles Trim, Joshua
    Browning, John Cooper, James Roberts, Elisha Parks, Willson Ver-
    millon, James Archdeacon, Thomas Neeley.

                    March Court 1781

126 Sales estate of Thomas Wisdom. Buyers: Thomas Yates, Martha
    Wisdom, Baze Newman, David Culbertson, Larken Wisdom.
128 Inv. estate of Nathaniel Harrelson by Dorcas Harrelson.
128 Account of sale of estate of David Robinson. Buyers: Thos.,
    James, and Saml. Robinson. By Thos. Robinson, adm.

                    June Court 1781

129 Sale of estate of Marye Maxwell. Sales to: Adam Sanders, Wm.
    Yates, John Lea, James Rainey, Edwd. Maxwell, Jno. Graves, Char-
    les Stephens, John Low, Thos. Graves, John Ogletree. By Edwd.
    Maxwell, adm.
131 Sale estate of John Cate sold by Thomas Neely, deputy sheriff.
    Buyers: Abram Hester, Robt. Berry, Bennett Williams, George
    Wagoner, David Webb, Charles Pirant, Henry Hambrick, Benjamin
    Harrelson, Wm. Aldridge. By James Benton, adm.
132 Inv. goods of Robt. McFarland.
    Inv. estate of Col. James Williams by Henry Williams, exec.
133 NATHANIEL HARRELSON -Will- w. 7 April 1781. Wife Dorcas; daugh-
    ter Mary Smith; sons Thomas, Forbus, Nathan, and Jeremiah;
    daughters Elizabeth and Sarah; Exec: wife and son Thomas. Test:
    John Payne, John Cochran.
134 ELKANAH HARRELSON -Will- w. 13 April 1781. Sons Jesse, Reuben,
    Micajah, Bradley, Hosea, Anderson, Hiram, Elkanah. Two sons
    apprenticed to Jacob Bull, one son with Michael Dickson; Exec:
    John Barnett and Henry Horley. Wit: Hugh Barnett, Elizabeth
    Wingfield, Margaret McFarland.
136 ROBERT HUSTON -Will- w. 23 Oct. 1778. Wife Jane; sons James,
    William, George; daughter Mary Cooper. Exec. wife Jane and
    son George. Wit: Robert McFarland, Henry Horley.
137 AMBROSE GATEWOOD -Will- (of Pittslyvania Co. Va.) w. 7 Oct.1769.
    Wife Martha to have estate her lifetime and to be returned to
    Dudley Gatewood; Nephew Dudley Gatewood. Exec: Dudley Gatewood.
    Wit: John Hambleton, Benj. Mosby. Proved on oath of Spillby
    Coleman.
138 JOSEPH SARGENT -Will- ND - Wife Ruth; son Daniel to get land
    bought of John Lea; daughter Elizabeth. household goods divided
    among all children. Exec: brother Stephen Sargent and Joseph
    Gold. Wit: Joseph Gold, Dan Sargent, Stephen Sargent.

                            6

Book A cont. 1781-1782
Page
139 HOSEA TAPLEY - Will - w. 24 Oct 1780. Wife Sarah; son in law
    John Short; Exec: wife and John Short. Wit: William Rankin,
    Ambrose Arnold. Proved on oath of David Mitchell.
140 JOHN JOHNSTON - Will - w. 16 Aug 1778. Wife Mary; son Daniel;
    daughters: Isabella wife to James Walker, Rachel wife to Joseph
    Walker, Jane wife to James Christie; sons William and James.
    Exec: son James and friend John Robertson. Wit: JerePoston, John
    Walker, John Herron.
142-143 Total tax assessments for 1780, 1781, 1782.

September Court 1781

144 HUMPHREY DONALDSON -Will- w. 5 Aug 1781. Wife Mary; daughters
    Jennett, Martha, Margaret, Rebecca; sons William, Andrew, Robert,
    Ebenezer, Humphrey; daughter Mary Richmond wife of James Rich-
    mond. Exec: wife & Wm. Richmond. Wit: Thomas Wiley, Laughlin
    McAlyea.
147 Div estate of Thomas Kimbro to: Eleanor, Robert, William, Thomas,
    John, and Graves Kimbro; John Bryant, Leonard Brown, Robert Bruce,
    Edwd. Nowel, Henry Turner for legacy to their wives; Caleb Carman.
150 Bill of sale: John Womack to James Anderson, sale of negroes.
    Wit: John Atkinson, Alex. Rose.
151 Jonathan Edwell orphan of 12 yrs. to Nath. Dickinson. /s/ Charles
    Burton, Chairman Inferior Court. Wit: Peter Smith,George Burton.
152,3,4 Sarah Edwell age 14, Judith Edwell age 10, Robert Edwell,14,
    apprenticed to Nathaniel Dickinson.
155 William Shearman orphan of 12 yrs. apprentice to William Wilson
    to learn art of shoemaking.
156,7 Francis Shearman age 7 yrs. 5 mos. and Charles Shearman orphan
    of 9 yrs. bound to Edmd. Alley. /s/ John Atkinson, Chairman CC.
158 William Frazier orphan of 5½ yrs. apprentice to Robert Willson.
159 Mary Todd orphan of 10 yrs. apprentice to Stephen Jones.
160 Polly Givins age 4½ yrs. apprentice (by her father's consent) to
    Jennet Douglass.
161 Elisabeth Frazier orphan of 18 months bound to David Vanhook.
162 Sarah George binds unto Richard Moore a mulatto child named
    Harbert age 2 yrs. 8 mos. 20 Aug 1781. Wit: L.Johnston, Richd.
    Smith, James Douglas.
163 THOMAS SPENCER - Will - w. 11 July 1781. Wife Elizabeth; sons
    Benjamin, John, Thomas; son John to get land adj. Roland Hughes;
    daughters: Francis, Betty, Bobby Pinnix, Mary, Susanna. Exec:
    wife Elizabeth and sons Benjamin and John. Wit: Arthur Lovens,
    John Henslee, Wm. Mitchell.
165 HENRY JESSE - Will - w. 20 June 1781. Wife; Exec: wife. Wit:
    James Roan, John Jesse, Frankey Jesse.
166 JOHN LEA - Will - w. 17 Aug 1778. Sons Elliott, Edmond, Carter
    (to get land on Richland Cr.), Owen (under 21, land on Hico);
    daughter Phebe to get plantation purchased of James Lea on Hico;
    daughter Millie; daughter Betty to have plantation purchased of
    Zachariah Lea, each daughter to get her share when she marries.
    Land (245 acres) to be saved on which Robt. Mitchell lives and
    deed made to him or his heirs and remainder to be conveyed to
    William Lea and John Lea Jun. if they pay for same. Exec:
    Andrew Caddell, Carter Lea. Wit: Moses Bradsher, John Henley,
    William Lea(Jurat).
168 GEORGE RAINEY -Will- w. 7 Feb 1779. Wife Mary; sons William,
    George; daughters Margret, Eliza, Mary, Sarah, Nancy. Children
    John and Martha received their share previously. Exec: wife.
    Test: Thomas Rice, Abraham Denton.

7

ROBERT BLACK -Will- w. 9 Aug. 1780. Wife Elizabeth; sons
George, Henry, John Black(who is my heir at law); youngest
son Thomas; daughter Elizabeth Fulkerson; Exec: son Henry and
son-in-law Abraham Fulkerson. Wit: Arch. Murphey, Jesse Duncan, Hannah Duncan.
171 Inv. estate of Robert Black by Henry Black.
172 Inv. estate of Henry Jesse by Elizabeth Jesse, exec.
172 Inv. estate of Moses Richardson on June 3, 1781. Approved on
oath of Susannah Richardson.

December Court 1781

173 THOMAS MCNEILL -Will - w. 20 Apr. 1781. Wife Ann; sons Thomas,
John, Benjamin; daughters Mary, Lois, Elizabeth Roberts, Nancy
Vermillon, Patsy Hubbard Lea. Exec: wife, son John, son in
law Willson Vermillion, and George Lea(son of William).
Wit: George Lea, John Clixby, Lucy Lea.
174 JOHN MOORE -Will- No date. Estate to wife for her life; then
to go to James Moore, son of David Moore. To the care of
Aaron Parker,Sen. Wit: John Eaken, Daniel Parker.
175 HUGH DOBBINS -Will- w. 10 Nov. 1781. Nephew Andrew Ferguson;
James Dobbins(my cousin Hugh Dobbins son); John Dobbins, brother to James; Elizabeth Coyle to get wife's clothes; Mary
Donaldson. Exec: Andrew Ferguson, Josiah Cole. Wit: Thomas
Wiley, Robert Long, James Long.
176 JOHN SCOTT -Will- w. 16 June 1781. Sons Robert, John, and
deceased sonWilliam; daughters Cathrine McAden, Mary McFarland; son in law Samuel Cunningham; son in law David Logan;
daughter in law Rebecca Scott; grandchildren:John and Hannah
Cunningham; David, Cathrine, and Mary Hannah Logan; Sarah,
Rebecca, Cathrine, Eamy, Elizabeth, Loften, and John Graham
Scott. Exec: sons Robert & John. Wit: Archibald Murphey,
Fred Debo, Jno. McAden.
178 Inv. estate of Richard Painter by Miles Duncan, adm.
179 Sales estate of Moses Farley.
180 Inv. estate of James Currie by John Currie.
181 Inv, estate of Jonathan Starkey taken 30 May 1781 by Jonathan
Starkey, adm.
182 Inv. estate of Danl. Duncan by Mary Duncan, adm.

March Court 1782

182 ALEXANDER STINSON -Will- w. 5 Jan. 1782. Daughter Nancy to get
land in Buckingham Co. Va.; Wife Sarah; any unborn child.
Personal estate left him by grandfather Childress to those
already named. Exec: father John Stinson and wife Sarah.
Wit: William Rainey, Hugh Dobbins, James Rainey.
183 JOHN RAINEY -Will- (From original at Archives) w. 26 Jan. 1782.
"Mr. John Rainey about to leave in search of his mare and had
not made a will desired that George Elliot and Jane Murphey
should bear witness to his request. He said William Rainey
was to have land on Hico where he formerly lived. The land on
Cane Cr. was his son James' and his son Thomas Rainey should
have land on Country Line Cr. His Negroes divided between
daughters Elizabeth and Jenny. Wife to have rest of estate."
184 RICHARD CARLON (Carlan) - Will - w. 10 Dec. 1781. Wife Mary;
unborn child to be named Richard or Mary; eldest brother John
Carlon, son of Mitchel Carlon, in Ireland, Dunegal County to
get estate if above heirs leave no heir. Exec: Robert Parks,
John Graves,Jun. Wit: Robt. Parks, David Dickey.

8

Book A cont. 1782
Page
185 SAMUEL WILKINSON -Will- w. 28 Oct. 1781. Wife; Sons Francis,
    John, William, Thomas, Nathan; daughters Ann, Mary, Catherine,
    Susannah. Exec: wife and son Thomas. Wit: John Ashburn and
    John Taylor. Daughters Fanny, Elizabeth.
186 Inv. estate of Christopher Brooks by Henry Williams, adm.
186 Acct. sale of William Wilkinson returned on oath of John
    Ogletree, adm.
187 Sale of estate of Richard Painter returned on oath of Miles
    Duncan, adm.
187 Acct. of sale of estate of James Currie.
187 Div. estate of Anthony Samuel to: Ann Samuel, widow; Molly,
    Sally, Anthony, Edmund, Benjamin, Samuel, Nancy, Betsy, and
    Josiah Samuel (orphans). 4 Dec. 1782. By Thomas Harrison,
    Robt. Burton, James Sanders.
189 Inv. estate of Humphrey Donaldson by Wm. Richmond and Mary
    Donaldson, exec.

June Court 1782

189 MATTHEW MANES -Will - w. 6 Mar. 1780. Wife Sarah; son Joseph;
    daughter Mary. Exec: father Samuel Mains and Joseph Cantrell.
    Wit: Robert Allison, John Hensley, Rachel Hensley. (Also
    spelled Mains).
191 THOMAS ROBERTSON-Will- (Recorded in Book A as ROBERTSON. Written
    on original as ROBINSON) w. 6 Apr. 1781. Wife; 2 youngest
    sons Mark and Alexander; son Thomas to get land adj. John
    Anthony and John Robinson; daughters Easter, Sarah, Gemina
    Pyerce; Robert Anderson; Exec: sons John and Thomas. Wit:
    John Anthony and Thomas Robinson.
192 CLAUD MUIRHEAD -Will- w. 17 Jan. 1782. Wife Elizabeth; unborn
    child to have residue of estate; if no child survives, estate
    to Nancy and Elisabeth Park, Orphans.of Wm.Park,decd.of Bute Co.
    Exec: wife, Arch Murphey, Josiah Cole. Wit: Hedgmont Warren,
    Henry Fulcher, David Ford.
193 Power of Attorney: William Kellow of borough of Winchester, Va.
    to Robert Dickens (to sell any land he may be entitled to).
    1 Aug. 1781. Wit: Benj. Rutherford, Edward McGuire.
193 Appraisal estate of Daniel Duncan by A. C. Murphey, Josiah Cole,
    and Hugh Dobbin.
196 Inv. estate of Claud Muirhead on 20 Apr. 1782 by Elisabeth
    Muirhead.
197 Allotment of land for widow of John Carman. Div. of estate of
    John Carman to: Hezekiah, John, and Caleb Carman; Hugh Reed;
    Robert Kimbrough; Jesse Kimbrough; James Turner; Abegail Carman;
    Andrew Carman; and Hugh Eagon. Div. by James Sanders, Thomas
    Slade, William Moore.
198 Acct. sale of estate of Jonathan Starkey.
198 Acct. sale of Richard Carlon.
198 Inv. of articles not mentioned in will of Jacob Robinson taken
    by Saml. Robertson.
199 Settlement estate of James Williams.
201 Inv. estate of Benjamin Goodman by Mariah Goodman, adm.
202 Inv. estate of Josiah Farley by Saml. Johnston, adm. (A true
    inv. except for ½ of the issue of a negro woman named Doll now
    in possession of old Wm. Farley in Virginia.)
203 John S. Brown, orphan of 12 years 7 mos., apprentice to Robert
    Payne to learn art of silversmith. /s/ Wm. Moore, Chairman
    County Court.

9

Book A cont. 1782
Page
204 William Taylor, orphan of 17 years, apprentice to Robert Payne
    to learn arts of blacksmith and silversmith.
205 Rebecca Cousins, free born negro, apprentice to Robert Davey.

September Court 1782

206 Amount of sale of estate of Matthew Manes approved on oath of
    Joseph Cantrel, exec.
206 Div. estate of Josiah Farley(minor) by James Lea, Richd. Esk-
    ridge, Stephen Sergent. Samuel Johnston to receive part for
    his wife's share. 29 July 1782.
207 Bond: To David Mitchell due from John Smith for timber.
208 Inv. part of estate of Col. James Williams by Mary Williams,
    exec.
208 Inv. estate of Daniel Williams by Mary Williams, adm.
208 Inv estate of Matthew Manes.
209 Inv. estate of William Corder by Chas. Taylor, exec.
209 Inv. estate of Joseph Sergent by Joseph Gold, exec.
210 Inv. estate of Stephen Hamblin by Thomas Cole, adm.
210 STEPHEN HAMBLIN -Will- w. 4 July 1781. To Thomas Cole: "Take
    care of my things until I return home again and you will much
    oblige your humble servant; and my mother take care of my
    clothes if she Please; and if I should not return I leave my
    mother part and rest divided among my Brothers and sisters."
    Proved on oath of Walter Ellis.
211 HENRY DIXON -Will - w. 18 Aug. 1778. Wife Martha; sons Wynne,
    Roger, Robert, Henry; daughters Elizabeth, Frances (land on
    Rutledge Cr. on south side of Dan River adj. the province line
    in Pittsylvania Co. Va.). Exec: wife and her brother Thomas
    Wynne, Charles Dixon. Wit: N.Dickerson,H.Reynolds,Sarah Sartin.
213 WILLIAM CORDER -Will - w. 2 Dec. 1780. Wife Pheby; children
    when they come of age; Exec: John Corder, Charles Taylor.
    Wit: James Barker, Miles Murphy, Lewis Corder.
214 JAMES GREYHAM - Will - w. 9 Feb. 1781. Wife; children: William,
    James, George, Thomas, Margret, Miller; grandson Reed Greyham.
    Exec: wife; Wit: Thomas Butler, Paul McClarney, Rose McClarney,
    Jno. Sammon.
215 MATTHEW DUTY -Will - w. 4 June 1782. Wife; sons William,
    Solomon(under 21), Richard(under 21); grandson William Owen;
    daughters Sarah Owen, Mary Duty, Ann Duty; sons John, Littleton,
    and Thomas. Exec: son William, John Adams, Charles Littleton.
    Wit: Richardson, James Stuart, Joseph Turner.
217 JOHN HARRIS — Noncupative will - w. 8 June 1782. John Clayton
    made oath that John Harris died 6 June 1782 and made this ver-
    bal will: Wife Ann to get entire estate. Wit: Elizabeth
    Clayton.
217 Indenture: Thomas Price, orphan of 5½ years, to James Farghar.
219 Indenture: Jerry Harrison, orphan of 17, to James Stringer.
220 James Harrison, orphan of 17, indenture to James Stringer.
221 Jacob Funk Stone,orphan of 1 year, indenture to John Douglass.
    /s/ John Moore, Chairman of County Court.
222 Judith Harrison, orphan of 9 years, indenture to Hannah Miles.
223 Johanna Harrison, orphan of 4½ years, indenture to Elizabeth
    Roberts. /s/ William Moore, Chairman of County Court.

Book A cont. 1782-1783 <u>December</u> <u>Court</u> <u>1782</u>
Page
224 Indenture: Robert Overstreet, orphan of 2 years, to Jacob Wright.
225 George Todd, orphan of 10 years, indenture to John Adams.
226 John Aldridge, orphan of 2 years, indenture to James Smith.
227 Bill of Sale: Benjamin Riden of Bedford County, Va., sale of
    negro, Gilbert, to Henry Williams of Mecklinburg, Co. 1 June
    1765. Wit: William Brown.
227 Assessment estate of Stephen Hamblin sold by Thomas Cole, adm.
    Sales to: T. Cole, James Guttery, Joseph Tate, Robt. Johnston,
    Henry McMullen, John McMurry. Test: Thomas Neely, D.S. (deputy
    sheriff).
228 Inv. estate of Alex Hayes by Elizabeth Hayes, adm.
228 Inv. estate of Richard Smithey by Nancy Smithey. adm.
229 Settlement estate of James Currie by John and Mary Currie, adm.
    and by Thos. Douglas and John Armstrong, guardians for Mary,
    John, James, Margaret, Joseph, and Jane Currie. Notes due the
    estate from Samuel McConkey and Andrew McCleary. Allotment for
    widow. 2 Dec. 1782.
230 Bill of sale: Susannah Stokes, sale of stock to Robert Donaldson
    for 1000 weight of inspected tobacco to be delivered at Halifax.
    Wit: Elizer Andrews, Rachel Donaldson.
231 Inv. Estate of Colo. Henry Dixon taken 2 Nov. 1782 by Charles
    Dixon, exec. Debtors to estate: Samuel Jones, Wm. Whitehead,
    John Southerland, Wm. Sanders, Col. Peter Perkins, Edward Gra-
    ham, William Armstrong, Malachia Dickerson.

March Court 1783

232 Indenture: Anderson Haralson, orphan of 7 years, to William Hus-
    ton.
233 Nathan Wingfield, orphan of 12 years, indenture to William Huston.
234 SAMUEL FARMER - Will - w. 30 Dec. 1779. Wife Cassandra; sons
    Daniel, William(land on Flatt River), Stephen, Nathan; daughters
    Rachael Wilson, Mary Wilson, Susanna Farmer, Ellenor McMahen,
    Jane Farmer. Exec: wife, Daniel Farmer, Richard Holeman.
    Wit: Richard Holeman, William Dennis, Jane Holeman.
235 WILLIAM NEELEY - Will- Statement of John Womack: William Neeley,
    deceased 21 Dec. 1782, made following will. Ellenor Neeley,
    widow, to get one-third part. Son Samuel; son Jacob(land on
    Flatt River). Children: John, Thomas, Samuel, Joseph, Jacob,
    Mary Pryor. Wit: William White, John Satterfield, James Mosser.
236 Bill of sale: Elling Harrison, sale of negro girl to Ailsey Win-
    stead. Wit: S. Harrison, Susannah Wheeler, Gabriel Davey.
237 Michael Dickson, release of bill of sale from James Gregory.
    Wit: Josias Dickson, Mary Dickson.
237 Power of Attorney: Isaac Brown to George Lea - to sign and ex-
    hibit unto John Jesse a deed of 550 acres on waters of South
    Hyco and Cobbs Cr. joining lines of Richard Lea. Thomas Carver,
    and others, as soon as Isaac Brown gets deed from State.
    7 Sept. 1783. Wit: Josiah Cole, Hugh Hemphill.
238 Deed of gift: Thomas Douglas to son Benjamin Douglas, a negro
    girl, Dinah, age 11. Wit: John Williams, A. E. Murphey.
239 Inv. estate of Charles Stephens by Elisabeth Stephens, adm.
240 Indenture: Lucy Day, orphan of 4, to David Allen.
241 Jesse Day, orphan of 3, indenture to David Allen.
242 Nancy Day, orphan of 2 months, indenture to David Allen.
243 Jesse Hood, orphan of 9 years, indenture to John Graves.

11

Book A cont. 1783

Page

244 Reuben Harralson, orpahn of 12 years, indenture to Jacob Bull.

245 Macajah Haralson, orphan of 11 years, indenture to Jacob Bull.

June Court 1783

246 JAMES STUART - Will - w. 31 March 1783. Wife Agness; sons
William and James; daughters Elizabeth, Rachel, Agness. Exec:
wife, Goodlow Warren, Robert Moore. Wit: Jeremiah Warren,
Eli Warren, William Duty.

247 THOMAS ROBERTSON - Will - w. 5 May 1783. Wife Penina;
children: Joab(youngest), Gideon(eldest), land adj. Archibald
Samuel; daughters Nelly, Patty, Rebecca, Penina, Keziah; Exec.
Jacob Hall,and wife Penina.

248 Sale of estate of Elkanah Haralson. Sales to: Henry Howard,
Stephen Austin, John Chambers, Peter Rogers, Bart Grier,
William Breekeen, Garrott Guttery, Banjamin Newton, Thomas
Neeley, Frances Scoggin, James Stringer, Charles Allen,
Charles Trim, William Link, Jacob Bull, William Fulcher,
James Archdeacon, William Stone, James Warren, Thomas Barnet
(HS), John Motheral, James Stuart, Ledford Parrot, Joel Pope,
John Cooper, Capt. John Moore, William Huston, James Rainey,
Jacob Davis, John Chambers, William Chambers Jun., Nathan Byas,
Benjamin Long, Seth Moore, Henry Horley, John Byas. By John
Barnett and Henry Horley, adm.

250 Sales estate of Claude Muirhead. Among buyers: William Muirhead, John Turner, Jno. Chambers, Henry McNeill, Archd. Campbell, John Link.

251 Inv. estate of William Corder. Allotment to widow Phebe.

252 Thomas Douglas and Abraham report settlement of estate of
Andrew Gibson between widow and 9 children. (Names not given.)

252 Div. estate of Charles Stephens to widow and child. Division
by Adam Sanders, David Shelton.

252 Inv. estate of Richard Norton by John Norton, adm.

253 Inv. estate of William Neeley by Samuel Neeley, exec.

253 Bill of sale: Archd. Campbell to Archibald Murphey.

254 Power of Attorney: Dorcas Wilkerson to John Anthony to convey
land on Negro Cr., waters of North Hyco, entered to Samuel Wilkerson by John Atkinson, entry taker.

255 Indenture: Solomon Parks Lea, orphan of 9 years, to William Lea.

End of Book A

Book B - Sept. 1783-March 1792

September Court 1783

Page
1 ROBERT JOHNSTON (Johnson on original)- Will - w. 12 Aug. 1783.
   Sons William, John, Robert, George, Benjamin. Philip; daughters
   Elizabeth Stuart, Judah Weake; Wife Frances; other children
   Lucy, Eliza, Dolla, Salley, Milly, Hampton, Phaney, Richard.
   Exec: wife and son Philip, and John Eakin, Thomas Cole.
   Wit: John Jackson, Sarah Hust.
2 ROBERT ATKINSON -Will - w. 7 June 1783. (From original)
   Sons John, Ransom; daughters Patsy, Mary, Aney, Jane, Sarah;
   Exec: sons John and Ransom, Joseph Moseley; Wit: Chas. Taylor,
   Edmond Browning, Richard Arvin.
3&4 Missing. The will of Robert Atkinson was partly on page 3.
5 Inv. estate Samuel Farmer.
6 Inv. estate of Peter Savory by Robert Dickens, adm.
6 Indenture: James Shearman, orphan of 5 years, to Alex. Wiley.
7 Jane Harrison, orphan of 11, apprentice to Chalton Ingram.
8 Sarah Harrison, orphan of 8, apprentice to John Miles.
9 Edward Upton and Jane his wife, bind her son William Long, a
   mulatto, to Samuel Bracken. Wit: Thomas Brooks, Thos. Rice.

December Court 1783

10 John Harrison, orphan of 6 years, apprentice to William Morgan.
12 Bill of Sale: John Bryant to Benjamin Hubbard, Sen. Test: Jonathan Low.
12 Obligation: John Bryant obligates himself to Hathey Shearman.
   "If Hathey Shearman marry Bryant, he agrees to give her and her
   heirs land and premises where he now lives". Wit: Benjamin
   Hubbard, Jonathan Low.
13 Power of attorney: John Bryant to Benjamin Hubbard to convey land
   on South Fork Country Line Cr. adj. William Sanders, Thomas
   Graves, Jonathan Low. /s/ John Bryant, Hathey Bryant.
14 Bill of sale: Joel Pope of Granville Co. to John Womack for one
   negro woman and child. Wit: John Tapley, Margret Tapley.
15 Power of attorney: John Ogletree to John Atkinson (to attend to
   all business and premises). 5 Nov. 1783. Wit: A. E. Murphey,
   John Chambers.
16 Power of attorney: Miles Duncan to John Ogletree. 13 Feb. 1783.
   Power granted to John Atkinson by Ogletree. 5 Nov. 1783.
17 Inv. estate of Robert Johnston by Francis Johnston,exec.
18 JAMES PAINE - Will - w. 4 Mar. 1782. Son William and Jean d. of
   William; son Robert and James son of Robert; son James Jun.and
   John son of James Jun.; son John and daughters Rebecca,Molly,
   and Nancey; Exec: sons John and Robert. Wit: John Clayton and
   Elizabeth Clayton.
18 Tax assessment for 1783.
19 Tax collected for building court house.
19 Marriage contract of John Cooper(widower) and Mary Gibson(widow).
   Cooper.will not interfere with her disposal of her property to
   her children and will make no claim on it. 10 July 1782. Wit:
   John Anthony, Thomas Douglass.

March Court 1784

20 List of estate of Robert Atkinson returned by Joseph Mosely.

13

22 ROBERT ALLEN(Allin) -Will- w. 6 June 1782. Wife Hannah; Lucy
McKissack wife of Thomas McKissack; Josiah Allen, son of Drury
Allen; son Drury;daughters Elizabeth Hutson, Agnes Williams,
Sarah Woody; Exec: Drury and Josiah Allen; Wit: Thomas Palmer
Jun., Elizabeth Allen.
25 Elizabeth Pryor, relinquishment of dower (land and mill sold by
her husband Hayden Pryor to John Baird of Prince George Co.
Va). 12 March 1784.
26 Amount sale estate of Spencer Prescod. Sold by Henry Howard,
adm. (Included shoemaker and sadler tools.)
26 GEORGE ROSEBROUGH -Will - w. 7 June 1782. Wife Jane; sons
Robert, William; daughter Margret; grandsons George Southard and
Allen Fuller. Exec: wife and Jonathan Skeen. Wit: Jno. Atkinson, Benj. Hatcher, Ann Chittingham.
28 Acct. sale of estate of William Man. Sales to : Elisabeth Man,
John Man, Samuel Greer, James Huston, Charles Allen, Charles
Trim, Thomas Barnett Sen., Pulliam Williamson, Benj. Long, John
Dowell, Robert McReynolds, Thomas Vanhook, Edmond Roberts, Wm.
Hargis, John Guthrie, John Payne, Thomas Palmer, John Douglas.
31 Inv. estate of Mathew Duty taken 10 Mar 1784 by Wm. Duty, exec.
32 SARAH BOWLES -Will- w. 1 Nov. 1783 & 31 Oct.   Son John;
daughter Mary Washington; granddaughters Sarah and Nancy Bowles;
daughter Oney Yeargin; Benjamin Yeargin and his brother John;
grandson Andrew Yeargin; Bartlett Yeargin; grandson Jordon Bowles;
Exec: son John and grandson Benjamin Yeargin; Wit: William·
Waite, Walter Oakley, John Cragg.
35 PATRICK FLYNN -Will- w. 9 Aug. 1781. Wife; sons John (land adj.
Long, Stephens, Crisp), Patrick; daughters Mary and Susannah.
Exec: wife and son John; Wit: James Roan, Mary Flynn.
36 Letter of Attorney: James Lea (the son and heir of William Lea,
decd.) of Caswell County to Thomas Phelps of same county to
"ask, demand, sue for as to obtain lawful title to tract of land
in King and Queen County, Va., 35 acres on waters of Matiponi
River near Maddison's Mill, said land falls to me by Heirship".
16 Mar 1784. Wit: H. Haralson, William Lea.
37 Indenture: James Hix voluntarily binds his son Richard Hix to
Thomas Hallyburton, Planter. Wit: James Jones, William Burton.

July Court 1784

38 WILLIAM CUMMINS -Will- w. 13 Mar 1784. Wife Martha; all my
children. Exec: friend Benjamin Johnston and wife Martha.
Wit: John Black, George Black, Thos. Black.
39 JOHN LYON - Will - w. 23 Apr 1784. Wife Jean; sons James, William,
Peter (land bought of Bennett Nolley), Henry (land adj. Reuben
Jourden); daughters Elizabeth Farrar, Mary Farrar, Frances
Bailey, Jane Anderson; grandson Richard Tankersly Lyon (land
bought of Joseph Cate); gran..daughter Salley Turner. Executor
make title Bennet Nolley for 350 acres "where I formerly lived"
called Rich Cove; son in law Samuel Anderson; Exec: John Womack,
John Farrar; Wit: James Mercer, Jemima Mercer, Ann Mercer.
42 HUGH McKEEN -Will - w. 30 Aug. 1781; wife Agness; 6 sons; John
Robertson, sister's son; oldest son Alexander McKeen. Exec:
wife and Thomas Robertson. Wit: Nathaniel Waddill, James Hubbard,
Thomas Robertson.
Probate: Washington County, North Carolina 6 May 1782
Probate: Caswell County, North Carolina July 1784
43 Report of valuation of one acre of land of William Lea on Country
Line Cr. at 2 lbs. 10 sh, and one acre on opposite side of Cr.
at 2 lbs. By David Shelton, Charles Stephens, James Long.

Book B cont. 1784 - 1785
Page
43 Inv. estate of Danl. Sanders by Adam Sanders, adm.
44 Inv. estate of John Scott by Robert Scott, exec.
44 Inv. estate of Patrick Flinn by Susannah Flinn, exec.
45 Inv. estate of Hugh Dobbin by J. Willson, adm.
45 Inv. estate of Thomas Robertson by Penina Hall and Wm. Hall, exec.
46 Sales estate of Benjamin Goodman on 8 Nov. 1782. Sales to:
    Mrs. Mariah Goodman, Samuel, Joseph, and Rhoda Goodman; William
    Brown (HB), John Williams, Hezekiah Rice, Lancelot Johnston,
    William Brown (cooper), Tyra Harris, Alexander Porter, Arthur
    Loving, Thomas Rice, Esq., William Swift.
46 Sale of property of William Berry on 27 Mar 1784. Sales to:
    Hudson Berry, John Brothers, Rebecca Berry, James Barker, Bluford
    Pleasant, Henry Davis, Jonathan Anthony, David Enocks, John Berry,
    James Murry, William Culberson, Joel Corder, Jonathan Murry,
    Bazewell Davis. Return by Benj. Douglas.
48 Inv. estate of Henry Hix. Debts due from Chas.Boulton, Benjamin
    Merritt, John Tarpley. By Eliz. Hix, adm.
49 Allotment of land for Elisabeth Mann from estate of William Mann.
    Land adj. Joseph Gill, Seth Moore. By John Paine, Gabl. Davey,
    John Lawson.
49 Acct. estate of Samuel Bumpass(Sept. 6, 1776),filed by Gabl.
    Davey. Bonds on Rimmer & Fowler, Partee & Philpot, Roberts &
    Rose, Caleb Brasefield, Cragg & Fowler, Merritt & Rose, Knowland
    & Roberts, Richd. Person & Merritt, Stephen Merritt, Hobgood &
    Fowler, Wm. Washington, Knowland & Langston.
    Cash paid to Thomas Murry, Doct. Burk, Wm. Washington for main-
    tenance of children, Moses Bridges, Jno. Anderson, Sarah Bowles.
    Bonds on Jno. Cooper, Wm. McDaniel.
51 Sales estate of Matthew Duty on 20 Apr 1874. Sales to: Benj.
    Debo, Robert Seymour, Jesse Duncan, John Clift, Wm. Duty, Henry
    Fielder, Wm. Harding, Thos. Barnett Jun., Byrd Wall, Joseph
    Gholston, Thomas Neeley, Sollomon Duty, Steven Stuart, Richard-
    son Owen, Mason Foley, James McKnight.
53 James Crumton Jun., son of James Sen., now of age, apprentice to
    Robert McReynolds. Wit: Henry McNeill, Ambrose Arnold.
55 Viney Gallispy, orphan 4 years old, apprentice to Thomas Palmer.
56 Isabella Gilasby, orphan of 6 years 4 months, apprentice to
    Thomas Palmer Sen.
57 Hiram Haralson, orphan of 7 years, apprentice to Lord Lord.
58 Assessments for 1784 and continental tax for 1784.
    Tax collected for building courthouse for 1784.

October Court 1784

59 Inv. estate of John Lyon that was lent to Jane Lyon his widow.
60 Div. estate of Hugh Dobbin(CL), to: Widow, Thomas Dobbin, Mary
    Dobbin, Elisabeth Dobbin, John Dobbin. By A. E. Murphey, Josiah
    Cole, John J. Farley.
62 Appraisal estate of Patrick Flynn.
62 Mary and Elizabeth Hewlett, age 12 years, children of Sarah Hew-
    lett, apprentice to William Morrow. Wit: Wm. Moore, James Grant,
    Jun.

January Court 1785

63 Bill of-Sale: John Black to Thomas Black, sale of 2 negroes, Patt
    and Patience. 12 Jan. 1781. Wit: Abram Fulkerson, Henry Black.
64 Sale estate of Presly Hunt by Henry Fuller.
64 Bill of Sale: Elen Harison to Samuel Harrison for negro girl, Lett.

Book B cont. 1785
Page
65 James Frazier, 7 years, bound by his mother Cathrine Frazier, to
   Thomas Vanhook.
66 DAVID VANHOOK -Will- w. 1 Oct 1781. Wife Lucy; sons Jacob(land
   adj. Breecken and Rose), Kendal (Bankes tract), David (land on
   S. Hico,McMennary Branch), Robert; daughter Sarah. Wit: Alex.
   Rose, John Womack, Wm. Glenn.
67 Power of attorney: George Black to Abram Fulkerson to execute
   deed to Josiah Cole for land on Cane Cr. 11 Oct 1779. Wit:
   Arch Murphey, Shadrack Hudson.
68 JOHN MOORE -Will- w. 22 Oct 1784. Daughters Elizabeth Lightfoot
   Moore, Lucy Moore, Mary Anderson Moore(under 18); sons John
   Moore, Patrick Henry Moore, William Moore; brother Joseph Moore
   to get land in Lunenburg Co. Va purchased of Wm. Williams;
   Wife Lucy. Exec: wife Lucy and brother Joseph, James Sanders
   and Arch. Murphey. Wit: John J. Farley, Rachel Dobbin, Josiah
   Cole.
71 FRANCIS HOWARD - Will - w. 6 Jan. 1784. Wife Sarah; son Francis
   (under 21); ten children: Henry,Groves, William, Francis, Larkin,
   Johnston, Rebeccah, Patty, Betty, Ann. Exec: wife and son Henry.
   Wit: Henry Howard Sen., Wm. Huston, Susannah Allen.
72 Indenture: William Cooper, orphan child, age 9, to Rowland Hewes.
   Wit: Zere Rice.
73 Hiram Cooper, 5 years old, bound to John Anderson.

April Court 1785

74 Inv. estate of John Roberts by John Warrin, adm.
74 Sale estate of James Landman on 8 Dec. 1784 by James Summers.
   Buyers: George Summers, James Summers.
75 Inv. estate of John Moore by Lucy Campbell and J. Campbell. Returned on oath of John Campbell.
76 Inv. estate David Vanhook by Jacob Vanhook, exec.
77 Inv. estate Francis Howard by Henry Howard exec.
78 Inv. estate of John Hodge by Hannah Hodge, adm.
78 MARY LEA - Will - w. 3 Nov. 1784. All my children; daughter
   Sarah Runnals; son George Lea. Exec: James Lea and son George
   Lea. Wit: Richard Eskridge(Jurat), James Lea(Jurat), Geo. Lea,
   Walter Brown.
80 ALEXANDER MILES - Will - w. 28 Sept. 1784. Wife Lucy to get land
   on Country Line Cr.; sons Thomas, John (Land on Rattlesnake Cr.),
   Jacob; daughter Elizabeth. Exec: wife, brother Jacob Miles, and
   John Shelton. Wit: Thos. Slade Sen., Thomas Slade, Jun.

July Court 1785

81 Inv. estate of Alexander Miles.
82 Elizabeth Farley, orphan of Moses Farley, guardian acct. with
   Samuel Johnston.
83 Power of attorney: Laughlin McIlyea to Charles Stephens to execute deed for sale of 330 acres land to William Richmond. Wit:
   William Moore, Meshack Morton.
84 JOHN CATE(S) -Will - w.6 Jan 1785. Granddaughter Ann Pyron;
   Margery Pyron; youngest son Thomas Cate; daughters Elizabeth
   Beary and Nancy Griffin; son Joshua Cate; grandson Joshua Cate;
   grandson Joshua Pyron; John Pyron; grandson John Cate, son of
   John; Wit: Thomas Cate, John Pyron, Jesse Robinson, Joseph Pogue.
85 Bond: Joel, Danl., Prudence, and Elizabeth Ledbetter of Caswell Co.
   and Shadrack Forrest of Orange Co.(all heirs of Henry Ledbetter,
   decd.) all agree to leave estate of decd. in possession of Eddy
   Ledbetter late wife of Henry. Wit: Wm. Glenn, Robert Hicks,
   Binghey Glen.

16

Book B cont. 1785-1786
Page
85 Peter Hamblin, adm. of Stephen Hamblin, returns acct. of estate.

86 FRANCIS SHACKLFORD - Will - w. 18 Feb 1780. Wife Eunice; son
   John; children Rebeccah, Armistead, Nancey, Henry, Absalom,
   Abner, Betsey. Exec: Col. James Sanders, Nathl. Dickerson,
   Olive Terry, Eunice Shacklford. Wit: Bazwell Willson, Thos.
   Jeffreys, Jas. Rainey, Chs. Kennon, James Gilasby.
87 JOHN MITCHELL - Will - w. 22 Sept. 1785. Wife Mary; Robert
   Mitchell Jun., James Simmons; Robert Mitchell son of Arthur
   Mitchell to get whole of estate. Exec: Robert Mitchell. Wit:
   Saml. McMurry, John McMurry.
88 CHARLES BURTON - Will - w.2 Aug 1785. Wife Jean; sons George,
   Edmond, Robert, Charles, Theoderick; daughter Dolly; land on
   north side of main road leading to Dixe's Ferry to be sold;
   land purchased of George Graham to be divided. Exec: wife
   Jean, Capt. Spillsby Coleman, Capt. Robert Payne. Wit: Chas.
   Dixon, Nath. Dickerson, Jonathan Greenhaw.
90 Tax assessments for 1785.
91 John Pearson, orphan of 17 years, apprentice to Robert Willson
   to learn mastery of blacksmith.

92 HENRY WILLIAMS - Will - w. 12 Apr 1785. Wife Elizabeth; sons
   Daniel, Joseph (land purchased from Henslee), Nathan (land pur-
   chased of Thomas Hart), Henry(McVier's old tract). daughters
   Nancy Rice, Elizabeth Williams, Susannah Rice, Ursley Duke
   Peoples, Salley Brookes, Jane Williams; granddaughter Mary
   Slade; son in law William Rice. Exec: wife and son in law Wm.
   Rice, and son Daniel when he arrives at 21. Wit: John Henslee,
   Wm. Brown, Thomas Rice.
96 Bill of sale: Reubin Taylor to Archibald Murphey, sale of negro
   girl Esther, age 19. Wit: James Willson, Thomas Palmer, Tavenor Hightower.
97 Bill of sale: William Stone to Arch. Murphey, sale of slave
   named Cesar, age 26 years. Wit: John J. Farley, John Monroe.
98 DARBY HENLEY - Will - w. 23 Aug 1784. Sons Edmund, James Dunbar
   Henley; daughter in law Lettice; son Darby; grandson Abner Henley, son of James Dunbar Henley; daughter Ann. Exec: sons
   Edmund and James. Wit: Loyd Vanhook, Willson Vermillion, Edmd.
   Roberts. Codicil 6 Nov. 1785: d. in law Lettice.
100 JAMES FLETCHER - Will - w. 10 Dec 1785. Wife Ursley; all children: William, James, Elizabeth, Mary, Sarah, Ursley, Grace;
   nephew Alexander Gray; nephew John Fletcher. Exec: son in law
   Alex Gray and Arch. Murphey. Wit: A. E. Murphey, Wm. Smith,
   Robt. Gray.
101 Elkanah Haralson, 7 years, apprentice to Hugh Barnett Jun.
102 Inv. estate of Francis Shacklford.
103 RICHARD SIMPSON - Will - w. 25 Nov 1783. Wife Mary; daughters
   Susannah Burton, wife of David Burton, Kesiah Buchanan(widow)
   to get land in Kentucky Co. Va., Margret Williamson wife of
   Jeremiah Williamson (land on Horsley Cr. purchased from Natha-
   niel Hart); son Richard Simpson; granddaughter Priscilla Poston; daughters Elizabeth Oldham wife of Jesse Oldham, Sarah
   Hart wife of Nathaniel Hart, Mary Ann Harris wife of Tyra
   Harris, Lidia Tate wife of Zacheus Tate, Ede Nunn wife of Wil-
   liam Nunn, Nancy Tate wife of Waddy Tate. Exec: wife, son
   Richard, son in law David Burton. Wit: John Williams, Jesse
   Oldham, Andrew Huse.

Book B cont. 1786
Page
105 Inv. estate of Charles Burton by Spill Coleman, exec.
106 Sale estate of Jane Davis by Robert Davis, adm.
106 Inv. estate of Jacob Browning by Elizabeth Browning, exec.
107 Sale estate of John Roberts. Buyers: John Warren, Daniel Evans,
   Henry Mitchell, Charles Crummell, Patrick Carnall, Christopher
   Hinton.
108 Inv. estate of James Fletcher by Alex Gray, exec.
109 Mary Davis, 5 years old, bound to Joseph Traylor.
110 List of number of Inhabitants of Caswell County 1786. See page iv.

April Court 1786

111 Inv. estate of Henry Williams by Elizabeth Williams, & Wm. Rice.
113 Bond: James Sanders Esq. appointed by law as Treasurer for County
   of Caswell.
114 Inv. estate of Richard Simpson taken by John Reid, adm. 7 Jan 1786.
115 Inv. estate of Sarah Bowles by John Bowles, exec.
   Sale estate of Sarah Bowles. Buyers: Andrew Yeargin, Jno. Washington, Edmund Colley, David Roberts.
116 Sale estate of John Dowell. Sales to: Henry Black, Mary Dowell,
   James Dowell, Nancey Dowell, Jane Dowell, Philip Hall, Johnston
   Webb, James Long, Nicholas Delone, John Guttery, Elisha Rowark,
   James Pullium.
116 Bill of sale: John Stone to Stephen Stuart, sale of negro named
   Isaac, 2 years old. Wit: Dudley Reynolds.
117 Letter of attorney: David Corbin of Culpepper Co. Va. to John
   Corder and Obed Florance to convey deeds for land which Corbin
   sold in Caswell Co. 4 Feb. 1786. Wit: Wm. McClanaham, justice
   of peace of Culpepper Co., John Bolling, Samuel McGuire, on oath
   of Moses Smith.
118 Bond of agreement between John Dowel and Elisha Rowark for money
   for land sold to Rowark from Dowel on Double Cr.
119 Receipt from Mary Dowell, adm., certifying Elisha Rowark paid for
   land. Wit: Abram Fulkerson.
119 DAVID HALL-Will- w. 26 Sept. 1778. Wife Dorcass; children: Francis, Sarah, William, Dorcass, Edy, Samuel, John. Exec: Edmund
   Alley and wife. Wit: Edmund Alley and Elisabeth Haddock.
120 Reuben Smithey, orphan, apprentice to John Warwick.
121 Jesse Haralson, 17 year old orphan, apprentice to Elijah Haralson.
122 Abram Holsonback, age 11, apprentice to James Jay.
123 Lydia Cate, orphan apprentice to William Bryan(t).
124 John Holsonback, age 16 the 6th June, apprentice to James Jay.
125 William Bush, base born child, apprentice to Robert J. Steele.
126 Bond for county treasurer, Archd. Murphey.
127-8 Bonds for Loyd Vanhook as Entry Taker for Caswell Co.
129 Bond for John Atkinson as Register of Caswell Co. 19 Jan. 1785.
130 A list of state fines collected.
131 Bond for Loyd Vanhook as Entry Taker of land. 17 Dec. 1783.

July Court 1786

133 WILLIAM WILLIAMS - Will- w.   Feb 1786. Son Tobias and his d.
   Priscilla; daughters Mary, Agness, Obedience; Agnes Williams,
   daughter of Obedience Williams (base born). Exec: Friend John
   Campbell and William Rainey.
134 BENJAMIN LONG - Will- w. 18 Apr 1786. Eldest son Benjamin;
   eldest daughter Sarah(land adj. Ambrose Hudgins and Robert
   Southard); 2nd d. Leah; 3rd d. Mary Barnett; 4th d. Martha;
   youngest son Reubin. Exec: son Reuben and son in law Thomas
   Barnett. Wit: Josias Dickson, A. Hudgens, Margaret Southard.

18

Book B cont. 1786
Page
136 JOHN ANTHONY -Will- w. 9 May 1785. Wife Ursley; sons Jonathan,
    James, Elijah, John, William, Joseph; daughters Sarah Berry,
    Nancy Stone, Jane Corder, Elizabeth Anthony. Exec: wife and
    sons Jonathan and Elijah. Wit: Clifton Allen, James Jones.
138 ROBERT RAY - Will - w. 20 Apr 1775. Wife Anns; daughter
    Susannah Ray; other children. Exec: wife, James Ray, William
    Ray. Wit: Arthur Brooks, John Brooks.
139 Inv. estate of David Hall by Dorcass Hall.
140 Additional survey of estate of John Roberts of assets in hands
    of John Warrin, adm. in right of his wife Elisabeth.
141 Inv. estate of John Moore Sen. by Joseph Moore and Montford
    McGehee.
142 Valuation of personal estate of Bartlett Yancey. Estate to be
    divided among widow and ten children. (Names not given.)
    15 July 1786. By John Williams, Robert Blackwell, Alex. Kerr.
143 Elijah Redman, orphan 1 year old, bound to William Swift.
144 Steven Bass binds himself to William Hudgens for rest of his
    life. 28 June 1786. Wit: John Willson, Betty Willson.
145 Lucy Pettiford, orphan of 6 years, bound to William Hudgens.
146 Polly Pettiford, 3½ year old orphan, bound to John Willson.
147 Stephen Pettiford, 1 year old orphan, bound to John Willson.
147 Bond for James Sanders appointed as sheriff of Caswell Co.
    21 July 1786.
148 Bond for James Sanders as sheriff for 1785.

October Court 1786

149 Inv. estate of Benjamin Long by Reubin Long & Thomas Barnett.
150 Inv. estate of John Anthony by Jonathan Anthony.
151 Inv. estate of William Rankin on 2 Oct. 1786 by William Lockhart,
    adm.
152 Acct. of sale of estate of Richard Simpson on 12 Aug. 1786.
    Sales to: Mrs. Mary Simpson, Richd. Simpson Jun., John Reid,
    Capt. Waddy Tate, David Burton, Capt. Zeppa Tate, Jerre William-
    son, John Pepper, Sherwood Nance, George Jackson, John Foote,
    Jesse Oldham.
153 Appraisal estate of Mathew Jouett on 24 Sept. 1782 by Wm. Moore,
    Robert Blackwell, and David Hart. Returned on oath of Thomas
    Brooks, exec.
154 Inv. estate of Gabriel Hews by Danl. Hews, adm.
155 JAMES PHELPS - Will- w. 5 Aug 1785. Wife Mary; sons William,
    Ambrose, Obidiah, Reuben, Thomas, Larken; daughters Lucy, Betty,
    Polly; Mother; Exec: wife and son William. Wit: Shadrack
    Hutson, James Williamson. Proved on oath of John Phelps and
    William Cromwell.
156 Bill of sale: Samuel Morris to James Rice, one negro girl named
    Beck. 19 July 1786.
156 Bill of Sale: John Lea Sen. to William Lea, sale of stock and
    household goods. 11 Aug.1786. Wit: John Rainey, Thomas Rainey.
157 Bill of sale: Stuart Farley to son Daniel S. Farley of Halifax
    Co. Va., sale of negro woman named Lucy "which was willed to me
    by John Farley deceased of Chesterfield Co. Va. at the death
    of his wife Mary Farley". Mary Farley(widow) of John.
    17 June 1786. Wit: Mason Foley, Reubin Graves.
158 Power of attorney: Michael Dixon of Wilks Co. Ga. to Josias
    Dickson to sell lands in Caswell Co. 16 Aug.1786. /s/ Michael
    Dickson.Wit: John Burnett, Isaiah Duest, Hugh Barnett, Thos.
    Barnett.
159 Alexander McIntosh, libel bill to Robert Parks. 13 Sept.1786.

Book B cont. 1786-1787
Page
159 James Shearman, orphan of 10 years, apprentice to Edmund Alley.

January Court 1787

161 Tax assessments for 1786.
161 Acct estate of Stephen Hamlin by Peter Hamlin adm.
162 TYREE HARRISS - Will - w. 1 Sept 1786. Daughters Nancy Aber-
    crombie, Frances Dabney wife of Cornelius Dabney; sons Tyree,
    Simpson, Robert(land in Rockingham Co. on little Troublesome
    Cr.), Christopher (land on High Rock Cr.,Rockingham Co.);
    daughters: Ede Harris, Liddy Harris; grandson William Chapman
    Abercromby. Exec: son Tyree and son Simpson and son in law
    Cornelius Dabney. Wit: John Jones, Jesse Oldham.
164 JOHN RICHMOND SEN. - Will - w. 7 Fab 1786. Wife Rachel; sons
    Joshua, Joseph (land on West end of land the Ridge Road from
    Martha to John to be dividing line); daughter Elizabeth (under
    age); Elder children To Witt Ellinor William Margret Mary John
    & John Langley Martha Jane. Exec: wife Rachael. Wit: Daniel
    McGilvery, Thomas Evans. (Original will has John Langley written
    on margin; has Mathew and Jean rather than Martha & Jane).
165 Agreement between Susannah Turner and Thomas Yancey for main-
    tenance of child. Wit: John Douglas, Robert Parks.
166 NICHOLAS BROWNING - Will - w. 23 Oct 1786. Wife Sarah; Joseph
    Jones to continue where he now lives; daughters Sarah, Jean;
    sons Enos, Francis, John, Charles; daughters Mary and Elizabeth.
    Exec: brother Edmund Browning and Joshua Browning. Wit: Isaac
    Corren, James Hopper. Proved on oath of Isaac Boren.
167 Inv estate of William Williams by John Campbell & William Rai-
    ney exec.
168 JOHN POWEL - Will - w. 16 Nov 1786. Wife; sons James, Charles;
    daughter Elizabeth; rest of children. Wit: Jacob Guttery, Char-
    les Powel, James Brown, Thomas Walters.
169 Mary Cooper alias Gibson in conjunction with James Gibson, acct.
    with Thomas Douglass, guardian for her 6 children. 29 Dec.1786.
169 Sale estate of Jacob Robertson.
170 Power of attorney: William Auston to Hudson Berry to prepare
    deeds for land for Thomas Summons, John Anthony, William Leake,
    Clifton Allen. 11 Nov 1786. Wit: John Yancey, Jonathan Anthony.
171 John Marshall of Warren Co. to John Shelton, sale of 3 negroes,
    Peg, Lucy, & Tom. Wit: Charles Dixon, Thomas Donoho,J Buckhanon.
172 Div estate of William Rankin by John Payne, James Farquhar,
    Robert Payne, and John Satterfield. Div to: Victory Rankin,
    widow; William McVey, James Rankin, Joshua Browning, Benjamin
    Hatcher, William Lockhart, William Robertson, Victory Rankin.
172 Acct sale by Penina Hall, exec. of ? (name not given). Sales to
    Robert Moore, James Bradley, William Hall, John Low, John Hip-
    worth, Charles Ferrell.
173 Gideon Johnston of Rockingham Co. to Archibald Murphey, sale of
    slave Peter age 12. Wit: Allen Walker, Douglas Oliver.
174 Inv estate of Fielding Lewis by Elizabeth Lewis adm.
175 Inv estate of James Phelps on 19 Apr 1786 by Wm. Phelps exec.
175 Money paid by exec of Thomas Robertson to people to whom he owed
    money: Joseph Talbert, Edmund Alley, James Bradley, Archibald
    Samuel, Wm. Rainey, Henry Black, Robert Moore (for schooling
    children), James Robertson, James Montgomery, Wm.Hews, James
    Randolph, James Williams. By Penina Hall exec.

Book B cont. 1786
Page
176 Money received by Penina Hall from debtors to Thomas Robertson:
Henry Black, John James Farley, Thomas Lea, John Rue, George
Samuel, William Gardner, Mr. Hightower.
176 Thomas Payne, 7 year old orphan, apprentice to Artha Brooks.
/s/ Stephen Moore, Chairman County Court.
177 Pryor Payne, 5 year orphan, apprentice to Artha Brooks.

April Court 1787

178 JAMES BRADLEY - Will - W. 15 Jan 1787. Wife Judith; sons
James (land on Dan River), Thomas, John, Edward; daughters
Mary, Susannah Shelton, Elisabeth Lea, Sarah Cochran wife of
David Cochran, Ann Hainey wife of William Hainey. Exec: wife,
sons James & Thomas. Test: James Sanders, Thomas Bradley,
John Bradley.
179 Inv. estate of Moses Moore by Anne Moore.
180 Sales of estate of Danl. Duncan on 30 Jan 1787. Buyers: Mary
Duncan, Jesse Duncan, Nathl. Duncan, Will Rainey, Reuben Newton,
Archd. Murphey, John Campbell, Daniel Merritt. By Mary Duncan,
adm.
181 Inv. of sale of Fielding Lewis and what Elizabeth Lewis, adm.
bought on 22 Feb 1787. Other buyers: John Givins, Wm. McDaniel,
David Allen, Stephen Auston, Jas. Hogue, Jacob Bull, Charles
Bostick, James Buchanan and his brother, Nathan Scoggins, Andw.
Buchanan, B. Newton, Reubin Newton, Byrd Wall.
182 Inv. estate of Tyree Harriss by Cornelius Dabney and Simpson
Harriss, exec.
183 Inv. Tyree Harriss estate by Tyree Harris taken 16 Apr 1787.
184 Acct. sale of estate of Francis Howard. Buyers: Henry Howard
Jun., Groves Howard,Jun., Groves Howard Sen., Peter Badgett,
Martha Howard, Henry Howard Sen., Thomas Owen Sen., Hugh Bar-
nett Sen., James Downey Sen., John Lawson Sen., James Hogue,
Joshua Coffee, Thomas Barnett Sen., Francis Howard, Henry Fullar, James Windfield, Samuel Glaze, Charles Allen, Wm. Allen,
John Long, Reuben Parrott, Reubin Long, Robert Southard, Benj.
Long, Thomas Barnett Jun., Wm. Hudgins, Hiram and Wm. Howard,
Paul Haralson Sen., Seth Moore, Andrew Bush, Charles Bostick,
Will Barnett (son of Hugh), Benj. Newton. By Henry Fullar and
Henry Howard, exec.
186 Memorandum of articles sold by H. Williams, exec. Returned on
oath of William Rice, exec.
187 Appraisal estate of John Richmond.
188 Inv. estate of Jacob Miles, decd. (son of Alex Miles, decd.) by
Joshua Carney. adm. One bond due from Jacob Miles Jun. 16
Apr 1787.
189 Power of attorney: John Smith to friend Benjamin Johnston to
recover from John Rogers his heirs and exec. and from John
Sykes and Yancey Bailey and from estate of Peter Rogers, decd.
of Halifax Co. Va. 31 Mar 1787. Wit: Jno. Moore, Joseph Turner, Abram Roger Turner.
190 Bill of Sale: John Robertson to James Hogue, sale of household
goods. 19 Jan 1787.Wit: Stephen Stewart, H. Haralson.
190 Bill of sale: Duncan Carmical to John Graves Sen., crop of
tobacco and all household furniture. 14 Oct 1786.
Wit: Aza Graves.

21

Book B cont. 1787

July Court 1787

191 STEPHEN WILLIAMSON - Will - w. 23 Mar 1787. Wife Elisabeth
and her 5 children; sons Benjamin and Henry E.; daughters Mary,
Lucy, Martha; daughter Nancy Harrison; Elisabeth Moore wife of
Samuel Moore to get stock bought of Richard Moore. Exec: sons
Benjamin and Henry E. Wit: Jerre Williamson, Nathan Garner.

192 Inv. estate of James Bradley by Judith Bradley, exec. Debtors
to estate: John and William Hainey.

193 Sale estate of Nicholas Browning by Edmund and Joshua Browning,
exec. 26 Jan 1787. Sales to: Horatio Cook, John Hopper,
Joseph Jones, Richard Arnold, Samuel Everett, John Cook, Edmund Browning.

194 Bill of Sale: Tavenor Hightower to John Dobbin, sale of all
household furniture and negro boy Simon, 5 years, negro girl
Abby, 5 years. 10 Dec 1785. Wit: H.J.(?)Taylor, John J.
Farley.

195 Bill of sale: William Stone of Burke Co, Ga., to James Robertson of Caswell County, sale of negro slave Isaac, age 6 mos.
26 Dec 1786. Wit: A. E. Murphey, Alex Murphey.

196 Bond: Elizabeth Guttery and Sarah Sheppard to John Monro and
Capt. John Summers. "Whereas John Sheppard a soldier belong-
ing to the 2nd Regiment of State of North Carolina in the said
Capt. John Summers Company died while in the service of his
country, and whereas Elizabeth Guttery and Sarah Sheppard are
Heirs to said John Sheppard and are entitled to the Wages of
said John for his services aforesaid". Wit: Thomas Tunks,
William Johnston. 1 Sept 1786.

197 Acct. of Elizabeth Farley, orphan, with Samuel Johnston. Cash
paid Andrew Ferguson for estate of Hugh Dobbin.

197 Certificate of acknowledgment; A letter to Court of Caswell by
wife Ede Jones. /s/ James Jones. Henry Willis(Jurat).
10 Jan 1786.

197 Receipt: William Stone receives from James Robertson 180 lbs.
for 3 negroes: Thom, Fanney, and Bek.

198 List of insolvents (required by tax law of 1781):

Nash District

James Archdeacon	B. Egerton	Jos. Shirely
Stephen Auston	Reuben Fletcher	John Shacklford
Edmund Archdeacon	Garret Guttery	David Warrick
Hudgens Burton	Robert Garrot	John Williams
John Cooper	Gabriel Hews	James Wray
Ambrose Christopher	Vincent Harrison	Robert Wray
B. Watson		John Willson

St. James District

William Ashley	Chas. Escride ?	Amos Parker
John Allison	James Floyd	Isabella Roberts
Henry Burnham	William Howel	John Clift
Robert Davis	Obediah Johns	John Hall
	Thomas Johns	

(Lists for remaining 6 districts not included in book.)

October Court 1787

199 "This day Benjamin Egerton of lawful age made oath that his
son John Egerton who was a soldier in the Continental Line
was born March the 5th 1760 and Died at his house in December 1780". 10 Aug 1787.

Book B cont. 1787-1788

Page

199 Bond: James Farquhar and William Lockhart to Justices of Coun-
    Court, 7 Dec 1787. James Farquhar had undertaken to build and
    maintain a bridge over Flatt River at a place known as South
    Fork of Flatt River, a good bridge for passengers and Carriages
    of every denomination for a period of 7 years.

200 A list of State fines collected: The State vs Cornelius Davis,
    Montford McGehee, Thomas Donoho, Richard Currier and wife,
    Henry and George Fullar, John Bradley, Joseph Armstrong, Benja-
    min Hubbard, James Summers, William Hainey, Wm. Moore,Esq.

200 State fines returned to Treas. for 1787: Henry Fullar Jun.,
    Benjamin Boswell, Henry McNeill, Samuel Kelley, John Atkinson,
    William Holderness, Joseph Smith, Byrd Rogers, Samuel Robert-
    son, James Guttery, William Hudgins, Cornelius Dabney,
    George Rudd.

201 Amt. sale of estate of John Moore on 11 Oct 1787. Buyers:
    Douglas Olliver, Wm. Addington, John Campbell; "one cow mention-
    ed in inv. given by John Moore Sen. to Elisabeth L. Moore, his
    granddaughter". By Jos. Moore, James Sanders, J. Campbell.

203 Acct..sales of John Moore Sen. on 13 Dec 1776 by Jos. Moore and
    Montford McGehee.

205 John Moore Jun. to John Moore's estate: accounts to Hugh Kelley,
    Thomas Stuart, George Darby, George Black, Thomas Gimbo, Edmund
    Alley, Henry McMullen, Henry and John Black, Richard Painter,
    Miles Duncan, William Powel, William Wiley, John Barnett, Ed-
    ward Bryant, Abram Rice, Edward Maxwell, Lloyd Vanhook, Mason
    Foley, Nathaniel Comer, William Fulcher, John Chambers, Richard
    Pendergrast, Josiah Shoemaker, Abram Fulkerson, Richard Esk-
    ridge, William Paschall, John Comer. Paid Nath. Venable in part
    legacy. By Joseph Moore and Montford McGehee, surviving exec.
    of John Moore Sen.

207 Power of attorney: Reubin Estis of Burke Co. to friend John Rice
    to manage and carry out lawsuit against Nathaniel Williams of
    Rockingham Co. Wit: Richard Estis, James Rice.

207 Div. estate of Henry Dixon to: Frankey, Susannah, Henry, and
    Robert Dixon; Mrs. Martha Dixon; Wynn, Roger, and Elizabeth
    Dixon. By John Summers, Henry Cobb, Nath. Dickerson.

208 Sales estate of Elkanah Haralson. Buyers: Hugh Barnett Jun.,
    William Breekeen, William Hill, James McNight, Hugh Barnett Sen.,
    Stephen Stuart, Joel Pope, David Womack, Wm. Chambers Jun.,
    Jane Haralson, Jonathan Skeen, Benj. Newton, Joseph Gill, Bart-
    lett Greer, Daniel Blackwell, Alexander Fowler. Debts to Henry
    Horley and John Barnett.
    Estate to be divided between 7 children: Jesse, Reuben, Micajah,
    Bradley, Anderson, Hyram, and Elkanah Haralson

211 William Croston, orphan 2 years old, bound to Hezekiah Rice.

212 Drury Nipper, age 10, son of William Nipper, bound to James Wilson.

January Court 1788

213 Edward Bryant (Doctor) of Caswell Co. sells to John Richmond
    one negro boy named Bob, age 9 years. Wit: William Milbank,
    H. Dobbin, William Richmond.

213 Bill of sale: Thomas Neeley to Robert Willson, sale of negroes.
    12 Jan 1788. Wit: H. Haralson, Thos. Stephens.

214 Bill of sale: John Woody to John Baird of Prince George Co., Va.
    for 73 head of cattle. 2 July 1787. Wit: Francis Ford; John
    Angus.

23

Book B cont. 1788
Page
214 Sale estate of Moses Moore by Anne Moore, adm. 19 Oct. 1787.
Sales to: Anne Moore, Sion Bobbitt, James Cuzzart, George Ander-
son, David Roberts, Daniel Meadows, Thomas Carrington, William
Mangum, Blackmon Pardue, Stephen Merritt, Nathaniel Carrington,
Phillip Pryor, Ephraim Moore, William Duke, Fowler Jones,
Thomas Horton, John Carrington Sen. and Jun., Frederick Rose.
EE paid John Manuel. CVD.
216 Deed of gift: Gideon Patterson to nephew James Sanders, "all my
goods and chattels", inc. negroes and household goods. 19 Jan
1788.
217 Estate of Henry Williams, accounts paid to Donaldson & Stott of
Petersburg, Charles Dixon, Lawrence Vanhook, Wyat Stubblefield,
John Rice Sen., P. Williamson, Benjamin Hubbard, John Windsor,
John McCully, Benj. Spencer, Edwd. Elam, Geo. Barker Sen.,
Lanslot Johnston, Empson Baird, James Gooch, Stephen Williamson.
Expenses paid for carriage of tobacco to Petersburg 5 lbs. 18sh.
Paid John McCulley for shoeing horses to carry tobacco to Peters-
burg 1 lb. 9 sh. 6p. 1786.
Additional accts paid to Richard Oldham, John Herbin, John Rice,
John Graves, Duncan Carmical, Joseph Patterson, Philip Vass,
Joel Rice.
218 CHARLES FERRELL - Will - w. 27 July 1787. Wife Maryann; daughters
Elizabeth, Catherine, Rosey; sons Charles and William. Exec:
wife, Charles Ferrell, Abram Dunaway. Wit: Joseph Swan, William
Yates, Edwd. Bryant.
218 Mary Daniel, base born age 4 years, bound to John Currie.
220 Taxable property for Caswell County for 1787
Acres of land 458006 including 15984 of which is western lands.
Polls 2550
Stud horses, value 17 lbs. 5 sh. 4 pence.
Wheels 14
825 gallons West India Rum
613 bushels salt
633 CT Brown Sugar

April Court 1788

221 Power of attorney: William Rainey to John Eacols Jun. of Halifax
County, Va. to sell and convey 2 tracts of Land in Green Co.,
N. C., 1300 acres on north side of French Broad River and the
other on an island in said river nearly opposite first tract.
21 Apr 1788. Wit: Nathan Farley?, Benj. Douglas, Saml.Johnston.
222 Lye Bill: Mary Taylor wife of Charles Taylor against William
Parks. March 10, 1788. Test: Robert Parks, Elizabeth Scott.
223 Power of attorney: Thomas Willingham to John Douglass to attend
to all personal affairs "the same as if I was present". Feb.
1788. Test: Loyd Vanhook, William Hainey.
224 Deed of gift: Ailsey Winstead to daughter Elizabeth Winstead,
a negro girl Judy. 4 Nov. 1787. Wit: Saml. Harrison.
224 Bill of sale: David Thomas to John Crisp, sale of livestock.
20 Dec. 1787. Wit: Charles Stephens, Robert Long.
225 Bill of sale: David Thomas to John Crisp, sale of negroes.
225 Bill of sale: Ollive Terry to Lancelotte Johnston (Surgeon),
sale of 382 acres land on both sides of Hogan's Creek, whereon
I now live, land purchased of Peter Smith adj. Jean Burton's
land. 4 Apr 1788. Wit: Saml. Watt, Richard Boggess, Hez. Rice.
227 Acct. of sale of estate of Gabriel Hughs 11 Nov 1786. Sales to:
Daniel Hughs, Missis Hews; by Daniel Hews, adm.

Book B cont. 1788
Page
227 Inv. estate of Mary Triplett 10 Feb. 1788 by George Summers, adm.
228 Estimate of debts paid for estate of Thomas Wisdom. Paid to
    James Watkins, William McCraw, Thomas Carson, James Turner,
    Marmaduke Stanfield, Isaac Reaves, David Blair. By Martha Wis-
    dom, adm. Payments to John Graves, William Shelton.
228 Inv. estate of Chas. Ferrell on 22 Apr 1788 by Maryann Ferrell,
    exec.
229 A true inventory (and no strategem) of estate of John Crisp by
    Betsy Crisp, adm. 17 Apr 1788.
230 James Smith, base born child 6 yrs. old, bound to John Currie.
231 Guardian acct.: Richard Simpson Jun. with John Reid. Acct. in-
    cludes going to Fairfax Co. Va. and returning 600 miles and
    expenses attending for 24 days, 9 lbs.; also for moving family
    to his plantation. 23 Apr 1788. By Robert Dickens, Thomas
    Rice, William Moore.
233 Francis Crisp, base born age 5 years, bound to Mary Womack.
234 JOSEPH POGUE - Will - ND   Wife Sarah; sons John, Joseph;
    all surviving children. Test: Peter Farrar (Jurat), James
    Farquhar (Jurat).

July Court 1788

235 James B. Watt, orphan 5 years old, bound to William Rudd.
236 Judith Bush, orphan 1½ years old, bound to John Gately.
237 John Chapman, orphan 13 years the 13 Oct. next, bound to
    William Atkins.
238 JOHN POTEETE - Will - w. 3 Jan 1786. Wife Ann; daughters:
    Elizabeth, Suckey Martin, Hannah Hail, Mary Vaun; sons William,
    Miles, James, John, Richard, Thomas Miles Poteete; grandchil-
    dren, son and daughter(John and Ruth) of son John. Wit: Jacob
    Miles Sen., Richard Cross.
239 Inv. estate of Joseph Pogue by Sarah Pogue, adm.
240 Power of attorney: Solomon Stansbury formerly of Caswell Co. to
    Mary Stansbury (widow) to execute to Thomas Graves and Jacob
    Miles Jun. a deed of tract of land which my Father left me.
    29 Sept 1786. Test: Jacob Miles Sen., Abraham Miles.
241 Inv. estate of Robert Burton on 19 July 1788 by Mary Burton.

October Court 1788

242 Contract of marriage: Richard Ward hath obtained license to be
    Joyned in hole matrimony with Lucy Hedgecock. 20 May 1787.
    Bondsman, Solomon Duty.
243 Taxable property totals for 1788. Included 15780 acres land
    given in on the Mississippi Waters.
243 Bill of sale: David Thomas to Jesse Carter, sale of negro girl
    Lyda. Wit: Thomas Jeffreys.
244 Bill of sale: John Lewis Sen. to exec. of Thomas Dobbin decd.,
    sale of negroes, 4 June 1788. Wit: James Saunders, John Poteet,
    Spill Coleman.
244 Bill of sale: Thomas Douglass to Thomas Evans, sale of negro
    girl Rachael. 2 Oct 1788. Wit: Thos. Neeley, Saml. Greer.
245 Benjamin and Henry E. Williamson, exec. of Stephen Williamson,
    decd., sale of negro girl Silvia, 11 years old, to Archibald
    Murphey.
245 William Lewis to Francis Howard, guardian, acct. filed.
246 Inv. estate of George Barker by Geo. & John Barker, exec.
247 Appraisal estate of John Poteete by Abram Miles, Jacob Miles,
    Thomas Slade Sen.

Book B cont. 1788-1789
Page
248 Bond: 22 July 1788 - Daniel Gold of State of Va. to Nicholas
Delone and William Lea. Whereas Delone and Lea have purchased
a tract of land of 295 acres lying on every quarter of a four
acre lot on which Caswell Court House stands, said land being
the real property of Daniel Gold, but now property of Golus
assignees. Wit: Jesse Carter, William Sawyers, Isaac Vanhook,
Thomas Vanhook.
249 Elizabeth Watkins, orphan 3 yrs. 9 mos. old, bound to John
Carman.
250 James Farrar, orphan of 11 yrs. the 4th of last June, bound to
William Glenn.
251 GEORGE BARKER - Will - w. 7 Mar 1788. Sons: Israel, John (land
known as Ephraim Logue tract and land purchased of Richard
Oldham), James, George (land adj. Orange Co. line known as Jno.
Murtree tract), William; daughters: Susannah Barker, Mary Taylor. Exec: sons George, James, John. Wit: John Henslee, John
Penix, Moses Oldham.
254 WILLIAM PARR SEN. - Will - w. 23 June 1787. Wife Mary; sons:
John (land on Andrew Branch adj. county line), William;
daughters: Elizabeth Brown, Rachael Walker. Exec: son William
Parr and John Walker. Wit: John Sammon, Edwd. Sammon.

January Court 1789

255 HENRY BLACK - Will - w. 21 July 1788. Wife Sarah; 8 children.
Exec: wife; Wit: Abram Fulkerson, Charles Haynie, George Black.
256 SAMUEL HARRISON - Will - w. 11 Oct 1788. Wife Joanah; daughter
Ezbel; my children. Exec: Benjamin Harrison, Sarah Harrison.
Jurat: Samuel Yarbrough, Susannah Wheeler.
256 Sale estate of Henry Williams by Elizabeth Williams, Wm. Rice,
and Daniel Williams, exec.
257 Inv. estate of Samuel Brown. Bonds on James and William Trigg;
taken by William Brown son to the deceased and adm.
257 Inv. estate of William Parr by Wm Parr exec.
258 From July Court 1787: Conditions for leasing by public outcry
bidder of county lots contignous to Court House:
Lot #1, East of Court House; lot # 2 on south side of road;
Lot # 3 bounded on east by court house lot and on west, north
and south by Col William Moore's land. Lots 1 and 2 to be used
for dwelling houses. Lot 3 to be built a good frame dwelling
House of 18 by 32 two stories, the House to be used for Commerce.
259 Acct. sale of Fielding Lewis on 22 Feb. 1787. Buyers: Nathan
Scoggins, Capt. John Given , James Windfield, John Cummins,
James Hogue, Byrd Wall, Charles Bostwick, James Buchanon, Wm
McDaniel, Henry McNeill, Capt. Joshua Coffee, Jesse Duncan,
Reuben Newton, John Noell, Stephen Auston, Jacob Bull, Nathl.
Duncan, Andrew Buchanon, John H. Pryor, Elizabeth Lewis. 1/7
part alloted to widow. By Robert Dickens, Joshua Coffee.
261 Bill of sale: Lewis Williams of Pittsylvania Co. Va. to William
Holt of Halifax Co. Va., sale of negro woman named Doll now in
possession of Richardson Owen. Wit: James Brooks, Martha Parker,
B. Mabrey. 29 July 1788. (Braxton Mabrey)
262 Bill of sale: Tapley Masten Lightfoot of South Carolina to
Richardson Owen, sale of negro woman named Doll, 20 years old.
10 Mar 1788. Wit: John Justis, James Gregory.
262 Bond: John Ragsdale to William Ragsdale Sen. John gives up part
of estate of Wm. Ragsdale for land already given him. 15 Dec.
1788. Test: Thos. Tarpley, Wm. Ragsdale Jun.

26

Book B cont. 1789
Page
263 Bill of sale: Jeremiah Williamson to Robert Blackwell, sale of
    negro man, Tom. Wit: James Williams, William Rice.
264 Deed of gift: William Lea to son in law John McNeill, gift of
    negro girl and her child Clary. 7 July 1788. Wit: J. Atkinson,
    Jean Caddell, Joseph Taylor.
264 Bill of sale: Josiah Chambers, to Arch. Murphey for one negro
    girl named Rachel. Wit: Philip Vass, James Gregory.
265 Bill of sale: Anne Tunks, Thomas Tunks, William Tunks to Herndon
    Haralson, sale of negro boy named Bob. Wit: Ailsey Tunks, A.E.
    Murphey, Benj. Deboe.
266 Tapley Duncan, an orphan 14 years old, bound to John Atkinson.
    Wit: H. Haralson DC (Deputy Clerk).

April Court 1789

267 Div. estate of George Barker by John Rice, Robert Blackwell,
    John Hensley. (Legatees not named.)
268 Bill of sale: Richardson Owen to Archibald Murphey, sale of
    negro girl Esther, 4 years next Aug. Wit: Joseph Taylor, H.
    Haralson.
268 Bill of sale; William Hall and wife, exec. to estate of Thomas
    Robertson,to Asa and Peyton Thomas of Pittsylvania Co. Va.,
    sale of negro woman Nell. Wit: Daniel Merritt, Jacob Pearson,
    Will Yeates.
269 Bill of sale: John Clayton Sen. to Coleman Clayton, sale of house-
    hold furniture and livestock. July 1788. Test: Daniel Clayton,
    John Harriss.
269 Inv. estate of Zachariah Long by Alexander Porter, John Foster.
    14 Mar 1789. Proved on oath of Richard Long.
270 Benj. Shelton, sale of 8 negroes,Mary, Simon, Jude, George, Dice,
    Dorias, Roda, and Lewis, to Armistead Watlington, also 100 acres
    land and all household furniture and livestock. 10 Feb. 1789.
    Wit: Greenwood Payne, John Payne.
271 Inv. estate of Elijah Haralson by Philip Vass, adm.
272 Solomon Cooper, orphan 6 years and 2 mos. old, bound to John
    McCullock.

July Court 1789

273 PATRICK CARNAL - Will - w. 19 May 1789. Wife Mary; sons: Richard,
    Patrick, Hubbard, Archibald, and Flemin(under 15 and youngest);
    daughters: Nancy Mitchel, Mary White, Mildred Olliver, Phanney
    Carnal. Son Patrick to get land bought of William Smith.
    Exec: wife, son Richard, Henry Mitchel and Thomas White sons
    in law. Wit: Thomas Miles, Randolph Buckley, Stephen Underdown.
275 WADDY TATE - Will - w. 14 Jan 1789. Wife Anne; all children.
    Exec: wife, friend Tyree Harriss, son William when he arrives
    at age 17 years. Wit: John Windsor, Richard Windsor, Rebeccah
    Windsor.
276 SHADRACK GREENE - Will - W. 17 Nov 1788. Zachariah Swallow the
    first son of daughter Mary Swallow wife to John Swallow;
    daughter Sarah Cranford wife of John Cranford; daughter Lucrecy
    Alberson wife of Archibald Alberson; son Thomas Humphries Greene;
    daughter Margaret Greene; Wit: Thomas Harrison, John Carmon,
    Cuthbert Thompson. Adm. of estate granted to Ann Greene.
278 Bill of sale: William Paschal, sale of livestock to Arch. Murphey.
278 Bill of sale: Reuben Long to John Paine, sale of negro named Amy.
    9 May 1789. Wit: James Williamson.
279 Power of attorney: Bazilla Human to John Graves to demand right
    of title to land on Reedy Fork, 200 acres. 18 Dec 1783. Wit:
    Thomas Graves, William Carrol.

Book B cont. 1789
Page
280 Inv. estate of Waddy Tate on 16 July 1789 by Ann Tate, exec.
281 Inv. estate of Richard Holman by Chas. Holeman, adm.
282 Power of attorney: Aaron Parker to Samuel Neely to deliver deed
    and convey land whereon Parker lives on both sides Flatt River
    adj. Jeffreys, Wm. Green, and Samuel Neeley unto James Jay.
    20 Oct. 1785. Wit: Robert Paine, Mathew Daniel.
283 Settlement estate of Francis Howard by Henry Howard, exec.
283 Deed: Elisha Rowark to John Hall - a tract of land Rowark bought
    of John Dowell,decd., adj. Philip Hall, James Pullium for Four
    Thousand weight of Tobacco and 50 shillings. 23 Oct 1788.
    Wit: William Richmond, John Sykes.
284 Return of accounts from Mr. Fulkerson to Mary Dowel, adm. estate
    of Jno. Dowel.
    Proved accounts against Jno. Dowel: Js. Williamson, John McMurry,
    Richard Curiar, Jean Dowel, Joseph Atkinson, Elisha Rowark,
    John Dukes, John McMullen, Samuel Woods, Charles Trim, Will
    Glenn, Joseph Palmer, John Paine, Gabriel Lea, Adams Sanders,
    Robert Mitchel, Thomas Douglass, William Hughs, Wm. McDaniel,
    Thomas Palmer, Joseph Armstrong, William Lea, Lawrence Vanhook,
    Richard Atkinson, John Douglass. Due Ann Greer 20 lbs.
285 Accounts paid by estate of John Dowell.
286 Joab Robertson, an orphan 8 years on 20 Oct 1788, bound to
    Philip Thomas.
287 Gideon Robertson, orphan 10 years old last June, bound to Moses
    Street.
288 Winney Simpson, orphan 5 years the 11 May, bound to Billy Hughs.
289 Tyree Harriss Jun.,in account with estate of Tyree Harriss,
    accounts paid to: Thomas Hayse, George Foote Sen., Melon Stacy,
    William Swift, Moses Oldham, John Pepper, Mary Simpson, Jepthah
    Rice, John Brown, John Buchanon, Lanslott Johnston, Jesse Car-
    ter, Mary Robertson, Benj. Spencer, Zephaniah Tate, Cornelius
    Dabney, John Jones, Mary Jones, Peter O'Neill, A. E. Murphey,
    Richard Simpson. Included "To sundrie expenses going down to
    Fayetteville with 5 H hds Tobacco, 25 lb. 2sh. 16 p.
    Acct.reviewed by Jerre Poston, John Rudd, James Williamson.
291 Settlement estate of Ezekial Haralson. Acct. paid to: Elijah
    Haralson, John H. Pryor, Nathan Byas, Thomas Douglass, David
    Boyd, B. Ridley, William Howard for schooling the children,
    Wm. McAden, Moses Walker, Paul Haralson, Edward Buckley.
    Approved by A. E. Murphey, Yancey Bailey.
292 Additional accounts of John Rogers, exec. to: Fielding Lewis,
    Reubin Newton, Henry Newton, Will and James Guttery, Nathan
    Scoggin, John Barnett Sen., Richard Escridge, John Ogletree,
    Samuel Warrin, Herbard Hawkins, Charles Bostwick, William Haw-
    kins Jun., Barnett Foley, Philemon Hawkins, Wm. Barnett, Solo-
    mon King, John Sutton, Henry Fullar, Wm. Stone, John Rogers
    Jun.&Sen., Arthur Brooks, Henry Willis, Wm. Southard, John
    Clift, Henry Clift, Joshua Johnston, Hackley Warren, James Kid.
293 Acct. estate of Daniel Sanders by Adams Sanders, adm. Acct paid
    to John Douglass, James Bradley Jun.

October Court 1789

294 RICHARD MINCEY- Will - (also written Minsey). w. 17 June 1789.
    Wife Judy. Exec. wife. Wit: Beverly Glenn, William Evans.
294 NATHANIEL FARLEY - Will - w. 16 May 1789. Wife Salley; sons
    Robert Burton Farley, Laban Farley, George Farley; daughters
    Elizabeth, Polly, Nancey. Exec: William Willson & John Burton.
    Wit: Will Keeling, Absolom Adams, William Willson.

28

Book B cont. 1789-1790
Page
296 Bill of sale: Thomas Palmer Jun. for 130 lbs. paid him by Thomas
    Palmer Sen. sale of livestock and household furniture also
    farming implements. 5 Jan 1789. Proved on oath of Joseph Pal-
    mer.
297 Bill of sale: Armistead Watlington to Benj. Shelton. (Reversal
    of bill of sale on page 270.) 20 Oct 1789.
298 Letter of attorney: Samuel Robertson about to leave the State
    with intent to move to Kentucky to David Shelton and James
    Robertson to convey tract of land on the main road by Col. James
    Sanders to Terry's back line, 125 acres, to Wm. Stephens.
    1 Sept 1789. Wit: Jacob Williams, James Willis,
299 Inv. estate of Patrick Carnal appraised by Goodloe Warren, Step-
    hen Olliver, Robert Moore. 24 Sept 1789.
300 Inv. estate of James Barker by Susannah Barker, adm.
301 Sales estate of Elijah Haralson. Sales to: Jacob Bull, Sarah
    Haralson,Widow; John Henry Pryor, John Chambers, Philip Vass,
    Robert Seymore, Stephen Stuart, James Paul, Wm. Jamison, Joseph
    Beedles, John Holloway, Arthur Brooks Jun.,Will Barnett, Josias
    Chambers, Will Chambers, John Burch, John Givens. By Philip
    Vass, adm.
302 Inv. estate of John Colman on 12 Oct 1789 by Elizabeth Colman,adm.
303 Inv. estate of Will Cummins on 19 Sept 1789 and acct. of sale.
    By Benj. Johnston, exec. and Isaac Bright in right of his wife
    Martha Cummins.
303 Inv. estate of Shadrack Greene by Ann Greene, adm.
303 Inv. estate of Aron Christenbury, on 19 Oct 1789 by John
    Christenbury, adm.
304 William Bush, orphan 5 years old last Xmas, bound to John Gately.
305 Elizabeth Bush, orphan of 10 months, bound to John Gately.
306 Taxable property for 1789.

                    January Court 1790

307 HANNAH DONALDSON - Will - w. 3 Aug 1789. Son Robert to get money
    in John Lawson's hands; daughters Mary, Rachel Dickson, Eliza-
    beth Noell, Hannah Breeze, Jane Ellison, Cateen Archdeacon, Sarah
    Wilkerson, grandsons Barnerd Donaldson and Thomas. Exec: John
    Lawson Sen. and his son David Lawson. Wit: Hugh Barnett, Fran-
    cis Lawson.
308 JOHN CURRIE - Will - w 20 Nov 1789. Wife and her son James;
    Sons: James (Nunns Cabbin tract), Hugh (Buckhill tract), William;
    daughters Mary, Elizabeth, Catherine, Martha, Margaret. Exec:
    3 sons. Wit: James Ray, Mary Currie Sen., Ann Murphey. Proved
    on oath of Mary Currie.
310 JOHN WALKER - Will - w. 14 June 1789. Wife Rachel; Son Thomas,
    youngest and under 16; children: Betsy, Benj.,William, Polley,
    Barbery, Thomas. Exec: wife, William Parr, brother Thomas Wal-
    ker. Wit: Saml. Paul, Judith Paul, Mary Parr.
311 JAMES GRAVES - Will - w. 9 Apr 1781. Sister Ann Yancey; brother
    Thomas Graves. Exec: brother Thomas Graves and Bartlett Yancey.
    Wit: Bazilla Graves, John Graves Sen. Proved on oath of Bazilla
    Graves and Azariah Graves who made oath that he believed John
    Graves Sen. was a concuring evidence to the said will at the
    time of executing same. Thomas Graves qualified as exec.
312 Inv. estate of Nathaniel Farley on 1 Nov 1789 by Wm. Willson.
313 Edith, Lydia, and Christopher Harriss, orphans of Tyree Harriss,
    guardians acct. with Cornelius Dabney. Reviewed by Thos. Donoho,
    Joshua Coffee, Stephen Moore.

Book B cont. 1790
Page
316 John Allison Sen. apprentices his son John Allison Jun. to John
Commins to learn art of slay making. Wit: Robert Gray, James
Commins.
317 Joshua Cate and William Person, one of the county of Warren and
other of county of Caswell, release quit claim unto Charles Holeman. 8 Jan 1790. Test: Richard Holeman.
318 Spillsby Coleman, treasurer's bond. Bondsmen: John Williams,
David Shelton, Will Rainey.
319 Bill of sale: John Minzes of Rockingham Co. to Archibald Murphey,
sale of livestock. 29 May 1789. Wit: John Lock, John Williams.
319 Bill of sale: Jesse Duncan to Archibald Murphey, sale of livestock.
320 Allotment to Simpson Harriss his part of negro from estate of
Tyree Harriss. By David Hart, Robert Blackwell, Benj. Spencer.
320 Acct. estate of Edward Bumpass by Hugh McVey. For clothing and
boarding 6 children, the orphans, for 1778-1789, 5 lbs. 2 sh.
10 pence per year.
321 Acct. of William Lea, trustee for Caswell County for 1787.
321 RICHARD BROOKS (spelled Brookes on original) - Will - w.3 Oct.1789.
Wife Ann; 4 youngest children William Bird Brooks (under 21),
Betsy Brooks, Frances Armstead Brooks, John Brooks; daughter
Ann Smith Graves; Exec: wife Ann and son in law Solomon Graves.
Wit: W. F. Smith, Israel Barker.

April Court 1790

323 THOMAS TUNKS - Will - w. 20 Nov. 1789. Wife Rachael to get land
adj. Rachael Love, John Chambers, Wm. Barnett; sons William,
Thomas, Philip; daughters Frances, Ann. Exec: wife and son
William. Wit: Jno. Chambers, Thomas Barnett, Benj. Deboe.
324 THOMAS BAXTER - Will - w. 24 June 1785. Wife Catherine;
son William (land adj. Paul McClarney's line); 3 young sons
John, James, and Robert; daughters Jane, Caty, Rachael; son
Thomas. Exec: wife Rachael and son William. Wit: John Sammon,
Caty McClarney.(Original will spelled Backster;exec.wife K Backster)
325 Div. lands of Benjamin Ingram, decd., between his 3 sons James,
John, and Charlton Ingram. Land on main road adj. Miles old
corner and Graves line. 8 Mar 1790. By Jerre Poston,surveyor,
Abram Miles, John Kennon, Samuel Henderson, Thos. Miles Sen.,
Joshua James.
326 Inv. Property of John Currie by James, Hugh, and William Currie,
exec.
328 Inv. estate of Stephen Williamson by Benj. Williamson, exec.
329 Acct. of Cornelius Dabney, exec. of Tyree Harriss. Acct. paid to
Doctor Johnston, Mary Simpson, Richard Simpson.
329 Inv. estate of John Walker on 15 July 1789 by Wm. Parr, exec.
330 Power of attorney: John Jackson to John Terrill to make deed to
convey land on Reedy Branch adj. Samuel McMurray, David Mitchell,
to Jonathan Terrill. 21 Apr 1787. Test: Thomas Cole, Hermon
Hopper, Thomas Willingham.
331 Power of attorney: Ann Tate, exec. of Waddy Tate, to John Reid to
go to Fairfax Co. Va. and receive from Richard Simpson, exec.
to Moses Simpson,decd., all legacy bequeathed to Ann by Moses
Simpson. 17 Apr 1790. Wit: Mary Simpson, Jerre Williamson,
George Foote.
332 Power of attorney: Thomas Brooks Sen. chosen by Henry Flipping,
orphan of Thomas Flipping late of Gloucester Co. Va. decd.,as
his guardian and was appointed by court of Caswell, appoints
trusty friend Thomas Brooks Jun. lawful attorney to demand and

Book B cont. 1790
Page
    receive from estate of Thomas Flipping decd. in Gloucester
    Co.. Va. all negroes, money, etc. due to said orphan. 20 Apr.
333 Estate of Moses Farley in acct. with Jno. James Farley, exec.
    (From 1775-1790). Accounts paid to: William Wiley, Capt. John
    Moore, John Williams, Geo. Farley, Abram Fulkerson, Mason Foley,
    James Phelps, Robert Scott, John Erwin, John Hodge, Wm. Thomas,
    James Brooks, Saml. Johnston guardian for Elizabeth Farley.
    Received from Charles Mason by wages in the Army 2 lbs, 13 sh.
    9 pence.
335 Same acct. as on page 333 recorded in error. /s/ A. E. Murphey.
336 William Lewis, an orphan 16 years old next Oct, bound to
    Thomas Owen.

July Court 1790

337-339 Deeds of trust and Bills of sale: John Lewis Sen.(M), John
    Lewis Jun.and Sarah Taylor wife of Philip Taylor (Sarah Taylor
    daughter of John Lewis Sen.) - sale of negro slaves to John
    Lewis Jun and Sarah Taylor. Wit: David Allen, N. Cuningham.
340 JOHN LEWIS of Halifax Co. Va. - Will - w. 8 June 1787.
    Wife Catherine; son John to have all land in Halifax Co. Va.;
    son John as trustee to daughter Sarah Taylor; daughter Apphea
    Allen . Exec. son John, Maj.David Allen, John Pettit.
    /s/ John Lewis Sen.(M). Wit: John Winters, Archer Walters,
    John Roper.
341 HENRY FULLAR SEN. - Will - w. 15 Fab. 1788. Wife Catharine;
    daughters Sarah Majors, Keziah Reynolds, Elizabeth Rankin,
    Mary Fullar, Anne Fullar; sons John, Peter, Henry, George,
    Abraham, Stephen, Isaac, Jacob, Isaiah. (Land on Stories Cr.)
    Exec: wife and son George. Wit: Josias Dickson, Chas. Mitchell,
    Michael Dickson.
344 THOMAS HARRISON SEN. - Will - w. 3 May 1790. 2 daughters Arsay
    Fuqua wife of John Fuqua, Magdalen McDugal; friend David Shel-
    ton. Tract of land to be conveyed to Thomas Jeffreys bounded
    by Bradley's line and Cochran's Spring branch. Exec: David
    Shelton. Wit: William Draper, Bowler Stephens, Samuel Pittard.
345 Sale estate of Tyre Harris on 8 Mar 1787. Sales to:
    Tyree Harriss Jun.

Joseph Montgomery	Michael Leathers	Hugh Robertson
Daniel Atkins	Joel Triplet	Joel Johnston
John Swift	Hezekiah Rice	John Johnston
Jeremiah Poston	Anthony Swift	Henry Dunlap
Jeremiah Tate	Joseph Dorris	Wm. Hornbuckle
Newton Foot	Geo.Foote Jun.	Nichols Smith
Peter Neill	Sherwood Nance	Cornelius Davis
Charles Hughs	Nathan Williamson	Richard Dill
John Jones	Benj. Spencer	Jepthah Rice
James Hughs	Martin Winsor	Richard Simpson
Thomas Swift	Malon Stacy	Joseph Street
George Summers	John McCullock	Prestley Harding
John Williams	Anderson Butler	Moses Oldham
John Herbin	Ede,Lydia,Robert,& Simpson Harriss.	

349 Acct.of Ede Harris with Tyree Harriss, guardian.
350 Div. estate of John Crisp among his heirs, namely: Elizabeth,
    Margaret, John, Mary Ann, Lucy, and Thomas Crisp. By Abram
    Fulkerson, Thos. Donoho, Will Richmond.

31

Book B cont. 1790
Page
351 Acct. and settlement estate of Mathew Jouet to legatees: John
Brown, John Jouet, Elizabeth Jouet, Jepthah Rice, Washington
Jouet, Armstead Rogers, Mary Jouet, Mathew Jouet, Thomas
Jouet. 19 July 1790. By Lancelotte Johnston, Robert Blackwell, Peter O'Neill, John Williams.
353 Inv. estate of Thomas Baxter on 3 Jan 1790 by Catherine Baxter.
353 Inv. estate of John Burch by Jane Burch, adm.
354 Sale estate of John Walker by William Parr on 18 June 1790.
Sales to: Findal Roland, Eliz. Walker, Col. Wm. Dix (John Winter security), Richd. Watson, Archd. Alverson, James Burton,
sheriff.
354 Bill of sale: David Mann, Sarah Mann, and William Ford Mann to
James Rankin, sale of negro woman Cloah. 5 Apr 1790. Wit:
John Paine, James Williamson.
355 Deed of gift: John SmithHurst to daughter in law Sarah Parker,
two negroes Newman and Dilce. 6 July 1790. Wit: Joseph
Taylor Sen., Joseph Taylor Jun.
356 Deed of gift: John SmithHurst to daughter in law Ann Parker,
two negroes Jobe and Tilla. 6 July 1790.
356 Bond: Thomas Brooks as High Sheriff of Caswell Co. Bondsmen:
John Brown, Thos. Donoho, Yancey Bailey.
358 Miss Elizabeth Farley, acct. with Samuel Johnston, guardian.

October Court 1790

359 WILLIAM SAWYER - Will - w. 16 Jan 1787. Sons: William(land
on east side Graves Mill road), Stephen, Absalom (plantation
I now live on). Wit: John Payne, Ann Sawyer, Dyce Sawyer.
360 Mournin (female), a mulatto orphan 3 years next March, bound to
Andrew Haddock.
361 Inv. estate of Robert Burton on 15 Oct 1790 by Joseph Dameron.
362 Thomas Sutton orphan 2 years old last Aug., bound to Edward
O'Neill. By Thomas Rice, Esq. on behalf of the Justices.
363 Bond: Thomas Brooks as Treasurer of Caswell Co. Bondsmen:
Thomas Rice, Benj. Williamson, Yancey Bailey, Daniel Williams,
Jethro Brown, James Williamson. 18 Oct 1790.
364 Bill of sale: Hannah Miles (widow) to Jacob Miles Sen., sale of
livestock, household goods, and "everything I possess", for
30 pounds. 18 Feb. 1790.
364 Sale of estate of Samuel Greer on 31 July 1790 by Margaret
Greer and Will Culbertson, adm. Buyers:

Margaret Greer	John Currie	John Turner
Samuel Motheral	Pemberton Burch	Alex McIntosh
John Low	Charles Taylor	James Smith
Joseph McReynolds	James Guttery	Robert Motheral
Richard Johnston	William Powel	Edwd. Nowel
John Atkinson	John Hightower	John Kimbrough
	William Culbertson	

365 Those receiving from adm. of estate of John Crisp: Baylor Burch,
James Wilson, Richard Burch Jun., John Crisp. Wit: William
Walker, John Crisp, William Brown, Baylor Burch. 4 Mar 1790.
366 Estate of John Walker in acct. with Will Parr, adm.
367 Inv. estate of Thomas Vanhook by Isaac Vanhook, adm.
367 Inv. of John Moor, decd. To John Campbell guardian for Mary A.
Moore (orphan).
368 Inv. of estate of Henry Fullar by George Fullar and Catherine
Fullar. 18 Oct 1790.

Book B cont. 1790-1791
Page
369 Inv. estate of Samuel Greer on 5 June 1790. By Margaret Greer
and William Culbertson, adm.
370 Power of attorney: Thomas Johnston of Shenandoah Go. Va. to
David Jones to convey 300 acres land on South fork Country Line
Cr. to Elizabeth Browning now living on the premises. 13 Aug
1790. Wit: John Carter, Moses Smith, James Johnston. By
John Hutcheson, Justice of Shenandoah Co.
370 Amt. sales of part of property of Henry Fullar. 30 July 1790.

January Court 1791

371 Taxable property for 1790.
371 Inv. estate of John Shy on 6 Nov. 1789. By Rachel Shy & Samuel
Shy, adm.
372 Sale estate of Thomas Harrison 4 Aug 1789. Sales to: David Shelton, Abner Qualls, Mathew Harriss, Edmund Alley, John J. Farley,
William Roper, Peter Harrill, John Low, Ralph Hubbard, William
Ragsdale.
373 Received of Major Greene, guardian of Elizabeth Jones Dilahay
and Nancy Gilliam Dilahay, orphans of Arthur Dilahay, household
articles for legacy left by said Arthur Dilahay. 17 Jan 1791.
374 Christopher Harriss, orphan, in acct. with Corn. Dabney. Payments to John Lenox, Richard Smith.
375 Power of attorney: Robert Culbertson, Laurence Co. South Carolina,
to Joseph Culbertson to convey land on Hico and Country Line
to William Culbertson. 17 Sept 1787. Wit: Edmund Browning,
Rob Ross.
376 Solomon Morgan, orphan 4 yrs. 8 mos. old, bound to Martin Cooper.
/s/ John Douglass, chairman county court.
377 William Gill, orphan 16 yrs. old, bound to Byrd Rogers.
378 Patsy Gill, orphan 12 yrs. old, bound to Byrd Rogers. /s/ Stephen Moore for the County Court.
379 State fines returned to Treas. for 1790-91 from:

Robert Moore	Henry Fullar	Henry McClarney
John Currie Jun.	James Gregory	Will Dix
Will Yellock	Thomas Yates	Hugh Dobbin
William Hainey	Robert Donaldson	John Reece
Thomas Stafford	Edwd. Doyle	James McClarney
James Messer	James Rankin	James Robertson
Jacob Williams	Paul Williams	Richd. Boggus
John Buckhanon	Robert I. Steele	Geo. Samuel
	John Maleer	

April Court 1791

380 Caswell Co. in acct. with William Lea, Trustee.
381 Estate of John Moore in acct. with James Sanders and Joseph
Moore, exec. from 1786-1790.
Payments to: John Low for Doctor Lancelotte Johnston

Jonathan Allen	Robert Moore	John Yancey
Col. Wm. Moore	George Wiley	Thomas Jeffreys
Edmund Lewis	George Black	Thomas Lipscomb
Thomas White	Ambrose Arnold	Josias Cole
Hugh Dobbin	Miss Rachel Dobbins	John Campbell for
Joshua Carney	Robert Willson	board of Betsy &
		Lucy Moore

By Adams Sanders & James Williamson

33

Book B cont. 1791
Page
383 Estate of John Moore decd. acct. since 1781 by John Campbell.
385 Estate of John Burch in acct. with Jane Burch, adm. Accts. paid
    to: James Lea, Andrew Warwick, Lewis Evans, Anthony Samuel,
    William Hainey, Elisha Rowark, William Warren, Joseph Atkinson,
    Elijah Reynolds, Thomas Dunn, **Pulliam Williamson**, Robert Mitchel,
    Elias Wallis, John Johnston(Taylor), William Dollarhide, James
    Robertson, Edward Doyle, Nicholas Delone, Thomas Neeley, Fulker-
    son & Black; approved by John Douglass, Adams Sanders, John
    McNeill.
387 Bond: John Man and William Man bind themselves to comply with
    the disposition by Andrew Barnett and Thomas N. Williams chosen
    as arbitrators to decide controversy with regard to a land dis-
    pute. Wit: William Sheppard, Danl. Hicks, Nimrod Ellis, Peter
    Fullar.
388 Arbitration between John Mann and William Mann: John Mann do give
    unto William Mann full possession of tract of land whereon widow
    Mann now lives, 152 acres, and that John Mann do give unto
    Thomas Mann when he arrives at age that tract of land which is
    believed to be his Father's property bought by him of John
    Cooper. 25 Jan 1791. By William Sheppard, Andrew Barnett,
    Thomas N. Williams.
389 AMBROSE LONG - Will - w. 10 Nov 1790. Wife Elizabeth; small
    children; daughters Elizabeth, Frances, Susannah; sons Reuben,
    John(land adj. Isiah Bull,Hugh Barnett, & Pryor), James(land
    adj. Trickey & Pryor), Jesse; daughters Anne Clift, Clary
    Harriss, Judith Carver. Exec: wife and son Reuben. Wit:
    Reuben Long, John Barnett, Rebecca Long.
390 Inv. estate of Andrew Enochs.
391 Sale estate of Andrew Enochs. Sales to: (Feb. 14)

Elizabeth Enochs	Charles Taylor	John Turner
Thomas Yancey	David Enochs	James Yancey
Benjamin Enochs	James Turner	Daniel Burford
James Culbertson	Joseph Culbertson	William Warren
William Dorriss	Thomas Graves	John Kimbrough
Jesse Robertson		Benjamin Shelton

392 Inv. estate of Edmund Gardner by Francis Smith, adm. 18 Apr 1791.
392 Part inv. estate of Samuel Harrison 18 Mar 1791 by Benjamin
    Harrison, exec.
392 Bill of sale: David Man to Isaac McCollum, sale of negro girl
    Aggie. 24 Feb 1791. Test: Alex Grayham, James Williamson.
393 Sundries sold by Vendue by adm. of John Shy 10 Feb 1791.
    Buyers:

Saml. Everet	James Guttery	John Shy
Rachel Shy(widow)	Thomas Yancey	Daniel Burford
Saml. Shy	Abram Hanks	William Leake
Jesse Scott	John Barnhill	Robert Stuart
John Millington	Polly Shy	John Brothers
Jonathan Anthony	Sally Shy	John McMenemay
Henry Davise Jun.	Richard Arnold	Larken Hearndon
James Byrd	Robert Mitchel	Will Pleasant
James Colman	Mary Linch	Andrew McClary

    Notes on Jesse Shy, Mary Shy, Samuel Shy, Samuel Everet, John
    Shy. Test: Samuel Shy, adm.
395 Inv. estate of John Shy on 3 Jan 1791. /s/ Martha Lay adm.
395 Amount sale of John Moore which feel into hands of John Campbell.

34

Book B cont 1791
Page
397 Inv. estate of Ezekiel Dollarhide 19 Apr 1791 by Robert Long
    and John McMullen, adm.
398 Div. estate of Jonas Parker decd. by John Day and William Yar-
    brough 16 Apr 1791. Legatees: Francis Parker, Abner Parker,
    Rebeccah Parker, Richard Parker, Stephen Parker, David Parker,
    Powel Parker, Jesse Allen, John Roberts, Martin Cooper,
    Joannah Parker.
400 Bill of sale: William Chambers to William Ervine, a negro named
    Dinah about 16 years old. 6 Oct 1790. NB: Ervine to deliver
    Dinah at Andrew Fergusons in the forks of Hico.
401 Power of attorney: Martha Fury to friend Jonathan Anthony to
    receive from Charles McIntosh amount of debt due Martha Fury.
    22 Apr 1791. Wit: Louis Vanhook, Jerre Poston.
401 Power of attorney: Jeremiah Williamson late of Caswell County
    to friend John Reed to bring suit and collect "my part of estate
    of Richard Simpson decd. of Fairfax Co. Va." 22 Nov 1790. Wit:
    John Jackson, Jesse Brintle(Jurat).
402 Oath of insolvency: On 8 Feb 1791 Edward Bryant was brought by
    Joaler and made oath the under amount is all that he is worth,
    working tools his wearing apparel and muster arms excepted.
    To 4 Dollars lent, small quantity of medicine, 3 small books.
    Wit: Jno. Douglass, Robert Payne, Thos. Douglass. Executions
    by Enoch Ferril, Will Ragsdale, Robert Burton.
403 Kinchen Goss, orphan of 7 years last Jan. , bound to Charles
    McMurray.
404 William Wyat, orphan of 5 years next March, bound to John
    Hipworth.

July Court 1791

405 Nancy Sutton, orphan 7 years old the 18 Sept. next, bound to
    William Waire.
406 Mary Sutton, orphan 9 years 28 Dec. next, bound to William
    Waire Sen.
407 ROYAL BOMAN - Will - w. 20 June 1791. Wife Elizabeth; sons Leah,
    Thomas(land adj. Sanders and Simon Roberts); son in law Simon
    Roberts; sons Joseph Royel Boman, Samuel Boman(land in Char-
    lotte Co. Va.), Leonard Boman, Robert Boman. Debt due Jesse
    Carter to be paid. Exec: John Zachary, Thomas Boman, Simon
    Roberts. Wit: William Sawyer(Jurat), Jonathan Starkey(Jurat).
409 THOMAS PALMER - Will - w. 11 May 1784. Wife Susannah;
    son Joseph; rest of children: John, Philip, Sarah Vanhook,
    Susanna Petters, Bashaba hale, Mary Wooden; son Thomas. "I
    order one acre of land never to be sold where son David is
    buried." Exec: wife and son Joseph. Wit: John Hall, Francis
    Howel, David Travis.
410 Bill of sale: Alexander Morrison to Hearndon Haralson, sale of
    negro slave Sally, 35-40 years old. 31 May 1791. Wit: A. C.
    Murphey, Benj. Deboe.
411 William F. Mann of Wilks Co. Ga. and John Mann of Amelia Co. Va.
    and David Mann ot Caswell Co., bill of sale to Jesse Satterfield
    for one negro boy named Jack. 19 Feb 1791. Wit: J. McCollum,
    James Rankin, Kindle Vanhook.
411 Bill of Sale: Joseph Atkinson to Laurence Lea, sale of livestock
    and household goods. 11 July 1791. Wit: William Lea, Zachariah
    Evans.
412 Bill of sale: John Robertson to Hugh Hemphill, sale of livestock
    and household furniture. 14 May 1791. Wit: H. Haralson, George
    Black.

Book B cont. 1791
Page
413 Bill of sale: John Atkinson to William Lea, sale of furniture.
Wit: Richard Atkinson, L. Lea.
414 Sale estate of Ezekiel Dollarhide on 13 May 1791. Buyers:

Elizabeth Dollarhide	Gabriel Murphey	Jesse Duncan
Mary Dollarhide	Willm. Ring	William Gallaher
John Hall	John Burch	Stephen Madden
Robert Long	Henry Cooper	Pulliam Williamson
William Dollarhide	Thomas Yates	James Wallox

By Robert Long and John McMullen, adm.
416 Appraisal estate of James Barker by Robert Parks, John Graves,
Thomas Graves. 15 Mar 1791.
417 Inv. estate of Thomas Clayton by Sarah Clayton, adm.
418 Sales of estate of Thomas Vanhook on 29 Nov 1790. Buyers:

John Christianbury	Loyd Vanhook	Samuel Motheral
John Hall	John McNeill	Thomas Steele
Widow Sally Vanhook	Philip Hall	Samuel Neeley
Isaac Vanhook	Joseph Palmer	William Everit
Benjamin Jacobs	Thomas Neeley	Jeremiah Samuel
Laurence Vanhook	Abram Hargis	Nicholas Delone

419 Inv. estate of Ambrose Long by Reuben Long, exec.
420 Sale estate of Samuel Harrison 6 May 1791. Buyers:

Osborne Jeffreys	John Winstead	Cotance Winstead
Samuel Wheeler	Benj. Harrison	Charles Winstead
Ellen Harrison		

421 The exec. of Henry Williams in acct. with Joseph Williams
orphans. 17 July 1791. Approved by David Hart, Lanslotte
Johnston, James Williamson.
422 Additional inv. estate of Thomas Vanhook;
One lottery ticket for Lott of land in Nicholas Delones and
Will Leas lottery in Leasburgh. Notes against Charles Bostwick,
Will Glenn, Wm. Dollarhide, John Sizemore of Halifax Co. Va.;
Willm. Carpenter for 25 bushels boiled salt to be delivered
on Bear Creek Onslow Co.
Among debtors on Book:

Nathan Cunningham	Samuel Evanse	Jesse Benton
Edward Clay	Henry Burton	Gabriel Davy
John Douglas	James Rankin	William Fullar
Henry Stephens	John Lea Sen.(Coun-	John Fullar
Moses Glidewell	try Line)	Archd. Fullar
Wat Harriss	Thomas Cates	Joseph Gold
Meshack Gentry	Reubin Newton	Wilson Vermillion
Lewis Greene	Richard Stiles	James Roberts
Archd. Carmeal	Joseph Palmer	Peyton Morton
John Lea	Jonathan Skeene	Nathan Scoggins
John Low	Charles Trimm	John Cushaw
Arthur Brooks	John Burch	Edmund Roberts
John Brooks	Joshua Browning	Henry McNeill
Josiah Chambers	John Clixby	Carter Lea
John Commins	Wm. McKnabb	George Black
Jacob Humble	James Reynolds	John Atkinson Car-
penter

424 Inv. estate of Solomon Thrift 19 July 1791 by Sarah Thrift, adm.
424 James Burn Watts, orphan 8 yrs. 6 mos., bound to Job Siddle.
425 Hannah Wyatt, orphan 3 yrs. old, bound to William Slade.

Book B cont. 1791
October Court 1791

Page
426 JOHN KERSEY of Cornwell Parrish in Charlotte County (Va.) -Will-
w. 26 Sept 1786. Wife Ursley; sons Thomas, John, Drury; William
son of Drury; daughter Elizabeth; Exec: 3 sons. "I desire my
estate should not be appraised". Wit: Drury Vaughn, Elizabeth
Runnolds, Erwin Wood.
427 SAMUEL DYER - Will - w. 20 Jan 1791. Wife Elizabeth to get land
at the place known as Hew Warry; sons Thomas, Samuel, Anthony;
daughters Catherine, Mary; Exec: William Stephens, Jerre Samuel,
Anthony Samuel. Wit: John Ragsdale, George Moore, Solomon
Merritt.
428 JOHN PERKINS - Will - w. 29 Dec. 1787. sons Martin(land on
Moons Cr.), Jesse; daughters Ann Foster, Sarah Mattocks,
Susannah Baker; wife Rachel. NB Son James Perkins.
Test: Wm. Morgan, Nancy Morgan.
429 MARY MONTGOMERY - Will - w. 26 May 1791. Sons Michael, James;
daughter Jane Maxwell; exec: Henry McAden. Wit: Thomas Ralph,
Henry McAden.
431 Inv. estate of Thomas Palmer by Joseph Palmer, exec.
431 Inv. estate of John Kersey by Drury and John Kersey, exec.
431 Estate of Ezekiel Haralson in acct. with John Rogers, exec.
Cash paid Geo. Vaughn for support of Elizabeth Haralson.
432 Deed of gift: William Jamison to beloved children David, William,
John Douglas, and Jean Jamison all my children now living - gift
of negro man named Tom. Trusty friend and Brother John Douglas
Esq. to see above deed carryed out in my absence. 22 July 1791
in the XVI year of our Independence.
433 Bill of sale: Isham Dalton to Maj. Tillman Dixon, 383 acres land
on both sides Hogans Cr. the Plantation said Dalton now lives on.
2 May 1791. Wit: Lancelotte Johnston, Jesse Carter.
433 Bill of sale: William Jamison to John Douglass, sale of household
goods and livestock. 10 Aug 1791. Wit: Mary Douglass, John
Maleer, Martn. Douglass.
434 Bill of sale: Thomas Palmer Sen. on 11 Dec 1790 gives unto six
children of Thomas Palmer Jun. household articles. Wit: Isaac
Vanhook.
435 Power of attorney: 2 June 1790 - John Motheral to trusty and loving friend Ann Greer to convey deed for that part of land left
me by my Father to any person the same as if I were there be-
cause I have sold the same unto her. Wit: John Simms.
435 Letter of attorney: Samuel Robertson late of County of Caswell
to my brother and trusty friend James Robertson to dispose of
land on which "I dwelled last when in said Co." 6 Sept 1790.
Wit: William Reed, William Keeling.
436 Acct. of John Campbell guardian to Mary A. Moore, orphan.
437 Estate of Thomas Robertson in acct. with Will Hall, exec.
Acct. paid to Elliner, Martha, Rebeccah, Kesiah Robertson;
William Powel, John Low, Thos. Stephens, Archey Samuel, Jacob
Pearson,James Williams attorney, Robert Moore, Allin Caldwell,
John Cochran, Robert Willson, James Robertson, Asa Thomas.
By James Sanders, Adams Sanders.

37

Book B cont. 1792

January Court 1792

Page
438 ANNE SMITH - Will - w. 17 Sept 1783. daughter Margaret Williams;
grandson William Williams, son of William Williams; granddaughter Elizabeth Williams (land on State line that divides
Va. and N. C.); granddaughters Anne and Kesiah Smith; Willis
Buckingham Smith to get plantation; granddaughter Nanney Riley;
Lettus Riley; grandson Mason Smith. Exec: grandson Mason Smith
and friend Archd. Murphey. Wit: George Conally, William Randolph, Abraham Randel. Amasa Smith qualified as exec.
440 FREEMAN LEATH - Will - w. 1 Dec 1791. Wife Susannah; heir
lawfully begotten by wife if she is delivered of a living child.
Exec: wife and George Barker.
441 ZACHARIAH LEA - Will - w. 28 Sept 1791. Wife Ann; daughters
Mary Bangston, Rachel Lea, Sarah Lea; sons Vincent, Henry,
George Lea. Children to receive portion as each comes of age
or marries. Exec: Moses Bradsher, Carter Lea. Wit: Thomas
Neeley, Thomas Carver, Mary Gould.
442 Div. estate of Josiah Farley between Sarah Johnston and Elizabeth Farley, Mother and Sister of said Josiah Farley. (Elizabeth Farley now Boulton). By Stephen Sargent, Richard Escridge,
James Lea.
442 Inv. estate of Mary Montgomery on 17 Jan 1792. H.McAden, exec.
443 Inv. household furniture of John Perkins by William Kennon and
Abram Perkins.
443 Contract between Nancy Butlar and John Robertson for support of
her child. Wit: William Rainey, George Black, Robert Bozwell.
21 Oct 1791.
444 Sale estate of Robert Burton on 1 Dec 1790. Buyers:

Jos. Dameron	Richard Walton	Dudley Gatewood
Andrew Harrison	Jacob Pearson	Philip Cox
Capt.Spill Coleman	Charles Price	Thomas Bennett
Benj. Williamson	James Burton	Jesse Carter
Jno. Southerland	Winn Dixon	William Ware
Alexander Lea	Col.Willm. Dix	Christopher Dameron
Jesse Robertson		

446 Acct. for orphans of Mr. Robert Burton. Payments for Lucy,
Jane, Sarah, Mary, Noel, and Andrew. By Joseph Dameron,
guardian.
447 Bill of sale: Thomas K. Wynne of Franklin Co., State of North
Carolina, to Henry Graves, sale of negro woman named Grace 18
years of age. 19 Aug 1791. Wit: Isham Melone, George Melone.
447 Bill of sale: James Hughs to Nicholas Delone, sale of livestock.
21 Jan 1791. Wit: Elisha Rowark, Laurence Vanhook.
448 Bill of sale: Robert Webb,Planter, to Nicholas Delone, sale of
mare heretofore pur'hased of John Holsonback. 3 Dec 1791.
Test: P. Williamson.
448 Inv. property of Jacob Porter on 17 Jan 1792 by Ann Greer, adm.
449 Joseph Morris orphan 5 yrs. old bound to Clifton Allin.
450 George Morris orphan 9 yrs. old bound to Clifton Allin.
451 Taxable property (total) for 1791.

March Court 1792

451 Letter of attorney: John Browning of Green Co. Ga. to David
Boran of same county to sell land in Caswell Co. N.C., formerly
property of Joseph Boran, decd., 206 acres and also to convey
title to James Smith of Caswell Co. 9 Jan 1792. Wit: Thos.
Houghton. By Ezekiel Parks, Esq. Clerk of Green Co.

38

Book B cont. 1792
Page
453 Caswell County's acct. with Alexander Rose, county trustee 1789.
Payments to:

Jethro Brown	Long Will Lea	Col.Stephen Moore
Ambrose Arnold	James Yancey	Capt. Will Lea
Spill Coleman	John Hall	John Surratt
Yancey Bailey	Nicholas Delone	Will Barnett
Hearndon Haralson	John Williams	Will Duty
Thomas Neeley	Greenwood Payne	George Farley
Archd. Murphey	William Hainey	

Received from Thos. Neeley for ground rent of his House at the
Court House and same from Willm. Hainey.
454 Inv. estate of James Lea on 30 Mar 1792 by Major Lea and John
Lea, exec.
455 JAMES LEA -Will - (of Orange County) - w. 28 Mar 1771.
sons William, John, and Major Lea to be executors. Wife Ann;
all my children. (Names not given). Wit: Thos. Camp Jun. and
Henry Lea. Proved by testimony of William Lea as by the disposition thereunto annexed. (See page 40 this book.)
456 ADAM STAFFORD - Will - w. 26 Aug 1791. Sons John, Samuel, and
youngest son Stephen (under 21); all my children. Exec: son
John and wife Susannah Stafford. Wit: Joshua James, Samuel
Stansbury, Benjamin Quine, Henry Howard.
457 WILLIAM QUINE - Will - w. 29 July 1791. Wife Sarah; daughters
Elizabeth Stafford, Sarah Quine; sons Jacob, Mordecai, Henry,
William. Exec: brothers Benjamin and Henry Quine. Wit: Henry
Howard, Samuel Stafford.
458 Inv. estate of Zachary Lea on 4 Feb 1792 by Moses Bradsher and
Carter Lea.
459 Inv. estate of John Graves Sen. taken at his dwelling house on
20 Mar 1792. A riding chair and Horse were given the widow
by consent of all legatees (extraordinary) also one Smiths
Anville and Bellows given Bazilla Graves by consent of legatees.
Legatees: Isbell Graves, Azariah Graves, Thomas Graves, Bazilla
Graves, John Kerr, Ann Yancey, John Graves, Thomas Slade, Solomon Graves. Inv. of that part of estate left to widow and of
part not yet divided. By Azariah, Solomon, John, and Thomas
Graves.
460 Inv. estate of Freeman Leath by George Barker, exec.
460 Acct. sales of Andrew Enoch by Robert Kimbrough. 10 Nov 1791

END OF BOOK B

39

The testimony of William Lea proving the will of James Lea was
not written into the Will Book. His testimony of March 1792
was discovered by the author filed with estate records of Person
County at the State Archives. After 1792 Capt. William Lea of
South Hico resided in the newly formed County of Person. His
disposition was made at the first session of the Court of Pleas
and Quarter Sessions for Person County. The will of Capt. Lea
was proved at the March Court 1804. The disposition if pictured
below.

June Court 1792

Page
1 BENJAMIN ENOCHS - Will - w. 5 Sept 1790. Wife Mary; 4 young
  sons Benjamin, Rice, John, Samuel; daughters Sarah, Mary Worson; son David; heirs of son Andrew decd.; Exec: wife Mary and
  son David. Wit: Charles Taylor, David Enochs, Robert Parks.
2 Bill of sale: William Carrol to George Carroll, sale of livestock. 25 Feb 1792. Test: Jesse Carter, James Gilaspi.
3 Eliz. Lightfoot Moore in acct. with James Sanders, guardian.
  Lucy A. Moore in acct. with James Sanders. 16 July 1791.
4 Estate of John Moore Jun. in acct. with the estate of John Moore
  Sen. (1786-91). Accts from: (Partial list)

Hugh Kelley	Thos. Gimbo	Richard Painter
George Darby	Rawley Dodson	Margaret Campbell
Elisha Bowdery	William Prowel	Thomas Stuart
John Graves	Edmund Alley	Doctor Johnston
George Rosebrough		Montford McGehee

7 Inv. estate of William Quine by Benj. and Henry Quine.
8 Settlement estate of Andrew Enochs by Robt. Parks, Azariah
  Graves, Thomas Graves. Elizabeth Enochs purchaser at sale;
  bonds on John Williams, Benjamin Enochs, James Colman.
9 Power of attorney: Joseph McKnight of Russell Co. Va. to Andrew
  Ferguson to convey 190 acres land in Halifax Co. Va. unto
  William Ervine. 13 Oct 1788. Wit: James Sargent, William Nash.
10 Bill of sale: William Hatcher to Robert Mayo, sale of livestock
  and furniture. 10 May 1792. Wit: James Mayo, James Landman.

September Court 1792

11 Bond: Jno. Sommers as Register for Caswell County. Bondsmen:
  John Brown, Wynn Dixon, John Grant.
12 Bond: Charles Dixon as coroner of Caswell County. Bondsmen: John
  Williams, Thomas Graves.
13 Patsy Atkinson orphan 3 years 6 mos. old bound to John Atkinson.
  /s/ Thomas Rice on behalf of the Justices.
14 Inv. estate of Benjamin Enochs by Mary Enochs.
15 Inv. estate of Adam Stafford by Jacob Miles Sen., Joshua James,
  Samuel Stansbury on 22 June 1792.
15 Mary Anderson Moore(orphan) in acct. with John Campbell guardian.
16 Acct. estate of Alex Cochran by John Cochran guardian for orphans.
17 Estates of Elkanah Haralsons orphans to James Chambers, guardian
  to Micajah, Bradley, and Elkanah Haralson.

December Court 1792

18 JAMES INGRAM - Will - w. 22 Oct 1792. Wife Mary; 6 children:
  Walter, Priscilla, Vachell, Clary, Benjamin, John. One lot
  to be laid off on Main Rd. nearest to Court House to each child.
  Exec: wife and friend Solomon Graves. Wit: John Ingram, Charlton
  Ingram.
19 Letter of Attorney: William Moore of Wilks Co. Ga. to William F.
  Booker to settle his business in N.C. 13 Sept 1792. Wit: Edward
  Moore, Tandy Dix, Saml. Moore.
20 David Hall orphan 15 years and 2 mos. bound to Robert Wilson.
21 Charles Boulton Jun. for his wife Elizabeth Boulton(late Elizabeth Farley) orphan and daughter of Moses Farley decd. release
  and quit claim unto Samuel Johnston late guardian for every
  legacy from estates of Moses and Josiah Farley decd. 9 Nov 1792.

Book C cont.1792-1793
Page
22 Release and quit claim: Samuel Johnston unto Charles Boulton.
   9 Nov 1792.
23 Rachel and Samuel Shy in acct. with estate of John Shy.
   Payments to:

Jesse Carter	Joseph Carney	Thomas McCulley
Greenwood Paine	John Walker	Empsom Byrd
Joseph Cantrill	John Atkinson	Thomas Cole
William Lea	William Hainey	Isaac Cantrill
John Forrest	John McMinemy	Nicholas Delone
Andw. McCawley		Stephen Madden

24 Acct. for orphans of Robert Burton. Board paid for Jean, Sarah,
   Mary, Noel, and Andrew Burton. Payments to Capt. Spill Coleman, John Sommers, Samuel Paul, Andrew Harrison.
25 Partrick Henry Moore, orphan's acct. with Thos. White, guardian.
   William and Lucy Moore, orphans of John Moore, acct. with Montford McGehee guardian. Bonds on Richard Carnal, William Everet,
   James Peterson, John Campbell.

January Court 1793

26 Bill of sale: John Maleer to Zachariah Evans, sale of household
   articles. 2 Dec 1792. Wit: John Johnston, Salley Malear.
27 Taxable property for 1792.

April Court 1793

26 GIDEON HOGG - Will - w. 7 Nov 1790. Wife Judith; sons Andrew,
   John, William, Gideon; daughters Ann Denton, Mourning Denton,
   Elizabeth Thomas, Agness Hogg, Judith Gibson, Rebeccah Shelton,
   Mary Yates. Exec: wife and son Andrew. Wit: Michael Cloe,
   Nicholas Cloe, Henry Baldwin.
27 Letter of attorney: Thomas Whitehead of Union Co. S.C. to Samuel
   Henderson to receive and sue for all debts due in N.C. 15 Oct.
   1792. Wit: Thos. Rice J.P., Jno. Grant J.P.
27 Letter of attorney: James Yates of county of Sumner in the
   Western Territory to Brother William Yates to recover money from
   John Blackwell of Granville Co. 1 Nov 1792. Wit: Jesse Evanse,
   Saml. Johnston.
29 Letter of attorney: Anne Tate,widow and exec. of Waddy Tate, to
   John Windsor to recover legacy due from exec. of Moses Simpson
   decd. of Fairfax Co. Va. 24 Apr 1793. Wit: Robert Williams.
30 Estate of John Moore Sen. in acct. with Josiah Shoemaker. Payments
   to wife and children (no names given).
31 Sales estate of James Lea on 17 July 1792. Buyers: James Robertson (CL), Maj. Lea, John Dobbin, Nathaniel Comer, Jerre Lea, John
   Hipworth, Obediah Sanders, John Lea(son of John), Nanney Haralson,
   Hearndon Lea, Joseph Peterson. By John Lea and Maj. Lea, exec.
32 Moses Watkins, orphan 5 yrs. old, bound to Bartholomew Dameron.
33 Robert Watkins, orphan 11 yr old, bound to Bartholomew Dameron.
34 Janney Watkins, orphan 9 yrs. old, bound to B. Dameron.
35 Isaac Watkins, orphan 7 yrs. ole, bound to B. Dameron.
36 Hezekiah Fanning binds his son William Fanning (by his own choice)
   to David Cochran(Taylor). 9 Mar 1793. Wit: Michael Montgomery.

July Court 1793

37 CHARNAL HIGHTOWER - Will - w. 6 Nov 1792. Wife Frances; exec:
   wife. Wit: John Puckett, Benjamin Hawkins.
38 RICHARD WINDSOR - Nunc. will - Estate to be divided between sisters
   and brothers. Wit: John Windsor, Thomas Reed. /s/ Richard Simpson, Justice.

Book C cont. 1793
Page
39 Estate of Mathew Jouit in acct. with John Brown. Payments to:

John Williams	Daniel Gwinn	James Dickie
Hawley Williamson	Jeremiah Poston	Thomas Simmons
Thomas Owen	Moses Armstead & Co.	Samuel Walker
Sarah Allen	Robert Parks	Robt. White
Timothy White	Jerre Williamson	William Moore
	Archibald Murphey	

Payment from Peter O'Neill.
40 Estate of Freeman Leath in acct. with George Barker, exec.
Payments to: Benj. Spencer, John Phenix, Montgomery & Love,
William Holderness for tax, Doct. Johnston, John Lennox,
Jethro Brown, John Baldwin. Approved by James Williamson
and Azariah Graves.
41 Estate of John Moore to John Campbell.
42 Isaac Vanhook, adm. of estate of Thomas Vanhook, debts incurred.
42 Robert Parks, esquire, County Trustee, in acct. with Caswell Co.
Claims allowed from Thomas Brooks, Laban Stafford, Hezekiah Rice.
43 Amt. of sales of John Powel, decd. by Joseph McClain, adm.
Buyers:

John Powel	Peter Smith	Charles Price
John Chilton	Nathl. Durham	Ezekiel Waters
Joseph McLaine	Jas. Powel	Robt. Harris
Tho. Bastin	Jepthah Rice	Simeon Ford
Will Lyon	Will Greenbough	Nat Dickinson
Paul Chappin		Tho. Dixon

44 Inv. estate of Gideon Hogg on 17 July 1793 by Andrew Hogg, Exec.
44 Feby. 1784 - Recd. of Mrs. Mary Duncan, adm. of Daniel Duncan 50
lbs. in full of legacy of said estate. /s/ Danl. Merritt for
Nancy Duncan.
44 Recd. of Mrs. Mary Duncan for legacy from Danl. Duncan. /s/ Nathl.
Duncan.
45 Frances Duncan to Mary Duncan, guardian acct.
45 Recd. of Mrs. Mary Duncan adm. of Danl. Duncan decd. for wife
Frances' legacy. /s/ Champess Madding. Wit: Elizabeth Duncan.
45 Mary Duncan(the younger) acct. with Mary Duncan (the Elder).
46 Rec. of Mrs. Mary Duncan wife Mary's legacy from estate of Daniel
Duncan. /s/ Benjamin Ragsdale.
46 Patience Wilkerson in acct. with Mary Duncan, adm.
47 Agness Jones orphan 6 yrs. old bound to Aron Anglin. /s/ James
Williamson on behalf of his fellow justices. /s/ Sarah Jones.

October Court 1793

48 CHARLES STEPHENS - Will - w. 18 July 1792. 3 sons Thomas, William,
and Benjamin; (land adj. Robert Long and land purchased of Thomas
Lea); daughters Elizabeth Wilson, Elizabeth Lea. Exec: 3 sons.
Wit: Robert Long(Jurat), Thomas Campbell(Jurat).
50 ABRAM PERKINS SEN. of District of Caswell and County of Caswell -
Will - w. 14 June 1793. Son Abram (land on Moons Cr. after
wife's death); wife Cisley; 5 children: Philemon Perkins, Molley
Grimes, Fanny Ware, Elizabeth Middlebrooks, Polly Perkins.
Exec: son Philemon. Wit: John Humphries, Philemon Perkins,
Alexander Nunalle, Martin Perkins.
51 WILLIAM HENSLEE - Will - w. 11 Oct. 1793. Elizabeth Mallory;
Susannah West; brothers and sisters. Exec: brothers John and
David Henslee. Wit: Malon Stacy, Aron Anderson, Nathan Williams.
52 Bill of sale: Nathaniel Durham to John Tinason, one negro man named
Bob formerly property of Isham Dalton. 3 Aug 1793. Test: John
Durham, James Grant Jun.

Book C cont. 1793-94
Page
52 Inv. estate of Richard Windsor by Jno. Windsor, adm.
53 Inv. estate of Waddy Tate by Richard Simpson adm.
54 Inv. personal estate of William Henslee.
54 Inv. estate of Charnal Hightower by Francis Hightower, exec.
55 Inv. estate of Abram Perkins by Philemon Perkins, exec.
55 Inv. estate Jacob Porter by Ann Greer, adm.
55 Inv. estate Charles Stephens.
56 Sales estate of William Barker 24 Oct 1793. Sales to:

John Barker	Joseph Barker	Israel Barker
David Barker	Thomas Mallory	Jonathan Poe
Charles Taylor	Susannah Leath	Thomas Taylor
John Turner		

/s/ Benj. Williamson DS for William Swift, Sheriff.
57 Mary Anderson Moore orphan acct. with John Campbell Guardian.
57 Certificate of insolvency: John Low made oath of his net worth
   excepting his working tools, muster arms and wearing apparel.
   (Case brought by adm. of estate of John Crisp.) 24 Nov 1792.
   /s/ Azariah Graves and Solomon Graves, justices.
58 Bond: John Campbell of Person County vs. James Sanders, Montford
   McGehee, Thomas White as guardian for legatees of John Moore,
   decd., and John Yancey as a legatee.
59 Estate of John Moore in acct. with John Campbell.
60 Subscribers appointed by General Assembly to lay off the seat for
   the Court House in Caswell County unanimously agree the Court
   House shall be fixed on the land of James Ingram and convenient
   to purchase 100 acres land for advantage of county and said land
   shall be divided in 4 equal lotts and sold to highest bidder for
   benefit of county. County to pay 150 pounds and expence of running the lines. /s/ John Graves, W. Stubblefield, Wm. Muzzle,
   Solomon Parks, David Shelton, David Hart.
   Following subscribers agree to receive and be answerable to James
   Ingram for above purchase. Friday 28 Sept 1792.
   /s/ James Williamson, Azariah Graves, Solomon Graves, Rich. Simpson, Jno. Grant, Wynn Dixon, Justices of Peace.

January Court 1794

61 Bill of sale: Buckner Wall, sale of stock and household furniture
   to Zachariah Evans. Wit: Wm. Haynie, Tho. Riggs.
62 Bond: Adams Sanders as tax collector.
63 Div. estate of John Perkins Jun. to Pleasant Perkins, Dicy Perkins,
   Sally Perkins, Nelley Grant, William Cannon. Div. by Spill Coleman, Charles Dixon, John Sommers, Wynn Dixon.
64 Sales estate of Waddy Tate on 15-16 Nov 1793. Buyers:

Mary Simpson	John C. Cox	Hugh Gwinn
Richard Simpson	Stephen Odear	John Windsor
William Tate	William Clark	John Reed
Nathaniel Williams Sen.	Duke Williams	Richard Tate
Joseph Smith	James Appleton	Nancy Reed
William Donoho	John Williams Esq.	Jerre Poston
Benj. Williamson	John Harbin	William O'Neill
Simon Carlisle	Solomon Allen	Jerre Williamson
Charles Hunter	Thomas Rice Esq.	William Holderness
William Park Swift	Robert Harris	Benj. Spencer
Robert Carson	Susannah Tate	Hugh O'Neill
Cornelius Dabney		

67 Inv. estate of David Hart by James Williamson and Thomas Hart adm.
68 Inv. estate of William Glaspy on 11 Nov 1793 by James Sanders, adm.

Book C cont. 1794
Page
69 Inv. estate of Thomas Brooks by Armistead Flippin, adm.
70 Caswell County in acct. with Alex Rose county trustee 1790.
Payments to:

Yancey Bailey	Nicholas Delone	Andrew Buckhanon
Hezekiah Rice	Stephen Sargent	John Henry Pryor
Ambrose Arnold,constable	Lord Lord	James Cochran
William Pulliam Williamson	Byrd Wall	John Yancey
Thomas Brooks, sheriff	John Surratt	Robert Boman

Thomas Neeley refuses to pay ground rent of a lott he rented of
the county whereon his house stands at old Caswell Court House.
William Hainey also refuses to pay balance of rent.
Cash received from Josias Chambers, George Farley, James Yancey.
Cash received from William Rainey for strays 19-14-4.
72 Person County in acct. with Caswell County. Included 20 pounds
paid James Cochran after division of county for his providing
Caswell County with a blank book for Registers office to
register deeds.

April Court 1794

74 Power of attorney: Purnell Ingram & Elizabeth Ingram (late Elizabeth Commens daughter of William Commens decd.) of Greenbrier
County, Va. to Archibald Murphey and Abram Dunaway to recover
part of estate of William Commens. 11 Nov 1793. Wit: Joseph
Hall, Reuben Gafford.
75 Bill of sale: Samuel Bullis to Reuben Cochran, sale of all property, livestock and household. 6 Oct 1793. Wit: John Bullis,
Simeon Cochran, Robert Bruce Jun.
75 Inv. remainder estate of Abram Perkins.
76 Sales estate of William Burch by Nancy Burch, adm. on 12 Feby
1794. (Buyers not given.)
77 Settlement estate of Anthony Samuel by Ann Samuel, adm. Legatees:
Anthony, Edmund, Benjamin, Josiah, Molly, Sally, Betsy, Nancy,
and Jenny Samuel.
78 Div. of negroes belonging to estate of Robert Burton between
Andrew, Noel, Mary, Sally, Jane, Lucy, and Robert Burton.
80 Joseph Dameron, adm., in acct. with estate of Robert Burton.
Payments to: William Dix, John Douglass, Spil Coleman, B. Ridley,
Jerre Poston, Jesse Carter, C. Dixon for taxes, John Graves,
Robert King, George Davis.
81 Sales estate of Col David Hart on 5-7 Feby 1794. Buyers:

Elizabeth Hart	John Graves	Abram Underwood
Armistead Rogers	Jepthah Rice	Cornelius Dabney
Col. John Williams	James Williamson	Richard Smith
Thomas Hart	Joseph Hart	William Cliften
John McCawley	William Hart	John Rice Sen.
Hezekiah Rice	Rebecca Hart	Thomas Nance
George Simms	Robert Kimbrough	Nath. Williams
James Orr	Robert Blackwell	Greenswood Payne
Cornelius Davis	Duke Williams	John Jackson
David Poyner	William Rice	Richard Simpson
George	Robert Williams	James Powel
Thomas Mallory	Jethro Brown	William Smith
John W. Jones	James Williamson for	Benj. Shelton
Robert Boman	A.Hart	Tyre Harriss
Joshua Boyd	Lanslot Johnston	William Bradley
Stephen Mallory	William Bradbury	Lewis Barton
John Kerr	/s/ James Williamson & Thomas Hart, adm.	

45

Book C cont. 1794

Page
86 Taxable property for 1793
    858 white polls   6 carriage wheels
    1006 black polls   4 ordinarys

July Court 1794

87 Receipt;. Received of Patrick Donoho 15 pounds for fine imposed for maintenance of child. /s/ Gincey Thomas. Test: William Lea. 24 May 1794
87 The estate of Alex Miles in acct. with Joshua Carney, exec., in right of his wife Lucy (for 1785).
Acct. paid to: Edmund Alley, Jacob Miles, Thomas Yates, Thomas Tarpley, Edwd. Swann, Jonathan Low, John Dobbin, Eppy Hightower, John Lea Jun., William Reed, John Lea Capt., Lanslotte Johnston, Tho. Slade.
88 Tyre Harris Jun. in acct. with Tyre Harris Sen. estate. Approved by John Reed, Richd. Simpson, James Williamson.
89 Mrs. Susannah Barker, adm. of Jas. Barker decd. Acct. paid to: Isaac Cantrill, James Colman, John Cooke, Jarrot Tool, David Barker, Benj. Spencer, John Buchanon, David Enoch, Jesse Scott, John Spencer. 22 July 1794.
Approved by Robert Parks, Richd. Simpson, James Williamson.
90 Simpson Harris settlement acct. with exec. of Tyre Harris.
92 Sales estate of William Glaspy on 11 Nov 1793. Sales to:

Jeremiah Samuel	Greenwood Payne	Fleetwood Gillaspy
James Glaspy	Wm. Shearman	John Walters
John Jeffreys	John Bennett	Archd. Samuel
John Winters	Champness Madden	James Robertson
John Browning	Joseph Gillasby	James Moore
Sophia Gillisby	Titus Benton	Ninian Martin
Samuel Pittard	Charles Shearman	Lucy Gillaspy
	Martha Gillaspy	

93 Bill of sale: David Dickey to John Dickey, sale of waggon, livestock, and furniture. 26 July 1794. Wit: John Crosset, James McCalif.
94 Settlement estate of Jacob Miles Jun decd. by Joshua Carney adm. Payment to orphans Thomas Miles, John Miles, Betsey Miles. 28 June 1784.
94 Inv. estate of Charles Allen, 28 July 1794 by Thos. Jeffreys,adm.
95 Inv. estate of Jehue Womack on 22 July 1794 by Josiah Womack, adm.

October Court 1794

96 JOHN RICE - Will - 13 Oct. 1794. Wife Susannah; (A debt due from John Stalcup.); nephews William Rice's son John and John Rice's son Simeon to get estate if wife has no child. Exec: wife Susannah, Brother Nathl. Rice and Brother William Rice. Wit: Robt. Mitchel, Mary Thomson.
97 THOMAS SIMMONS - Will - w. 5 Oct 1794. Wife Priscillah; daughters Martha, Priscilla, Keziah, Sarah, and Hannah Graves; sons Thomas, Alexander. Exec: Thomas Graves, and son Thomas Simmons. Wit: Charles Taylor, Butlar Murphey.
99 RICHARD HAMBLETT - Will - w. 11 Oct. 1794. Wife Caty; children: Robert, William, Sarah, Richard, Hannah, Elizabeth, and Byrd. Exec: Samuel Neeley and Robert Hamblett. Wit: Samuel Neeley, Staple Malone.
100 Inv.estate of John Rice by Nathaniel Rice.
101 Inv. estate of Thomas Simmons on 29 Oct 1794.

Book C cont. 1794-95
Page
102 Eliz. Jouit in acct. with John Brown guardian. Payments to Lewis
    Pike, John Lenox, John Buckhanon, Jepthah Rice.
103 Sale estate of Jehue Womack by Josiah Womack, adm.
103 Residue estate of William Burch - 3 negroes Dinah, Paul, Israel.
104 Settlement estate of John Crisp by George Black adm. Payments to:

Joshua Carney	Isaac McCullom	Eliz. Ashburn
Thomas Phelps	John Smithey	John Crisp Jun.
Philip Vass	Henry Cooper	Baylor Burch
Duncan Carmical	Jesse Benton	James Wilson
J. Farley for 1788 taxes	Joseph Taylor	John Johnston
J. Yancey for 1789 taxes	William Nash	Thomas Bradley
Robert Long	James H. Keys	Andrew Warwick
William Richmond	John Low	

Cash received from:	George Burch	Charnal Hightower
Jesse Carter	Joseph Hicks	Larkin Wisdom
John Justice	Thomas Lea	James Phelps
Jacob Pearson	M. Morton	James Lea
Thomas Yates	John Peterson	Shadrock Roberts
Absolem Roberts	Jos. Peterson	Benj. Evanse
Z. Evanse	John Lea	
Elisha Evanse	Peyton Morton	

January Court 1795

106 Letter of Attorney: James Wisdom to Brother Larkin Wisdom to
    recover estate due from Francis Wisdom decd. of Pittsylvania
    County, Va. 6 Jan 1795. Test: William Rainey JP, John McMullen.
106 Letter of attorney: Sarah Wisdom and Martha Wisdom to Brother
    Larkin Wisdom to recover from estate of Francis Wisdom their
    decd. grandfather of Pittsylvania Co. Va. such property now in
    possession of Dr. Crawford Williams. 26 Jan 1795. Test: James
    Robinson.
107 February Election for Congress 1795
    At election held 12 & 13 Feby. 1795 to elect member of Congress
    to represent our third Division, the number of votes is
    Jesse Franklin 206 and Joseph Winston 101. /s/ Adams Sanders,
    Sheriff, A. E. Murphey, Jas. Yancey.
107 Inv. estate of Richard Hamlett by Robert Hamlett exec.
107 Inv. estate of Jehu Womack.
108 Richard Tate orphan 18 years the 9th last Dec. apprentice to
    to Hudson Brown.
109 WILLIAM MITCHELL - Will - w. 4 Jan 1795. daughters Sarah, Mary,
    Susannah, Sicily, Nancy, Elizabeth Cary; sons John, William
    Henslee, James; Exec: friend John Henslee, son John Mitchell.
    Wit: David Henslee, Nathan Williams, John Anderson.
110 Taxable property for 1794
    White polls 870   Carriage wheels 10
    Black polls 1012   Ordinarys 10
    Tavern Keepers: David Cochran, Zachy Evans, Will Lea, James
    Yancey, Robert Boman, Sally Hargis, Jesse Carter, James
    Robertson, Law Vanhook.

April Court 1795

111 Letter of attorney: William Otwell of State of South Carolina
    and county of Pendleton, to friend Thomas Arnett of Stokes Co.
    N.C. to settle all debts owing to me and convey deed; also to
    ask for papers Paul Chappin hath in his possession.
    9 Mar 1795. Wit: John Arnett, William Farish, John Hellon.

47

Book C cont. 1795
Page
112 DAVID PORTER - Will - w. 18 Dec 1794. son Alexander; grandsons
William Porter, John Johnston; daughters Mary Kelly, Rebeccak
Johnston; Exec: son Alexander. Wit: John Grant, Thomas Kimbrough.
113 MICAJAH POOLE - Will - w. 4 Apr 1791. Son George; Micajah Pool
son of Thomas Pool. Exec: son George Pool and Chloe Pool his
wife. Wit: Andw. Haddock, Daniel Gwinn, Thomas Leake.
114 JEREMIAH POSTON - Will - 1 Feb 1795. Wife Elizabeth (land in
Caswell and Rockingham Co. adj. Nath. Williams); rest of
estate in N.C. and in state of Maryland divided among children: Priscilla Dickens, William, Katy, Betsy, Henry, Polly,
Anna, Richard, Francis and unborn child; Exec: wife and son
William when he arrives at age and friend John Coates Cox.
Wit: Jno. C. Cox, Wm. H. Rice.
115 Inv. and sales of Elizabeth Boman on 15 Dec 1794 by Robert Boman,
adm.
116 Sales estate of Thomas Brooks Jun. on 18 Feby 1794. Sales to:
Jane Brooks   Edmund Williamson   Will Page Sen.
Armstead Flippin   Jonathan Brooks   Azariah Graves
Charles B. Brooks
By Jane Brooks and Armistead Flippin, adm.
117 Inv. estate of William Mitchel.
118 Inv. estate of John Shearman by Pemberton Burch, adm.
118 Inv. goods and chattels of Mary Gibson. A note on Nathaniel
Dickerson; goods in possession of James Gibson all but one
pewter dish which he refuses to give up. Payments due to:
Eppehroditus Stone and Mary Crisp. Others mentioned: James
Williamson, James Fullington, John and Richard Gibson.
By Joel Gibson, adm.
119 Sales estate of Royel Boman by John Zachary and Simon Roberts,
exec.
120 Acct sale of estate of Jean Mullin by James Coils adm.
Sales to:
Polly Mullen   James Coils   Joshua Mullins
John Lea Sen.   John Stafford   Fuller Long
James Lea   Joseph Peterson Sen.   Watson Winters
Mary Riddle   Thomas Campbell
/s/ James Kiles, adm. 5 Mar 1795.
121 Sale estate of Charles Allen by Thomas Jeffrey, adm. Simon negro
man sold to Thomas Jeffreys, also Pett and her children Sarah
and Beckey. "Since sale the adm. has been furnished with copy
of will of Drury Smith decd. of Mecklenburg Co. Va. that above
negroes Simon, Pett, and her issue were given to the issue of
Charles Allen by the Daughter of said Drury and wife of said
Allen and no legal right was in the said Allen". Adm. would be
compelled to give up negroes.
121 Paul Watlington gives free privilege to Robert Boman and Stephen
Roberts to join his Mill Dam to north side of Country Line Cr.
and said mill for use of public. 25 June 1794. Wit: George
Wiley, Jesse Poyner.
122 James McGolly 15½ years of age bound to George Pendergrast.
/s/ Azariah Graves, chairman of inferior court.
123 Power of attorney: Edmund Haggard to sons David and Rice Haggard.
10 Sept 1792. Wit: Roland Milam, James Barton.
124 Bill of sale: George Reed to Jesse Carter, sale of livestock and
household goods. 27 Jan 1795. Test: W. W. Cunningham, H. Atkinson.

Book C cont. 1795
Page
125 Bond: Hugh Dobbin and Thomas Jeffreys unto Reubin Taylor, conveyance of deed of Land adj. Abram Dunaway on Kilgore's
Branch to John Hall's corner.

July Court 1795

126 Letter of attorney: Mary Burriss to James Arnett (shortly in-
tending to go into state of Maryland) to recover from estate of
Jonathan Partridge of Dorset Co. Maryland. 25 July 1795. Wit:
Bartholomew Bower, Francis Moss, William Moss.
127 Letter of attorney: Ursley Anthony to son Elijah Anthony to recover from Edmund Anderson of Hanover Co. Va. 28 July 1795.
Wit: David Jones, Robert Parks.
128 Sales estate of Jeremiah Poston. Sales to:

Elizabeth Poston	John Windsor	William Dickens
William Bradberry	John O'Bannock	Nathl. Williams
John Cox	John Nance	Rollen Milam
Danl. Allen	Will Hornbuckle	Geo. Summers
John Jenkins	Henry Harding	Jno. Buckhannon
James Appleton		

129 Inv. estate of Micajah Pool by Geo. and Chloe Pool.
130 Estate of Alex Miles in acct. with Jacob and Lucy Miles exec.
For boarding orphans Thomas, John, Elizabeth, and Lucy Miles
from 1784-85 exec paid 20 pounds.
131 County of Caswell in acct. with Alex. Rose late trustee (1790)
Cash paid to Robert Parks, Yancey Bailey, John Maleer, John
Hall; paid William Waite for surveying the county after divi-
sion, William Hainey for overpayment of ground rent and re-
leasement of Tho. Neeley and Hainey from ground rent.
Paid Person County ½ received from Maj. George Lea, Charles
Dixon, and Will Lea on acct. strays; paid first payment for
Court House, Joal, and 2 acres land.
Paid to Person County ½ received of Stephen Moore; paid Capt.
Lea, late county trustee, ½ cost of buying weights and measures
and lawbooks for use of this county. Paid William Cocke, Esq.,
Sheriff, balance due for taxes.
132 Received of William Lea first payment in part of old Caswell
Court House and Jail with 2 acres land. Sold by Charles Dixon
and Maj. George Lea.

October Court 1795

134 Taxable property 1795
White polls 891
Black polls 1073
Tavern licenses at 2 pounds each from William Lea, Thos. Jeff-
reys, David Cochran, Jesse Carter, Nicholas Delone, Joshua
Hudson, Robert Boman, John Graves.
134 ISAAC BELEW - Will - w. 11 Sept 1794. daughters Jemima Harvel
and Mary Belew; son Daniel Belew (land adj. Jerre Samuel);
Exec: daughter Mary and friend Stephen Sargent. Wit: A. E.
Murphey, Reuben Gafford, Betsy Murphey.
135 HENRY DIXON - will - w. 4 Aug. 1795. Wife Elizabeth;
sons Charles, Tilman; granddaughter Francis Dixon d. of Henry
Dixon decd. Exec: 2 sons. Wit: W. Dixon, N. Williams Jun.,
G. Cunningham. Proved on oath of Wynn Dixon.

49

Book C cont. 1795-96
Page
137 ROBERT BRUCE - Will - w. 16 Oct 1795. Wife to have money owed
by James Carrell; daughter Betsy; all daughters;
Sons Thomas (land adj. James Carrol and Joseph Bush),
William (land adj. Joseph Bush); John, and Robert. Exec. wife;
Wit: John Payne(Taylor), James Carroll. The executor qualified
and no name given.
138 Inv. estate of Roger Dixon 22 Oct 1795 by Mary Dixon, adm.
139 Inv. estate of Robert Bruce by Elizabeth Bruce, exec.
140 Sale estate of Henry Williams 22 Sept 1795 by William Rice exec.
Sales to:

William Rice	Elizabeth Williams	Malon Stacy
Samuel Dickie	Charles Brooks	Humphrey Roberts
Richard Oldham	Thomas Slade	Eli Stacy
Joseph Williams	Nathan Williams	William H. Rice
David Gooch	James Yancey	George Poe

141 Inv. estate of Isaac Belew 11 Sept 1795 by Mary Belew alias
Winters, exec.
141 Inv. estate of John Mallery by John Mallery adm.
142 Estate of David Hart in acct. with James Williamson adm.
Acct. paid to Elizabeth, Thomas, Rebecca, and William Hart;
Dr. Lanslotte Johnston, Geo. Jackson, Daniel Allen, Will H. Rice,
Geo. Simms, John Lenox, Thomas Jeffreys, Doct. John Cox.
143 Letter of attorney: "Sarah Williams exec. of Joseph Williams late
of Granville Co. N.C. to Matthew Clay of Pittsylvania Co. Va.
to collect and recover a Judgment obtained in Pittsylvania Co.
in May 1788 by Exec. of said Joseph Williams against Daniel
Williams Jun. and Elizabeth Williams Exec. of Henry Williams
decd. who was exec. of James Williams decd. for the sum of 58
pounds which is 345 lbs tobacco". 11 Sept 1795.
Wit: Greaf Barksdale, Jno C. Russell, John Dawson.
144 Edmund Smith a (Black) base born orphan 4 years and 2 mos. old
bound to John Baynes.

January Court 1796

145 PLEASANT PERKINS - Will - w. 24 Nov 1795. Sisters Sally Perkins,
Dicey Colman, Lucy Grant. Exec: Charles Dixon and Cornelius
Grant. Wit: W. Dixon, Jesse Perkins, James Perkins.
Charles Dixon and Neeley Grant qualified as exec.
147 ANN GILLASPY - Will - w. 1 Oct 1791. Son James; clothes to be
divided between Sally Crigg, Betsy Haddock, and Jane Howard.
Exec: son James. Wit: Dudley Gatewood, Berriman Watkins,
John Bennett.
148 Inv. estate of Charles Leath by Thomas Spencer adm.
Inv. of property Thomas Spencer has received of Charles Leath
decd. in his lifetime: one negro girl, one bed and furniture.
Susannah Leath widow and relict of Freeman Leath decd. made
oath her decd. husband in his lifetime received from Charles
Leath decd. one cow which is all her husband received from his
father. /s/ Richard Simpson JP
149 Inv. estate of William Ware 23 Jany 1796 by Jno Ware and Will
Ware adm.
150 Inv. estate of Michael Nichols by Martha Nichols adm.
151 Inv. estate of Pleasant Perkins.
151 Inv. estate of Washington Jouet (land on Country Line Cr. adj.
John Brown, Col. John Williams, William Nash Esq. and one
negro girl Dinah 10-11 years old. By Thos. Jouet adm.

Book C cont. 1796
Page
152 Letter of attorney: Hugh Dobbin to William Rainey to attend
    to all business in North Carolina and Virginia. Hugh Dobbin
    about to travel to the western waters. 10 Dec 1795. Wit:
    William Jeffreys, Will McAden.
153 Nancy Sutton orphan of 11 years 3 mos 7 days bound to Thomas
    Ware.
154 Mary Sutton 13 years old on 28 last Dec bound to Martha Ware.
    /s/ Gabriel Lea Esq. on behalf of the Justices.
155 Robert Farley orphan of 16 next April bound to Groves Howard.
156 James Smith orphan 13 years 9 mos. old bound to James Currie.

April Court 1796

157 Estate of James Lea in acct. with Major Lea and John Lea exec.
    Division and settlement with payments to:
    Clerk for recording will; for coffin and paid cryer of sale.
    Cash paid Jacob Miles Jun for voucher #1, Luke Lea #2,
    Joseph Henderson #3, Will Lea by John Lea #4, Joseph Henderson
    #5, Isabella Graves #6, Paul Haralson #7, John Lea exec & Lega-
    tee, Major Lea Exec. & legatee.
    27 Apr 1796. By A. E. Murphey, James Sanders, William Lea.
    (Note from KKK- Some one has scratched over Joseph Henderson
    #3 and written Joseph Peterson in pencil. The original of
    this report is filed at State Archives with estate records
    of James Lea. The original gives Joseph Peterson #3. It
    appears the recorder made a mistake.)
158 Sale of Personal property of William Ware 20 Mar 1796. Sales to:
    William McCollum   Peter Smith   Martha Ware
    John Ware   Abner Parrott   Thomas Ware
    John O'Neal   Joel Kennon   William Ware
    Dudley Gatewood   John Bullock   Moses Ware
    James Whalebone   Bond due from Jonatius Tennison
    By John Ware, adm.
161 Joseph McClain, adm. estate of John Powell. Payments to:
    Grant & Summers; Isham Dalton, lawyer's fee (Col Williams),
    John Tennison, John Wilson.
161 Inv. estate of George Allin Davis by Charity A. Davis, adm.

July 1796

162 Sales estate of Michael Nicholson by Martha Nicholson, adm.
    Sales to:
    Martha Nicholson, Thomas Johnston, Capt. Robert Paine, William
    Rainey; "6 head of sheep run away before the day of sale; 3
    barrels corn made use of in the family before day of sale; 40
    lbs. cotton and 1 chissel lost; about 2000 lbs tobacco not
    sold; part in a stud horse in Va. no account of." 27 Feb. 1796.
164 Sales estate of John Shearman 10 Nov 1795. By Pemberton Burch,adm.
    Sales to: Drury Clark, Mrs. Shearman, William Wallis, Jeremiah
    Brooks, John Burch, William Gallaugher, John Christenbury,
    Willson Jones, Joseph Neeley, Will Hews.
165 Sales estate of Charles Leath 16 Feb 1796 by Thomas Spencer, adm.
    Sales to:
    Mason Leath   Thomas Spencer   John Dawson
    Robert Lackey   William Carter   Garland Sneed
    John Kerr   John Mallery   James Mallory
    Samuel French   John Henslee   Nathan Williams
    David Henslee   Thomas Mallory   Richard Hornbuckle
    Henry Harden

Book C cont. 1796
Page
167 List of sales of Mesheck Morton 19 Feb 1796. Sales to:

Jesse Carter	Mary Morton	Anderson Morton
Robert Kimbrough	Thomas Yancey	Edward King
Thomas Graves	Robert Bowman	Josiah Morton
James Turner	Samuel Boman	Anderson Morton
John Kimbrough	John Hightower	James Kitchen
William Lea merchant	William Sawyers	Major Lea
John Graves Jun.	Thomas Wiley	
By Jesse Carter adm.		

168 Inv. estate of Meshack Morton.
168 JAMES LONG - Will - w. 21 Jan 1796. Wife Priscilla; daughter Mary   Dollarhide widow of Ezekiel Dollarhide; children now living: Robert Long, Agness Maxfield, Mary Dollarhide, Jeane Upton, Rebreeah Branham widow of David decd.; son Robert to have Bible the confession of faith and Isaac Ambrose. Exec: wife and son Robert. Wit: Thomas Stephens, John Warwick.
170 Inv. estate of James Long 20 June 1796.
171 JOHN CROSET - Will - w. 22 Oct 1795. Wife Jeane; son William; rest of children: Charity, Margret, James, Jeane, Elizabeth, and the young child(all under age). Exec: wife, and Margaret Greer. Wit: Jas. Currie, David Dickey, Sarah Currie.
172 Settlement estate of Elijah Harrelson. Payments to Thomas Barnett, Henry Howard, John Johnston, Reuben Haralson, Bradley Haralson, Jno Rogers guardian of Jesse Haralson orphans.

October Court 1796

172 Letter of Attorney: Tyree Harriss to Richard Hornbuckle to convey land to Robert Brown and Thomas Hornbuckle. 1 Oct 1796. Wit: Robt. Mitchel, George Alexander Swift.
174 Elizabeth Starkey, base born girl 3 yrs. 5 mos. old bound to Rachel Shy (widow). 28 Apr 1794. /s/ Thomas Rice Esq., chairman of Inferior Court.
175 Spott Pearce orphan 12 years 5 mos. old bound to Job Siddle. 28 Apr 1794.
176 Nancy Hall orphan 2 yrs. 10 mos. old bound to Mary Currie.
177 William Starkey, orphan 7 yrs. old the 6th Oct 1793 bound to Jonathan Starkey. 28 Apr 1796.
178 Letter of attorney: David Enochs to Clifton Allen to deliver unto Thomas Graves Sen. a deed to 180 acres land on Country Line Cr. adj. Thomas Yancey, Thomas Graves, and David Jones part of tract known as Kelly's land. 14 Sept 1796.
178 Inv. estate of William Morgan by Susannah Morgan adm.
179 Inv. estate of Edward Mills on 22 Apr 1796.
180 Inv. estate of Boler Stephens on 22 Oct 1796 by Nancy Stephens adm.
181 Letter of attorney: William F. Booker of Columbia Co. Ga. to Edward Moore of Wilkes Co. Ga. to travel and dispose of all land in N.C. 13 Sept 1796. Wit: Chs. R. Carter.
182 Acct. by John Barker with estate of William Barker. Approved by Sol. Graves, W. Dixon.
182 Sales estate of Abram Perkins 7 Oct 1796 by Jesse Perkins adm. Sales to:

John Dennis	Abraham Perkins	James Perkins
Robert Boman	George Smith	Jesse Morgan
Joshua Hudson	Thomas Baxter	William Ware
Jesse Perkins Jun.	Isaac Middlebrooks	Peter Smith
Henry McClarney	Henry Perkins	Charlton Ingram
William Standard	Robert Mayo	William B. Burton

Book C cont. 1796-97
Page
182 cont. sale of Abram Perkins
    William Morgan   Ignatius Tennison   Robert Dixon
    John Ingram   John Bullock   Wynn Dixon
    John Perkins
185 Division lands of the late John Hodge among male heirs of said
    decd.
    (all present and of lawful age)
    Isaac Hodge (land adj. Nathaniel Comer, James Willson, and
    Hearndon Haralson)
    Samuel Hodge (adj. Absolem Roberts, Haralson, and James Roam)
    David Hodge (adj. Roberts, Charles Stephens)
    10 Sept 1796. By Saml. Johnston, Nathl. Comer, Gabriel Lea.
187 Sales estate of John Mallory 16 Nov 1795. Sales to:
    John, Stephen, James, Salley, Rebecca, Thomas, and Henry Mallory

Jeremiah Jackson	Benjamin Gibson	Josiah Payne
Samuel French	Richard Jones	William Carter
Theodorick Carter	Clifton Allen	John Mitchel
John Sawyer	Butler Murphey	David Henslee
Jeremiah Williamson	Lewis Pike	Benjamin Kid
Robert Kimbrough	John Scogings	Jonathan Brooks
Joseph Carter	Charles Hunter	Lewis Sheppard
Robert Lacky	Malon Stacy	John Payne(Taylor)
Raleigh Vickers	George Robinson	Nathaniel King

190 Sales estate of William Mitchel by John Henslee and John Mitchel
    Exec. Sales to:

John Mitchel	Hudson Brown	Solomon Jackson
Robert Lacky	Richard Tate	James Polston
Jethro Brown	John Hastings	Elizabeth Williams
John Hensley	Edmund Browning	John Mallory
William Nash	Benjamin Gibson	Nathan Williams
Richard Jones	John Dawson	Benjamin Kid
Susannah Mitchel	William Tate	Alexander Lacky
Lewis Foster	John Bush	Andrew McCully
Thomas Spencer	William Ballard	Absolem Sawyer
William Brooks	John Anderson	Zachariah Hastings
Russell Sullivant	William Brown	Jeremiah Jackson
William Edwards	James Brown Jun.	Raleigh Vickers
Cuthbert King	John Jones	Clifton Allen
John Sawyer		

194 Robert Parks county trustee in acct. with Caswell County.
    Balance due county per contra:

Greenwood Payne	John Dickey	Jesse Carter
Laban Stafford	Thomas Donoho	James Sanders Jun.
James Robinson	Thomas Yancey	Charles Dixon
Archibald Murphey	Elisha Paschal	John Atkinson's
Alex Porter	William Swift	estate
Saml. Johnston	Azariah Graves	James Burton
John Reid	Richard Simpson	Adams Sanders
Hezekiah Rice	John Adam Wolf	William Rainey
Solomon Graves	William Sawyer	William Sanders

January Court 1797

197 JOHN RICE - Will - w. 14 Nov 1796. Wife Lettisha; Susannah Rice
    widow of son John Rice decd.; daughter Anna Williams and her
    children; sons Thomas, William, Nathaniel; daughter Mary.
    Exec: sons William and Nathaniel, and son in law John Rice.
    Wit: Robt. Mitchell(Jurat), John Henslee (Jurat).

Book C cont. 1797
Page
198 Samuel Motherals ear mark - a crop and slit in the right ear and
    a crop in the left.
198 Inv. estate of Andrew Burton on 2 Jan 1797 by James Burton adm.
199 Inv. estate of Peggy Kinchen by W. Nash adm. Money in hands of
    Wm. Kinchens exec.
199 Sales estate of John Rice Jun. Sales to David Hensley, Mahlon
    Stacy, Benjamin Kid, William Rice, Lancelot Johnston, Nathaniel
    Rice, John Rice, Bartlett Estis, Susannah Rice, Nathan Williams,
    Robert Kimbrough.
200 Sales estate of James Smith by D. Dickie adm. Sales to:

Sarah Smith	George Farley	Benjamin Warren
David Dickie	James Greer	Sol. Smith
William Culbertson	James Currie	John Atkinsom
John Dickie	George Eubank	Aquilla Compton
John Hightower	William Howard	William Warren
Thomas Jackson	Larkin Wisdom	William McMan
Samuel Motheral		

202 Inv. estate of Hezekiah Rice on 21 Oct 1796 by Ibzan Rice adm.
202 Inv. estate of John Grant by J Grant Jun. adm.
203 Sales estate of Edward Mills.
204 Inv. estate of John Rice on 17 Jan 1797.
206 Alexander Green Hall orphan of 16 yrs. and 16 days bound to
    Elijah Barton. By Robert Parks chairman of county court.
207 Joshua Butler, base born child 6 yrs. old the 15 of next Aug.,
    bound to Jacob Ahart.
208 James McGauley orphan 16 yrs. and 9 mos. old bound to Robert
    Willson.
209 William Wyatte orphan 11 yrs. old bound to William Willson.
210 Betsy Ballard, orphan 13 yrs. old, bound to Henry Dickens.
211 Matthew Mills orphan of 14 yrs. the 6 day of next month bound
    to Devereux Inge.
212 Sales estate of Boler Stephens on 24 Nov 1796. Sales to:

Nancy Stephens	Abner Robinson	George Samuel
Jeremiah Samuel	David Kersey	Joshua Draper
James Rainey	Robert Willson	Peter Ragsdale
George Stephens	James Rainey	Frances Stephens
Anthony Stephens	Archibald Samuel	Samuel Kersey
Andrew Bryant	David Cothran	Doctor McAden
Hearndon Haralson	David Thomas	Andrew Bryant
Darling Wray	William Cunningham	George Reid

214 Estate of Meshack Morton in acct. with Jesse Carter and Mary
    Morton adm.
215 Taxable property for 1796.

April Court 1797

216 Gardner Ballard 8 years old the 2 day of next June bound to
    Jesse Brintle.
217 Robert Turner 15 yrs. and 7 mos. old bound to John Murry, Black-
    smith.
218 John Ballard age 9 yrs. Oct next bound to John Jackson.
219 Execution of deed: Hugh Dobbin in 1793 did bid for and buy tract
    of land of John Low and sold said land to Thomas Roberts.
    Dobbin gives power of attorney to William Rainey to act "for me
    as I am about to go to Western Country". Test: Nicholas Delone
    (Jurat), William Lea Jun., Thomas Evans, Robert Long.

54

Book C cont. 1797
Page
220 Letter of attorney: Tilman Dixon to brother Charles Dixon to convey to Wynn Dixon deed to tract of land on Hogan's Cr. given
me by my father also tracts purchased of Isham Dalton, Oliver
Terry, and Peter Smith (Roundhill) and Nathaniel Dickinson.
2 Nov 1796. Wit: Ibzan Rice, Danl. Burford, Thos. Jouett.
221 Inv. estate of Mathew Richmond by Ann Richmond adm.
222 Additional inv. of Peggy Kinchen by W. Nash adm.
222 Francis Smith adm. acct. with estate of Edward Guardner.Approved
by A. Graves and Thos. Kimbrough.
223 James Sanders in acct. with estate of William Gillaspie. Acct.
paid to Thomas Jeffreys, Capt. Robert Willson, Thomas Akin,
Eliza Haddock, Gideon Patterson, David Shelton. Approved by
C. Dixon, Jas. Burton, William Lea.
224 James Lea in right of his wife as adm. of estate of William
Burch final acct. (1794). Payments to:

George Hugston	George Reynolds	John Crisp
William Breeze	Durrett Richards	John Whitloe
John Wallace	Robert Motheral	Laban Stafford
Buckner Wall	Andrew Warwick	John Warwick
Joshua Carney	Elias Wallace	Richard Johnston
Thomas Kilgore	Pemberton Burch	John Winningham
James Cochran	John McAden,Doct.	William McNabb
Thomas Roan		

226 Robert Kimbrough and Elizabeth Enochs adms. of Andrew Enochs.
Vouchers paid to James Coleman, Benjamin Enochs, H. Haralson,
Ambrose Arnold, Col. Murphey, and Robt. Kimbrough guardian to
Elizabeth Enochs. Approved by Jas. Yancey and William Gooch.

July Court 1797

227 Letter of attorney: Duke Williams to friend Tyree Harris (who
shortly intends to remove to State of Tennessee) to receive
money due from any person in Tenn.; also to demand 3 slaves
Sarah, Bob(age 15-16) and Duke, formerly property of Cornelius
Dabney who removed from the county and bought at a sale by
Duke Williams. 25 July 1797. Wit: Betsy Williams, John
Williams (Jurat).
228 Letter of attorney: John James Farley obtains judgment against
John Lewis (M) for money owed and whereby Lewis removed to
Georgia, Farley gives letter of attorney to Seaborn Jones of
state of Georgia to recover debt from Lewis. 27 July 1797.
229 JOHN HIPWORTH - Will - w. 16 Feb 1793. Wife Mary to get whole
estate and after her death estate divided betwixt Walter
Winters and William Winters. Exec: wife Mary and E. Hightower.
Wit: Hearndon Lea, Epproditus Hightower(Jurat).
230 Letter of attorney: Jane Mills (widow) of Rockingham County, N.C.
to John Price Sen. of Caswell County to sell thirds of land
left by husband Edward Mills to Thomas Arnett. 11 Mar 1797.
Wit: Charles Price, Tanday Walker.
231 Letter of attorney: Hugh Dobbin to William Rainey to take charge
of all business in NC "as my business calls me to State of
Tennessee". 6 Apr 1797.
232 JOHN JOHNSTON SEN. - Will - w. 30 May 1796. Wife Hannah;
sons Thomas, John, William(under 14), James, Samuel;
daughters Jean, Elizabeth, Mary, Sarah, Hannah; land 2 rods
square the burying ground near old Barn not to be sold or disposed of; exec: wife, John Warwick, son Thomas. Wit: Sam Johnston, John Warwick, Robert Thomas.

Book C cont. 1797
Page
234 Inv. estate of Martha Lay by Peter Lay adm.
234 Inv. estate of John Johnston by exec.
235 Caswell County in acct. with John Somers - payment for 3 books
    purchased.
235 Sales' estate of William Morgan 2 Dec 1796. Sales to:
    Susannah Morgan   Nathan Holloway   Roger Atkinson
    Thomas Jeffreys   Richard Ogilby   Joseph Flipps
    William Rainey   Hearndon Haralson   Gabriel Gunn
238 Robert Martin in acct. with estate of Moses Richardson.
    Vouchers paid to:
    William Moore   Unity Richardson   Zebrou Hix
    Chloe Smith   Thomas Poor   James Ingram
    William Sawyer   James Landman   John Low
    William Gwynn   David Shelton   James Long
239 Sales estate of Mathew Richmond 30 June 1797. Sales to:
    Ann Richmond   Thomas Phelps   John Kimbrough
    Nicholas Delone   Alexander Murphey   Isaac Rainey
    Thomas Boman   Jonathan Starkey   Lewis Malone
    Christopher Dameron Bartholemew Dameron Daniel Melton
    Edward Nowell   Robert Donaldson   Daniel Malone
    William Richmond   John Forguss   Henry Thomas
    Joshua Hudson   John Richmond Jun.   James Roan
    James Nowell
241 Estate of John Shearman in acct. with Pemberton Burch. Payments
    to : Mildred Shearman, Amess McNeill for bond and interest,
    Washburn and Shearman note. Other payments:
    John Burch   Samuel Motheral   Willson Jones
    William Wallace   John McMurry   Adam McNeeley
    David Mitchell   Robert Motheral   Abram Buttery
    William Mitchell   Richard Johnston   John Yancey
    Pulliam Williamson   Henry Cooper   James Thompson
    William Hargis   Thomas McNeill   William Lea
    Approved by Isaac Rainey, John Graves, Robert Blackwell,
    Jas. Burton.
243 Alexander Green Hall orphan 16 yrs. old bound to Durreau Inge.
244 Stephen Jones orphan 16 yrs. bound to Joseph Arnett.
245 Champness Hall, son of Judith Hall, 18 yrs. and 7 mos. old
    bound to Phillip Pearce.
246 Robert Parks in acct. with County of Caswell. Vouchers paid to:
    Thomas Yancey   Archibald Murphey   Will Rainey
    Richard Simpson   Azariah Graves   John McMullen
    William Sanders   Greenwood Payne   Hezekiah Rice
    Solomon Graves   William Muzzle   William Lea
    David Mitchell   Charles Dixon   James Burton
    Thomas Donoho
    Approved by Jesse Carter, David Gooch

            October Court 1797

247 Receipt: Tyree Harris receives a bond of Benjamin Spencer and
    Thomas Spencer for 300 lbs. tobacco due 1st of January and
    received by Harris as guardian for Christopher Harris.
    11 Nov 1791. Wit: John Windsor (Jurat)
248 Letter of attorney: William Anglin Sen. adm. of Cornelius
    Anglin decd. of Caswell Co.,to son Aaron Anglin to recover all
    titles to land in Tennessee. 25 Oct 1797. Wit: James Williamson.
248 William Hargis Sen. mark To Wit A crop and a slit in each ear.
248 Larkin Wisdom's ear mark for his stock "A carap and underkeel
    in each ear"

Book C cont. 1797
Page
249 PETER SMITH - Will - w. 18 Apr 1793. Daughter Elizabeth to have
articles now in her and her husband's possession; daughter
Martha; sons Jesse, Moses, Aron; rest of sons James, William,
Presley W., George, John B., Elias, Elijah; "My negro man
Anthony who though not absolutely free, I will that he have
liberty to have his own free choice to serve which of my children he shall choose and not to be confined to any particuler
but if ill treated by one to have free liberty to go to another
and not to be sold to any other person". Exec: John Windsor,
Richard Hornbuckle, son William W. Smith. Wit: James Grant Jun.,
Jepthah Rice, Henry Ferrel.
250 JOSEPH WATERS - Will - w. 20 Sept 1797. Wife Rebeccah;
daughters Susannah Hobbs, Chloe Waters; my 9 children: Priscilla
Harbin, Zeph. Waters, James Waters, Lyddy Broody, Judith Waters,
Benjamin Waters, Keziah Waters, Joseph Waters, Pheby Goldsmith;
3 youngest children Pearson, Anna, Loyd Waters. Exec: wife and
Isaac Hobbs. Wit: Griffin Gunn, William Gunn, John Shuckleworth.
251 JAMES RANDOLPH SEN. - Will - w. 15 June 1797. Wife Mary;
son John to get land and plantation when he reach 21. If son John
does not reach maturity land to go to son Nimrod; son Randolph;
daughter Rebecah; if wife remarry her share to sons Jeremiah
and Nimrod; son Robert to take son John if wife dies before
young sons come of age and William should take Nimrod.
Exec: son James and son-in-law William Dye. Wit: A. E. Murphey,
Wm. Gordon, John Carter.
252 Inv. estate of Bartholomew Bowers by J Grant Jun. adm.
253 Letter of attorney: Martha Dixon widow of Henry Dixon decd. to
Nathaniel Williams Jun. to recover any sums of money from any
person in United States said Martha may be entitled to.
5 Sept 1797. Wit: N. Williams Jun.
254 Letter of attorney: Jonathan Anthony of Christian County, Ky.
to Obed Florence to deliver deed of conveyance to Joseph McReynolds for land in Florence's tract adj. land where McReynolds
lives. 22 Aug 1797. Test: Thos. Yancey (Jurat), Elijah Anthony.
255 Inv. estate of Joseph Waters 20 Oct 1797 by Rebecca Waters and
Isaac Hobbs.
255 James Burton adm. of Andrew Burton decd. in acct. with estate.
256 Inv. estate of James Roan by Janney Roan adm.
257 Inv. estate of Peter Smith by Richard Hornbuckle, exec.
258 James Leath orphan of Charles Leath in acct. with Mason Leath
guardian. Coleman, Isaac, and Betsy Leath, orphans of Charles
Leath acct. filed with Mason Leath. Approved by Rich. Simpson,
Jas. Yancey.
260 James Williamson adm. in acct. with estate of David Hart.
Vouchers paid to: Benjamin Williamson, John Graves, Thomas
Kimbrough, William H. Rice, William Hart, Elizabeth Hart,
Jethro Brown.
261 Settlement estate of Andrew Enochs. Elizabeth Enochs guardian
to orphans and widow to get ½ part. 24 Oct 1794. Returned to
court by Jas. Yancey, Zaphaniah Tait, William Gooch Jun.
262 Christopher Williams Brooks orphan in acct. with William H. Rice
guardian. Cash paid to George Somers, William Holderness; tax
paid for 1795 & 96.
263 Taxable property for 1798
White polls 844   Stud horses value 11 lbs.7 sh. 6 p.
Black polls 1079

57

Book C cont. 1798
Page

January Court 1798

264 RACHEL DOBBIN, wife of Thomas Dobbin decd. - Will - w. 15 July
1797. Sons Hugh and John; daughters Margaret Comer, Betsy
Escridge and her son John, Rachel Vanhook; daughter Nancy Leas
son John C. Burch to have negro boy Archer and Archer to live
with James Lea and Nancy Lea till his master comes of age.
Exec: sons in law Robert Vanhook and Nathaniel Comer. Wit:
Moore Comer, Christopher Dameron Jun. (Jurat), John Flyn.
"In the 34 line it is mentioned that negro boy Archer is to live
with James Lea his said Master's guardian and to work for his
said masters maintenance John Campbell Burch till he comes of
age."
266 Letter of attorney: John Connally of Caswell County, Charles
Connally of Elbert County, Ga. to friend George Connally of
Nottaway County, Va., to recover all debts and bequeaths, lega-
cies due in said state of Virginia. 1 Nov. 1797. Wit: A. E.
Murphey, Richd. Sanders, J. Yancey.
267 Sales estate of James Roan 11 Nov. 1797. Sales to Jane Roan,
Pulliam Williamson, Andrew Gibson, Christopher Dameron, Edward
Clay, Elijah Reynolds; by Jane Roan adm.
269 Allotment to widow and orphans of James Roan 31 Oct 1797 by
Gabriel Lea, Samuel Hodge, Vines Mathis, William Stevens.
270 Inv. estate of Robert Harriss 13 Jan 1798. Notes on Joseph
Montgomery, John Copeland, Joseph Hicks, Isaac Jackson, William
Ellet, Wm. Thomas, Jacob Harris, Andrew and Robert Ray, Daniel
Allen. Tobacco sold at Danville, Va. By Agness Harris adm.
271 Sale of part of estate of James Randolph 1 Nov 1797. Sales to:
Abner Robinson, John Hall, Thomas Fisher. By James Randolph
Jun. and William Dye exec.
272 JOHN YATES - Will- w. 24 Aug 1797. Oldest son Allen (all land
including that bought of David Hall), son Alford (land bought of
Samuel Dyer formerly owned by Archibald Samuel and Thomas
Robinson); 5 daughters Betsy Yates, Milley Yates, Dolley Yates,
Salley Yates, Anny Yates. Exec: Robert Willson, Archibald
Murphey, Asa Thomas. Wit: Archd. Samuel (Jurat), William Yates
(Jurat).
273 Joseph Dameron adm. estate of Robert Burton acct. filed. Estate
to be divided among 7 children. (Names not given.)
274 Sales part of estate of John Rice 7 Feb 1797. Sales to:

Edmund Rice	Nathaniel Rice	Robert Lackey
Letisha Rice	James Love	William Clifton
John Cox(Doctor)	Thomas Mallory	David Poyner
John Goodloe	William Rice	Robert Thompson
James Brown	Bartlett Estis	Nathan Slade
Robert Kimbrough	Thomas Jones	

276 Div. land of Washington Jouette decd. to legatees John Jouette,
Armistead Rogers and 5 lots purchased by Jethro Brown from other
legatees. Division by James Cobb, Lewis Barton, George Sims,
Lanslot Johnston, Robt. Blackwell.
277 Sales estate of Peter Smith to:

Priestley Whaler Smith	James Simpson	Wm. Payne
George Smith	Jepthat Rice	Charles Price
James Powell	Ignatius Tennison	Lanslot Cheatwood
Joseph McClain	James Arnette	John Royall
Robert Dixon	Peter Smith	Simeon Ford
Elizabeth Parrot	Jesse Dalton	Martha Smith

Book C cont. 1798

Page

278 & 9 Sales eatate of Peter Smith cont. Sales to:

Nancy Waters   Henry Durham   Thomas H'arold
Mrs. Brackin   Samuel Brackin   William Smith(BS)
Richard Hornbuckle Edward Bauldin   Nathaniel Dickerson Jun.
James Vaughan   Simon Adams   Sarah Mills.
By Richard Hornbuckle exec.

280-297 Missing pages - The index in Book C does not include any
documents that would have been recorded on these pages. It
appears the clerk made a mistake in numbering the pages.

April Court 1798

298 Letter of attorney: Benjamin W. Burford to Daniel Burford to
receive pay, to sell, and to discharge all matters relative
to estate of Colin Persons decd. late of Southampton County,
Va. 11 Nov 1797. Wit: Robt. Martin, John Mallory, David
Henslee.

299 Letter of attorney: Joseph Hart, Reubin Hart, Archibald Hart,
and Elizabeth Hart - and Elizabeth Hart as guardian for orphans
of David Hart decd. to wit John, Nathaniel, David, Susannah,
Mary, and Elizabeth - to William Hart of State of Kentucky to
convey real estate said David Hart decd. situate in Kentucky
or Tennessee. 25 Oct 1798. Wit: W. Nash.

300 The property of Widow Lay decd. sold 20 Dec 1798 to:
Peter Lay, Daniel Gwyn, William Anglin, Mary Lay, Thomas Rice,
James Browning, Will Browning Sen., Will Browning. By Peter
Lay adm.

301 Gabriel Lea, guardian for orphans of Meshack Morton decd. sells
land to Thomas Wiley. 24 Apr 1798.

301 Div. estate of Andrew Burton decd. by James Burton adm.
Legatees: Mary Dameron mother of the decd., Robert Burton,
Lucy Martin, Jane Burton, Salley Burton, Mary Burton, and Noel
Burton, brothers and sisters of decd. 10 Feb 1798. By C. Dixon,
Berryman Turner, Dudley Gatewood.

302 Gabriel Lea, guardian orphans of Meshack Morton, acct. filed.
Vouchers paid to Wm. Lea, Wm. Norwood, 27 Apr 1798.

303 THOMAS SLADE - Will - (from original will) w. 10 Apr 1798.
Wife Hannah; daughter Hannah Lea; grnaddaughter Nicey Lea to
get her mother's portion who is decd.; grandson Devereu Hightower to get his mother's portion who is decd.; son Lem
Slade; daughter Catherine Lea; land to be divided among all
living children; tobacco to be sold to Jesse Carter; Exec:
spouse H Slade, sons Thomas and William. Wit: Thomas Gunn Jun.
and James Gunn.. Hannah Slade and William Slade exec. qualified.

305 Bond: James Burton guardian of Noel Burton orphan of Robert
Burton and adm.of Andrew Burton to pay proportionate part
of debts of Andrew Burton decd. Proved on oath of Henry Atkinson.

305 Joseph Dameron for his wife and guardian for Jane, Salley, and
Polly Burton orphans of Robert Burton shall pay their part of
debts of estate of Andrew Burton decd. Bonded by John Martin.

306 John Martin for his wife Lucy shall pay his part of debts against
estate of Andrew Burton.

307 Spillsby Coleman guardian to Robert Burton shall pay his part of
debts of said estate. 28 Dec 1793. Wit: Dudley Gatewood, C.
Dixon (Jurat).

307 Mordecai Burgess Ear Mark to wit one smooth crop in the right
ear and a slope the underside the left ear.

Book C cont. 1798
Page
308 Settlement estate of Thomas Brookes Jun. Payments to:

Jesse Carter	Thomas Swift	John Lea
Jethro Brown	Geo. A. Davis	Paul Watlington
William Holderness	Daniel Gwyn	Benj. Williamson
Elizabeth Gardner	Lancelott Johnston	Will Rice
Thomas Jeffreys	Jonathan Brookes	Archibald Murphey
Grant & Somers	Patrick Magonigal	

Expenses to and from Raleigh 5 lbs.
By Jane Brooks and Armstead Flippin adm. Examined by John
Yancey, Jesse Carter, James Burton.
310 Letter of attorney: James Ray to son James Ray Jun. to sell land
on Stoney Creek (being part of larger tract sold to Bondville
Brown), also to sell corn and other articles. 17 Oct 1797.
Wit: Anthony Swift (Jurat), John Henslee.
310 Letter of attorney: Thomas Bradley to William Norton to demand
and receive any money owed or any money due in N.C. 15 Oct 1796.
Wit: T. Dixon, David Poyner (Jurat).
311 Div. estate of Andrew Burton decd. by James Burton adm.
Legatees: Joseph Dameron for his part; Joseph Dameron guardian
for Jane, Salley, and Mary Burton; John Martin for his wife's
part; Robert Burton for his part; Noel Burton as per acct.
311 Allotment to widow and children of John Harrison decd. (Names not
given). By J. Currie, Solomon Parks, John Pleasant.
/s/ W. Muzzle J.P.
312 Inv. estate of Thomas Slade 24 Apr 1798 by Hannah Slade and
Willm. Slade adm.
313 Sale estate of Mathew Richmond - Repeat of pages 239-240.
316 Caswell County in acct. with Richard Simpson, Treas. of Public
Buildings. 26 July 1797. Cash paid Devereau Inge undertaker
of the Jail; cash received of John Haywood public treasurer
pursuant to act of Genl. Assembly, 200 lbs.
316 Sales estate of John Harrison 13 Mar 1798. Sales to:

James Turner	Sarah Ashford	Mrs. Nancy Harrison
John Groom	Thomas Vaughan	John Barnhill
Luke Pendergast	Charles Taylor	Andrew McClarney
William Pleasant	Charles Groom	John Morrow
Mrs. Ashford	Saml. Everett	John Pleasant

By Nancy Harrison, adm.
318 JOHN SCOTT - will - w. 21 Jany 1795. Wife Mary; daughters Jane
Bell and Polley Strader; son in law John Wall; son James Scott;
Martha Johnston; son Joseph Scott to get land "whereon I live";
Exec: son Joseph; Wit: Will Bethell (Jurat), Richd. Bethell.
319 Inv. property of Buckner Wall by John Whitlow adm. Tobacco in
hands of Thomas Phelps.

July Court 1798

320 SAMUEL WALKER - Will - w. 28 Oct 1797. Wife Eleanor; 2 grandsons Saml. Walker and James Walker (land I now live on);
5 children: Elizabeth Cob, Jane King, James Walker, Muriel Orr,
Elinor Walker. Exec: Robert King, and son James. Wit: John
Watt, Margaret Watt, Henry Cob.
321 Letter of attorney: Wm. McIntosh to friend Solomon Parks to
recover wages due from State of N.C. to Cornelius Anglin a late
soldier in the continental line of N.C. to which wages "I suppose myself entitled as his heir at law and said Solomon should
compromise with the person that hath drawn the wages".
29 Jany 1798. Wit: Danl. Burford, John Appleton, James Appleton.

Book C cont. 1798
Page
322 Estate of Francis Shackelford in acct. with Nathl. Dickenson,
exec. (1785-92) Payments to:
James Grant   Lancelott Johnston   Ben Williamson
James Galloway   James Montgomery   William Wilkerson
George Adams   John Sammons   Richd. Sanders
Thomas Dobbins   Blow & Barksdale   James Sanders
322 Sale estate of Thomas Slade 25 May 1798. Sales to:
Capt. John Graves   Jacob Miles Jun.   William Sawyers
John Lea Jun.   Reubin Cox   William Ray
David Kersey
323 Settlement estate Nathl. Haralson decd. by Will Donoho and
wife Darcus, exec. to: Thomas Forbus, Jeremiah Haralson,
Joseph Smith, and Thomas Turner, legatees. 25 July 1798.
Div. by Jas. Burton, C. Dixon, Thos. Bouldin.
324 James Williamson, Commr., in acct. with Caswell County.
Amt. received from sale of lots   784 lbs.
Cash paid John A. Wolf   333, 59, & 51 lbs.
   "   "   Mary Ingram   150 lbs.
   "   "   Jere Poston   15 lbs. 10 sh.
   "   "   Capt. C. Dixon   7 "   10 "
   "   "   Howard Cash   3 "
   "   "   J. Williams   3 "

Balance in hands of Jas Williamson 101 lbs. 9 - 3
Balance due county   "   "   "

325 Fanney Morrow, orphan 5 yrs. old last June 7th day, bound to
Geo. Samuel. /s/ Jesse Carter,Esq., Chairman county court.
326 William Rainey and John Stafford having built 3 bridges,
one across Country Line Cr. at Jesse Carter's, another across
same creek at John Graves Mill, other across Hogan's Cr. at
Bullocks Old fish Trap, said Rainey and Stafford shall repair
and maintain bridges for 7 years and county not responsible
for any breaches.
327 Ordered that Tax of nine pence be laid on the poll and 3 pence
on every 100 acres land for the support of the poor.
Test: Thomas Gunn, Jun., Clk.
327 Sale estate of Buckner Wall to:
John Whitlow   Nancy Wall   John Whitlow
Larkin Wisdom   William Whitlow   Jesse Whitlow
Daniel Malone   Lewis Ashburn
By John Whitlow adm.
328 William Rainey in acct. with County Court of Caswell.
Amt. of stray money collected   258 lbs. 10 - 2
Vouchers paid: James Forgher for bridge, Alexander Rose,
John Campbell, Edmund Browning, Jesse Pearce, James Swainey.
For building Caswell old Goal   80 lbs.
329 Letter of attorney: Nathl. Hart, acting exec. of Nathl. Hart
decd., to Richard Simpson to recover all debts due to said
estate. 5 Aug. 1797. Wit: Jo Hart. Proved on oath of
Joseph Hart.

October Court 1798

330 JOHN SIDDALL - Will - w. 22 Aug 1794. Wife Esther; 2 sons and
son in law Job Siddall, Ira Siddall and Ephraim Nowell;
daughters Martha Siddall, Amey Siddall, Betsy Anglin, Nancy
Siddall; sons Jesse and Stephen one shilling sterling each.
Exec: son Job and wife, and Ephraim Nowell. Wit: Azariah
Graves, Samuel Merton.

Book C cont. 1798
Page
331 MARY SIMPSON - Will - w. 6 Nov 1797. Daughters Margaret William-
son wife of Jerre Williamson, Keziah Reed wife of John Reed;
son Richard Simpson; grandchildren the children of Nathaniel
Hart and Tyree Harris decd.; granddaughters Polly Pratt wife of
James Pratt and Betsy Currie wife of Hugh Currie; daughters
Elizabeth Oldham wife of Jesse Oldham, Lydia Tait wife of
Zacheus Tait; granddaughter Priscilla Dickens wife of William
Dickens; the 3 youngest children of Waddy Tait decd. (Edy,
Zedekiah and Jesse); the 5 children of David Burton by his
first wife namely Zera, Chinai, Polly, John, and David.
Exec: son Richard. Wit: Benjamin Burford, Forister Stanback.
332 Inv. goods of Samuel Walker by Robt. King exec. 20 Oct. 1798.
333 Sale property of Bartholomew Bowers decd. 2 Oct 1797 by James
Grant Jun. adm.
333 Rent of plantation to John Mitchell and hire of negro woman
and child to David Hensley they being the property of estate
of Willima Mitchell decd. By John Hensley and John Mitchell,
exec.
334 Appraisal of negroes of Andrew Enocks decd., negro boy Cuff at
150 lbs. and negro woman Lucy at 50 lbs. Widow to receive her
part. 27 Sept 1798. By David Gooch, William Culbertson, Obed
Florance.
335 William Crosson 13 yrs. old bound to Edmund Rice.   /s/ William
Rainey Esq., Chairman of County Court.
336 Reubin Childress 10 yrs.old bound to Larkin Warrin.
337 David Morrow orphan 7 yrs. 9 mos. old bound to Reubin Cox.
338 Sales estate of John Rice on 16 Jan 1798 by Nathaniel Rice exec.
Sales to:

William Rice	John Kerr	Salley Jones
Nathaniel Rice	Alexr Kerr	John Morrow
David Hensley	Archibald Rice	Susannah Rice
William Clifton	Bartlett Estis	John Hensley
Howell Massey	James Sheppard	William Kimbrough
John Scoggin	Lewis Sheppard	Booker Sheppard
Benony Rosson	Anderson Williams	James Ray
Mary Strader	Anne Brooks	John Graves
John Jackson	Joseph Tait	Charles Shanks
Elijah Holder	William Slade	William Anglin
Lancelot Johnston	John Weeden	Robert Thompson
Thomas Vinson	Nathan Slade	Joseph Street
Sarah Thompson	Thomas Foster	Elisha Evans
Elizabeth Williams	Zeph. Tait	John Berry
Lewis Corbitt	Thomas Taylor	Thomas Richardson
Andrew McCullock	Charnal Hightower	William Ballard
Robert Martin	Elizabeth Thompson	Joseph Pogue
Joseph Chandler	William Brown(Sawyer)	Joseph Tait
Wm. B. Brooks	John Mallory	John Mitchell
Robert Sawyer	Alexander Porter	Richard Hensley
Thomas Mallory	John Mother(al)	Richard Estis
Henry Brewer	Nathan Williams	Frank Smith
James Yancey	Mary Thompson	Elizabeth Gardner
Robert Kimbrough	Robert Brown	Henry Rice
Samuel Dickey		

345 On 13 Mar 1798 Thomas Harrison gives to son William K. Harrison
500 acres land adj. land purchased by Wm. K. Harrison of James
Overstreet. Wit: Andrew Harrison, George B. Dameron, Jurat.

Book C cont. 1798-99
Page
345 Inv. estate of Neely Grant by Lucy Grant adm.
346 Sales estate of James Merritt decd. by Solomon Merritt adm.
28 July 1798. Sales to:

James Rainey	James Farley	William Gordon
George Thomas	Benjamin Howell	Thomas Boulten
Mathew Terry	Enoch Duneway	Letty Merritt
Jesse Robinson	Priestly Carter	Solomon Merritt
James Randolph	Thomas Madding	James Robinson
Theodorick Johnston		

Bonds on Thomas Fisher, Daniel S. Farley, Asa Thomas, Priestly
Carter, Henry Clift.

January Court 1799

348 Russell Kennon orphan 13 yrs. old last Nov. bound to Nicholas
Coils. (Also spelled Coyles).
349 John Darnell an orphan age 16 yrs. bound to Elijah Barton.
350 Eli Sharp orphan 6 yrs. old bound to Samuel Brackin.
351 George Sharp orphan 8 yrs. old bound to Greenbury Voss.
352 THOMAS HARRISON - Will - w. 20 Jan 1799. "It is my wish and
desire if Laws of North Carolina should ever take place for
freeing slaves for them to be set at Liberty". Land to be
divided among following sons on which each had built: William,
Andrew, Thomas, Charles, John, and Robert; daughters Elizabeth,
Jean, Mildred, Patsey; Wife; Exec: wife and sons William and
Andrew. Wit:Andrew Harrison Sen., Jeane Harrison (Jurat), Jane
Harrison (Jurat). Proved on oath of Jane Harrison and Jean
Harrison (the younger).
353 JOHN BROWN - Will - w. 7 June 1798. Wife Sarah; daughters Nancy
Harper, Elizabeth Swift, Sally Brown; sons Bedford, Jethro,
Robert, John, William, Green; grandson Bedford Brown; 4 young-
est children: Sally, Johnny, Billy, and Green. Exec: sons Bed-
ford, Robert, and John. Proved on oath of Doct. Lancelott
Johnston and Thomas Brooks.
354 MARTHA WARE - Will - w. 2 Apr 1797. Daughter Martha McCollum;
exec: William McCollum and his wife Martha. Test: John Thrasher,
John Johnston, Vachel Ingram. Proved on oath of Vachel Ingram.
355 GEORGE FARLEY - Will - w. 30 Nov 1798. Wife Catharine; daughter
Parthenia Farley; if Parthenia dies before she comes of age,
land to go to brothers John Farley and Henry Farley; brothers
and sisters; sister Mary Farley. Exec: wife, Henry Burton, and
David Mitchell. Wit: H. Burton, Mary Farley, Martha Wilson,
Kesiah Burton, John Wisdom.
356 ARCHELAUS CARLOS - Will - w. 10 July 1798. Wife Fanny Carlos
to get land purchased of Peter Smith and John Powel; daughters
Elizabeth and Nancy; children: Polly Dixon, William Carter
Carlos, Dolley Rice, Robert Cole Carlos, Elizabeth Boman, Nancy
Carlos. Exec: wife Fanny; Wit: C. Dixon, David Powel, James
Powel.
358 WILLIAM BOYD SEN. - Will - w. 2 Jan 1799. Son Armested Boyd to
get land in Halifax Co. Va. on waters of Miry Creek; son William
Boyd Jun. (land in Halifax Co. Va. on Dan River; son Stephen
Williamson Boyd (land in Halifax Co. Va. known as Double Cr.);
Wife Mary Boyd (land on Hogan's Cr.); Exec: Henry Cook and James
Chalmers(Va.)Sons Armistead and Benjamin. Wit: Dudley Gatewood,
Joel McDaniel, Jane Huston.

63

Book C cont. 1799
Page
360 JOHN HUGHES - Will - w. 31 Aug 1798. Wife Mary; sons Andy, John,
Gibson; daughter Obedience; unknown heir; Wit: Thomas Brinsfield, Samuel Fielder, Thomas Johnson.
362 Bond: David Hart to George Sims 7 Jan 1789 concerning deed of
land Sims resides on adj. Abner Powel & Turky pen Branch.
Test: Thomas Hart
363 Allotment to Sarah Brown widow of John Brown decd. By C. Dixon,
Lancelot Johnston, Robt. Blackwell. 22 Nov 1798.
364 Letter of Attorney: Elizabeth Enoch to Thomas Kimbrough to rent
her dower and take up writ as Thomas Kimbrough is guardian to
orphans of Andrew Enochs decd. Wit: James Yancey, Alex. Murphey. 24 Jan 1799.
365 Appraisal and allotment to 6 legatees of James Ingram:
John Ingram, Benjamin Ingram, Clary Ingram, Vaychel Ingram,
Moses Allen, Walter Ingram. By Samuel Henderson, John Graves,
and Jos Burton.
366 Sale estate of Jean Mullins by James Coyles adm.
367 Div. of slaves of Richard Brooks decd. to Ann Brooks, William B.
Brooks, James Shepperd in right of wife Frances, John Brooks.
By James Williamson, Nathaniel Rice, John Henslee. 14 Nov 1798.
368 Joseph and Mary Mains orphans of Matthew Mains in acct. with
Robert Mitchell guardian. Payment to Henry Davis for boarding,
clothing, and schooling from April 1782 til 7 Nov 1798.
369 Mary A. Moore orphan acct. with John Campbell guardian. 26 Jan
1799.
370 The estate of Matthew Mains in acct. with Joseph Cantrill.
Cash paid to James Dickey, Ephraim Bird, A. Murphey, John
Williams, to Henry Davis for one-third part as his wife's thirds.
14 Nov 1798. Approved by James Williamson, James Yancey,
Nathan Williams.
370 James Yancey's mark,cross and slit in the wright and slitt in the
Left year (ear).
371 Inv. estate of John Siddall given in by Ephraim Noel an exec.
372 Noel Burton in acct. with Jos.(or Jas) Burton guardian.
372 Inv. and sale of estate of Jno. Yates. Buyers:

Catharine Yates	Abner Robinson	James Samuel Sen.
William Williams	Reubin Phelps	Miss Frances Step-
Richard Gates	Bias Williams	hens
Jeremiah Samuel	Robert Wilson	George Samuel
Daniel S. Farley	James M. Williams	Archd. Samuel
James Samuel Jun.	John Brunt	John Burton
Crofton Williams	George Thomas	Lewis Vaughn
William Yates	Joseph Swan	Enoch Dunaway

Test: Daniel S. Farley, Archd. Samuel
376 Taxable property for 1798 - 850 white polls, 1129 black polls
376 THOMAS HORNBUCKLE - Will - w. 29 Mar 1799. Wife Nancy;
Sons Richard, William, George; daughters: Milly Windsor wife of
Thomas Windsor, Elizabeth Hardin wife of Henry Hardin, Susannah
Windsor wife of John Windsor, Sally Simpson wife of James
Simpson, Frances Rogers wife of William Rogers(land on Haw R.);
Nancy Keen wife of John Keen; grandson William Keen.
Exec: wife Nancy, son Richard, son in law James Simpson.
Wit: Samuel Cobb, Thomas Brinsfield, Owin Ballard.
Proved April Court 1799.

Book C cont. 1799

April Court 1799

Page
378 Sales estate of Samuel Greer. Sales to William Fitch, David Boren, William Lea, Henry Williams. By Margaret Greer, adm.
379 Inv. estate of Thomas Harrison Sen. on 20 Feb. 1799. Bonds on William Kennon, William and John Dix. By Wm. K. Harrison and Andrew Harrison exec.
381 Inv. estate of Archelaus Carlos 2 Apr 1799 by Fannie Carlos, exec.
382 Inv. estate of William Boyd by Armsted Boyd and Benjamin Williamson 27 Feby 1799.
383 Inv. of effects of George Farley 19 Apr 1799 by Catrine Farley.
384 Inv. estate of William Boyd HH formerly of Halifax Co. by James Chambers exec. 15 and 16 Apr 1799. Div. of slaves to Armistead Boyd and William Boyd.
387 Inv. estate of Thomas Graves 20 Apr 1799 by Azariah Graves adm. Included 26 slaves.
388 List of estate of Mary Simpson and sales to:

Thomas Hornbuckle	Russell Sullivant	James Hargrove
David Barker	Jere Lea	Jeremiah Buck Jun.
Joseph Walker	William Clifton	Benjamin Williamson
Robert Brown	David Hensley	Zachariah Hastings
Richard Simpson	Duke Williams	Samuel Cobb
William Brannock	John Scoggin	Jesse Rayne
William Tait	William Dickens	Owen Ballard
Henry Dickens	Richard Hornbuckle	Nathan Williamson
John Reed	James Ray	David Taylor
Joseph Benton	John Goodloe	Edward Noles
Benjamin Gibson	Thomas Mallory	John Nance
Simon Carlile	William McCullock	George Hornbuckle
Jeremiah Williamson	Samuel French	Jesse Brintle
William Noles	Charles Brooks	Malon Stacy
John Paschal	John Thomas	Rawling Vickers
Jesse Hollis		

390 Sale estate of John Yates 20 Mar 1799. Sales to:

William Yates	James Robertson	William Williams
Capt. George Samuel	Archd. Samuel	John Roper
Jeremiah Samuel	Enoch Dunaway	

391 Samuel Morris age 15 years and 6 mos. bound to Thomas Pendergast. /s/ Michael Montgomery, Chairman County Court.
392 Power of attorney: Sarah Brown to son Thomas Jouett to attend to all affairs and to settle with exec. of her decd. husband. 11 Mar 1799. Wit: John Byron, Green Lee Brown.
393 Sales estate of John Siddall by Job Siddall exec. Sales to:

Nancy Siddall	Ephraim Nowell	Nicholas Coyles
George White	Joseph Lewis	James Nowell
Job Siddall	Ira Siddall	Thomas Campbell
James Kimbrough	John Lea	Robert Long

July Court 1799

394 Sale estate of Thomas Graves 16 and 17 May 1799 at his late dwelling house by Solomon Graves, Azariah Graves, and Thos. Gunn adm. Sales to:

Hannah Graves	Thomas Gunn Jun.	James Graves
Jacob Graves	Nancy Graves	Solomon Graves
John Graves Jun.	Thomas Graves	James Turner
James Turner Jun.	Isbell Graves	Azariah Graves Sen.
Thomas Kimbrough	Azariah Graves Jun.	Alex Murphey
Groves Howard	John Graves Sen.	Richard Bennett

Book C cont. 1799
Page
394 Sale estate of Thomas Graves cont. Sales to:
    Thomas Yancey   John Kimbrough Sen.   Robert Kimbrough
    Thomas Morris   Jourdon Whitlow   Edmund Harper
    Thomas Simmons   Milner Bennett   John Bruce
    James Gunn   Charles Shanks   Robert Brown
    John Kimbrough Jun.
399 Appraisal and div. negroes belonging to the late Thomas Graves
    to following legatees: Hannah Graves, widow; Jacob Graves,
    John Graves, James Graves, Thomas Gunn, Nancy Graves, Thomas
    Graves, Isbell Graves, Azariah Graves, Lewis Graves, Majah
    Graves. Each legatee 155 lbs. 18 sh. 2 pence. Two negroes
    Hannah and Peter not appraised nor alloted on account of
    being demanded by George Barker. 25 slaves alloted.
    Div. by John Graves, Alex Murphey, Saml. Morton, Bazzley
    Graves.
400 July 11, 1799 - Received of David Gooch $476 being in full of
    his account as guardian for me. /s/ Henry Williams.
401 Inv. estate of Thomas Hornbuckle and of part to be divided to
    following legatees: Mrs. Nancy Hornbuckle, Betsy Hardin wife
    of Henry, Sally Simpson wife of James, Susannah Windsor wife of
    John. By Richd. Hornbuckle exec.
402 Inv. estate of John Brown by John H. Brown exec.
403 Inv. estate of John Rice 18 July 1799 by John Adams. Wit: Jett
    Burton.
403 Inv. balance of property of Jno Harrison 22 July 1799 after one
    year's allotment. By Thomas Pendergast.
404 William Glaspy orphan of 16 yrs. and 11 mos. and 8 days bound
    to Robert Donaldson.
405 Pharis Sommers orphan 10 yrs. bound to George Sommers.
    /s/ Archibald Samuel Esq., Chairman County Court.
406 Zere Sommers orphan 12 yrs. old bound to George Sommers.
407 Sally Hughs age 7 yrs. the 16 next Oct bound to Sarah Hughs.
408 Mary Harvill age 11 yrs the 1st last Jany bound to Andrew M.
    Bryant.
409 HENRY BALDWIN SEN. - Will - w. 14 Jan 1799. Wife Elizabeth;
    sons Henry, John, Edward, Luke; daughters Lucisy Clove, Betsy
    Baldwin, Priscilla Bastin, Hannah Baldwin; son Lazarus;
    Exec: wife Elizabeth; Wit: Thomas Duncan, Andrew Hogg (Jurat),
    Ephrain Russell(Jurat).
410 HENRY DAVIS - Will - w. 25 Oct 1798. Wife Mary Norman Davis;
    Exec: wife. Wife to pay each child, sons and daughters,
    5 sh each within 1 yr. Wit: Anthony Horton, Andrew McClary.
411 WILLIAM THOMAS - Will - w. 17 Apr 1798. brothers Philip Thomas,
    Asa Thomas to get land; Exec: James Sanders, William Moore,
    Asa Thomas. Wit: Jesse Robertson, Nathaniel Pass, Theod.
    Johnston.

October Court 1799

412 Inv. estate of John Hughs by Mary Hughs adm.
412 Inv. estate Henry Baldwin by Elizabeth Baldwin exec.
413 Inv. estate of Stewart Farley by John Burton and Hez. Farley.
415 Inv. property of Henry Davis on 18 July 1799 given in by Mary
    Norman Davis. Cash due from James Hughs, Anythony Horton.
415 Amt. of rent of plantation and hire of negro woman belonging to
    estate of William Mitchell decd. William Scoggin to rent of
    plantation, Robert Lackey to hire of woman. By John Hensley and
    John Mitchell, exec.

66

Book C cont. 1799 - 1800
Page
416 STEWART FARLEY - Will - w. 21 Mar 1798. Wife Mary Farley;
son Hezekiah (tract of land I live on);John Burton (negroes
Bob, Dick, Sall); Henry Burton; remainder of estate to be sold
and divided between Daniel S. Farley, Hezekiah Farley, John
Burton, and Henry Burton. Exec: Daniel S. Farley, John Burton,
Hez. Farley. Wit: Durrett Richards, Ambrose Arnold.
417 Charles Craddock in Amealey (Amelia) County (Va.) to Stewart
Farley to balance of bond left in hands of William Cross Craddock to collect, amt. not ascertain.
James Farley Sen., Nottaway County (Va.) to Stewart Farley to
a part of a legacee left to me by John Farley the amt. not ascertain, an inventory will be found amongst my papers of the
goods. James Wilkerson Halifax Co. Va. to Stewart Farley to note
to be found in my papers.
The above accounts I give to John Burton provided he leave to
collect them. /s/ Stewart Farley. 21 Mar 1798. Wit: Durrett
Richards.
417 BENJAMIN SHELTON - Will - w. 4 Mar 1799. Wife Rebeckah;
sons Leonard, Clever; black people should have privilege of
choosing their master; Exec: wife; Wit: Peter Ruark(Jurat),
John Price Sen. Rebeckah Shelton widow and relict qualified
as exec.
418 Mourning Gilaspy orphan 10 yrs. 6 mos. old bound to James Sin-
clear.
419 Mary Jones orphan 4 yrs and 4 mos old bound to Robert Parks.
/s/ John McMullen Esq., Chairman County Court.
420 Sale residue of estate of John Harrison. By Thomas Pendergast.
421 Sale estate of John Rice on 10 Aug 1799. Buyers: Esther Rice,
John Adams, Peter Smith, Joel McDaniel, William Gomer.
By John Adams, adm.

January Court 1800

423 Sale estate of George Farley by H. Burton and Catharine Farley,
exec. Buyers:

Catharine Farley	William Mansfield	Bayly Byrd
Thomas Neely	Henry Fuller	Jeremiah Brooks
David Mitchell	James Warren	James Birk
Abraham Holsonback	Thomas Barnett	William Stewart
Henry Burton	Hackley Warren	Alexander Wiley
John Wisdom		

425 List of sale of Sarah Brown decd. sold by Jeptha Rice adm. Buyers:

Robert Blackwell	George Sims	Thomas Jouett
Jeptha Rice	Robert Boman	James Shelton
Lancelot Johnston	Edmond Rice	John Brown

426 Sale of property of Robt. Harris by Duke Williams adm. Sales to:
Duke Williams, Richard Simpson, John Cox Doctor, Jeremiah William-
son.
427 Inv. estate of William Abel on 15 Nov 1799 by Thomas Bastin adm.
428 Allotment of land of Thomas Graves to said legatees:
John Graves -land adj. Dr. Johnston.
Jacob Graves - land adj. Thomas Yancey, widow's dower, & Mill Cr.
James Graves - adj. widow's dower and North fork Country Line
Cr. & Mill Cr.
William Moore - land called Carrols tract.
Azariah Graves - land called Red land fork adj. Thomas Kimbrough
and Country Line Cr.
Major Graves - land called Williams tract at Ridg Path crossing
the creek.
cont. next page   67

Book C cont. 1800
Page
429 Allotment of land of Thomas Graves cont.
   Thomas Graves - land called French's tract on North fork of
     South fork of Country Line Cr. adj. Alex Murphey and Kim-
     brough's line to small hickory near old Court house Road.
   Thomas Gunn - land called Joneses Tract adj. Widow Browning
     old line along Ridg Path.
   Esbel Graves - land called new survey adj. Alex Murphey, Jno.
     and Thomas Kimbrough.
   Lewis Graves - land called Wiley's Tract adj. Thomas Wiley,
     John Richmond, and Shadden's corner, and aj. John Graves
     Jun.
   Div. by Alex Murphey, John Graves, Barzillai Graves. State-
   ment with legatees of Thomas Graves:

John Graves	214 acres	Lewis Graves	350 acres
Jacob Graves	282 "	Major Graves	188 "
James Graves	128 "	Thomas Graves	210½ "
William Moore	183 "	Thomas Gunn	212 "
Azariah Graves	354 "	Esbell Graves	376 "

   Total acres 2497½
   Total value 1552 lbs., 10 sh. 6 pence.
431 Div. of negroes belonging to John Brown decd. among legatees:
   Sarah B. Brown, John H. Brown, William Brown, Green L. Brown.
   14 Nov 1799. Div. by Lancelot Johnston, Robert Blackwell,
   Samuel Moore, John Buchannon.
432 Div. negroes of Robt. Harris decd. between A. Duke Williams in
   right of his wife and Robert Harris an infant of Robert Harris,
   decd. Comm: A. Graves, James Williamson, John Reid, Lancelot
   Johnston, Jno. Sommers, Robert Blackwell.
433 Appraisal negroes of Thomas Slade estate and drawing of negroes
   by following legatees:

Thomas Slade	Josiah Slade	Susannah Talbert
William Slade	Ezekiel Slade	Catherine Lea
Nathan Slade	Nancy Graves	Hannah Lea

   Div. by Thomas Donoho, Sol Graves, Thomas Bouldin.
434 Green Smith a base born child age 3 yrs. next June bound to
   Robert Smith.
435 DEVERUX INGE - Will - w. 15 June 1799. Matthew Terry and
   Alexr. Hall to divide working tools if said Hall finished his
   indenture with Terry and if not Terry to have all.
   Exec: Matthew Terry. Wit: D. Richards (Jurat), John Stanfield.

April Court 1800

436 Letter of attorney: Mary Burrows exec. of estate of John
   Burrows decd late of Dorset Co. Md.,and James Brockman and
   Betsy Brockman wife of James and daughter of John Burrows to
   James Arnett of Caswell County to demand and receive of Jonathan Patridge or Dorset Co. all estate and property due them
   from estate of said John Burrows. 1 May 1800. Wit: Benj.
   Williamson JP, R. Hill JP.   (Name may be Burrous.)
437 Letter of attorney: Ursley Anthony to friend Elijah Anthony to
   recover money, debts, goods due from estate of William Anthony
   in State of Tennessee, Sullivan Co., and in State of Virginia,
   Henry Co. or else where he the said William died, said Ursley
   being exec. of John Anthony brother to said William Anthony.
   28 April 1800. Wit: Thos. Simmons, William Bird (Jurat).

Book C cont. 1800
Page
438 THOMAS RICE - Will - w. 13 Apr 1800. Wife Abegail; son Zeri
    Rice; 6 children or heirs: Zeri Rice, George Sims, Robert
    Blackwell, Lancelot Johnston, Daniel Gwyn, Tench Vannoy;
    negro Lydia to choose her master; Margaret Lackey; land on
    Country Line where John Payne (Taylor) formerly lived to be
    sold; surveying instruments to be sold; after wife's death
    land to be divided among her children; each child to have
    a horse as it comes of age. Exec: Robert Blackwell, Lancelot
    Johnston. Wit: Thos. Slade (Jurat), Zear Gwyn. Codicil: Four
    youngest sons to have blacksmith tools. 13 Apr 1800.
439 SALLY PERKINS - Will - w. 18 Apr 1800. Mother Usley Cannon;
    sister Lucy Grant; nephew Pleasant Perkins Coleman.
    Exec: friend Ellis Evans. Wit: Joseph Dameron, Daniel Gossage.
    Ellis Evans qualified as exec.
440 Fanny Morrow orphan 7 yrs. old bound to Benjamin Howell.
441 James Watson orphan 12 yrs. and 2 mos. old bound to Elijah
    Carman.
442 Alexr. Walton orphan 8 yrs. old bound to Whitehead Page.
443 James Alverson orphan of 14 yrs. 3 mos. bound to Matthew Terry.
444 Settlement estate of John Womack decd. by Josiah Womack adm.
    Cash received from Charlton Ingram, Wyatt Stubblefield, Clara
    Stone. Cash paid to Jethro Brown, W. Bethell, Col. J. Willson,
    John Lenox, James Grant, Thomas Jeffreys, J. Philpot, Mrs.
    Mills, Leven Downs, I. Griffin, James M. Burton, D. Burton,
    C. Ingram.
    Approved by C. Dixon, Jas. Somers, John Cobb.
445 Thomas Pendergast, adm.,settlement estate of John Harrison.
    Approved by James Yancey, William Pleasant, Solomon Parks.
446 Estate of Andrew Burton decd. in acct. with Jas. Burton adm.
    Payments to leagatees: Thomas Harrison, John Martin, Joseph
    Dameron,guardian for Latty Burton, guardian for Polly Burton,
    Robert Burton, James Burton, guardian for Noel Burton.
446 Deed of gift: Robert Burton to William B. Burton, gifts of live-
    stock and household furniture for to discharge any debts
    against his estate. Wit: John McAden, Richard Goin, Richard
    Kiggins.
447 Deed of gift: Robert Burton to sisters Lucy Martin, Jane Harri-
    son, Sally and Polly Burton, gifts of slaves.
448 Inv. estate of Peter Lay decd. taken 20 Jan 1800 by Thomas Slade,
    adm.
448 Sales estate of Peter Lay Feb 1800. Sales to:

Richard Boman	Patsey Lay	John Pogue
James Cinclair	Solomon Graves	Thomas McFarling
Mary Lay	John Smithy	Jacob AHart
Francis Smith Jun.	Bird Lay	Thomas Rice
George Stovall	William Bruce	Zachariah Groom
John Graves Sen.	John Terry	

July Court 1800

450 Letter of attorney: Margaret Greer adm. and William Culberson adm.
    of estate of Samuel Greer decd. to Jonathan Davis of Greenville
    Dist. South Carolina to ask for and receive money due by Samuel
    Kelly of aforesaid Dist. S.C. 24 Mar 1800. Wit: A. Murphey,
    John Burton.

Book C cont. 1800
Page
451 Acct. of estate of Samuel Greer by Margaret Greer and Wm. Cul-
berson adm. Cash paid sheriff for costs in suit on the adm.
of Samuel Kelly; cash paid to Beauford Pleasant, James Guttery,
James Kitchen, Edmund Browning, James Currie, Joseph McReynolds,
John White, Margret Man, Fanny Man, James Coleman, Jonathan
Nichols, Thos. Sloan.
452 Bond: Hezekiah Rice to Richard Henson - Rice to procure Richard
Henson lawful deed for 200 acres land whereon Henson lives.
Wit: Anderson Butler, Thos. Swift, Lewis Pike.
Bond assigned from Henson to David Poyner for value received.
20 Oct 1788. /s/ Richard Hinson. Test: Morgan Ponder, James
Walker.
453 Letter of attorney: Edmund Haggard late of Caswell Co. now of
Kentucky to John Swift to demand money or institute suit.
2 Nov 1799. Wit: DK Williams, Nathan Williamson.
453 Inv. and sales estate of Robert Dixon decd. taken 26 Apr 1800
by C. Dixon adm.
454 HUGH DOBBINS of Clark Co. state of Tennessee - Will - w. 29 July
1797. Wife Ann Dobbins to get one-sixth part; 640 acres land
in Clark Co. to wife during her life; sons John and Thomas
Dobbins; daughters Elizabeth, Margaret, and Rachel; lots in
Clarkswell ? Co. TN to be sold; sloop in Baltimore port called
Eliza commanded by Captain Johnson Messick of New York to be
sold on July 1 next and money used in purchase of slaves;
money in a gentleman's hand at Petersburg, Va. Exec: wife Ann,
son John, and friend James Moore. Wit: Samuel Freeman, David
Chapman, Elizabeth Chapman.
Proved 15 Aug 1799 in Baltimore County on oaths of Samuel Free-
man and David Chapman. /s/ Wm. Buchanan, Register of Wills of
Baltimore Cty.
Proved in Orphans Court for Baltimore County, Md. 11 June 1800.
Written copy proved in Caswell County July 1800.

457 BARKLEY ELAM - Will - w. 20 Mar 1800. Wife Mary J. Elam;
son William Wilson Elam(under lawful age); daughters Mary J.
Harris, Phebe B. Elam, Nancy Elam; land and mill to be sold.
Exec: friends William Gordon, Jesse Carter Esq., Robert H.
Childers. Wit: Simon Roberts (Jurat), Thomas Roberts,
Robert H. Childers.
458 Inv. estate of Thomas Rice taken 3 May 1800 by Lancelot Johnston and Robert Blackwell exec.
459 Inv. property of James Martin decd. by John Martin adm.
460 Inv. estate of Sally Perkins taken 14 June 1800 by Ellis Evans,
exec. Bonds on Levi Blackwell, John Denis, James Richardson.
Sale of estate of Sally Perkins to William Kennon.
461 Sally Harvell orphan 8 yrs. old bound to Elijah Barton.
462 Allen Harvell orphan 5 yrs. old bound to Elijah Barton.
463 Bond: Whereas David Mason hath undertaken the Building of addition to End of the Bridge at Capt. John Graves Mill agreeable to
order directed to John Graves Sen. and John Yancey commissioners to let building of same and bid was let to Mason for 3 lbs.
and Mason will keep bridge for 5 years. Wit: J. Yancey, John
Graves.
464 Robert Parks, Trustee of Caswell County, in acct. with Caswell
County. 1796-1798.
467 Adm. of James Smith decd. acct. with the estate. Voucher paid to
David Dickey. By Sarah Smith and David Dickey adm. of James
Smith. Approved by David Mitchell, William Warren, James Yancey.

Book C cont. 1800

Page
468 Letter of attorney: John Thomas of Pittsylvania County, Commonwealth of Va., to friend Henry Cook of Hallifax Co. Va. to
bargain and sell tract of land in Sumner County, Tennessee on
Cumberland River, 250 acres, said land purchased from James
Dix on 14 Oct 1799. 29 Oct 1800.
469 Letter of Attorney: Ann Dobbins of Caswell County exec. to last
will of Hugh Dobbins decd. to friend and brother James Moore of
Montgomery County, Tennessee to demand and receive from persons
in Tenn. or Kentucky that may be in any way indebted to Hugh
Dobbin. 24 Oct 1800.
470 Letter of attorney: Thomas Bouldin and John Willson, Merchants
and partners of Caswell County to Joseph Payne and James Turner
of same county to institute suits, recover and demand all debts
due. 13 Oct 1800. /s/ Thomas Bouldin for Bouldin and Willson.
471 Disposition taken of Peter P. Thornton by William Scott and
Thomas Humphreys. A case involving Davis Booker as Pltff. and
Daniel S. Farley and John Burton as defendents. In 1784 after
returning from sermon in Halifax Co. to Mr. William Oliver's
to Dinner, Daniel S. Farley came to Mr. Olivers and enquired
for Reubin Thornton. Brother of said Thornton was within.
Peter Thornton signed for his brother receipt for benefit of
Farley against a bond in favor of Davis Booker. Brother Reubin
Thornton married the widow of William Munford who was Sister of
Henry Ward mentioned in the receipt.
Above disposition proved Campbell Co. Va. - "that Peter P.
Thornton made disposition at Tavern of Charles Hoyle in town of
Lynchburg at 5 O'clock, Friday 24 day Oct 1800." /s/ Wm. Scott
and Thos. J. Hunphreys.
Receipt: April 10, 1784 - Rec. of Mr. Henry Ward in favor of
Daniel S. Farley 1060 lbs crop tobacco it being in full of bond
given Davis Booker. /s/ Reubin Thornton. Test: Peter P.
Thornton. Recorded Caswell Co. Oct. term 1800.

473 THOMAS WILSON - Will - w. 11 Oct 1800. Wife Keziah Wilson;
four daughters Rachel, Mary, Keziah, and Elizabeth; daughter
Rebekah Foote; sons Johnston Wilson (land adj. Askridges line
and Samuel Johnstons line), Abner (adj. Johnston Wilsons line),
William, Henry, Jeremiah (home tract on North Hico); 3 last
sons under lawful age and of last wife. Exec: wife and Gabriel
Lea and John Warrick. Test: Wm. Gordon, Thos. Kendrick, Thos.
Stafford. /s/ Thomas Willson.
Codicil: Thomas Wilson; wife; daughters Rachel Wilson, Mary
Reed, Keziah Wilson, Elizabeth Wilson. 13 Oct 1800.
Keziah Wilson and John Warrick qualified as exec.

476 ABRAHAM WOMACK - Will - w. 15 Sept 1796. sons William, Josiah;
daughters Mary Benton, Nancy Engram, Lucy Engram, Sinie Brackin,
Elizabeth Womack. Exec: son Josiah and friend William Bethell.
Wit: William Bethell, Jeremiah Stubblefield, Nancy Bethell.
Josiah Womack qualified as exec.

477 John Hinton minor orphan age 12 yrs. 3 mos. bound to Freeman
Hubbard. /s/ Azariah Graves Esq. Chairman of County Court.
22 Jan 1798.

END OF BOOK C

Taxable Property for 1799

	Acres of Land	White Polls	Black Polls	Tax Horses
Richmond District	74933	923	459	468
Caswell District	33385½	130	159	501
Gloucester District	53039	221	236	100
St. Davids District	61746⅜	266	363	220
Total Amount	223104	818.11	95	£20.16.8

Test: A. Murphey Clk

Taxable Property for 1800

	Acres of Land	White Polls	Black Polls	Tax Horses
Richmond District	76987½	242	505	98
Caswell District	62643½	179	711	60
Gloucester District	59124	220	282	138
St. Davids District	5746½	240	322	133
Total Amount	236018	881	1330	8.4

Test: A. Murphey Clk

Book D - Page 11

Book D - October 1800 - April 1803

October Court 1800 cont. from Book C

Page
1 THOMAS HINTON - Will - w. 25 Aug 1800. Has given to all children except son Sterling Hinton; all property bequeathed to son
  Christopher Hinton requesting him to take charge of son Sterling. Exec: son Christopher. Wit: Jas. Gunn, Ralph Hubbard,
  Freeman Hubbard.
2 Sales estate of James Martin decd. by John Martin adm.
2 Amt. rent of plantation and hire of negro belonging to estate of
  William Mitchell.
3 Inv. estate of Barkley Elam taken 25 Oct 1800 by Jno. Wilson adm.
4 Inv. and sales perishable part estate of Aquilla Stansbury decd.
  taken on 17 May 1800. Sales to:
  Capt. Richard Simpson   Auston Browder   Henley Hunphreys
  Jacob Wright Jun.   William Underwood   John Keen
  Jeptha Rice   Chalton Ingram   Robert Mullins
  Luke Stansbury
5 Inv. goods and chattels of Hugh Dobbin decd. taken 24 Oct 1800
  by Ann Dobbin exec.
5 Inv. estate of Robert Burton decd. by William B. Burton adm.
6 Bond: William Muzzall esq. as Sheriff of Caswell Co. 29 July
  1800. Bondsmen: Richd. Simpson, Azariah Graves.
7 Bond: William Muzzall as tax collector.
8 Henry Quine orphan 14 yrs. 9½ mos. old bound to Michael Montgomery.
9 William Nipper 13 yrs old bound to Joseph Eddings.
  /s/ Michael Montgomery esq. Chairman County Court.
10 Alsey Hudson, female child of colour, orphan 2 yrs. old, bound
   to Zephaniah Tait.
11 Taxable property for 1799 and 1800. (See page 72 this book.)

January Court 1801

12 DAVID SHELTON - Will - w. 31 Mar 1800. Wife Susannah Shelton.
   daughter Elizabeth Shelton (under age) (land on South side
   Country Line where I formerly lived adj. James Lea, Joseph Swann);
   oldest son by present wife named James Shelton (land adj. Jesse
   Carter and Jacob Wright purchased of Col. William Moore);
   son David (under age) (land adj. Alexander Dobbin decd.);
   daughter Nancy Shelton (land adj. Nicholas Matlock and land purchased of George Rudd and Jesse Carter);
   youngest son Henry Shelton (land adj. Wm. Yates, Jesse Carter);
   Land willed to devisor by Thomas Harrison now at law for with
   Col James Sanders to be sold and divided among 5 children.
   Tract of land in Tenn. on Deer River 3000 acres out of which
   Col James Robinson is to have 1000 acres and John Barnett 666;
   land on Red River (grant not obtained) to go to 5 children;
   150 acres called Stalk field, 254 acres part of 1000 acre tract,
   300 acres in Daniel Boons hands, 2200 acres in David Conneleys
   hand, 1658 acres part claimed by Doctor Hager and 50 acres on
   Cumberland River all to go to 5 children.
   Exec: wife Susannah, friend Herndon Haralson, and grandson David
   Southerland. Wit: Nicholas Matlock, Elizabeth Cunningham,
   Elizabeth Matlock, John Kersey.
   Codicil: 3 children not mentioned by first wife: John Shelton,
   Agnes Southerlin, Lucy Carney had already received their part.
   30 Apr 1800. Wit: Joseph Hall, William Cunningham, Mary Haralson.

73

Book D cont. 1801
Page
16 LAWRENCE VANHOOK - Will - w. 6 Apr 1797; wife Mary (land adj.
Joseph Carney); if Zachariah Jones and wife Elizabeth die with-
out issue, negro woman lent them to go to 5 children of devisor:
Loyd Vanhook, son in law William Lea, Aron Vanhook, Lawrence
Vanhook, son-in-law Thomas Hargis; Exec: Loyd Vanhook and Wil-
liam Lea. Wit: William Hargis Sen., William Lea, Elizabeth
Hargis.
Codicil: Business to stand as actually finished.
Proved on oath of Wm. Lea Jun. and Eliza Hargis.

18 JOHN MCMINAMY (McMinnamy) - Will - w. 12 Sept 1800.
Son Alexander and his son John; daughter Sarah Motheral and her
daughters; daughter Jeane; son William to have plantation and
rent of place on Eno. Exec: sons Alexander and William.
Wit: Thos. Pendergast, John Pendergast.

19 WILLIAM MCKEE - Will - w. 23 Apr 1799. Wife Martha;
son Robert (land with house on which he lives); daughter Mary
(land where I live adj. Robert), Jesse; daughter Agness.
Exec: John McMinimay, James Clark, son Robert.
Wit: William McCord, Ann Dunn, John Rainey Jun.

20 Jenne Johnston's ear Mark: a swallow fork in each ear.

21 THOMAS GUNN - Will - w. 13 Nov 1800. Wife Eloner Gunn;
sons John, Allen, Sterling, Daniel, Thomas; son in law Ellis
Evans; sons James, Griffin, Anderson, Pickney; daughters Sally
Burton, Prsicilla Gunn. Exec: James Burton and son Griffin Gunn.
Wit: C. Dixon, Moses Ingram, Ann Green.

22 Sale part of property of Samuel Paul decd.   Sales to:

Richard Kigins	James Paul	Thomas Finn (Feans)
Freeman Hubbard	Jenne Hodge	Thomas Harrison
William Payne	Andrew Harrison	Robert Paul
Ralph Hubbard	Calib Carmon	Wm. B. Burton
Edward Lewis	Benjamin Walker	Elijah Ingram
Richard Hill	Benjamin Hooper	Kitt Hinton
Mary Alverson	Charles Dixon	Benjamin Quine
Meredith Price	Joseph Dameron	Darling Ray
John Martin	Michael Montgomery	Epp Stone
Joel McDaniel	George White	Thomas Ray
William Gordon	Daniel Price	William Knight
John Everett	Samuel Dameron	Archibald Alverson
Peter Smith	Wm. K. Harrison	Findal Rowland
Charles Payne	Judith Paul	Daniel Coleman
John Dix	Molly Alversom	John Nipper
Thomas Baxter	Henry Howard	Spilby Coleman
Noel Coleman	Garland Hill	Richard Hill
Groves Howard	John Lea	

By James Paul adm.

27 Sales estate of Robert Bruce decd taken 5 Nov 1800.   Sales to:

Malicha Holloman	Elijah Burton	Daniel Gunn
James Carrol	Henry Atkinson	Jeptha Rice
William Moore	Robert Bruce	Starling Carrol
John Payne (Taylor)	Thomas Kimbrough	James Graves
Richard Martin	Clever Shelton	John Kimbrough
John Graves	Jacob Graves	Josiah Morton
Wm. Bruce (1 Bible)	Solomon Graves	Frances Rice
James Turner	Ann Yancey	Thomas Smith
Barzillai Graves	Alex Murphey	

By James Carrol adm.

Book D cont. 1801
Page
30 Sales of property of William Quine sold 13 Nov 1800. Sales to:

James Burton	John Martin	Adam Stafford
Reubin Cox	John Ingram	James Claymore
Richard Haddock	Chalton Ingram	Caleb Carmon
George Powell	Edward Waddleton	Forbes Mann
James Gunn	James Richardson	Benj. Quine
Thomas Gunn Jun.	Elijah Carmon	Groves Howard
Jesse Bever	William Carmon	Henry Howard
Jacob Miles	Jacob Quine	Francis Howard
John Forgus	Woodley Hooper	William Kennon

By Benjamin Quine, exec.

32 Bond: Joseph Hart, Archibald Hart, Eliz. Hart and Duke Williams
bound unto James Kinnebrew and Benj. Joans of Sussex County, Va.
to make deed to 365 acres land sold by Joseph Hart to Kinnebrew
and Joans on waters of Country Line Cr. and Stony Cr. surveyed
by David Hart decd. 27 Jan. 1801. Test: James Moore, William
Hargrave, John Swift. Bond delivered to Wm. Kinnebrew 20 May
1804.
33 Inv. estate of Samuel Paul by James Paul adm. on 22 Nov 1800.
Included 4700 ? tob° pased at Danville; judgments against
Benjamin Hardister; bond on Ellis Evans.
34 Inv. estate of Abraham Womack taken Nov 1800 by Josiah Womack.
34 Inv. estate of Thomas Willson decd. by John Warrick exec.
35 Zephaniah Campbell orphan 18 yrs. old on 25 Dec next bound to
Freeman Hubbard.
36 Aron Smith orphan 17 yrs. in Apr next bound to Richard Hornbuckle.

April Court 1801

37 Power of attorney: John Thomas of Pittsylvania Co. Va. to friend
Durrett Richards of Caswell Co. to ask for and obtain any money
or debts due to Thomas. 15 Apr 1801. Test: John Rodgers, Shad-
rick Taylor, William Fuqua, William Wilkerson.
38 Allotment to Sarah Mayhan Relict of William Mayhan decd. 14 Feby
1801. Wit: John Anderson, Thomas Loyd.
39 Sales estate of Thomas Gunn 6 & 7 Febry 1801 by Jas. Burton and
Griffin Gunn exec. Sales to:

Elinor Gunn(widow)	Maj. Richard Sanders	Benjamin Hooper
James Gunn	Griffin Gunn	William White
John Gunn	Wynn Dixon	Freeman Hubbard
Sterling Gunn	Henry Atkinson	David Thomas Sen.
Elisha Winn	Alexander Murphey	Jacob Wright
Daniel Gunn	Richard Bennett	Daniel Gossage
Thomas Harrelson	James Turner(Constable)	John Graves Jun.
Thomas Gunn	Richard Haddock	George Southerlin
Capt. John Graves	Daniel Jennings	Robert H. Childers
Daniel Gwyn	George B. Dameron	Epoproditus Stone
James Burton	Jesse Bever	Robert Woodlief
William Carmon	James Richardson	Hooper

48 Inv. estate of Thomas Gunn taken 15 Dec 1800.
50 Inv. perishable property of estate of William Mayhan decd. taken
28 Feby 1801 by Sarah Mahan adm.
51 Sales of part of estate of William Mahan 20 Mar 1801. Buyers:

Sarah Mahan	Col° Robert Parks	Thomas Simmons
Samuel Dickey	Thomas Mallory	John Mallory
John Hensley	Robert Mitchell	

Book D cont. 1801
Page
53 Deed of Gift: Ambrose Foster of Halifax Co. Va. to grandchildren
Robert McCain, Polly McCain, and John Foster McCain, gift of
negro girl named Lucy and her increase, said slaves to live with
children and their father Alexander McCain until John Foster
McCain obtain full age. 31 Jan 1801. Wit: A. E. Murphey, Sol
Debow.
54 Debtors to estate of Saml. Paul: Ellis Evans, Benjamin Hardester,
William Knight.
Div estate of Saml. Paul to Jesse Bennett who married Pattey Paul,
to Richard Kiggans who married Rachel Cox the daughter of said
Saml. Paul, to Robert Paul, to David Roper, to James Paul, and to
Judith Paul widow. 3 Feb 1801. Div by Dudley Gatewood, Richd.
Sanders, Starling Gunn.
55 Schedule of property of Allen Gunn orphan in hands of Griffin Gunn
his guardian. Schedule of property of Priscilla Gunn orphan of
Thomas Gunn decd. in hands of James Burton guardian.
55 William Woods ear mark with which he marks his stock to wit: an
under keel in each ear.

July Court 1801

56 Settlement estate of John Rice decd. Bonds on Bartlett Estis,
Nathan Slade; cash in hands of Wm. and Nathanl. Rice.
57 Inv estate of William Stephens by Anthony Stephens adm. 20 July
1801.
58 Inv estate of Nathaniel Rice decd. by Jas. Yancey and Susannah
Rice adm.
59 Estate of George Farley decd. Accts. paid to William Lea Sen.,
James Cochran, Simeon Cochran, Mary Cooper, Samuel Motheral,
John McMullen, Phillip Sneed, John Stafford, Elizabeth Hargis,
Lawrence Lea, Lancelott Johnston, Thomas Simmons, Wm. Lea Jun.,
David Mitchell, John Brown, Thomas Jeffreys, John Woods. Commrs:
L. Lea, J. McMullen, Isaac Rainey.
59 Ordered that 6 pence be laid on the poll and two pence on every
100 acres land for support of the poor in 1801. Test: Thos.
Gunn, Clk.
60 Allotment to Abigail Rice widow of Thomas Rice decd. (land adj.
Thomas Slade). By Jethro Brown, Saml. Moore, John Buchanon,
John Graves.
61 Estate of John Siddall: accts. paid to John McAden, John Lea,
Azariah Graves, John Graves, Carter and Burton, Job Siddall,
Ephraim Nowell. Notes on John Ferguson, Cobb Wright, Robert Boman.
By Job Siddall and Ephraim Nowell, exec.
62 Sale of property belonging to John Martin, Ellis Evans, Henry Lewis,
George Martin, William P.G.M.Martin. 6 Sept 1800. Sold by John
Martin and Ellis Evans.
63 Valuation personal estate of Nathaniel Rice decd. by John Henslee,
Malon Stacy, Thomas Johnston commrs.
65 Settlement estate of Aquilla Stansbury by Luke Stansbury adm.
17 May 1800. Cash received of William Clemson and William Dixon.
Accts. paid to Jacob Wright, John Willson and son, William Speller, Jas. Colquehon; bonds due from Richard Simpson; notes due
from Chalton Ingram and Henley Humphries; judgment in James
Turner's hands against Jeptha Rice; acct. due from James M.
Burton.
66 Inv estate of David Shelton on 9 Mar 1801 by Susannah Shelton and
H. Haralson exec.

Book D cont. 1801
Page
67 Inv estate of Laurence Vanhook.   Debts or notes on:

Phillip Sneed	Philip Hall Sen.	Thomas Miles
Thomas Hargis	Abraham Hargis	John Milner Jun.
Loyd Vanhook	Richd. Hamlet	Nath. Norfleet
William Lea	Thomas Hargis	James Nelson
Richd. Carnal	William Hargis	John Parker
John Ashburn	John Johnston	Thomas Riggs
William Brekeen	John Holsonback	Thomas Roan
Pemberton Burch	Betsey Hargis	George Runnolds
Jacob Grider	Zach Jones	Duncan Rose
Patrick Carnal	William Lea Sen.	William Stevens
Joseph Carney	Lawrence Lea	Mary Vanhook
John Dameron	Wm. Lea Jun.	Lawrence Vanhook
Barth Dameron	James Lea	Aron Vanhook
Christr. Dameron	Rachel Lesley	Jacob Vanhook
George Darby	Reubin Long	Willis Wells
James Dollarhide	John McFarlan	Thomas Word
Lewis Evans	Robert Malone	Abner Willson
Richd. Eskridge Jun.	James McMurray	Kindle Vanhook
George Eskridge	Staple Malone	Pulliam Williamson
William Herley	John Miles	William Yalock
		Vincent Warren

68 Inv estate of William McAden decd. by Jane McAden adm.

70 MACKSFIELD HENSLEE - Will - w. 31 Dec 1794. Wife Martha;
sons John, David(land known by name of Wm. Henslee);
daughter Mary Henslee; granddaughter Sarah Henslee Thomson;
daughter Susannah Oldham; daughter Nancy Payne; granddaughter
Elizabeth Cary Mitchell. Exec. sons John and David. Wit: Nathan
Williams, Eli Stacy. John Henslee refused to qualify exec. and
David Henslee the other qualified.

73 Statement of sales of estate of John Rice.
73 William Price adm. of Edward Mills decd., accts paid by Allen
Nichols and Thomas Longville. Commrs: Richard Hill, William
Moss, Joseph Arnett.
74 Settlement estate of Edwd. Mills. Payments to:

Mary Burrows	Absolem Sawyer	James Colquehon
Simon Ford	Gregory Durham	Benjamin Nichols
James Powell	John Willson	John Price
John Nichols		

Paid widow Mills for her part of estate; paid William Mills
for his part of estate.

75 THOMAS EVANS - Will - w. 8 Apr 1801. Wife Mary; youngest son
William; daughter Frances Ashburn wife of D. Anderson Ashburn;
son Jesse Evans to get mathamatical books and Scale of Dividing;
daughter Pherilee Evans wife of Daniel Evans; son Lewis Evans;
daughter Pheeby Malone wife to Staples Malone; Exec: friend
John Warrick and Gabriel Lea Esq. Wit: Robert Thomas, Thomas
Langley.

77 Bond: Gabriel Lea esq. as Sheriff of Caswell County. 29 July 1801.
Wit: Robt. Williams.

October Court 1801

78 Bond: Gabriel Lea as sheriff and Tax Collector. Bonded by Wm.
Muzzle, Daniel Darby.

Book D cont. 1801-1802
Page
79 Sales estate of Macksfield Henslee. Sales to:

John Henslee	Charles Brooks	John Scoggins
Mary Henslee	Thomas Mallory Sen.	James Simpson
David Henslee	Thomas Mallory Jun.	James Mallory
Rawley Vickers	Robert Sawyers	Nathan Williams
John Pinix	Lancelott Johnston	William Cantrill
Jesse Brintle	Robert Lackey	Samuel French
Aron Simpson	Henry Williams	Wm. Scoggins
Thomas Foster	Edmund Ballard	Jesse Payne
James Sheppard	Lewis Barton Jun.	James Ray
Lewis Foster	Henry Robertson	Joel Leath
Thomas Morean	Aron Anglin	John Mitchell
William Nash	Ezekiel Jones	
John Goodlow	Malon Stacy	

81 Amt. of rent of plantation and hire of negro woman belonging to
   estate of William Mitchell. Wm. Scoggins for rent of plantation;
   Lewis Foster for hire of negro woman.
82 Inv estate of Macksfield Henslee on 10 Aug 1801 by David Henslee exec.
83 Armsted Phillips a mullatto boy age 5 yrs. and 6 mos. bound to
   Epp⁰ Stone.
84 Nancy Phillips a mulatto girl 8 yrs. old on 15 March next bound to
   Eppophroditus Stone.

January Court 1802

86 Letter of attorney: John Zachary to William Browne to attend to
   all business as if I were present. 27 Jan 1802. Wit: Lancelott
   Johnston, Robt. Blackwell.
87 Letter of attorney: Anderson Ashburn of Knox Co. Tennessee to
   Lewis Ashburn of county and State aforesaid to sell tract of
   land that Rachel Wallis now lives on in Caswell Co. N.C.   11 July
   1798. Wit: Charles Clary. Recorded Knox Co. July 1798.
   Approved by John Sawyers, Justice of the Peace, Knox Co.
   Recorded Caswell Co. N.C.. Jan 1802.
88 Allen Harvill orphan of 6 yrs. and six mos. bound to Daniel Darby.
   /s/ William Rainey, Chairman County Court.
89 Sales estate of William McAden decd. by Jennett McAden, adm.
   Sales to:

Capt.Robert Willson	Jenett McAden	James McNeill
Col⁰ James Sanders	James McAden	John Mason
Duncan Rose	Samuel Curl	Labon Stafford
William Rainey	John. Pearson	Obediah Sanders
Hezekiah Farley	John McAden	Nathaniel Pass Jun.
Joseph Hall	Daniel S. Farley	Jesse Elmore
John Burton	William Yates	Catherine McAden
Abner Burton	Epephroditus Hightower	William Willson
Thomas Jeffreys	Hugh McAden	

92 Sales estate of John Hughes decd. Sold on 22 Nov 1801 by Thomas
   Morean guardian to the orphans. /s/ Thomas Mareign.
   Sales to: Henry Harden, Thomas Mareign, John Windson, Moses
   Simpson, William Boswell, John Brinsfield, Richard Hornbuckle,
   Robert Hatrick.
93 Inv estate of James Mallory decd by Sarah Mallory and Ezekiel
   Jones adm.
93 Sale of balance estate of William Mahan to Sarah Mahan adm.

Book D cont. 1802
Page
94 Sale estate of William Stephens by A. Stephens adm. Buyers:
Robert Willson, Samuel Stephens, Frances Stephens, James
Samuel, Hezekiah Tucker, Anthony Stephens, George Carrol.
95 Inv estate of Pemberton Burch in my house as adm. /s/ Daniel
Malone, adm.
96 Notes in possession of John Hughes when he died on: John McKinney, John Underwood, Bartholomew Zachary, Henry Martin, William
Madkin, John Madkin, Absolem Harvey, Thomas Johnston.
To cash: 30 dollars which was in cash when he dyed. Above a
true account to best of my knowledge. $40 which I made use of
in my widowhood. /s/ Mary Mareighn.

96 Taxable property for 1801

Richmond District		213	white polls	504	black polls
Gloucester	"	246	"	317	"
St. David's	"	270	"	429	"
Caswell	"	129	"	145	"
Totals		858	"	1395	"

April Court 1802

97 JOHN PETERSON - Will - w. 20 July 1795. Tract of land on Country
Line Cr. and all stock and household goods divided between
Thomas Peterson and John Peterson sons of James Peterson;
100 acres land to James Peterson. Exec: James Peterson for his
sons John and Thomas. Wit: Gregory Hightower, Thomas Hightower.
James Peterson and Thomas Peterson qualified as exec.

98 Power of attorney: Whereas John Reason departed this life intestate being then of Amelia Co. Va. and had one female child
Judith Bentley Reason, said estate having no adm. and no guardian, Joseph Holsclaw having intermarried with said Judith Bentley gives power of attorney to John Burton of Caswell Co. to
sue for and recover from said estate. 22 Dec 1801. Wit: Henry
Holsclaw, Abner Burton.
99 Power of attorney: John Windsor to friend Simpson Harris of
Davidson Co. Tennessee to sue and receive from exec. of John
Rice decd. 200 acres land agreeable to his bond. 27 Apr 1802.
99 Inv. estate of Thomas Robertson decd. taken 29 Apr 1802 by Solomon Graves adm.
100 Inv estate of Thomas Evans by John Warrick and Gabriel Lea.
101 Sales estate of Thomas Evans. Sales to:

Staples Malone	Thomas Miles	Hamilton Reynolds
William Evans	James Dollarhide	John Womack
Daniel Malone	James Johnston	Robert Hamblett
John Ashburn	William Warren	Garnett Neeley
Thomas Stephens	George Huston	Thomas Kendrick
William Stewart	Daniel Evans	John Miles
Lewis Evans	George Rennalds	George Lea
Mary Evans	William Haralson	Loyd Vanhook
Richard Meleer	Lawrence Lea	Kindle Vanhook
Thomas Verlines	John Price	

102 Inv estate of Thomas Graves Jun. decd by Thos. Gunn adm.
103 Power of attorney: Godfrey Crowder of Mecklinburg Co. Va. to
John Holloway of Person Co. N.C. to demand and receive sums
of money due to me as exec. of last will of David Shelton decd.
in right of wife. 26 Apr 1802. Wit: Wm. Rainey, John Bradsher.
103 Allotment to Sarah Mallory relict of James Mallory decd. 9 Feby
1802. Commrs: Nathan Williams, Zephaniah Tait, Robert Mitchell,
and John Henslee.

Book D cont. 1802
Page
104 Estate of David Shelton decd. in acct. with Herndon Haralson and
    Godfrey Crowder, exec: Payments to John Lowry atty. in Ky.;
    Sarah Crowder, Nicholas Matlock, Job Siddall, Henry Patillo for
    funeral (5 lbs.); Joseph Dameron for schooling children;
    3 gallons whiskey for the sale at 10 sh; county taxes 11 lbs,
    9 pence. Approved by William Rainey, Solomon Graves, Jesse
    Carter.
    Sales estate of David Shelton - cash received of William Parker,
    William Horley in Ky., David Kersey, Alexander Murphey, William
    Suit, William Montgomery, Thomas Donoho.
105 Settlement estate of Mathew Richmond by Ann Richmond adm. - met
    at Leasburg on 5 Feb 1802 to make inv. Commrs: William Richmond,
    Gabriel Lea, L. Lea.
106 Robert Parks county trustee tax report: 223,104 acres land at
    8 pence; 2013 polls at 2 sh.

106 List of insolvents for year 1799
        WP White polls   BP Black polls

Drury Rhodes	1WP	1BP	John McElroy	1WP	
Jesse Morgan	1		Stephen Roberts	1	
Alexander Nunley	1		Wm.Underwood	1	
John Neal	1		George Robbins	1	
Alexander Lyon	1		Devereau Inge	2	
Wm.Carter Carlos		2	Edmond Rice	1	1BP
Johnston Bever	1		Wm. Gordon	1	
John Wootch	1		Jane Johnston		1
Leroy Howell	1		Warren Roberts	1	
John Johnston	1	2	Sandy Smith	1	
Richard Allen	1		Samuel Boman	1	2
William Smith	1		John Durham	1	
Joseph Walker	1	3	James Sammons	1	
Anthony Horton	2	1	James Frost	1	
Alexander Porter	1		Thomas Roberts	1	
Field Nichols	1		John Bush	1	
John Bruce	1		Calib Fisher	1	
Samuel Everett	1		James Hughes	1	
Timothy ?	1		George Smith	1	5
John Golson	1		Benj. Williamson	1	2
William Longat	1		Thomas Jouitt	1	7

108 JOHN DICKEY - Will - w. 14 Jan 1802. Oldest son Zachariah Dickey;
    oldest daughter Frances Douglass; 2nd son John (land adj. Wil-
    liam Currie); 3rd son; 2nd daughter Rebecah (land where mansion
    house stands). Exec: son David Dickey and Rebeccak Dickey.
    Wit: William Warren, Rebeccah Douglass. Rebeccah Dickey quali-
    fied as exec.
109 Sales estate of James Mallory on 20 Feb 1802. Sales to:
    Sarah Mallory   Malon Stacy   Maxfield Henslee
    Thomas Mallory Jun.   Richard Jones   Henry Williams
    Raleigh Vickers   Lewis Foster   Edward Boswell
    Joel Leath   John Henslee   Henry Davis
    Stephen Mallory   John Mallory   Thomas Mallory Sen.
    Ezekiel Jones   Thomas Foster   Nathan Sims
    John Jones
110 Acct. sales of parcal of tobacco and one half of stud horse of
    the estate of Michael Nichols returned by adm. to July Court
    1796. By Lewis Sheppard in right of his wife. Tobacco sold to
    Frame & Love and to John Warrick.

Book D cont 1802
Page   of
111 John Hudson son/Joshua Hudson of voluntary will apprentices
    himself unto Francis Smith (carpenter) Jun. Wit: Azariah
    Graves, Phillip Pearce.
112 William Jones base born child 3 yrs. old the 5 of March next
    bound to John Enochs.
113 Allen Caswell mulatto boy 19 yrs. old Jany. last bound to Henry
    Atkinson.

July Court 1802

114 Inv. estate of Berryman Grayham decd. taken 13 Apr 1802 by Peggy
    Grayham adm.
114 Inv estate of John Dickey decd. by David Dickey and Rebekah Dic-
    kie, exec.
115 Inv. estate of John Kimbrough Jun. decd. by A. C. Murphey adm.
116 Part of estate of Thomas Graves decd. for 1799-1802.
    Bonds on Lacy Moore for board, Isaac Johnston for hire of negro,
    John Graves for hire of Peter; judgment on Samuel Henderson.
    Payment from Jacob Graves for one negro woman named Hannah,
    William Slade for negro boy Peter, Thomas Kimbrough for negro
    girl Cile.
    Receipts of Jacob, John, and James Graves for what was received
    during their father's life time; same from Thomas Gunn.
    1801 Hannah Graves paid for hire of Hannah, John Graves for hire
    of Hannah in 1802.
117 Ordered that 9 pence be levied on every poll and 3 pence on every
    100 acres land for support of the poor.
118 Settlement estate of William Abell decd. by James Grant and Wil-
    liam Dye with Thomas Bastin adm. Paid debts as follows:
    Judgment against William Abell in behalf of Samuel Allen; paid
    Turner Patterson for crying property at sale; judgment by
    Richd. Gibson and C. Price. 20 July 1802.
118 William Quine age 14 yrs. Christmas next bound to Francis Howard.
    /s/ James Williamson Chairman of County Court.
119 John Nunn orphan 19 yrs. old bound to George Williamson to learn
    art of a cabinet maker. /s/ David Gooch esq. Chairman of County
    Court.

120 EDWARD NOEL - Will - w. 8 June 1802. Wife Susannah; daughters
    Nancey, Ellenor, Margret, Betsy, Martha; sons Reubin, William,
    Thos. Edward, Jas., and Joel. Exec: wife Susannah. Wit: Thos.
    Kimbrough. Susannah Noel qualified as exec.

121 RICHARD ESTIS - Will - w. 23 Aug 1799. Wife Sarah; daughters
    Elizabeth, Annah, Francis, Mary, Martha, Sarah, Nancey; sons
    Bartlett (100 acres land whereon he now lives), Richard Bennett,
    and Micajah. Wit: William Gooch, William Slade.

123 Solomon Graves and Mary Ingram exec. of James Ingram decd, settle-
    ment of estate. One bond on Commissioners appointed by act of
    Assembly for purpose of fixing on a place for erecting the pub-
    lic buildings for Caswell County, 150 lbs. Approved by Henry
    Atkinson and James Williamson. 28 July 1802.

October Court 1802

123 HANNAH GRAVES - Will - w. 27 July 1802. Sons Azariah and Major;
    my 4 children Isbell, Azariah, Lewis, and Major Graves, and Is-
    bell Moore if in case Isbell Moore should die before lawful age
    then to return to my 4 children; Exec: trusty friend and rela-
    tions Thomas Yancey, John Graves Capt. and Thomas Simmons. Wit:
    J.G.Murphey, Anne Yancey, William Moore. Approved on oath of John
    Green Murphey.

Book D cont. 1802 - 1803
Page
125 Sales estate (livestock) of Edward Noel decd. by Susannah Noel.
125 William B. Burton adm. estate of Robt. Burton decd.,acct. sales
     of estate to Noel Coleman, Richard Keggin, Daniel Price, James
     Paul, Meredith Price, John Washam, Charles Paine, Francis Ray.
     Dec 1800.
125 List of Insolvents for 1800 by Wm. Muzzall, Sheriff. (No names)
126 Amount of hire of negro woman and rent of plantation of William
     Mitchell.
126 Inv. estate of Booker Sheppard decd. by Lewis Sheppard. Money
     due from George Stovall.
126 Sales estate of Thomas Robertson decd. by Solomon Graves adm.
     Sales to: James Burton, Rebekah Robertson, John Graves, John
     Foster, Richard Long, Henry Atkinson, Archibald Alverson, Solo-
     mon Graves, Jesse Beaver, Jacob Quine.
127 Sales estate of John Kimbrough Jun. decd. taken 21 Aug 1802.
     Sales to: Isbell Kimbrough, Alexander Murphey, Anne Yancey,
     Benjamin Sewell, James Yancey, William Kimbro, Isaac Johnston,
     John Graves, James Graves, Robert Browning, Jordan Whitlow.
     By Alex Murphey adm.
129 Acct. of estate of William Quine decd. by Benjamin Quine exec.
     Vouchers paid to: Jesse Carter, Lancelot Johnston, John McAden,
     Forgus Man, William Cook, Lewis Yearley, Benjamin Quine.
     Jan. 1801.

                    January Court 1803

130 WILLIAM GOOCH SEN. - Will - w. 5 Nov 1801. Wife Frances;
     12 children: William, James, David, Nathaniel, John,and Thomas
     Gooch, Mary Sneed, Elizabeth Kimbrough, Nancy Benton, Sarah
     Rice, Cisley Gooch, Polly Williams; 5 oldest children: Mary, Jas.,
     Elizabeth, Nancy, William; legacy left to wife by last will
     of John Rice decd. (Mary Sneed widow of John Sneed, Nancy Ben-
     ton widow of Jesse Benton, Sarah Rice wife of William H. Rice,
     Polly Williams wife of Henry Williams.) Land adj. Robert
     Martin and J nes Yancey. Exec. sons Wm. David, and John. Wit:
     Alex Murphey, Henry Williams.

132 ARCHIBALD HART - Will - w. 12 Sept 1802. Brother Joseph Hart
     (land on Green River in Ky.); mother Elizabeth Hart; sisters
     Susannah, Polly, and Elizabeth Hart; Polly and Archibald Dixon,
     children of Wynn and Rebeccah Dixon. Exec: Elizabeth Hart.
     Wit: Henry Atkinson, William Hart.

133 Further inv. estate of William Boyd decd. in Va. of property
     that could not be found for first inv. A suit by Mary Boyd and
     others against James Chalmers Esq. in Halifax Co. Va. court.
     April 1799.
134 Sale property of Booker Sheppard by Lewis Sheppard adm. on 22
     Nov 1802. Sales to: Lewis Sheppard, Anderson Williams, George
     Stovall, Stephen Chandler, John Pinson, Thos. Sheppard, Jas.
     Sheppard.
135 Sales estate of Thomas Simmons decd. after the death of Pris-
     cilla Simmons by Thos. Simmons exec. Sales to:

William Moore	Thomas Yancey	Thomas Gooch
Zephaniah Tait	James Yancey	John Jones
Thomas Compton	Bartlett Estis	James Birk Sen.
Aquilla Compton	Fanney Gooch	James Wisdom
William Jopling	John Love	John Yancey
William Farrar	Benjamin Sewell	Milner Bennett
Jacob Graves	Alex Murphey	James Birk Jun.

Book D cont. 1803
Page
136 Sales estate of Thomas Simmons cont. Sales to:
   William Malone   Thomas Simmons   Berry Hunt
   Robert Brown   Jordan Whitlow
137 Sale estate of Buford Pleasant decd. taken 11 Nov 1801 by James
   Melton and William Pleasant, adm. Sales to:
   John Pleasant   Auston Stalcup   Cornelius Dollarhide
   William Pleasant   James Piles   Thomas Baughan
   Robert Parks   Alexander Benson   Samuel Everet
   Lewis Corbitt   James Murphey   John Wells
   Gabriel Murphey Jun. Rachel Shy   George Horton
   James Turner(Hico)   John Stalcup   Stephen Pleasant
   James Melton   John Eubank   Michael Pleasant

139 Sales estate of Nathan Rice decd. by Williamson Rice adm. Sales to:
   Jeremiah Rice   Patsey Allen   Edmond Rice
   Sarah Rice   Stephen Mallory   James Cobb
   Williamson Rice   James Orr   William Clifton
   Nathan Rice   George Sims   John Keen
   William Nash   Henry Dunlap   Richard Simpson
   Hezekiah Boswell
141 Sales estate of Thomas Hornbuckle decd. Sales to:
   Nancy Hornbuckle Nancy Phillips   Anthony Horton
   Solomon   "   James Simpson   Owen Ballard
   Henry Harden   John Keen   William Scrivener
   Jeremiah Williamson George Smith   John Bruce
   Richard Hornbuckle James Raye   John Allen
   John Windsor Jun.   William Brintle Jeptha Rice
   Thomas Hornbuckle John Scoggins   Joseph Allen
   Ann Simpson   Abner Powell   John McKinney
   Archibald Hart   Absolem Harvey   Richard Sorinson
   Samuel Boman   George Hornbuckle David Boyar
   John Goodlow   Simon Carlile   Robert Williams
   John Royall   Benjamin Gibson John Zachary
   Nathaniel Williams Jere Jackson   Hudson Brown
   William Poston   John Bush   Lewis Pike
   John Lenox   Thomas Windsor John Dawson
   John Dickey   William Aldriss

144 Sales estate of Hugh Dobbin decd. by Kindle Vanhook on 25 Jan 1801.
144 Inv estate of Hugh Dobbin. Notes on Kindle Vanhook, James
   McMurray, Benjamin Douglass.
144 Sale estate of Bereman Greyham decd. by Peggy Greaham adm. on
   16 Sept 1802. Sales to:
   Peggy Greahan   Herberd Greaham Carter Dalton
   Ezekiel Waters   John Arnett   James Guinnings
   Thomas Weatherford Cager Greaham   William Underwood
145 Sales estate of Hannah Graves decd. sold 11 Nov 1802. Buyers:
   Zephaniah Tait   Johnston Birk   William Moore
   John Graves Jun.   Jordan Massey   Elijah Barton
   Samuel Morton   Thomas Yancey   Isbel Graves
   Thomas Simmons   Jordan Whitlow   William Jopling
   James Birk   Henry Scott   Richard Arnold
   Christopher Dameron John Payne(Taylor) Elisha Evans
   Robert Martin   Robert Scott   William Farrow
   Jacob Graves   Henry Scott   Azariah Graves(son
   Barzillai Graves   James Turner   of Thomas)
   Samuel French   John Morton   Absolem Johnston
   James Yancey   Absolem Lea   John Eubank
   Bartlett Yancey   James Graves   Robert Mitchell

Book D cont. 1803
Page
146 Estate sales Hannah Graves cont.   Sales to:
    William Wilmouth   Jesse Morton   William Turner
    Susannah Noel   James Vaughan   William Ricketts
    John Murray   Thomas Kendrick   John Graves Sen.
    Charles Hunter

149 Allotment of negroes of Thomas Simmons decd. to legatees:
    Thomas Yancey, Thomas Simmons, William Anthony, Alexander
    Simmons, and heirs of Hannah Graves decd.
    "There is owing to Joshua Taylor and William Leak legatees of
    said Thomas Simmons in right of their wives who were daughters
    of said decd. or to their heirs the sum of one hundred and six
    pounds to be paid by other legatees agreeable to their allot-
    ments which is 1/7 part of the whole".   17 Jan 1803.
    Commrs: Alex Murphey, Edmond Browning, John Kimbrough.

150 Amt. sales of estate of Hugh Dobbin.
150 Inv. estate of Thomas Simmons by Thomas Simmons exec.
153 Acct. estate of Thomas Simmons decd.   Accts. paid to Zeph Tait,
    John Buchanan, William Gooch, David Gooch, Thomas Kimbrough,
    Andrew McCawley, John Berry, James Yancey, William Cantril,
    Obediah Martin, Elijah Anthony, Lewis Corder, Samuel Shy,
    John Shy, James Poe, William Leak, Joshua Taylor.
    Acct. of adm. of Thomas Graves decd. and Thomas Simmons sur-
    viving exec. of Thomas Simmons decd.

154-5 John Adams adm. of John Rice decd. acct with the estate;
    Settlement to widow Esther Rice thirds of said estate, to
    Francis Garner and James Rice their part.

154 Release: Lewis Pike Sen. on 1 Nov 1802 received of W. Nash
    acknowledgement for $218 and 1/3 dollar which was balance due
    from Nash for land sold him.   3 Jan 1803.   Wit: David Poyner,
    Jeremiah Jones.

155 Thomas Vanhook orphan 14 yrs. old 26 Nov last bound to Reuben
    Jones.

156 Letter of attorney: John Harrill to Jesse Carter to demand and
    recover from exec. of the late Step Roberts decd. any legacy
    due him by virtue of his marriage with Martha Harrill daughter
    of said Step Roberts.   24 Jan 1803.   Wit: Henry Atkinson,
    Andrus Harrison.

157 Inv. estate of Hugh Dobbin.

April Court 1803

158 Sales estate of Darling Ray decd. sold 16 Nov 1802.   Sales to:
    Jesse Carter   Widow Ray   Mrs. Morton
    Richard Bennett   Freeman Hubbard   James Peterson
    George White   David White   Francis Ray
    Anderson Morton   Herndon Lea   John Hinton
    Meshak Morton
    By Jesse Carter, adm.

159 Inv. estate of Darling Ray taken 16 Nov 1802.

159 William Rainey, Sheriff, protests against the goal as being
    insufficient to hold prisoners as some persons have made their
    escape from custody of the proceeding sheriff.

Book D cont. 1803
Page
160 Inv. estate of Thomas Langley decd. taken on 3 Feb 1803 by
    Mary Langley adm.
    Accts. due to Thomas Langley for 1802-3 from:
    Allen Burton   James Wisdom   Mathew Tanner
    Robert Donaldson   John Westbrook   James Richmond
    Thomas Roberts   James Nelson   Daniel McGillvery
    Abner Wisdom   John Waterfield
162 Sales estate of John Brown decd. sold 22 Nov 1798 by John H.
    Brown exec. Sales to:
    Sarah Brown   William Brown   Jesse Rice
    Thomas Jouett   Garland Key   Joseph Benton
    Russell Sullivant   Green Lea Brown   Richard Smith
    James Russey   John H. Brown   Samuel Boman
    Charles Brooks   Wm. McFarland   Thomas Rice Esq.
    Jethro Brown   H.E.Williamson   John Goodloe
    Robert A. Brown   Jep Rice   Joseph Roe
    Anthony Swift   Benj. Williamson   Lewis Sheppard
    Francis Smith   Nathan Rice Jun.   George Williamson

165 James Burton adm. of Andr Burton decd. in acct. with estate;
    rent of land due from Thomas Fearn; accts. paid to Fearn, Noel
    Burton, Evans Knight, William Richardson.

166 Inv. estate of William Gooch decd. Sales on 5 Feb. 1803 to:
    Wm. H. Rice   Jordan Whitlow   David Gooch
    Nathaniel Gooch   John Yancey   Wm. Gooch Sen.
    Abner Gooch   James Burk   Lewis Sheppard
    John C. Gooch   William Moore   Wm. Gooch Jun.
    Francis Gooch   Henry Williams   Sarah Estis
    John Graves Jun.   Malichi Holloman   James Turner
    William Bruce   Francis Rice
        By Wm. and David Gooch exec.

168 James Burton adm. estate of Andrew Burton, accts. paid(1799) to:
    Jo Dameron, Sally Burton, Polly Burton, Thomas Harrison, Jno.
    Martin, Noel Burton, Robt. Burton.
    Accts. paid for 1800 to Sally Knight and others as in 1799.

169 Inv. estate of Jesse Moore decd. by Nathaniel Pass adm.
170 Sales estate of Jesse Moore to:
    Sally Moore   Nathaniel Pass   William Williams
    William Cates   John Pass

171 Joseph Elam orphan 7 years the 2nd day of Aug. bound to William
    Clemson (also spelled Climpson). /s/ Samuel Johnston, Chair-
    man of the County Court.

172 Estate of Thomas Hornbuckle decd. in acct. with Richd. Horn-
    buckle and Jas Simpson exec. Payments to legatees:
    George Hornbuckle, John Keen, William Keen;
    Vouchers paid to Thomas Bradford, John Douglass, George Horn-
    buckle, Thomas Hornbuckle, Richd. Hornbuckle, Thomas Windsor.

172 Lewis Sheppard adm. Michael Nicholson decd.;
    tobacco sold to Fraim and Love; cash paid Nicholas Delone,
    William Lea, Nicholas Coil, James Williamson, Aaron Sherrin,
    John Stafford, John Yancey, Pulliam Williamson, Daniel Darby.
    Acct. approved for Lewis Sheppard adm. of Michael Nicholson
    decd. right of his wife.

Book D cont. 1803
Page
174 JAMES GIBSON - Will - w. 11 Nov 1802. Wife Frances;
daughters Conny Harriss, Nancy Gibson; son Nathan Gibson;
my small children: daughters Triss, Isbal, Dicey; sons John,
Elijah, Ralia. Exec: wife Frances; Wit: Thomas Duncan,
Richard Gibson.

"Amen to this book. I wish it had three times as
many leaves in it.
A^d Murphey"

Unrecorded Will

With the original wills at the State Archives is a will for

JOHN DAMERON - w. 6 Mar 1804. Wife Mary; daughter Eliza;
unborn child. If wife and children die, estate divided between
brothers Christopher and Bartholomew Dameron and sisters
Ann M. Mathis, Sally Mathis, Patsey McDaniel, Patience Clark,
Polly Dameron, and Caty Dameron. Exec: wife, friend Gabriel Lea.
Wit: Joshua Richmond, William Morgan, Bartholomew Jackson.

"Jurors dont suppose this to be the last will of John Dameron decd."
Test: Wm. B. Harrison.

April Court 1803 cont. from Book D

Page
1 John H. Brown exec. of John Brown decd. Notes on Thomas Jouett, William Wilkinson, Elijah Brown, Richard Simpson, Capt. Waddy Tait, and David Poyner.
1 Francis Morrow age 9 yrs. the 11 of June next bound to James Moore.
2 John Brown estate cont.: payments to Thomas Rice, Doct. Johnston, Mrs. Williamson, Solomon Hornbuckle, Joseph Roe, Robert Brown, William Norwood, Ezekiel McCollester, John Lenox, John Graves, Adam Sanders, John Zachary. (Partial list)
3 Joseph Sharp, orphan 8 yrs. old next May, bound to Jonathan Starkey. /s/ David Gooch, Chairman County Court.
3 Lewis Watkins,base born of colour now 2 yrs. and one mo. old, bound to Daniel Elam.

4 JOHN SOMERS - Will - w. 7 Mar 1803. Wife Catherine (land adj. Ibsan Rice); sons John, Ardon, Ira, James; all lands in State of Tennessee to go to 4 sons; daughters Abijah, Ann, and Sarah Somers. Exec. to make deed of conveyance to John Donaldson or his heirs of part of military lands in Tenn. which was to be given him for locating and surveying same. Exec: wife and Brother James Somers and son John Somers. Wit: C. Dixon, Dolley Rice, Fanny Carlos(Jurat).

5 JOHN LEA - Will - w. 10 Mar 1803. Wife Winneyfred; 6 children: James, John, Benjamin, Jeremiah, Nancy, and Sally; part of land "I leave to daughter Frankey forever"; daughter Betsy Evans. John and Solomon Graves to appraise and divide estate. Exec: sons John, James, Benjamin, and Jeremiah. Wit: Solomon Graves, Barzillai Graves, John Graves. /s/ John Lea Sen. James Lea and Jerre Lea qualified.

6 WILLIAM ANGLIN SEN. - Will - w. 26 Mar 1798. Wife Ann; son John to get obligation on Benjamin Kidd for 51 lbs. 12 sh. son in law William McIntosh; son in law James Barton; sons William and Aron Anglin; daughters Sally Anglin, Catharine Browning. Exec: wife. Wit: James Williamson, Ann E. Williamson, Benjamin Kidd.

July Court 1803

8 GIDEON PATTERSON - Will - w. 10 Mar 1803. Slaves Aggie and Merrier not to be held in Bondage and exec. to procure their Liberation. Son Gideon to have negro man Isaac. Exec: son Gideon Patterson and James Sanders. Wit: Joseph Pulliam, James Sanders.

8 Allotment for one year to widow and family of Thomas Langley. Commrs. Gabriel Lea, James Nelson, Abner Wisdom, Joseph Dameron.
9 Richard Hornbuckle and William Smith exec. to estate of Peter Smith decd. 7 legatees to divide estate and one legatee being dead and his share to be divided. 27 July 1803.
9 Allotment to Sarah Chapman widow of James Chapman decd. for her and her family. By James Orr, Joseph Scott, Jos. Roe, Thos. Humphries.

Book E cont. 1803
Page
10 Inv. goods and chattels of John Somers decd. by Catharine Somers, exec.
11 Inv estate of William Anglin decd. taken 28 Apr 1803 by Ann Anglin exec.
11 Inv estate of James Vinson decd. by George Hornbuckle, adm.
12 Inv estate of Hezekiah Carmon decd. taken 7 May 1803 by Elijah Carmon adm.
12 Inv estate of James Chapman by Sarah Chapman.
13 On May 10, 1803, inv taken at the late Dwelling House of John Lea Sen. decd.: 1 bond on Major Lea Sen. for 15-12-9 baring date of 25 Mar 1796. By James Lea and Jerre Lea, exec.
14 Sales estate of John Lea Sen. made 7 June 1803. Sales to:

William Parker	Samuel Evans	Solomon Graves
Jeremiah Samuel	David Thomas	Jeremiah Lea
Elisha Evans	James Darby	James Lea
Robert Sanders	Francis Lea	John Lea (CB)
John Roan	Thomas Cambel	Thomas Lea
Freeman Hubbard	John Long	John Roper
William Sawyer	Thomas Donoho	Jesse Carter

16 Inv estate of William Kerr decd. taken 13 May 1803.
Sales estate of William Kerr decd. by Mary Kerr adm. Sales to:

Mary Kerr	Benoni Rawson	Malon Stacy
Richard Jones	Robert Sawyer	John Jones
Ezekial Jones	Nathl. Gooch	Robert Sawyer
Mary Stadler	Ed Browning	Alex Kerr
Jesse Hollis	Joel Leath	Caswel Tait
Zephaniah Tait	Maxfield Henslee	Thomas Simmons
Benj. Lea	John Kerr	George Barker
Jere Lea	Alex Vinson	Rease Enoch
John Enoch	John Love	Thomas Mallory
Conoly Walker	Thomas Davis	Thomas Loyd
Hiram Cooper	William Brown	William L.Webb(Doct)

18 Amt. of sale of James Chapman decd. Sold to Sarah Chapman and Samuel Chapman.
19 State of North Carolina, Rockingham Co. On 7 May 1803 estate of Hezekiah Carmon decd. was sold at public auction. Sales to:

James Smith	Cornelius Burris	Peter Byson
John Wilson	Jonathan Murrey	George Hornbuckle
William Hutcherson	Thomas Humphreys	Nicholas Chut
Isaac Pritchett	John Herbin	Isaac Crowder
Richard Burris	John Mareen	Joel Johnson
Elijah Carmon	Joseph Pritchett	Jonsey Wilson
Charles Payn Sen.	Peter Uersillott	
Elijah Flack	Joel Stallions	
Nicholas Smith	Jeremiah Pritchett	

By Elijah Carmon adm.
21 Estate of John Hughs decd. in acct. with Thomas Marain and Mary his wife who is adm. with will of said Hughs her late husband. Accts. paid to Peter Byson, John Douglass; cash received from Bart Zachary, Wm. Matkins, John Matkins, John Underwood, Absolem Harvey, John McAden, Thomas Tomlinson, Henry Martin. (Marain also spelled Mareign.)
21 Amt. of estate of William Gooch decd. sold at auction 18 May 1803. Sale of 1 little negro Milley to William H. Rice.
22 Allotment to Mary Kerr widow of William Kerr decd. for herself and child. 4 Apr 1802. By Thomas Loyd and William Cantrill.

Book E cont. 1803
page
23 Insolvents for 1801

William Barnett	Elisha Wynn	Richard Royel
John Cochran Jun.	Richard Boggess	John Roberts Sen.
James Clemson	Warren "	Simon Roberts
Thomas Climer	Samuel "	Mary Curry
Robert Farley	Charles Price	
John Petters	John Price Jun.	

                By William Lea   D Shff.
23 One shilling laid on the poll and four pence on every 100 acres
   land for support of poor for 1803.
24 Bond: Robert Parks esq. as county trustee. /s/ Robert Parks, John
   McMullen, John Yancey.
24 Bond: William Rainey as the appointed sheriff of Caswell County.
25 At election held 11 and 12 Aug 1803 at court house of Caswell
   County for member of Congress to represent the ninth district,
   following is number of votes to each candidate:
       Anthony Brown   2
       Theo Lacey   135
       William Nash   82
       Marmaduke Williams   601
   /s/ Wm. Rainey, sheriff; George Williamson and Starling Gunn,
   inspectors; Robert H. Childers and James Gunn, clerks.
26 Taxable property for 1802

		White polls		Black polls
St. David's Dist.		216		317
Caswell	"	193	"	228 "
Gloucester	"	269	"	340 "
Richmond	"	247	"	489 "

        344 acres land subject to double tax.

October Court 1803

26 ELIZABETH POSTON - Will - w. 1 July 1803. Land to be divided
   between all children; household goods to children as they come
   of age as follows: William Poston, Caty Poston, Elizabeth Smith,
   Henry Poston, Polly Poston, Richard Poston, Franky
   Poston, Jeremiah Poston. Exec: son William Poston and son in
   law William Smith. Wit: Simon Carlile, Wm. H. Rice.

27 CHARLES BOULTON - Will - w. 14 Feby 1803. Wife Elizabeth(land on
   Dan River with mansion house); son Lent Boulton; daughter
   Judith Thomas and her 2 sons Icabod and John Thomas; 3 sons Char-
   les, Thomas, and William; John Boulton's children; Obediah Wynn's
   children by daughter Aney; son John Boulton's sons. Exec: William
   Boulton, Thomas Gatewood, Lent Boulton. Wit: Elizabeth Combs,
   James Dix.

29 HEZEKIAH RUDD of County of Chesterfield,Virginia - Will -
   w. 3 Sept 1803. Estate to be kept together until youngest child
   reaches 10 yrs; then to be divided equally among following
   children: Viney Pinchback; Jeremiah, Nancey, James, Bidsey, David,
   and Rebeccah Rudd. William Pinchback and wife Viney to keep
   children with them. Exec: William Pinchback, Jeremiah Rudd.
   Wit: A. Gordon, Levi Fuller, Frankey Rudd.
31 Inv. estate of Walter Garner by John Garner and Hezekiah Bozwell
   taken 29 Oct 1803.
32 George Hornbuckle received of Richard Hornbuckle exec. to Thomas
   Hornbuckle his part of personal estate. 14 June 1803.

89

Book E cont. 1803 - 1804
Page
33 John Windsor of Rockingham Co. received his share of personal estate of Thomas Hornbuckle. 14 June 1803.
35 Henry Hardin received his share of estate of Thomas Hornbuckle.
36 Thomas Windsor received his share of estate of Thomas Hornbuckle.
37 Allotment to Isbell Kimbrough widow and relict of John Kimbrough
   Jun. 6 Aug 1802. Commrs: David Gooch, Edmund Browning, Saml.
   Morton, William Culberson.
38 Insolvents in Caswell County in 1802

	White Polls	Black Polls		White Polls
John Bennett	1	3	Edward Waldrop	1
John Bradsher	1		Mourning Ballard	1
Edward Brown	1		Chamberlain Enoch	1
Lewis Cox	1		George Foot	1
Presley Draper	1		James Wray	1
Robert Elam	1		Jepthah Rice	1
James Johnston(BS)	1		John Coumon	1
William Kersey	1	1	William Underwood	1
William Johnston	1		Josiah Boman	1
Elijah Miller	1	1	William Mansfield	1
Solomon Newcom	1		Richard St.John	1
William Phelps	1		Ress Stuart	1
William Wray	1		John Westbrook	1
Elijah Alverson	1		James Powell	1
Richard Boggess	1		Hackley Warren	1
Elisha Conway	1		Tolbert Gibson	1
Robert Conway	1		William McCubbins	1
Jesse Conway	1		Allen Nicholas	1
Paul Chappin	1	4	Henry Stone	1
Henry Ferrell	1		Arthur Toney	1
Joseph Arnett	1		Thomas Birch	1
Robert Clark	1			
Thomas Fitzgerald	1			

39 Inv. estate of Gideon Patterson on 27 Oct 1803 by Gideon Patterson exec.
40 Thomas Slade adm. of Peter Lay in acct. with estate.

January Court 1804

41 Inv estate of Thomas Yancey decd. Bonds on James Turner, William
   Leak, Nathan Williams, Alexander Murphey, Thomas Simmons.
   Open accts. on William Moore and James Birk Jun. By Bartlett
   Yancey and James Yancey adm.
42 Sales estate of Thomas Yancey on 17 Nov 1803. Sales to:

Elizabeth Yancey(Relict)	Robert Mitchell	James Kimbrough
James Turner (CL)	John Graves Jun.	Charles S. Hunter
John Paine (F)	Jesse Morton	James Birk Sen.
Isaac Johnston	Bartlett Estis	Doct.Wm.S.Webb
Thomas Simmons	Thomas Haralson	Thomas Turner
Jacob Ahart	William Moore	Nathaniel Slade
James Turner(Payne)	Jordan Whitlow	Jacob Graves
Jesse Womack	Bartlett Yancey	James Yancey
Ann Yancey	James Graves	James Birk Jun.
Jesse Robertson	William Ricketts	Robert Malone
Capt. John Graves	William Byrd	Nathaniel Snipes
Richard Martin	Daniel Gunn	Fanney Yancey

Book E cont. 1804
Page
45 Sales estate of Thomas Yancey cont. Sales to:

John Yancey	William Malone	Elisha Evans
John Morton	William Rudd	Charles Turner
John Pinson	Alexander Murphey	William Clemson
William Bruce	Lewis Shepherd	Josiah Turner
William Turner	Francis Smith Sen.	Richard Vaughan
James Scott	Micajah Estis	John Weedon

48 Acct. of property and sale of estate of Thomas Langley taken
18 Aug 1803. Sales to:

Mary Langley	Johnson Birk	John Hightower
Abner Wisdom	David Thomas Jun.	Benjamin Warren
Thomas Johnson	Mordecai Burgess	William Whitehurst
Jesse Womack	William Brooks	Joseph Chandler
Moses Langley	John Waterfield	William Brandon
Joseph Langley	Thomas Turner	Elizabeth Roberts
James Nelson	William Turner	Thomas Jackson Sen.
Daniel Malone Jun.	Jacob Graves	James Richmond
Samuel Motheral	Daniel Hightower	Charnal Hightower
Bartholomew Dameron Sen.	Charles Gordon	John Yancey
Matthew Tanner Jun.	Staples Malone	William Forrest
James Wisdom	James Birk Sen.	Daniel McGillivery
Richard Maleer	Henry Burch	Frances Brandon
Benjamin Suit	Jesse Morton	Alexander Wiley
Robert Martin	Lot Egman	Joseph Carney
Jordan Whitlow	William Oen	Thomas Miles
Lewis Shepherd	Larkin Wisdom	Thomas Boman
Matthew Tanner Sen.	David Haddock	James Burress
John Graves Jun.	Lewis Wisdom	Nancy Roberts
William E. Fox	Thomas Jackson	Daniel Darby
William Evans	David Burton	
Jeremiah Samuel	John Langley	

By Mary Langley adm.

58 Inv estate of Richard Estis taken 19 Apr 1802 by Bartlett and
Micajah Estis.
58 Inv. estate of Elizabeth Poston on 15 Aug 1803 by Wm. Poston exec.
59 Sales estate of James Vinson to:

Thomas Brinsfield	William Hamblett	Elias Loveless
George Hornbuckle	John Madkins	Peter Byson
John Pricherd	Thomas Merain	William Dickens
William Madkin	David Robertson	Charles Payn
Joseph Rumley	Jesse Payn	James Busick
William Vinson	Henry Harden	Richard Hamblett
Sarah Vinson	Isaac Davis	

By George Hornbuckle adm.

61 Div. of negroes belonging to estate of Thomas Yancey decd. to:
Elizabeth Yancey, James Yancey, Tryon Yancey, Priscilla Yancey,
Nancy Yancey, Artilia Yancey. 12 Nov 1803. Tryon Yancey indebted to other legatees. Commrs: William Gooch Sen., Thos Harrelson, Alex Murphey.
62 Div of negroes and crop of corn and tobacco of estate of John Lea
agreeable to clause in will to legatees: James Lea, William
Zachary, Benjamin Lea, Thomas Les, Jeremiah Lea, John Lea.
63 Sales estate of Henry Dixon Jun. left to his wife during her life.
Sales to: John Williams, C. Dixon for H.Dixon, John Bizor, Nat
Williams. One negro boy John in hands of Armistead Flippin which
legatees agreed he shall keep for his share of estate.

91

Book E cont. 1804
Page
64 Settlement estate of Thomas Gunn.
68 Estate of Barkley Elam in acct. with John Wilson adm. Payments to:

William Norwood	Peyton Morton	Duncan Cameron
David Elam	Simon Robards	William Lea
William Gordon	James Kitchen	Doctr Vaughan
Gabriel Lea	Robt. H. Childress	John Graves & Sons
(Partial list)		

71 Second sale of John Lea on 16 Nov 1803. Sales to:

James Wisdom	William Parker	John Lea Sen.
Jesse Carter	Mary Hipworth	James Lea
Bart Dameron	Isaac Jackson	Jeremiah Lea
Lott Egman	Free Robin Watkins	Benjamin Lea
Robt. Dameron	Thomas Lea	Capt. John Graves
Nicholas Coils	Ephraim Nowel	Frances Lea
James Peterson	Elisha Evans	William Winters
John Johnston	John Long	Hearndon Lea
Thomas Peterson		

73 Estate of Jeremiah Poston in acct. with John Cox exec. Accts.
paid to: James Appleton for crying sale, Henry Harding, Benj.
Williamson sheriff, Benj. Spencer, Wilson & Galloway, John Cox.
Paid cash to: Tyre Harris, John Lenox, Jethro Brown, John Yancey
sheriff, Thos. Jouett, J.Fields sheriff Rockingham, John Nance,
William Holderness, Nat Williams.
75 Received of Joseph Anthony $54 it being Penney Anthony part of
first div. of John Anthony estate. /s/ Asa Paul. Test: Samuel
Dickie.
76 John Cox adm. Jeremiah Poston: sales collected from James Adams,
Paul Chappel, Mrs. Nelson, Anthony Swift, Rob Mitchell, Jethro
Brown.
77 Prison Bounds laid off adj. garden formerly occupied by Henry
Atkinson. By John Graves, Sol.Graves, Henry Atkinson, Thos.
Haralson.

April Court 1804

78 Inv. property of Thomas Graves Jun. at sale held at Hannah Graves
on 7 May 1802. Sales to: Isbell Graves, Hannah Graves, Thomas
Simmons, John Graves, William Moore, William Kimbrough, Elijah
Barton, Absolem Lea, James Graves, Alex Murphey, Daniel Gunn.

79 JOHN CLIBOURNE GOOCH' - Will - w. 4 Apr 1804. Mother Frances Gooch.
Nephew John Gooch son of Nathaniel Gooch; brothers William,
David, James, Nathaniel, and heirs of Thomas Gooch; sisters
Sarah Rice, Polly Williams. Exec: brothers William and David;
Wit: Wm. Gooch Sen., Anderson Birk, Alinor Gooch.

82 Inv. estate of Jas. Willson. Notes on Azariah Graves, Thomas
Neeley, Pleasant Hardwick, William Dye. Cash in hands of John
Willson in Pittsylvania. By Margret Willson adm. and D. Henslee,
adm.
83 Settlement estate of Tho. Graves Sen.
85 Estate of John Rice Sen. in acct with William Rice exec. Cash
paid Thomas Rice, Danl. Williams, Frances Gooch, Anthony Thompson, Mary Thompson.
87 Settlement estate of Thos. Evans by Gabriel Lea and John Warwick,
exec.
89 Div estate of Thomas Graves Sen. and Jun. to: Hannah Graves, Jacob
Graves, John Graves, James Graves, Thomas Gunn, William Moore in
right of wife, Isbell Graves, Azariah Graves, Lewis Graves,
Major Graves, Thomas Graves Jun. decd. 6 Apr 1804.

Book E cont. 1804
Page
93 Estate of Thomas Rice decd. Vouchers paid to: Jesse Carter,
   Jethro and John Brown, Reubin Cochran, James Saintclair, Armistead Watlington, Wm. Muzzall, Thomas Johnston, Lancelot Johnston, Jonathan Starkey, Bouldin & Willson, Robert King exec.,
   Samuel Walker, Frances Smith; to Lancelot Johnston for riding
   to Halifax Court, to Red House, to Milton, and 8 days at Caswell Court.
96 Settlement estate of Thomas Rice. Receipts from: John Terry,
   Zere Gwynn, Ziza Rice, Elijah Graves, John Payne, George Stovall, Daniel Gwynn, James StClair, Aquilla Barton, Charles
   Turner, Major Thomas Donoho, Jonas Sykes, Thomas Slade.
97 Thomas Gunn adm. Thomas Graves Jun., acct. with estate.
   Legatees: Jacob, John, James Graves; Thomas Gunn in right of
   his wife sister to decd.; William Moore in right of his former
   wife sister of decd.; Isbell, Azariah, Lewis, Major Graves.
98 Estate of Booker Shepard decd. in acct. with Lewis Shepard adm.
   Cash received of George Stovall. Cash paid to: Murphey & Lea,
   Lewis Shepard, Nathan Williams, Thomas Shapard, Rhoda Bush,
   John Graves Sen., Doct Wm. Webb, John Graves & Sons.
99 George Burton by act of General Assembly empowered to expose
   to Publick sale lands on which his father Charles Burton owned-
   this obligation void if Burton does sell land and distribute
   proceeds. /s/ Geo. Burton, Maraday Price, Joel McDaniel, J.
   Grant, John Tennison, Silvs. Stokes. 1 May 1804.
100 Inv property of John Fargerson on 18 Feby. 1804 by Jesse Carter
    adm.
100 Acct. sale of John Kimbrough Jun. Sales to: Alex Murphey (1 log
    and frame house), John Graves Jun. Cash collected of Polly
    Fury; judgment on James St John.
101 Sales estate of John Fargerson on 18 Feb 1804. Sales to:
    Richard Bennett, Jesse Carter, Jacob Wright Jun., Josiah Mor-
    ton, Polly Fargerson, Freeman Hubbard, Jacob Wright Sen., Calib
    Wright, Lot Egmon.

                    July Court 1804

103 Inv. estate of Beuford Pleasant by William Pleasant and James
    Melton adm.
104 Div. estate of Beuford Pleasant to legatees: William Pleasant,
    James Melton in right of his wife, Lewis Corbit in right of his
    wife, Alexander Benson in right of his wife, James Piles in right
    of his wife, John Stalcup in right of his wife, Austin Stalcup
    in right of his wife, James Turner(Hico) in right of his wife,
    Lucy Pleasant widow and Relict. Micajah Pleasant and John
    Pleasant sons and heirs of Beuford Pleasant decd. refused to
    give in what they had received of the estate of their father.
    We have not devised them any part of the balance. 14 June 1804.
105 Acct. sales of estate of Gideon Patterson.
106 Sale property of James Wilson on 1 June 1804. Sales to:
    Margaret Wilson, Thomas Stafford, John Wilson, William Nash,
    John Delap, Zachariah Hasten, Henry Dunlop Sen., Abner Wilson,
    William Wilson, Gours Whitemore, David Henslee. (Partial list)
    Cont. on page 109 sales to Johnson Wilson, Wiley Yancey, Ann
    Brooks, Edmond Hearndon.
108 James Harrison orphan 16 years old the 1 of Feby next bound to
    John Landers. /s/ Archd. Samuel, Chairman of County Court.
110 Robert Harrison orphan 15 years old bound to Jesse Carter.
111 Lelia Manuel orphan 7 years old next April bound to Joshua
    Beaver. /s/ William Nash, Chairman County Court.

                            93

Book E cont. 1804
Page
112 Sales estate of John C. Gooch on 5 May 1804. Buyers: Francis
    Gooch, John Morton, Nathaniel Gooch, Wm. Gooch Sen., Wm. L.
    Webb, David Gooch, Richard Jones, James Birk Jun., Henry Wil-
    liams. Cash received of Andrew McCawley.
113 Election for representative to Congress on 9 & 10 Aug 1804.
    Marmaduke Williams   679 votes
    Mr. Branson   1 vote   Mr. Lacey   9 votes
114 Settlement estate of William Kerr with Mary Kerr adm.
115 Report of Robert Parks, county trustee.
118 Allotment to Margret Wilson widow of James Wilson decd. and to
    her family.
119 Bond: Samuel Johnston as sheriff of Caswell County.
121 Valuation estate of Elizabeth Poston decd. by John Reid, Richd.
    Simpson, James Williamson.
122 Thomas Simmons exec. of Thomas Simmons decd. acct with estate.
123 Sales estate of Walter Garner on 11 Nov 1803. Sales to:
    Abner Powell   Thomas Mallory   Chlos Garner
    Owen Ballard   Alexander Bruce   Peter Madkins
    Hezk. Boswell   Thomas Kellow   Edward Boswell
    George Hornbuckle   Craven Bozwell   John Boswell
    Walter Madkins   William Brintle   Theo Carter
    David Bruce   Robert Bruce   John Garner
    George Herbin
125 ANDREW WARRICK - Will - w. 5 Apr 1802. son John Warrick;
    daughters Jennett Roan, Mary Warrick(land known as Narrow Pas-
    sage), Elizabeth Stephens; children of Margaret Thomas.
    Exec: son John; Wit: Saml. Johnston, Gabriel Lea.
127 Inv estate of Colwell P. Pool decd. by Richard Bennett adm.
    12 May 1804.
128 Taxable property for 1803
    St. David's Dist.   232 white polls   380 black polls
    Caswell Dist.   178   "   222   "
    Richmond Dist.   282   "   512   "
    Gloucester   264   "   325   "
129 Settlement estate of William Boyd.
131 Settlement estate of John Kimbrough Jun. by Alex Murphey adm.
    Paid vouchers of Robert Browning, Mgry Kelly, Milner Bennett,
    John Graves, Doctor John McDowell, Isaac Johnston.
133 Bond: Robert Parks as county trustee.

                    October Court 1804

133 Ordered one shilling to be laid on every poll and four pence on
    every 100 acres land for support of the poor for 1804. /s/
    Azariah Graves, Clk.
134 Power of attorney: Joseph Chandler to George Stovall and son
    William Chandler to sell estate (except lands willed to sons
    William and Stephen Chandler); 20 Oct 1804. Test: William
    Gooch Sen., Barzillai Graves.
134 JAMES BARNETT SEN. - Will - w. 16 Aug 1804. Wife Ann Barnett;
    sons William, Thomas, John; daughters Betsy Woolfolk and
    Nancy Campbell; money due from Micajah Davis of Richmond;
    requests no appraisal of estate. Exec: sons John, William,
    Thomas. Wit: Ro Payne, Wm. Clarke, Currie Barnett(Jurat).
    Codicil: Money due by bond to go to wife. 9 Sept 1804. Wit:
    Currie Barnett, Wm. Quenily, John Quenily.

                          94

Book E cont. 1804 - 1805
Page
136 ROBERT LYON - Will - w. 23 Oct 1804. Wife Rebecca;
6 children: Jane Johnston, Ann Daniel, Mary Middlebrooks,
William Lyon, Robert Lyon, John Lyon, Temperance Poteat and
their heirs; heirs of Mary Middlebrooks; grandson Edmond Lyon;
granddaughter Betsy Lyon. Exec: James Burton, Henry Howard.
Wit: Starling Gunn, Daniel Chandler, John Gunn.

137 THOMAS RICE - Will - w. 20 Mar 1804. Sons Elisha, Joel, William
H. Rice; daughters Rebecca Windsor, Sarah Gwyn, Marsy Nunn,
Leucy Scoby; daughter in law Sally Rice widow of Nathan Rice
decd.; daughter Mary Oldham's children. Slave Sarah not to be
sold and to live with family member of her choosing. Exec: son
William H. Rice and John Windsor Senr. Wit: James Williamson,
G. Williamson, William Poston, Christopher Brooks(Jurat).

139 JACOB MILES SNR. - Will - w. 10 Feb 1800. Wife Hannah Miles.
son Jacob (land on Rattlesnake Cr.); granddaughter Martha Gunn
(land on Rattlesnake Cr.); daughter Priscilla Henderson; 6 of
my grandchildren: Jacob Graves, John Graves, James Graves,
Thomas Miles, John Miles, Elizabeth Cimbro. Exec: son Jacob
and Thos. Gunn Jun. Proved on oaths of Jacob Miles Jun., Starling Gunn, Thomas Slade Sen., John Graves Sen.

139 GEORGE HUMPHREYS - Will - w. 12 June 1804. Sons George, Benja-
min, William; son Leer(Zeer)? Humphreys; son in law John
Nicholas; daughter Elizabeth Owens, Polly Lions, Frances
Humphreys. Exec: sons George and Benjamin. Wit: Robt. West,
Smith Lawson, Peter Smith.

141 RACHEL SHY - Will - w. 7 Oct 1804. Sons Samuel, Jesse, Robert,
and Eli Shy; daughter Patsey Everett and her daughters Hannah
and Polly; friend Elizabeth Starkey; daughters Polley Vissage,
Sally Enoch, Anney Enoch. Exec: Richard Arnold and son Eli Shy.
Wit: W. L. Webb, Richard Arnold, Mary Arnold.

142 Inv property of estate of John Dameron on 28 July 1804 by Mary
Dameron adm.
142 Inv estate of George Humphries on 24 Oct 1804.
143 Inv estate of Thomas Rice (C.Branch) decd. taken 30 Oct 1804
by Wm. H. Rice and John Windsor Sr. exec. (Cabin Branch?)
144 Obligation: "This shall oblige me and my Heirs to let my Father
and Mother James and Ann Barnett live on in Joyful possession
of land and tenements bought of Wynn Dixon in Caswell County
during their lives allowing me to build a mill and make improvements". /s/ Tho Barnett. 9 May 1804. Wit: Currie Barnett,
Silas Heston.
144 Inv estate of William Murphey and sales on 25 Aug 1804. Among
buyers: Lucy Murphey, widow; James Murphey, John Murphey,
Josiah Thomas, Larkin Herndon, David Herndon, Erasmus Compton,
Daniel Malone, Thomas Morris.
145 Inv estate of Ann Eddings 29 Oct 1804. Judgments against Abner
Quarles. By Charles Sherman adm.
145 Rent of plantation of William Mitchell to Alex Lackey.
145 Nathaniel Gooch's Ear Mark of his stock To Wit A crop and a Slit
in the Right Ear and a crop in the left.

January Court 1805

146 William Rainey to put into repair bridge across Country Line
Creek near Jesse Carter's. Wit: Jas Burton.

95

Book E cont. 1805
Page
146 Settlement estate of Abraham Perkins by Jesse Perkins adm.
   Cash paid to Abram Perkins Jr., Isaac Middlebrooks, Aquilla
   Swann, William Ware, Peyton Wade, Mary Perkins widow of Phil
   Perkins.
147 Power of attorney: John and Anderson Middlebrooks of Hancock
   Co. Ga. to Zere Middlebrooks of same county to recover from
   estate of Robert Lyon decd. of Caswell Co. NC legacy left to
   Zere and Anderson Middlebrooks by Lyon. Wit: A.M.Devereau,
   T. Hamilton. /s/ Jno W. Devereau,noty., Hancock Co. Ga. at
   Sparta Ga. 15 Dec 1804.
148 Settlement estate of John Kimbrough. Div. to Isbel Kimbrough,
   widow; Sally, John, Patsey, Tabitha Kimbrough, orphans of John.
   8 Nov 1804.
149 Sales estate of John Dameron. Buyers: Mary Dameron, Christopher
   Dameron, Edward Clay, Lewis Malone.
150 Sales estate of Thomas Rice decd. taken 15 Nov 1804. Among
   buyers: William Nash, Hugh Gwyn, John Windsor Sen., Solomon
   Debow, Sarah Rice, Samuel Paschal, Wm. H. Rice, John Watt,
   Lucy Scoby, Josiah Paschal, Leonard Sartain, Nathan Rice, John
   Windsor, John Goodloe, Wm. Berry, Rhoda Gibson, Garland Key,
   John Nance, Thomas Key, John Tapscott, Edney Tapscott, John
   Hays, Henry Delop, Williamson Rice, Christopher Brooks.
153 Sale estate of George Humphreys. Sales to: Benjamin Humphreys,
   Peter Smith, Rosaner McClarney, Simon Adams, George Humphreys,
   Paul Chappel, Greenbury Voss, William Lynn, Daniel Gossage,
   Jesse Dalton, Wm. West, Edward Ruark, Elijah Sims, William Hun-
   phreys, James Robertson, Carter Blackwell, John Chilton,
   Obedier Holloway, James Grant.
157 Sales of Robert Lyon on 19 Nov 1804. Among buyers: Mrs. Rebecca
   Lyon, John Payne, William Lyon, James Vaughan, Joel Kennon,
   Jeremiah Beaver, Philip Pearce, John Knight, Benjamin Gomer,
   Rober Randolph, Richard Haddock, Jacob Quine, John Baxter,
   Isaac Wright, Capt. John Graves, Epophroditus Stone, James
   Curtice, Archer Alverson, James Ray, Joshua Grant, Thomas
   Yearley, Ibzan Rice. Acct. rendered by James Gatewood for
   James Colquehown and Co; bond on John Southerland.
161 Inv of Robert Lyon taken 8 Nov 1804.
162 John Woods and Catherine his wife, adm. estate George Farley,decd.,
   div. to John and Catherine.
163 Sales estate Nathaniel Rice 23 & 24 Nov 1804. Sales to:
   Wiley Yancey, Isaac Johnston, Anderson Birk, Archibald Rice,
   William Scoggins, Bartlett Estis, Robert Thompson, John Scoggins.
   (Partial list)
167 Allotment to Nancy Rudd widow and relict of Aldridge Rudd decd.
   10 Nov 1804.
167 Allotment to Mary Dameron widow of John Dameron decd. 10 Nov 1804.
167 Allotment to widow and children of William Poteat decd. 2 Nov.
168 Estate of Hezekiah Carmon, payments to: Hannah Carmon, Cornelius
   Boroughs, Johnston Herbin. By Elijah Carmon adm.
168 Ear Mark that Jepthah Parks gives cattle Hogs and Sheep is a
   Swallow ford in each ear and under bit in the right ear.
   30 July 1805.

Book E cont. 1805
Page
168 JOHN WILLIAMS - Will - w. 31 May 1798. Wife Betsy (land on Horsley Cr. at Nash's line to mouth of Dill Branch); son Duke;
granddaughter Betsy Williams Simpson (under 21) and her brother
John Kincholoe Simpson; granddaughter Betsy Williamson Williams
and her brother John Williams; granddaughter Nancy Lea Graves
(under 21) and her brother John Williams Graves; daughter Betsy
wife of Azariah Graves; daughter Henrietta Simpson wife of Richard Simpson(land purchased of Lewis Pike and Hall Williamson);
daughter Betsy(land on Horseley's Cr. adj. Tubbs Branch to
Brown's and Goodloe's lines). Exec: son Duke Williams, son in
law Richard Simpson, and Azariah Graves. Wit: Signal Akeen,
Jerre Williamson.
171 Robert West flesh mark a Crop in left Ear and whole in right Ear.

April Court 1805

172 Received of Robert Mitchell guardian of Mathew Mains orphan by
the hands of Samuel Dickie the sum of 45 lbs. Received by me
/s/ Thomas Shanks. Feb 1799.
172 Amt. rent of plantation belonging to orphans of James Mallory.
By William Sawyer guardian.
172 Sale of horse to Lewis Burton that widow of James Wilson was
allowed by commrs.
172 Inv estate of John Williams. Feb 1805.
173 Settlement estate of James Vinson by George Hornbuckle adm.
Approved by Anthony Swift, Hezekiah Boswell, Thomas Garrett.
173 Inv estate of William Poteet taken 31 Oct 1804 by John Poteet.
174 Sales estate of William Poteet. Buyers: Mary Poteet, Daniel
Gwinn, John Graves Sen., Daniel Gunn, Joshua Pogue, John Starkey,
Miles Poteet, Jeremiah Beaver, James Poteet, Martin Perkins,
Elam Knight, William Quissonbury, David Haddock, Cary Sawyer,
William Sawyer. (Partial list)
176 George Hornbuckle guardian acct. with orphans of John Hughs.

177 JAMES GRANT SEN. - Will - w. 8 Dec. 1801. Sons John, Dirkin,
William, James Jr., Reubin, Joshua; daughters Elizabeth Fitzgerald, Marg Lemon, Rachel as she and her only child is dead;
wife Ann Grant; grandson John son and heir of son Neely Grant
decd.;one-half claim to lands in Stafford and King George Counties, Va. Exec: sons James Jr. and Joshua. Wit: Edward Watlington, Washington Weaver, Thomas Fitzgerald.

178 WILLIAM B. BURTON - Will - w. 6 Jan 1805. daughter Jane Burton
Richardson (under 18); brothers James Burton; sister Nancy Bennion,
niece Patsey Winston. Exec: brother James Burton and friend
Thomas Winston. Wit: Moses Ingran, John Gunn, Griffin Gunn.

179 JAMES SAMUEL - Will - w.18 July 1801. Wife Sarah; children:
James and Leah Samuel, Fanny Dameron, Walker and Josiah Samuel;
4 grandchildren Lucy, Herndon, John, and James Hill. Exec:
Archd. Samuel and William Yates. Wit: James McNeely, John Yates.

179 JAMES ARNETT - Will - w. 11 June 1800. Wife Mary Ann Arnett;
sons James (house and lot in Danville), Joseph (lot in Danville);
daughters Peggy Durham, Sary and Mary Arnett (2 youngest).
Wit: John Price Sen., Major Brockman, James Brockman.

180 David Hutson, male child of colour, one yr. old Aug. next, bound
to William Cantrell. /s/ James Rainey, Chairman County Court.
181 Betsy Hutson, child of colour, 3 yrs. Aug. next, bound to William
Cantrell.

97

Book E cont. - 1805
Page
182 William Hannah, orphan 16 yrs. old the 11 of June next, bound
    to Nicholas Thompson to learn mastery of saddle and harness
    making.
183 Wiley Robinson orphan 7 yrs. the 22nd of this Instant bound to
    John Gomer. /s/ John Yancey, Chairman of County Court.
    30 May 1805.
184 William Robinson, 12 yrs. old next June, orphan, bound to John
    Gomer.
185 Pleasant Robinson orphan of 5 yrs. next Aug. bound to John Gomer.
186 Sales estate of Aldridge Rudd on 16 Nov 1804. Sales to:
    Nancy Rudd widow, W. S. Webb, Polly Rudd, Josiah Morton, Fanney
    Rudd, William Pinchback, Daniel Gunn, William Rudd, Capt. John
    Graves, Jeremiah Samuel, James Turner(P), Jacob Ahart, Groves
    Howard, Alex Murphey, Robert Martin, William Turner, Thomas
    Turner, Barzillai Graves. By Alex Murphey and Groves Howard,adm.
188 Inv. estate of Aldridge Rudd taken 10 Nov 1804.
189 Settlement estate of James Mallory.
190 Inv estate of James Samuel in presence of Thomas Fisher, John
    Stanfield, and Daniel S. Parley by Archd. Samuel exec.

July Court 1805

190 Sale estate of Neeley Grant on 11 Aug 1798. Buyers: Lucy Grant,
    widow; Joshua Grant, Samuel Boman, Thomas Fitzgerald, Peter
    Smith, Charley Price, Richard Long, John Ferry, William Kennon,
    Richard Estes. By Joshua Grant adm.
191 Inv estate of James Grant.
192 Sales estate of William B. Burton July 20, 1805. Sales to:
    Thomas Winston, Benjamin Walker, Benjamin Quine, James Burton,
    Samuel Henderson Jun., Charles Payne, John Payne, Elizabeth
    Lewis, Henry Dix, Peter Smith.
193 Inv property of William B. Burton.
194 Inv estate of Thomas Kimbrough on 4 May 1805 by Thomas Graves
    and Groves Howard adm.
195 Sales and inv estate of Robert Lyon. Sales to John Payne, James
    Burton, Thomas Winston, Archibald Alverson.
195 Inv estate of James Arnett on 27 July 1805 by Mary Arnett adm.
196 Inv estate of Israel Barker by George and James Barker.
197 Insolvents for 1804 given in by Samuel Johnston high Sheriff.
    (Each assessed for 1 white poll unless name is followed by
    a number indicating more than 1 poll.)

Thomas Goins	James Carrol 2	Dudley Ballard
Malichi Holoman	Stephen Chandler	John Berry
James Kimbrough	David Evans	John Delap
David Tulloch	James Gooch	Henry Dickens
Moses Ingram	Randolph Buckley	Benjamin Gibson
John Brooks	Elijah Reynolds 2	John Goodloe 4
Watson Winters	Jesse Morton	Nathan Sims
Thomas Elam	John Briggs	Richard Swift 2
Norris Compton	John Coleman	William Waldrop
James Burnwatts	Trustram Fisher	Gower Whitemore
Jacob Burch	John Jenings	Micajah Estes
William Alders	William West 2	Simon Carlile
William Bruce	Edward Waldrop	Robert Donaldson

198 Div estate of James Smith decd. to 7 legatees: Sarah Smith widow;
    Janny(Fanny?) Jackson wife of Thomas Jackson, George and Robert
    Smith sons of decd., Sarah, Nanney and Elizabeth Smith daughters
    of decd. 17 July 1805.

Book E cont. 1805
198 Insolvents for 1803 given in by William Rainey Esq. sheriff.
(Each assessed for 1 poll unless followed by another number.)

Thomas Burch	Robert Watkins	Ben Gibson
William Cunningham	Demsey Womble	George Hornbuckle
Enoch Dunaway	John Briggs	Pleasant Johnston
Robert Elam	Luke Boulain	John Thomas
Jesse Elmore	Elisha Conway	Thomas Merain 2
John J. Farley	John Coleman	Charles Payne
Charnell Hightower 2	John Farrell	John McCalester
Ambrose Lea	John Jenings	Charles Payne
Roderick McDaniel	James Murphey	John Patrick
John Ponds	Ephraim Russell	Howel Leroy
Josiah Pullium 2	Wheeler Smith	John Johnston
Thomas Swaynnie	Edward Waldrop	David Nelms
James Wright	Pleasant Childress	Susannah Noel
William Williamson	George Foot	Robert Thomas

199 Allotment to Temperance Poteat widow of James Poteat decd.
31 May 1805.
199 Allotment to Betsy Kimbrough widow and relict of Thomas Kimbrough decd. 17 May 1805.
200 Sol Graves TPB (Treasurer Public Buildings) reports the Jael in
a situation by no means sufficient for safe keeping of debtors
and the underpining of this Court house ought to be repaired.
200 Letter of attorney: Henry Strater to William King to act in all
business. 25 Mar 1805. Wit: James Orr JP, Jos. Murphey.
201 Div property of Thomas Yancey by James Yancey and B. Yancey guardians to: James Yancey Jun., Tryon Yancey, Priscilla Yancey,
Nancy Yancey; property received by Elizabeth Yancey and
Attilia Yancey. 31 July 1805.
202 Settlement estate of Thomas Yancey.

202 JOHN PLEASANT - Will - w. 7 May 1805. Son Beauford; daughter
Martha; children to take care of their brother William or Lewis
Corbit and sister Nancy should take William. Exec: friends
Micajah Pleasant and Thomas Pendergast. Wit: Lewis Corbit,
James Melton.

204 JOHN VAUGHAN - Will - w. 20 Apr 1805. Wife Jerusa; children
under age; sons Sterling and Thomas; children: Tabitha, Salley,
Jerusha, Lissa, Sterling, Thomas, and unborn child. Exec:
Solomon Graves, Thomas Pendergast, and wife Jerusha. Wife may
desire to remove to Nottaway or Lunenburg Co. Va.
Wit: L. Johnston, William Pleasant, Thomas Vaughan.
Jerusha Vaughan widow qualified.

205 ISRAEL BARKER - Will - w. 3 Jan 1804. Sons George and James;
sons Burnley, John, Israel, and Isaac Newton; Exec: 2 oldest
sons George and James. Wit: John Pinnix, George Barker, John
Henslee.

October Court 1805

207 James Kimbrough base born child age 3 yrs. the 22 of Aug last
bound to Andrew Kimbrough.
208 Goolsby Wattson orphan 4 yrs. old bound to Michael Montgomery.
/s/ Joshua Richmond, Chairman County Court.
209 Archibald Ransom orphan of 15 yrs. bound to Philip Pierce. /s/
Philip Pearce.
210 Edmund Lyon orphan 18 yrs. old the 15 Mar next bound to Thomas
Harrelson.

Book E cont. 1805 - 1806
Page
211 Sales estate of Israel Barker on 24 Sept 1805. Sales to:

Hiram Cooper	James Haydon	Thos. Shanks
James Barker	John Penix	Baz Kerr
George Barker	Anderson Burk	William Johnston
John Barker	Mrs. Brooks	John Garner
William Brintle	Peter McKinney	William Rudd
Burnly Barker	Jonathan Brooks	Henry Williams
Elisha Barton	Wiley Yancey	Zachariah Groom
Lewis Foster	Judith Penix	Willis Davis
Capt. Tait	George Barker Jun.	(Partial list)

214 Inv estate of Thomas Boswell on 20 Oct 1805 by John Yancey adm.
215 Report of William Rainey Sheriff in acct. with Robert Parks,
    county trustee.
216 Sales estate of Robert Lyon on 22 Oct 1805 to William Lyon. Bond
    due from Jno. Hoomes.
217 Inv estate of John Vaughan by William Pleasant, Gabriel Murphey
    Sen., and Thomas Prendergast.
218 Inv property Robert Lyon.
218 Sales estate of James Samuel on 20 Sept 1805 by Archd. Samuel.
    Sales to Walker Samuel, Sarah Samuel, Jeremiah Samuel.

January Court 1806

219 William Huston base born child 8 yrs. old the 18 of July last
    bound to William Parker.

220 EDMUND ALLEY - Will - ND. Bequeaths to Charles Shearman, Lewis
    Vaughan, Capt. John Burton, Maj. Robert Willson, and Mr. John
    McCain. Exec: Capt. John Burton. Wit: Isakiah Farley, W.Willson.

220 SAMUEL ENOCH - Will - ND. Wife Elizabeth Enoch; child Sarah
    Enoch. Exec: wife Elizabeth. Wit: Andrew Kimbro, W. S. Webb,
    William Smith.

221 CHARLES DIXON - Will - w. 24 Nov 1805. Major Tilman Dixon of
    Tennessee to get 7 slaves; Henry Dixon son of decd. brother
    Henry Dixon (land in Caswell Co.); Americus Dixon son of Bro-
    ther Tilman Dixon (all land in Tenn.). Exec: Maj. Tilman Dixon
    of Tenn. and Henry Dixon. Wit: Joseph Bracken, Thomas Swann,
    Saml. Dabney.

222 Inv. estate of Samuel Enoch by Elizabeth Enoch on 28 Jan 1806.

222 RACHEL SULLIVANT - Will - w. 21 Aug 1805. Sons Drury, Isaac,
    Jesse, Russell, and Jordan; daughters Patsy and Nancy. Exec:
    friends Solomon Brintle and Anthony Swift. Wit: Anthony Swift,
    George Sims, Solomon Brintle.

223 Div property of William B. Burton 22 Nov 1805 to: James Burton,
    Nancy Benion, Patsy Winston. Commrs: Joseph Bracken, John Cobb,
    Henry Howard, Jesse Perkins, Silvanus Stokes.
224 Sales estate of Robert Lyon by John Gamble adm. Open accts. on
    David Pen, Danl. S. Farley.
225 Inv estate of John Pleasant. Property devised to Beuford and
    Martha Pleasant.
227 Div of negroes of Thomas Harrison to 8 legatees: Samuel Smith,
    John Harrison, Charles Harrison, Robert Harrison, William Harri-
    son, Andrew Harrison, Jane Harrison, Thomas Harrison.
228 Sales estate of Thomas Bozwell to Juday Bozwell and Salley
    Bozwell. By J. Yancey adm.

Book E cont. 1806
Page
229 JOSEPH CHANDLER - Will - w. May 1800. Sons William and Stephen
(land near George Stovall's spring); 9 children: James, Betty,
Sucky, Joseph, Lucy, Edmund, Sally, William, Stephen.
Exec: David and William Gooch, Barzillai Graves. Wit: William
Gooch, James Gooch.

230 Settlement estate of Joseph Chandler. Estate indebted to George
Stovall. Div to 9 legatees: James Chandler, John Pinson, George
Stovall, Joseph Chandler, William Pinson received nothing,
Edmund Chandler, Willm. Mitchell, Willm. Chandler, Stephen
Chandler.

231 Legatees of Jos Chandler empower George Stovall to proceed with
administrating remainder of estate.

231 Power of attorney: Joseph Chandler, Edmund Chandler, William
Pinson, and William Mitchell to James Chandler to receive from
estate of Joseph Chandler. 15 Oct 1805. Given from Franklin Co.
Georgia. Test: Stephen Chandler.

232 Julius Gibson of Pendleton County, South Carolina gives power of
attorney to Peter Smith to receive and recover from Joel Gibson
of Pittsylvania Co.Va. and his sureties in Caswell County.
19 Aug 1805. Wit: Robt. West.

233 Power of attorney: Robert Lyon of Lincoln Co. Ga. to friend and
brother John Lyon to recover from James Burton and Henry Howard,
exec. of Robert Lyon decd., father of said Lyons. Proved in
Laurens District, S. C. by J. A. Elmore and William Null.
16 Dec 1805.

235 Power of attorney: John Lyon of Laurens District, S. C. to
Alexander Murphey to receive legacy of his decd. father Robert
Lyon for him and on behalf of his brother Robert Lyon. 25 Nov
1805. Wit: Josiah Farmer.

236 Power of attorney: Nehemiah Daniel of Patrick Co. Va. to William
Lyon (son of Robert Lyon) of Caswell Co. to receive Ann Daniel's
part (his wife) in estate of Robert Lyon. 29 Jan 1806.

237 Joseph Bracken hath petitioned the court that negro slave named
Arnos (Arnes), property of Bracken, may be liberated and become
free. Should Arnes ever become chargeable to the county, said
obligation should be voided.

238 Towney Elam orphan 19 yrs. old the 10th day of Oct last bound to
Charles L. Hunter. /s/ Solomon Graves, Chairman County Court.

April Court 1806

239 Estate of John Fargusan decd. in acct. with Jesse Carter adm.
240 Estate of John C. Gooch in acct. with William Gooch exec.
241 Sales estate of Samuel Enoch by Betsy Enoch adm.
241 Allotment to Mary West widow of John West decd. and her family.
242 Estate of John Lea in acct. with James & Jeremiah Lea exec.
243 Estate of Nathaniel Rice in acct. with Wylie Yancey in right of
his wife Susannah and James Yancey adm. of estate of Nathan
Rice decd.

244 Div estate of Nathan Rice to 6 children and widow:
Wiley Yancey for wife Susannah; Archibald Rice, Anderson Birk
in right of his wife Nancy, William Scoggins in right of his wife
Patsey, Nathaniel Lacey Rice orphan, Edmund Butler Rice orphan,
James Rice orphan. 24 Apr 1806.

245 Power of attorney: Ann Garner of Fauquier Co. Va. to Daniel Garner
to recover and receive property in Caswell County. 10 Oct 1805.
Wit: Joannah Barnett, Judith Barnett, Joanna Hampton, John Barnett, Anbrose Barnett.

246 Inv property of Charles Dixon.

101

Book E cont. 1806
Page
247-8 Inv estate of James Poteat. Sales by John Poteat adm.
249 Inv and sale estate of Edmond Alley decd. by John Burton exec.
    Sales to Robert Wilson, John Farley, John Burton, Nannie Durham,
    William Wilson, William Yates, Jesse Elmore.
250 Inv estate of John West decd. Provisions laid in for widow
    and children. 29 Apr 1806 by Robert West adm.
251 Sales estate of Charles Dixon on 24 Feb 1806. Sales to Henry
    Dixon, William Aiken, Isaac Wright, Benjamin Quine, John Ferrell,
    Epephorditus Stone, Whitehead Page, Meredith Price, Benj. A.
    West, Alexander Ferguson, Simon Adams, Levi Blackwell.
253 Mary Woods in acct. with estate of Samuel Woods decd. Sales to
    Mary Woods, Lewis Malone, David Rainey, William Richmond,
    Samuel Woods, James Murphey, James Woods, Thomas Woods, John
    Woods, Matthew Macklin, Isaac Rainey, Phillip Wadkins, Staples
    Malone, James Bowman, William Woods, John Rainey, William Ferrell,
    Barnard Kemp, John Goodloe Warren, Thomas Dollarhide, John Malone.
255 Sale property of Thomas Kimbro 15 May 1805 to Elizabeth Kimbrough,
    John Graves Sen., James Graves, Henry Turner, W. S. Webb, John
    Martin, James Vaughan, Joshua Beaver, Jacob Graves, Lewis Corbit,
    John Yancey, Robert Browning, Azariah Graves Jun., Lot Egman,
    William Farmer, Groves Howard, William Glasby, William Rudd,
    Abram E. Morton, Richard Arnold, Alex Wiley, William Kimbro,
    James Currie.
259 Additional inv estate of Thomas Kimbro on 20 Apr 1806 by Thomas
    Graves and Groves Howard adm.
259 Mourning Gillaspy girl of colour age 17 yrs. the last day of
    March last bound to Jacob Ahart.
260 Inv estate of Natha¹ Rice. Bond due of Anderson Williams.
260 Littlebury Gwinn and Major Price - bonded to build bridge cross
    Hogan's Creek, 12 ft wide and 104 ft long of good timbers.
    15 Mar 1806. Wit: William Rainey, Joel McDaniel.

July Court 1806

262 Asa Thomas and Nathan Williams, Judges for election, certify that
    MDuke Williams got 675 votes and Thos Lacey got 145. Election
    held 14 and 15 Instant.
262 Betsy Watkins age 2 yrs. last Sept., child of colour, bound to
    Christopher Dameron.
263 Lewis Watkins child of colour, age 5 yrs. last March, bound to
    Christopher Dameron.

264 RICHARD HORNBUCKLE - Will - w. 17 June 1806. Wife Elizabath;
    sons Simpson, Hiram. Exec: Aaron Simpson and wife Elizabeth.
    Wit: Thomas Garrett, Ersania Taite.

265 WILLIAM PAGE - Will - w. 11 Mar 1805. Wife Elizabeth;
    daughters Rachel, Salley, Elizabeth, Jane, and Polly Waters;
    son John. Exec: son John. Wit: Robert H. Childers, James Page,
    Edward Loofman(Loosman).

266 Inv estate of Johnston McDaniel taken 28 July 1806 by Susanna
    McDaniel adm.
267 Mary Dameron exec. estate of John Dameron - commrs. met at
    Leasburg and approved accts. Approved by Gabriel, S., and
    William Lea.
268 William Pinchback and Jerre Rudd exec of Hezekiah Rudd, in acct.
    with estate. Sales to William Robertson, James Dollarhide;
    bonds on Charles Nunnally, Francis Page. Payments to sheriff
    of Chesterfield, Morris Pilkenston, Peter Rowlett, Dr. McAden,
    Nancy, Jerre, James, Biddy, David, & Rebecca Rudd.

Book E cont. 1806
Page
270 Additional inv estate of James Willson by D. Henslee adm.
271 Crafton Williams has received of William Rainey $20 for damage
which Wm. Rainey's mill on Country Line Creek has done to "me
and my hereafter" by same being four inches higher than the same
is at this day. Wit: Danl. S. Farley.
272 Hezekiah Boswell in acct. with estate of Walt Garner. Accts.
paid to Jethro Brown, John Garner, Abner Powell, William Bruce,
Robert Bruce, Jonathan Murray, Mary Roberson, Ann Hornbuckle,
Samuel Johnston for tax, John Lenox, Alex Bruce, Owen Ballard.
274 Taxable property for 1804-5
 1804   993 white polls   1539 black polls   18 retailers
 1805   961   "   1517   "   18   "
275 Insolvents for 1804

Jeremiah Lutrall	Brockman White	Elijah Carman
James Lawrence 2	Marmaduke Ingram	Joshua Phillips
Wm. Moss Jun. 3	Richard Going	Jesse Evans
Thomas Moss	Stephen Bloyd	John Burchett
Smith Sutton	John Caw	Jesse Morton
George Smith	James Ridley	William Wallace
Julos Sanders		Ibzan Rice

275 Christopher Dameron Sen. not to remove two free children of
colour, Lewis and Betsy Watkins, from Caswell County and
should deliver them to Court when they arrive at age.

October Court 1806

277 John Carrole orphan 9 yrs. old bound to George Carrole.
278 Edward Carrole orphan 6 yrs. old bound to George Carrole.
279 Sales estate of Nathaniel Hart. Buyers: Elizabeth Hart,
guardian to Nathl. Hart, John Hart, MDuke Williams, Duke
Williams Capt., Thomas Poyner, James Jennings, John White,
Jepthah Rice, Capt. Wynn Dixon. Bond on Maj. Azariah Graves.
280 Sales balance estate of William Mitchell to: Nathan Williams,
Thomas Foster (150 acres land), Evan Jeffrey, Joseph Benton.
281 James Carrole adm. estate of Elizabeth Bruce. Cash paid for
vouchers of Robert Bruce, Frances Smith, Elijah Graves, William
Muzzall, Charles Turner, Robert Mitchell. Sale in 1801.
Paid legacies to: William Hall, John Travis for David Tolloch,
John Payne (Taylor), James Hayes, James Carrole. (Settlement
estate of Robert Bruce decd.) 15 Sept 1804. Approved by Jas.
Yancey, Alex Murphey.
282 Power of attorney: Isham Dalton to Marmaduke Williams to act in
his name concerning tract of land in Hanover Co. Va. 20 Oct.
1806. Test: Jesse Dalton.
282 William Rainey to build bridge across Hico at Love's ford.
Bond by Gabriel Lea, Daniel Darby, Samuel Love.
284 Power of attorney: John Lyon of Laurence Dist, S. C. (Laurens)
to Zera Middlebrooks to recover and receive from James Burton
and Henry Howard exec. of his father Robert Lyons estate in
Caswell Co., said estate now in hands of Rebecah Lyon step
mother. Attorney should first pay debt due from Lyon to Mathew
Tanner for $2086. 30 July 1806. /s/ William Burnside and Wm.
Null JP, Laurens Dist, S.C; Elihu Creswell CC.
285 Power of attorney: Drury Rhodes to John Standfield and Durrett
Richards to conduct business in a suit against Michael Mont-
gomery as defendant in Hillsborough Dist. respecting 5 negroes,
Chance, Dick, Tom, Jack, and Sam. 18 Sept 1806. Test: Asa
Thomas, Thos. Gatewood, Smith Kinesel, John Scott, Charles Ray,
William Yates Jun.

Book E cont. 1806 - 1807
Page
285 Addition to Power of attorney given by Drury Rhodes to Standfield
and Richards empowers them to settle dispute by sending case to
court of Equity. 21 Oct 1806.
287 Insolvents for 1805

Jacob Chilton	William Underwood	Nathan Rice
James Cannon	Thomas Smith	James Shelton Jun.
John Terrill	David Bruce	John Smithey
Byrd Gomer	John Bush	Russell Sullivant
Isaac Hodge	Jeremiah Bush	Nathan Sims
Isaac Hobbs	Richard Chuning	Robert Sawyer
William Lay	William Clark	Charles Turner
Levy Middlebrooks	John Corr	Jere Walker
Wm. W. Moss	Robert H. Childers	Jesse Elmore
Spencer Moss	Enoch Chamberlain	Gabriel Gunn
Robert Overstreet	Hyram Cooper	Pleasant Farley
George Powell	Henry Davis	John Whittington
Joseph Price	John Dickens	Charles Hubbard
Peter Ruark	John Dickey	Abraham Hargis
William Moss	John Darnold	Richd. Matthews
Edward Ruark	William Fulars	Garnett Neely
Timothy Ruark	Humphrey Griffin	Joshua Phillips
Joseph Swann	John Hensley	William Rather
George Smith	Ezekiel Jones	George Roper
Joshua Trigg	John Jackson	Lewis Ashborn
George Broach	William Poston	Burton
Hugh Currie	James Ray	James Wallace
James Greer	William Pruitt	John Wisdom
John Hubt?	Henry Turner Sen.	John Wallace
Abell Horn	Chas Turner	

288 WILLIAM LEA SEN. of Leasburgh - Will - w. 14 Mar 1804. Wife
Catharine (4 rooms in dwelling house in Leasburgh and land
purchased of Thomas Hargis); son Lawrence (land on Cobb Cr.
purchased of Wm. Hargis and on Kilgore's Br, also lots in Leasburgh containing store house and saddle shop);
son James Lea (land on Kilgore's Br. where he now resides);
son in law William Donoho to have one-fourth profit from mercantile business; dry goods to be obtained from Petersburgh;
5 rooms in east end of dwelling house in Leasburgh to Wm.Donoho.
Exec: son Lawrence and son in law Wm. Donoho. Wit: Loyd Vanhook,
John McAden, Nicholas Thompson.

291 JOHN CHILTON - Will - w. 16 July 1806. Sons John (land on fall Br.),
Lemuel, William; my 6 children: James, William, John, and Lemuel
Chilton, Polly Travis, and Sally Travis. Exec: sons James &
William. Wit: Benjamin Williamson, Simon Adams, Sally Thompson,

292 Balance of sale estate of William Mitchell.

January Court 1807

293 JOHN COCHRAN SEN. - Will - w. 12 July 1803. All children: David,
Robert, John, William, Reubin, James, and Simeon Cochran,
Peggy Williams, Esther Hubbard, Sarah Barker, Mary Barton, Tabi-
tha Bruce. Exec: sons John, Reubin, James, Simeon. Wit: Groves
Howard, Edmund Harper, John Cochran Jun.

Book E cont. 1807
Psge
296 VINES MATTHEWS - Will - w. 25 Oct 1806. Land bought of William
and James Lea be sold; Wife Nancy; estate to be kept together
until youngest child is of lawful age; all my children;
sons Drury Matthews, Thomas; legacy may come from Father's estate. Exec: wife and friend William Lea of Leasburgh.
Wit:Isaac Jackson, Bartholomew Dameron, Vincent Lea.
/s/ Vines Matthis.

298 Inv estate of Vines Matthews by Ann M. Mathews and William Lea.
299 Balance sale of Nat Hart estate by John Hart.
300 Inv estate of Richard Hornbuckle by Betsy Hornbuckle exec.
301 Inv estate of John Vaughan decd. by Thom. Vaughan and James
Yancey.
302 Cornelius Willson, male child of colour 4 yrs. old last Feb,
bound to Edward Swann.
303 Susanna McDaniel adm. in acct. with estate of Johnston McDaniel.
Notes on John McDaniel, Steples Malone, Ann Evans, Bartholomew
Jackson, James Johnston Sen, Jeremiah Fletcher.
304 Estate of Jeremiah Poston in acct. with John C. Cox exec. Sale
of land on Stony Creek to John Windsor, also in Rockingham.
304 Received on 10 May 1806 of Wilie Yancey adm. in right of his
wife of estate of Nathaniel Rice decd. 179 lbs. in full of
legacy of decd. Father's estate. /s/ Archabal Rice.
305 Sales estate of John Vaughan to:

James Vaughan Sen.	John Millington	Josiah Thomas
Thomas Vaughan Jun.	Samuel Everett	John Wells
Nicholas Vaughan	Thomas Vaughan Sen.	Thomas Pendergast
James Vaughan Jun.	Isaac Johnston	Andrew McClarney
Mary Riddle	James Turner(Hico)	William Mansfield
James Yancey	Samuel Smythy	John Murrey
Micajah Pleasant	Josiah Turner	William McMinamy
William Turner	Thomas Coleman	Robert Malone
Ransom Hagwood	John Word	
George Horton	Willis Ashford	By Thomas
Richard Vaughan	John Pleasant	Vaughan and James
Robert Scott	Ely Shie	Yancey adm.
Edmond Browning	Bleuford Pleasant	

309 John Freeman a free black man of Caswell County indebted to
Durett Richards and Josiah Samuel obliges to serve Richards for
term of 6 years. Wit: William Yates Jun., John Hall, Ambrose
Butt. 11 Dec 1806.
309 Receipt of William Scoggins in right of his wife Patsey for his
part of estate of Nathaniel Rice.
310 Inv estate of Joshua Richmond on 6 Dec 1806 by Phebe Richmond and
William Richmond exec. Debts due the estate for schooling from
Allen Burton, Christopher Dameron, Ann Richmond, William Mitchell,
John Flynn, Josiah Boman, John Waterfield, Absolem Bass, Mordecai
Burgess, Vines Matthews.
312 Note: William Phenill to Durett Richards of Richard & Samuel.
4 Feb 1806. Wit: John Hall, Drury Rhodes, James Bouldin, George
O. Connally.

313 JOSHUA RICHMOND - Will - w. 22 Sept 1806. Wife Phoebe;
children: Warren, John, and Robert Richmond. Exec: wife Phoebe
and brother William Richmond. Wit: W. S. Webb, Joseph Richmond.

314 Execution of deed of trust from Edward Jordan to Henry Dixon and
Joseph Barnett for sale of stud horses. Wit: Elizabeth Burton.

Book E cont. 1807
Page
315 Div land of Mary Gibson decd. among her 10 children:
Hannah Lay(land on state line), Richard Gibson, Lucretia Burchfield, William Gibson, Julius Gibson, Omey Hogg, James Gibson,
Susannah Lay (adj. Henry Atkinson), John Gibson, Joel Gibson.
Commrs: Silv Stokes, Mereday Price, Gregory Durham, Greenbury
Voss, Joel McDaniel. Survey by Danl. S. Farley, surveyor.
317 Allotment to Susannah McDaniel widow and relict of Johnston
McDaniel decd.
317 Receipt: Wiley Langley receives of Thomas Wiley guardian 164
lbs. in full his part of estate of Thomas Langley decd.
23 Sept 1806. Test: Joseph Langley.
318 Receipt: Anderson Birk receives from Wiley Yancey adm. for wife
Nancy's legacy in estate of Nathaniel Rice.
318 Power of attorney: William Poston to John Windsor Jun. to settle
with Col⁰ Richard Simpson exec. of Mary Simpson decd. for money
due Poston as a legatee. 20 Nov 1806. Wit: John N. Dobbin,
Henry Poston.
318 Power of attorney: Zedekiah Tate to John Windsor Jun. to settle
with Col⁰ Richard Simpson as exec. of his grandmother Mary Simpson decd.

April Court 1807

319 SPILLSBY COLEMAN - Will - w. 14 July 1806. Wife Elizabeth (land
adj. Obey Holloway); son Nowel(or Noel) (land on Hogan's Cr.);
daughter Patsy Winston and her children; grandson Coleman
Winston(land in Sumner Co. TN on Cumberland River); granddaughter Elizabeth Burton Winston. Exec: Nowel Coleman, James
Burton, Dudley Gatewood, Thomas Winston, Elizabeth Coleman.
Wit: Benjamin Williamson, Benerman Walker, Edward Lewis.

321 SMITH SANDERS - Will - w. 14 Jan 1807. Wife Patsey; youngest
son Smith Sanders; son Moses; daughters: Frances, Betsy, Patsy,
Zella, Polley, Salley, and Anna Sanders. No signature.
Paper purporting to be last will but not signed offered for probate by James D. Taylor who drew the writing. Court ruled it
was will as to personal property but not to real property.

322 GRIFFIN TUGGLE of Chatham Co. N.C. - Will - w. 11 Nov 1798.
son Nicholas Tuggle; wife Frances; exec: wife Frances and
William Berry her son. Wit: William Paschal, Drury Stokes, Leroy Poyner, David Walker.

323 Power of attorney: John W. Mann of Halifax Co. Va. to Joel Mann
to receive from a law suit against William Rainey and to collect
from John Pentecost late of Caswell Co. a judgment against him
by John W. Mann. 29 Oct 1804.
324 Settlement estate of Berryman Greyhan decd. by Margret Greyham
adm. Accts paid to Sarah Greyham, William Bethel, Paul Chappel.
325 Inv and sale of property of Vines Matthews on 7 Feb 1807.Sales to:
Lawrence Lea, Isaac Jackson, Daniel Darby, Samuel Evans, Thomas
Riggs, Ann M. Matthews widow.
327 Sales estate of John Chilton on 18 Nov 1806. Sales to:

James Chilton	Daniel Price	Benj. Humphries	Rose McClarney
William Chilton	Wm. Trigg	Gregory Durham	Wm. Gossage
John Chilton	Timothy Adams	Thomas Swann	Daniel Gossage
Robert Lauton	John Travis	John Swann	Wm. Lyon
Joseph Arnett(Big)	James Travis	Meredith Price	Elijah Yates
Simon Adams	Benj.C.West	Robert West Esq.	Wm. Holloway
Martin Clark	Francis Ray		

Book E cont. 1807
Page
330 Inv estate of John Chilton.
331 Estate of William Poteat in acct. with John Poteat adm. Payments
   to Benjamin Quine for crying sale, Saml. Johnston for tax, Jesse
   Carter, Doctor Webb, John Bennett, Widow Poteat.
332 Inv property of Elender Greer by Samuel Greer adm.
332 Estate of Joshua Richmond: negro woman Isbel sold to John McMurry
   for 333 dollars.
333 Adm of James Willson in acct with legatees. No names given.
334 Inv estate of John Cochran Sen. and list of sales (partial list):

Barzillai Graves	Jos Bush	Richd. Haddock
James Cochran	Francis Smith	Henry McNeill
Groves Howard	Thomas Boman	Lewis Corbit
Phillip Watkins	William Chandler	Zachariah Groom
Arquilla Burton	Robert Cochran	William Parker
John Graves Sen.	Simeon Cochran	Freeman Hubbard
David Barker	John Pinson	William Singleton
James Tollar		

   Bequeaths to David, John, Robert, James Cochran, and to
   Mary Barton.
339 Received of William Rainey full amount of my brother John W.
   Mann's judgment. /s/ Joel Mann. Test Danl. S. Farley.
339 Settlement estate of Aldrage Rudd by Alex Murphey and Groves
   Howard adm.
341 James Mann orphan age 9 yrs. the 24 Oct next bound to Moses
   Richardson.
341 John Mann orphan of 7 yrs. the 6 day of Sept. next bound to
   Moses Richardson.

July Court 1807

342 MORDECAI BURGESS - Will - w. 10 June 1807. Wife Mary;
   son Joseph is under age; my 3 sons; my 6 children: Elinor,
   Elizabeth, William, John, Joseph, and Jenny. Exec: John Langley and wife Mary Burgess. Wit: Joseph Langley, Abner Wisdom.

343-5 Bonds for John Stamps as sheriff of Caswell County.
346 Bond for Robert Parks as county trustee.
346 Taxable property for 1806.

347 EDMOND BROWNING - Will - w. 19 Apr 1807. Wife Mary Ann Browning;
   son John; son Calebs Heirs; daughter Nancy McReynolds;
   son Joshua Browning sons Beedy and Joshua; daughter Elizabeth's
   children; daughter Mary Culberson; sons Robert and Nimrod;
   daughter Racheal Browning; granddaughter Nancy Bowren;
   Exec: son Robert and Alex Murphey. Wit: J Zachary, Thomas
   Browning.

348 Inv estate of Edmund Browning on 23 May 1807.

350 WILLIAM BROWN - Will - w. 10 June 1807. Niece Martha Brown;
   sister Sally B. Brown; brother John H. Brown; store shall be
   carried on by brothers Jethro and John Brown. Exec: Jethro and
   John Brown. Wit: Ransom Boswell, Elizabeth Moore.

350 Allotment to Mary Melton widow of James Melton decd. 13 May 1807.
351 Sales estate of James Melton on 22 May 1807. Sales to Polly
   Melton, Thomas Turner, Barnett Kemp, Wallis Ashford, Lewis Corbit,
   William S. Webb.
352 Inv estate of Mordecai Burgess on 24 June 1807
353 Inv property of Griffin Tuggle by William Berry exec.
354 Acct. sales of Robert Lyon.

Book E cont. 1807
Page
354 Additional inv. of Samuel Grier. Judgment received from Samuel
    Kelly in South Carolina.
354 Inv property of James Melton decd. by William S. Webb and Mary
    Melton adm.
355 Div of negroes of Charles Boulton to legatees: William Boulton,
    Thomas Boulton, Lent Boulton, Chas.Boulton, John Boulton, Obad
    Wynne. 7 May 1807. Commrs: Tho. Bouldin, James Rainey, James
    Dix, Asa Thomas, Rich Saunders.
356 Power of attorney: Drury Rhodes to Messrs Durrett Richards and
    John Stanfield to sell negroes now in possession of Michael
    Montgomery to satisfy debt due to Montgomery. 12 Nov 1806.
    Wit: Tho Bouldin, Jas Dix, John C. Collier.
357 Acct estate of Robert Lyon by James Burton and Henry Howard.
    Special legacy to Temperance McClain, to William Lyon guardian
    to Edwd Lyon, Betsy Lyon; to Robert Lyon as per will, to John
    Pyron and Rebeccah Lyon. Bond on John Southerlin.
358 Inv and sales estate of Elender Grier by Samuel Grier adm.
    Sales to Samuel Greer, Nancy Greer, Peggy Grier, Beauford Plea-
    sant, Charity Crosset.
359 Estate of James Poteat in acct with John Poteat.

October Court 1807

360 MARY BOYD - Will - w. 11 July 1807. Two brothers;
    some relations Elizabeth Harrison and three sisters Mary, Martha,
    and Nancy,Stephen Moore, Edwd Moore, Alfred Moore, Seanea Moore;
    Elizabeth, Martilla and Samuel Moore Jun.; Mary Brown, Thomas
    Harrelson Jun., Eliza Harrelson; Mother to have servant Hart-
    well and after mother's death he should be sold to his Father in
    Halifax Co. Va. Dispute over land with Armistead and William
    Boyd. 2 sisters Martha Harrelson and Elizabeth Moore.
    Exec: Thomas Harrelson and Benjamin Williamson. Wit: Francis
    Harrelson, Elizabeth Harrelson.

361 Sales estate of Spillsby Coleman to Noell Coleman, Mrs. Elizabeth
    Coleman, John Baxter, Benj.C.West, Obediah Holloway, John Ingram,
    Joseph Farguson, Thomas Winston, Robert West, Stephen Ingram,
    Molly Alverson, Starling Ruffin, William Lynn, David Womack,et al.
364 Inv property of Spillsby Coleman on 30 Mar 1807.
365 Inv estate of Philip Cox decd. Bond on Lewis Cox. Debts due from
    William Anderson, Thomas Brown, Reason Benton, Thomas Barnett,
    Randolph Buckley, Reuben Cox, George Crittendon, William Dix,
    Samuel French, Armstead Shackleford, Noel Waddill, Thomas Ward,
    William Towns Sen., et al. By Lewis Cox adm.
369 Towns Elam orphan of 11 yrs. the 10 Oct bound to John Tennison.
370 Power of attorney: Lucy Moore of Person Co. to trusty friend John
    Yancey of Caswell Co. to demand and recover negro man names Jess
    now in possession of Thomas Jeffreys, negro woman Jude and her
    child Mary now in possession of Alexander Cunningham which
    her deceased father John Moore lent to her mother. Other negroes
    in possession of John Campbell of Abeville Dist. S.C. 5 Aug 1807.
    Wit: Ad Murphey and Hugh Shaw.
371 Power of attorney: Thomas Spencer of Williamson Co. Tenn. to John
    Spencer of same place and John Pennix of Caswell Co. NC to recover
    money due as a legatee of William Mitchell decd. of Caswell Co.
    (given in right of his wife Mary). 30 Sept 1806.
372 Receipt: Received of John Henslee exec of Wm. Mitchell decd. 112
    lbs. in full of Thomas Spencer's wife's part of her Father's
    estate. /s/ John Pennix as lawful attorney. 1 Sept 1807.

Book E cont. 1807 - 1808
Page
372 Among insolvents for 1806:

Alex Allen	Frances Powell	Jacob Gryder	Wm. Gomer
John Coleman	Lewis Strader	James St.John	Wm. Harvell
Jesse Conway	John Duncan	Geo Kelly	Theo Johnston
Wm. Clark	Benj. Kidd	Elij.Kimbrough	Tho Johnston
John Ferrell	Leger Merchant	John Martin	Oba Phelps
Tho Greer	Daniel Spencer	Moses Brooks	Wm. Pinchback
Isaac Hobs	Jos Shaddock	Alex Ford	Wm. Pryor
Walter Ingram	Geo Ward	Charnel Hightower	Saml.Stephens
Joshua Jefferson	Tho Dollarhide	Josiah Earp	David Thomas
Wm. Kingston	Tho Colier	Ro Elam	Drury Rhodes
Geo Lay	James Corder	Jas S. Farley	Thomas Rainey

373 Estate of Henry Dixon Jun. in acct with Charles Dixon. Accts. paid
to Dr. Johnston, Absalom Tatom, Benj. Hubbard, Sophia Runnals,
Wm. Blount, Mr. Hill for funeral sermon 2 lbs., Shadrak Jackson.
374 Charles Dixon decd. exec. of Henry Dixon Jun. decd. in acct. with
legatees of Henry: included 75,000 in certificates issued for
soldiers bounty at 8800 for one.
Div among 8 legatees: Martha Dixon widow, Wynn Dixon, Roger Dixon's
heirs, Robert Dixon, Nathaniel Williams in right of his wife
Frances, John Williams in right of his wife Susannah, Henry Dixon.
Paid John Bysor for heirs of Roger Dixon.
376 Settlement estate of Henry Dixon Jun. Bond on Malachi Dickerson
(1792). 28 Oct 1807. Commrs: Alex Murphey, Thos. Donoho,
So Graves.

January Court 1808

379 ANN BROOKS - Will - w. 4 Mar 1806. Son William B. Brooks;
9 grandchildren: Wm.B Brooks sons John, Robert, & William and
daughters Betsy, Ann, & Joanna; Frances A. Sheppard's daughters
Ann, Betsy, and Polley. Exec: son Wm. B. Brooks. Wit: Sol
Graves, S. Graves, John L. Graves.

379 JAMES KITCHEN - Will - w. 30 Oct 1807. Wife: 9 children: Joseph,
Esther, Moses, James, Sally, Stephen, Elizabeth, Daniel, and John.
Exec: wife. Wit: Thomas Roberts, Judith Richmond, Mich.Montgomery.
Elizabeth Kitchen qualified exec.

380 ELIZABETH SMYTHE - Will - w. 8 Jan 1808. Son Samuel;
Nancy Dickie, Elizabeth Aldress, John Smythe, William Smythe.
Land bought of James Turner to be divided between 2 youngest
children Ann Smythe and Reuben Smythe. Exec: friends Samuel
Smythe and Richd. Henslee. Test: William Pleasant, Martha Plea-
sant, Margret Grier, Samuel Grier.

381 CHRISTOPHER DAMERON - Will - w. 10 Nov 1807. Wife Sarah;
daughters Polly and Caty Dameron; sons Christopher (unmarried)
and Bartholomew; daughter Nancy Matthews; grandchildren: Eliza
Ingram Dameron and Patsy Depee Dameron; daughter Sally Matthews;
daughter Patsey Anderson; children of Sally Matthews.
Exec: uncle Joseph Dameron and cousin Joseph Dameron with
son Bartholomew Dameron. Wit: John T. Curl, Robert H. Jackson,
Bart. Dameron Sen.

382 Inv estate of William Boulton decd. 15 Dec 1807 by Mary Boulton.
383 Inv estate of Elizabeth Smythe by Saml. Smythe exec.
383 Sales balance estate of James Melton to Mary Melton and Wm. S.Webb.

Book E cont. 1808
Page
384 Sale property of Mordecai Burgess to Thomas Burton, Mary Burgess,
    Larkin Wisdom, John Price, John Langley, David Brandon, David
    Haddock. By John Langley and Mary Burgess exec.
384 Inv property of Ann Brooks by William B. Brooks.
385 Welldon Hardy orphan 2 yrs old last Nov bound to William Orr.
385 Harrell Hardy orphan 7 yrs. old last June bound to William Orr.
386 Power of attorney: Robert Cochran to Richard Haddock to receive
    from exec. of John Cochran decd. all money due as legatee of
    John Cochran. 16 Jan. 1808. Wit: Robt. Browning, Elisha In-
    gram.
387 Allotment to Elizabeth Cox widow of Philip Cox decd. for herself
    and her family. 25 Jan 1808.
389 Bond: Ephraim Nowel to build bridge across Country Line Cr. on
    road from Jesse Carter's store to Leasburg and Nowel to keep
    bridge in good repair for 7 years passable for carriages and
    horses.
390 Lewis Watkins orphan of colour 7 yrs. old bound to Gregory
    Hightower. Betsy Watkins orphan of colour 3 yrs. old bound to
    Gregory Hightower.
391 Edmund McCubbins orphan of colour 14 yrs. next July bound to
    Benjamin C. West.

March Court 1808

392 ROSANNAH McCLARNEY - Will - w. 23 Oct 1807. Desired clothes di-
    vided between Caty Ferrell, Elizabeth Holloway, and Caty
    Ferrell's four children; grandson James McClarney son to Caty
    Ferrell; son Henry McClarney. Exec: Capt. Meredy Price. Test:
    Robert West, Polly Price. Meredith Price qualified.

392 Inv estate of Christopher Dameron decd.by Joseph Dameron Jun.exec.
393 Sales estate of Christopher Dameron on 19 Feb 1808. Sales to
    Thomas Jackson, Bart Dameron Jun., Samuel Hodge, William Gould,
    George B. Dameron, Bartholomew Jackson, Ann Matthis, John Lea,
    John T. Curles, Benj. Stephens, Charles Matthis, Isaac Jackson,
    Sally Dameron, Susannah McDaniel, John Richmond, Brittain Moore.
395 Inv estate of Mary Boyd by Thomas Haralson. Sales estate of Mary
    Boyd.
396 Inv property of Mason Leath by Joel Leath.
397 Div land of Philip Cox to legatees:
    Philip Cox (land adj. Thomas Gatewood); Amy Cox (land on State
    line); John Cox; Lucy Cox; Susannah Cox intermarried with
    Nathaniel Shaw (land adj. State line and Crittendon's corner);
    Rachel Cox; Elizabeth Cox intermarried with Ludwell Worsham;
    Lewis Cox; Mary Cox intermarried with John Burgess; Reuben Cox;
    Gabriel Cox. Commrs: Danl. S. Farley, Richard Sanders, Holloway
    Pass, Andrew Harrison, Wm. K. Harrison.
399 Inv property of Mrs. Rose McClarney on 22 Jan 1808 by Meredith
    Price exec.
400 Sales estate of Jas. Aldridge held 16 and 17 Feb 1808. Sales to:

John Aldridge	Nicholas Vaughan	John Graves Jun.
Alsey Aldridge	Joseph Tait Jun.	Robert Murray
Zephaniah Tait	Joseph Tait Sen.	John Murray
John Kerr	Elijah Kimbrough	Wilie Yancey
James Wilder	Richard Jones	Drury Dunn
Sarah Aldridge	Thomas Shanks	John Fitch
Elizabeth Aldridge	Caswell Tait	William Faucett
Hosea McNeill	John McHorney	John Wilder
Thomas Belsire	James Hughs	Richard Bird
James Tait		

Book E cont. 1808
Page
403 Inv personal property of James Aldridge.
405 Sale personal property of Ann Brooks in Feb 1808. Sales to:

William B. Brooks	Park Swift	Caswell Tait
Thomas Shanks	Archibald Rice	Dennard Brinsfield
John Pinnix	Equiller Barton	Jonathan Brooks
Wilie Yancey	Thomas Belsiah	Elizabeth Gardner
Lewis Barton	Anderson Birk	William Chandler
William Clifton	John &Burnly Barker	Frederic Stovall

408 Inv estate of Elizabeth Smythe and sales to:

John Smythe	Nathaniel Malone	Thomas Morris	Abram St.John
Anne Smythe	John Murphey	Thomas Miles	James Eubanks
John Dickie	Willis Ashford	William Warren	John Terrell
John Johnston	John Sanders	Reuben Smythe	
Samuel Smythe	Stephen Malone	William Pleasant	

409 Sales estate of John Gomer by Jeremiah Beaver adm. Sales to:

Nicholas Willis	Andrew Haddock	John Gomer
Nancy Gomer	John Foster	Philip Cook
William Henderson	Daniel Gwyn	Starling Carrol
Solomon Beaver	Robert Foster	Sucky Gomer
Jesse Beaver	Nathaniel Wilmouth	William Gomer
Benjamin Hooper	Polly Gomer	Jeremiah Beaver
Jacob Henderson	Jacob Quine	
Azariah Graves Jun.	Thomas Graves	

411 Sales estate of Edmund Browning on 3 Sept 1807. Sales to:

Richard Erwin	Abraham St.John	Hiram Culberson	Nathl.Jones
Wm.S.Webb	David Barnwell	Richard Arnold	Lot Egmon
Mumford Ford	William Jopling	Wm. Muzzall	Wm.Compton
David Haddock	Thomas Vaughan Jun.	Thomas Morris	Barnet Kemp
Robert Browning	Richard Hightower	Hasten Bartlett	Bailer Byrd
Philip Walton	William Culberson	Rachel Browning	Wm.Price
Thomas Turner	Maryann Browning	John Zachary	Jos.Colier
John Barnwell	John Browning	Thomas Villines	Wm. Rudd
John Wells	John Ward	Nimrod Browning	et al

417 Estate of Chs Dixon in acct. with Henry Dixon exec.

June Court 1808

418 LAWRENCE LEA of town of Leasburg - Will - w. 15 Apr 1808.
Wife Phebe; son Washington under 17 yrs. (lots where store house
and lumber house stand); son William H. Lea; daughters Artimeria
and Pheby Ann; son Madison; Mother; Exec: wife Phebe, friend
William Donoho, and Loyd Vanhook. Test: A. Vanhook, N.Thompson,
Loyd Vanhook. Proved on oath of Alfred Vanhook.

420 ISAAC JACKSON - Will - w. 21 Apr 1808. Wife Patsey Jackson;
all my children. Exec: Joseph Dameron Jun., Robert H. Jackson,
Daniel Jackson. Wit: James C. Smith, James Lea, George B.Dameron.

421 ISAKIAH FARLEY - Will - w. 29 Apr 1808. Youngest son William S.
Farley and youngest daughter Martha under 21 yrs.; wife Martha;
children: Catherine Durham, Joseph Farley, John B. Farley, Rachel
Farley, Martha Farley, Wm.S.Farley; son in law Newman Durham.
Exec: James Lea, James Rainey. Test: Tho Jeffreys, John Burton.

422 JOHN TENNISON - Will - w. 18 Dec 1807. Wife Elizabeth; her five
children Asariah, Reubin Polly Harriott Gregory Nancy; 5 last
children are my five last children; my 3 sons Levi, John, and
James; daughter Coos?; 4 daughters: Elizabeth wife of Henry Cobb,
Anna wife of William Cobb, Catherine wife of Asa Cox, and Ceacy.
Exec: son Levi; Wit: David Powell, Turner Patterson, Wm.Tapscott.

111

Book E cont. 1808
Page
424 Sale estate of Rosetta McClarney by Meredith Price exec. on 27
May 1808. Sales to William Richardson, Obediah Holloway, Wm.
Ware, Findal Rowland, Major Price, Mrs. Catherine Ferrell.
424 Appraisal and div estate of Edmund Browning to William Culberson
and Rachel Browning.
425 Bond: William Rainey to keep in order bridge over Kersey's ford
on Country Line Creek.
426 Taxable property for 1807

Gloucester Dist.	250	white polls	392	black polls
Caswell Dist.	198	"	250	"
Richmond Dist.	260	"	636	"
St.David's Dist.	223	"	413	"
total	919?		1691	

426 Allotment to widow of James Aldridge decd.

September Court 1808

427 Power of attorney: David Jones to Azariah Graves Jun. to commence
suits. 27 Sept 1808. Wit: B. Yancey.

427 ANN GRANT widow and relict of James Grant decd. - Will - w. 16
Aug. 1807. Sons Joshua, James; heirs of son John Grant decd.;
sons Dishan(or Dirhan), William; heirs of son Neeley Grant; son
Reuben; daughters Elizabeth Fitzgerald, Marget Lemon, and heirs
of daughter Rachel Tennison. Exec: son James; Wit: David Lawson,
John Durham, Ann Durham.
428 Will of Isakiah Farley repeated.

429 WILLIAM SWIFT - Will - w. 5 May 1804. Wife Frances; sons John,
Thomas, Anthony, Richard, William Park, and George Alexander
Swift; daughters: Sarah Williamson, Frances Swift, Susanna
Harris, Margret Williamson decd.(to be divided among her child-
ren Nancy Caleb and Archibald Cotnam, William Williamson, Peggy
Russell, Park Williamson). Exec: wife, sons Thomas & George
Alexander Swift. Wit: John Pinnix, George Barker.

431 Sales estate of John Gomer on 9 Feb 1808. (Repeat of page 409)
433 William H. Rice and John Windsor Sen. exec. of Thomas Rice decd.
Legacies paid to Hugh Gwyn, Sarah Rice, Lucy Scoby.
433 Inv estate of Isaac Jackson by Joseph Dameron adm.
434 Inv estate of Benjamin Quine on 19 Aug 1808 by Henry Quine adm.
435 Allotment to Hester Quine widow of Benjamin Quine decd. Commrs:
Henry Howard, Starling Gunn, David Womack, William Knight.
436 Accts. due estate of Vines Mathews decd. from Richard Burch,
Absolom Johnston, James Bayley, William McKissack, William
Whitfield, John Waterfield, Simeon Cochran, William Stephens;
by William Lea exec.
436 Inv estate of Lawrence Lea merchant late of Leasburg.
By Phebe Lea & Loyd Vanhook exec.
437 Inv goods and chattels of John Tennison decd. Bonds on William
Walker, John Allen, Daniel Allen, William Hatcher, James Pucket,
Joseph Montgomery, Alexander Ferguson, Elijah Sims, et al.
439 Moses Surratt orphan of 10 yrs last Aug bound to William Eddings
to learn art of a Taylor.
440 Edmund Butler Rice, 15 yrs old the 21 of July last, bound to
William Bird.
441 Pleasant Robinson age 10 yrs the 6 of Aug next bound to Jeremiah
Beaver.
442 Townsey Elam orphan 14 yrs old bound to James Holder.

End of Book E

Book F - December 1808-April 1814.

December Court 1808

113

Book F cont. 1809

March Court 1809
Page
19 CONRAD STRADER - Will - w.7 Oct 1808. Marget Daywatt, Mary
Shelly, Katy Lewis, Ester Elmore; 3 grandchildren Marget Nichols,
John and Frances Nichols (money to be collected of Elijah Withers);
my 6 children: Barbery Shelly, Henry Strader, Peter Strader,
Lewis, Christian, and David Strader; wife. Exec: Peter Strader,
Christian and David Strader. Wit: Elijah Withers.

20 BARTHOLOMEW DAMERON - Will - w. 3 May 1804. sons Christopher and
Alexander; daughter Patsey Jackson; granddaughter Polley;
daughters Sally Dameron, Hanny Morton. Exec: brother Joseph
Dameron, son Christopher and son-in-law Isaac Jackson.
Wit: Francis Hightower, Fanney Johnston.

21 ELIZABETH WILLIAMSON - Will - w. 2 Sept 1804. Daughter Martha
Harrill; sons Benjamin and Henry E. Williamson if they live till
death of Mrs. Elizabeth Daughtry wife of Jeremiah Daughtry part
dowry in land of estate of brother John Edmons decd.;
living sons and daughters. Wit: John Swann, Simon Adams, Whita-
ker Cox.

22 GEORGE SIMS - Will - w. 18 Jan 1806. Daughter Jane Hendly Sims;
daughter Henrietta Brown three children Allotha, Jane Hendly and
Lucinda Brown; daughter Allotha Sawyers three children John,
Henrietta, and Nathan Sawyers; son George Sims Jun. lawful heirs;
sons and daughters: Zilpah, Jacky, Frankey, Lorainah, Nathan,
Zeruiah, Edward, and Mary. Exec: Nathan Sims and Thomas Malory
Sen. Wit: James Williamson, Anthony Swift, Hezekiah Boswell.

23 Inv estate of William Donoho decd. and sales of estate.
24 Inv estate of William Donoho surviving partner of Lea and Donoho,
Merchants.
27 Balance due firm of Lea and Donoho. By Duncan Rose adm.
34 Report of Robert Parks county trustee.
35 Inv estate of James Hughs decd. taken 2 Feb 1809.
37 Inv personal estate of William Nash decd. Bond on Robert, Marmaduke, and Duke Williams; one on Benjamin Burnsides. Books included law dictionaries, public statutes, Blackstone commentaries.
38 Inv estate of Noel Coleman on 28 Nov 1808 by Jos Burton exec.
39 Inv of Joel McDaniel decd. by Maredy Price exec.
39 Sales of Noel Coleman decd. on 1 Feb 1809 to: Capt. John Graves,
John Harrison, James Burton, Elisha Alverson, Thomas Winston,
James Richardson, Thomas Baxter, et al.
41 Sales estate of John Tennison decd. by Levi Dennis exec.
42 Sales estate of Joshua Richmond on 26 Jan 1809. Sales to:
Daniel Darby, Joseph Langley (lot of books), John Lipscomb,
Moses Langley, Jno Richmond Jun., Robert Jackson, John Bateman,
Rhobartis Carney, Charles Mathis, Joseph Richmond, Daniel Rich-
mond, Alex Wiley, John Langley, Thomas Wiley, et al. By William
Richmond exec.
44 Sales estate of Alexander McNeill to Mary McNeill, Wm.S.Webb,
Thomas Bell, William Walker(farmer), et al. Notes due on Joshua
Grant, Henry McNeill, Abraham St.John, William O'Neal, Hillard
Hall.
46 Sales estate of James Hughs to Sarah Hughs, Andrew Hughs, etal.
48 William S. Webb and Mary Melton adm. of James Melton decd. acct.
filed with estate.

Book F cont. 1809
Page
49 Allotment to Enice Donoho widow of William Donoho decd.
49 Allotment fo Sary Hughes wife of James Hughs decd.
50 Power of attorney: James Gooch of Warren County, Kentucky to
friend Drury Gooch of same county to recover money due him as
heir or legatee of William Gooch decd formerly resident of Caswell County and from estate of his brother John C. Gooch of Caswell Co. 27 Jan 1809.
Barren County, Kentucky -approved by Henry Miller and Tho
Dickerson.
51 William Rhodes orphan of 12 yrs the 3 of Oct next bound to
William Swann. /s/ William Webb, Chairman County Court.
51 John Sammons orphan 15 yrs the 31 Dec next bound to William
Patterson. /s/ James Yancey,Chairman County Court.
52 Received 17 July 1805 89 lbs in full my proportionable part in
right of my wife of the estate of James Smith decd. (Rec. of
Sarah Smith adm.) /s/ Thomas Jackson.
52 Power of attorney: Robert Bruice of Sumner County, Tenn. to William
S. Webb of Caswell Co. to receive legacy left by father in law
John Cochran Sen. decd. 5 Feb 1808. Wit: Sol Debow, H.Haralson.

June Court 1809

53 Inv estate of George Sims decd. Bonds on Williamson Rice, Robert
Sawyers; notes on Nathan Sims, Edward Sims, Lewis Barton, Thomas
Foster, Lewis Foster. By Thomas Mallory, exec.
54 Inv estate of Bartholomew Dameron Sen. by Joseph Dameron exec.
55 A catalogue of debts due estate of William Lea, merchant.
58 Amt. sales of land of Israel Barker sold to Burley Barker.
58 Sale of horse property of Hudson Brown by William Brown adm. 26
July 1809.
58 Election commissioners met at the house of Daniel Hightower in
Gloucester District to receive tickets given to elect members of
Congress and electors for President. 20 May 1809.
59 Sales estate of Bartholomew Dameron on 18 Apr 1809. Among buyers:
William Anderson, Robert Jackson, Bart Jackson, Joseph Dameron Jun.
& Sen., Patsey Jackson, Bart Dameron Jun., Salley Dameron, George
B. Dameron, Drury Mathis, John Bateman, Robert Long, Thomas Jackson,
Thomas Mathis, William & Susannah McDaniel, Thomas Riggs, Drury
Burton.
60 Settlement estate of Phillip Cox by Lewis Cox adm.
61 George and James Barker in acct. with legatees of Israel Barker.
62 List of hire of negroes of the estate of Vines Mathis by Wm.Lea exec.
62 Place of election in Richmond District to be at house of Mr. Thomas
Connally in town of Milton; at the house of Mr. Gregory Durham's
in Caswell District.
63 Plat of land of James W. Smith on N. Hico adj Mrs. Willson's land
and Major Farley's late entry. John Dobbin forbid the placing of
markers for plat. By John Burton processioner.
64 Power of attorney: Elisha Loony of Bedford Co. Tenn. to friend
Samuel Coplinger of Willson Co. Tenn. to recover sums of money
from estate of Andrew Enochs in Caswell Co. 26 Sept 1805.
/s/ Elisha Luna. Approved by William Babb and Jeremiah Brown JP.
and by John Allcorn CWC.
65 Taxable property for 1808.

September Court 1809

65 William Robinson orphan 16 yrs old the 12 of June last bound to
Nicholas Willis.

Book P cont.1809
Page
66 Harvey Turner child of color 4 yrs old the 25 of Feb last bound
   to William V. Brown.
67 Joseph Payne Hall orphan 14 yrs the 15 of July last bound to
   John Scott.
67 Wylie Robertson orphan of 12 yrs on 22 Apr last bound to Humphrey
   Roberts.
68 William Morrow of Orange Co. N.C. puts out and binds his sons
   Alfred age 5 yrs 26 of last Aug and John age 3 yrs the 27 of ?
   to George Prendergast.
69 WILLIAM P. SWIFT - Will - w. 27 Feb 1809. Wife Salley; children:
   Susannah, Mary, John, Fanney, George, Salley, Anthony;
   Exec: wife and brother Thomas Swift, Anthony Swift, Anthony Tate.
   Wit: Thomas Windsor, Samuel Fielder.
70 WILLIAM GRAYHAM SEN.. - Will - w. 20 June 1807. Daughter Charity
   Allen Davis, Lidda Elmore; daughter Polly Elmore's heirs;
   sons Edward, William, George, John, Peter; grandson Herrington.
   Grayham; negroe woman Venus to be freed from service and to have
   15 acres land. Exec: son John, William Weatherford, Thomas
   Weatherford. Wit: W. Morgan, James Murphey. Proved on oath of
   William Morgan.
71 Sales estate of Noel Coleman by Jas Burton exec.
73 Inv estate of Noel Coleman on 28 Nov 1808. Bonds on William Rich-
   ardson, Leonard Henderson, Thomas Mitchell, John Harrison, Edward
   Swann.
73 Settlement estate of Abraham Womack decd. and of receipts of Josiah
   Womack exec. - every legatee has received legacy and is satisfied
   except David Benton who refused to accept his.
74 Sales of estate of George Sims. Among buyers: Benjamin Lane, Cobby
   Foster, Jane Sims, Thomas Garrott, Samuel Cobb, William Clifton,
   Nathan Sims, Pleasant Childress, Wyatt Ballard, Jesse Payne, Aaron
   Simpson, Buckner Duke, John & George Simmons, Wylie Yancey.
79 Sales estate of Joel McDaniel in Jan & Feb 1809. Among buyers:
   Meredith Price, Lock Atwell, John Norman, Martin Clack, William
   Penix, Jacob Quine, James Martin, Sarah Thompson, Clorey Coleman,
   William Coleman, Samuel Pullen, William Lynn, Richard Atwell,
   John Atwell, Leger Merchant, Edmund Sparks, William Beaver, Levim
   Downs, David Lay, William Astin, Joseph Mason, Joseph Arnett,
   Caleb Anglin, Smith Coleman, Samuel Ford.

December Court 1809

81 Allotment of negroes of estate of James Hughs to heirs as follows:
   Elizabeth, Andrew, Samuel, Martha, William, and Sarah. 23 Nov 1809.
   Commrs: Zephaniah Tait, Obed Florance, Thomas Loyd, Quinten Anderson.

82 HENRY TURNER - Will - w. 9 May 1807. Wife Anne; sons John and Henry;
   sons Billey, Thomas, James; daughters Elizabeth Lipscomb, Frankey
   Martin, Milley Jones, Nancy Kimbrough, Sally French, Mary Cochran;
   grandson Yancey Turner; granddaughters Mary French, Fanny Turner,
   Delila Turner and Nancy Turner daughters of John Turner; daughter
   Susannah Donoho. Exec: sons James and Thomas. Wit: W. S. Webb,
   William Kimbrough.

83 THOMAS JACKSON - Will - w. 13 Sept 1809. Wife Mary; children Joshua,
   Robert H., Daniel, John, Agness; widow & children of Thomas Jackson'
   (land which Joshua sold to his brother Thomas); daughter Sally
   Smith. Exec: sons Robert H. and Daniel. Wit: Joseph Dameron,
   Gregory Hightower, William P. Jackson.

116

Book F cont. 1809 - 1810
Page
85 JOSEPH BUSH - Will - w. 27 Apr 1804. Wife Maryann; son Zenas (land
    adj Robert Martin and James Carroll); 6 children of deceased daugh-
    ter Nancey Haralson, Fanny, Betsy, Nathaniel, Sally, Dorchas, and
    Nancy; grandson Bennett Haralson; daughters Betsy Flemming, Rhoda,
    Zebba, Merah, Lowas, and Mary Bush; daughters Nancy Haralson and
    Frankey Harrelson. Exec: son Zenas and friends Barzillai Graves
    Sen. and Solomon Graves Sen. Wit: B. Yancey, John Ogilley
86 Inv estate of William P. Swift.
86 Allotment to Phebe Lipscomb widow of John Lipscomb decd.
87 Inv estate of Thomas Jackson Jun. decd. by Jane Jackson adm.
87 Inv estate of Jane Harrison by Andrew Harrison Jun. adm.
88 Inv estate of William Terry decd taken 23 Sept 1809 by J. McMullin,
    adm.
88 Inv balance estate of James Hughes.
89 Allotment to Nancey Terry widow of William Terry.
89 Allotment to Jane Jackson widow of Thomas Jackson Jun. 13 Oct 1809.
89 Inv estate of Catherine McAden decd by John McAden adm. 25 Dec 1809.
91 Sales estate of John Lipscomb on 23 & 23 Nov 1809. Among buyers:
    Phebe Lipscomb, James Vaughan, Zadock Rice, William Russell, Isaac
    Johnston, Lot Egmond, Joseph Richmond, John Richmond, William
    Herritage, James & Daniel Richmond, Allen Hightower.
93 Report of Robert Parks county trustee.
93 Inv estate of Thos. Vanhook decd. Judgment on Philip Walton;
    note on George Darby. Sale of cows to Thomas Villines, Thompson
    McKissock. By Daniel Darby adm.
94 Div of negroes belonging to estate of Noel Coleman to: Elizabeth
    Graves, Spillsby Coleman Winston, Elizabeth Burton Winston, Noel
    Coleman Winston, Joseph Barrett Winston. (Capt. John Graves
    received for Elizabeth Graves.)
95 Crafton Williams complains that William Rainey in 1805 raised his
    mill 4 inches higher than the dam and Rainey failed to pay
    damages as directed. 9 Jan 1808.
96 Sales estate of John Gray decd. on 2 Nov 1809. Among buyers:
    Susannah Gray, William McMinemy, Thomas Compton, John Mitchell,
    Nathaniel Norfleet, Thomas Wiley, Miles Wells Sen., Norris Compton,
    Thomas Wilkerson, John Mansfield, Abraham Villines, William Cros-
    sett, Thomas Coleman, Hazelwood Wilkerson, Robert McKee, Joseph
    Taylor, Absolem Johnston, James Milliner, Jonathan Terrell. By
    David Mitchell adm.
99 Sales estate of James Hughes to Sarah Hughes, Robert Faucett, et al.
99 Sales property of William Terry to Nancy Terry, Reuben Jones, Wil-
    liam Brumit, William Hughes, Samuel Evans, John Buttery, Abner
    Wisdom, George Houston, Thomas Matthews, Jeremiah Broughton,
    Rollin Terry, et al.
101 Nancy Owens female infant of color 15 yrs. old last Sept bound to
    Daniel Hightower.

April Court 1810

101 Allotment to Nancy Bird widow of Temple Byrd. 18 Jan 1810.
102 Balance sales of estate of John Lipscomb to Thomas Peterson, John
    Peterson, Phebe Lipscomb, John Lea (CB), Elisha Evans.
102 Settlement estate of Vines Mathews for hire of negroes; legacy
    received from sale of land in Brunswick Co. Va. to Creed Huskins.
    Aug 1809. By William Lea exec.
103 Inv property of David Ford decd. by Rebecca Ford adm.
103 Sales estate of David Ford to Mrs. Ford, Robert Martin, James Page,
    John Gooch, Mumford Ford, Elizabeth Ford, Pleasant Rudd.
104 James Dickie age 12 yrs. the 13 of Aug next bound to James Crosset.

Book F cont. 1810
Page
105 John Dickie age 9 yrs the last day of Nov bound to James Crosset.
    /s/ Solomon Graves, Chairman County Court.
106 Inv estate of Henry Turner.
107 Sales estate of Henry Turner on 15 Feb 1810. Sales to: Wm. S.
    Webb, Jacob Vanhook, Martha Atkinson, George Martin, Richard
    Martin, Ann Turner, Mary Stadler, George Horton, Azariah Graves
    Jun., Benjamin Sewel, et al.
109 Sales estate of Joseph Bush to Maryann Bush, Zenas Bush, Thomas
    Harrelson, Betsy Flemming, John Simmons, Archibald Rice, Stephen
    Ingram, Bartlett Yancey, Jacob Ahart, Jordan Whitlow, John
    Payne (Taylor), Thomas Holderness, Edmond Herndon, Henry Willis,
    Zachariah Groom, Daniel Chandler, Hosea McNeill, Charles Brooks,
    et al.
115 Inv property of Temple Byrd by Nancy Byrd on 10 Jan 1810. Sales
    estate of Templain Bird to George Smith, William Golliher, Abram
    Holsenback, Vincent Lea, Baylor Byrd et al.
116 ALSTON (AUSTIN) STALCUP - Will - w. 27 Nov 1809. Wife;
    daughter Sylvira (under age); sons William and Levi. Exec: wife.
    Test: William Bird, James Johnston. /s/ Austin Stalcup.
    Patsey Stalcup widow and relict qualified.
117 Hack Brown boy of colour age 9 yrs the 6 of Feb last bound to
    James Warren.
118 Inv property of Joseph Bush decd. by Zenus Bush.
119 Appraisal of property due Maryann Bush widow of Joseph Bush.
120 Sales estate of Thomas Jackson Sen. Buyers: Mary Jackson, Robert
    H. Jackson, Agness and Daniel Jackson, Patsy and Josiah Jackson,
    John T. Curl, Joseph Langley, Ransom Dollarhide, et al.
124 Inv property of Thomas Jackson Sen. on 10 Jan 1810.
126 Sales estate of Thos Jackson on 3 Oct 1809.
129 Balance inv of Catharine McAden.
130 Jennet McCaden adm. of estate of William McCaden, accts. filed for
    1801-3.
130 Sales balance estate of John Gray to Absolem Johnston, William
    Mansfield. Acct. on Alexander Gray.
131 Inv property of John Foster decd. by Robert Foster.
132 Allotment to Ann Turner wife of Henry Turner decd. 29 Dec 1809.
133 Power of attorney: Dennard Brinsfield to loving friend Thomas
    Brinsfield of Caswell Co. to receive and recover money and attend
    to all business. 8 Feb 1809. Test: Thomas Slade Jun., Anthony
    Swift.
134 Inv estate of Austin Stalcup by Elizabeth Stalcup exec. Notes on
    Richard Whitmore, John Stalcup; cash due by Lucy Ashford and
    John Pleasant.

July Court 1810

134 Settlement estate of Thomas Vanhook by Daniel Darby adm.
135 Sales estate of John Foster decd. taken 25 May 1810. Sales to
    John Horton, Simon Adams, Commal Ward, Tilman Stone, John Pucket,
    Ira and John Somers, John Standley, William Haley, James Winn,
    Berry Worsham, Ibzan Rice, Bartlett Yancey, John Ferry, Jeremiah
    Fletcher et al. By Robert Foster adm.
137 Sales estate of Catherine McAden to John and James McAden, Adam
    and Henry Stafford, George M. Willson, Jane McAden, William Jones,
    Daniel S. Farley, John Hall, William Climpson, Newman Durham etal.
140 Taxable property for 1809.
       980 white polls   1760 black polls
       10 stores   14 retailers spirits

Book F cont. 1810 - 1811
Page
140 Sales and inv estate of Peter McKinney decd. by Thomas Payne adm.
141 Jefferson Artis free boy of colour of age of 3 yrs. bound to
    Peggy L. Nash.
141 List of strays returned on Ranger's book taken up by:
    Andrew Harrison - 1 sheep   Aaron Simpson - sow & 9 pigs
    Wm. P. Swift - 1 steer   Nicholas Vaughan - sorrel mare
    John Roper - 1 bay mare   Jesse Womack - gray mare
    Robert Willson - 1 bull   James Yancey - 1 cow & calf
    James Shelton - 1 cow   James Simpson - yellow bay mare
        By William Lea, Ranger
142 Settlement estate of Thomas Kimbrough by Thomas Graves and Groves
    Howard adm.
143 Insolvents for 1808 returned by John Stamps, high sheriff.

October Court 1810

145 Nathan Williams orphan of age of 15 yrs. bound to Howell Whitmore.
145 Ordered 2 shillings be laid on every poll and 8 pence on every
    100 acres land for support of poor for 1810.
146 Inv estate of George Eubank by Nathaniel Malone adm.
147 Inv property of Capt. John Moore. Bonds on Thomas Worsham,
    Spencer Lyon, Polley Olliver, William Ferrell, Robert Holloway,
    Richard Ogilby, John D. Moore, Nath. Comer. By Thomas Jeffrey,
    adm.
148 Estate of John Vaughan by Thomas Vaughan and James Yancey adm.
    acct. filed.
149 Estate of John Gomer - accts paid to Thomas Bouldin and John
    Graves & Son. By Jeremiah Beaver adm.

January Court 1811

150 Allotment to Lucretia Eubank, widow,for herself and her family.
    Commrs: Isaac Rainey, John Crisp, Miles Wells.
150 Allotment to Lucy Mansfield widow for herself and family.
151 Sales estate of Spillsby Coleman.
151 Inv balance of property of Noel Coleman by James Burton exec.
152 Sale estate of William Mansfield on 14 Nov 1810 by James Broach,
    adm. Sales to: Lucy Mansfield, John Mansfield, James Woods,
    Barnett Kemp, Mary Mansfield, Benjamin Bowdoin, Simion Cochran,
    Robert McKee, Thomas Burch, Isaac Rainey, James Broach.
153 Sale estate of George Eubank to: Staples Malone, Miles Wells Jun.,
    James Eubank, Lucretia Eubank, David Rainey, et al. By Nathaniel
    Malone adm.
154 Power of attorney: Robert L. Harrison late of Caswell Co. to
    Griffin Gunn to confirm lease of land with Daniel S. Farley and
    attend to all business. 14 Oct 1810. Wit: Goodwin Evans, Jurat.
154 Valuation of 240 acres land willed by Thomas Hornbuckle to Thomas
    Windsor at death to Nancy Hornbuckle to be $325.
155 Settlement estate of Lazarus Bouldin by John Bouldin adm. 28 Oct.
156 Obligation: Robt. Browning and Alex Murphey exec of Edmund Browning
    decd. paid over to bounden Nimrod Browning 189 lbs. in full legacy
    due him from his deceased Father Edmund Browning. Wit: Solomon
    Parks.
157 Bedy Browning heir and devisee of Joshua Browning decd. who was
    one of the children of Edmund Browning received his share of es-
    tate of Edmund Browning. Wit: John Thomas.

119

Book F cont. 1811
Page
158 JAMES SIMPSON - Will - w. 11 Nov 1810. Wife Salley Simpson (land on Stony Cr.); sons Levy, William, and James; daughters Nancy Brown, Susanna Simpson; daughters Delila, Elizabeth, Sally, Milley, Polly (land on Caswell Road adj Thomas Garrett and Griffin Gunn on Country Line Cr.). Exec: wife and Thomas Windsor. Wit: William Robertson, William Shelton, Richard Smith(Jurat).

April Court 1811

160 List of strays turned in by William Lea, Ranger:
Alfred Parks - 1 ewe
Nicholas Medlock - 4 hogs
Phebe Lipscomb - 3 barrows & 2 sows
Miles Wells Sen. - 1 calf
Jenney Jackson - 1 barrow

160 Joshua Browning heir and divisee of Joshua Browning decd. one of children of Edmund Browning received his share of estate paid into Edward King attorney.

161 Edmund Browning bequeathed to daughter Haney McReynolds wife of Joseph McReynolds a legacy; McReynolds appoints William Whitsett his attorney to collect $400 and exec. has paid same. Bonded by Mary McNeill, Solomon Parks.

162 Edmund Browning bequeathed to heirs of Calib Browning. Elijah Browning for himself and attorney for Tolliver, Henry Browning, John Flynn and his wife Lucy, Molley and Jenney Browning children and heirs of Calib Browning.

163 James Burton exec estate of Noel Coleman.

164 Allotment to Nancy Foster widow and relict of John Foster decd. 22 Apr 1810.

165 Allotment to Beddy Strader widow of Peter Strader decd. 4 Mar 1811.

166 Sarah Hughs and Wm. S. Webb adm of estate of James Hughes acct filed with legatees. Judgment on Robert Patton; bond on Benjamin Spencer for 4000 lbs tobacco and Spencer has gone from this country.

167 Additional inv estate of John Gray - 2 negroes born since death of John Gray.

168 Settlement estate of Christopher Dameron decd. by Joseph and Bart Dameron exec.

170 Sales estate of Alexander Walker decd. by Jethro Brown adm. to:

Charles Brooks	Garland Key	Zere Somers
Samuel Watt	Thomas Poyner	James Cobb
Mary Walker	Leonard Certain	James Orr
John Wall	William Kermichael	John Rice
Francis Smith	Williby Mustain	Lewis Certain
James Taylor	Jepthah Rice	Signor Ahorn
Rhodeham Loveless	John Walker	William Berry
James Knott	William Morgan	Wiley Sanders

172 Inv estate of Alexander Walker on 5 Feb 1811 by Jethro Brown.

173 JOHN JONES - Will - w. 3 Mar 1811. Wife Susannah Jones; sons Ezekiel and Richard (land on Toms Creek, adj. Zephaniah Tait); daughters Mary Corder, Susan Lane, Sally T. Sawyers, Elizabeth Leath, Frances N. Henslee. Exec: wife and 2 sons; Wit: W.S.Webb, William Smith.

174 JAMES McMILLION - Will - w. 15 Mar 1810. Wife Amy; all my children; land adj. Ezekiel Waters and Judah Edwell. Exec: wife Amy; Wit: J. Grant, Henry Durham.

120

Book F cont. 1811
Page
174 Younger Hardwick orphan 17 yrs of age the 26 Feb last bound to
William Climpson to learn the art and mastery of a Hatter.
175 Sale property of John Dickey on 23 Apr 1811 by William Currie adm.
Sales to: Zachariah Dickey, Lucy Payne, Nathaniel Snipes, George
Horton, George Roberts, John Smithey, Abraham Holsenback, Wm.
Currie, Daniel Baldridge.
176 Div of 11 negroes of estate of Jane Harrison to: John Ware,
William Harrison, heirs of Thomas Harrison, heirs of Mildred
Moore, heirs of Elizabeth Kennon, Joseph Dameron, Andrew Harrison Sen.
177 Inv property of Thomas and Ann Hornbuckle sold by James Simpson,
exec and adm. Thomas Windsor adm. signed the return.
178 Bond: John Swift in right of his legacy received of Thomas Swift
and George A. Swift exec of William Swift decd. one negro boy
Martin. Wit: Francis Harris.
178 Estate of Jane Harrison in acct with Andrew Harrison adm.
179 Sale property of Thomas and Nancy Hornbuckle on 16-18 Aug 1810 to:
James Simpson, James Sutton, James Heydon, Thomas Garrott, John
Reed, Aaron Simpson, Andrew Ballard, James Brown sailor, Roger
Simpson, William Vincent, James Cooper, Leroy Gossett, Oliver
Simpson, William Keen, Nicholas Chubb, John Keen, Elizabeth
Hornbuckle, et al.
182 Sales estate of John Foster by Robert Foster adm. Sales to:
Robert Foster, Nancey Foster, William Gillaspy, Thomas McFarland,
Thomas Foster, Zachery Groom, Jonathan Brooks, Nicholas Willis,
John Gomer, John Swann, William Adkins, Edward Watlington, Benjamin Ponds, John Ferry, Drury McKinney, Bartlett Yancey, et al.
186 Bond: Nathan Williamson in right of wife Sarah received from estate
of William Swift decd. his legacy.
187 Inv estate of James Simpson by Sally Simpson adm. List of bonds
and notes.
189 Francis Swift received legacy of estate of William Swift.
190 Sales estate of James Simpson on 21 Feb 1811 to: Green L. Brown,
Henry Standard, Thomas Mallory, Abraham H. Morton, et al.
191 Sales estate of Peter Strader to: Rawley Karnes, Sanday Newell,
John Rains Sen., Robert W. Stubblefield, David and Biddy Strader,
James Rawley, John Arnett, Christian Strader, Caleb Anglin, et al.
193 Inv estate of Peter Strader. Money due from estate of Conrad
Strader. Bond on Paul Chappin date 6 Mar 1807; bond on William
Shearman date 1794; one on Paul Chappin date 1 Mar 1801.
By Christian and David Strader adm.
194 Div negroes of estate of John Foster to heirs as follows: Salley
Foster; Widdow Foster; Jesse, John, Richard, Robert, Thomas,
Polley, and Azariah Foster; Richard Gunn and wife, John Cates
and wife. Commrs: Griffin Gunn, Tho Graves, Jno Burton, Saml.
Dabney.
196 James Burton and Thomas Winston exec last will of William B.
Burton acct with estate filed.

197 RICHARD BENNATT - Will - W. 30 Nov 1810. Son Ambrose L. Bennett;
grandson James Bennett and granddaughter Nancy Vaughan (children
of James Bennett decd.); 2 granddaughters Mary Bennett and Nancy
Bennett (daughters of John Bennett decd.); granddaughter Nancey
Scryer (daughter of Richard Bennett decd.); Molly and Betsy Bennett daughters of Richard Bennett decd.; son Milner Bennett ;
daughter Nancy Waller decd. and her children; granddaughter Agness O. Dickerson daughter of John; Molley Graves and Betsy
Byson (or Bysor). Exec: son Milner and Ambrose L. Wit: Gregory
Hightower, William Donoho, Jno. W. Caldwell.

Book F cont. 1811
Page
199 Power of attorney: Joseph McReynolds of Sumner Co. Tenn. to
William Whiteside of Orange Co. NC to receive of Alex Murphey
and Robert Browning exec of Edmund Browning his legacy from the
estate. 11 July 1808. Approved by William Trigg and Edwd.
Douglass of Sumner Co. /s/ David Shelby, Clk of Court.
200 Power of attorney: Joshua Browning of Bedford Co. Tenn. to Edward
King to receive legacy from deceased grandfather Edmund Browning.
17 Nov 1810. Test: Bedy Browning. /s/ Leonard Henderson, Judge
Superior Court.
201 Power of attorney: Tolliver Browning, Henry Browning, John Flynn
intermarried with Lucy Browning, Milley Browning, and Jenney
Browning to Elijah Browning their Brother to receive legacy left
them as heirs of Calib Browning decd. by will of Edmund Browning
decd. of Caswell Co. Approved by Wm. McMillan and D. Hampton,
JP's of Clark Co. Ky. 27 Sept 1810.
202 Taxable property for 1810
975 white polls   1760 black polls.
10 stores   17 retailers of spirits

July Court 1811

203 Insolvents for 1809.

204 EPEPHRODITUS STONE - Will - w. 17 May 1811. Wife Lucy;
children: Tilman, John, Robert, Peter, and James Stone.
Exec: friends Major Price, Silvanus Stokes. Wit: Robert West,
Thos. Penick.

204 LABAN STAFFORD SEN - Will - w. 16 May 1811. Son Henry (land at
Cobb Cr and Hico where he now lives); sons Laban, Eli, Adam and
Joseph (youngest); daughter Nelly wife of Joseph Feshee, Sally
wife of Ransom Cook, Delilah wife of Johnston Cook, Tabbitha
wife of Joseph Taylor; 7 sons John, William, Laban, Eli, Henry,
Adam, Joseph; sons Thomas and James. Exec: William Lea of Leasburg, Samuel Smith, Edward D. Jones. Wit: Saml. Johnston, William Willson, William Rainey.

206 Inv estate of Richard Bennatt 19 May 1811 by A. L. Bennett exec.
207 Sales estate of Richard Bennatt decd. on 10 May 1811. Among buyers:

Milner Bennatt	Peter Pysor	Thomas Graves Capt.
A. L. Bennatt	James Bennatt	William Peterson
Thomas Hightower	John Graves Capt.	Thomas Peterson
Jacob Scryer	Martin Clerk	James Peterson
Caleb Wright	Jeremiah Fletcher	George Manley
John H. Barker	John Lea (CB)	Joseph Knight
Maj. Thomas Donoho		John Lea Capt.

Bonds on Peter Bysor, Haddock & Alverson, Reed & Yearley.
210 Inv on 12 Mar 1811 estate of Richard Estes by Bartlett Estes adm.

210 ANTHONY SWIFT - Will - w. 8 Nov 1809. Wife Elizabeth; nephews
Thomas Williamson, Anthony Williamson. Exec: wife and nephew
Thomas Williamson. Wit: Andrew Robinson, Benjamin Lane.

211 Inv estate of John Jones decd. taken 7 May 1811 by Susannah Jones
and R. Jones exec.
212 Inv property of Robert Long by Elizabeth Long adm.
213 Joseph Payne Hall orphan 16 yrs. old 16 of July bound to Wm. Lyon.
214 Settlement estate of Mordecai Burgess by John Langley and Mary
Burgess exec.
215 Sales estate of Richard Estes to Lewis Shepherd, Bartlett Estes,
William Rudd, Joseph Stafford, William & Peter McKinney, James
Page, Wiley Yancey, Zenus Bush, John Pinson, Martin Browning,
Sarah Estes et al.   122

Book F cont. 1811
Page
217 James Lea esq. in acct with Hezekiah Farley's estate. Judgments
    on Daniel S. Farley, Hugh Shaw.
218 Meredith Price adm of Joel McDaniel decd. acct filed.
220 Estate of John Tennison decd. acct with Levi Tennison exec.
222 William Warren orphan age 6 yrs. last Mar bound to George Roberts
    to learn art of a blacksmith.

October Court 1811

223 Power of attorney: William Rainey to Edward D. Jones, attorney at
    law, to receive and demand money coming to me in State of Virginia
    in my own or the right of my wife Lucy A. Rainey, formerly Lucy
    A. Jackson of Amelia Co. Va.(To receive from estate of Mrs.
    Elizabath Jackson decd. of Amelia Co. on waters of Surat Home Cr,
    money mow in hands of commrs. in Notaway Co.) 28 Oct 1811.
224 Inv estate of Anthony Swift on 16 July 1811.
225 Notes belonging to estate of Anthony Swift.
234 Sale property of Anthony Swift. Sales to: Peter Bysor, James
    Birk, Nathan Rice, Jethro Brown, Elizabeth Dye, Ibzan Rice,
    William Smith, Hezekiah Boswell, Elizabeth Swift, Thomas Wil-
    liamson.
235 Levy Fuller in right of his wife Susanna adm. estate of Johnston
    McDaniel, settlement of estate.
236 List of bonds returned to court by Sally Simpson exec of James
    Simpson decd. on: Thomas Jouett, Jeremiah Jones, Henry Dunlap
    Sen., Jos. and Alexander Murphey, George Foot.
236 Inv estate of Eppeproditus Stone taken 17 July 1811. Bonds on
    Peter Smith, Levy Stone, Henry Baldwin (to Eppe Stone as adm. of
    Philip Stone decd.), Jack Hatcher. Money received in Knoxville,
    Tenn. $305.64. By Major Price exec.
237 Sales estate of Eppe Stone on 3 Oct 1811. Sales to Meredith Price,
    Major Price, Jeremiah French, Elijah Martin, Evans Shaw, John
    Wosham, William Penix, Levin Downs, Silvanus Stokes, Isaac West,
    John Ruark, Bartlett Yancey, Mathew Mills, David Lay, et al.
238 William and David Gooch exec in acct with estate of William Gooch
    decd. Legacy paid to James Gooch.
239 Estate of John Gray decd. in acct with David Mitchell adm. Judg-
    ment in hands of adm. vs William Mansfield decd.
240 Estate of Benjamin Quine in acct with Henry Quine adm. 17 Sept
    1811.
240 Div of 5negroes willed to James Bennett and William Vaughan in
    right of his wife Nancy by Richard Bennett decd.
241 Settlement estate of John Tennison by Levi Tennison exec. Lega-
    cies left for 5 youngest children. 27 Oct 1811.

242 SUSANNAH LEATH - Will - w. 6 July 1811. Son Freeman Leath and if
    he die before age 21, estate to go to Brother John Barker and
    after his death to be divided between James Taylor, Hiram Taylor,
    and Susannah Taylor. Exec: brother John Barker. Wit: Robert L.
    Mitchell, James Brown.

243 WILLIAM RICHARDSON - Will - w. 18 Sept 1811. Land in Halifax Co.
    Va. to be sold; estate to be kept together by brother in law
    Noel Burton; land on Hogan's Cr.; wife and children; horses
    bought of Capt. Price to be sold. Exec: Noel Burton and brother
    James Richardson. Wit: Andrew Harrison Sen., Dan L. Farley,
    Edward Busey.

Book P cont. 1811 - 1812
Page
244 JOSEPH FARLEY - Will - w. 9 Sept 1811. Legacy left by Father
Hezekiah Farley to be divided to: 2 brothers John B. Farley and
William S. Farley, 2 sisters Rachel Roper and Martha Farley and
(my relation) Polly Lea (daughter of Sally Lea) the supposed
child of my father Hezekiah Farley. Mother Martha Farley.
Judgment on Newman Durham. Exec: friends Dr. John McAden,
Samuel Smith, and uncle Abner Burton. Wit: John Burton, Stephen
W. Burton, George Farley.
245 Inv estate of Laban Stafford decd taken 20 Sept 1811.
246 Sales estate of Robert Long decd sold 20 Sept 1811. Buyers:
Elizabeth Long, John Long, Salley Long, Mary Long, Robert Long,
William Stephens, Bart Dameron, John Crisp, Lewis Malone, Jonathan Starkey, John Lea, Thomas Comer, Daniel Richmond, John Richmond, William Richmond, Josiah Chandler, John Roan, James Dollarhide, Thomas Villines.

January Court 1812

248 In Nottaway County, Va. court 5 Dec 1811, Hampton Waller is
appointed guardian to his children Richard, Ephraim, Thomas,
Elizabeth, Nancy, Polly, and Ambrose Waller. By Francis
Fitzgerald Jun., CC.
248 On 3 Jan 1812 John Fuqua, William Welsh, and William Minor for
Ralph Fuqua sign agreement with Godfrey Crowder. Crowder has
paid lawyers fees for recovery of tract of land in Caswell Co.
of Col. James Sanders. Wit: Henry Geter, Edwin Reaney.
249 Inv estate of Joseph Farley.
249 Inv estate of John Warrick taken by Jno. Roan and William Stephens.
250 Inv property of Susanna Leath. Bonds on Benjamin Cantril, James
and John Cooper.
250 Allotment to Salley Sewell widow and relict of Benjamin Sewell
decd. 12 Nov 1811. Commrs: Jas Yancey, William Gooch Sen.,
Elisha Evans, Alex Murphey.
251 Allotment to Mrs. Mary Walker of a part of estate of Alex^r Walker.
By A. Graves, David Poyner, James Orr.

251 JOHN WARRICK - Will - w. 6 Feb 1811. Nephew John Roan; nephew
William Stephens; sister Margret Thomas widow. Exec: John Roan
and William Stephens Jun. Wit: Daniel Darby, Isaac Vanhook.

252 Sales estate of John Warrick to: Robert Hamlett, David Thomas,
Thomas Loftin, Gabriel Lea, George Smith, John Roan, William
Stephens, Charles L. Hunter, William Evans, Gabriel B. Lea,
Lemuel Bowers, James Darby, Richard Maleer, Benj. Stephens,
Christopher Mathis et al.
253 Sale balance of property of Bartholomew Dameron to Joseph Dameron
Jun. and Daniel Malone.
253 Additional property of estate of Richard Bennett sold to Milner
Bennett, George B. Dameron, Thomas Hightower.
254 Sales personal estate of William Park Swift. 2 Nov 1811.
254 Inv property of Benjamin Sewell taken 12 Nov 1811 by James Graves
and Stephen D. Watkins adm. An acct on Barnet Kemp.
255 Sales estate of Benjamin Sewell 21 Nov 1811. Sales to:
Salley Sewell(Mrs.), Salley Sewell(Miss), William Smith, Charles
G. Cock, James Martin, Vincent Griffin, Daniel Sewell, Barnett
Kemp, Thomas Graves(son Jacob), Jacob Graves, Jerre Rudd, Bartlett
Estes, Azariah Graves, James Graves, Isaac Pinson, Stephen D.
Watkins, et al.

Book F cont. 1812
Page
256 Sales property of James Simpson on 19 Nov 1811. Sales to:
Oliver Simpson, Jethro Brown, Hedley Harrison, Edney Tapscott,
George Williamson, et al. By Salley Simpson exec.
257 Obligation: Archibald Curles of Madison Co. Ky. to Susannah
Crowder, Godfrey Crowder in right of his wife, and to Herndon
Haralson. Wit: Archibald Haralson, Jonathan Haralson.
/s/ Arch^d Curle.
258 Power of attorney: Henry Poston to James Orr to settle with
John C. Cox exec of Jesse Poston decd. and also as former guardian to receive as legatee of Jerre Poston decd - also as attorney
for brother William Poston. 1 June 1809. Test: Jno Humphries,
Robert Orr.
258 Power of attorney: Rebecca Lyon of Caswell Co. determined to remove to Caroline Co. Va. to friend Richard Haddock to sell and
dispose of household goods loaned by her husband Robert Lyon.
and to rent land whereon she lives and hire out negroes. 2 Aug
1811. Wit: Sol Graves, B. Yancey.
259 Power of attorney: Alston Solomon, John Clift, James Price,
John Gibson all of Bedford Co. Tenn. legatees of Elizabeth
Browning decd. legatee of Edmund Browning decd. to George Browning of same county to receive from estates in Caswell Co.
260 George Browning attorney for Auston Solomon in right of his wife
Phebe, John Clift in right of his wife Delilah, James Price in
right of wife Milley, and John Gibson in right of wife Elizabeth
of Bedford Co. Tenn. (all legatees of estate of Edmund Browning)
and children of Elizabeth Browning daughter of said Edmund to
William Kimbrough to discharge all debts.
261 Caleb Browning of Bedford Co. Tenn.(child of Elizabeth Browning)
obligated to Jacob Graves to discharge debts of Browning estate.
262 Thomas Windsor adm. estate of Nancy Hornbuckle, settlement of
estate.
263 Alcey and John Aldrage adm of estate of James Aldrage decd. acct
filed.
264 Robert West adm of John West decd. Estate sales to Mary West,
David L. West, Robert West.

April Court 1812

265 Power of attorney: John T. Street of Williamson Co. Tenn. to
Zephaniah Tait to settle ratible (ratable) part of the estate
now in hands of Ann Vincent. 15 Feb 1812.
266 Power of attorney: Craven Bozwell of Henderson Co. Ky. who has
power of attorney of Wynn Dixon and Joseph Cowen exec of will of
Elizabeth Hart decd. to John Windsor Sen of Caswell Co. to
collect all monies due and money due exec from Malahn Stacy of
Caswell. 26 Mar 1812.
267 Inv property of David Preston by Rebeckah Preston adm.
267 Second inv of Laban Stafford.

268 SAMUEL BRACKEN - Will - w 18Feb 1812. Wife Rebecah;
son John (land bought of Peter Smith); daughters Jane Cobb, Margret Sanders; son Joseph; daughter Hannah Murphey decd., 2 grandchildren John Murphey and Martha Ector Murphey; daughters Izbell
Blackwell, Martha Ector Haralson, Sina, Uarca, Gripina Bracken.
Exec: sons Joseph and John. Test: W. Morgan, Isaac King, Robert
I. King.

269 Amt. of sales estate of Isaac Jackson.
269 Allotment to Elizabeth Long wife of John Long decd. for her and her
family. 13 Feb 1812. Commrs: James Lea, Wm. Richmond, Samuel Hodge,
James Darby.

Book F cont. 1812

Lage

270 Allotment to Polley Muzzall widow of William Muzzall decd. 25
Feb 1812. Commrs: Jas Yancey, Robt. Browning, Nathl. Gooch,
James Graves.

271 Inv property of John Long decd taken 25 Jan 1812 by Elizabeth
Long and John Roan adm.

272 Inv estate of William Richardson decd taken 21 Mar 1812.
Bonds due estate from John Dix, Sherod Gowen, William Gattis,
Joshua Wall, James Ware, Terry Dickerson, Fendal Roland, Evans
Knight, Rich R. Kennon, William Quine, James Paul, John Farger-
son, Edmund Richardson, et al.

273 Inv estate of William Muzzall decd taken 4 Feb 1812 - includes
sundry articles of old store goods; allotment to overseer and
to James Eubank who is building barn on plantation of decd by
contract before his death. Payments from estate to Slade &
Yancey, Stephen Ellis, Samuel Madden, John Porterfield, et al.

276 Sales estate of William Muzzall on 25 & 26 Feb 1812. Sales to:
Nathaniel and Joseph Muzzall, James Barnwell, Richard Arwin,
Thomas Compton, William Currie, Thornton Malone, Thornton Banes,
James Rudd, Samuel Greer, Henry Turner, Thomas Coleman, Robert
and David Barnwell, William Fitch Jun., Polly Muzzall, Alsolem
Lea, Nathaniel Norfleet, James Yancey Jun. bought 2 dozen marbles
for 12½¢, Jonathon Terrell, John Roan, Robert Faucett, Miles
Wells, James Bird(Stiller), Caswell Tait, Abraham Villines, James
Vaughan Sen., Barzillai Graves Sen., Richd. and Charnell High-
tower, Robert Scott, Christopher Thomas, Salley & Betsy Muzzall,
Abner Wisdom, William Jopling, Jepthah Parks, Hasten Bartlett,
William Turner, et al.

282 William Lea in acct with estate of Vines Matthews for hire of
negroes for 1812 to Daniel Jackson, Major Wallis, Jack Baitman,
Nancy Matthews, Samuel Woods. One-third allotment to widow,
other part to orphans.

283 Total sales of property of Laban Stafford Sen. sold 20 Sept 1811.
Allotment of negroes to: Laban, Adam, Henry, Ely, Thomas, and
Joseph Stafford. By William Lea exec.

284 Sales estate of James Currie on 11 Apr 1812. Sales to: Isham
Malone, James & John Currie, Thomas Villines, Philip Baynes,
Allen Cooper, James Crossett, George Roberts, Hugh & William
Currie, William Ashford, Thomas Miles, et al. Rent of John
Dickie's land for year. By William Currie adm.

285 Sales estate of Eppy Stone by Major Price exec on 14 Nov 1811.
Sales to: Capt. Barzillai Graves, Thomas & Robert Ware, F. Berry-
man Worsham, Lucy Stone, Presley Carter, William Ware Jun. & Sen.,
James Richardson, Thomas Penix, George Sharp, Ludwell Worsham,
Luke Palmer, Elijah Duncan, et al.

288 Allotment and div of negroes Rachel, Lucy, and Jerry between
William Hubbard, James Hubbard, and Daniel Smith in right of
his wife Sally, the negroes given to them by their Father Ralph
Hubbard by deed of gift.

289 Settlement estate of William Terry decd by Capt. John McMullen adm.

290 Joseph Dameron Sen. exec estate of Bartholomew Dameron acct filed
for 1810-12.

291 Deed of trust: Hasten Bartlett hath borrowed of John Kimbrough
$25. Bartlett sells slave girl 4 yrs. old, Celah, to Alexander
Murphey. Wit: Robert Browning. 23 Sept 1811.

292 Solomon Graves, Treas. of Public Buildings, reports publick jail
is in an unfit situation to retain prisoners. Court ordered
Maj. Thomas Donoho, John Stamps, Solomon Debow, Jesse Carter,
James Yancey, Bartlett Yancey, Alex Murphey, & Philip Pearce

Book F cont. 1812
Page
        to examine repairs and draw plan for same. Jan 1812.
        April 14, 1812 - Above committee report necessary to build a
        room fronting Jail Door of 16 ft. long and 14 wide with chimney
        of stone or brick for purpose of a Jailor's room.
292 List of strays returned by
        William Penix - 1 sow   Samuel Pittard - 1 sow
        Joseph Arnett - 5 hogs   Jacob Ahart - 1 mare
293 Spencer Ball bound to George O. Connally for term 3 yrs. & 6 mos.
294 Robert Ball bound to George O. Connally for term of 7 yrs.
295 Sales estate of John Long decd. by Elizabeth Long and John Roan
        adm. Sales to: Elizabeth Long, John Lea (C.B.), Nathaniel Comer,
        Salley Long, Job Siddall, Thomas Comer, William Suit, Benjamin
        Stephens, Nicholas Coils, John Richmond, Fielding Lewis, Benja-
        min Ponds, Daniel & William Richmond, Joseph Langley, John Comer,
        William Coventon, Thomas Coventon, et al.

                    July Court 1812

298 Inv personal estate of Samuel Brackin decd. by John Brackin exec.
        Bonds on Nathl. Murphey, William Long, William Weatherford.
        Bequeaths in will to Sinah, Uarky Bracken and to wife Rebecah.
299 Sales estate of Samuel Bracken on 13 May 1812 to: Rebeccah, John,
        and Joseph Bracken, N.P.Mimms, John Cobb, William Weatherford,
        Ibzan Rice, Joseph Lane, James Somers, Christian Strader, Alex
        Paschal, Edward Ruark, Thos. North, Levi Blackwell, et al.
300 Allotment to Elizabeth Long widow of Robert Long decd.
        Commrs: Gabriel Lea, William Richmond, William Lea.
301 Matilda Garrot, girl of colour, age 3 yrs. the 4 Apr last, bound
        to Danl. Darby.
302 Allotment to Mary McKee widow of Jesse McKee decd. 2 May 1812.
        Commrs: W. Warren, Miles Wells, Thomas Morris, John Hewlett.
302 Jeremiah Hinton age 12 yrs Jan next bound to Barnett Kemp.

303 JOHN KERSEY - Will - w. 22 Feb 1812. Son Drury; daughter Dicy
        Jones; 3 children: Marthy, Sarah, and Alexander. Exec: son Alex
        Kersey. Wit: William Jones, John Gamble.

303 Inv property of James Birk Jun. taken 4 May 1812 by Thomas Turner
        and Anderson Birk. Notes on William Collier Jun., Ira Copeland,
        Thomas Neely.
304 Sales estate of James Birk Jun. on 7 May 1812. Sales to:
        Nathaniel Gooch, Quentin Anderson, Polly Birk, Abraham Lambrick,
        Thomas & Henry Turner, James Yancey, Hugh Walker, John Slade,
        Thomas Belsiah, Abner Walker, James Graves, Christopher Brooks,
        Elijah & Barz Graves, Nathaniel L. Rice, Mumford Ford, Nathl.
        Gooch Jun., Mark Collier, James Miles, Willis Ashford;
        Thompson, Anderson, and Benjamin Birk.
306 Inv estate of George Samuel decd taken 20 June 1812 by Rowsee
        Samuel adm.
307 Allotment to widow of George Samuel decd. 20 June 1812.
        (Index lists allotment to Johanna Samuel.)
308 List of part of sale of James Simpson - 1 negro man Solomon sold
        to Sally Simpson for $500.
308 Inv property of Jesse McKee decd by Robert McKee adm. Note on
        Thomas Forest.
309 Settlement with Jane Jackson adm of Thomas Jackson Jun. decd.
        Payments made to Joseph Langley, Vincent & William Lea, James
        C. Smith, Robert H. Jackson, Alexander Griffin, Daniel Darby
        for crying sale, Barnett Kemp, Joshua Jackson, et al. By Greg
        Hightower and Joseph Dameron Jun.

Book F cont. 1812 - 1813
Page
310 Settlement with Nancy Bird adm of Temple Bird decd. Payments to: John McCaden, Gabriel & Vincent Lea, Abraham Holsonback for Crying sale.
310 William Scribner base born child in his 14th yr. bound to William Walker.
311 Allotment to Mary Birk widow and relict of James Birk decd. 21 Apr 1812. Commrs: W. S. Webb, Nath Gooch, Joseph Collier, Abner Walker.
312 Insolvents for 1810.
313 Sales estate of Robert Long taken 20 Sept 1811. Sales to: Elizabeth Long, John & Mary Long, William Stephens, Bart Dameron, John Crisp, Lewis Malone, John Whitlow, William Gordan Jun., Jonathan Starkey, William Richmond, John Lea (CB), Thomas Comer, Daniel & John Richmond, David Hodge, Loyd Vanhook, Thomas Donoho, Josiah Chandler, David Harris, James Montgomery, Joshua Carney, Thomas Riggs, Thomas Waterfield, James Vaughan, William Hicks, John Burton, Parum Jackson, John Roan, James Dollarhide, James Peterson, John Swann, Thomas Villines. By Elizabeth Long adm.
316 Estate of John Somers in acct with John Somers and Catharine Somers exec. Payments to: John Keen, Peter Elmore, Doct. Patton, Doct. Webb, Paul Chappel, Richard Underwood; John Somers exec for expenses and other charges in Tenn. Land sold Robt. Blackwell. Debts collected of Joel McDaniel, Arthur Tony, Abraham Underwood. Commrs: Saml. Dabney, James Orr, John Cobb.
318 Taxable property for 1811
     925 white polls   1858 black polls
     11 stores   15 retailers
            October Court 1812
319 Sales estate of George Samuel decd taken 25 Sept 1812. Sales to: Anner & Lewis Samuel, Samuel Pittard, Archibald & Rowzee Samuel, Jeremiah Samuel, John Davis, William Morton, William Randolph, Jeremiah Fletcher, Abner Qualls, Joshua Siddall, Richard Haddock, Amos Saterfield, Anderson Morton, Henry Roper, Thomas Persail, William Jones. By Rowzee Samuel adm.
320 Inv property of John Kersey decd taken 8 Oct 1812. By Alex Kersey exec.
321 Sales of James Simpson to Jethro Brown, James Knott; Sally, Aaron, and Moses Simpson.
322 Appraisal personal estate of Anthony Swift 6 Oct 1812.
324 Sales estate of George Sims by Thomas Mallory and Nathan Sims exec.
325 Report of William Muzzall county trustee for 1807-9. Included payments to Richard Henderson, solicitor; (William Muzzall decd. late county trustee acct approved by B. Yancey, Azariah Graves, James Yancey.)

            January Court 1813
331 Sales estate of John Moore decd. sold 3 Nov 1810. Sales to: Newman Durham, Asa Thomas, John Pass, Susanna Williams, Samuel Curl, Richard Ogilby, James Boulain, et al. By Tho Jeffreys adm.
332 Div of negroes belonging to estate of Robert Long to: Elizabeth Long widow, Robert and John Long, Mrs. Nancy Maxfield, Sally and Mary Long. Commrs: Jesse Carter, Jno Burton, B.Yancey.
333 Power of attorney: John Ogilby of Oglethorpe Co. Ga. guardian to orphans of John Moore of Caswell Co. decd. to friend Richard Ogilby to adjust with Thomas Jeffreys all business relating to estate of John Moore decd. 16 Dec 1812. Approved by Isaac Collier clerk Inferior Court of said Co. and George Hudspeth,esq.

                        128

Book F cont. 1813

Page

334 Div of negroes belonging to William Mitchell Jun. to the estate of John Gray decd. Legatees of John Gray: Widow Susannah Gray; Yancey, John, Lethy, Alexander, and Fanny Gray. 26 Dec 1811.

334 Inv goods and chattels of Henry Turner Junr. decd. Part bond on James Stewart. By J. Turner adm. 12 Oct 1812.

335 Sales remaining property of John Long.

335 Sales estate of John Hightower decd sold 5 Nov 1812. Sales to: Agness Hightower, James Nelson, Eppy Moore, John Jackson; Daniel, Devereu, James Hightower; John Thomas, Alexander Wiley, Abner Wisdom, Barnett Kemp, Elijah Morton, Nicholas Thompson, Joseph Langley, et al. By Daniel Hightower adm.

337 Inv estate of John Hightower on 31 Aug 1812.

338 Allotment to Agness Hightower relist of John Hightower.

338 Inv property of Robert Long Jun. on 12 Jan 1813 by John Roan adm.

339 Sales property of the orphans of Saml. Enochs decd sold 2 Jan 1813. Sales to Elizabeth Enochs, William Barnwell, Joseph Pinnix, John Murry, et al.

339 Inv and sale estate of Jesse McKee sold 5 May 1812 to: Polly McKee, Robert McKee, Absolem Lea, Joseph Armstrong, et al.

341 Jethro Brown adm estate of Alex Walker, acct filed. Accts paid to Ellimor Payne, Mrs. Peggy L. Nash, William Bethell, Doct. Edwd. M. Foulds, et al.

342 Acct of rent of land of John Dicky decd for 1813 by Wm. Currie adm.

April Court 1813

343 Alfred McCubbins base born male child age 6 yrs. the 8 of July next bound to John Bauldin. /s/ James Rainey, Chariman County Court.

344 Thompson Porter orphan age 18 yrs the 20 May next bound to Thomas Poyner.

345 Silvester McCubbins base born child age 8 yrs the 3rd Oct next bound to John Bauldin. (Also spelled Bauldwin). By Alex Murphey D.C. (Deputy clerk)

346 ROBERT BLACKWELL - Will - w. 28 Nov 1812. Wife Zillah; sons Robert and John; children: Carter Blackwell, Nancy Malone decd., Levi, Thomas, and Garland Blackwell; Polly Watt, Kitturah Watt, no heir of deceased daughter Betsy Malone decd. Exec: wife Zillah, Thomas and Robert Blackwell. Wit: Charles Mitchell, Chas. Brooks.

348 Estate of William Stephens in acct with Anthony Stephens adm.

349 Inv property of Robert Long Jun. decd taken 25 Feb 1813 by James Lea adm.

349 Sales estate of Robert Long Jun. to Elizabeth Long widow, Capt. John Burton, John Maleer, Daniel Richmond, Thomas Riggs Jun., Drusus Riggs, John Hodge.

350 William Barnwell in right of his wife Elizabeth exec of Samuel Enochs decd. Payments to Thomas, Reece and Mary Enochs, et al.

351 Bond: 6 Apr 1813 - William Richmond an exec of will of Joshua Richmond decd hath paid over to Phebe Lipscomb as guardian to orphans of Joshua Richmond amount due orphans and to Phebe Lipscomb from John Lipscomb's estate as late widow of said Joshua decd. Wit: Joseph Richmond.

352 William Richmond and Phebe Lipscomb exec of will of Joshua Richmond acct filed. Paid exec of Step Roberts, Lott Egmond, Joseph Langley, et al. 27 Mar 1813.

353 Estate of George Eubanks decd in acct with Nathaniel Malone and L. Eubanks.

Book F cont. 1813
Page
355 Settlement estate of Isaac Jackson decd. by Joseph Dameron and
Robert H. Jackson exec.
356 Estate of John Dickey by Wm. Currie adm. Note to Rebeccah Dickey.
357 Second sale estate of Robert Long Sen. to Elizabeth Long (widow
of Robert Long Sen. decd.), et al.
358 Estimate of property advanced by Robert Long in his life time to:
John Long, Nancy Maxfield now Nancy Harris, Salley Hodge, Mary
Riggs, Elizabeth Long widow of Robert Long decd. and Robert Long
Jun. 9 Apr 1813.
359 Acct estate of Vines Matthews by William Lea. Sale of negro man
Isaac.
360 Joseph Collier guardian in acct with Sally and James Collier her
husband formerly Sally Kimbrough, orphan of John Kimbrough Jun.
360 Alexander Wiley maketh oath that the mark which he designates his
stock is a crop off right ear and an underlick taken out of
left ear.
361 Div and allotment of negroes of estate of William Donoho decd to:
Eunice Long late widow of said Donoho, William C. Donoho, Alex
Donoho. Commrs: Moses Bradsher, Cary Williams, Ish Edwards.
362 List of strays returned
Stray sow and pigs taken up by Francis Smith; dark bay mare by
Edward Watlington.

July Court 1813

362 Return of Congressional election held 30 Apr 1813 -
Gloucester Dist: Bartlett Yancey 214, James Martin 1; In Milton:
Bartlett Yancey 138, James Martin 7; at Gregory Durhan's:
Yancey 107, Martin __; at tavern house of Jethro Brown: B Yancey
251, James Martin Jun. __.

363 LEWIS MALONE - Will - w. 17 June 1813. Sons Carter, Robert, Good-
ley, Nashvail, Michael, Lewis Green, and Sandy Malone;
daughter Elizabeth. Exec: Thomas Blackwell, Daniel Malone, Carter Malone. Test: Gabriel Lea, Samuel Pittard.

364 Insolvents for 1811.
366 Addtional acct sales estate of Samuel Bracken.
366 Allotment to Libby Parks widow and relict of Jephthah Parks decd.
14 May 1813. Commrs: Jas. Yancey, William Walker, James Currie,
Lewis Corbit.
367 Bartlett Estes exec in acct with estate of Richard Estes decd.
368 Bartlett Estes adm in acct with Sarah Estes decd.
369 Settlement estate of Thomas Jackson decd by Robert H. Jackson and
Daniel Jackson exec.
370 Inv property of Robert Blackwell decd taken 25 Apr 1813 by Thomas
and Robert Blackwell exec.
371 Sales estate of Robert Blackwell on 7 May 1813. Among buyers:
Garland, Robert, John, Levi, Thomas, Carter Blackwell; Nathl.
Mims, Zillah Blackwell, James Watt, James Cobb, James Paschall,
Charles Brooks, James D. Taylor, John Ferry.
372 Estate of Richard Bennett in acct with A.L.Bennett exec. Payments
to: Rev. William Moore for funeral services $8, Dr. James C.Smith,
Darcus Donoho, William Peterson, Thomas Ruffin as coundil for
estate, Bartlett Yancey attorney, James Lea(son of Capt.),
Capt. John Lea, Thomas Purcell, Dr. McAden.
373 Taxable property for 1812
892 white polls   1875 black polls

Book F cont. 1813 - 1814

Page   October Court 1813

373 HANNAN SLADE - Will - w. 3 May 1813. Sons Ezekiel(land includ-
ing his dwelling house), Josiah, Thomas; all children: William,
Nathaniel, Susannah Tolbert, Catharine Lea, Hannah Lea.
Exec: son Thomas. Wit: James Miles, Richard B. Gunn.

373 ANNER SAMUEL - Will - w. 26 June 1813. Sons Rowzee and Lewis;
daughters Susannah Satterfield and her children, Mildred Morton,
and Lettey Morton. Exec: son Rowzee. Wit: Andrew Harrison,
Samuel Pittard.

375 Sterling Vaughan orphan 14 yrs old the 9 of Jan last bound to
James Holder. /s/ Meredith Price, Chairman County Court.

376 Charles Connally orphan age 18 yrs the 1 of Jan next bound to
James Holder until he attain age of 21 yrs to learn art of a
sadler.

377 Inv estate of David Womack decd by Azariah Graves adm.
Bonds on Abner Walker, Polly Birk, Anderson Birk.

378 Power of attorney: Godfrey Crowder acting exec of last will of
David Shelton decd to William B. Stokes of Mecklenburg Co. Va.
to transmit all business between estate of David Shelton and
estate or heirs of Thomas Harrison Sen decd. 8 Oct 1813. Test:
Miles T. Crowder, Henry Shelton.

379 Inv estate of Lewis Malone decd. Notes on Thomas Johnston,
Robert Foster, Thomas Villines, Barzillai Graves, Jesse Womack,
John Whaley, William Malone, Patrick Moore. Open book accts on
Richard & John Maleer, John Roan, Joshua Carney, et al.

381 Messrs. Atkinson and Carter in acct with Thomas Bouldin, discharge
and receipt for bond.

381 Inv estate of William Jones decd. taken 11 Oct 1813 by P. Clayton
Jones adm.

382 Sales of perishable estate of Asa Thomas sold by Durrett Richards
adm on 4 and 12 May 1813. (No names given)

       January Court 1814

387 ALEXANDER KERR - Will - w. 7 Apr 1810. Son John Kerr to get all
land; son in law Geroge Barker; sons in law William Gooch and
William Slade; daughters Sally Gooch, Nancy Spencer, Susannah
Taylor, Patsey Slade, Frances Barker; 4 daughters of deceased
daughter Molly Spencer; Negro man James to be sold among heirs
and not out of family; deceased daughter Betsy Richey and her
heirs. Exec: son John, sons in law William Gooch and George
Barker. Wit: John Henslee, Betsy Henslee.

389 BARTLETT HATCHETT - Will - w. 5 Oct 1813. Wife Peggy Archeaken
Hatchett; Children: Polly, Edward Russell, John, and Bartlett
Hatchett. Exec: Gabriel B. Lea and Gabriel Lea Sen. Wit:
Joshua Carney, Gabriel Lea Sen. Executors refused to qualify
and adm of estate with will annexed granted to William Russell.

389 Nathan Lambert orphan 8 yrs old the 2 Apr next bound to James
Orr. /s/ Jethro Brown, Chairman County Court.

390 Allen Aldrige orphan age 5 yrs the 3 May next bound to Joshua
Beaver to learn art of stone mason.

391 Inv estate of Alexander Kerr decd taken 7 Jan 1814. Notes on
John Simmons, Robert Martin, Wylie Yancey, James Yancey.
Accts on Jeremiah Lea, John Kerr; by John Kerr and George
Barker exec.

392 Inv estate of Washington Wright decd taken 13 Jan 1814 by
Azariah Graves adm.

131

Book F cont. 1814
Page
392 Inv estate of Anner Samuel decd taken 11 Jan 1814 by Rowzee
Samuel exec.
393 Inv estate of Jepthah Parks Nov 1813 by Quentin Anderson adm.
393 Allotment to Delilah Womack widow of David Womack decd for support of her and her family.
394 Sales estate of Jeptha Parks sold 4 Jan 1814. Buyers: William
Culberson Sen. & Jun., James Bird, Howell Whitmore, Aquilla
Compton, David Mitchell Jun., Thomas Arnold, William Price.
395 William Lea exec in acct with orphans of Vines Matthews decd. for
hire of negroes for 1814.
395 Inv property of Elizabeth Williams taken 15 Oct 1813 by Nathan
Williams adm.
395 Inv some property of Jesse McKee and sale to Robert McKee adm.
396 Acct of sale: Sold to Nathan Williams the interest of Henry Williams decd. 1000 acres land in Tenn., Murray Co., on waters of
Big tom or Indian Cr. /s/ Elizabeth Williams exec. 10 Mar 1813.
396 Inv estate of Hannah Slade decd and sale of negro girl Sally to
John Lea.
396 Memorandum of 30 negroes and remaining estate of Col^o William
Nash decd valued 3 Jan 1814 by Jethro Brown, John H. Brown,
James Knott.
398 Peggy L. Nash exec of Col^o William Nash decd in acct with estate.
Div of negroes to James Whitted, Farmesia Nash, William Nash,
Alfred Moore Nash, Eliza Nash, Abner Nash, - one lot left for
widow. 5 Jan 1814.
400 Sales estate of David Womack decd. to: Delilah Womack widow,
James White, Jesse & Elisha Alverson, Richard Gunn, James Rich-
ardson, Benj. C. West, James Ingram, Azariah Graves Jun., Frances
& Groves Howard, William Graves, Jeremiah Rudd, Elijah Graves,
David Hailey, Thomas & John Baxter, Jacob Quine, Benj. Loafman,
John Scott, John Graves, James Davis, James Faucett. Open accts
on Stephen Ingram. By Azariah Graves adm.
403 Settlement estate of James Currie decd by William Currie adm.
Debts on Thomas Miles and John Zachary.
404 Sales estate of Phebe Lipscomb taken 4 Nov 1813 by John and Joseph
Richmond adm. Sale made at plantation whereon she died.
Among buyers:

Joseph Richmond	John Peterson	Jesse Richmond
James Bowling	Thomas Turner	Daniel Richmond
William Hundley	John Richmond	James Nelson
Lott Egmon	(widow son)	John Johnston
William Suit	William Evans	Thomas Boman
George O. Connally	Daniel Darby	John Thomas(Waggoner)
Thomas Connally	Elizabeth Kitchen	Archibald Rice
Elisha Evans	Zadock Rice	Samuel Pittard
Ibzan Rice	William Sawyers	Wm.Richmond Sen.
John C. Jones	Joseph Kitchen	Alexander Wiley
Kendal Vanhook	John Langley	Moses Langley
Robert Jackson Jun.	Joseph Langley	Abner Wisdom
John Richmond Jun.&Sen.	Joseph Chandler	James Yancey Jun.
Robert H. Jackson	James Graves	Ira Siddall
Geroge B. Dameron	Wm.Richmond Jun.	

408 James Graves and Stephen D. Watkins adm of Benjamin Sewell decd
acct filed. Payments to: Daniel Sewell, Solomon Graves attorney,
Barnett Kemp for judgment. 12 Jan 1814.

Book F cont. 1814
Page
409 JOHN DOBBINS - Will - w. 25 Nov 1813. Wife Elizabeth; land adj
   Samuel Smith; daughters Aletha, Salley; sons Hugh, Azariah,
   Archibald, and James to receive land as each comes of age.
   Exec: friends Daniel Darby and Thomas Comer. Test: Isaac Vanhook, John Comer.
   Daniel Darby qualified exec. Thomas Comer appeared and relinquished all pretentions to qualify.
410 Garland Shackleford bound to Gabriel Cox to learn art of a Tanner.
410 Hugh Cox age 17 yrs bound to Gabriel Cox.
411 Levi Murphey orphan age 13 yrs the 26 June next bound to Jonathan
   Terrell to learn art of a planter.
412 Amy Phillips, girl of colour, 2 yrs old in Sept next bound to
   Joseph Knight.
413 Daniel Phillips boy of colour 4 yrs old the 22nd Instant bound to
   Joseph Knight.
413 Frederick Phillips boy of colour age 6 yrs last Mar bound to
   Ellis Evans.
414 Dilcey Phillips girl of colour age 9 yrs next Sept bound to Ellis
   Evans.
415 Inv estate of James Kitchen decd taken 6 Apr 1814 by Wm. Sawyers.
416 Inv of sundry notes due exec of Lewis Malone decd. Daniel Malone
   exec.
418 Sales estate of Elizabeth Williams decd sold 24 Jan 1814. Buyers:
   Elizabeth Williams, Charles Brooks, James Graves, Zachariah Neill,
   Nathaniel L. Rice, Hosea McNeill, John Henslee. By Nathan
   Williams adm.
419 Inv property of Robert Lyon decd after the decease of Rebecca Lyon.
   By James Burton and Henry Howard exec. Acct due by Richard Haddock attorney for Rebecca Lyon; acct due by John P. Harrison and
   Griffin Gunn for hire of negro Charles.
419 Sales property of Robert Lyon sold 28 July 1814 to Peter Powel,
   John Lyon, Griffin Gunn, Joseph McClain, John Powel.
419 Amt of estate of Washington Wright decd taken 16 Feb 1814. Sale
   of negro girl to Major Thomas Donoho. By Azariah Graves adm.
420 Settlement estate of Jesse McKee by Robert McKee adm. Payments
   to Dr. Robert Mitchell, Simon Cochran, Barnett Kemp, John Madden,
   Norris Compton, James Eubank, Isaac Rainey, Andrew Madden, also
   to widow.
420 Settlement estate of Peter Strader decd. Approved by Elijah
   Weathers, James Powell, John Hudnall.

End of Book F
April Court 1814 continues in Book G

N

Caswell	Richmond	St. Lawrence	Nash
		×	
St. David's	Gloucester	St. Luke's	St. James

Caswell County 1777-1792 with 8 districts.
X indicates Caswell Court House the name being
   changed to Leasburg in 1788.
Person County was formed in 1792 from the eastern
   part of Caswell. The districts falling into
   Person were St. Lawrence, St. Luke's, Nash,
   and St. James.
The districts in Caswell after 1792 were Richmond,
   Caswell, St. David's, and Gloucester.

The first tax list for Caswell County 1777 was included
in a book of compilations by the author in 1977.

CASWELL COUNTY 1784 TAX LIST
Book C.R.020.701.1
State Archives

Compiled by Henry E. Kendall

Following name is number of acres of land, where the "land lyeth" is
given for some districts, then number of white polls and number of
black polls. (Ratl. is Rattlesnake Cr., CL is Country Line Cr.

Richmond District

Alley Edmond 192 Country Line 1-0
Adams John 0   1-0
Atkinson Roger 1375 Dan R   0-5
          500 Lumpkins R
          175 Old Mill Cr
Belew Isaac 325 Country Line 1-0
Baxter Peter 320 Rattlesnake 1-0
Bradley James Sen. 940 Dan R. 2-5
Burton John 200 Hico 1-1
Bolton Charles 500 Dan R. 1-6
Boulton John 200 Stink Shole 1-0
Barnett John 167 C Line 1-0
Crisp John 0-1-2
Coram Robt. 329 Moons Cr 1-0
Coyle Elisabeth 320 C Line 1-0

Comer Nathl. 600 Hico 2-1
Carman Hezekiah 143 Ratl. 1-0
Cameron John 0-1-0
Cochran David 150 Little Cr 2-1
Conaly George 112 C Line 0-0
Carman John 117 Ratl. 1-0
Carman Caleb 150 " 1-2
Cole Josiah 0   3-2
Carmichal Archd. 0 - 1-0
Dobbin Catharine 313 C.Line 0-0
Dobbin John 313 0 - 1-0
Dunaway Abram 450 Mill Cr 1-0
Donoho Thomas 100 CL & Ratl. 2-2
Duncan Elijah 0 -   1-0
Daviss John 100 Ratl. 1-0

134

Daviss John Sen. 120 Ratl. 1-0
Daviss Hezekiah 100 " 1-0
Dyer Samuel 0 1-0
Dobbin Rachel 250 Hico 0-3
Dobbin Hugh 2660 Hico & CL 1-5
Dobbin John 500 Hico 2-4
Eskridge Richard 250½ Hico 1-3
Flynn John 300 No Hico 1-0
Fulkerson Abram 200 Hico 2-4
Farley John James 334 CL 1-2
Ferrell Charles 300 CL 1-0
Gillaspy William 0-1-0
Grant James 0-1-0
Gardner Edward 100 CL 1-0
Gillaspy James 250 Cane Cr 2-0
Hightower Charnall 160 CL 1-1
Hodge John 752 SHico&Reedy Fk 1-0
Hodge Isaac 225 Reedy Fk 1-0
Hightower Epaph[S] 557 CL 1-3
Hurtt William CL 1-0
Hall David 200 CL 1-0
Hall John 100 CL 1-0
Hix Betty 127 CL
Hix Zebedy 416 Ratl. 1-0
Harrison Thomas Esq. 3020 Dan' R
       and Moon's Cr 1-9
Harrison Ninian 640 Moons Cr 1-2
Harrison Andrew 1100 Dan R 2-9
Hudson Joshua 612 Ratl. 1-1
Harrison Thomas 1400 Little 1-0
Holcom William 120 Dan R 1-0
Hubbard Benjamin 433 CL 1-0
Hinton Christopher 100 CL 1-0
Hipworth John 0- 1-0
Haralson Gideon 112 CL 1-0
Hightower Tavener 0- 1-0
Henderson Samuel 352 Ratl. 1-2
Hudson Shadrack 260 Wyne Cr 0-0
Hall William 100 Little Cr 1-0
" for Robinson estate 800 CL
Jeffreys Thomas 125 Little Cr 1-0
Ingram Benj. 640 Ratl. 1-5
Ingram Charlton 0-1-0
Johnston Peter 100 Ratl. 1-0
Johnston Daniel 170 Ratl. 1-0
John Johnston Sen. 277 Hico 1-0
Jean Phillip 0 -1-0
Johnston Samuel 1477½ Hico
          Wynn Cr. 1-2
Johnston John 200 Hico 1-0
James Joshua 100 Ratl. 1-0
Kersey John 840 CL 1-0
Low John 505 CL 1-0
Lea John (of Wm.) 0 1-0
Lea Thomas 140 CL 1-0
Lea William 1052 CL 1-2
Lea John Sen. 648 CL 2-3
Lea Major 431 CL 1-3
Long James 360 N Hico 1-1
Leek James 100 Reedy Fk 1-0

Lewis John(Byrd) 1100 Dan R 0-14
Lewis Robert 0 - 5-0
Lewis Charles 0 - 4-0
Long Robert 510 Reedy Fk 1-3
Lea Gabriel 417 Hico 1-0
Merritt Benj. 144 CL 1-0
Merritt Daniel 75 CL 1-0
Montgomery Michl 575 Ratl. 2-1
Merritt Ann 460 Mill Cr 0-2
Miles Jacob Sen. 547 Ratl. 1-4
Moore William Col. 1714 CL 1-9
        360 acres Hogans Cr
        250 " Rutledge Cr
        320 N Hico
        295 Cobb Cr
        990 Randolph County
Miles Jacob Jun 340 Ratl 1-0
Morrow Robert 200 Ratl 1-0
Matlock Nicholas 208 CL 2-1
Morrow William Sen.160 Ratl.1-0
Morrow William Jun. 100 Ratl 1-0
Melton Joseph 525
Moore Robert 0 - 2-0
Moore Jesse 0 -1-0
" for Wm. Moore 450 CL
Meadows William 140 CL 2-0
Miles Alexander 607 CL 1-1
McDaniel William 300 Hico 1-0
McAden Catharine 760 Hico
Murphey Archd.Col.1110 Hico 1-4
"   3210 near Miss.R.
Montgomery James 237 Ratl. 1-1
Oxford Edward 300 Ratl. 1-0
Peterson John 198 CL 1-0
Peterson James 100 CL 1-0
Powell William 100 Ratl 1-0
Peterson Joseph 205 CL 2-0
Poteat John 330 Ratl 1-1
Phelps James 292 Mill Cr 2-0
Pass Nathaniel 434 Mill Cr 3-0
Pond Walter 0 - 2-0
Page Nathaniel 0 - 1-0
Pearson Jacob 300 CL 1-0
Quine Henry 200 Moons Cr 1-0
Randolph James Sen. 90 CL 2-0
Randolph William 90 Mill Cr 1-0
Randolph James Jun 95 CL 1-0
Reese John 100 Ratl 1-0
Roan James 250 Hico 1-0
Robinson James 150 CL 1-0
Ragsdale William 662½ CL 1-3
Ray Thomas 100 CL 1-0
Reece William 0 -1-0
Roper William 360 Ratl. 1-0
Rice John 320 Moons Cr 2-0
Ralph Lewis 0-1-0
Rainey William 1650 Western waters
                915 Hico 2-0
Raleigh, James 0-1-0
Roberts John 250 Hico 1-0

1784 tax list cont. Richmond & Caswell Dist.

Robinson Samuel 300 CL 1-0
Ragsdale John 0-1-0
Runals Dudley 640 CL 2-1
Reed George 0-1-0
Stokes Mace 200 Mill Cr 1-0
Sawyer William 0-1-0
Stansbery Mary 384 Rattl.
Stephens Charles 650 Reedy Fk
 & N Hico 2-1
Shelton David 1088 Ratl,CL 2-4
Shelton John 364 Ratl 1-1
Swann Edward 88 CL 1-0
Samuel George 255 CL 1-5
Samuel Jeremiah 0-1-0
Samuel Anthony 260 Ratl 1-2
Samuel Ann 0-0-3
Slade Thomas Jun 100 Ratl 1-2
Slade Thomas 580 Ratl 1-3
Sanders Adam 820 CL 1-1
Starkey Jonathan 600 CL 1-1
Shackelford Francis 0-1-2
Stephens William 300 CL 2-0
Sanders Richard 350 Dan R.1-4
Samuel Archd. 200 CL 1-1
Sanders Wm.Jun. 500 Dan R.2-4
Smith Joseph 640 CL 1-0
Simmons Thomas 270 Ratl 1-2
Stafford Laban 1232 Hico 1-0
Smithey Nancy 102 Hico
Shelton David 3000 west land
 on fork of Dan R.

Sanders James Col 1650 Dan R 1-10
Tarpley Thomas 440 Little Cr. 1-0
Thomas Phillip 57 CL 1-1
Thomas David 513 N Hico 1-1
Taylor Reubin 1150 Mill Cr 1-2
Tarpley John 100 Dan R 1-0
Tolbert Joseph 515 Ratl 1-1
Upton Edward 184 Ratl 2-0
Wright Jacob 643 Ratl 1-2
Willson James (TB) 867 N Hico 1-2
Willson William Capt. 97 CL 1-0
 "   James Capt 194 CL 1-0
 "   Robert 283 CL 1-0
Willis Henry Sen 100 Ratl 1-0
Warwick Andrew 844 N Hico 1-0
Wright Abram 50 Ratl 1-0
Willis Joseph 100 Ratl 1-0
Welsh Saml. 0-1-0
Williams Jacob 300 Ratl 1-0
White George 0-1-0
Willson Thomas 300 Hico 1-2
Yates John 100 CL 1-1
Yates William 220 CL
(by Arch Samuel)

Taken by James Sanders

Caswell District

Abbr: Ho Hogans Cr. - WIC Wolf Island Creek. - Rutl. Rutledge Cr.

Allen Davis 75 Ho Cr 1-0
Arnall Andrew 572 WIC 1-0
Akin Will Jun 640 - 1-0
Avery Isaac 50 Ho Cr 1-0
Brackin Samuel 533 Moons Cr 1-0
Beasley Richard 840 --- 1-5
Bullock Samuel 237 Ho Cr 1-0
Boggus James ---1-0
Broach Jones ---1-0
Brown James 540 Rutl. 1-1
Boggus Richard 242 -- 1-0
Burton Charles 1641 1/3 Ho Cr
 1-7
Baldwin Henry 400 - 1-0
Baxter Thomas 347 WIC 1-0
Brown William 0-1-0
Collins John 300 --1-0
Cannon John 166 --1-0
 "   William 521 Moons Cr 1-3
Cockrill William - 1-0
Coram William 100 Ho Cr 1-0
Coleman Spillsby 375 Ho Cr 1-9

Dixon Tillman 640 Ho Cr 1-1
Durham Isaac 258 WIC 1-0
Dickinson Nath. 940 Ho Cr 1-1
Dixon Henry 640 Ho Cr 1-6
 "   Charles 210 Ho Cr 1-0
 "   Henry (estate) 360 Ho Cr 0-2
Embry Robert 531 - 1-0
Elliot James 641-1-0
Ellmon Charles 200 - 1-0
 "   Peter 236-1-0
Foster John 0-1-0
Ferrall Henry 0-1-0
Foster Thomas 110-1-0
Ford Simon 500 Ho Cr 1-0
Gatewood Dudley 385 Ho Cr 1-8
Graham William Sen 242 Ho Cr 1-2
Grant James 502 -1-3
 "   John 231 1-0
 "   William 0-1-0
Graham John 0-1-0
 "   Edwd. 250 Ho Cr 1-0
Gibson James 190 -1-0

136

1784 tax list cont. Caswell Dist

Gibson John 110 -1-0
Graham Wm. Jun. 0-1-0
Greenbough Jonathan 300 1-0
Humphries George 500-1-0
Horton Townsen 0-1-0
Hogg Gideon 135 WIC 1-0
" Andrew 0-1-0
Hitt Peter 150 Moons Cr 1-0
Hainey Charles 0-1-0
Huston Christopher 637 -1-0
Hopkins James 0-1-0
Holloway Obediah 100 Ho Cr 1-0
Hainey William 0-1-0
Ingram John 906 -1-0
Jones Joshua 0-1-0
Jackson Shadrack 200 -1-0
Johnston Alexander 172 Ho 1-0
Ingram James 200 Ho Cr 1-0
King Robert 300-1-0
Leek William Sen 230 Moons Cr 1-0
Lyon Robert 250 Moons Cr 1-2
Leek Wm. Jun. 0-1-0
Midlebrooks Anne 445 Ho Cr 1-0
" Isaac 195 " 1-0
" John 232 " 1-0
McCubbin William 0-1-0
Miles Abram 640 Ho Cr 2-2
Morgan Samuel 300 Ho Cr 1-0
Miller James 900 Ho Cr 1-0
McCullom ____ 160 Ho Cr 1-0
Moss William 1200 Ho Cr 1-1
Morgan William 300 Ho Cr 1-0
Miles John 100 Ho Cr 1-0
McGonagall Patrick 0-1-0
Perkins Abram 280 Moons Cr 1-2
Powell John 82 Ho Cr 1-0
Porter Alexander 320 -1-2
Parr John 0-1-2
" William Jun. 0-1-1
Perkins John 309 Moons Cr 1-1
Philpott ____ 0-1-0
Parr William Sen. 553-1-0
Pendergrass 100-1-0
Perkins James 0-1-1
Page Nathaniel 0-1-0
Paul Samuel 737 Moons Cr 1-6
" Robert 0-1-1
Quine William Jun. 316-1-0
" William Sen. 200-1-0
" Benjamin 315-1-0
Roberts John 200-1-0

Taken by Chas. Burton

Richardson Lawrence 250-1-0
" Moses 323½-1-0
" James 379-1-0
" Thomas 0-1-0
Rogers Adenston 0-1-0
Runals Dudley 395 WIC 1-0
Strader Conrad 731 Ho Cr 1-0
" Henry 258 Ho Cr 1-0
Swann Thomas 300 Rutl. 1-0
Stublefield Wyatt 1487 Ho Cr 1-5
Stanfield William 420 -1-2
Smith Peter (Wago^r) 100 Ho Cr 1-1
Snow James 250 WIC 1-0
Summers George 755-1-0
Smith William 0-1-0
Smith Peter (RH) 266 Ho Cr 1-3
Stringer James 234 Moons Cr 1-0
Slade William 0-1-0
Summers James 0-1-0
Sawyers Stephen 0-1-0
Terry Olive 266 Ho Cr 1-0
" Sarah 607
" Rebeccah 0-2-0
Thomas Cuthburt 0-1-0
Trigg William 640-1-0
Tucker Obediah 0-1-0
Turner Beryman 0-1-5
Whalebone Thomas 0-1-0
Watherford William 0-1-0
Watts Thomas 25 Ho Cr 1-0
Watherford Thos.Sen.120-1-0
Waters Ezekiel 100-1-0
Whitton George 552 Ho Cr 1-0
Wair John 210 Ho Cr 1-0
Watkins James 0-1-0
Waters Thomas 50 Ho Cr 1-0
Walker John 330 Ho Cr 1-1
Whitehead William 1150 Ho Cr 1-1
White Robert 342-1-0
Wair William Sen. 334 Ho Cr
Womack Abram 382-0-2
Weatherford Thomas 0-1-0
Wair Thomas 0-1-0
Wright Asa 0-1-0
Wair William Jun. 140-1-0
Wright John 0-1-0
Sammon John 414-1-1
McClarney Paul 100
Dixon Henry estate 3240 Ho & Moons
Knighton William 150-1-0
Powell James 340 Ho Cr 1-2

1784 tax list cont. Gloucester Dist.

Gloucester District

List did not include location of land. Following name is no. of acres of land, no. of white polls, no. of black polls.

Akins James 400-1-0
Anthony John 900-1-1
"   Jonathan 0-1-0
Allin Clifton 250-1-0
Auston William 250-1-0
Ashburn John 30-1-0
Arvin Richard 0-1-0
Ashburn Anderson 200-1-0
Armstrong John 1003
(for Currie orphans)
Adcock John 100-1-0
Aswell Pearn 0-1-0
Burrough Henry 300-1-0
"   Willis 50-1-0
Bryant James 0-1-0
Browning John 929-1-0
"   Joshua 908-1-0
Boran Isaac 400-1-0
Browning Edmd. 472-1-0
Berry Hudson 900-1-1
Benton James 300-1-0
Browning Jacob 300-1-0
Barnwell William 350-1-0
Barker James 356-1-1
Browning Saml. 100-1-0
Boush Joseph 260-1-1
Browning George 0-1-0
Brothers John 300-1-0
Bates J.Jeffreys 150-1-1
Bruce Robert 460-1-1
"   Alexander 200-1-0
Breeze William 0-1-0
Carney Joseph 300-1-0
Cochran John 220-1-2
"   Reubin 90-1-0
Culbertson William 250-1-0
Cooper Henry 236-1-0
Culbertson David 150-1-0
Corder John 300-1-0
Corder Lewis 0-1-0
Cochran William 400-1-0
Culbertson Robert 200-1-0
Cole Thomas 250-1-0
Carney Joshua 510-1-0
Cantrell William 180-1-1
Corder Joel 150-1-0
Culbertson James 610-1-0
Crumpton Aquilla 300-1-0
"   Thomas 0-1-0
Currier James 200-1-0
"   Richard 200-1-0
Carroll William 100-1-0
Currie John 618-1-0
"   James 1619-1-0

Dickey John 374-1-0
"   David 0-1-0
Donoho William 830-1-2
Dollarhide Ezekiel 600-1-0
Davis Boswell 250-1-1
"   Jonathan 200-1-0
"   Henry Sen. 200-1-0
"   Nicholas 0-1-0
Dollarhide Aquilla 0-1-0
"   Francis 0-1-0
Evans Thomas Jun. 290-1-0
"   David 100-1-0
"   Thomas Sen. 179-1-0
Enochs Benjamin 300-1-0
Evans Thomas(schoolm.) 327-1-0
Elliot William 0-1-0
Evans Zachariah 80-1-0
Ellis Walter (Delingt.) 0-1-0
French Samuel 150-1-1
Florance Obediah 320-1-0
Fuller Henry 850-1-0
Ford Colvin 450-1-0
Fuller Elijah 0-1-0
Goloher William 0-1-0
Graves Barzilla 400-1-0
Gooch G. Billy 0-1-4
"   James 0-1-0
"   William Jun. 0-1-1
Greer Samuel 550-1-0
Graves John Jun. 2000-1-4
"   Thomas 954-1-3
Gold Daniel 300 --
Gooch William 1529-1-3
Hews Billey 200-1-0
Huston George 437-1-0
Hopper James 247-1-0
"   John 200-1-0
Harvey Andrew 0-1-0
Hearndon David 200-1-0
Johnston Richard 400-1-0
"   James 440-1-0
Jones Thomas 100-1-0
"   Thomas Jun. 0-1-0
"   David 450-1-1
"   William 430-1-1
Jewill Absolem 60-1-0
Jackson John 250-1-0
Johnston Francis 200- -
Jones David for Richard Jones
    decd. 0-1-5
Kerr John 100-1-0
Kimbro Thomas 350-1-2
"   William 475-1-1
Kelly Samuel 300-1-0

1784 tax list Gloucester Dist. cont. & St. David's Dist.

Kelly William 0-1-0
King Nathaniel 200-1-0
Kimbro John 408-1-2
 "   Eleanor 350-0-3
Kilgore Thomas 455-1-0
Kimbro Robert 775-1-2
King Edward 200-1-0
Langley Thomas 640-1-0
Low Jonathan 440-1-0
Lea James 470-1-0
Love Jane(widow) 300-0-1
 "   Samuel Jun. 216-1-0
Love Saml.(Hatter) 0-1-0
Lea William 300-1-0
McIntosh John 400-1-0
Motheral Joseph 105½-1-0
 "   Saml. 110-1-0
Murphey Gabriel 890-1-0
 "   John 0-1-0
Morton Meshack 320-1-0
McGillvery Daniel 0-1-0
McIntosh Charles 0-1-0
 "   William 50-1-0
McReynolds Joseph 0-1-0
McMin John 200-1-0
McMinamy Alex. 710-1-0
 "   William 200-1-0
McIntosh Thomas 290-1-0
Martin Richard 440-1-0
McReynolds Rowland 379-1-1
McCluskey Edwd. 400-1-0
McCoy Neal 154-1-1
McMullen Henry 470-1-1
 "   John 185-1-0
Melton Daniel 500-1-0
 "   Benjamin 100-1-0
McIntosh Alex. 200-1-0
McReynolds Saml. 0-1-0
Nowell James 200-1-0
 "   Ephraim 0-1-0
Night John 100-1-0
Nowell Edward 640-1-0
Pleasant Bluford 600-1-0
Pearce Moses 218-1-0

Pendergrass Luke 1970-1-0
Pleasant John 100-1-0
Poe Jonathan 250-1-0
Parks Solomon 1030-1-0
Porter Christopher 250-1-0
Payne John 200-1-1
 "   Josiah 0-1-0
Phelps Thomas 1084-1-0
Parks Robert Esq. 1902-1-0
Riddell James 0-1-0
Rice John 400-1-0
Robinson Thomas 0-1-0
Ray James 250-1-1
Richmond John Jun. 650-1-2
Robinson John 580-1-0
Richmond William 1150-1-1
Rice Jonathon 0-1-0
 "   James Esq. 474-1-0
 "   Thomas 255-1-0
Richmond John Sen. 500-1-0
Roan Thomas 35-1-0
Richmond Mathew 248-1-0
 "   James 100-1-0
Shy John 350-1-0
Smith Moses 130-1-0
Scott John 100-1-0
Sargent James 55-1-2
Shaw Ralph 150-1-0
Sanders William Capt. 1280-1-4
Sargent Thomas 127-1-0
Tanon Thomas 0-1-0
Taylor Charles 424-1-1
Turner Henry Sen. 300-1-3
 "   Henry Jun. 0-1-0
 "   James 200-1-0
Vanhook Aaron 300-1-0
Wilie Thomas 632-1-0
 "   Alex. 417-1-0
Warson Henry 250-1-1
Wisdom Martha 150-1-0
 "   Larkin 0-1-0
Wallace John Sen. 200-1-0
Yancey Bartlett 883-1-6
Yates Thomas 150-1-0

Taken by Robert Parks Esq.

St. David's District

Anglin William 410 CL 1-0
Adcock Edmund 150 Ho 1-0
Anderson Jno 450 Stony Cr. 1-0
Brown William(Cooper) 500 Stony 1-0
 "   John(son of cooper)0-1-0
 "   Leonard 616 CL 1-0
Barton Lewis 325 CL 1-0
 "   James 75 CL 1-0
Barker George 0-1-0
Brown William 250 Jordan Cr 1-0

Abbr. Ho Hogan's Cr.; CL Country
  Line; Hors Horsley Cr.

Brothers John 450 Jordan 1-0
Burton David 300 Stony 1-0
Brooks Charles 0-1-0
Barker David 0-1-0
Berry John 210 Stony 1-0
Brown John 1650 CL 1-9
 "   Thomas 259 CL 1-1
Brownin William 75 CL 1-0

139

1784 tax list cont. St. David's Dist.

Brownin John 0-1-0
Blackwell Robert 940 Moons 1-3
Barker Israel 305 CL 1-1
Burton Samuel 300 Stony 1-0
" Cuthbert 180 Stony 1-0
Brooks Thomas 810 Moons 1-2
Barker George Sen. 477 CL 1-7
" John 0-1-0
Cobb Noah 301 Moons 1-0
" Henry 504 Moons 1-3
" John 100 Moons 1-0
Cantrel Joseph 340 Stony 1-4
Davise Henry 80 Jordan 1-0
" Henry Sen. 200 Jordan 1-0
Dill John Sen. 222 Hors 1-0
" Annals 100 Hors 1-0
" John 150 Moons 1-0
" John (HT) 286 Moons 1-0
" Richard 100 Hors 1-0
Dickens James 0-1-0
Dennis John 100 CL 1-0
" Ignatius 0-1-0
Davis Baswell 250 Jordan 1-0
" Jonathan 100 Jordan 1-0
" Nicholas 0-1-0
Estis Richard 500 CL 1-0
Eak William 400 CL 1-0
Foot George Jun. 131 Hors 1-1
" George Sen. 413 Hors 1-6
Gwyn William 50 Moons 1-0
" Daniel 81 Moons 1-1
Graves John 1690 CL 1-13
Holderness William 0-1-0
Hughes James 300 Moons 1-0
Hayes John 100 CL 1-0
Haddock Andw. 200 CL 1-0
Herbin William 77 Moons 1-0
Harding Presly 0-1-0
" John 800 Moons 1-0
Herbin John 120 Ho 1-0
Hensly Maxfield 214 Stony 1-1
Hughes Charles 288 Stony 1-0
" James 250 Stony 1-0
" David 200 Stony 1-0
Hagard Edmond 640 CL 1-0
" David 0-1-0
" William 0-1-0
Hensly John 113 Stony ·1
Hughes Rowland 1390 Stony 1-2
Harris Tyra 662 Stony 1-14
Hart David 2583 CL 1-7
Jones James 620 CL 1-2
Johnston James 202 Moons 1-0
" Lanslotte 200 CL 1-4
Lovins Arthur 200 Stony 1-0
Kerr Alexander 928 CL 1-6
Lawson John 0-1-0
Lackey John 400 Stony 1-0

Lay John 300 CL 1-0
Martin George 0-1-0
Mitchell George 120 CL 1-0
Mallory John 0-1-0
" William 0-1-0
McCulley John 200 Stony 1-0
Murry Jonathan 0-1-0
Murphey John 0-1-0
Moore Samuel 0-1-2
Mitchell William 531 CL 1-0
Murry James 0-1-0
McClusky Edward 400 Stony 1-0
Mahon William 100 Stony 1-0
Mallory John Sen. 200 Stony 1-2
Nunn Elijah 0-1-0
Nance Thomas 30 Hors 1-0
" Sherwood 0-1-0
Oldham Richard Sen. 0-1-0
" Richard 600 Stony 1-0
" John 640 Stony 1-1
Orr James 220 Moons 1-0
Oldham George(Major) 1-7 Stony 1-0
" Jesse 670 Stony 1-2
" Richd.(of Jesse) 0-1-0
" Moses 890 Stony 1-1
" James 250 Stony 1-0
Ponder Morgan 0-1-0
Poston Jerre 350 CL 1-0
Pinex John 100 Stony 1-0
Payne Greenwood 200 CL 1-1
Paine John 300 CL 1-0
" John 0-1-0
Pike Lewis 150 Moons 1-0
Rice William 0-1-2
Reed Nathaniel 500 Stony 1-0
Rice Thomas (CB) 350 CL 1-3
" H. William 55 CL 1-0
" Nathan 300 CL 1-0
" John Sen. 640 CL 1-3
" John (of Jno Rice) 0-1-0
" Thomas Esq. 820 CL 1-4
" Zeri 0-1-0
" Jephthah 0-1-1
" Nathaniel 0-1-0
" Hezekiah 816 Moons 1-2
Rainey Mary 200 CL 0-0
Simpson Richard 2708 Stony 1-7
Smith Richard 282 Moons 1-0
Smith Nicholas (Mol) 0-1-0
Swift William 809 Stony 1-6
" John 320 Moons 0-0
" Anthony 0-1-0
Scott James 188 Ho 1-0
Spencer John 400 Stony 1-0
" Benjamin 482 CL 1-0
" Elizabeth 444 Stony 0-0
Swift Thomas 600 Moons 1-3
Sims George 1030 CL 1-1
Sawyers William 300 CL 1-0

1784 tax list - St. David's Dist. cont. - St. Lawrence Dist.

Sawyers John 300 CL 1-0
Scott John 350 Moons 1-0
Triplett John 200 Hors 1-0
Taylor James 100 CL 0-0
Tate Waddy 320 CL 1-2
Tubb William 0-1-0
Triplett Nimrod 110 Hors 1-0
Walker Samuel 400 Moons 1-0
"   James 0-1-0
Warson William 0-1-0
Williamson Stephen 3740 CL 1-11
Williams John Att. 1500 CL 1-6

Taken by William Swift Esq.

Williamson Jerre 270 Hors 1-0
White Timothy 50 Hors 1-0
Wright William 100 CL 1-0
Williamson Nathan 375 CL 1-2
"   Hall 0-1-0
Williams Henry 2016 Stony 1-13
"   Henry 1500 Western waters
Windsor John 243 CL 1-1
Willis Henry 66 CL 1-0
Whitlock Robert 100 CL 1-0
Walker Daniel 0-1-0

St. Lawrence District

Abbr: Stor Story's Cr.; Sarg Sargent's Cr.; Richl Richland Cr.

Atkinson John Esq. 2860 Richl. &
  Stor; 1880 Sugartree Cr.,
  85 Adams Cr; 303 Cobb Cr.
  400 Rutl.; 450 Haw R.
  320 Stor Cr.
  3 white polls,7black polls
Atkinson Roger 250 Hico
             649 Stor Cr.
Baswell Robert 0-2-0
Black John 503 Hico 1-0
Barnett Hugh Jun.250-Adams Cr.1-0
"   Thomas (of Hugh) 118-1-3
"   William Sen. 150-1-0
Barnett Thomas 500 Stor 1-0
Bull Jacob 210 Stor 1-0
Barnett Thomas Jun.0-1-0
Buckley Edward 33-1-0
Black George 269 Hico 1-1
"   Thom. 272 Sarg 1-1
"   Henry 305 Cobb Cr 1-1
Bradsher Moses 150 Hico 1-0
"   John 300 Hico 1-0
Barnett Hugh Sen.381 Adams 1-2
"   William Jun. 0-1-0
Chambers Josias 280-1-0
"   John 375 Gents Cr.1-0
Carver William 940 Stor 1-0
Clay Edward 740 Richl Cr. 1-5
Carroll George 0-1-0
Chambers William 100 Henly's 1-1
Campbell Arch. 668 Hico 1-3
Chambers William 354 Stor 1-2
Clift John 300 Stor 1-1
Campbell John 918 Cobb Cr,CL 1-7
Camp Benjamin 0-1-0
Carmichal Duncan 100 Hico 1-0
Childers Abram 200 -1-0
Carver Thomas 277-1-0
Chambers James 0-1-0

Duest Hezekiah 600-1-0
Dinwoody John 400-1-0
Duncan Jesse 0-1-0
Duty William 156-1-0
Deboe Benjamin 250 Hico 1-0
Duncan Mary 811 Hico 0-2
Deboe Frederick 360 Cane Cr 1-1
Douglas Thomas 227 Cobb Cr
"   '   365 Richm.Dist 1-2
" for John Armstrong 227½-0-0
Douglass Benjamin 355 Hico & Cane
                          1-1
Doyl Edwd. 249 -1-0
Darby George 350-2-0
Dobbin & Campbell 261
Dollarhide Ezekiel 0-1-0
Edington William 0-1-0
Elliott George 209 Wynn's Cr 2-0
Ellmon Travis 300 Wynns 2-0
Fuller John Jun. 200-1-0
"   William Jun. 238-1-0
Fulcher Henry 0-1-0
Foley Mason 0-1-3
Fuller Peter 0-1-0
"   James 250-1-0
"   William 126-1-0
Fletcher James 375Cane Cr.1-0
"   James Jun. 0-1-0
Fuller Henry Sen. 365-1-0
"   George 0-1-0
"   Henry Jun. 0-1-0
"   John 400 Stor 1-0
"   Peter Jun. 102-1-0
Ferrol Enock 0-1-0
Goff Thomas 0-1-0
Gold Joseph 448 Hico 1-0
Going Gutrich 175 Cane 1-0
Golson Joseph 338 Cane 1-3
Gregory James 666661-0

141

1784 tax list - St. Lawrence Dist. cont.

Haralson Jane 536 -0-4
Hatcher Benj. 465-1-1
Howard Henry 657 Hico 1-12
Harris John 0-1-0
Howard Hiram 0-1-0
Haralson Elihah 360-1-0
Hinton Thomas 200-1-0
Howard Francis 0-1-1
Harding William 500-1-2
Hemphill Hugh 520-1-0
Hamblett James 1000 Cane 1-5
Haralson Herndon 1000-1-0
Henly James D. 304-1-0
" Edwd. 200-1-0
" Darby 0-1-0
Johnston George 169-1-0
" Benj. 300 Sarg 1-0
" William 160 Cobb 1-1
Jesse John 631 Hico 1-0
& Moravian land
Johnston William 0-1-0
" John 0-1-0
(not given in)
Long Benjamin Jun 220-1-0
" Benjamin Sen.1095 Stor 2-0
Love Rachel 408 Gents 0-0
Long Ambrose 514 Jents Cr.1-0
Lewis Edmund 300 Hico 1-0
Long James 0-2-0
Lea James 198 Hico 1-1
" William 126 Hico 1-0
" Richard 150 Hico 1-0
" John 126 Hico 2-0
" George 268 Cobb Cr. 1-4
" Barnett 112 Cobb Cr 1-0
" John - Cobb Cr.1-0
" Edmd. 228 Hico 1-0
" Zachariah 290 Hico 1-1
" Owen 180 Hico 1-1
" Ambrose 0 Hico 1-0
" Carter 242 Hico 1-2
" Elliot 53 Hico 2-1
" William(Capt.) 756 Hico 1-4
Mitchell John 87 Hico 1-0
McKnight Andrew 0-1-0
McDowell Benjamin 282 Hico 1-0
McFarland Danl. 389 Hico 1-2
McGhee Mumford 666 Hico 1-7
Monroe John 0-1-0
Murphey Alex. 163½ Cane 1-0
McKnight James0-1-0
Moore Robert 690 Hico 1-4
Mitchell Arthur 550 Cobb 1-0
McFarland John 272 Cobb 1-1
McDaniel Elizabeth 320 Cane 0-1
McKeen Agness 960 Hico & Kil-
          gore Branch 0-0
Moore Joseph 1820 Hico 0-0

Miles Thomas 385 Hico 2-2
McNeil John 400 Hico 1-1
" Ann 450 Hico 0-2
Moore John Esq. 390 Hico 1-7
Newton Benjamin 408 Hico 1-2
Nash Edward 100 Hico 1-0
Newton Reubin 500 Hico 1-0
Neely Thomas 306½ Hico 1-3
Newton John 0-1-0
Nash Thos.Jun. 200-1-0
Oliver Douglas 100-1-0
Paschell William 0-1-0
Pendergras Richd. 217 Hico 1-0
Pride Woolsey 383 Cane 1-1
Potter Ephraim 0-1-0
Robinson James,Capt. 463 Cain Cr.&
          Guilford Co. 1-0
Rogers John Jun. 0-1-0
Robinson Joseph 0-1-0
Rainey John 60-1-0
" Elizabeth 300 Cane 0-1
Roberts James 0-1-0
Roberts Edward 120-1-1
Robinson Thomas by Geo. Black 393
          Sarg Cr.
Sargent William 425 1-0
Stewart James 640 Ghents Cr.1-1
" Stephen 300 " 1-0
Skeene Peter 0-1-0
Stuart Agness 200 Hico 0-0
Southard Robert 0-1-0
" William 400-1-0
Seymore Robert 282 Hico 1-0
South Benjamin 177 S.Hico 1-1
Stone William 375-2-5
Sargent Daniel 300 Kilgore Br.1-0
" Stephen 500-2-0
Stokes Silvanus 0-1-0
Stewart William 950 Hico 1-0
Skeen Johnthan (not given in)
Tricky Giles 220-1-0
Tunks Thomas 200-1-1
Turner Joseph 218 Hico 2-2
Vermillion William 100-2-0
Vanhook Thos. 210-1-0
" Loyd 1000 Hico 1-0
" Lawr. 1370 (his polls given
          in Washington Co. Vrg.)
Warson James 0-1-0
Warren John Jun. 50-1-1
Womack Abram 305 Stor 1-4
Walter Paul 400 ----
Williams Tobias0-1-0
Waller John 0-1-0
Williams William 163½ Cane 1-0
Wright Clayborn 140-1-0
Watson Benjamin 0-1-0
Warren John 750 Wynn & Hico 1-0

142

1784 tax list - St. Lawrence Dist. cont. - St. Luke's Dist.

Wright John 182 1-1   Warren Hedgman 285 Hico 1-0
  "   Richard 186 1-0   Wall Byrd 525 Hico 1-4
Warren John (Virg.) 363   Fulcher Wm. Sen. 238 Hico 1-0
  "   Goodloe 1409 Cane 1-0   Patterson David 200 Stor 1-0
       Taken by John Moore Esq.

St. Luke's District

Abbr: Dbl Double Cr.; Richl Richland Cr.; Flat R(iver)

Alston William 2436 Flat R. 1-7   Gately Thomas 0-1-0
Atkinson John 100 Flat 1-0   "   Joseph 50 Flat 1-0
Allin Drury 640 Flat 1-2   "   William 100 Flat 1-0
Arnold Ambrose 0-1-0   Howell Francis 250 Hico 1-0
Bryant James 150 Flat 1-1   Hall John 150 Hico 1-0
  "   William 350 Flat 1-0   Hargiss Richard 480 Flat 1-0
Blake John 0-1-0   Hall Phillip 400 Dbl 1-0
Badgett Thomas 500 Dbl 1-0   Holeman Richard 1200 Flat 1-4
Brown William 206 S.Hico 1-1   Hargiss Thomas 700 Flat 1-0
Bailey William 340 S.Hico 1-4   "   Abram Jun.300 Flat 1-0
Broadaway John 0-1-0   "   Abram Sen. 200 Flat 1-0
Brown Abrahm. 570 Flat 1-3   "   William 340 Flat 1-0
Blackhard Chas. 194 Flat 1-0   " Shadrack 685 Flat 1-0
Burch Pemberton 484 Flat 1-0   2100 Black River 1-0
Breekeen William 300 Dbl 1-0   Jones Francis 940 Hico 0-4
Cadall Andrew 320 Dbl 1-0   "   Drury 300 Hico 1-1
Clark James 16- Flat 1-0   Jacobs Richard 0-1-0
Cate Thomas 0-1-1   "   Benjamin 0-1-0
Crumpton James 0-1-0   Kelly Edmond 384 Hico 1-0
Combs Thomas 0-1-0   Lockhart William 400 Flat 1-0
Christanbery Nicholas 307 Dbl   Lister Lyles 0-1-0
       1-0   Lyon Peter 747 Flat 2-4
Cooper John 100 Dbl 1-1   Lowther William 200 Hico 1-0
Christanbery Mary 399½ Hico 0   Mitchell David Jun. 300 Hico 1-0
Cate Joshua 300 Flat 1-1   "   David 300 Hico 1-2
Douglas John 260 Hico 1-1   McKissick John 320 Hico 2-2
Dollar Ambrose 0-1-0   McMurry John 472 Hico 1-2
Dollarhide Cornelius 0-1-0   McKissick Thomas 320 Hico 1-1
Dowell John 17½ Dbl 1-0   Melone Nathaniel 256 Hico 1-3
  "   James 0-1-0   "   Daniel 656 Hico 1-2
Ferrall John 0-1-0   McCarver James 350 Lincoln Co.
Farrar Joseph 200 Flat 1-1   "   350 Hico 2-0
  "   John 200 Flat 4-1   McAlister John 200 Hico 1-0
Fisher Risdom 200 Flat 1-0   Moore Abram 200 Flat 3-2
Foshee Charles 100 Dbl 1-0   McAlister George 0-1-0
Farquhar James 450 Flat 2-1   Moore Demsey 1950 Flat 1-3
Farrar Peter 346 Flat 2-4   McMurry Samuel 722 Hico 1-2
  "   William 0-1-2   Messer James 640 Flat 1-0
Farmer Thomas 212 Flat 1-0   McReynolds Robt. 186 Flat 1-0
Franklin Edmd 0-1-0   McNeill Henry 1170 Flat 1-4
Gillson William 200 Flat 1-0   McReynolds Joseph 0-1-0
Guthrie John 0-1-0   Oldridge Joseph 200 Flat 3-0
Gately Isham 0-1-0   Pyrant Charles 245 Flat 1-0
Glenn William 517 Flat 1-1   Pope Joel 560 Arons Cr 1-1
Graves Thomas 181 Hico 1-0   137 Flat R.
Goins Edward 100 Hico 1-0   Pyrant William Jun. 0-1-0
Gillson David 600 Flat R. &   Palmer Joseph 400 Montgomery Co.
  Little R. in Orange 1-0   307 Hyco 1-0

143

1784 tax list St. Luke's Dist. cont. - Nash Dist.

Palmer Thos. Jun. 2116 Mont-
   gomery Co. & Flat R. 1-0
Pogue Joseph 250 Flat 1-0
Price John 200 Hyco 1-0
Pogue John 0-1-0
Pyrant William Sen. 150 Flat
   1-0
Pulliam James 380 Dbl 1-0
Palmer Thos Sen 640 Dbl 1-0
Rankin William 460 Flat 1-4
Rainey John 400 Hyco 2-0
Robertson David 680 Flat 1-0
   "   Charles 200 Flat 1-0
Ragsdale Thomas 0-1-0
Rankin James 250 Richl 1-0
Rose Alexr 993 Richl 1-3
Simmons John 0-1-0
Surratt Joseph 506 Hyco 1-0
Smith James 876 Flat 1-0
   "   Robert 200 Flat 1-0
Surratt John 0-1-0

Stanfield Robert 350 Hyco 1-0
Sikes John 260 Hyco 1-0
Trimm Charles 240 Hyco 1-0
Terrill John 400 Hyco 1-2
Vanhook David 1196 Hyco & near
   the Ct House 1-2
Webb Robert
   "   Johnston
Winningham Thomas 200 Hyco 1-0
Williamson Wm.P. 150 Hyco 1-0
   "   Thomas 20 Hyco 1-0
Wood Saml. 516 Hyco 1-0
Willson John 400 Flat 2-1
Williamson Henry 0-1-0
Walton Jesse 0-1-0
Womack John 890 Flat; 420 Dbl.Cr.
   200 Hyco; 350 Mayo 1-6
Waite William 5577 & 3/4 1-0

Taken by John Womack Esq.

Nash District

Abbr: Dnd Donaldson's Cr., Blw Bluwing or Blewing or Bluewing Cr.;
   Dwt Dishwater Cr.; Ctl Castle Cr.

Andrew Eleazer 400 Dnd 1-0
Adams John 571 Blw 1-2
Archdeacon James 0-1-0
Allen Drury 940 Mayo Cr.2-6
Archdeacon Edmund 100 Mayo 1-0
Allen Charles 904 Adams Cr. 1-2
   "   David 0-1-4
Bostick Charles 308 Ctl Cr.1-1
Buckhannon Andw. 200 Ctl 1-0
Barnett David 250 Mayo 1-0
Brooks Artha 450 Bowls Br. 2-1
Bright Simon 320 Dnd Cr. 1-0
   "   Robert 300 Dnd 1-0
Brooks John 415 Bols Br 1-0
Bozwell James 385 Blw Cr. 1-0
Breedlove Charles 200 Blw 1-0
Barnett John 356 Adams Cr.1-0
Bailey Yancey 400 Dwt,Adams1-2
Baird John 7670 Nayo 2-21
Barnett Sarah 366 Adams Cr. 0-1
Brooks Tabitha 0-1-0
Barnett Agness 50 Mayo 0-0
Coffee Joshua 400 Ctl Cr. 1-6
Coleman Richard 300 Mayo 1-2
Clayton John Sen. 700 Mayo 1-0
   "   John Jun. 0-1-0
Caraway Thomas 0-1-0
Clayton Thomas 565 Mayo 2-2

Cunningham Nathan 525 Mill Cr. 1-0
Canady John 0-1-0
Dickens Josias 440 Adams Cr. 1-1
Donaldson Robert 250 Rambo Br.1-0
   "   Hannah 157 Mayo 1-2
Dickson John 0-1-0
Demney Zachariah 200 Adams Cr.1-0
Dickson Jacob 249 Blw 1-0
Day John 454 Tarr R. 1-0
Davey Robert 250 Mayo 1-2
   "   William 500 Mayo 1-0
   "   Gabriel 1000 Mayo 1-4
   "   "   for Samuel Bumpass
   orphans 700 Tarr R.
   "   for Edwd Bumpass orphans 196
   Tar River
Dixon Michael 1100 Adams Cr
Glaze Samuel 242 Hyco 1-2
Glass Josiah 0-1-0
Gentry Shadrack 0-1-0
Guttery Garrott 250 Adams 2-0
Gunn Mary 600 Mill Cr 0-2
Gentry Allen 0-1-3
Gunn Thomas 200 Mill Cr 1-0
Gwinn John 378 Mill Cr 1-4
Horley Henry 447 Ctl 1-0
Harrison Samuel 250 Mayo 1-2
Halliburton Charles 100 Blw 1-0

144

1784 tax list - Nash Dist. - St. James Dist.

Halliburton John 250 Blw 1-0
Hudgins William 100 Adams 1-0
Huston William 842 Adams 1-0
Harriss Samuel 300 Mayo 1-0
Huston James 280 Adams 1-0
Haralson Jonathan 105 Admas 1-0
Howard Francis 500 Adams 1-2
Hallfburton Wm. 730 Admas 2-1
Hudgins Ambrose 300 Adams 1-0
Holloway John 1530 Mayo 1-1
Halliburton David 300 Blw 1-0
Haralson Paul Jun. 0-1-0
"   Paul Sen.1165 Adams 1-1
Harrison Vincent 250 Mayo 1-0
Hague James 200 Ctl 1-0
Hooper Obediah 0-1-0
Howell Joseph 0-1-3
Hix David 0-1-0
Johnson Joseph 0-1-0
Jones Stephen 381 Blw 1-0
Jones Richard 350 Dnd 1-1
James John (Hyco) 300 Bould Br.1-0
"   John(Mayo)200 Mill Cr 1-0
Jones James 1660 Blw 1-4
Layton John 200 Adams 1-0
"   James 100 Adams 1-0
Lewis Fielding 132 Ctl 1-1
Lawson John 532 Mayo 1-3
Lord Lord 351 Bould Br.1-0
Mitchel John 388 Adams 1-9
McDaniel William 193 Mayo 2-0
Mann John 802 Adams 1-0
Morries John 0-1-0
Moore Seth 783 Adams 1-4
McFarland James 0-1-1
"   Margaret 794 Ctl 0-3

Mann Elizabeth 75 Adams 0-0
Pryor J. Henry 575 Hyco 1-4
Patterson Gideon 485 Hyco 1-5
Pryor Hadon 200 Mill Cr.1-2
Pool William Petty 150 Mill 1-0
Pittman Joseph 100 Arons Cr. 1-0
Pettiford George 300 Mill 1-0
Ragon Jesse 100 Blw 1-0
Ragon Owen 150 Blw 1-0
"   Nathan 150 Mayo 1-0
"   John 0-1-0
Ramsey Daniel 0-1-0
Self Abraham 300 Buck Mt. 1-0
Street Moses 681 Mayo 1-1
Scoggin Nathan 250 Mill 1-0
Sanders Richd 0-2-0
Tate Nathan 0-1-2
Vass Phillip 610 Blw 1-6
"   Thomas 100 Blw 1-1
Vanhook Isaac 122 Mayo 1-1
Wilson John 250 Adams 1-1
Wray Robert 0-1-0
Wilkerson John 250 Dnd 1-0
Wilson James 400 Mayo 1-1
Walton James 0-1-0
Walker Jesse 0-1-0
"   Moses 320 Ctl 2-3
Winstead Samuel 900 Mayo 2-2
"   Ailsey 50 Mayo 0-1
"   Cotance 0-2-0
Wheeler Samuel 100 Buck Mt.1-1
Williams John 0-1-0
Womack David 300 Ctl 2-6
Yarbrough Jno 850 Mayo 1-2
"   Saml. 238 Mayo 1-2

Taken by Gabl. Davey Esq.

St. James District

Abbr: Richl Richland Cr.

Anderson George 100 Cubb Cr. 1-0
"   James 100-1-0
Bumpass John 209 Deep Cr.1-0
Baughn Zachariah 400 Cubb Cr.1-0
(name possibly Vaughn)
Bowls John 140 Cubb 3
Cochran James 60 Cub.
Commins John 342 Flat River 1-1
Cruze Hardy 881 Deep Cr. 1-0
Cochran John 262 Flat 1-0
Cates Robert 1000 Flat 1-2
Cozart John 100 Napper Reeds 1-0
"   Peter 100 "   1-0
Cash John 548 Cubb 1-0
Crumer Absalom 0-1-0
Clayton Daniel 640-1-0
Clixby John 600 Deep Cr.1-0
Day Francis 250 Tarr R. 2-0

Daniel Matthew 200 Richl 1-0
Davis Robert 150 Tarr
Duncan H. Abraham 200 Tarr 1-0
Dickens Robert 16077 In Caswell
Co. on sundry waters 1-10
Farmer Casandra 402 Flat
Fowler William 0-1-0
Floyd James 0-1-0
Farmer Daniel 178 Flat 1-0
Glen William 150 Deep 1-0
"   Beverly 257 Deep 1-4
Griffin Andrew 1280 Deep 1-0
Goss Thomas 250 Deep 1-0
Green Lucy 100 Little Cr.
Gill Robert 0-0-2
Hester Robert 0-1-2
Hubbard Joseph 151 Richl. 1-0

145

1784 tax list - St. James Dist.

Hust Smith John 2131 Flat 1-3
  (Smithhurst?)
Hicks John 100 Mud Br. 1-0
  "   Daniel 0-1-0
Harrison Benjamin 0-1-1
Harris Goldman 640 Orange Co.
  1-0
Jones Richard 193 Tarr 2-3
Jay James 220 Flat 1-0
Jeffreys Osborne 3236 Flat 1-1
  "   Paul 1256 Flat 2-9
Jones Nicholas 300   ?Cr. 1-0
Johnston Joshua 340 Flat 1-0
Kenady James 267 Cubb Cr. 1-0
Ledbetter Daniel 362 Deep Cr. 1-0
  "   Henry 136 Deep 1-1
  "   Joel 150 Deep 1-0
Mason Thomas 133 Cubb 1-0
Moore Stephen 2285 Flat R. & Deep
  Cr. 2-3
Minshew Richard 200 Flat 1-0
Mooney Jacob 0-1-0
Meddows Daniel 100 Little Cr. 1-0
Mederias Abraham 292 Cubb 1-0
Moore Moses 500 Little 1-0
  "   Alexander 0-1-0
  "   Arthur 2104 sundry waters
  1-0
Neeley Samuel 100 Richl 1-0
Nichols Willis 937 Flat 1-0
Oakley Walter 200 Cubb 1-0
  "   John 300 Cubb 1-0

Pryor Ann 400 Flat 0-2
Payne John Esq. 4618 Deep Cr.&
  Flat R. 1-13
Parker Aaron 50 Flat 1-0
Payne William 1424 Mill Cr. 1-1
Pratt William 250 Tarr 1-2
Pryor Matthew 200 Flat 1-0
Parker Richard 815 Tarr 3-1
Powell Nehemiah 0-1-0
Paine Robert 1899 Richl.& Hico
  1-7
Roberts James 0-1-0
  "   John 0-1-0
  "   David 450 Cubb 1-0
Rutherford William 360 Flat 1-1
Reeves George 0-1-0
Rimmer George 0-1-0
Satterfield John 200 Richl 1-1
  "   Bedwell 175 Deep Cr.1-0
Scoggin Francis 50 Richl 1-0
Swainey John Sen. 266 Deep 1-0
Smith Mercer Conrad 289 Flat 1-0
  (name may be Messersmith)
Swainey John Jun. 100 Deep 1-0
  "   James 0-1-0
Tapp William 1397 Tarr 1-3
Tinsley Abraham 106 Flatt 1-0
Thomas John 0-1-0
Traylor Joseph 67 Deep 2-0
Webb David 230 Tarr 1-0
Williams Bennett 231 Deep 1-0
Wren Benjamin 0-1-0 .
White William Esq. 350 Spring &
  Tapley Cr. 1-5
Yarbrough William 294 Tar 1-3

Taken by William White Esq.

146

CASWELL COUNTY GUARDIANS' ACCOUNTS
Book CR 020.510.1 at the State Archives

Guardian	Orphan

Page

1794

1	Andrew Harrison	Lucy Burton
1	Joseph Dameron	Orphans of Robert Burton decd.
3	Spillby Coleman	"
4	Montford McGehee	Miss Lucy Moore
	"	William Moore
5	"	Patrick Moore
5	Joshua Carney	Thomas, Betsy, John Miles, orphans of Alexr Miles
7	John Campbell	Mary Anderson Moore

1795

7	Clifton Allen	Orphans of Saml. Morris - inc. expenses for sending to Va. for record of will
8	Joseph Dameron	Jane, Sally, Polly, Noel, Andrew Burton
9	Andrew Harrison	Lucy Burton
10	Susannah Leath	Freeman Leath, orphan of Freeman Leath
10	John Campbell	Mary Anderson Moore

1796

11	Thomas Taylor	Elizabeth and James Barker of James Barker decd.
13	Mumford McGehee	Patrick, William, Lucy Moore
15	Robert Kimbrough	Joseph Williams orphan of Henry Williams

1797

19	Elizabeth Enochs widow	Orphans of Andrew Enochs
20	Mason Leath	James, Coleman, Isaac, Betsy Leath, orphans of Charles Leath
22	William H. Rice	Christopher Williams Brooks
22	Robert Mitchell	Joseph and Mary Mains, orphans of Matthew Mains

1799

24	Azariah Graves	Miss Lucy Moore

1801

32	Walter Ingram	Clary Ingram
32	Richd. Hornbuckle	Aron Smith, orphan of Peter Smith

1802

34	Griffin Gunn	Allen Gunn
35	James Burton	Miss Priscilla Gunn

1803

38	Sterling Gunn	Miss Barbery Walker
40	Thomas Marain	Andy, John, Obedience, Gibson, Mary Hughes, orphans of John Hughs

1804

46	Mary Boyd	Stephen W. Boyd
46	James Burton	Wife of John Payne
48	Jacob Quine	Pickney and Anderson Gunn

Guardians' Accounts cont.

Page	Guardian	Orphan
	1805	
50	Griffin Gunn	Allen Gunn
54	John Graves	Lewis Graves orphan of Thomas Graves
56	James Graves	Major Graves " " "
58	Azariah Graves	Azariah Graves " " "
62	George Hornbuckle	Orphans of John Hughes
65	Sarah Smith	Sarah, Nancy, Elizabeth Smith, orphans of James Smith
65	Richard Hornbuckle	Uzziah Tait
67-69	"	Jane M. Tracy, Endoxey Tait, Zenas Tait, orphans of Zacheus Tait
70	Sarah Smith, Mother	George Smith, orphan of James Smith
	1806	
74	William Lyon	Edmund Lyon (legacy from Robert Lyon decd.)
78	William Lyon	Elizabeth Lyon
83	Jesse Carter	Wilson W. Elam, Nancy Elam
84	John Warrick	John Roan
84	Levi Blackwell	Aron Smith
85	Solomon Graves	Isbell Graves (receipt signed by William Graves)
85	Thomas Wiley	Wiley Langley (money received from Mary Langley adm. of Thomas Langley)
86	Mary Kerr	Zephaniah Tait Kerr
86	Richard Hornbuckle	Zephaniah Tait
87	Thomas Slade	Patsey Lay, orphan of Peter Lay
88	James & Bartlett Yancey	James Yancey Jun., Tryon Yancey, Priscilla Yancey, Nancy Yancey, orphans of Thomas Yancey (Paid tuition 1804 for Tryon Yancey at Caswell Academy, in 1805 pd. Azariah Graves for tuition.) (Priscilla Yancey pd. John Zachary for tuition.)
90	Catharine Somers	Nancy and Sally Somers
91	William Sawyer	Nancy, William, Susannah Mallory, orphans of James Mallory
92	Elizabeth Yancey	Attelia Yancey, orphan of Thomas Yancey
93	Joseph Collier in right of his wife Isbell	Sally, John, Patsy, Tabitha Kimbrough, orphans of John Kimbro Jun.
94	John Woods in right of his wife	Parthenia Farley
95	John Windsor(in Rockingham co.)	Zedikiah Tate
97	Christopher Dameron	Eliza Ingram Dameron, Patsy Dameron, orphans of John Dameron
98	Jno. Windsor	Jesse Tate
99	Daniel Darby	Thomas Vanhook
100	Henry Atkinson	John Ingram Jun.
101	William Corder of Clarke Co. KY	George, Joseph, Nancey, Amea Morris, orphans of Samuel Morris

Guardians' Accounts cont.

Page	Guardian	Orphan
	1807	
108	Andrew Harrison	Jane Harrison orphan of Thomas Harrison
108	Jesse Carter	Robert L. Harrison
109	Lewis Sheppard	Sally P., Polly, and Elizabeth M. Nicholson orphans of Michael Nicholson
112-3	Sarah Smith	Nancy, Sary, Elizabeth, and Robert Smith orphans of James Smith
115	Wilie Yancey	Edmond B. Rice, Nathaniel L.Rice, James Rice, orphans of Nathl. Rice
118	William Lyon	Elizabeth and Edmund Lyon
119	Wm. Gordon	Nancy, James, David, Rebeccah, and Bidsey Rudd, orphans of Hezekiah Rudd
119	Nathaniel Gooch	John Gooch son
121	Richard Hornbuckle	Jane M. Tracy, Zenas and Eudoxy Tate
124	William Willson	Jeremiah and Henry Willson, orphans of Thomas Willson
125	John Yancey	David, Elizabeth, and Sarah Enoch, orphans of Andrew Enochs
126	William Chilton	Estate of Lemuel Chilton
	1808	
132	Joseph Bracken	Patsey and Robert Dixon heirs of Robert Dixon (land in TN)
133	Solomon Debow	Nathaniel Lacy Rice
134	Thomas Windsor	Beazey, Gilson, Polly, Andrew, and John Huse (from estate of John Huse) Also spelled Hughes
136	Thomas Windsor	Jonas Tate
139	James Yancey	Priscilla, Nancy, Artelia Yancey
143	Alexander Wiley on behalf of his wife Polly	Zephaniah Tait Kerr
144	Nathaniel Gooch	John Gooch
	1809	
163	Alex Murphey & Solomon Graves	7 orphans of John Vaughan: Tabitha, Sally, Jerusha, Sterling. Elizabeth, Thomas, and John Vaughan
165	Polly Poteat	Nancy, John, and Miles Poteat (of William Poteat decd.)
168	Thomas Slade	Patsey Yearley (formerly Patsey Lay) Wife of Charles Yearley (or Yearby)
169	William Gold	Orphans of John Dameron
169	John Yancey	Polly Loony wife of Elisha Loony and daughter of Andrew Enochs
170	John Yancey	Samuel Coplinger gives receipt for legacy due his wife as heir of Andrew Enochs
	1810	
184	John Harrison	William P. Martin

Guardian's accounts cont.

Page	Guardians	Orphan
	1810 cont.	
190	Griffin Gunn	Robert L. Harrison
192	Mary Melton	James, David E., Nancy, Martha Melton (from estate of James Melton)
194	Jennett McAden	Cynthia A. Hall; James, Catharine, Margaret McAden, orphans of William McAden
194	Peggy Grayham	Heirs of Berreman Grayham
200	John Woods	Parthenia Farley, orphan of George Farley
201	Turner Patterson	James Dennis
	1811	
201	Elizabeth Kimbrough	6 children: Nancy, Polly, Duke, Elijah, Azariah Kimbrough, orphans of Thomas Kimbrough. (Only 5 named. son Vincent)
202	Joseph Collier	Sally, John, Patsey, Tabitha Kimbrough orphans of John Kimbrough
205	Barzillai Graves	Lewis Graves. Accts. pd to Dr. Starbuck and Dr. W. L. Webb
206	William Sawyer	Nancy, William, Susannah Mallory, orphans of James Mallory
208	James Graves	Major Graves orphan of Thomas Graves
209	Groves Howard	Miss Polly Bush,(legacy from Joseph Bush)
209	Alexander Wiley	Zephaniah Tait Kerr orphan of William Kerr. (Paid David Davis for schooling)
211	William Lyon	Elizabeth Lyon
212	Nathaniel Gooch	John Gooch an infant
	1812	
223	Thomas Slade	Yancey, Jno., Lethe, Fanny Gray, orphans of John Gray
224	Wylie Yancey	Edmund B. and James Rice
226	Thomas Harrison	Charles Harrison
234	Thomas Windsor	Biddey, Gilson, Polly Hughes
235	Wm. S.(or L..) Webb	Martha, Samuel, Elizabeth, and William Hughes
237	Sarah Smith	Sarah Warren wife of Thomas Warren (Sarah legatee of James Smith)
238	Solomon Debow	7 orphans & widow of James Aldrage: Sally, Joseph, James, Susannah, Ricard. (only 5 named)
	1813	
245	Andrew Hughs	Orphans of James Hughs decd., acct. with Samuel & Elizabeth Hughs
246	William Graves	Isbel Moore
249	Nathan Williams	Levi Simpson orphan of Jas.Simpson (Paid Thos. Garrett & Watlington for schooling)
250	Nathan Williams	William and James Simpson, orphans of James Simpson
253	Levi Fuller	Nancy and Johnston M. McDaniel
253	William Willson	Henry Willson

Guardian's Accounts cont.

Page	Guardian	Orphan
	1813 cont.	
255	Thomas Wiley	Alexander Gray
257	Azariah Graves	Receipt from Aza Graves in full payment
261	Joseph Collier	Sally Collier and James Collier her husband formerly Salley Kimbro orphan of John Kimbrough
	1814	
262	Robert H. Jackson	Agness Jackson
263	Elizabeth Long	Robert Long Jun. decd.
268	James Yancey	Attelia Yancey orphan of Thomas Yancey. (Paid William Gooch for schooling)
272	William Barnwell	Salley Enoch
274	Thomas Wiley	Alexander Gray
277	John McMullen	Orphans of William Terry: James, Kerr, Rowling, Elizabeth, Gideon, Thomas, and Mitchell Terry
280	Meredith Price	Estate of Joel McDaniel. Expenses for William and John McDaniel(exp. for carrying tobacco to Lynchburg)
285	Estate of Phebe Lipscomb	Warren, John, and Robert Richmond
290	John Woods	Samuel Brown and wife Parthenia Farley, receipt of payment
	1815	
294	John Brackin	
	John Cobb,(former guard.)	Yuarka and Greppena Brackin
297	Mrs. Dililah Womack	John, Green, Nancy, Vashty, Henry, and Elizabeth Womack
298	Robert McKee	Nancy McKee
298	John Brackin	Sina Brackin
300	Joseph Collier	Receipt from William Collier for part of wife Patsey Collier (former Patsey Kimbrough) estate from father John Kimbrough
302	Nathan Williams	Levi, James, and William Simpson
	1816	
319	George B. Dameron	Susannah Matthews orphan of Vines Matthews
319	Joseph Dameron Jun.	Joshua Jackson
320	George B. Dameron	Anny M., Patsy B., and Luke Matthews orphans of V. Matthews
322	George B. Dameron	Receipt from Lewis Yealock for payment from estate of Linsey Matthews
	1817	
324	Hezekiah Boswell	Peggy and Matthew Garner
332	Richard Hamblett	Gilson Hews (Cash advanced 50 sh. to Gilson to pay a Gentleman whom Gilson had traveled from the South with.)
333	Andrew Hughs	Samuel Hughs
334	Isaac Rainey	Orphans of George Eubank

Guardians' Accounts cont.

Page	Guardian	Orphan

1817 cont.

Page	Guardian	Orphan
335	John Stamps	Russell, Polly who married Daniel Gwynn, and Bartlett Hatchett (received from estate of Bartlett Hatchett
337	James Yancey	Angus McNeill Pd. Gregory Hightower for schooling. Pd. Wm. B. Meroney and Robert H. Childers for schooling.
341	Alexander Murphey	Nancy Muzzall now Nancy Mitchell. Orphan of Wm. Muzzall. Balance due D. Mitchell and wife.
341	Alexander Murphey	Nathaniel G. Muzzall
343	Alexander Murphey	Edward Bartlett and wife Elizabeth heirs of Wm. Muzzall
344	Thomas Slade	Joseph W. Muzzall (received from estate of Wm. Muzzall)
345	Alexander Murphey	Francis and Will A. Muzzall (Mrs. Polly Muzzall widow of Wm. Muzzall)

1818

Page	Guardian	Orphan
348	Daniel Hightower	Stephen Hightower
348	Daniel Price	John McDaniel orphan of Joel McDaniel
350	Daniel Hightower	William Hightower
352	John Stamps	Muzzall children
356	Hezekiah Boswell	Matthew Garner
357	John P. Freeman	Thompson Harden
362	R. M. Sanders	Archibald G., Mary C., Susan S., and Jesse Carter (received from estate of Jesse Carter)
366	Sally B. Carter	Elizabeth B., and William B. Carter (Estate of Jesse Carter)
367	Sylvanus Stokes	Wm. & John McDaniel
374	Thomas Gunn	Polly Finley (cash received from Wm. Taylor former guardian of Rockingham)
375	Joseph Roe	Linda, Thomas, and William Swift (Pd. tuition at John Stamps school and at McNeal"s school)
377	Whitehead Page	Samuel and Nancy King orphans of Isaac King
378	Daniel Hightower	John, Elizabeth, Daniel, and Lucy Hightower
379	Stephen Kitchen	James Kitchen
382	Joseph Dameron	Joshua Jackson
383	John Kitchen	Moses Kitchen
383	John Comer	William, Polly, Bezel M., John R., and Elizabeth G. Long, children of John and Elizabeth Long

1819

Page	Guardian	Orphan
389	Major Price Sen.	Major Price Jun.
394	Hosea McNeill	Nancy, Alexander, Ellender, Jamima, Susannah, Joseph, and Isaac Cantrill, (received from estate of Benjamin Cantrill)
398	William W. Price	Susannah, Nancy, Daniel, Polly, Pinkney, Washington, and Anderson Price

152

INDEX TO WILL ABSTRACTS

Asterisk indicates original will is filed at State Archives.

Index to will abstracts cont.

Index to will abstracts cont.

155

In the name of God Amen I Hugh McKun being
of a low State of Health, but of Sound and Perfect
Memory but being uncertain of this Mortal Life
I do make this my Last Will and Testament
I also do leave and bequeath unto my Loving wife
Agness McKun my Land and Household furniture
Consisting of Plows, Horses and Hoes and to Clear and to Clear
what Ground she likes, and if she likes to Marry
again to have it During her Lifetime and then
that to be Equally Divided amongst my six sons
and John Robertson my Sister son I also leave and
bequeath unto my Oldest son Alexander McKun
one Black Mare, and all Books to be left in the
Executors hands, I do appoint my Loving wife
Agness McKun & Thomas Robertson to be my Executors
Given under my hand this 30th day of October 1781.

Test: Nathaniel Waddill
James Hubbard
Thomas Robertson

Hugh McKun

State of North Carolina
Washington County
This day Nathaniel Waddill, James Hubbart
and Thomas Robertson Personally came before me Charles Allison a
Justice for the County aforesaid and made Oath that this is the Last
Will and Testament here above Written of Hugh McKun
Sworn to the 6th day of May 1782
Charles Allison

July Court 1784
Caswell County
The Execution of this Will was Produced in
Court and upon Consideration thereof it was
Ordered to be recorded
Test
R G Murphy

INDEX

by

MARY FRANCES KERR DONALDSON

(SURNAMES only - A name may appear more than once on any given page.)

BANKES 16
BARKER 10, 15, 24-27, 29, 30, 36, 38,
  39, 43, 44, 46, 52, 65, 66, 88, 98-
  100, 104, 107, 111, 112, 115, 122,
  123, 131, 138, 139, 140, 147, 153
BARKSDALE 50, 61
BARNET or BARNETT 1, 2, 4-6, 12, 14,
  15, 17-19, 21, 23, 28-30, 34, 39,
  52, 67, 73, 89, 94, 95, 101, 105,
  108, 134, 141, 144, 153
BARNHILL 34, 60
BARNWELL 111, 126, 129, 138, 151
BARTLETT 111, 126, 152
BARTON 45, 48, 54, 58, 63, 70, 78, 83,
  87, 92, 93, 100, 104, 107, 111, 113,
  115, 139
BASS 19, 105
BASTIN 43, 66, 67, 81
BATEMAN or BAITMAN 114, 115, 126
BATES 138
BAUGHAN or BAUGHN 83, 145
BAXTER (also see BACKSTER) 30, 32, 52,
  74, 96, 108, 114, 132, 134, 136, 153
BAYNES or BANES 50, 126
BEAR CREEK 36
BEASLEY 136
BEAVER or BEVER 75, 80, 82, 93, 96, 97,
  102, 111, 112, 116, 119, 131
BEDFORD COUNTY, TENN. 115, 122, 125
BEDFORD COUNTY, VA. 11
BEEDLES 29
BELEW 49, 50, 134, 153
BELL 60, 114
BELSIRE or BELSIAH 110, 111, 127
BENNETT or BENNATT 38, 46, 50, 65, 66,
  75, 76, 81, 82, 84, 90, 93, 94, 107,
  121, 122, 123, 124, 130, 153
BENNION or BENION 97, 100
BENSON 83, 93
BENTLEY 79
BENTON 1, 2, 4-6, 36, 46, 47, 65, 71,
  82, 85, 103, 108, 116, 138
BERRY or BEARY 6, 15, 16, 19, 20, 62,
  84, 96, 98, 106, 107, 120, 138, 139
BETHEL or BETHELL 3, 4, 60, 69, 71, 106,
  129
BIG TOM CREEK, TENN. 132
BIRCH 90
BIRD 64, 68, 110, 112, 117, 118, 126,
  128, 132
BIRK 67, 82, 83, 90-92, 94, 96, 101, 106,
  111, 123, 127, 128, 131
BIZOR 91
BLACK 3-5, 8, 14-16, 18, 20, 21, 23, 26,
  33-36, 38, 47, 141, 142, 153
BLACKS (also see SLAVES)
  Rebecca Cousins - free born 10

BLACKS (continued)
  John Freeman - free black man 105
  Aggie and Merrier-freed by Patterson
  Arnos - freed by Bracken 101
  Venus - freed by Grayham 116
BLACK RIVER 143
BLACKHARD 143
BLACKWELL 19, 23, 27, 30, 32, 42, 45,
  56, 58, 64, 67-70, 78, 96, 102, 125,
  127-130, 140, 148, 153
BLAIR 25
BLAKE 143
BLUEWING, BLUWING, or BLEWING CREEK 144,
  145
BLOUNT 109
BLOW 61
BLOYD 103
BOBBITT 24
BOGGESS or BOGGUS 4, 24, 33, 89, 90, 136
BOLLING 18
BOLTON 134
BOMAN 35, 45, 47-49, 52, 56, 63, 67, 69,
  76, 80, 83, 85, 90, 91, 98, 105, 107,
  132, 153
BOOKER 41, 52, 71
BOONS 73
BOREN or BORAN 20, 38, 65, 138
BOROUGHS 96
BOSTICK or BOSTWICK 21, 26, 28, 36, 144
BOSWELL, BASWELL, or BOZEWELL 23, 38,
  80, 83, 89, 94, 97, 100, 103, 107,
  114, 123, 125, 141, 144, 151, 152
BOULAIN 99, 128
BOULDIN 61, 68, 71, 93, 105, 108, 119, 1.
BOULTON or BOULTEN 15, 38, 41, 42, 63,
  89, 108, 109, 113, 134, 153
BOWDERY 41
BOWDOIN 119
BOWERS or BOWER 49, 57, 62, 124
BOWLES or BOWLS 14, 15, 18, 145, 153
BOWLING 132
BOWLS, BOLS, or BOULD BRANCH 144, 145
BOWMAN 52, 102
BOWREN 107
BOYAR 83
BOYD 28, 45, 63, 65, 82, 94, 108, 110,
  147, 153
BRACKEN or BRACKIN 5, 13, 58, 63, 71,
  100, 101, 125, 127, 130, 136, 149,
  151, 153
BRADBURY or BRADBERRY 45, 49
BRADFORD 85
BRADLEY 20-23, 28, 31, 45, 47, 60, 134,
  153
BRADSHER 7, 38, 39, 79, 90, 130, 141
BRANDON 91, 110
BRANHAM 52

158

BRANNOCK 65
BRANSON 94
BRASEFIELD 15
BREEDLOVE 144
BREEKEN, BREEKEEN, or BREKEEN 6, 12,
   16, 23, 77, 143
BREEZE 29, 55, 138
BREWER 62
BRIDGES 3, 15
BRIGGS 98, 99
BRIGHT 29, 144
BRINSFIELD 64, 78, 91, 111, 113, 118
BRINTLE 35, 54, 65, 78, 83, 94, 100
BROACH 104, 119, 136
BROADAWAY 143
BROCKMAN 68, 97
BROODY 57
BROOKS or BROOKES 4, 9, 13, 17, 19, 21,
   26, 28-32, 36, 43, 45, 48, 50, 51,
   53, 57, 60, 62-65, 67, 78, 85, 91,
   93, 95, 96, 98, 100, 109-111, 113,
   118, 120, 121, 127, 129, 130, 133,
   139, 140, 144, 147, 153
BROTHERS 15, 34, 138, 139
BROUGHTON 117
BROWDER 73
BROWN or BROWNE 2, 3, 6, 7, 9, 11, 15-17,
   20, 26, 28, 32, 39, 41, 43, 45, 47,
   50, 52, 53, 57, 58, 60, 62-69, 76,
   78, 83, 85, 87-90, 92, 93, 97, 103,
   107, 108, 113-115, 118, 120, 121, 123,
   125, 128-132, 136, 139, 143, 151, 153
BROWNING or BROWNIN 4, 6, 13, 18, 20, 22,
   33, 36, 38, 46, 53, 59, 61, 68, 70,
   82, 84, 87, 88, 90, 94, 102, 105, 107,
   110-112, 119, 120, 122, 125, 126, 138,
   139, 140, 153
BRUCE or BRUICE 2, 7, 45, 50, 66, 69, 74,
   80, 83, 85, 91, 94, 98, 103, 104, 115,
   138, 153
BRUMIT 117
BRUNSWICK COUNTY, VA. 117
BRUNT 64
BRYANT 2, 6, 7, 13, 18, 23, 24, 35, 54,
   66, 138, 143
BUCHANON, BUCHANAN, BUCKHANON, BUCKHANNON,
   or BUCHANNON i, 17, 20, 21, 26, 28, 33,
   45, 46, 47, 49, 68, 70, 76, 84, 144
BUCK 65
BUCK MOUNTAIN 145
BUCKHILL 29
BUCKINGHAM COUNTY, VA. 8
BUCKLEY 27, 28, 98, 108, 141
BULL 6, 12, 21, 26, 29, 34, 141
BULLIS 45
BULLOCK 51, 53, 61, 136
BUMPASS 1, 3, 15, 30, 144, 145, 153

BURCH 29, 32, 34, 36, 45, 47, 48, 51, 55,
   56, 58, 77, 79, 91, 98, 99, 112, 143
BURCHETT 103
BURCHFIELD 106
BURFORD 34, 55, 59, 60, 62
BURGESS 1, 59, 91, 105, 107, 110, 113,
   122, 153
BURKE or BURK 3, 15, 85, 100
BURKE COUNTY 23
BURKE COUNTY, GA. 22
BURNET 19
BURNHAM 22
BURNSIDE or BURNSIDES 103, 114
BURNWATTS 98
BURRIS or BURRESS 49, 88, 91
BURROWS, BURROUS, or BURROUGH 68, 77, 138
BURTON iv, 2, 4, 7, 9, 14, 17, 18, 19,
   22, 24, 25, 28, 32, 35, 36, 38, 42, 52,
   53-64, 66, 67, 69, 71, 73, 74-76, 78,
   79, 82, 85, 91, 93, 95, 97, 98, 100-
   108, 110, 111, 113-116, 119-121, 123,
   124, 128, 129, 133, 134, 136, 137,
   139, 140, 147, 153
BUSEY 123
BUSH or BOUSH 18, 21, 25, 29, 50, 53,
   80, 83, 93, 104, 107, 117, 118, 122,
   138, 150, 153
BUSICK 91
BUTE COUNTY 9
BUTLER or BUTLAR 10, 31, 38, 54, 70
BUTT 105
BUTTERY 56, 117
BYAS 12, 28
BYRD 34, 42, 67, 90, 111, 117, 118
BYRON 65
BYSOR or BYSON 88, 91, 109, 121-123

C

C. or CABIN BRANCH 95
CADALL 143
CADDELL 7, 27
CALDWELL 37, 121
CALEB 112
CAMERON 92, 134
CAMP 39, 40, 141
CAMPBELL or CAMBEL 4, 5, 12, 16, 18, 20,
   21, 23, 32-34, 37, 41-44, 48, 61, 64, 65,
   75, 88, 94, 141, 147
CAMPBELL COUNTY, VA. 71
CANADY 144
CAIN or CANE CREEK 1, 8, 16, 135, 141,
   142
CANNON 44, 69, 104, 136
CANTRELL, CANTREL, CANTRILL, or CANTRIL
   9, 10, 42, 46, 64, 78, 84, 88, 97,
   124, 138, 140, 152
CARRAWAY 144

COLEMAN or COLMAN (continued) 30, 34,
  38, 39, 41, 42, 44-46, 50, 55, 59,
  69, 70, 74, 82, 98, 99, 105, 106,
  108, 109, 113, 114, 116, 117, 119,
  120, 126, 136, 144, 147, 153
COLLEY 18
COLLIER or COLIER 108, 109, 111, 127,
  128, 130, 148, 150, 151
COLLINS 136
COLQUEHON or COLQUEHOWN 76, 77, 96
COLUMBIA COUNTY, GA. 52
COMBS 89, 143
COMER 23, 42, 53, 58, 119, 124, 127,
  128, 133, 134, 152
COMMINS or COMMENS 30, 36, 45, 145
COMPTON 54, 82, 95, 98, 111, 117,
  126, 132, 133
CONNALLY, CONALLY, CONALY or CONNELEY
  38, 58, 73, 105, 115, 127, 131,
  132, 134
CONWAY 90, 99, 109
COOK or COOKE 3, 5, 22, 46, 63, 71,
  82, 111, 122
COOPER 6, 12, 13, 15, 16, 20, 22, 27,
  33-36, 47, 56, 76, 88, 100, 104,
  121, 124, 126, 138, 143
COPELAND 58, 127
COPLINGER 115, 149
CORAM 134, 136
CORBIN 18
CORBITT or CORBIT 62, 83, 93, 99,
  102, 107, 130
CORDER 10, 12, 15, 18, 19, 84, 109,
  120, 138, 148, 153
CORNWELL PARISH 37
CORR 104
CORREN 20
COTNAM 112
COUMON 90
COUNTIES, see Amelia, Baltimore, Bed-
  ford, Brunswick, Buckingham, Burke,
  Bute, Campbell, Caroline, Caswell,
  Charlotte, Chatham, Chesterfield,
  Christian, Clark or Clarke, Columbia,
  Cornwell Parish, Craven, Culpepper,
  Davidson, Dorset, Dunegal, Elbert,
  Fairfax, Fauquier, Franklin, Glouces-
  ter, Granville, Green, Greenbrier,
  Guilford, Halifax, Hancock, Hanover,
  Henderson, Henry, Kentucky, King and
  Queen, King George, Knox, Laurence,
  Lincoln, Lunenburg, Madison, Mecklin-
  burg, Montgomery, Murray, Nottaway,
  Oglethorpe, Onslow, Orange, Patrick,
  Pendleton, Person, Pittsylvania,
  Prince George, Randolph, Rockingham,
  Russell, Shenandoah, Southampton,

COUNTIES (continued) Stafford, Stokes,
  Sullivan, Sumner, Sussex, Union,
  Warren, Washington, Wilkes, William-
  son, Willson.
COUNTRY LINE CREEK i, 8, 13, 14, 16,
  33, 36, 48, 50, 52, 61, 66, 68, 69,
  73, 75, 79, 95, 103, 110, 112, 120,
  134, 135, 136, 139-141
COURT OF PLEAS AND QUARTER SESSIONS
  i, 2
COURTHOUSE i, ii, 13, 15, 26, 39, 41,
  44, 49, 68, 99, 144
COUSINS 10
COVENTON 127
COWEN 125
COX 38, 44, 48-50, 58, 61, 62, 75, 76,
  90, 92, 105, 108, 110, 111, 113-115,
  125, 133
COZART 145
CRADDOCK 67
CRAGG 1, 14, 15
CRANFORD 27
CRAVEN COUNTY, S. C. 4
CREEKS, see Adams, Andrew Branch, Arons,
  Bear, Big Tom, Bluewing, Bowl's
  Branch, Cain or Cane, Castle, Cobbs,
  Cochran's Spring Branch, Country
  Line, Cubb, Deep, Dill Branch, Dish-
  water, Dixe's Ferry, Donaldson's,
  Double, Gents, Henly's, Hico, High
  Rock, Hogan's, Horsley, Indian, Jor-
  dan, Kilgore's Branch, Little,
  McMennary Branch, Mayo, Mill, Miry,
  Moon's, Mud Branch, Napper Reeds,
  Negro, Old Mill, Owens, Rambo Branch,
  Rattlesnake, Reedy Branch, Reedy Fork,
  Richland, Rutledge, Sargent's Spring,
  Stink Shole, Stoney, Stories, Sugar-
  tree, Surat Home, Tapley, Tom's,
  Troublesome, Tubb's Branch, Turkey-
  pen Branch, Western Waters, Whet-
  stone Branch, Wolf Island, Wynn's.
CRESWELL 103
CRIGG 50
CRISP 14, 24, 25, 31, 32, 44, 47, 48,
  55, 119, 124, 128, 134
CRITTENDON 108, 110
CROMWELL 19
CROSS 25
CROSSET, CROSET, or CROSSETT 46, 52, 108,
  117, 118, 126, 153
CROSSON or CROSTON 23, 62
CROWDER 79, 80, 88, 124, 125, 131
CRUMER 145
CRUMMELL 18
CRUMPTON or CRUMTON 15, 138, 143
CRUZE 145

CUBB CREEK 145, 146
CULBERTSON or CULBERSON 6, 15, 32-34,
   54, 62, 69, 70, 90, 107, 111, 112,
   132, 138
CULPEPPER COUNTY, VA. 18
CUMBERLAND RIVER, TENN. 71, 73, 106
CUMMINS 14, 26, 29, 153
CUNNINGHAM or CUNINGHAM 8, 31, 36, 48,
   49, 54, 73, 99, 108, 144
CURL 78, 109, 118, 128
CURLES 110, 125
CURRIE or CURRY 8, 9, 11, 24, 25, 29,
   30, 32, 33, 51, 52, 54, 60, 62,
   70, 80, 89, 102, 104, 121, 126,
   128, 130, 132, 138, 153
CURRIER or CURIAR 23, 28, 138
CURTICE 96
CUSHAW 36
CUZZART 24

                    D

DABNEY 20, 21, 23, 28-30, 33, 44, 45,
   55, 100, 121, 128
DALTON 37, 43, 51, 55, 58, 83, 96,
   103
DAMERON 2, 32, 38, 42, 45, 56, 58,
   59, 60, 62, 69, 74, 75, 77, 80,
   83, 85-87, 91, 92, 95-97, 102,
   103, 105, 109-112, 114-116, 120,
   121, 124, 126-128, 130, 132, 147,
   148, 149, 151-153
DAN RIVER 10, 21, 63, 89, 134-136
DAN RIVER TOWNSHIP ii
DANIEL 24, 28, 95, 101, 145
DANVILLE, VA. 58, 75, 97
DARBY 23, 41, 77, 78, 85, 88, 91, 103,
   106, 114, 117, 118, 124, 125, 127,
   132, 133, 141, 148
DARNELL 63
DARNOLD 104
DAUGHTRY 114
DAVEY or DAVY 1, 3, 10, 11, 15, 36,
   144, 145
DAVIDSON COUNTY, TENN. 79
DAVIS, DAVISE, or DAVISS 4, 12, 15,
   18, 22, 23, 31, 34, 45, 51, 60, 64,
   66, 69, 80, 88, 91, 94, 100, 104,
   116, 128, 132, 134, 135, 138, 140,
   145, 150, 153
DAWSON 50, 51, 53, 83
DAY 5, 11, 35, 144, 145
DAYWATT 114
DEBOW, DEBO, or DEBOE 1, 2, 5, 8, 15,
   27, 30, 35, 76, 96, 115, 126, 141,
   149, 150
DEEP CREEK 145, 146

DEER RIVER, TENN. 73
DELAP or DELOP 93, 96, 98
DELONE i, 18, 26, 34, 36, 38, 39, 42,
   45, 49, 54, 56, 85
DENNEY 144
DENNIS or DENIS 11, 52, 70, 114, 140,
   150
DENTON 7, 42
DEVEREAU 96
DEWEESE 1, 153
DICKENS i, 1, 3, 9, 13, 25, 26, 48,
   49, 54, 62, 65, 91, 98, 104, 140,
   144, 145
DICKERSON 3, 4, 10, 11, 17, 23, 48, 59,
   109, 115, 121, 126
DICKEY, DICKIE, or DICKY 8, 43, 46, 50,
   52-54, 62, 64, 70, 75, 80, 81, 83,
   92, 97, 104, 109, 111, 117, 118,
   121, 126, 129, 130, 138, 153
DICKINSON or DICKENSON 7, 43, 55, 61,
   136
DICKSON 6, 11, 18, 19, 29, 31, 144
DILAHAY 33
DILL 31, 140
DILL BRANCH 97
DINWOODY 141
DISHWATER CREEK 144
DISTRICTS, see Caswell, Gloucester,
   Hillsborough, Nash, Richmond, St.
   David's, St. James, St. Lawrence,
   St. Luke's.
DIX 4, 32, 33, 38, 41, 45, 65, 71, 74,
   89, 98, 108, 113, 126
DIXE'S FERRY 17
DIXON 2, 10, 11, 17, 19, 20, 23, 24, 37,
   38, 41, 43-45, 49, 50, 52, 53, 55-61,
   63, 64, 69, 70, 74-76, 82, 87, 91,
   95, 100-103, 105, 109, 111, 125, 136,
   137, 144, 149, 153
DOBBINS or DOBBIN 3, 4, 8, 9, 15, 16,
   22, 23, 25, 33, 42, 46, 49, 51, 54,
   55, 58, 61, 70, 71, 73, 83, 84, 106,
   115, 133-135, 141, 153
DOCTOR 67
DODSON 41, 113
DOLLAR 143
DOLLARHIDE 34-36, 52, 77, 79, 83, 102,
   109, 118, 124, 128, 138, 141, 143
DONALDSON ii, 7, 8, 9, 11, 24, 29, 33,
   56, 66, 85, 87, 98, 144, 153
DONALDSON'S CREEK 144, 145
DONOHO 20, 23, 29, 31, 32, 44, 46, 53,
   56, 61, 68, 80, 88, 93, 104, 109,
   111, 114-116, 121, 122, 126, 128,
   130, 133, 134, 138
DORRIS 3, 31, 34
DORSET COUNTY, MARYLAND 49, 68

DOUBLE CREEK 18, 63, 143, 144
DOUGLASS or DOUGLAS i, 1-3, 7, 10-15,
20, 24, 25, 28, 33-37, 40, 45, 80,
83, 85, 88, 122, 141, 143
DOWELL or DOWEL 14, 18, 28, 143
DOWNEY 21
DOWNS 69, 116, 123
DOYLE or DOYL 33, 34, 141
DRAPER 31, 54, 90
DUEST 19, 141
DUKE or DUKES 24, 28, 116
DUNAWAY or DUNEWAY 24, 45, 49, 63-65,
99, 134
DUNCAN 4, 8, 9, 13, 15, 21, 23, 26,
27, 30, 36, 43, 66, 86, 109, 126,
134, 141, 145
DUNEGAL COUNTY, IRELAND 8
DUNLAP or DUNLOP 31, 83, 93, 123
DUNN 34, 74, 110
DURHAM 43, 59, 77, 80, 97, 102, 106,
111, 112, 115, 118, 120, 124,
128, 130, 136
DUTY 10, 12, 14, 15, 25, 39, 141, 153
DYER or DYE 37, 57, 58, 81, 92, 123,
135, 153

E

EACOLS 24
EAGON 9
EAK 140
EAKEN or EAKIN 8, 13
EARP 109
EAST 5
ECHOLDS 113
EDDINGS 73, 95, 112
EDINGTON 141
EDMONS 114
EDWARDS 53, 130
EDWELL 5, 7, 120
EGERTON 22
EGMAN, EGMON, or EGMOND 91-93, 102, 111,
117, 129, 132
ELAM 24, 70, 73, 85, 87, 90, 92, 98, 99,
101, 108, 109, 112, 148, 153
ELBERT COUNTY, GA. 58
ELLET 58
ELLIOT or ELLIOTT 8, 136, 138, 141
ELLIS 10, 34, 126, 138
ELLISON 29
ELLMON 136, 141
ELMORE 78, 99, 101, 102, 104, 114, 116,
128
EMBRY 136
ENGRAM 71
ENO RIVER 74
ENOCH, ENOCHS, ENOCK, or ENOCKS 15,

ENOCH, ENOCHS, ENOCK, or ENOCKS (continued)   34, 39, 41, 46, 52, 55,
57, 62, 64, 81, 88, 90, 95, 100,
101, 115, 129, 138, 147, 149, 151,
153
ERVINE 35, 41
ERWIN 31, 111
ESKRIDGE, ESCRIDE, or ESCRIDGE (also
see ASKRIDGE) 10, 16, 22, 23, 28,
38, 58, 77, 135
ESTIS or ESTES 23, 54, 58, 62, 76, 81,
82, 85, 90, 91, 96, 98, 122, 124,
130, 140, 153
EUBANK or EUBANKS 54, 83, 111, 119,
126, 129, 133, 151
EVANS or EVANSE 18 20, 25, 28, 34-36,
42, 44, 47, 54, 62, 69, 70, 74-77,
79, 83, 87, 88, 91, 92, 98, 103,
105, 106, 117, 119, 124, 132, 138,
153
EVERETT, EVERET, or EVERIT 22, 34, 36,
42, 60, 74, 80, 83, 95, 105

F

FAIRFAX COUNTY, VA. 25, 30, 35, 42
FANNING 42
FARGERSON or FARGUSON 93, 101, 108, 126
FARGHAR 10
FARISH 47
FARLEY iv, 4, 8-10, 15-17, 19, 21, 22,
24, 28, 29, 31-33, 38, 39, 41, 45,
47, 51, 54, 55, 63-67, 71, 76, 78,
89, 96, 98-100, 102-104, 106, 107,
109-113, 115, 118, 119, 123, 124,
135, 148, 150, 151, 153
FARMER 11, 13, 101, 102, 143, 145, 153
FARQUHAR 20, 23, 25, 143
FARRAR or FARROW iv, 14, 25, 26, 82,
83, 143
FARRELL 99
FAUCETT 110, 117, 126, 132
FAUQUIER COUNTY, VA. 101
FAYETTEVILLE 28
FEANS 74
FEARN 85
FERGUSON 8, 22, 35, 41, 76, 102, 112
FERRELL, FERREL, FERRALL, FERRIL, FER-
ROL 20, 24, 25, 35, 57, 90, 102, 109,
110, 112, 119, 135, 136, 141, 143,
153
FERRY 98, 118, 121, 130
FIELDER 15, 64, 116
FIELDS 92
FINLEY 152
FINN 74
FISHER 58, 63, 80, 98, 143

FITCH 65, 110, 126
FITZGERALD 90, 97, 98, 112, 124
FLACK 88
FLAT or FLATT RIVER 2, 11,-23, 28,
 143-146
FLEMMING 117, 118
FLETCHER 17, 18, 22, 105, 118, 122,128,
 141, 153
FLIPPING or FLIPPIN 30, 31, 45, 48,
 60, 91, 113
FLIPPS 56
FLORENCE or FLORANCE 18, 57, 62,
 116, 138
FLOYD 22, 145
FLYNN, FLYN, or FLINN 14, 15, 58,
 105, 120, 122, 135, 153
FOLEY 15, 19, 23, 28, 31, 141
FOOTE or FOOT i, 19, 28, 30, 31,
 71, 90, 99, 123, 140
FORBUS 61
FORD 3, 9, 23, 43, 58, 77, 109,
 111, 116, 117, 127, 136, 138
FORGHER 61
FORGUS or FORGUSS 56, 75
FORREST or FOREST 16, 42, 91, 127
FOSHEE or FESHEE 122, 143
FOSTER 27, 37, 53, 62, 76, 78, 80,
 82, 100, 103, 111, 115, 116,
 118, 120, 121, 131, 136
FOULDS 129
FOWLER 15, 23, 145
FOX 91
FRAME or FRAIM 80, 85
FRANKLIN 47, 143
FRANKLIN COUNTY, GA. 101
FRANKLIN COUNTY, N. C. 38
FRAZIER, FRAZER, or FRASER 2, 7,
 16
FREEMAN 70, 105, 152
FRENCH 51, 53, 65, 78, 83, 108, 116,
 123, 138
FRENCH BROAD RIVER 24
FROST 80
FULCHER 9, 12, 23, 141, 143
FULKERSON 4, 8, 15, 16, 18, 23, 26,
 28, 31, 34, 135
FULLER, FULLAR, or FULARS 6, 14, 15,
 21, 23, 28, 31-34, 36, 67, 89,
 104, 123, 138, 141, 150, 153
FULLINGTON 48
FUQUA 31, 75, 124
FURY 35, 93

G

GAFFORD 45, 49
GALLAHER or GALLAUGHER 36, 51
GALLOWAY 61, 92
GAMBLE 100, 127
GARDNER or GUARDNER 21, 34, 55, 60, 62,
 111, 135.
GARNER 22, 84, 89, 94, 100, 101, 103,
 151, 152
GARRETT, GARRET, GARROTT, or GARROT 5,
 22, 97, 102, 116, 120, 121, 127, 150
GATELY 25, 29, 143
GATES 64
GATEWOOD 2, 4, 6, 38, 50, 51, 59, 63,
 76, 89, 96, 103, 106, 110, 113, 136,
 153
GATTIS 126
GENERAL ASSEMBLY OF N. C. i
GENTRY 36, 144
GENTS, GHENTS, or JENTS CREEK 141, 142
GEORGE 7
GEORGIA 55
GETER 124
GHOLSTON 15
GIBSON 3, 12, 13, 20, 42, 48, 53, 58,
 65, 81, 83, 86, 90, 96, 98, 99, 101,
 106, 125, 136, 137, 153
GILCHRIST 113
GILL 15, 23, 33, 145
GILLASPY, GILLASPIE, GILASBY, GILLASBY,
 GILLISBY, GILASPI, GILASPY, GALASPY,
 GALLISPY, GLASBY, or GLASPY 1, 15,
 17, 41, 44, 46, 50, 55, 66, 67, 102,
 113, 121, 135, 153
GILLSON 143
GIMBO 5, 23, 41
GIVINS, GIVENS, or GIVEN 7, 21, 26, 29
GLASS 144
GLAZE 21, 144
GLENN or GLEN 2,5, 16, 26, 28, 36, 143,
 145
GLIDEWELL 36
GLOUCESTER COUNTY, VA. 30, 31
GLOUCESTER DISTRICT i, iv, 72, 79, 89,
 94, 112, 115, 130, 134, 138, 139
GOFF 141
GOINS, GOIN, or GOING 69, 98, 103, 141,
 143
GOLD 2, 6, 10, 26, 36, 138, 141, 149,
 153
GOLDSMITH 57
GOLLIHER or GOLOHER 118, 138
GOLSON 80, 141

GOMER 67, 96, 98, 104, 109, 111, 112, 119, 121
GOOCH iv, 2, 24, 50, 55-57, 62, 66, 81, 82, 84, 85, 87, 88, 90-92, 94, 95, 98, 101, 115, 117, 123, 124, 126-128, 131, 138, 149-151, 153
GOODLOE or GOODLOW 58, 65, 78, 83, 85, 96-98
GOODMAN 5, 9, 15
GORDON 57, 63, 70, 71, 74, 80, 89, 91, 92, 128, 149
GOSS 35, 145
GOSSAGE 69, 75, 96, 106
GOSSETT 113, 121
GOULD 38, 110
GOWEN 126
GRAHAM, GRAYHAM, GREYHAM, GREAHAM, GREYHAN 2, 10, 11, 17, 34, 81, 83, 106, 116, 136, 137, 149, 153
GRANT 15, 41-44, 48, 50, 51, 54, 57, 60-63, 69, 81, 93, 96-98, 112, 114, 120, 135, 136, 153
GRANVILLE COUNTY, N. C. 13, 42, 50
GRANVILLE, LORD 4
GRAVES i, 1, 2, 6, 8, 11, 13, 19, 21, 24, 25, 27, 29, 30, 34, 36, 38, 39, 41, 43-46, 48, 49, 51-53, 55-57, 61, 62, 64-71, 73-76, 79-85, 87, 88, 90-99, 101-103, 107, 109-112, 114, 117-119, 121, 122, 124-128, 131-133, 138, 140, 143, 147-151, 153
GRAY 17, 18, 30, 117, 118, 120, 123, 129, 150, 151
GREEN or GREENE 27-29, 33, 36, 74, 145, 153
GREEN COUNTY, GA. 38
GREEN COUNTY, N. C. 24
GREEN RIVER, KY. 82
GREENBOUGH 43, 137
GREENBRIER COUNTY, VA. 45
GREENHAW 17
GREENVILLE DISTRICT, S. C. 69
GREGORY 11, 26, 27, 33, 141
GRIDER 77
GREER or GRIER 1, 12, 14, 23, 25, 28, 32, 33, 37, 38, 44, 52, 54, 65, 69, 70, 104, 107-109, 126, 138
GRIFFIN 16, 69, 104, 124, 127, 145
GRIMES 43
GROOM 60, 69, 100, 107, 118, 121
GRYDER 109
GUILFORD COUNTY, N. C. 4, 5, 142
GUINNINGS 83
GUNN 5, 6, 56, 57, 59, 61, 65, 66, 68, 73-76, 79, 81, 89, 90, 92, 93, 95, 97, 98, 104, 112, 119, 120,

GUNN (continued) 121, 131-133, 144, 147, 148, 150, 152, 153
GUTHRIE 14, 143
GUTTERY 11, 12, 18, 20, 22, 23, 28, 32, 34, 70, 144
GWYNN, GWINN, or GWYN ii, 43, 44, 48, 56, 59, 60, 69, 75, 93, 95-97, 102, 111, 112, 140, 144, 152

H

HADDOCK 1, 18, 32, 48, 50, 55, 75, 91, 96, 97, 107, 110, 111, 122, 125, 128, 133, 140
HAGER 73
HAGGARD or HAGARD 48, 70, 140
HAGUE 145
HAGWOOD 105
HAIL 25
HAINEY 21-24, 33, 34, 39, 42, 45, 49, 137
HALE 35
HALEY or HAILEY 118, 132
HALIFAX 11
HALIFAX COUNTY, VA. 19, 21, 24, 26, 31, 36, 41, 63, 65, 67, 71, 76, 82, 93, 106, 108, 123
HALL 12, 15, 18-22, 27, 28, 35-37, 39, 41, 45, 49, 52, 54, 56, 58, 68, 73, 77, 78, 103, 105, 114, 116, 118, 122, 135, 143, 150, 154
HALLIBURTON or HALLYBURTON 14, 144, 145
HAMBLETON 6
HAMBLETT 46, 79, 91, 142, 151, 154
HAMBLIN 10, 11, 17, 154
HAMBRICK 6
HAMILTON 96
HAMLETT or HAMLET 47, 77, 124
HAMLIN 20
HAMPTON 101, 122
HANCOCK 5
HANCOCK COUNTY, GA. 96
HANKS 34
HANNAH 98
HANOVER COUNTY, VA. 49, 103
HARALSON, HARRALSON, or HARRELSON i, 4, 6, 11, 12, 14, 15, 17, 18, 21, 23, 27-29, 35, 37, 39, 41, 42, 51-56, 61, 73, 75, 76, 79, 80, 90-92, 99, 108, 110, 115, 117, 118, 125, 135, 142, 145, 154
HARBIN 44
HARDEN or HARDIN 51, 64, 66, 78, 83, 90, 91, 152
HARDING 15, 31, 49, 92, 140, 142
HARDISTER or HARDESTER 75, 76
HARDWICK 92, 121

165

HARDY 110
HARGIS or HARGISS 14, 36, 47, 56, 74, 76, 77, 104, 143
HARGROVE or HARGRAVE 65, 75
HAROLD 59
HARPER 63, 66, 104
HARRILL 33, 84, 114
HARRIS or HARRISS 10, 15, 17, 20, 21, 27-31, 33, 34, 36, 43-46, 52, 55, 56, 58, 62, 67, 68, 70, 79, 85, 92, 112, 121, 128, 130, 140, 142, 145, 146, 154
HARRISON 1, 2, 9, 10, 11, 13, 15, 22, 24, 26, 27, 31, 33, 34, 36, 38, 42, 60, 62, 63, 65-67, 69, 73, 74, 84-86, 93, 100, 108, 110, 113, 114, 116, 117, 119, 121, 123, 125, 131, 133, 135, 144-147, 149, 150, 154
HART 6, 17, 19, 30, 36, 44, 45, 50, 57, 59, 61, 62, 64, 75, 82, 83, 103, 105, 125, 140, 154
HARVELL, HARVEL, or HARVILL 49, 66, 70, 78, 109
HARVEY 79, 83, 88, 138
HASTEN 93
HASTINGS 53, 65, 113
HATCHER 14, 20, 41, 112, 123, 142
HATCHET or HATCHETT 3, 131, 152, 154
HATRICK 78
HAW RIVER 64, 141
HAWKINS 28, 42
HAYDON or HEYDON 100, 121
HAYES 11, 103, 140
HAYNIE 26, 44
HAYS or HAYSE 3, 5, 28, 96
HAYWOOD 60
HEARNDON or HERNDON 34, 93, 95, 118, 138
HEDGECOCK 25
HELLON 47
HEMPHILL 3, 11, 35, 142
HEMRICK 3
HENDERSON 30, 42, 51, 64, 81, 95, 98, 111, 116, 122, 128, 135
HENDERSON COUNTY, KY. 125
HENLEY or HENLY 7, 17, 142, 154
HENLY'S CREEK 141
HENRY COUNTY, VA. 68
HENSLEE, HENSLEY, or HENSLY 7, 9, 17, 26, 27, 43, 44, 47, 51, 53, 54, 59, 60, 62, 64,-66, 75-80, 88, 92, 93, 99, 103, 104, 108, 109, 120, 131, 133, 140, 154
HENSON OR HINSON 70
HERBIN 24, 31, 88, 94, 96, 140
HERLEY 77
HEROT 1

HERRITAGE 117
HERRON 7
HESTER 6, 145
HESTON 95
HEW WARRY 37
HEWES or HEWS (also see HUGHES) 16, 19, 20, 22, 24, 51, 138, 151
HEWLETT 15, 127
HICKS 16, 34, 47, 58, 128, 146
HICO CREEK 7, 8, 11, 12, 16, 33, 35, 40, 71, 93, 103, 105, 115, 122, 134, 135, 136, 141-146
HIGH ROCK CREEK 20
HIGHTOWER 17, 21, 22, 32, 42, 44, 46, 47, 52, 54, 55, 59, 62, 78, 79, 91, 99, 109-111, 114-117, 121, 122, 124, 126, 127, 129, 135, 152, 154
HIGHTOWERS TOWNSHIP ii
HILL ii, 23, 68, 74, 77, 97, 109
HILLSBOROUGH DISTRICT 103
HINTON 18, 71, 73, 74, 84, 127, 135, 142, 154
HIPWORTH or HIPSWORTH 20, 35, 42, 55, 92, 135, 154
HITT 137
HIX 14, 15, 56, 135, 145
HOBBS or HOBS 56, 57, 104, 109
HOBGOOD 15
HODGE 16, 31, 53, 58, 74, 104, 110, 125, 128-130, 135
HOGAN'S CREEK 24, 37, 55, 61, 63, 102, 106, 123, 135-137, 139, 140
HOGARTY 5
HOGG 42, 43, 66, 106, 137, 154
HOGUE 21, 26
HOLCOM 135
HOLDER 62, 112, 131
HOLDERNESS 23, 43, 44, 57, 60, 92, 118, 140
HOLEMAN or HOLMAN 11, 28, 30, 143
HOLLIS 65, 88
HOLLOMAN or HOLOMAN 74, 85, 98
HOLLOWAY 29, 56, 79, 96, 106, 108, 110, 112, 119, 137, 145
HOLSCIAW 79
HOLSENBACK or HOLSONBACK 18, 38, 67, 77, 118, 121, 128
HOLT 26
HOOD 11
HOOMES 100
HOOPER 74, 75, 111, 145
HOPKINS 137
HOPPER 2, 20, 22, 30, 138, 154
HORLEY 6, 12, 23, 80, 144
HORN 104
HORNBUCKLE 31, 49, 51, 52, 57, 58, 64-66, 75, 78, 83, 85, 87-91, 94, 97, 99,

167

168

LONG (continued) 65, 77, 82, 88, 92, 98, 115, 122, 124-130, 135, 142, 151, 152, 154
LONGAT 80
LONGVILLE 77
LOONY 115, 149
LORD 15, 45, 145
LOVE 30, 43, 58, 80, 82, 85, 88, 103, 139, 142
LOVELESS 91, 120
LOVENS or LOVINS 7, 140
LOVING 15
LOW 5, 6, 13, 20, 32, 33, 36, 37, 44, 46, 47, 54, 56, 135, 139
LOWRY 80
LOWTHER 143
LOYD 75, 88, 116
LUMPKINS ROAD 134
LUNA 115
LUNENBURG COUNTY, VA. 16, 99
LUTRALL 103
LYNCHBURG, VA. 71, 151
LYNN 96, 108, 116
LYON or LYONS 14, 15, 43, 80, 95, 96, 98-101, 103, 106-108, 119, 122, 125, 133, 137, 143, 148-150, 154

Mc

McADEN or McCADEN 8, 28, 37, 38, 51, 54, 55, 69, 76-78, 82, 88, 102, 104, 117, 118, 124, 128, 130, 135, 150
McALISTER, McCALESTER, or McCOLLESTER 87, 99, 143
McALYEA or McILYEA 7, 16
McCAIN 76, 100
McCALIF 46
McCAN 1
McCARVER 143
McCAWLEY 42, 45, 84, 94
McCLAIN or McLAINE 43, 51, 58, 108, 133
McCLANAHAM 18
McCLARNEY, McCLEARY, or McCLARY 10, 11, 30, 33, 34, 52, 60, 66, 96, 105, 106, 110, 112, 137, 154
McCLUSKEY or McCLUSKY 139, 140
McCOLLUM or McCULLUM 34, 35, 47, 51, 63, 137
McCONKEY 11
McCORD 74
McCOY 139
McCRAW 25
McCUBBINS or McCUBBIN 90, 110, 129, 137
McCULLOCK 27, 31, 62, 65

McCULLY or McCULLEY 24, 42, 53, 140
McDANIEL 15, 21, 26, 28, 63, 67, 74, 86, 93, 99, 102, 105, 106, 110, 114-116, 123, 128, 135, 142, 145, 150-152
McDONALD or McDONNEL 3, 4, 154
McDOWELL 94, 142
McDUGAL 31
McELROY 80
McFARLAND, McFARLIN, McFARLING, or McFARLAN 1, 2, 5, 6, 8, 69, 77, 85, 121, 142, 143, 154
McGAULEY 54
McGEE 4
McGEHEE or McGHEE 1, 19, 23, 41, 42, 44, 142, 147
McGILLVERY or McGILLIVERY 20, 85, 91, 139
McGOLLY 48
McGONAGALL 137
McGUIRE 9, 18
McHORNEY 110
McINTOSH (also see MACKINTOSH) 19, 32, 35, 60, 87, 139
McKEE 74, 117, 119, 127, 129, 132, 133, 151, 154
McKEEN 14, 142, 154, 156
McKINNEY 79, 83, 100, 119, 121, 122
McKISSACK, McKISSICK, or McKISSOCK 14, 112, 117, 143
McKNABB or McNABB 36, 55
McKNIGHT or McNIGHT 15, 23, 41, 142
McMAHEN 11
McMAN 54
McMENNARY BRANCH 16
McMILLION or McMILLAN 120, 122, 154
McMIN 139
McMINEMY, McMINNAMY, McMINAMY, or McMENEMAY 34, 42, 74, 105, 117, 139, 154
McMULLEN or McMULLIN 11, 23, 28, 35, 36, 47, 56, 67, 76, 89, 117, 126, 139, 151
McMURRAY or McMURRY 11, 17, 28, 30, 35, 56, 77, 83, 107, 143
McNEAL'S SCHOOL 152
McNEELEY or McNEELY 56, 97
McNEILL, McNEIL, or MacNEILL 5, 8, 12, 15, 23, 26, 27, 34, 36, 56, 78, 107, 110, 113, 114, 118, 120, 133, 142, 143, 152, 154
McREYNOLDS or McRUNNOLDS 2, 14, 15, 32, 57, 70, 107, 120, 122, 139, 143
McVEY 20, 30,
McVIER 17

169

M

MABREY or MABERY 3, 4, 26
MACKINTOSH (also see McINTOSH) 2
MACKLIN 102
MADDEN or MADDING 36, 42, 43, 46, 63,
126, 133
MADDISON'S MILL, VA. 14
MADISON COUNTY, KY. 125
MADKINS or MADKIN 79, 91, 94
MAGONIGAL 60
MAHAN, MAHON, or MAYHAN 75, 78, 140
MAJORS 31
MALEER or MELEER 33, 37, 42, 49, 79,
91, 124, 129, 131
MALLORY, MALORY, or MALLERY 43-45,
50, 51, 53, 58, 59, 62, 65, 75,
78-80, 83, 88, 94, 97, 98, 114,
115, 121, 128, 140, 148, 150
MALONE or MELONE 38, 46, 56, 61, 77,
79, 83, 90, 91, 95, 96, 102, 105,
111, 119, 124, 126, 128-131, 133,
143, 154
MAN or MANN 14, 15, 32, 34, 35, 70,
75, 82, 106, 107, 145
MANES or MAINS 9, 10, 64, 97, 147,
154
MANGUM 24
MANLEY 122
MANSFIELD 67, 90, 105, 117-119, 123
MANUEL 24, 93
MAREIGN, MAREIGHN, MARAIN, MAREEN,
MERAIN, or MOREAN 78, 79, 88,
91, 99, 147
MARSHALL 20
MARTIN 25, 46, 56, 59, 60, 62, 69,
70, 73-76, 79, 82-85, 88, 90, 91,
98, 102, 109, 116-118, 123, 124,
130, 131, 139-141
MARYLAND 48, 49
MASH 6
MASON 31, 70, 78, 116, 146
MASSEY 62, 83
MATHIS or MATTHIS 58, 86, 105, 110,
114, 115, 124
MATKINS 88
MATLOCK 73, 80, 135
MATTHEWS or MATHEWS 104-106, 109,
112, 117, 126, 130, 132, 151, 154
MATTOCKS 37
MAXFIELD 52, 128, 130
MAXWELL 6, 23, 37
MAYO 41, 52
MAYO CREEK 144, 145
MEADOWS or MEDDOWS 24, 135, 146
MECKLINBURG COUNTY 11

MECKLENBURG COUNTY, VA. 48, 79, 131
MEDERIAS 146
MEDLOCK 120
MELTON 56, 83, 93, 99, 107-109, 114, 135,
139, 150
MERCER 14
MERCHANT 109, 116
MERONY 152
MERRITT 15, 21, 24, 27, 37, 43, 63, 135
MERTON 61
MESSER 33, 143
MESSERSMITH 146
MESSICK 70
MIDDLEBROOKS or MIDLEBROOKS 43, 52, 95,
96, 103, 104, 137
MIDDLETON 2
MILAM 48, 49
MILBANK 23
MILES 3, 4, 10, 13, 16, 21, 25, 27, 30,
32, 41, 46, 49, 51, 61, 75, 77, 79,
91, 95, 111, 126, 127, 131, 132, 135,
137, 142, 147, 154
MILL CREEK 67, 134-136, 144-146
MILLER 2, 90, 115, 137
MILLINGTON 34, 105
MILLS 52, 54, 55, 59, 69, 77, 123
MILNER or MILLINER 77, 117
MILTON 1, 93, 115, 130
MILTON TOWNSHIP ii
MIMS or MIMMS 127, 130
MINCEY or MINSEY 28, 154
MINOR 124
MINSHEW 146
MINZES 30
MIRY CREEK, VA. 63
MISSISSIPPI RIVER 135
MISSISSIPPI WATERS 25
MITCHELL or MITCHEL 7, 10, 17, 18, 27, 28,
30, 31, 34, 46-48, 52, 53, 56, 62-64,
66, 67, 70, 73, 75-79, 82, 83, 90, 92,
95, 97, 101, 103-105, 108, 116, 117,
123, 129, 132, 133, 140, 142, 143, 145,
152, 154
MONROE or MONRO 17, 22, 142
MONTGOMERY 20, 31, 37, 38, 42, 43, 58,
61, 65, 73, 74, 80, 99, 103, 108, 109,
112, 128, 135, 154
MONTGOMERY COUNTY 143, 144
MONTGOMERY COUNTY, TENN. 71
MOONEY 146
MOON'S CREEK 37, 43, 134-137, 140, 141
MOORE 1, 1, 2, 4, 6-10, 12, 15, 16, 19-26,
29, 31-34, 37, 39, 41-44, 46, 49, 52,
56, 64, 66-68, 70, 71, 73-76, 81-83,
85, 87, 90, 92, 93, 107, 108, 110, 119,

170

MOORE (continued) 121, 128-131, 135,
140, 142, 143, 145-147, 150, 154
MORGAN 13, 33, 37, 52, 53, 56, 80,
86, 116, 120, 125, 137
MORRIS or MORRIES 19, 38, 65, 66, 95,
111, 127, 145, 147, 148
MORRISON 35
MORROW 15, 60-62, 69, 87, 116, 135
MORTON 16, 36, 47, 52, 54, 58, 66,
74, 83, 84, 90-94, 98, 102, 103,
114, 121, 128, 129, 131, 139
MOSBY 6
MOSELEY or MOSELY 13
MOSS 49, 77, 103, 104, 137
MOSSER 11
MOTHERAL 12, 32, 36, 37, 54-56, 62,
74, 76, 91, 139
MOURNIN 32
MUD BRANCH 146
MUIRHEAD 9, 12, 154
MULLEN, MULLIN, or MULLINS 48, 64, 73
MUNFORD 71
MURPHEY or MURPHY 1, 1-4, 8-13, 15-18,
20-22, 25, 27-31, 35, 36, 38, 39,
43, 45-47, 49, 51, 53, 55-58, 60,
64-66, 68, 69, 72, 74-76, 80-84,
90-95, 98-103, 107-109, 111, 113,
116, 119, 122-127, 129, 133, 135,
139, 140, 142, 149, 152, 156
MURRAY, MURREY, or MURRY 15, 54, 84,
88, 103, 105, 110, 129, 140
MURRAY COUNTY, TENN. 132
MURTREE 26
MUSTAIN 120
MUZZALL or MUZZLE 44, 56, 60, 73, 77,
82, 93, 103, 111, 126, 128, 152

N

NANCE 19, 31, 45, 49, 65, 92, 96, 140
NAPPER REEDS 145
NARROW PASSAGE 94
NASH 41, 47, 50, 53-55, 59, 78, 83,
84, 89, 93, 96, 97, 113, 114, 119,
129, 132, 142, 145, 154
NASH DISTRICT 1, iv, 22, 134, 143
NEAL 80
NEELEY or NEELY i, 4, 6, 11, 12, 15,
23, 25, 28, 34, 36, 38, 39, 45,
46, 49, 51, 67, 79, 92, 104, 127,
142, 146, 154
NEGRO CREEK 12
NEILL 31, 133
NELMS 99
NELSON 77, 85, 87, 91, 92, 113, 129, 132
NEWCOM 90
NEWELL 121
NEWMAN 6

NEWTON 12, 21, 23, 26, 28, 36, 99, 142
NEW YORK 70
NICHOLAS 90, 95
NICHOLS 50, 70, 77, 80, 114, 146
NICHOLSON 51, 85, 149
NIGHT 139
NIPPER 23, 73, 74
NOBLES 113
NOELL or NOEL 26, 29, 64, 81, 82, 84,
99, 154
NOLES 65
NOLLEY 14
NORFLEET 77, 117, 126
NORMAN 116
NORTH 127
NORTON 12, 60
NORWOOD 59, 87, 92
NOTTAWAY or NOTAWAY COUNTY, VA. 58, 67,
99, 123, 124
NOWELL or NOWEL 1, 2, 6, 7, 32, 56, 61,
65, 76, 92, 110, 139
NULL 101, 103
NUNLEY 80
NUNN 17, 29, 81, 95, 140
NUNNALLY or NUNALLE 43, 102

O

OAKLEY 14, 146
O'BANNOCK 49
ODEAR 44
OGILBY or OGILLEY 56, 117, 119, 128
OGLETHORPE COUNTY, GA. 128
OGLETREE 6, 9, 13, 28
OLD MILL CREEK 134
OLDHAM 3, 17, 19, 20, 24, 26, 28, 31,
50, 62, 77, 95, 140
OLDRIDGE (also see ALDRIDGE) 143
OLIVER or OLLIVER 1, 20, 23, 27, 29,
71, 119, 142
O'NEAL 51, 114
O'NEILL 28, 32, 43, 44
ONSLOW COUNTY 36
ORANGE COUNTY, N. C. i, 2, 5, 16, 26,
116, 122, 143, 146
ORR 45, 60, 83, 87, 99, 110, 120, 124,
125, 128, 131, 140
OTWELL 47
OVERSTREET 11, 62, 104
OWEN, OWENS, or OEN 10, 15, 21, 26,
27, 31, 43, 91, 95, 117
OWENS CREEK 5
OXFORD 135

P

PAGE 48, 69, 102, 113, 117, 122, 135,
137, 152, 154

PAINE, see PAYNE
PAINTER 8, 9, 23, 41
PALMER 5, 14, 15, 17, 28, 29, 35-37, 126, 143, 144, 154
PARDUE 24
PARKER 3, 6, 8, 22, 26, 28, 32, 35, 77, 80, 88, 92, 100, 107, 146
PARKS or PARK i, 6, 8, 9, 19, 20, 24, 36, 38, 41, 43, 44, 46, 49, 53, 54, 56, 60, 67, 69, 70, 75, 80, 83, 89, 94, 96, 100, 107, 113, 114, 117, 119, 120, 126, 130, 132, 139
PARR 26, 29, 30, 32, 137, 154
PARROTT or PARROT 12, 21, 51, 58
PARTEE 15
PARTRIDGE or PATRIDGE 49, 68
PASCHALL, PASCHAL, or PASCHELL 23, 27, 53, 65, 96, 106, 127, 130, 142
PASS 66, 78, 85, 110, 124, 135
PATILLO 80
PATRICK 99
PATRICK COUNTY, VA. 101
PATTERSON 24, 55, 81, 87, 90, 93, 111, 115, 143, 145, 150, 154
PATTON 120, 128
PAUL 29, 42, 74-76, 82, 92, 126, 137
PAYNE, PAINE, or PAYN i, iv, 6, 9, 10, 13-15, 17, 20, 21, 27, 28, 32, 35, 39, 42, 45, 46, 50, 51, 53, 56, 58, 69, 71, 74, 77, 78, 82, 83, 88, 90, 91, 93, 94, 96, 98, 99, 103, 116, 118, 119, 121, 129, 139, 140, 146, 147, 154
PEAD 4
PEARCE, PIERCE, or PYERCE 9, 52, 56, 61, 81, 96, 99, 126, 139
PEARSON 17, 27, 37, 38, 47, 78, 135
PELHAM TOWNSHIP ii
PELL 113
PENDERGRAST, PENDERGAST, PENDERGRASS, PENDERGRAS, or PRENDERGAST 23, 48, 60, 65-67, 69, 74, 99, 100, 105, 116, 137, 139, 142
PENDLETON COUNTY, S. C. 47, 101
PENIX, PENNIX, or PENICK (also see PINNIX) 26, 100, 108, 113, 116, 122, 123, 126, 127
PENN or PEN 3, 100
PENTECOST 106
PEOPLES 17
PEPPER 19, 28
PERKINS or PERKYNS 2, 11, 37, 38, 43-45, 50, 52, 53, 69, 70, 96, 97, 100, 137, 154
PERSAIL 128

PERSON or PERSONS 3, 15, 30, 59
PERSON COUNTY, N. C. ii, 40, 44, 45, 49, 79, 108, 134
PETERSBURG, VA. 24, 70, 104
PETERSON 42, 47, 48, 51, 79, 84, 92, 117, 122, 128, 130, 132, 135, 154
PETTERS 35, 89
PETTIFORD 19, 145
PETTIT 31
PHELPS 14, 19, 20, 31, 47, 56, 60, 64, 90, 109, 135, 139, 154
PHENILL 105
PHILLIPS or PHILLIP 78, 83, 103, 104, 133, 135
PHILPOT or PHILPOTT 3, 15, 69, 137
PIKE 47, 53, 70, 83, 97, 140
PILKENSTON 102
PILES 83, 93
PINCHBACK 89, 98, 102, 109
PINNIX, PINIX, or PINEX (also see PENIX) 7, 78, 99, 111, 112, 129, 140
PINSON 82, 91, 101, 107, 122, 124
PITTARD 31, 46, 127, 128, 130-132
PITTMAN 145
PITTSYLVANIA COUNTY, VA. 4, 6, 10, 26, 27, 47, 50, 71, 75, 92, 101
PLEASANT 15, 34, 60, 69, 70, 83, 93, 99, 100, 105, 108, 109, 111, 118, 139, 154
POE 44, 50, 84, 139
POGUE 16, 25, 62, 69, 97, 144, 154
POLSTON 53
PONDER 70, 140
PONDS or POND 99, 113, 121, 127, 135
POOL or POOLE 48, 49, 94, 145, 154
POOR 56
POPE 12, 13, 23, 143
PORTER 15, 27, 38, 44, 48, 53, 62, 80, 129, 137, 139, 154
PORTERFIELD 126
POSTON i, 4, 7, 17, 28, 30, 31, 35, 43-45, 48, 49, 61, 83, 89, 91, 92, 94, 95, 104-106, 125, 140, 154
POTEAT, POTEET, or POTEETE 25, 95-97, 99, 102, 107, 108, 135, 149, 154
POTTER 142
POWDRY 1
POWELL or POWEL 5, 20, 23, 32, 37, 43, 45, 51, 58, 63, 64, 75, 77, 83, 90, 94, 103, 104, 109, 111, 133, 135, 137, 146, 154
POYNER 45, 48, 58, 60, 70, 84, 87, 103, 106, 120, 124, 129
PRATT 1, 62, 146
PRESCOD 14
PRESTON 125
PRICE 10, 38, 43, 54, 58, 67, 74, 77,

172

RIVERS (continued) Deer, Eno, Flat or
   Flatt, French Broad, Green, Haw,
   Little, Matiponi, Mississippi,
   Red, Tar
ROAN ii, 7, 14, 53, 55-58, 77, 88,
   94, 124, 126-129, 131, 135, 139,
   148
ROBARDS 92
ROBBINS 80
ROBERSON 103
ROBERTS 3, 6, 8, 10, 14-19, 22, 24,
   35, 36, 47, 48, 50, 53, 54, 70, 80,
   84, 85, 89, 91, 109, 116, 121, 123,
   126, 129, 135, 137, 142, 146
ROBERTSON 3, 7, 9, 12, 14, 15, 20-23,
   27-29, 31, 33-35, 37, 38, 42, 46,
   47, 65, 66, 78, 79, 82, 90, 91, 96,
   102, 116, 120, 144, 155, 156
ROBINSON 2, 5, 6, 9, 16, 47, 53, 54,
   58, 63, 64, 73, 98, 112, 115, 122,
   135, 136, 139, 142, 155
ROCKINGHAM COUNTY, N. C. 20, 23, 30, 48,
   55, 88, 90, 92, 105, 148, 152
RODGERS 75
ROE 85, 87, 152
ROGERS 12, 21, 23, 28, 32, 33, 37, 45,
   52, 58, 64, 137, 142
ROLAND 32, 126
ROPER 31, 33, 65, 76, 88, 104, 119, 124,
   128, 135
ROSE 7, 15, 16, 24, 39, 45, 49, 61, 77,
   78, 114, 144
ROSEBROUGH 14, 41, 155
ROSS 2, 33
ROSSON 62
ROUNDHILL 55
ROUNTREE 2
ROWARK 18, 28, 34, 38
ROWLAND 74, 112
ROWLETT 102
ROYALL or ROYEL 58, 83, 89
RUARK 67, 96, 104, 123, 127
RUDD 23, 25, 28, 73, 89, 91, 96, 98,
   100, 102, 107, 111, 117, 122, 124,
   126, 132, 149, 155
RUE 21
RUFFIN 108, 130
RUMLEY 91
RUNNALS, RUNALS, or RUNNOLDS 16, 37,
   77, 109, 136, 137
RUSSELL 50, 66, 99, 112, 117, 131
RUSSELL COUNTY, VA. 41
RUSSEY 85
RUTHERFORD 9, 146
RUTLEDGE CREEK 10, 135-137, 141

S

SAINTCLAIR 93
ST. DAVID'S DISTRICT i, iv, 4, 72,
   79, 89, 94, 112, 134, 139, 140,
   141
ST. JAMES DISTRICT i, iv, 22, 134, 145,
   146
ST. JOHN 90, 93, 109, 111, 114
ST. LAWRENCE DISTRICT i, iv, 134, 141,
   142, 143
ST. LUKE'S DISTRICT i, iv, 134, 143,
   144
SAMMON or SAMMONS 10, 26, 30, 61, 80,
   115, 137
SAMUEL 2, 3, 9, 12, 20, 21, 33, 34,
   36, 37, 45, 46, 49, 54, 58, 61, 64-
   66, 79, 88, 91, 93, 97, 98, 100,
   105, 127, 128, 131, 132, 136, 155
SANDERS 1, 2, 6, 9, 11-13, 15-19, 21,
   23, 24, 28, 29, 33-35, 37, 41, 42,
   44, 47, 51, 53, 55, 56, 58, 61,
   66, 73, 75, 76, 78, 87, 88, 103,
   106, 110, 111, 120, 124, 125, 136,
   139, 145, 152, 155
SARGENT, SARJENT, or SERGENT 2, 6, 10,
   38, 41, 45, 49, 139, 142, 155
SARGENT'S CREEK 141, 142
SARTIN or SARTAIN 10, 96
SATTERFIELD or SATERFIELD 11, 20, 35,
   128, 131, 146
SAUNDERS 25, 108
SAVORY 13
SAWYER or SAWYERS 26, 32, 35, 52, 53,
   56, 61, 62, 77, 78, 88, 97, 104,
   114, 115, 120, 132, 133, 136, 137,
   140, 141, 148, 150, 155
SCARLET i
SCOBY 95, 96, 112
SCOGGIN, SCOGGINS, or SCOGINGS 12, 21,
   26, 28, 36, 53, 62, 65, 66, 78, 83,
   96, 101, 105, 145, 146
SCOTT 1, 8, 15, 24, 31, 34, 46, 60,
   71, 83, 87, 91, 103, 105, 113, 116,
   126, 132, 139, 140, 141, 155
SCRIBNER or SCRIVENER 83, 128
SCRYER 121, 122
SEAGROVE ii
SEAL 5
SEATON or SETON 1
SELF 145
SEWELL or SEWEL 82, 118, 124, 132
SEYMOUR or SEYMORE 15, 29, 142
SHACKLEFORD, SHACKLFORD, or SHACKELFORD
   17, 22, 61, 108, 133, 136, 155
SHADDOCK 109
SHANKS 62, 66, 97, 100, 110, 111

SLAVES (continued)
GIFTS OF SLAVES: (continued)
Newman and Dilce - Smithurst
to Parker 32
Sarah - Rice to Rice 95
Slaves - Burton to Burton 69
Slaves (7) - Dixon to Dixon 100
Tom - Jamison to Jamison 37
HIRE OF:
Charles - Harrison and Gunn to Lyon 133
Negro - Johnston 81
Negro - Mitchell 73
Negroes - Lea 126
Negroes - Mathews 117
Negroes - Matthews to Lea 132
Negroes - Mathis 115
Negro Woman - Mitchell 82
Negro Woman - Mitchell to Foster 78
Negro Woman - Mitchell to Lackey 66
Negro Woman and Child - Mitchell to
Hensley 62
SALE OF SLAVES*:
Abby - Hightower* to Dobbin* 22
Aggie - Man to McCollum 34
Amy - Long to Paine 27
Beck - Morris to Rice 19
Bob - Bryant to Richmond 23
Bob - Durham to Tinason 43
Bob - Tunks to Haralson 27
Celah - Bartlett to Murphey 126
Cesar - Stone to Murphey 17
Cile (girl) - Graves to Kimbrough 81
Cloah - Man to Rankin 32
Dinah - Chambers to Ervine 35
Doll - Lightfoot to Owen 26
Doll - Williams to Holt 26
Esther - Owen to Murphey 27
Esther - Taylor to Murphy 17
Gilbert - Riden to Williams 11
Grace - Wynne to Graves 38
Hanna - Dix to Gatewood 4
Hannah - Graves to Graves 81
Isaac - Matthews 130
Isaac - Stone to Robertson 22
Isaac - Stone to Stuart 18
Isbel - Richmond to McMurry 107
Jack - Coleman to Moore 2
Jack - Mann to Satterfield 35
James - Kerr 131
Lett - Harrison to Harrison 15
Lucy - Farley to Farley 19
Lyda - Thomas to Carter 25
Mary, Simon, Jude, George, Dice, Dorcas,
Roda, Lewis-Shelton to Watlington 27

*First name is the seller; second name is
the buyer.

SLAVES (continued)
SALE OF SLAVES: (continued)
Milley - Gooch to Rice 88
Negro Girl - Harrison to Win-
stead 11
Negro Girl - Wright to Donoho 133
Negro Woman and Child - Pope to
Womack 15
Negro Slaves - Lewis to Taylor 31
Negroes - Lewis to Dobbin 25
Negroes-- Neeley to Willson 23
Negroes - Thomas to Crisp 24
Nell - Hall to Thomas 27
Parice - Coleman to Moore 2
Patt and Patience - Black to
Black 15
Peter - Graves to Slade 81
Peter - Johnston to Murphey 20
Peg, Lucy, Tom - Marshall to
Shelton 20
Pett, Sarah, Beckey - Allen to
Jeffreys 48
Purchase of Slaves - Dobbins 70
Rachel - Chambers to Murphey 27
Rachel - Douglass to Evans 25
Sarah, Bob, Duke - Dabney to
Williams 55
Sally - Morrison to Haralson 35
Sally - Slade to Lea 132
Silvia - Williamson to Murphey 25
Simon - Allen to Jeffreys 48
Simon - Hightower to Dobbin 22
Slaves (4) - Dobbins to Fulkerson 4
Slaves - Rhodes to Montgomery 108
Slaves - Womack to Anderson 7
Solomon - Simpson to Simpson 127
Tom - Williamson to Blackwell 27
Tom, Fanney, Bek - Stone to Rob-
ertson 22
OTHER:
Chance, Dic, Tom, Jack, Sam -
involved in lawsuit - Rhodes
vs. Montgomery 103
Hannah and Peter - demanded by
Barker from Graves 66
Jess - Moore recovered from Jef-
freys 108
Jude (woman) and Mary - Moore
recovered from Cunningham 108
Slaves - Moore recovered from
Campbell 108
SLOAN 70
SMITH 1, 2, 4, 6, 7, 10, 11,17, 18,
21, 23-25, 27, 30-34, 38, 43-45,
48, 50-52, 54-59, 61-63, 67-70, 74,
75, 80, 81, 83, 85, 87-89, 91, 93,
95, 96, 98-101, 103, 104, 107, 111,

176

SMITH (continued) 115, 116, 118, 120,
122-127, 130, 133, 136, 137, 139,
140, 144, 146-150, 155
SMITHEY, SMITHY, SMYTHY, or SMYTHE 11,
18, 47, 69, 104, 105, 109, 111,
121, 136, 155
SMITHHURST 32, 146
SNEED 51, 76, 77, 82
SNIPES 90, 121
SNOW 137
SOLOMON 125
SOMERS or SOMMERS (also see SUMMERS)
41, 42, 44, 56, 57, 60, 66, 68, 69,
87, 88, 118, 120, 127, 128, 148, 155
SORINSON 83
SOUTH 142
SOUTHAMPTON COUNTY, VA. 59
SOUTHARD 14, 18, 21, 28, 142
SOUTH CAROLINA 26, 47, 108
SOUTHERLAND or SOUTHERLIN 4, 11, 38,
73, 75, 96, 108
SPARKS 3, 116
SPARTA, GA.96
SPELLER 76
SPENCER 6, 7, 24, 28, 30, 31, 43, 44,
46, 50, 51, 53, 56, 92, 108, 109,
120, 131, 140, 155
SPRING CREEK 146
STACY 28, 31, 43, 50, 53, 54, 65, 76-
78, 80, 88, 125
STADLER 88, 118
STAFFORD 33, 39, 41, 43, 48, 53, 55,
61, 71, 75, 76, 78, 85, 93, 118,
122, 124-126, 136, 155
STAFFORD COUNTY, VA. 97
STALCUP 46, 83, 93, 118, 155
STALLIONS 88
STAMPS 107, 113, 119, 126, 152
STAMPS SCHOOL 152
STANBACK 62
STANBURY 155
STANDARD 52, 121
STANDLEY 118
STANFIELD or STANDFIELD 25, 68, 98,
103, 104, 108, 137, 144
STANSBURY 3, 25, 39, 41, 73, 76, 136
STARBUCK 150
STARKEY 8, 9, 35, 52, 56, 87, 93, 95,
97, 124, 128, 136
STEELE 18, 33, 36
STEPHENS 6, 11, 12, 14, 16, 23, 24, 29,
31, 36, 37, 43, 44, 52-54, 64, 76,
79, 94, 109, 110, 112, 124, 127-129,
136, 155
STEVENS 58, 77
STEWART 1, 2, 21, 67, 79, 129, 142
STILES 36

STINK SHOLE 134
STINSON 8, 155
STOKES 4, 11, 93, 100, 106, 122, 123,
131, 136, 142, 152
STOKES COUNTY, N. C. 47
STONE 10, 12, 17-19, 22, 28, 48, 69,
74, 75, 78, 90, 96, 102, 118, 122,
123, 126, 142, 155
STONEY or STONY CREEK 60, 75,-105, 120,
139, 140, 141
STONY CREEK TOWNSHIP ii
STORY'S or STORIES CREEK 31, 141-143
STOTT 24
STOURGEN 3
STOVALL 69, 82, 93, 94, 101, 111
STRADER or STRATER 60, 62, 99, 109,
114, 120, 127, 122, 133, 137, 155
STREET 28, 31, 62, 125, 145
STRINGER 1, 4, 10, 12, 137, 155
STUART 10, 12, 13, 15, 18, 23, 29, 34,
41, 90, 142, 155
STUBBLEFIELD or STUBLEFIELD 4, 24, 44,
69, 71, 121, 137
SUGARTREE CREEK 141
SUIT 80, 91, 127, 132
SULLIVAN COUNTY, TENN. 68
SULLIVANT 53, 65, 85, 100, 104, 155
SUMMERS (also see SOMERS) 16, 22, 23,
25, 31, 49, 51, 137
SUMMONS 20
SUMNER COUNTY, TENN., WESTERN TERRI-
TORY 42, 71, 106, 115, 122
SURAT HOME CREEK 123
SURRATT 39, 45, 112, 144
SUSSEX COUNTY, VA. 75
SUTTON 28, 32, 35, 51, 103, 121
SWAINEY 61, 146
SWALLOW 27
SWAN or SWANN 24, 46, 64, 73, 96, 100,
104-106, 114-116, 121, 128, 136,
137
SWAYNIE 99
SWIFT 15, 19, 28, 31, 44, 52, 53, 60,
63, 70, 75, 85, 92, 97, 98, 100,
111-114, 116-119, 121-124, 128,
140, 141, 152, 155
SYKES 21, 28, 93

T

TAIT or TAITE (also see TATE) 57, 62,
65, 73, 79, 82-84, 87, 88, 100, 102,
110, 111, 116, 120, 125, 126, 148
TALBERT 20, 68
TANNER 85, 91, 103
TANON 139
TAPLEY 7, 13, 155

177

WAKEFIELD 3
WALDROP 90, 98, 99
WALKER 5, 7, 20, 26, 28-30, 32, 42,
  43, 55, 60, 62, 65, 70, 74, 80,
  88, 93, 98, 104, 106, 112-114,
  120, 124, 127-131, 137, 141, 145,
  147, 155
WALL 15, 21, 26, 44, 45, 55, 60, 61,
  120, 126, 143
WALLACE 55, 56, 103, 104, 139
WALLER 121, 124, 142
WALLIS 34, 51, 78, 126
WALLOX 36
WALOCK 3
WALTERS or WALTER 20, 31, 46, 142
WALTON 38, 69, 111, 117, 144, 145
WAR BETWEEN THE STATES ii
WARACK 3
WARD 25, 71, 108, 109, 111, 118
WARE, WAIRE, or WAIR 35, 38, 43, 50-
  52, 63, 96, 112, 121, 126, 137,
  155
WARF 113
WARREN or WARRIN 9, 12, 16, 18, 19,
  28, 29, 34, 54, 62, 67, 70, 77,
  79, 80, 90, 91, 102, 111, 118,
  123, 127, 142, 143, 150
WARREN COUNTY 20, 30
WARREN COUNTY, KY. 115
WARRICK 22, 71, 75, 77, 79, 80, 94,
  124, 148, 155
WARSON 139, 141, 142
WARWICK 18, 34, 47, 52, 55, 92, 136
WASHAM 82
WASHBURN 56
WASHINGTON 1, 3, 14, 15, 18
WASHINGTON COUNTY, N. C. 14, 156
WASHINGTON COUNTY, VA. 142
WATERFIELD 85, 91, 105, 112, 128
WATERS 43, 57, 59, 83, 102, 120,
  137, 155
WATKINS 25, 26, 42, 50, 87, 92, 99,
  102, 107, 110, 124, 132, 137
WATLINGTON 29, 48, 60, 93, 97, 121,
  130, 150
WATSON 22, 32, 69, 99, 142
WATT or WATTS 3, 24, 25, 36, 60, 96,
  113, 120, 129, 130, 137
WEAKE 13
WEATHERFORD or WATHERFORD 83, 116,
  127, 137
WEATHERS 133
WEAVER 97
WEBB 6, 18, 38, 88, 90, 93-95, 98,
  100, 102, 105, 107-109, 111, 114-
  116, 118, 120, 128, 144, 146, 150
WEEDEN or WEEDON 62, 91

WELLS 77, 83, 105, 111, 117, 119, 120,
  126, 127
WELSH 124, 136
WEST 43, 95-98, 101, 102, 106, 108, 110,
  122, 123, 125, 132
WESTBROOK 85, 90
WESTERN WATERS 135, 141
WHALEBONE 4, 51, 137
WHALEY 131
WHEELER 11, 26, 36, 145
WHETSTONE BRANCH 2
WHIPPLE 5, 6
WHITE 11, 27, 33, 42-44, 65, 70, 74, 75,
  84, 103, 132, 136, 137, 141, 146
WHITEHEAD 11, 42, 137
WHITEHURST 91
WHITEMORE or WHITMORE 93, 98, 118, 119,
  132
WHITESIDE 122
WHITFIELD 112
WHITLOCK 4, 141
WHITLOW or WHITLOE 55, 60, 61, 66, 82,
  83, 85, 90, 91, 118, 128
WHITSETT 120
WHITTED 132
WHITTINGTON 104
WHITTON 137
WILDER 110
WILEY or WILIE 7, 8, 13, 23, 31, 33, 48,
  52, 59, 67, 68, 91, 102, 106, 114,
  117, 129, 130, 132, 139, 148-151
WILKERSON 12, 29, 43, 61, 67, 75, 117,
  145
WILKINSON 9, 87, 155
WILKES or WILKS COUNTY, GA. 19, 35, 41,
  52
WILLIAMS 3, 5, 6, 9, 10, 11, 14- 24, 26,
  27, 29-34, 36, 38, 39, 41-45, 47-51,
  53-55, 57, 61, 62, 64-68, 70, 75, 77-
  80, 82, 83, 85, 89-94, 97, 100, 102-
  104, 109, 113, 114, 117, 119, 128,
  130, 132, 133, 136, 141, 142, 145-147,
  150, 151, 155
WILLIAMSON 14, 17, 19, 22, 24, 25, 27,
  28, 30-36, 38, 43-46, 48, 50, 53, 56-
  58, 60-62, 64, 65, 67, 68, 70, 77, 80,
  81, 83, 85, 87, 89, 92, 94, 95, 97,
  99, 104, 106, 108, 112, 114, 121-123,
  125, 141, 144, 155
WILLIAMSON COUNTY, TENN. 108, 125
WILLINGHAM 24, 30
WILLIS 22, 28, 29, 111, 115, 118, 121,
  136, 141
WILLSON or WILSON 1, 3, 7, 11, 15, 17,
  19, 22, 23, 28, 29, 32, 33, 37, 41,
  43, 47, 51, 53-55, 58, 63, 64, 69,
  71, 73, 75-79, 88, 92-94, 97, 100,

179

WILLSON or WILSON (continued) 102,
103, 105, 107, 115, 118, 119,
122, 136, 144, 145, 149, 150,
155
WILLSON COUNTY, TENN. 115
WILMOUTH 84, 111
WINCHESTER, VA. 9
WINDFIELD or WINGFIELD 6, 11, 21, 26.
WINDSOR, WINSOR, or WINDSON 24, 27, 31,
42, 44, 49, 56, 57, 64, 66, 78, 79,
83, 85, 90, 95, 96, 105, 106, 112,
116, 119, 120, 121, 125, 141, 148-
150, 155
WINN 75, 118
WINNINGHAM 55, 144
WINSTEAD 4, 5, 11, 24, 36, 145
WINSTON 47, 97, 98, 100, 106, 108,
113, 114, 117, 121
WINTERS or WINTER 31, 32, 46, 48, 50,
55, 92, 98
WISDOM 6, 25, 47, 54, 56, 61, 63, 67,
82, 85, 87, 91, 92, 104, 107, 110,
117, 126, 129, 132, 139
WISEMAN 3
WITHERS 114
WOLF or WOLFF 1, 53, 61
WOLF ISLAND CREEK 136, 137
WOMACK 2, 7, 11, 13, 14, 16, 23, 25,
46, 47, 69, 71, 75, 79, 90, 91,
108, 112, 116, 119, 131, 132, 137,
142, 144, 145, 151, 155
WOMBLE 99
WOODEN 35
WOODS or WOOD 28, 37, 76, 96, 102,
119, 126, 144, 148, 150, 151
WOODY 14, 23
WOOLFOLK 94
WOOTCH 80
WORD 77, 105
WORSHAM 110, 113, 118, 119, 123, 126
WORSON 41
WRAY 22, 54, 90, 145
WREN 146
WRIGHT 3, 11, 73, 75, 76, 93, 96, 99,
102, 122, 131, 133, 136, 137, 141,
142, 143
WYATT, WYAT, or WYATTE 5, 35, 36, 54
WYNN or WYNNE 4, 10, 38, 89, 108
WYNN'S, WYNN, or WYNE CREEK 135, 141

Y

YALOCK, YEALOCK, or YELLOCK 33, 77, 151
YANCEY 1, 1, 6, 19, 20, 29, 33, 34, 39,
44, 45, 47, 50, 52, 53, 55-58, 60,
62, 64, 66, 67, 69, 70, 74, 76, 81-85,
89-93, 96, 98-103, 105, 106, 108, 110,

YANCEY (continued) 111, 112, 115-119,
121-128, 130-132, 139, 148-152
YANCEYVILLE, N. C. i
YANCEYVILLE TOWNSHIP ii
YARBROUGH 26, 35, 145, 146
YATES or YEATES 3, 6, 24, 27, 33, 36,
42, 46, 47, 58, 64, 65, 73, 78,
97, 102, 103, 105, 106, 136, 139,
155
YEARGIN 14, 18
YEARLEY or YEARBY 82, 96, 122, 149

Z

ZACHARY 35, 48, 78, 79, 83, 87, 88, 91,
107, 111, 132, 148

180

INDEX
PLACES, STREAMS, ETC.

CASWELL COUNTY NORTH CAROLINA WILL BOOKS 1814 - 1843

Guardians' Accounts 1819-1847
1850 & 1860 Census Mortality Schedules
Powers of Attorney from Deed Books
1777-1880

Abstracts
by
Katharine Kerr Kendall
Index by
Mary Frances Kerr Donaldson
1983

In 1979 the author published her abstracts of the Caswell County, North
Carolina, Will Books 1777-1814. This volume covers the years 1814-1843. The
Will Books are at the office of the Clerk of Court, Caswell County Courthouse,
Yanceyville, NC 27379. The books are actually record books. In addition to wills
each book contains estate inventories, accounts, sales, settlements; indenture
bonds, letters of attorney, plus reports of various county officers and commissions.

Extant original wills of Caswell County are filed at the NC State Archives,
Raleigh, NC 27611, file number CR 020.801.1-7. On pages 197-8 of this volume is
a list of 272 wills abstracted. An asterisk preceding the testate indicates the
original will is filed at the State Archives.

The books of Guardian Accounts 1819-1847 are at the State Archives filed under
CR 020.510.2-4. Such accounts are germane to probate records of this volume. The
Mortality Schedules of 1850 and 1860 Federal Census are on pages 179-182. The
books are at the State Archives. Powers of attorney from the Caswell County Deed
Books 1777-1880 were abstracted from the books at the Caswell County Courthouse,
office of Register of Deeds.

Caswell County began its history in 1777 when it was formed from northern
Orange County. The first session of the County Court of Pleas and Quarter Sessions
met on June 10, 1777 at the house of Thomas Douglass near present day Leasburg, at
that date the center of the county. In 1791 Person County was formed from the
eastern portion of Caswell County and a site for a new seat of government was laid
out as near the center of the county as possible. From 1792 until 1833 it was
known as Caswell Court House. In 1833 the name was changed to Yanceyville to honor
James Yancey a leader in establishing a good and sound county government and the
first permanent chairman of the County Court of Pleas and Quarter Sessions. He
was a Representative in the General Assembly of North Carolina in 1802 and intro-
duced the bill creating the first school of Caswell County, the Caswell Academy.
In his obituary in the RALEIGH REGISTER, Dec. 3, 1829, it was stated that he
served as a worthy Representative for many years in the General Assembly, and in
his death the County of Caswell has sustained considerable loss".

Katharine Kerr Kendall
2814 Exeter Circle
Raleigh, NC 27608

ABBREVIATIONS USED IN ABSTRACTS

adm administrator(s)
acct account
adj adjoining
CC Caswell County(used in power of attorney from deed books)
commrs commissioners
d daughter
div division
exec executor(s)
inv inventory
ND No Date
Test Testifier(s)
w. written - indicates date a will was written. The
          probate date of a will is the month and year
          in which it was proved and listed by the
          County Court.
wit witness(es)
Water courses
 Br Branch
 Cr Creek
 R River

Other books by the author:

CASWELL COUNTY, NORTH CAROLINA - Historical Abstracts of Minutes of
    Caswell County 1777-1877. Published 1976; reprint 1977. Out of print.

CASWELL COUNTY NC Land Grants, Tax lists, apprentice bonds, and a list of
    estate records. Published 1977; reprints 1978, 1980. Price $10.00.

PERSON COUNTY COMPILATIONS - Land grants, tax lists, wills books from 1792
    until 1820. Published 1978; reprint 1982. Price $12.00.

CASWELL COUNTY NC WILL BOOKS 1777-1814 - Abstracts of 290 wills, guardian
    accounts 1794-1819; 1784 tax list showing location of land.
    Published 1979. Price $15.00.

CASWELL COUNTY NC MARRIAGE BONDS 1778-1868 - Contains 5000 marriage bonds
    with name of bride and bondsman or witness, over 15000 names. Listed
    in alphabetical order by name of groom. 59 of these bonds had been
    mistakenly filed in Stokes County records. Published 1981. Price $16.00

    All books are indexed by Mary Frances Kerr Donaldson.

CASWELL COUNTY WILL BOOKS

Book G - April 1814 - Jan. 1817

April Court 1814

Page
1 William Wall of Orange County binds his son William Wall 9 yrs.
old on or about the 11th of Aug next to William V. Browning of
Caswell County . 3 Mar 1814. Wit: Wm. Rainey, James Malone.
2 Power of attorney: Joseph McReynolds of Sumner Co. Tenn. to
Thomas Willson of county and State aforesaid to demand and to
receive of exec of Edmund Browning decd of Caswell County monies
due as part of legacy left McReynolds. 23 Dec 1813.
Approved by John Lauderdale and William Trigg, JP's of Sumner Co.;
David Shelby, Clerk; Edward Douglass presiding JP, Sumner Co.
4 Bond: Joseph McReynolds by his attorney Thomas Wilson of Sumner Co.
Tenn. and John Browning of Orange Co. NC bound unto Solomon Graves
Chairman of Caswell County Court of Pleas and Quarter Sessions on
condition that McReynolds shall refund his part of debts and
charges recovered from Robert Browning and Alex Murphey exec of
last will of Edmund Browning. Wit: Richard Browning.
5 Thomas Haralson surviving exec of last will of Mary Boyd decd in
acct with estate. Vouchers paid of Graves & Gunn, Wm. S. Webb,
John & Nathl. Wilson, Thomas Fearn, Jno. Somers.
6 Acct against sundries for strays taken up by rangers:
Elijah Graves 1 barrow(2.50)   John Bastin 1 bay horse ($17)
Asa Thomas 1 horse ($50)   William Smith 1 black horse
Thomas Swift 1 barrow   Benj. C. West 2 sows
William Brown 1 bull yearling

July Court 1814

6 MILNER BENNETT - Will - w. 4 Feb 1814. Wife Mary; daughter Mary
Bass Bennett (under 21); son Richard Henry Lea Bennett (under 21);
son Ambrose Lea Bennett (under 21); all surviving children:
Lucy Lea Sawyer, Nancy Hatcher Henderson. Exec: brother Ambrose
Lea Bennett and Thomas Graves brother-in-law. Wit: Thos. Gatewood,
Jas. Holder, Ch. Willson. Proved on oath of Charles Willson and
Ambrose L. Bennett qualified.

9 Power of attorney: Godfrey Crowder of Mecklinburg Co. Va. to Miles
T. Crowder of same county to transact business in NC and in Caswell
County. 3 July 1814. Wit: Edwin Reamy, Henry Shelton.
10 James Jeffreys age 14 the 14 Feb last bound to Jesse Harper. Jesse
Harper doth covenant and agree to teach and instruct said James
Jeffreys or to send him to school 9 months also the art of house
carpenter and Shop Joiner and that he will constantly find and
provide for said apprentice sufficient diet, washing, lodging, and
apparel fitting for an apprentice and servant until he attains
age of 21 years. /s/ Michael Montgomery, Chairman County Court.
(Note: Similar conditions and requirements appear on most apprentice bonds and are not repeated in abstracts.)
11 Inv property of Bartlett Hatchett decd by William Russell adm with
will annexed. Notes on Abraham Dunaway, William Willson, James
Henley, James Dollarhide, John Durham, William Breekeen, Philip
Echols,Samuel Jones, Richel Link, George Eskridge. 5 negroes left
in possession of Peggy Hatchett widow.

1

July 1814
Page
13 Acct sales personal estate of Bartley Hatchett to:
   Peggy Hatchett   Parks Beman   John Glenn
   Hugh Darby   John Howard   John Graves
   Solomon Graves   William Russell   Barzillai Graves
   John Taylor   Richard Smith
   By William Russell adm.
14 Sales estate of James Kitchen on 17 May 1814. Sales to:
   William Graves   Hugh Darby   Alexander Wiley
   Howell & Crews   Allen Hightower   Moses Langley
   Elijah Graves   James Vaughan   John Langley
   David Mitchell   Thomas Peterson   John Kitchen
   James Williams   Solomon Graves Esq. Nathl. Muzzall
   Abner Wisdom   Romolus Sanders   William Smith
   Jonathan Starkey   Joseph Kitchen   Fielding Lewis
   James Nelson   Thomas Langley   Elizabeth Kitchen
   Stephen Kitchen   Joseph Langley   Barnet Kemp
   Churchill Jones   Reubin Cox   John Carver
   John Comer   William Chandler   Nicholas Coils
   Cleator Jones   Daniel Chandler   Josiah Chandler
   Daniel Kitchen   James Graves   William Richmond Jun.
   James Martin   Sally Kitchen   John Hodge
   John Bateman   Thomas Bowman   William Patterson
   Wm.Sawyer Sen.&Jr. Step Roberts   Moses Kitchen.

21 JOHN TERRELL - Will - w. 8 Feb 1814. Wife Ann; sons Jonathan,
   Joseph, James (to get plantation after wife's death); daughters
   Peggy, Fanny, and Mary Terrell; daughters Lucy Murphey, Betsy
   Herndon, Patsy Murphey, Sally Murphey, and Isabella Moore.
   Exec: sons Jonathan and James. Test: Isaac Rainey, John Currie,
   Betsy Rainey.

23 ABNER BURTON - Will - w. 24 Feb 1807. Niece Polly Burton;
   brother John Burton. Exec: brother John. Wit: Thomas J. Moore,
   Barz Graves.

24 Sales estate of John Kersey 18 Dec 1812 to: Geo. M. Wilson, James
   Holder, Abraham Stanfield, Robert Randolph, Robert Tate, William
   Parker, Benjamin Matlock. By Alex Kersey.

25 Sales estate of David Preston by Rebecah Preston adm. to:
   Mose Stokes, George Ellot Sen., Smith F. Kent, Miss Nancy Preston,
   Miss Rebecca Ellot, Nathaniel Pass Sen., Samuel Burch, William
   Chambers, Thomas Phelps, Richard Barsdil, James & William Taylor,
   John Hall, James Navarre.

26 William Lea exec estate of Vines Matthews acct filed. Money received from land sold in Brunswick Co. Va. Accts paid to Elizabeth Ashburn, John Love, Bat Jackson, Jas Dameron, Moses Langley,
   Richard Burch, Nancy Robinson, Labon Stafford, John Breekeen et al.

30 Elizabeth Long adm of Robert Long Sen decd. Cash paid to Jesse
   Carter, G.B.Lea, N. Thompson, Elijah Morton, D.S.Farley, Jas
   Holder, D. Richmond, Jno Lea, Dr. McAden, B.Yancey, Thos. Jeffreys.

32 John Rone (Roan) exec estate of John Warrick. Accts paid to G & V
   Lea, Janett Roan, Robert Hamblett, Allen Burton, Jos. Richmond.

35 Sales estate of Joshua Jackson to: Robert Jackson, Daniel Hightower, Thomas Burton, James Nelson, John Bateman, Daniel Jackson;
   bonds on Richard and Daniel Hightower, Robert H.Jackson.

36 James Lea adm of Robert Long Jun. decd settlement of estate:
   To Sally Hodge due in div of negroes of estate; to Mary Riggs,
   David Harris, Nancy Harris for same; to Elizabeth Long for hire of
   negroes while she was guardian for the decd. 21 Jan 1814.
   Approved by Griffin Gunn and Jesse Carter.

Book G 1814-1815
Page
37 Taxable property for 1813
    230373 acres land
    904 white polls   1191 black polls
    9 stores   15 retailers of spirits
    amt for stud horses 15.15

October Court 1814

39 Thomas Turner and Anderson Birk adm of James Birk decd.
    Received cash of John Murray. Paid cash to William Street,
    Elijah Graves, Stephen & Benjamin Watkins, William Gooch Jun.,
    David Womack, Richard Jones for crying sale, Bartlett Estes for
    judgment, Thomas Turner, Christopher Thomas judgment; paid for
    sundries for widow of decd.; judgment on McClary. Recd. cash from
    Aquilla Compton, Thomas Jouett, Richard Hightower.
42 Estate of Sam Bracken in acct with John Bracken exec. Payments to
    Jeremiah Harrelson, Center Blackwell, Thomas Ruffin, Sam Dabney,
    William Grant, John Cobb, Robert King, Rodam Loveless, Jethro
    Brown, Doct. Foulkes.
43 Inv on 7 Oct 1814 of property of John Terrell decd by Jonathan
    and James Terrell.
44 Inv estate of Milner Bennett by A.L.Bennett exec on 20 Aug 1814.
44 Inv property of Abner Burton on 18 July 1814. Bond on Moses Taylor;
    note on Daniel S. Farley; note from William Lea to Wm. Taylor.
    Receipt on Geo Farley deputy sheriff for note on Jno. Hubbard;
    bonds on Newman Durham, Walker Samuel, Anthony Stephens;
    acct anti Martha Farley.
46 Sales property of John Dobbin decd by Daniel Darby exec. Notes
    on John Burton, Daniel Darby, William Evans, Capt.Wm.Gordon,
    Thomas Matthews, Adam Stafford, John Roan, Will Rainey, James
    Darby, Samuel Smith, Christopher Hinton.
47 Shadrach Ballard of age of 10 yrs. April next bound unto Solomon
    Brintle. /s/ Solomon Graves,Chairman Court of Pleas and Quarter
    Sessions.
48 Power of attorney: Anderson Smith to friend Allen Gunn to rent
    land and receive pay during "my absence while a soldier in US
    Army". 19 Sept 1814. Wit: Griffin Gunn, Azariah Graves.
49 Rent of land for 1815 for orphans of John Dickie decd -$25.50.
    By James Crossett.

January Court 1815

49 Div of negroes belonging to estate of William Muzzall decd to
    legatees: Mrs. Polly Muzzall, Edward Bartlett, Nathaniel G.
    Muzzall, Joseph W. Muzzall; Nancy, Frances, and William A. Muz-
    zall. 23 Nov 1814.
50 Evert Dawson Green Carter son of Braxton Carter,age 10 yrs.,
    bound by consent of his father to John M. Glenn.
    /s/ James Yancey, Chairman County Court.
52 Amt of hire of negroes of estate of John Hightower decd for 1813.
    Payment to James Hightower, Robert H. Jackson, John Thomas,
    Fielding Lewis, Nicholas Hightower.
52 Joseph Dameron Jun. guardian for Joshua Jackson acct filed.
53 Inv property of Isaac King decd by W. King adm.
54 Debts due Elizabeth Harden adm of Henry Harden decd. from
    Edwd M. Jones and Robert Holderness, Sam Cobb, James Bruce, Nathan
    Sims, Thomas Holderness, Wm.Buttery, James Cobb, Iverson Gwynn,
    Edney Tapscott, Zachariah Neal, Robert Brown, Joseph Allen, John
    Dillard, John Rice, John Windsor, Samuel Fielder, John Nance Jr.
    One years allowance for widow.

3

Book G 1815
Page
56 James Broach adm of William Mansfield decd acct filed. Pd vouchers
   of Baylor Burch, Barnett Kemp. Debtors to estate: Robert & Pheby
   McNab, Thomas Malone, Geo. Eubank.
57 Sales estate of John Terrell by Jonathan Terrell exec. Buyers:

Robert Hester	Lewis Terrell	Elisha Ruark
James Terrell	Willis Wells	Massey Terrell
John Murphy	Nathaniel Snipes	Janney Terrell
James Murphy	John Bateman	Abraham Villines
Jonathan Terrell	Clifton Jones	Thomas Verlines
John Roan	Lock Martial	William Evans
James Martin	Miles Brown	Robert Wade
John Eskridge	Britain Moore	Thornton Banes
John Sanders	William Owen	Joseph Smith
John Mansfield	Elijah Morton	William Mansfield
Major Wallis	Samuel Woods	Elijah Hyler
Joab Overby	Timothy Warren	Robert Jackson
William Leigh	Samuel Warren	Alexander Golerher

58 Allotment to Rachel King widow of Isaac King decd.
58 Inv of personal estate of James Culberson decd in hands of Wm.
   Culberson adm. 10 Jan 1815. Recd from John McFarling 8 Nov 1814.
59 Div of negroes belonging to estate of John Vaughan decd to following heirs: Elizabeth Vaughan widow; Alexander M. Long for his
   wife Tabitha; Jerusha, Sally, Thomas, Starling, and John Vaughan.
   Commrs: Jas Yancey, Thos Turner, William Gooch, Nathl Gooch,
   James Graves.
60 Sales estate of Thomas Stuart decd by William Stuart Sen adm.
   Sales to: Thompson McKissack, Thomas Burton, Robert Waid(Wade),
   George Thomas, Thomas Villines, Barnet Kemp, Stephen Stuart,
   James Stuart.
61 Acct estate of Conrad Strader by Christian and David Strader exec.
61 William Lea exec in acct with orphans of Vines Mathis decd for hire
   of Jenney and her six children for 1815, sum of $43.75.
62 Allotment to Elizabeth Harden widow of Henry Harden decd. 12 Dec
   1814.
62 Inv estate of John Coats decd and allotment to widow.
63 Allotment to Patsy Coats widow of John Coats. (Also spelled Courts).
   13 Dec 1814. By Thomas Swan, Greensbury Voss, and John Bolding.
   Test: William Robertson J.P.
64 John Burton exec of Abner Burton decd in acct with estate of Joseph
   Farley decd. Pd Mrs. Martha Farley her legacy from will; notes on
   James Holder, Thomas Jeffreys; pd Alex Kersey for making coffin $3.
   Pd Edward D. Jones atty.
65 Insolvents for 1812

John Baxter	Abner Perkins	Bartholomew Ellis
James Kanaday	Isaac West	Joseph Guess
Joshua Coleman	Lemuel Worsham	Bidsey Hughs
John Coleman	Benjamin Williamson	Hendly Humphreys
Sterling Caroll	William Carroll	James Leath
Henry Evans	Ro Elam	Geo Loyd
Larkin Ford	James Flipps	Isaac Mahan
Allen Kelly	Pleasant Hall	Henry Perkins
David Geleason	Danl Smith	Thomas Shanks
John Nichols	Isaac Wilkins	Samuel Tapscott
John Payne	Anderson Birk	Dempsey Ashford
Rich Perkins	Azariah Bruce	Thompson Birk
John Perkins	Ro Bruce	James Brawton
James Perkins Jun.	Samuel Boman	William Burch

4

Book G 1815
Page
65 cont.Insolvents for 1812 cont.

Robert Bevell	Alex Griffin	Charles Mathis
Windle Cook	Jno Haraway	Nicholas Vaughan
George Eubank	Elijah Kimbrough	Richd Vaughan
James Fowler	Jordan Massey	Jno Warren.
Tho Forest	Miles Scott	

66 Insolvents for 1813. (Repeats from 1812 not included)

Larken Ballard	William Newell	James K.Daniel
Joseph Burrows	Thomas Poteat	Saml Everett
Elijah Duncan	Daniel Smith	John Fitch
John Farell	Robert Sanders	James Johnston Jun.
Andrew Haddock	Caleb Wright	Joel Leath
Samuel Jelton	John Grayham	Ambrose Lewis
George Lay	John Horseford	John Murry
Thomas Langwell	John Noles	Ro McNab
Jno Nicholas	William Timberlake	Tho Morris
Jno Travis	Joseph Broadway	Abram Price
Fennel Willson	Philip Baynes	William Prewet
Absolem Bass	Henry Burch	Paschall Roberts
Jesse Elmore	Benj. Birk	Job Compton
Jno Howard	Enoch Collins	Zaeby Powell

Return by John Stamps late sheriff.

67 Estate of Robert Blackwell in acct with Thomas and Robert Blackwell exec. Pd Parson Moore for preaching funeral $2. Pd Francis
Smith for venduring $1. Payments to Samuel & James Watt, Daniel
Malone exec of Lewis Malone, legacy to Thomas & Robert Blackwell,
Levi, Carter, and Guarnold Blackwell; Pd John Keen for making
coffin; pd to Dr. Foulks, Rhodeham Lovelace.
68 Griffin Gunn trustee in acct with Caswell Co. reports for 1811-2.

April Court 1815

70 Sales estate of William Muzzall on 25 Sept and 18 Nov 1812. Buyers:

Polly Muzzall	Christopher Thomas	Absolem Lea
Nathaniel G. Muzzall	Daniel Hightower	Hosea McNeill
Thomas Turner	William Jopling	Thomas Pendergast
Thomas Compton	Betsy Muzzall	William Culberson
James Crossett	William Rudd	Azariah Graves Jun.
William Turner	James Turner(Hico)	Solomon Atkinson
Nathaniel Malone	Stephen Malone	Robert Jackson
Barnet Kemp	Lewis Corbett	Gregory Hightower
Robert Browning	Thomas Jouett	By Alex Murphey adm.

74 Inv estate of John Kimbrough Jun. decd due him from his guardian
Joseph Collier. 10 Apr 1815.
75 Bill of sale: James Bennett of Nottaway Co. Va. to Ambrose L. Bennett of Caswell County for negro slaves Aggy and her 2 children,
Kennon and Sarah. 11 May 1813.

76 SALLY KERSEY - Will - w. 18 Dec 1814. Brother Alex[r] Kersey to get
land left by father; sister Dicy Jones and Will Jones her husband
to have rest of estate to be divided later to their children:
John, Benj., William, Salley, Anny, Lucy, James, and Betsy Jones.
Exec: brother Alexander Kersey. Wit: Geo. M. Willson, Thomas
Gossett.

5

Book G 1815
Page

77 JOHN HUDNALL - Will - w. 23 July 1814. "I desire to distribute
all my property amongst my children". Granddaughter Elizabeth
R. Courts (land bought of Joseph Arnett); Lewis Whittemore and
his wife (land where I now live); Loosy Pitts; Eliza Clark,
Jemima and Betsy Clark; John Hutcheson and Molley his wife;
Scytha Withers; John Jeffries 3 daughters; land bought of El-
more, Hill, and Withers; balance of money to Scytha Withers;
balance of negroes to George Courts and Elijah Withers.
Exec: George Courts and Elijah Withers. Test: James Rawley,
Daniel Rawley.

79 WILLIAM JOHNSTON - Will - w. 25 Nov 1801. Uncle Samuel Johnston;
aunt Pheby Johnston; 3 sisters Elizabeth, Susannah, and Jane
Raney; land to step mother Elizabeth. Exec: uncle Samuel Johnston. Test: Loyd Vanhook, Lawrence Vanhook, Wm. McDaniel.
The exec refused to qualify and John Johnston named adm with the
will annexed.

80 Tempy Ballard of the age of 6 yrs the 25th of Dec. last bound to
Thomas Barton until she reach 21 yrs.

81 Zachariah Ballard, age 2 yrs July next, a boy of colour, bound
to Simon Denny.

82 Silvey Ballard, age 13 yrs next July, bound to Burnley Barker.

83 Greene Cary base born child of Sally Cary, 4 yrs the 15th March,
bound to George Burch.

84 Inv and sales estate of Lazarus Baldwin decd by John Baldwin adm.
11 Feb 1815.

87 Joseph Smith age of 8 yrs the 24 of Feb last bound to Thomas Swann.

88 WILLIAM UMPHREYS - Will - w. 18 Dec 1814. Wife Mary to have all
estate during her life; children: Elizabeth, Patsy, John, Jensey,
and Susannah Umphreys. Exec: wife Mary; Wit: Wm. Robertson,
Obediah Holloway, Elizabeth Holloway.

89 Sale estate of Lazarus Bouldin. Among buyers: Anguish Shaw, James
M. Dayley, Luke Bouldin, Henry Bouldin, John Bouldin, Thomas
Henderson, Littleberry Worsham, Alexander Ferguson, Robert Payne,
David Murphey, John Bastin, Richard Hill, Levin Downs, George
Adams, James Ransom, Levi Dennis, James Astin, John Royal,
Obediah Owen, John Brim, Instant Lay, Edmund Sparks.

90 Inv estate of Daniel Kitchen on 20 Jan 1813 by Stephen Kitchen adm.
Land purchased of Moses Kitchen; recd from estate of James Kitchen decd.

91 Sales estate of Daniel Kitchen to: Joseph Kitchen, Gregory Hightower, John Richmond, Freeman Hubbard, John Boman, William Sawyer
Sen., John Kitchen. Notes on A.L.Bennett, James Vaughan.

92 Sales of property of John Coats decd to: Peter Smith, Gregory Dur-
ham, John Brockman, Patsey Courts, Benjamin Loafman, John B.
Tennison, Edward Ruark, Williamson Price, Robert Coats, William
Bethell, John Powell, Rawley Kerns, Richard Hill. 31 Jan 1815.

94 Quinton Anderson adm of estate of Jephthah Parks, acct filed.
William Culberson guardian to orphans.

96 Acct of strays returned by William Lea county ranger for 1815.
Wm. Richmond Jun. - 1 cow   Richard Smith Senr. - 1 mare
Lewis Barton Sen. - 1 steer   David Mitchell Jun. - 1 horse
Joseph Arnett - 1 horse   William Kennon - 1 horse

Book G 1815

July Court 1815

97 Inv of Matthew Walker decd against the United States $19.93 by
   William Walker adm. 8 July 1815.
97 List of rents of land of L Malone by Daniel Malone adm to:
   plantations to Samuel Pittard and Richard Maleer.
   separate field to Daniel Malone Jun.
   legacy Robert Blackwell decd.
98 Sales or property of Hedley Harrison decd. Sales to Archibald
   Coleman, Thomas Brinsfield, Sarah Simpson, Hezekiah Boswell,
   Simpson Hornbuckle, Moses Simpson, James Cooper. By Salley
   Simpson adm. 9 May 1814.
99 Allotment to Ellenor Quine for years provisions. Debt due from
   John Martin for $12. 18 May 1815. Commrs: Michael Montgomery,
   James Burton, Robert Ware, John Ingram.
100 Inv property of William Humphreys on 10 June 1815 by Polly
    Humphries exec.
101 Inv property of Elizabeth Long Junr. decd by John Comer adm.
102 Inv property of James Knighton decd by William Walker adm. Re-
    quest to court to allot years provisions to widow.
103 Inv property of Jacob Quine decd by Elisha Ingram adm. 22 Apr
    1815. Acct due on John Martin. Acct due by Daniel Hailey;
    bond due by Littlebery Worsham in 1817; 1 hoe and bell said to be
    at Presly Carter's shop.
104 Inv estate of John Hudnall of property specially willed (888 acres
    land); inv property sold by George Courts and Elijah Withers;
    notes due on Josiah Womack, Miles Murphey Sen & Jun; Richard
    Hill; accts on Joseph Murphey, David Murphey, William Murphey,
    and George Courts.
106 Inv estate of William Johnston decd and amt of sales by John John-
    ston adm. Bonds on Johnston son of Widow, James Johnston black-
    smith, James Lea, John McMurry, James Johnston Sen., William
    Edins, Frances Burton.
108 Taxable property of Caswell County for 1814
       787 white polls   8 stores
       1847 black polls   14 retailers spirits

October Court 1815

108 ROBERT PARKES - Will - w. 1 Aug 1815. Wife Mary; daughter Celah
    Malone(land adj Hiram Culbertson, Richard Arvin to VanHooks line
    then by Spencer's and George Prendergast's line); son Alfred
    (land on blue creek at a ford called Arvin's road and adj land
    given to son Jepthah); son Jeptham (land adj Culbertson, Solomon
    Parkes, and Hiram Parkes); son Alfred to have land given to wife
    Mary after her death; clothes and books to be divided between sons
    Hiram and Alfred. Exec: son Alfred; sons William, Hiram, Robert,
    heirs of son Laban, heirs of son Jepthah to have $1 each;
    daughters Rachel, Elizabeth, Susannah, and Sarah $1 each.
    Wit: Richard Arvin, William Florance. /s/ Robert Parks.

111 JOHN KEEN - Will - w. 30 Aug 1815. Wife; son Thomas; all children;
    son William and Daughter McClain; daughters Elizabeth Grayham,
    and Sally Potter; sons James and David; daughters Nelly, Nancy,
    and Susannah; young children under age. N.B. My wife to will her
    chest and Table and clothes to who she pleases.
    Test: Jos. Roe. No exec named.

7

Book G 1815 - 1816

112 Sales property of Jacob Quine on 4 Aug 1815 to:
    Ellenor Quine   James Miles   John Baxter Jun.
    Velinda Alverson   James Davis   Joshua Jeffers
    Maraday Price   James Matlock   Stephen Chandler
    Wm. W. Price   Reuben Kennon   James Ingram
    Edward Jones   Mary Alverson   James White
    John Mimms   Peter Powell   Presly Carter
    Andrew Haddock   Absolem Sawyer   James Burton.
    Woodlief Hooper   Elisah Ingram
      By Elisha Ingram adm.
115 Inv property of John Keen by Thomas Humphreys, Ransom Boswell,
    and David Poyner.
116 James Burton and Henry Howard exec of Robert Lyon decd. acct
    filed. Cash received from Richard Haddock, John P. Harrison,
    Griffin Gunn.
117 John Jeffreys age 13 yrs the first of June next bound to Jesse
    Harper. James Yancey, Chairman of County Court of Caswell Co.
118 Betsy Roads age 6 yrs the 4th of April next bound to Jacob Ahart.
119 Allotment to Peggy Knighton and family of one years provisions,
    she wife of James Knighton decd. Test: William Robertson J.P.
120 Power of attorney: William Stafford of Jackson Co. Tenn. to Brother
    John Stafford of same county to receive legacy of Father Laban
    Stafford decd. 18 Sept 1815.
120 Received on 27 Jan 1814 of Thomas Barton 10 lb.14 sh. 8 p. being
    full balance against the estate of decd husband William Able.
    /s/ Milly Able. Test: William Robertson.
121 Receipts of Jesse Abel and Sarah Abel for part of their father's
    estate. Thomas Barton adm. 12 July 1815. Test: John Powel,
    Josh Montgomery.
121 Receipt of Agness Jackson for legacy of Thomas Jackson Senr. decd.
    of Robert H. Jackson guardian.
122 Rent of land of John Dickie's orphans for 1816 - $35.01.
122 Transfer of property: Nuam Johnston in right of wife to Robert
    Lyon for her part from estate of Robert Lyon decd. 30 Sept 1815.
123 Receipt of Nuam Johnston for legacy left his wife after death of
    Rebeccah Lyon decd. Wit: Richard Haddock.

January Court 1816

124 RICHARD ESKRIDGE - Will - w.21 Mar 1809. Wife Elizabeth;
    sons Thomas, Burdet, John, William; daughters Rebecca, Anne, and
    Martha; other children: George, Richard, Samuel, Elizabeth Price,
    Sarah Coils, and Mary Stafford all are married and have been
    given their portions. Exec: wife Elizabeth, Burdet Eskridge,
    and Vincent Lea of Leasburg. Wit: Gabl. Lea, Vincent Lea.
    Burdet Eskridge qualified.

126 JESSE CARTER - Will - w. 30 Sept 1815. House and lot in Peters-
    burg, Va., to be sold; wife Sally Carter (land bought of Thomas
    Donoho and Jacob Wright Sen.); wife to have all negroes which
    she had before marriage; nephew Jesse Thompson; children to get
    land and Tavern House west to Wm. Sawyer's line; daughter Rebekah
    P. Sanders; son John P. Carter; Payton Morton released of all
    debts and to continue living where he resides; Ralph Hubbard and
    David Thomas Sr. released from debts. Exec: son-in-law Romulus
    M. Sanders and friends John H. Brown and John P. Harrison, and
    son John P. Carter. Wit: Griffin Gunn, William Sawyer.

Book G 1816

128 ROBERT BLACKWELL - Will - w. 6 Dec 1815. Wife Matilda;
daughter Martha Blackwell under age to get land willed by
Father and where his Mother now lives; brother John; brothers
and sisters to share estate if Martha departs life before age
or marrying. Exec: wife, brother Thomas Blackwell. Test: Joseph
Roe, Zillah Blackwell. Thomas Blackwell qualified.

130 HENRY QUINE - Will - w. 1 Jan 1816. Sister Sariah Camron*wife of
William Camron; brother William Quine; Mrs. Jane Montgomery wife
of Michael Montgomery Esq.; Catherine Quine eldest daughter of
Jacob and Nelly Quine his wife; Goolsby Quine; Michael Montgom-
ery son of Michael Montgomery Esq. to get silver watch; Miss
Elizabeth Montgomery daughter of Michael and Jane; saddle bags to
Alexander Montgomery; brothers Mordecai and William Quine; sister
Elizabeth Stafford wife of John Stafford. Exec: Francis Howard.
Test: Laban Farley, Michael Montgomery Junr., Alexander Mont-
gomery. Francis Howard qualified.*(Carman or Carmon)

131 NATHANIEL PASS - Will - w. 12 Jan 1811. Sons Holloway(eldest), and
Nathaniel; daughters Sally Moore, Jemimah Williams, Mary Phelps,
Ellis Taylor, Rebekah Burton, Fanny Taylor; sons John and Thomas;
grandson William Moore; granddaughters Patsy Pass Williams,
Fanny Ellis Gann, Nancy Burton; grandsons John Felps, Thomas
Taylor, and Henry Taylor. Wife Ulsey to have land during her
life and then to go to son Thomas. Exec: son Thomas Pass.
Wit: Ad. Murphey, John G. Murphey, H. Harrelson.

133 NATHAN WILLIAMSON JR. - Will - w. 10 July 1815. Sisters Patsy,
Sally, and Polly P. Williamson; all sisters and brothers:
George, Thos., J., Swift, and Anthony; Fanny Prather, Patsy,
Sally, Polly P., Betsy Smith, and Peggy Simpson. Exec: brothers
Thos. and Swift Williamson. Test: Thomas Poyner, Thompson Porter.

134 CHARLES H. BROOKS - Will - w. 7 Oct 1815. Wife Sally Brooks to
raise children and dispose of estate at her discretion.
Exec: Brother-in-law Nathan Williams, son George Brooks.
Wit: Henrietta Rice, Jesse Payne.

136 Acct current of Durett Richards adm of Asa Thomas. Commrs: Archd
Samuel, Geo. M. Willson, Thos Gatewood, Warner Williams.

137 Sales estate of Elizabeth Long decd by John Comer adm. Sales to:

George B. Dameron	Jeremiah Willson	John Roan
William Dameron	John Lea	Drucis Riggs
Nicholas Coils	Edly Campbell	Wm. Hinton
Archibald Rice	James Vaughan	Peter Crowder
Walker Samuel	James Fullington	Jannet Roan
Fieldin Lewis	Robert Martin	Daniel Richmond
John Hodge	Charles Mathis	Abel Fulks
Freman Hubbard	William Stephens	David Northington
Romulus Sanders	Hutchen Burton	Jesse Robertson
William Campbell	Wm. Peterson	Wm. Long - Wm. Lewis
Samuel Hodge	Mary Hinton	Thomas Boman
Hiram Herley	Wm. Richmond	John Peterson
Jeremiah Rudd	Joseph Kitchen	Asa Oliver - Polly Long
Elisha Evans	Brittain Moore	Wm. Whitlow - John Comer
Thomas Comer	David Hodge	James Darby - James Swan
Daniel Hicks	Nathaniel Comer	Anderson Burk
Charnal Hightower	Thomas Riggs	Abijah Rolen
Lewis Ferrell	Isaac Vanhook	John Chandler
Joseph Richmond	Isaac Richmond	John Johnston

9

Book G 1816
Page
144 William Lea exec in acct with orphans of Vines Mathis decd for
    hire of negroes for 1816.
145 Sales estate of Carter Malone by Daniel Malone adm. Notes on
    Thompson McKissack, Young Burt, Joseph Muzzall, Thomas Villines,
    George Thomas, Richard C. Ward, Charnal Hightower; judgment on
    Garnet Neely.
146 Inv property of Col⁰ Robert Parks decd by Alfred Parks.6 Jan 1816.
147 Rent of land for 1815 of estate of Lewis Malone by Daniel Malone.
147 Ordered that 20 cents be laid on every poll and 6 cents on every
    hundred dollars worth of landed property for use of the poor for
    1815. Azariah Graves, Clk.

                April Court 1816

148 THOMAS SWIFT - Will - w. 15 Mar 1816. Sons Harvey, Robert, John,
    Wesley, Milton, Williams B., and Thomas; daughters Betsy Shelton,
    Polly Tate, Susanna Swift, Lindy Swift; wife Peggy Swift to have
    estate during her life. Exec: wife, Caswell Tate, and John
    Stamps. Wit: Jethro Brown, Alvis Clifton. John Stamps qualified.

151 ANN RICHMOND - Will - w. 20 Feb 1814. Sons Jesse, Isaac(lands
    from legacy due them from father's estate); daughters Peggy and
    Agness; sons James and Joel. Exec: sons James and Jesse.
    Wit: John Langley, William Richmond, John Richmond.

153 THOMAS LEACHMAN - Will - w. 22 Jan 1816. Wife Susannah all
    property during her life and then divided among children:
    Littleton, John, Citty, Elizabeth, and Thomas Leachman.
    Exec: wife and John Boswell. Wit: Samuel Fielder, Joseph Carter.
    Susannah Leachman qualified.

154 GREGORY DURHAM - Will - w. 4 July 1815. Wife Peggy to have estate
    during her life or widowhood; sons James and Isaac; daughters
    Salley Durham,Patsey Buncy (or Burns?). Exec: wife and William
    Robertson. Wit: W. Patterson, Isaac Patterson.

156 JOHN PENIX - Will - w. 27 Mar 1816. Wife Barbara; daughters
    Elizabeth, Susannah, Ann; sons Thomas, John, Benjamin, Milton,
    and Joseph. After wife's death estate to all children. Exec:
    Wife Barbara and friend Nathan Williams Esq. Wit: John Henslee,
    Macksfield Henslee. Nathan Williams qualified.

157 ELIZABETH LONG SENR. - Will - w. 23 May 1815. Daughter Mary Steph-
    hens two daughters Katharine Hightower and Betsy Stephens;
    daughter Elenor Whitlow; daughter Sally Hodge(wife of John) and
    her 2 children Gabriel and Betsy; daughter Mary Riggs son Robert
    Long; orphans of son John Long decd (4 eldest and the youngest
    Betsy). Legacy for Robert Long put to interest until he is 21
    years. Exec: Daniel Hightower. Test: Greg. Hightower, William
    Whitlow.

159 Sale estate of Charles B. Brooks on 29 Jan 1816. 1 sorrel mare
    and 1 bay horse sold to George Brooks.
160 Inv estate of Nathan Williamson decd taken 5 Jan 1816 by Thomas
    and Swift Williamson, exec.
161 Sales property of William Hailey decd sold 16 Feb 1816 to:
    Mrs. Hailey, John Lea, Geo Williamson, N. Lea, Chas. Hunter,
    Pope Crowder. By John Lea adm.
162 Inv estate of Lewis Foster by Joseph Benton adm. Bonds on Free-
    man Leath, Anthony Foster.
164 Inv personal estate of Richard Eskridge decd by Birdet Eskridge,
    exec. 16 Apr 1816.

                        10

Book G 1816

Page
165 Inv estate of Henry Quine by Francis Howard. Bonds on George
Findley, Alex Montgomery, Rowzee Samuel, John Payne.
166 Acct of strays returned by county Ranger for 1814:
Wyatt Stubblefield - a sorrel horse
William Rainey - a young bay mare
166 Inv property of Robert Blackwell 25 Jan 1816. Notes on Edward
M. Jones, Thomas Smith, Carter Blackwell, Phil Neal, Matilda
Blackwell, William Cobb, Levi Blackwell, James Cobb, Richard
Smith, James Scarborough, Jonathan Murry, William Bradbury.
168 Inv property of Elizabeth Williams decd. by N.Williams adm. A
memo on Nathan Williams; bonds on George Brooks, Susanna Rice,
Henry Williams, Benjamin Spencer (this bond doubtful). 7 Apr
1816.
170 Inv estate of Henry Williams decd by N. Williams adm.
170 Inv and sales estate of Nathaniel Pass Sen. on 9 Feb 1816. Sales
to Thomas Pass, John Pass, Lewis Hall, Rebecca Burton, Nathaniel
Pass, Jeremiah Samuel, William Williams, John Hubbard; bonds on
John Pass, William Singleton, John Hubbard, William Gattis, Thomas Connally. By Thomas Pass exec.
172 Sale property of Nathan Williamson on 6 Feb 1816 to: Thomas Fielder,
Thos Williamson, John Pennix, John Barker Sen., Freeman Leath.
173 Sales property of John Garner on 1 Feb 1816 to:

Mary Garner	David Douglas	Aaron Simpson
Susannah Garner	Malon Stacy	Thomas Fielder
Thomas Garner	Jesse Payne	Caleb Willson
Freeman Leath	Joel Leath	Buckner Duke
Hezekiah Boswell	James Taylor	William Jones
Zachariah Hasting	Nathan Sims	

By Freeman Leath adm. Cash received of Geo Brooks by hands
of Nathan Williams.
175 Additional sales of estate of Bartley Hatchett to Hugh Darby,
Ibzan Rice, John Howard, James Adkins, William Gillaspie, William
Graves, Zeri Gwyn, James Rudd, Ziba Rice, Zachariah Groom, Richard Smith, Polly Hatchett, Zadock Rice, Elisha Stanley, John G.
Warren, Samuel Evans, Elijah Martin.
177 Amt of hiring of negroes of B. Hatchett decd by William Russell,
adm to Richard Ogilby, John Graves, Elijah Martin, John Mims,
H. Lipscomb, John Cobb, Joseph Stafford, Richard Haddock, Jourdon Whitlow, Jacob Ahart.
178 Statement of property of Charles B. Brooks decd. Note against
Edmund Rice due 1815. By Nathan Williams and George Brooks,exec.
179 Sales estate of Elizabeth Williams on 12 Jan 1816 to:

Henry Williams	Thomas Christmast	Thomas Arnold
Nathan Sims	William Turner	Henry Collier
Joseph Lane	Henry Hailey	Peter McKinney
Ira Siddle	Daniel Sewel	William Smith
Willis Ashford	Richard Smith Jun.	Nathan Williams
Jesse Payne	Ibzan Rice	

180 Sales estate of Elizabeth Williams on 29 Jan 1816. Among buyers:

William Hargraves	Zachariah Groom	Sally Brooks
James Graves	Robert Swift	Malon Stacy
George Brooks	William Henslee	Philip Pearce
Joseph McCully	Thomas Henslee	George Simmons
John Sawyer	John Henslee	William Slade
Charles Cox	William H. Rice	Samuel Fielder
Elisha Barton	Nathaniel L. Rice	George Oldham

11

Book G 1816
Page
180 Sales estate of Elizabeth Williams cont. Sales to:

Charles Mitchell	Thomas Stacy	Devreu Hightower
David Barker	William Glasby	Jesse Hollis
Samuel Estress	Thomas Belsiah	Hosea McNeill
Ransom Boswell	Madison Birk	George Shelton
Wyley Yancey	John Pinson	James Kinnebrew
Joel Leath	James Taylor	Christopher Brookes
James Bird	James Shepherd	Thomas Foster
James Vaughan	Mumfor Ford	Hugh Darby
James Page	John Penix	Robert Brown
John Hastain	Robert Martin	John Anderson
Bartlett Estress	Jourdan Massey	
John Stadler	Thomas Poyner	
William Chandler	Williamson Rice	

Sale of slaves: Tilmon to Malon Stacy, Simon to James Yancey, Sall to James Graves.
    By Nathan Williams adm.
193 Sale estate of Henry Williams on 29 Jan to:John Pinson, Howel
    Massey, Peter Powel, Jeremiah Lea, et al. Nathan Williams adm.
194 Inv personal property of Jesse Carter decd at his north, middle,
    and south quarter and of slaves not including negroes given to
    Romulus Sanders; inv at mansion house; 1 Nov 1815. By Romulus
    Sanders exec.
196 Inv goods, wares, merchandise at store of Jesse Carter decd.
    14 Oct 1815.

    THERE IS MISTAKE IN THE NUMBERING OF PAGES. PAGE NUMBER REVERTS TO:
182 List of balances due Jesse Carter. 8 pages of store accounts.
191 Inv of goods bought by Maj. John H. Brown for Jesse Carter.
197 List of property of Jesse Carter sold 1-5 Feb 1816. Among buyers:

Josiah Samuel	David Northington	James Rudd
John Lea (CB)	John Meadows	Peter Crowder
Major Thomas Donoho	Maj.Thomas Graves	John Horton
Richard Jones overseer	Vincent Peterson	Wm.Gilasby
Richard Jones(Hogan's Creek)	Archibald Samuel Esq.	Herndon Samuel
Henson Alverson	Nathaniel Meadows	Sol Sute
Wid Martha Jackson	Nicholas Willis	John Hodge
Wm. T. Glascow	Gen.Barzallai Graves	Alex Gordon
Robert Randolph	William Lea of Capt.	Jacob Ahart
Capt. Warner Williams	Philip Pearce	John Poteet
James Lea of Capt.John	William Lyon Sen.	Miles Poteet
William Kirk	Pleasant Chandler	Wm.Parker
William Herritage	Josiah Chandler	John Hinton
Henry Hooper	Romulus Sanders	
Wid. Sarah Carter.		

Property retained by Wid Sarah Carter, John P., Mary C., Archibald G., Susanna S., Jesse, Elizabeth B. and William Carter.

202 Div of slaves of Jesse Carter to Romulus Sanders for his wife
    Rebecca, to widow Sarah Carter, and to 7 children named above.
    Value of slaves $28161; total about 100 slaves. 20 Jan 1816.

207 William Lea Esq. in acct with estate of Laban Stafford decd.
    Div to sons Jno., William, Labon, Ely, Adam, Joseph, and Henry
    Stafford.

210 Allotment to Sisley Foster widow of Lewis Foster decd and to
    orphans of Lewis Foster. Capt. Joseph Benton to pay her $50 from
    estate , he being acting adm. Commrs: John Pennix, John Barker,
    Mahlon Stacy. 1 Feb 1816. Nathan Williams J.P.

Book G 1816
Page
211 William Furgurson, an orphan of age of 10 yrs last Aug., apprenticed to Roswell Burross. Nathan Williams, Chairman Co. Court.
212 William Gibson orphan age 7 yrs and 4 mos. bound to Charles
Keesee. James Yancey, Chairman County Court.
213 George Draper an orphan age of 19 yrs last Oct bound to Elijah
Carmon.
214 William Sawyer Sen. exec. in acct with estate of James Kitchen,
decd. Payments to Doct Smith, Attorney Suttle. 10 Apr 1816.
214 Receipt of Beauford Pleasant for $284.83 for balance in full part
of estate of his Father. Recd. from Micajah Pleasant and
Thomas Pleasant exec. 2 May 1812.
215 Receipt of William Florence for $295 for his part of estate of
John Pleasant decd in right of his wife. 2 May 1812.
215 William Lea exec in acct with orphans of Vines Mathews decd for
hire of negroes.

July Court 1816

216 SAMUEL JOHNSTON SEN. - Will - w. 17 Jan 1811. Son John to have
goods which he has already received and the eastern tract of land
given in deed 2 Feb 1810; son Samuel to have remaining western
land; daughter Sally Holder and her husband James Holder;
daughter Suckey Gordon; daughters Polly, Phoebe, and Charlotte.
Exec: sons John and Samuel. Test: Loyd Vanhook, John Johnston.
Codicil: Changes allocation of slaves to Sally, Polly, Phoebe,
Charlotte, Susannah. 10 Apr 1816. Samuel Johnston qualified.
219 Additional inv of estate of Betsey Sloan decd by Samuel Grier adm.
Money due her from Margaret Grier and William Culbertson adm
of Samuel Greer, decd. (Name possibly Stoan or Stone.)
220 Inv property of Gregory Durham decd on 22 Dec 1815 by Peggy Durham
and William Robertson exec. Bonds on William Burns, James Arnett,
Joel Gilson, John Alverson (South Carolina), David Lewis.
221 Inv estate of Lewis Corbet decd by James Yancey adm.
222 Inv estate of John Penix decd taken 16 Apr 1816 by Nathan Williams
exec. Bond on Joseph Lane.
223 Inv property of Francis Gooch decd taken 1 May 1816 by Nathl.
Gooch adm. Included $4 found in Desk after the sale by William
H. Rice.
225 List of balance of property of Jacob Quine decd, $57.02 his Wages
as a soldier in the United States Service. Elisha Ingram adm.
9 May 1816.
226 Inv estate of John C. Gooch decd by William Gooch adm. 1 May 1816.
227 Inv estate of Thomas Campbell decd taken by Hugh Campbell adm.
"Edley Camal Detor to his father."
228 Inv estate of Elizabeth Long decd widow of Robert Long decd by
Daniel Hightower exec. 30 Jan 1816.
229 Inv property of George Walker decd taken 16 Feb 1816. Bonds in
presence of William Florence and Aqul. Compton. By Hugh Walker.
230 Inv estate of William Walker decd by Deborah Walker and Joseph
McCulloch. Book accts against Joshua Walker, Joseph McCullock,
Ashford Walker, Howel Whitmore, Charnal Hightower, Anderson Birk,
Beny Hunt, John Fitch Sen.
232 Inv property of Solomon Childers decd taken 9 Apr 1816 by Hosea
McNeill adm.
232 Power of attorney: Nancy Turner of Wayne County, Ky., to friend
William Gunn of county aforesaid to recover from estate of grandfather Henry Turner decd of Caswell Co. that part willed to her.
15 Feb 1815.

234 Power of attorney: James Donoho of Sumner County, Tenn., to friend Yancey Turner of county aforesaid to recover from estate of Henry Turner decd of Caswell Co. 1 Oct 1814. Wit: John Barr, Elijah Simpson. David Shelby, Clerk of Court.

236 Power of attorney: John Cochran of Robertson Co., Tenn., to friend Thomas Gunn of Logan Co., Ky., to receive of Thomas Turner of Caswell Co. exec of his father's estate and Cochran a legatee of same. 12 Aug 1813. Archer Cheatham, preciding Justice of Robertson Co.

237 Inv and sales of subjoined personal estate of Richard Eskridge decd sold 1 May 1816.

238 Sales estate of John C. Gooch decd on May 2 & 3, 1816. Among buyers: Christopher Brooks, Nathaniel Gooch, William Chandler, Jeremiah Graves, Stephen Rice, Henry Williams, Wilie Yancey, James Vaughan.

239 Sales estate of William Gooch decd by William Gooch exec. Among buyers: Elisha Evans, Joseph Morton, John Zachary, James Graves, Nathaniel Gooch, William Bruice, James Page, Nathaniel L. Rice, Henry Williams, William Gooch, Thomas Haralson, James Yancey, Christopher Brooks, Devreau Hightower, Abner Gooch, Howell Boswell.

240 Sale of property of Lewis Foster decd taken 8 Feb 1816. Sales to:

Susannah Foster	Anthony Foster	John Hasting
Cisley Foster	Thomas Foster	William Barker
Aaron Simpson	George Oldham	Spencer Jackson
Coleby Foster	John Lea	John Barker
Joseph Benton	Malon Stacy	William Hasting
William Sawyer	Larken Ballard	Polly Foster
John Mitchell	William Jones	Freeman Leath
David Douglas	James Sawyer	By Joseph Benton adm.
Thomas Fielder	Hezekiah Boswell	

243 Sale of property of Christopher Dameron taken 1 May 1816. Sales to:

Isaac Watkins	John Lea (CB)	Parim Jackson
Druce Riggs	Samuel Loven	David D. Nutt
Joseph Swan	James Darby	Williamson Dameron
Robert Hamblett	William Dameron	Christopher Matthews
George B. Dameron	Charles Matthews	By Joseph Dameron &
David Hodge	Robert H. Jackson	Batt Dameron exec.

245 Sale of property of Solomon Childers decd sold on 27 Apr 1816 to:

Thomas Williamson	Thomas Poynor	James Taylor
Lewis Ballard	Nathan Sims	Elish Brown
Solomon Brintle	Hosea McNeill	Thomas Jackson
By Hosea McNeill adm.		

246 Sales estate of Richard Burch by B. Kemp adm. Sales to:

Polly Burch	John Hulett	William McManamy
George Horton	Edmun Burch	Samuel Woods
Richard Burch	George Burch	Robert McKee
Baylor Burch	William Mansfield	Barnet Kemp

248 Sale of property of Ann Richmond on 2 May 1816 to:

Peggy Richmond	John Langley	Joseph Richmond
Isaac Richmond	William Burgess	Joseph Kitchen
John Richmond Jun.	William Ware	John Long
Joel Richmond	Daniel Darby	Walker Samuel
Moses Kitchen	Isaac Watkins	John Mathis
Daniel Richmond	Thomas Waterfield	Martin Morton
William Richmond Jun.	John Roan	Elijah Morton
Joseph Langley	Bird Wisdom	Ambrose L. Bennett
Daniel Malone	James Nelson	William Lea

Book G 1816
Page
248 Sales of Ann Richmond cont.
   William Whitlow   Adams Richmond   William Stephens Jun.
   Step Roberts   William Dameron
      By James and Jesse Richmond exec.
251 Sale of property of Sarah Dameron 1 May 1816 to:
   James Darby   Luke Mathis   George B.Dameron
   Patsey Jackson   Charles Mathis   John Hodge
   William Dameron   Bird Wisdom   Samuel Hodge
   Ann Moorhead Mathis   Thomas Waterfield
      By Batt Dameron
253 Sales of part of estate of William Walker by Deborah Walker and
   Joseph McCulloch adm. 8 July 1816.   Sales to:
   Deborah Walker   James Graves   Pleasant Corbet
   Thomas Loyd   Charles Cocks   Thomas McCullick
   Joseph Bradford   Elizabeth Walker   George McCullock
   James Byrd   William McCord   Patsey Erwin
   George Walker   Hugh Walker   John Weedem
   James Barnwell   Andrew McCullock Sen. Thomas Turner
   John Walker   "   Jun.   et al
   Robert Martin   Joseph McCullock
259 Sales estate of Lewis Corbet sold 27 June 1816. Sales to:
   Anney Corbet   James Yancey   John Zachary
   Joseph McCullock   Jarrett Figgans   William Turner
   Joseph Aldridge   Jesse Corbet
      By James Yancey adm.
261 Sales estate of John Keen decd by David Poynor Jr. adm.   30 Dec.
   1815. Sales to:
   William Maroney   James Curtis   Nathan Rice
   James Foster   John Shackelford   John Winsor
   James Orr   John Cobb   James Maby
   William Orr   Ellen Keen   James Keen
   Thomas Poynor   Molly Keen   Thomas Humphreys
   Richd. Smith   Benjamin Elmore   Charles Mitchell
   John Grant   Samuel Luterall
   Philip Neal   John Rice
   Robert Orr   David Walker
   Wm.Paschal Sen.
262 Sale of perishable property of Alexander Kerr Jun. decd by order
   of April 1816 Court. By James Kerr adm.   9 July 1816
   Note on Benjamin Lea with Solomon Kerr, security.
    "   " Solomon Kerr   " Benj. Lea   "
    "   " Hosea McNeill " Wm. V. Brown   "
    "   " Larkin Ballard " Macksfield Henslee "
    "   " Pleasant Childers with Benjamin Lea security
    "   " Barz.Kerr with Solomon Kerr security.
263 Inv property of Alexander Kerr Jun. decd: 1 negro boy Stephen,
   1 horse, a few farming tools.
263 Debts due on books of Asa Thomas decd with the State of NC.
   By Durrett Richards adm.
264 Sales estate of Francis Gooch sold 2 May 1816. Among buyers:
   Nathl. Gooch, James Miles, George Shelton, John Pinson, Wm.H.
   Rice, Joshua Rudd, Polly Egmon. (List is 6 pages long)
271 Inv of sales of Elizabeth Long by Daniel Hightower exec.
   Among buyers: Bart Dameron, Daniel Darby, John Whitlow, William
   Whitlow, William Stephens Sen., John Comer, Nathl. Comer Sen.&
   Jun., Druis Riggs, Samuel Love, Samuel Hodge, Daniel Hodge,
   Pason Jackson, Jesse Robertson, Thomas Mathis, Daniel Hicks,
   James Swann, Philip Day, Lewis Yealock.

15

Book G 1816
Page

277 Property sold at late dwelling house of George Walker decd by
   Hugh Walker adm. on 18 and 19 Apr 1816. Sales to:

James Bird	Willis Reaves	Jacob Graves
Abner Walker	Joseph McCullock	James Graves
James Walker	William Douglas	Gear Graham
Ashford Walker	William Smith Jun.	William Walker,Org.
Aquilla Compton	Dev Hightower	Aze Graves
William McCord	Joshua Walker	Richard Arwin
James Miles	Thomas Malone	James Baulden
Thomas Arnold	Joseph Smith	William Street
Richard Jones	James Faucett	David Fulton
James Currie	Geo Walker	William Davis
Christer Spencer	Reese Enoch	John Murray
Zachaus Paul	John Stadler	Howel Whitmore
John Walker	William Jopling	Absolem Nutt
Vines Grey	Willis Ashford	Abel Foulkes
Job Walker	Elizabeth Stalcup	Wylie Yancey
Wilie Massey Sen.	William Maughan	Will McCawley
John Shaw	Buford Pleasant	Geo McCawley
David Davison	Henry Collier	John T. Ray
William Bird	James Collier	John Weedon
John Fitch Sen.	Benjamin Birk	Colby Foister
Thomas Page	Elisha Brown	John Fitch Jun.
William Miles	Jeremiah Lea	

284 Taxable property for 1815
   912 white polls   11 stores
   2087 black polls   14 retailers spirits

285 Allotment to Polly Burch from estate of Richard Burch decd. By
   Thomas Slade, Samuel Woods, Jonathan Terrell. 3 May 1816.
285 Sales estate of Benjamin Cantrill decd sold 29 Apr 1816 by James
   Yancey adm. Sales to:

Richard Browning	William Brannock	Jeremiah Lea
John Sawyer	William Cantrill	John Armstrong
James Vaughan	Robert King	Sarah McCullock
Edmund Rice	Robert Martin	John Hasting
Luke Hicks	Samuel Edmundson	Jonathan Davis
Isaac Cantrill	Mary Stadler	Joseph Benton
Hosea McNeill	Thomas Christmast	William Sawyer Jun
Henry Davis	Richard Martin Sen.	Nathan Moore
Lewis Barton	Richard Martin Jun.	John Sawyer Sen.
John Henslee	Doct. John Mebane	James Yancey
Freeman Leath	Nathan Sims	Joseph Armstrong
John Underwood	Samuel Estes	Alfred Moore
Simon Davis	Barzillai Kerr	Robert Browning
Jesse Hollis	James Simmons	
Thomas Foster	Bennett Estes	

291 Allotment of negroes of estate of William Walker decd to: George
   Walker by Hugh Walker guardian; Joseph McCullock in right of his
   wife Nancy; Elizabeth Walker by her guardian Hugh Walker; Deborah
   Walker. 17 Apr 1816. By Q. Anderson, C. W. Brooks, Wm.Florance.
292 Allotment to Deborah Walker widow of William Walker.
293 Allotment to Ann Corbet for year's maintenance for her and children. 27 June 1816. By W. Warren J.P., James Bouldin, Thos Pendergast, Thomas Turner.
294 Allotment to wife and family of Benjamin Cantrill decd. 27 Apr
   1816. By Thomas Williamson, Wm.V.Brown, Hosea McNeill, Jesse
   Hollis, William Sawyer.

Book G 1816
Page
294 John Carter Horseford,orphan age 10 yrs. the 27 Dec last, bound
to Pryor Loveless.
296 Elizabeth Horseford, orphan age 2 yrs. the 15 March last, bound
to Pryor Loveless.
297 William Russell adm of Bartlett Hatchett decd with the will attached paid to Polley Gwin, Russell Hatchett, John Hatchett, and
Bartlett Hatchett all remaining estate now in hands of John
Stamps guardian of said children legatees of Bartlett Hatchett.
299 Inv estate of Benjamin Cantrill decd. Notes on Samuel Dickey,
Robert Lackey, William Davidson, Thomas Phillips, Arthur Lovens,
William Wallis(to estate of Alexander Robbs), George Brown, Benjamin Simpson, Sarah Freeman, James Hart, Thomas Maraen, Wiley
Whiteheart, George Horner, Samuel Beasley; James Taylor for at-
tending as witness in suit vs Henry Davis. By James Yancey adm.

October Court 1816

301 JOHN HENSLEE, SEN. - Will - w. 20 Mar 1816. Land to be divided
between 4 sons and one daughter, Richard, William, John, Benjamin,
and Sarah; already given to sons Macksfield and Thomas; daughters
Eleanor Ray, Keziah Ray, and Betsy Pleasant. Exec: Nathan
Williams Esq., son Richard Henslee, and son-in-law Beauford
Pleasant. Wit: John Pennix Sen., Thomas Pennix, John Pennix Jun.
Nathan Williams qualified.

303 SAMUEL SMITH - Will - w. 3 June 1816. Wife Elizabeth to keep estate together; son Samuel H. Smith to manage plantations in Caswell and Person; children to have portion of estate as each marries or reaches 18 yrs. Exec: wife, sons Samuel H. and John,
brothers William Smith, Maurice Smith, and Alexander Smith of
Granville County.
"Confirmed as noncupative will by verdict of Jury and Judgment
of the Court. Saml. H. Smith qualified. (See minutes of Octo
T(erm) for verdict)"

306 MOLLEY PARKS - Will - w. 30 July 1816. Son Alfred Parks to have
whole estate; grandson Robert Parks the son of Hiram Parks;
clothes to children of Alfred Parks; daughter Celah; granddaughter Polly Parks daughter of Jepthah Parks. Exec: James
Nelson. Wit: William Florance, John Murray.

307 WILLIAM KENNON HARRISON - Will - w. 17 Nov 1798. Wife Mary H.
Harrison to have 700 acres land on Dan River; if there are heirs
wife to have her dower,and if no heir wife to dispose of property as she is disposed to.
On oath of John McCadin, Andrew Harrison, and John P. Harrison
that will and hand writing was of the decd, it was admitted to
probate. Mary H. Harrison qualified.

308 Inv of goods, chattles of John Bateman decd by James Darby adm.
14 Oct 1815. Debtors to estate: Thomas McKissack, William
Herritage, William Whitlow, Giles Rogers, Thomas Wright.
309 Inv estate of Jourdan Whitlow decd. Notes due from Nicholas
Willis, John Stamps. By Romulus M. Sanders, adm.
310 Inv of John Burtons property. Bonds on Solomon Debow, Stephen
W. Burton, Samuel Burch, William Rainey Jun., John Garner; judgment on Daniel S. Farley in Caswell Court Insolvement.
312 Inv estate of John Kerr Senr. decd by John Kerr an adm. 16 negroes.
Cotton sold in Richmond $388 subject to deduction for carriage
to Richmond and for necessary articles purchased there for the
family; sale of corn to Elisha Brown, Mahlon Stacy, Jerry Lea,
Jno Sawyer, Jno Underwood. Note on Wiley Yancey given to Alexan-

17

Book G 1816
Page
312 cont.
    der Kerr Sen. decd.
314 Inv of property of Obed Florence decd taken 3 Apr 1816. By William
    Florence and Toliver Florence adm.
316 Inv of Richard Gibson on 10 Sept 1816 by Anor Gibson administra-
    trix (his wife).
316 Sales property of Jourdan Whitlow decd to:

John Howard	William Groom	Josiah Morton Jun.
Nicholas Willis	Joshua Butler	Polley Whitlow
William Turner	Josiah Morton	James Browning
Elijah Martin	Martin Browning	Barz Graves Sr.
Joshua Rudd	William Willis	Barz. Graves, Genl.
Abel Foulks	John Whitlow Jun.	By Romulus Sanders,
Thomas McFarlin	William Bruce	adm.

317 Sale of property of John Bateman on 30 July 1816 by James Darby,
    adm. Sales to:

Susannah Bateman, widow	Luke Matthews	John Richmond
Zachariah Evans	John Smith	William Campbell
Daniel Darby	David D. Nutt	Joseph Langley
Williamson Dameron	Charles Matthews	Daniel Richmond
Thomas Comer		

319 Sales property of Tho Swift by John Stamps exec. Sales to:

John Swift	Hugh Cobb	Rhodeham Loveless
William Shelton	John W. Graves	Thomas Christmas
Wesley Swift	Milton Swift	William Ferrell
Suckey Swift	Ira Siddall	Wm. B. Merony
Elijah Weathers	John Keesee	Ibzar Rice
Daniel Scott	James Atkins	Robert Swift et al

322 Amount of sale of Thomas Campbell decd by Hugh Campbell adm.
323 Acct estate of John Hightower by Daniel Hightower adm. Commrs:
    William Lea, Joseph Dameron, William Warren, Joseph Langley.
325 Inv property of Thomas Swift decd taken 16 Apr 1816 by John Stamps
    exec. Included 1 Whitfield Sermons, 3 vol. Wesley's notes;
    19 slaves.
327 Receipt of Elijah Kennon to Mr. Groves Howard for 122 pounds for
    full legacy due from estate of Joseph Bush decd to wife the
    daughter of Joseph.
328 Sales estate of Obed Florence taken 30 Apr 1816. (Buyers not inc.)
332 Allotment to widow and family of John Bateman for year's provisions.
333 Allotment of negroes of John Hightower decd to: William, Agnes,
    Daniel, Stephen, Nicholas, James, Lucy, Elizabeth, and John
    Hightower. 5 Oct 1816.
334 Durett Richards adm of Asa Thomas acct current.
335 Div estate of John Hudnall decd into 8 parts. (Names not given)
336 Adm of William Muzzall decd in acct with estate. Accounts paid to
    James Yancey, Slade & Yancey, Doct. Wm. S. Webb, William Kirkland,
    Thomas Compton, Absolem Lea, Daniel S. Farley; paid Mrs. Williams
    for curing negro Absolem's sore foot; pd Thomas Henderson, Printer,
    for ad in the Star; pd William Lockhart tax for Orange land for
    1814. Notes on Nimrod Ellis, John St.John, John Paul, and
    Darling Ray (insolvent and decd), Solomon Newcom (insolvent and
    gone), Robert Clark (insolvent and gone); pd Robert H. Jackson
    for coffin for Egbert N. Muzzall. Commrs: Azariah Graves, and
    William Lea.
341 John Roan adm of estate of John Long decd final acct. Allowance
    made for Elizabeth Long decd during her lifetime.
343 Distribution of estate of Henry Harden decd to: James Foster, John
    P. Freeman, Thompson Harden, and Elizabeth Harden. 15 Oct 1816.
    Elizabeth Harden adm.

Book G 1816-1817
Page
343 Hire of negro Adam belonging to Joshua Jackson by Joseph Dameron.
344 Asa Russell, orphan age 11 yrs the 19 Apr last, bound to Major
    Brockman.
345 Joseph William Dawson Green Carter , age 9 yrs the 13 Sept last,
    bound to John Keesee. Gabriel Lea, Chairman County Court.
346 Receipt: Alexander Murphy gives receipt to Groves Howard for money
    as adm of Aldridge Rudd decd, Mrs. Nancy Rudd widow.

January Court 1817

347 JOHN H. BROWN - Will - w. 11 Sept 1816. Wife Nancey; son William B.
    Brown (under 18) to get land purchased of John Endsley of Stokes
    County with Jonathan B. Watlington; son William to have all lands
    after mothers death and he should have a good classical education
    at Chapel Hill or some other good seminary. Exec: wife Nancey and
    nephew Bedford Brown (son of Jethro Brown), and brother-in-law
    Alfred M. Bethell. NB If son William die without heir, all land to
    go to Nancy.

350 ELIZABETH SWIFT - Will - w. 16 May 1816. Sister Sarah Carter to get
    all estate. Exec: brother John H. Brown and sister Sarah Carter.
    Wit: Thomas Williamson, Anthony Williamson, Caty Chamberlin.

351 JAMES WARREN - Will - w. 31 July 1809. Wife Sarah to have estate
    during her life or widowhood; son Thomas; daughters Fanney and
    Nancey (land on Panther Creek); all children Elizabeth Holt
    together with the rest. Exec: sons William and Boswell Warren.
    Wit: Reuben Jones and James Crosset.

353 Allotment to widow of W.B.Meroney for support for herself and
    family. 4 Dec 1816.
354 Allotment to Martha Burton of estate of John Burton decd. 8 Nov
    1816. Commrs: Richard Ogilby, Alex. Kiersey, Geo. M. Willson.
354 Inv of bonds and cash of Elizabeth Williams decd. Bonds on Henry
    & Nathan Williams, George Brooks, Susanna Rice, Benjamin Spencer
    due 1794 considered of no value (he insolvent and non-resident),
    Daniel Williams due 1787 of no value. By Nathan Williams adm.
355 Inv estate of Wm. B. Merony decd taken by Jethro Brown. 11 Nov.
356 Inv and sales estate of Alexander Kerr Jun. decd sold 15 Nov 1816.
    Sales to: Christopher Brooks, Elisha Brown, Barzillai Kerr, Free-
    man Leath, Jeremiah Lea, Guilford Childers, Pleasant Childers,
    James Vickers, Benjamin Lea, Samuel Estes, Buckner Duke, John
    Kerr Jun. By James Kerr adm.
357 Sales estate of John Kerr Senr. on 14 Nov 1816 to: Jeremiah Lea,
    Joseph Penix, John Sawyer, William Hart, Hosea McNeill, Christopher
    Brooks, George Martin, et al. By James Kerr & John Kerr adm.
358 Inv property of Zephaniah Tait decd taken 20 July 1816 by Nathaniel
    Gooch adm. Notes on Thomas Jouett, John Barker, Robert Martin,
    Jeremiah Lea, Absolem Nutt, Benoni Rawson (desperate); accts on
    Richard Arnold Sen. & Jun., James Bird (Caswell), Guilford
    Childers et al.
362 Sales of Capt. John Burton decd sold 8 Nov 1816 to:

James Fullington	Henry Burton	Edward Kiersey
James Lea Esq.	John E. Ogilby	Wm. Roberts
Richard Ogilby	James Farley	Peter Crowder
Noel Burton	Thomas Pass	E.D.Jones
Stephen Burton	Robert Tait	Henry Roper
Jeremiah Samuel	Burwell Bevil	William Lea
Henry Mahon	Peter W. Farley	Josiah Samuel
John Hubbard	Wm. Williams	Mrs. Tucker

19

Book G 1817
Page
366 Sales estate of Thomas Swift 6 Aug 1816 by J. Stamps exec. to:

Wesley Swift	Milton Swift	John Foster
John & Robert Swift	Suckey Swift	John Stanley
Philip Pierce	Joseph Roe	Mrs. Sally Brooks
William Shelton	Caswell Tait	Robert Dupey
Edward Watlington Sen.	Joseph Cobb	James Curtice
Brooks Watlington	Henry Glass	Joel Leath et al.

371 Bartlett Yancey ear mark of his stock a crop and a slit in left
ear and the right ear foxed.
372 Sales estate of Zephaniah Tait sold 7 Nov 1816 by Nathaniel Gooch,
adm. Among buyers:

Henry Tait	Nathaniel Gooch	Richard Arnold
Anthony Foster	Brice Collins	William Barnwell
John Shaw	Reddick Dishonugh	William Mise
Daniel Payne	William Street	Willis Reeves
Alexander Wiley	Elijah Flack	Solomon Kerr
Zachariah Patillo	Nathaniel Snipes	Tapley Horn
Lucinda Tait	Wesley Debulor	William Vincent
Elizabeth Yancey	Juhu Bird	Freeman Leath
Francis A. Tait	James Graves	Edmund Herndon
William Slade	Jacob Graves	

380 Inv estate of Solomon Simpson decd who departed this life 17
Sept 1816. By Gabriel Lea adm.
381 Sales estate of John Henslee decd. Among buyers. Thomas Poyner,
Buford Pleasant,Richard Henslee, Macksfield Henslee, William &
Thomas Henslee, John Mitchell, Joseph Lane, Joseph Penix, James
Massey, Mahlon Stacy, Larken Ballard, Thomas Barton, Sally Henslee, Cesile Foster, Joseph Benton.
385 Sale of property of William B. Merony decd by Jethro Brown adm. to:
John Swift, Jethro Brown, John H. Pickard, John Rice, James Paschall, James Cobb, William P. Hall, Mrs. Merony, James Barker,
Claborne Dalton, Thomas Merony, Zachariah Neal, William Herritage,
Richard Smith purchased 1 gig for $12.25.
387 Inv estate of Samuel Smith decd. Land in Caswell Co. on Dan River,
in Person Co. on Hico and Adams Creeks, in Tenn. not particularly
known. Large amount of books inc. Methodist guides, Wesley's
works, biographies "well bound and 50-60 old school books and
phamplets". By Samuel H. Smith exec. Bonds on Samuel J. Harrison,
James Pullington, Jos Dickson, Dennis O'Briant; acct on Cary
Williams.
391 Div of negroes of Thomas Swift decd to: Harvey, Lucinda, Robert,
Wesley, William, John, and Susanna Swift; to William Shelton and
his wife Betsy, to Milton Swift.
392 Allotment of estate of Zephaniah Tait to: Brice Collins, Alexander
Wiley, Lucinda Tait, Elizabeth Yancey, Fanny Tait, Nathaniel Gooch,
Henry Tait. 8 Nov 1816. Commrs: James Yancey, Jere Lea, E.Brown.
394 Estate of Daniel Kitchen in acct with Stephen Kitchen adm.
395 John Lea adm. estate of William Hailey decd acct. filed. Allowance to Mrs. Hailey; paid George Williamson for crying sale.
Accts pd to R.M.Sanders, Jesse Robertson; judgment on Thomas
Jeffreys vs William Hailey.
396 Power of attorney: Ezekiel Jones of Montgomery Co., Tenn., to
Nathan Williams Esq. of Caswell Co. to demand from Richard Jones
of Caswell County exec of John Jones decd all money due from estate. 22 Oct 1816.
397 Thomas Phillips a boy of colour age 2 yrs. bound to William Kennon.
/s/ William Cannon.

Book G 1817

Page

398 Rachel Phillips a girl of colour age 5 yrs the 9th of Sept last
bound to William Kennon. (seal) William Cannon.

399 William Howell, boy of color age 12 yrs. last Sept, bound to
Thomas Kennon.

400 Peter Huston, boy of color, age 2 yrs. bound to William Douglas.

401 Henry Mann age 11 yrs bound to Robert Smith.

402 Appraisal and Div estate of John Kerr decd. A list of property
given to following during his lifetime:
James Kerr for Alexander decd.
Benjamin Lea for William Kerr decd.
Jeremiah Lea, Benjamin Lea, Christopher Brooks, John Kerr Jun.,
Joseph Pennix, Barzillai Kerr, James Kerr, Solomon Kerr.
Allotment to widow of decd. Commrs: Q. Anderson, Hugh Walker,
Thomas Lloyd.

End of Book G

Taxable Property for 1816

Names of Destrict	N° acres of Land	Amount of Valuation	White Polls	Black Polls	Stores	Retailers
Richmond	80603	338311~33	251~	860~	8~	10~
St. Davids	58504½	156892~37½	215~	515~	6~	6~
Caswell	47309½	149666~38	172~	313~	1~	1~
Gloucester	64213~½	173959~32½	303~	488~	5~	7~
Total Am.t	250630	818829~41	941~	2176~	20~	24

Book H-Page 79

21

April Court 1817

Justices present: Gabriel Lea, James Rainey, Archibald Samuel, Esqrs.

Page

1 JAMES WILLSON - Will - w. 13 Nov 1816. Wife Nancey all property
during her life; sons George M. Willson(land after wife's death);
2 grandchildren Nancey Vaughan and Maurice Vaughan; son-in-law
Lewis Vaughan. Exec: George M. Willson, John Lea Jun., and George
Washington Jeffries. Wit: John Gamble, Nancey Howell.

2 CATHARINE CURRIE - Will - w. 5 Feb 1816. Sister Mary Willson;
brother Hugh Currie; sisters Elizabeth, Martha, and Margaret Currie;
part of land of James Currie decd to brother William Currie.
Exec: brothers Hugh and William. Wit: Ezekiel Warren, John Westbrooks, John Mitchell. William Currie qualified.

3 Additional inv estate of Anthony Swift by Thomas Williamson surviving exec. 25 Mar 1817. Cash from sale of John Dawsons land to
Hezekiah Boswell.

4 Acct current of sales of Anthony Swift decd to: Thomas Williamson,
Abraham Simmons Jun., Anthony Foster, John Rice, Acquilla Barton,
James Cobb, Nicholas Chub, Drury Pinson, Richard Smith, Nathan
Rice, Jesse Brintle, Lewis Barton, John Chamberlain, James Bird,
Williamson Rice, Spencer Jackson, John Williamson Jun., William
Carmichael, George Simmons, James Massey, John Smithey. Feb 1817.

6 Residue of estate of Henry Harden sold 12 Feb 1817 to: Thomas
Brinsfield, John Windsor, John P. Freeman, Jeremiah Rice. By
Jeremiah Rice adm.

7 Sales estate of John Kiersey Sen. decd. Mar 15, 1817. Sales to:
Wiley Johns, Alexander Kiersey, Martha Kiersey, George Findley,
and Thomas Jeffreys.

7 Property sold by Joseph Benton adm of Lewis Foster decd to:
Cisley Foster widow; judgment against Robert Lackey and John T.
West; notes on Aron Simpson and Nathan Williams.

8 Sales estate of Thomas Baxter decd sold 4 Apr 1817 by Jane Baxter,
adm. Sales to: Mrs. Jane Baxter, John Baxter Jun., Nathan Slade,
Thomas Ware Jun., Robert Ware, Peter Smith, James White, James
Richardson, William Ware Sen & Jun., William Ferrell (son of Henry),
Thomas Kennon, John Cobb, James McClarney, Henry Terrell, Daniel
Scott, John Baxter Sen.

9 Inv goods of Brown, Watlington and Co. Mar 1817 by Alfred Bethell,
exec of John H. Brown. Bonds of George Williamson and Nathaniel
Rice.

12 Inv goods belonging to firm of Bethell and Brown on 30 Mar 1817
by Alfred M. Bethel exec of John H. Brown.

19 Solomon Graves adm in acct with estate of William McKinney decd.
Accts due of William Cook, Thomas Kennon, Absolem Sawyers, Eleanor
Quine, John Ingram, Starling Gunn, Nathaniel Harrelson, F.B.
Phillips. Note pd Richard Haddock due Thomas Skates.

19 Inv balances due Jesse Carter. Among debtors:

Miss Yankey Sawyer
Stephen Kitchen
John Love(son of Samuel)
Francis Hightower(widow)
Capt. William Richmond
Major Graves(Capt. James Graves guardian)
Mary Poteat(widow)

John Morton(son of Pey-
ton)
James Lea Jun.
William Lea Jr.
William Lea of Capt.
Azariah Graves of Thom.
Jacob Graves

Book H 1817
Page
19 cont. - Debtors to Jesse Carter:
Widow Long spo of Robt. decd.   William Shareman
Lewis Graves   Charles Shareman
Betsy Campbell of Tho.   William Suite Jr.
William Cunningham(Tennessee)   Daniel Sewell
Miss Patsy Beaver   Thomas Yearly
McNeill & Kirkland   Tryon Yancey
Thos Kennon son of Joel   John Meadows
John Payne(Taylor)   Rev. William Moore
John Payne(Person Co.)   Sherrod Owen
Robert Sanders   Epps Moore   et al
     (The list is 9 pages.)
28 Sales estate of Jesse Carter decd by Romulus Sanders adm.
30 Alexander Kiersey exec of John Kiersey decd - sales to Thomas
   Jeffrey, William Moore, Doct. John McCaden, George Williamson,
   sheriff, John Stamps sheriff.
31 William Williams orphan age 7 yrs. next Aug bound to Benjamin
   Johnston.
32 William Forguson orphan age 13 yrs. next Aug bound to James Ware.
33 Daniel Elam orphan age 12 yrs. the 10 of last Mar bound to
   Alexander Kiersey.
34 Daniel Philips orphan, a boy of colour, age 8 yrs. bound to Edwin
   Raimey.
35 Sale property of Meradith Price decd sold 7 Feb 1817 to:
   Polly Price   William Gossage   Jesse Alverson
   Daniel Price   James Travis   James D. Patton
   Benjamin C. West   Stephen Coleman   Henry Haley
   James Robertson   Wesley Cook   Levin Downs
   Wm.W. Price   Thomas Penix   Little Beny Gibson
   Greenbury Voss   William Lea   et al.
37 Inv property of Meradith Price decd. Bonds on Charles Keesee,
   Julius Allen, John Ross, James D. Patton, John and James May,
   John Mims, Woodlief Hooper, Hugh Stubblefield, William Dodson,
   David Lay et al.
38 Inv estate of William K. Harrison taken 8 Jan 1817.
39 Amended inv of John Kerr Sen. decd. Note on John Sawyer Jr.
40 Allotment to Hannah Bastin widow of Thomas Bastin decd for herself
   and family. 30 Jan 1817. Commrs: James Orr JP, Josiah Womack,
   William Walker, John Cobb.
40 Settlement estate of John Grant to 4 distributees and the widow.
   (No names given.) By W. P. Hall and William Robertson.
41 Clayton Jones adm in acct with estate of William Jones decd. Paid
   George Ubanks (Eubanks?) exec vs said Jones.
41 Return of rent of land by William Currie guardian of orphans of
   John Dickie decd.
42 Acct of strays returned by William Lea county Ranger:
   Wm.K.Harrison 1 bay mare $40   George Lea 1 Brindle heifer
   David Walker 1 bay mare $20   William Smith 2 ewes & 2 lambs
   Richard Martin 1 black steer $6.50 William Smith 1 bay mare $10
42 Alexander Murphy adm of estate of William Muzzall decd and guardian
   to orphans, acct filed.

July Court 1817

Justices present: Gabriel Lea, William Robertson, Thomas Boulden.

23

Book H 1817
Page
43 ROBBIN KING SEN. - Will - w. 25 Mar 1817. Daughters Jane King and
   Ellen King; sons Robbin J.(or I) King, Joseph King (land adj
   Joseph Isaac King); land given to children of son Isaac King;
   land on Moon's Creek to go to wife for her life and then to son
   Robbin. Exec: sons Joseph and Robbin J.(or I). Test: W. P. Hall,
   Carter Blackwell, Levi Cobb.
44 Allotment to Polly Price widow of Meredith Price for her & family.
45 Inv goods of William King decd by John Watt adm.
45 Amt of money left in hands of Mr. Elijah Graves and received from
   said Graves $71.08 belonging to Joseph Boman decd. Geo. Brooks,
   adm.
46 Inv Catharine Currie decd and her part of lands of James Currie decd.
   Included land in Orange Co. in dispute, also land in western territory adj Thomas Mulholland entered by Edward Willson and James
   Currie. By William Currie exec.
46 Inv of Robert Mitchell Capt of the 10th Reg^t of U.S.Infantry as far
   as has come to my hands - one pair of Horseman's Pistols, quantity
   of books and medicine. By William Mitchell adm.
46 Examined accts. of Isaac King decd in hands of John Watt adm of
   William King decd. Bonds on Whitehead Page and John Page.
   Whitehead Page guardian to children of Isaac King decd. 23 Apr 1817.
47 Inv estate of Stephen Stewart decd by Robert Hughston adm.
47 Inv property of Thomas Bastin decd taken 1 May 1817 by Major Brockman Jun. adm.
48 Sales estate of James Knighten decd by William Walker adm. 28 June.
49 Sales estate of Thomas Bastin by Major Brockman Jr. adm. to:

Hannah Bastin	John Bauldin	Peter Adams
John W. Grant	John Bastin	G.W.Stubblefield
John Powel	Benjamin Norman Sen.	Randol Rhoads
Lewis Whitmore	Benjamin Norman Jun.	Edward Beusey
Isaac Patterson	Richard Hill	Brockman Nicholds
James Walker	Henry Strader	Peggy Sanders
Peter Stubblefield	Greenbury Willson	Noah Cobb
Major Brockman Sen.	Sarah Nicholds	James Abel
Thomas Bastin	Cotton Nun	Susannah Sims et al.

52 Inv of notes of estate of Benjamin Cantrill decd. Notes on:
   Howell Massey, Coleman Leath, Maxfield Henslee, Joseph Pennix, Ann
   Vinson, James Wilder, Jonathan Davis, David Davis et al.
   Cash received of John Hastin, John Berry, Edmund Herndon, Milie
   Whitehart, judgment against Alen Faddis and Arthur Lovens, Samuel
   Beasley, Hannah Freeman, Samuel Love, Thomas Morain.
53 Sales estate of William King decd by John Watt adm to: Obediah
   Nunley, Robert King, Joseph King, Polly King, George W. Stubble-
   field, John Dalton, Samuel Hill, et al.
55 Acct sales of John Toler decd to George Toler, Downey Wade, Robert
   D. Wade, George Hughston. By Nancy Towler adm.
56 Settlement estate of Anthony Swift decd by Thomas Williamson.
   (Eleven pages of debtors and interest due the estate.)
67 Sales property of Anthony Swift.
68 Div estate of Anthony Swift to each legatee: Thomas Williamson,
   Anthony Williamson, Sarah Carter.
68 Allotment to Nancy Towler 2 Nov 1816. By William Mitchell Jun.
   and Robert D. Wade.
69 Settlement estate of Zephaniah Tait decd and div to legatees by
   Nathaniel Gooch adm. Payments to: Henry Tait, Fanny Tait, Lucinda Tait, Alex Wiley, Brice Collins, Elizabeth Yancey.

24

Book H 1817
Page
71 Acct estate of Nathaniel Pass decd by Thomas Pass exec. Payments
    to: Abel Taylor his legacy, Nathl. Pass Jun., John Pass, William
    Moore Jr., Thomas Taylor, William Williams' daughters legacy,
    Rebecca Burton's children, Holloway Pass, John Phelps acct.
72 This day Daniel Merritt of Caswell Co. of proper age made oath
    before William Rainey JP that he was at a settlement between
    Daniel Goodrum and Thomas Pass relative to a Hh of Tobacco said
    Pass sold Goodrum belonging to estate of Nathaniel Pass decd for
    $10 but tobacco did not reach contract and was settled at $8 and
    only 992 pounds. 7 June 1817.
72 Allotment of one year's provisions for Anne Stewart widow of Step-
    hen Stewart decd and to her family. 21 Apr 1817. Commrs: J.Mc-
    Mullen JP, William Owens, James Lea, William Mitchell.
73 Acct current and settlement estate of George Samuel decd by Rowzee
    Samuel adm. Payments to Thomas Jeffreys, John Lea, Andrew Harri-
    son, Willson & Williamson, Daniel Farley et al.
73 Acct estate of Lewis Foster decd by Joseph Benton adm. Payments to:
    Jethro Brown for bond, James Shepard, Anthony Foster, Cisley Foster
    (allowance),Freeman Leath acct., Robert Foster.
74 Daniel Darby exec estate of John Dobbin acct with estate. Deduct
    Christopher Hinton's bond Insolvent. Judgments on William Gordon
    Jun., Abram Villines, Thomas Riggs; accts paid of John Lea, James
    Lea, George Lea et al.
76 Nathaniel Gooch adm in acct with estate of Francis Gooch. Cash in
    hands of Wm. H. Rice, Henry Williams, Nathaniel Gooch. Paid vou-
    chers of Edmund E. Rice, Nathan Williams, Thomas Ruffin, Q.Ander-
    son, Richard Jones, Amos Ford, William Brown. 6 June 1817.
77 Griffin Gunn county trustee in acct with Caswell County 1813-15.
    Report examined by A.K.Ramsey, Henry Hooper.
78 Randolph Rhoads orphan age 5 yrs. the 15 of May last bound to
    William Parker. Test: Alex Murphey D.C.(Deputy Clerk), Gabriel
    Lea Chairman County Court.
79 Taxable property for 1816. Picture on page 21.
80 William Howel a boy of colour age 12 yrs. last Sept. bound to
    William Kennon. /s/ William Cannon.
81 Power of attorney - Benjamin French of Madison County, Mississippi
    Territory, to James Kimbrough of Giles County, Tenn. to recover
    and receive all monies owing or accruing to French. 5 Sept 1814.
    German Lester clerk of Giles Co.; John Dickey presiding Justice
    for said county.
82 George Williamson sheriff reports returns of votes for 15th Con-
    gress from polling places:

Polling place	Thomas Settle	Romulus Sanders
Caswell Courthouse	3	113
Daniel Hightowers	14	6
James Sanders linns old field	61	22
Milton	8	145
Jethro Brown's Tavern	21	215
Total	107	501

14 Aug 1817

October Court 1817

Justices present: Andrew Harrison, Ambrose L. Bennett, Thomas
Bouldin.

25

Book H 1817
Page
83 NATHANIEL COMER - Will - w. 13 Sept 1817. Wife Peggy; sons
Nathaniel, Thomas, John; daughters Frances Roan, Nancey Richmond,
Peggy Comer; orphans of daughter Betsey Long; 3 sons to get all
land aside of dower; land in Halifax Co. Va., on Peter's Creek
511 acres to be sold; property willed to wife to be divided to
all legatees at her death. Exec: friends Thomas and John Comer.
Wit: Edwd. M. Foulkes, John E. Brown, Wm.S.Farley. Thomas Comer
qualified.

85 AMACE STOKES - Will - w. 30 Aug 1817. Wife Susannah to get land,
mansion house, and mill during her life or widowhood, then all
land to son Moore Stokes; daughter Miliand Stokes (also spelled
Melina, melinda); daughter Elizabeth Barsdale; grandsons William
Burch and Amace Stokes Burch sons of Samuel Burch and Peggy M.
Burch his wife; 3 granddaughters Lucinda, Elizah, and Susannah
Burch (under 16); Bird Barsdale. Exec: wife, son Moore Stokes,
and friend William Moore, Sen. Wit: Durett Richards, Robert
Smith, Thomas Sadler.
N.B. Daughter Nancy Connally $1.00
         "   Kezziah Prewet $1.00

87 MARGRET GRIER - Will - w. 30 Apr 1816. Daughter Nancy Compton;
heirs of daughter Margret Horton; heirs of daughter Elizabeth
Stone; son Samuel Grier. Exec: son Samuel. Wit: James Crosset,
Henrietta Compton, Jno Sanders, Starling Warren.

88 Acct current estate of John Courts with W. H. Burns in his wife's
right adm. of said estate. 11 Oct 1817. Commrs: W.P.Hall,
Silvs. Stokes.

88 Inv property of Thompson McKissack decd by Thomas Villines adm.
15 Sept 1817.

89 Articles of agreement between Sarah Carter (widow) and Romulus M.
Sanders for self and wife and as guardian for John P. Mary C.,
Archibald G., Susan S., and Jesse Carter, all minors under 21.
Sarah Carter relict of Jesse Carter did dissent from will of
Jesse Carter. She agrees to take certain lands in lieu of dower
to wit:mansion house (land purchased of William Moore, of Jacob
Wright Sen., and of Thomas Donoho). William B. and Elizabeth B.
Carter children of Sarah & Jesse Carter.3Mar 1817. Test: George
Williamson.

91 Additional inv estate of Obed Florence. Notes on John and William
Fitch.

91 Inv property of Robert King decd by Joseph and Robert J. King exec.

92 Inv property of Henry Tapscott decd by Winefred Tapscott adm.

92 Power of Attorney -Elisha Brown of Caswell Co. to James Love of
same county to make deed in trust to James Brown Jun. to cover
crop and livestock. 13 Oct 1817. Wit: Hosea McNeill, Jesse Hollis

93 The Grand Jury have examined apartment of the Jail as directed by
law, they are kept sufficiently clean and due regard paid to prisoners health but they recommend Door of Debtors Room be repaired
and likewise a window in same Room. Jail is in good order and
Jailor deserves much credit. B.Brown foreman.

93 Report of Bridge Committee - repairs let to David Douglas for $74.4"

93 Rent of land of heirs of John Dickey decd.

94 Allotment to Elizabeth Massey widow of Howel Massey decd for her and
family.

94 Allotment to Nancey McKissack and family. By J.McMullen, John
Thomas, Major Wallis, John Woods.

26

Book H 1817-1818
Page
95 Allotment to Phebe Nelson late widow of William Nelson decd. 5
   Aug 1817. Commrs: Joseph Dameron, Abner Willson, Joseph Langley.
95 Sales property of Howel Massey decd taken 5 Aug 1817 to Elizabeth
   Massey and John Massey.
96 John Comer adm estate of John and Elizabeth Long decd acct filed.
   Part of acct previously returned by Mr. Roan.
96 Daniel Malone exec estate of Lewis Malone acct filed for rent of
   land.
97 Sales estate of William Nelson decd by Phoeby Nelson adm to:
   Young Burt   John Johnston   Christopher Matthews
   Goodloe Warren   John Love   Alexander Griffin
   Joseph Aldridge   John S. Hutcheson   Daniel Malone
   Charles Cook   Charles Matthews   Ambrose Nelson
       Bonds on Thomas Villines, Wm. & Quentin Anderson.
98 Acct sales of Stephen Stewart decd sold 23 Aug 1817 by Robert
   Huston adm. Sales to: Anna Stewart, George Huston Sen., William
   Gallaugher, Mrs. Leak, Robert H. Childers, Zera Huston, George
   Huston.
99 Acct current estate of John Hightower by Daniel Hightower adm.
101 John T. Blake orphan age 15 yrs the 5 Aug last bound to Jethro
    Brown. Solomon Graves chairman county court.
102 John Durham orphan age 15 yrs the 25 Sept next bound to Benjamin
    Elmore. Michael Montgomery chairman county court.
103 Allotment of dower lands to Nancey McKissack from husband Thomp-
    son McKissack decd. Land adj John McMullen, George Whitfield.
    6 Oct 1817.
103 Valuation and allotment of negroes of Obediah Florence decd.to
    Phebe Florence decd widow one-seventh part; rest to 6 legatees,
    the children. (no names). 25 Aug 1817.

           January Court 1818

105 Inv personal estate of Mary Morton decd by Martin Morton adm.
    Crop rented to William and Mishoe Morton.
106 Inv estate of Amace Stokes decd.
107 Inv goods and chattels of James Williamson decd taken 6 Nov 1817.
    By Geo Williamson adm.
107 Inv property of Margret Grier by Samuel Grier. 7 Jan 1818. Bond
    on Thomas Slade; judgment on John Fitch.
108 Inv property of Nat Comer decd by Thomas Comer exec.
108 Inv estate of Thomas Bastin decd by Major Brockman Jr. adm.
109 Acct sales of Henry Tapscott by Winefred Tapscott adm. Sales to:
    Winefred Tapscott   Polly Tapscott   Hezekiah Boswell
    John Tapscott   Edney Tapscott   Ransom Dolihide
    Elizabeth Tapscott   Starkey Smith   Nicholas Chubb
    George F. Thomas   Arvey Scott   William Tapscott et al.
       One negro man York crippled and no bid; 1 negro man Shadrack
       blind and no bid; 1 old negro woman Pat no bid; 1 blind boy
       Ned no bid.
110 List of sales of Thomas Bastin decd to John, Hannah, and Thomas
    Bastin; to Brockman Nicholds, James Burns, Lewis Whittemore et al.
111 Sales of Joab Overby decd sold 7 Nov 1817 to Susannah Overby,
    Rebecca Overby, Elizabeth Overby, William Whitlow, Siras Riggs,
    Benjamin Stephens. By William Owen adm.
112 Sales estate of Nathaniel Comer decd. Among buyers: John Roan,
    James Fullington,Thomas Burk, James Crosset, James Fuller, Lewis
    Vaughan, William Matthews.

                        27

Book H 1818
Page
113 Sales property of James Williamson sold 6 Nov 1817 to: Ann E.
Williamson, William Cobb, Ibzan Rice, Aquilla Barton, William
Russell, John Dalton, Zadock Rice, Peggy L.Nash, George William-
son, James Knott, John Stamps.
114 Daniel Malone in acct with estate of Carter Malone. Notes on
Charnal Hightower, Richard Word, George Thomas insolvent.
115 Elisha Ingram adm to estate of Jacob Quine decd. Payments to:
Jesse Carter, Thomas Graves, Stephen Ingram, John Ingram, Drury
McKinney, Samuel Dabney et al.
116 Freeman Leath and Thomas Garner adm in acct with estate of John
Garner decd. Cash received of George Brooks for tobacco. Accts
paid to Roger Simpson, Thomas Poyner, Hosea McNeill, John Piron,
Thomas Garner et al.
117 Settlement estate of Ann Richmond by James and Jesse Richmond exec.
Vouchers paid of John & Isaac Richmond, James C. Smith, Joseph
Langley, Darby for crying the sale, William Richmond, Vincent Lea,
Gabriel Lea.
117 William Steward in acct with estate of Thos Steward decd.
118 George Brooks adm estate of Joseph Boman. Acct filed for cash
received of Elijah Graves.
118 Romulus M.Sanders adm estate of Jourdan Whitlow. Cash paid to
Russell on note, John Payne, Francis Smith, J.Carter decd.
Note on Nicholas Willis doubtful.
119 Acct current estate of Gregory Durham decd. Peggy Durham exec
of estate has passed to William Robertson exec receipt for full
amount of all property. 2 Dec 1817. Commrs: W.P.Hall, Lewis
Whittemore, Elijah Withers.
119 Allotment to Winefred Tapscott widow of Henry Tapscott decd.
31 Oct 1817. By Thomas Williamson JP, Hezekiah Boswell, Thomas
Garrott, Thomas Brinsfield.
120 Div of negroes belinging to estate of Meredith Price to legatees:
Joel Price, Mrs. Price; to Susannah, John, Polly, Daniel, Meredith, Nancy, Addison, Pinckney, Major, William W., and Washington Price. By Elijah Withers, Dudley Gatewood, Benj. C.West,
William Pennick.
121 Allotment to Rebecca Overby late widow of Joab Overby decd for
herself and family. By Gabriel Lea, Samuel Hodge, John Whitlow,
Daniel Malone.
122 Allotment of negro slaves of estate of Bartlett Hatchett decd to
heirs and devisees (to wit): Bartlett, and Edward R.Hatchett; to
Daniel Gwyn and wife Polley, and to John Hatchett.
123 Allotment and div personal estate of Joel McDaniel decd between
William and John McDaniel heirs at Law. By Jas Burton, Luke
Palmer. 22 Dec 1817.
124 Henry Legan a boy of colour,14 yrs. old the 10th of Mar next,
bound to William Sawyer.
125 Betsy Legan, girl of colour, age 12 yrs. the 5th of Apr next,
bound to Anderson Morton.

126 ARCHIBALD MURPHEY - Will - w. 8 Mar 1816. Wife to have land and
plantation during her life and one-eighth part forever. Sons
Archibald D. and Alexander; children of son Alexander, Archibald
D., and John G.; children of daughters Polly Haralson, Betsy
McCaden, Nancy Debow, and Lucy Daniel; Dr. John McCaden, Herndon Haralson, and John Daniel to receive shares for their children. Exec to hold part for children of Nancey Debow. Money due
from John Bysor of Tenn. Exec: sons Alexander and Archibald D.
Wit: James Rainey, William Rainey, William Hundley, Nath. Pass.
(cont on next page)
28

Book H 1818
Page
128 Archibald Murphey will cont.
    Codicil: 20 Oct 1817. Daughter Lucy Daniel has departed this
    life and exec to hold her part in trust for her children.
    Son John G. Murphey has removed to land conveyed by James
    Sanders on Bradley's lick Creek of Stone's River. Dr. John
    McAden to be added as exec of will. The 3 exec qualified.

130 JOHN WINDSOR SEN. - Will - w. 30 Sept. 1810. Son John(land in
    Rockingham Co. on Country Line); son Thomas (Virginia money);
    daughters Sarah Tapscott(land where she lives bought of Tait),
    Rebekah Windsor; son Joseph (the Manes plantation where I now
    live with mill and still); daughter Frances Windsor; John Taps-
    cott son of Sarah. Exec: sons John, Thomas, and Joseph. Wit:
    Thomas Williamson, Anthony Williamson.
    Witnesses testified a part of will was mutilated or destroyed
    by fire. James Rice and Thomas Garrott testified this to be
    true copy as they had read same before its destruction. It was
    admitted to probate.

132 RICHARD PENDERGRASS - noncupative will - W. 25 Dec 1817.
    Daughter Sally Roe of Person Co. to have small trifle due to
    testator's affection for her; daughter Nancy Curtis of Caswell
    Co. to have whole of estate; rest of children already provided
    for. Wit: Edmond Rice, Henry Curtis. James Curtis appointed
    adm with said will annexed. 2 Jan 1818.

133 CHARLES LEWIS - Will - w. 22 May 1806. House and lot in Milton
    to be sold or slaves to be sold to pay expenses; women to be
    sold convenient to husbands and not separate small children
    from Mothers. Wife Gatne (or Galne) Hood to have part during
    her widowhood; son Nicholas (land called Fennys plantation
    south to Dan River on Island ford); daughters Elizabeth and
    Lucy. Exec: Saml. Dabney, Capt. James Dix, Asa Thomas, Andrew
    Harrison Jun., John Stamps Jun. Wit: George Dabney Jr., Will
    Boulton, Daniel S. Farley, Shad Johnson, Charles Harrison.
    Codicil - 20 Oct 1817. Wife, son Nicholas, daughter Lucy,
    son-in-law Warner Williams(land where old Mr. Boulton lived).
    Exec: Warner Williams, William Stamps. Wit: Andrew Harrison,
    John Russell, William Walters. Proved Pittsylvania Co. Va.
    17 Nov 1817. Proved Caswell Co. Jan 1818.

                April Court 1818   Second Monday
    Justices present: James Yancey, John Stamps, Elijah Withers

137 Power of attorney: John Jeffries of Culpepper Co. Va. to Meredith
    Jeffries of county aforesaid (John guardian for his two daughters)
    to recover legacies made by John Hudnall of Caswell County.
    26 Feb 1818. John Jeffries guardian of Fanny and Jannian Jef-
    fries. Receipt of Meredith Jeffries for $400 their part of
    estate of John Hudnall. 21 Mar 1818.
139 Power of attorney: Anderson Middlebrooks of Morgan Co. Ga. to
    brother Zera Middlebrooks of Newberry Dist. SC to collect legacy
    left by grandfather Robert Lyon of Caswell Co. 2 Jan 1817.
140 Power of attorney: Robert Lyon of Jasper Co. Ga. to Zeri Middle-
    brooks of SC to collect from estate of Robert Lyon. 2 Dec 1816.
141 The strays by William Lea county ranger taken up by:
    James Vaughan, 1 mare; William Walker, 1 yearling
    Josiah Morton, 1 heifer; Goodloe Warren, 1 mare.

                            29

Book H 1818
Page
141 Inv property of the late Col. Archibald Murphey taken 12 Nov
1817. Lists articles given to Mrs. Jane Murphey widow forever
by will of decd. Included lots in Milton on Dan River, land in
Rutherford Co. Tenn. and Clay Co. KY (subject to law suit).
Land conveyed by Murphey to Henry Rutherford of Williamson Co.,
Tenn., for locating and surveying land. Bonds on William Irvin,
James Rainey, Newman Durham.
143 Receipt of Nuam Johnston for wife's legacy left her by Robert
Lyon decd except what is to come to her after decease of Rebecca '
Lyon, James Burton and Henry Howard exec. 20 Oct 1807.
144 Receipt of William Lyon for legacy left him by Robert Lyon.
11 Oct 1815.
144 Receipt of William Lyon for money received for Nehemiah Daniels
legacy left him by Robert Lyon decd. 14 July 1808.
144 Receipt of Nehemiah Daniel for wife's legacy from Robert Lyon after
death of Rebecca Lyon decd. 10 Feb 1816.
145 Receipt of Zeri Middlebrooks for legacy left John Lyon by Robert
Lyon decd. 20 Nov 1809; and after death of Rebecca Lyon 12 Aug
1817. Receipt of Robert Lyon for same legacies.
146 Receipt of Joseph McClain for legacy left his wife after death of
Rebecca Lyon. 31 Aug 1816.
146 Inv estate of John Windsor decd. Notes on John WindsorJun.,
Nicholas Chub, William Rice, Duke Williams. Bond on Thos Sullivan. By John and Joseph Windsor exec.
147 Additional inv estate of John H. Brown.
148 Acct current of John Windsor. Sales to:

Major John Reed	John Walker	Enoch Chamberlain
Henry Tapscott	John P. Freeman	Benjamin Elmore
John Tapscott	John Lea	Samuel Moore Jun.
John Horseford	Samuel Hill Sen.	Edney Tapscott
John Windsor	Pryer Loveless	George Loveless
Joseph Windsor	John Matkins	Nathan Sims
John Smithy	James D. Taylor	et al

151 Hosea McNeill adm in acct with estate of Salmon Childress decd.
Payments to Nathan Williams, George Barker's execution, et al.
4 Apr 1814.
152-164 Romulus M. Sanders exec in acct with estate of Jesse Carter
decd. (Cash receipts cover 12 pages.) Paid cash to Sarah B.
Carter for legacy. Cash retained due the 4 oldest children of
the Testator for cash received by said Testator of Richard
Atkinson adm of Susan Payne decd. 28 Sept 1808.
165 Bond: John Hudnall late of Caswell Co. left property willed to
John Hutcherson who agrees to pay his part of all debts against
Hudnall. Bonded by William W. Moore. Test: James Rawley.
166 Bond:24 June 1815. Eliza Clark wife of William Clark (Eliza
legatee of John Hudnall), Clark agrees to pay ratiable part of
all debts. Bonded by Robert Courts. Test: Sithey Withers,
Lewis W. Whittemore. John Jeffries agrees to pay his part of
debts of Hudnall's estate.
167 Lucinda Pitt and William Pitt, she a legatee of John Hudnall,
agree to pay part of debts.

168 DAVID DAVIS - Will - w. 3 Feb 1818. Brother Jonathan Davis to
have all estate. Exec: brother Jonathan. Wit: Susannah Brown.

30

Book H 1818
Page
168 JOSEPH DAMERON - Will - w. 26 Jan 1818. Wife; children; negroes
which came by last wife to go to her and to her last 6 children.
Charles to have his choice sold or hired yearly and being a
publick speaker for God he should have one-third of his income
to support him as a preacher and 2-3rds to go to first wife's
children. Exec: George B. Dameron, John P. Harrison.
Test: Thos Gunn, Starling Gunn, J.C.Smith.

169 GEORGE M. WILLSON - Will - w. 22 Nov 1817. Daughters Elizabeth
Ann Willson and Mary Lea Willson (under age); should children
die before marriage or adulthood, estate to be divided between
Lewis Vaughan's two children Nancy and Morris, and the heirs of
John Lea (CB) whose daughter Polly was wife of testator.
Exec: George Williamson, Nathl. Lea. Wit: Joel Thomas, Catharine
Durham, John Gamble.

171 MARY MORTON - Will - w. Mar 1817. Children: Martin, Hezekiah,
Polley, and Nancey Morton; son Jacob Morton. Exec: son Martin.
Test: Nathaniel Meadows, John Roberts.

172 Bird Gomer orphan now 17 yrs old the 26 of Sept bound to Thomas
Turner.

July Court 1818

173 Power of attorney: John Stephens of Robertson Co. Tenn., to
friend Thomas Fisher of same place to convey 239 acres land in
Caswell County on Dan River adj Bleuford Reid and James Matlock,
land left by Father Bowler Stephens. 11 Mar 1818.

174 Taxable property for 1818:
totals: 938 white polls - 2232 black polls - 20 stores

174 Inv estate of James Willson decd by Geo Williamson and Nathl. Lea
exec of George M. Willson decd who was exec of said James Willson.

175 List of property belonging to estate of Maj. Robert Willson decd
by Ch. Willson adm.

175 Inv estate of Wilie Tendall by adm William Currie on 2 May 1818.
"To amount of cash received by hands of the Honbl. James S. Smith
of the Government of the United States $24.70."

176 Inv estate of George Willson decd. Bond on George W. Jeffreys.

176 Additional inv of John Bateman decd. Payments from James Peterson,
Thompson Matick, William Herritage, William Whitlow, Thomas
Wright.

177 John and Joseph Richmond adm estate of Phebe Lipscomb acct filed.
Inc. Phebe Lipscombs part of cost in suit of Russell.

178 Barnet Kemp in acct with estate of Richard Burch decd. 9 July 1818.

178 Sales estate of Joseph Dameron decd to: Absolem Benton, William
Dameron, Charles Beusey, Severn Beusey, Geo. B. Dameron, Henry
Shelton, Benjamin Dameron, et al.

179 Inv of goods and chattles of Jeremiah Willson decd and acct of
sales to: Henry W. Willson, John Hinton, Levi Fuller, William
Morgan, Archibald Rice, William Long, Kezziah Willson, Booker
Boman, Henry Mahon, et al. By Henry Willson adm.

180 Joseph McCullock and Deborah Walker adm of William Walker decd
acct with legatees. Received by McCullock previous to death of
Walker.Equal share to 4 legatees; cash paid to William Smith in
right of his wife Elizabeth; paid accts of Elizabeth, Deborah,
and George Walker; pd Hugh Walker guardian. By Jas Yancey,
William Gooch, James Graves.

181 Settlement estate of William King decd by John Watt adm.

Book H 1818
Page
182 James Kerr adm of Alexander Kerr Jun. decd acct with estate. Paid
Hezekiah Bozwell for crying the sale; pd Womack for surveying;
pd adm expenses to oppose a road running through land of decd;
pd expenses at Superior Court Spring 1818. Note on Thomas Paddis.
183 Power of attorney: William Jopling of Green Co. Tenn., to Thomas
Smith of county aforesaid to demand of Thomas Smith of Caswell Co.
a negro woman Hannah and her child now in possession of Thomas
Smith. 4 Oct 1817.
184 Power of attorney: William Smith of Caswell Co. but on way to
State of Tenn. to friend John Richmond Jun. of Caswell County
to attend to all business and to prosecute suit pending against
Thomas Burton. 20 Apr 1818. Wit: Alex Murphey, Azariah Graves.
185 Inv estate of Joseph Dameron. Debt due from John Dameron.
186 Tilmon Chance a youth bound for 6 yrs and 5 mos to Dennis Willson
until he reach 21 yrs.
187 Thomas Chance a youth bound to Dennis Willson for 4 yrs. until
he reach 21.

188 FRANCIS HIGHTOWER - Will - w. 3 Apr 1818. Son Joshua; granddaughter Francis Peterson; son Gregory. Wit: David Northington,
Peter Crowder.

188 Abraham Pope born in Town of Tanton (Taunton?), England aged
22 years on 7 Jan 1818 a British subject formerly; came to United
States on 1 Sept 1816 and intends in future to reside in North
Carolina and to become a citizen thereof. 15 July 1818.

189 JESSE HOOD - Will - w. 30 Apr 1818. Wife Mary to have all land
and personal property. Wit: Thomas Bolton, Patsey Hubbard,
Ailsey Tullock.

190 Whereas William Gordon was guardian to minor legatees of Hezekiah
Rudd decd and recovered judgment against William Pinchback and
Jeremiah Rudd exec;and David Rudd one of wards and minor legatee
died several years ago; William Willson and Adam Stafford intermarried with Nancy and Bidsey Rudd, two legatees of Hezekiah.
Willson and Stafford release to Pinchback and Rudd their right
and interest in above judgment if the latter two release claim
on estate of David Rudd decd. 11 Jan 1814. Test: E.D.Jones.
The handwriting of E.D.Jones proved by Alex Murphey as Jones
not an inhabitant of this State. 1818.

October Court 1818

191 Power of attorney: Samuel H. Smith and John Smith acting exec of
Samuel Smith decd of Caswell Co. to James W. Smith of Jackson
Co. Tenn., to collect all monies due to estate in State of Tenn.
11 Oct 1818.
192 Allotment to Providence Haddock and family for a yrs provisions.
By James Montgomery, Samuel Pittard, Thomas Harrison.
193 Inv property of Richard Haddock decd by Stephen Haddock adm.
193 Settlement estate of Elizabeth Long decd by Daniel Hightower exec.
Payments to Drusis Riggs, William Whitlow, James C. Smith, et al.
Wit: William Warren, William Anderson.
194 James Yancey adm estate of Benjamin Cantrill decd in acct with
estate. Pd accts to Collector of Revenue of Orange and Caswell;
to Prudence Davis, Negroe James, Jesse Hollis, James McCray,
Sarah Youngers bond, Cobby Foster, Henry Brannock, Thomas Foster,
Bartlett Yancey fee, Richard Browning in part of the first
widow's allowance, State Bank of NC, et al. Examined by Alex
Murphey, William Gooch.

Book H 1818
Page
196 Noel Burton exec in acct with estate of William Richardson decd.
    Payments to Elisha Alverson, James Richardson, William Ware,
    Greenbury Voss, James H.Pass, Elijah Carman, James Paul, Elisha
    Ingram, Edmund Richardson; cash paid Bios a slave of Evans Knight;
    cash pd to Billy and George, slaves.
198 Capt. David Poyner Jr. in acct with estate of John Keen decd.
    Payments to John Shackleford, Robert Blackwell, Jere Rice, William
    and Susannah Keen, Rhoadham Loveless, Ellen Keen, Joseph Roe,et al,
200 James Richardson exec estate of William Richardson decd. From
    James Richardson's store acct. July 1, 1814 - Sept. 30, 1818.
201 Jethro Brown adm in acct with estate of William B. Merony. Pro-
    visions for Mrs. Merony.
202 James Darby adm in acct with estate of John Bateman decd. Notes
    on Samuel and Sarah Smith; made widow's allowance. 12 Oct 1818.
    Examined by Gabriel and William Lea.
203 Sales personal estate of Mary Morton decd made on 14 Nov 1817 by
    Martin Morton exec. (Buyers names not included in book.)
204 Inv estate of Isaac Hodge decd taken 17 July 1818. Money in hands
    of A. Harrison and Romulus Sanders; corn entitled to Charles
    Bucey. Sales of estate to: Severn Bucey, Clarles Bucey, David
    Hodge, Miss Judy Hodge, Miss Hannah Hodge, Joseph Knight, John
    Everet, Allen Jones, Daniel S. Farley, Forbus Harrelson, Elisha
    Alverson, Thomas Evans, Archer Samuel, David Kiersey. By John P.
    Harrison adm.
206 Insolvents returned by George Williamson D Sheriff for 1814

Joshua Jeffreys	Philip Ubank (Eubank)	Anderson Smith
John Alverson	Theoderick Johnston	John Ferrell
Cobb Anglin	Benjamin Price	James Miller
George Ford	John Barnwell	William Brown Jr.
Enoch Ford	Thomas Bell	Nathan Browning
John Payne Esq.	Solomon Compton	Peter Harvel
Edward Ruark	Jonathan Hunt	James Willson
Edward Sparks	James Johnston	John Payne
George Cook	James Jones	Philip Baynes
Bartholemew Egmon	James Roper(no such man)	James Kelley
Richard Horseford	Alexander Madden	Paschal Roberts
James Luttrell	James Paschall	
Levi Tennison	Jesse Perkins	

207 Insolvents for 1815

John Farley Sen.	James Jackson	Archibald Cole-
Peter Harvel	John Keton	man
Iskmail Bauldwin	John Mansfield	Samuel Cobb
John Foster	Pilemon Tapley	Levi Denison
John Humphreys	James Vaughan Jr.	William Fryer
Jesse Perkins	William Wilkins	Lewis Foster
Edwin Ruark	William Brown(son of Wm)	Wm.Garrison
William Swan	John Brown, son of Jas.	John Garner
Benjamin Birk	Lewis Ballard	John Hughes
James Ferrell(no such man)	James ?	David Humphreys
Alexander Golaher	Alexander Barker	Lewis Humphreys
Reuben Jeffries	Green L.Brown	James Ray

207 Insolvents for 1816

John Martin	John Berry	Jesse Payne	Robert Randolph
Daniel Pogue	John Brown	Nathan Dalton	Joseph Stafford
Bird Reed	Green S.Brown	James Dalton	John Shackleford
Hardy Brewer	Solomon Brown	Elijah Dawson	Stephen Bastin
Thomas Jouett	Henry Hailey	Moses Grant	George Grayham
George Thomas	James Lutrell	Joseph Jones	David Hailey(given in twice)

33

Book H 1818-1819
Page
207 cont. Insolvents for 1816

James Kennaday	Moses Charles (no such man)	John Swan
George Lyon	William Murry	Henry Ruark
Timothy Longwell	John Perkins	William Swan

208 Claybourn Williams 6 yrs old bound to Joshua Beaver.
209 Shadrack Bush age 14 yrs bound to Moses Simpson.
210 Booker Williams, a girl age 10 yrs., bound to Peggy L. Nash.

211 ANN YANCEY - Will - w. 29 Apr 1816. Son Bartlett; granddaughters Nancey Yancey, Priscilla Howard; daughters Elizabeth Slade, Isbel Collier; granddaughter Salley Rice; sons John, James, and Bartlett; daughter Nancey Johnston or her children to have income from hire of negroes; residue divided between grandson Yancey Wiley and granddaughter Sally Rice (one-eighth part at age 21); daughter Mary Graves otherwise Mary Biddle*or her children. Exec: sons John, James, & Bartlett. Wit: So Graves, Barzillai Graves. Bartlett Yancey qualified.(* Riddle on original)

213 Inv personal estate of Daniel Jones decd by John G. Willson adm. Money received from United States due for services in army $93.35 which is all effects found belonging to Jones.

January Court 1819

214 Inv estate of Robert Dupuy taken 23 Oct 1818 by Silvs. Stokes adm. Bonds on John Cobb, John Grant, Henry Cobb. Acct against James Martin of Pittsylvania Co. Acct on Joshua Stone Jr. desperate; bonds on Elizabeth Motley and James Anderson. Acct due from William Crews.

214 Div negroes of estate of Anthony Swift to Thomas Williamson, Anthony Williamson, and Sarah Carter. 15 Jan 1817. Does not include negroes in possession of exec of William Swift decd.

215 Inv and sale of Robert Tate decd. Sales to: Thomas Riggs, Edward Dunnavent, William Hinton, Elizabeth Tate widow, Tinsley Lea, Lott Egmon, Joel Tate, Henry Roper. By R.M.Sanders adm.

215 Sale of parcel of corn belonging to estate of Isaac Hodge decd to James Paul.

216 Inv estate of Ann Yancey by B. Yancy exec. Money given to Nancy Johnston.

216 Receipt of Thomas Winston guardian of Spilsby C. Winston to James Burton exec of Noel Coleman decd for legacy, also for legacy of Elizabeth B. Winston, Joseph B. Winston, and Noel C. Winston. Guardian appointed by Rockingham Court for said children at Feby. Term 1810.

217 Receipt of Thomas Winston to James Burton exec of Wm.B.Burton decd for full part of estate.

217 Receipt of John Binion to James Burton and Thomas Winston exec of Wm.B.Burton for negro alloted from estate.

217 Receipt of John Graves to James Burton exec of Noel Coleman decd for negroes Archer and Lucy which he has had in his possession since 1808.

217 Receipt of Thos Winston guardian for Winston children's part of estate of Noel Coleman.

217 Receipt of John Graves for wife's part of estate of Noel Coleman. 13 Jan 1819.

Book H 1819
Page
218 Sales estate of Richard Haddock 30 Nov 1818 to : Providence Haddock;
Polley, Elizabeth, and Stephen Haddock; George Williamson, James Richardson, Woodlief Hooper, Anselem Haddock, James Ingram, Elisha Ingram,
James Ware, Michael Montgomery, Walker Samuel, et al.
220 Sales estate of Jane Jackson sold 20 Nov 1818 to:

Dolly Smith	Charnal Hightower	Jerry Jackson
Robert Smith	Bart Dameron	Joseph Langley
John Murphey	Ambrose Nelson	Parum Jackson
Polley Jackson	John Jackson	Alexander Wiley
Wm. Burgis	John S. Hutchinson	Nathaniel Snipes

By Robert H. Jackson and George Smith
222 Additional inv of estate of George M. Willson decd. Bonds and assets received of Thomas Jeffreys of whom he was a partner; from James Daniel,
Jarrett Feagans, James Fullington, Benjamin Howel, John Lea Sen., Har-
bart Samuel, Robert Tate, John Lea CB, Watson Winters, William Ashford,
Rucker Lea, David Northington, Samuel Curls, John Atwell, Elizabeth Dobbins, Burrell Bevell, William Humdley, Henry Royster, et al.
223 Sales property of Robert Dupuy decd sold 19 Nov 1818 to:
Chaney Dupuy, Henry Glass, William Crews, Joseph Cobb, Dennis Willson,
John Bastin, Elijah Davis, Henry Baldwin, et al.
225 Sales estate of Ann Yancey sold 7 Nov 1818 to: Bartlett Yancey, Nathaniel
Slade, Joseph Collier, James Yancey, John P. Harrison, Thomas Washburn,
Elijah Martin, John Graves, Charles G. Cock (or Cook), Azariah Graves (son
of Thomas), William Lyon Jr., James Vaughan.
226 Sales of property of George M. Willson sold 3 Nov 1818 to:

John Lea	Richard Gates	Elizabeth Elam
Maj. Thomas Donoho	John Davis	Andrew Johnston
John Sledge	Thomas Lea	Sherrod Owen
Jeremiah Graves	John Hubbard	John P. Sledge
William Glasgow	William Parker	George Carroll
Wiley Jones	John Johnston	William Mutry
Lewis Shirley, et al.		

228 Receipt of Thornton Black for his part of estate of Hiram Black in Tenn.
Receipt to Joseph McDowel. 20 Nov 1818.
229 John Kerr and James Kerr adm of John Kerr decd. acct with estate. Cotton
sold in Richmond. Accts paid to Daniel Farley for surveying; bonds due
Andrew McCawley, Doct. Edwd. M. Foulkes, et al. A debt due from the estate
of Susannah Taylor and the daughters of Mary Spencer decd., $214.24.
230 Release of James Rudd and Jeremiah Jacobs to Jeremiah Rudd and Jeremiah
Jacobs. William Gordon guardian to minor legatees of Hezekiah Rudd decd.
Jacobs intermarried with Rebecca Rudd, daughter of Hezekiah.
231 Hugh Walker adm of George Walker decd. in acct with the estate.
231 Allotment to Chana Dupuy and family. 16 Nov 1818.
232 William Parker Peterson an orphan age 7 years bound to Joseph Peterson.
233 Hijah Gates age 11 years next May bound to Henry Mahon to learn art of
shoe and boot maker.
234 Power of attorney - Edward Bauldwin of Hopkins Co., Ky., to son Hiram
Bauldwin of county aforesaid to receive from estate of decd. Brother
Lazarus Bauldwin of Caswell County and to receive from legal represen-
tatives of Clement Trigg late of Caswell Co., decd. Father-in-law. 25
Sept. 1818. Alexander Ashley JP and William Wilson JP of Hopkins Co. Ky.

Book H 1819
Page
236 LEVIN DOWNS - Will - w. 7 Nov 1818. All estate to go to wife Ann.
   Exec: wife Ann. Wit: Ro Payne, Geo Lay, Instant Lay.

April Court 1819

237 Acct of strays taken up by Abraham Sanders.
237 GEORGE CONNALLY - Will - w. 5 May 1818. Three sons, Thomas, George O.,
   and William J. Connally; wife Frances Connally; daughters: Rebecca
   Brandon, Sarah Bouldin, Ann Richmond, Kitty Montgomery; heirs of son
   John Connally; heirs of son Charles Connally; daughter Angelico Gattis;
   daughter Fanney Bouldin.
   Exec: wife Frances, and sons Thomas & George O.
   Test: D. Richards, John Hubbard, Jno. Smith. Thomas Connally qualified.
239 Allotment to Betsey Bartlett widow and relict of Edward Bartlett decd.
   Met at house of Mrs. Polly Muzzall. 5 Feb 1819.
239 Allotment to Martha Blackwell for provisions from her decd husband's estate.
   4 Feb 1819.
240 MATTHEW HUBBARD- Will - w. 14 Mar 1813 at cantonment near Salisbury, NC.
   "Of the second regiment of Artillery in army of United States, in perfect
   health but calling to mind the uncertainty of life especially in my new
   profession" and "at this early period of life have nothing except what I
   may acquire". Land promised to dutiful soldiers by the Government to
   go to brother Ralf Hubbard of Caswell County, NC together with all other
   personal property. Wit: S. Donoho, Jas Faul, Nathl. Henderson.
   Proved on oaths of Gen. Barzillai Graves and Ambrose L. Bennett that signature of Sanders Donoho was his proper handwriting and said Sanders Donoho
   and other witnesses are beyond the limits of the State.
   Ordered committed to record.
241 Inv estate of Jane Jackson decd. Notes on James and Daniel Hightower.
   By Robert H. Jackson and George Smith, adm.
241 Inv property of William H. Cook decd by Phillip Cook, adm.
241 John Baxter Jun. in acct with Jane Baxter adm of Thomas Baxter, decd.
   Payments to Rachel, Patsey, Delila, Polly, Dolley, and Caty Baxter.
242 Jane Baxter adm of Thomas Baxter accts paid of John and Nathaniel Willson,
   James Richardson, Priestly Carter, James Ingram, James Burton.
243 Inv estate of David Hailey taken 20 Jan 1819 by Iverson Graves, adm.
   Accts. on William Lyon Jun., Charles Harrison.
243 List of property of William Williams decd. Sales to Thomas Phelps, Durrett
   Richards, George Taylor, Anderson Hughes, Hiram Phelps, Nathaniel Williams,
   John Hall, Kindal Bozwell, Mathew M. Smith, John Pass, William Moore, Jr.;
   By John Pass.
244 Div estate of William Boulton decd. to Mrs. Boulton; and to William, Charles,
   E. D., and Mereweather Boulton. Old Man James and old Woman Nancey to be
   supported by legatees.
   Commrs: Warner Williams, Jas Holder, Richd Ogilby, P. H. Inge, JP.
245 Allotment to Betsey Tait wife of Robert Tait decd. By John Gamble, Henry
   M. Clay, James Rainey JP. Nov 1818.
245 Sales estate of David Hailey decd by Iverson Graves adm on 20 March 1819.
   Sales to Lucy Hailey, Edmund McCubbins, Iverson Graves, Miss Martha Crow,
   Col. Thomas Graves, Richard Foster.
246 Div negroes of estate of William Donoho decd. between Dr. Edward Donoho
   and Capt. John C. Elliott in right of his wife Polly, heirs of the decd.
   13 Apr 1819. Div by Sol Graves, Azariah Graves.

Book H 1819
Page
247 Bird Eskridge exec in acct with estate of Richard Eskridge.
247 Inv property of Ann Downs decd taken 8 Mar 1819. Bond on Swan Cox; amt
     against estate of Richard Walthall; acct anti Instant Lay. Sales property
     of Ann Downs to: Charles Harrison, Zeri Gwyn, Henry Bouldin, Nancey Downs,
     Levin Downs, Chainey Thomas, George Lay, Instant Lay, Edwin Raimey, Ann
     Gibson, Peter B. Stubblefield, Peter Smith, Elizabeth Downs, Wm. W. Price,
     James Eudaley, Jonathan Foxdale, Charles Beusey, John Keesee, Greenbery
     Voss. By Levin Downs, adm.
249 Inv and sales estate of Levi Blackwell to:

Martha Blackwell	Richard Jones	John Mimms
Marshall Blackwell	Joseph Montgomery	Charles Mitchell
Abner Miles	Warren Weatherford	Edmund Rice
William Morgan Jun.	Benjamin Ashley	Dennis Wilson
William Morgan Sen.	Hiram Weatherford	John Blackwell

          By Martha Blackwell, adm.
251 List of sales of Edward Bartlett property on 5 Feb 1819 to:

Elizabeth Bartlett	Alex Murphey	Charles Murry
William Miles	John Murphey	Polley Muzzall
John Jackson	William Barnwell	Nathl. G. Muzzall
David Mitchell	Joseph Aldridge	Col. Wm. Mitchell
Christopher Thomas	Samuel Dameron	Miss Susan Bartlett
John Everett	Elisha Evans	Matson Birk
Pleasant Lewis	Robert Browning	Benjamin Pleasant
Robert H. Jackson	Thomas Slade	Nath. L. Rice
Capt. Thomas Turner	Richard Arvin	Larkin Warren
Thompson Bartlett	William Florence	Sarah Muzzall
William Turner	William Slade	Robert Martin

     Debts due Edward Bartlett from Miles Brown, Carter Malone, William Jopling
     (all desperate). One year's allowance to Elizabeth Bartlett and children.
     By Thomas Slade, adm.
253 Inv and sales property of George Connally decd sold 4 Feb 1819 to:

William Childs	William Gattis	Frances Brandon
Thomas Burch	John Wood	Samuel Curl
Anthony Terrell	David Brandon	Thomas Gordon
Thomas Connally	William B. Collins	Walker Samuel
Joseph Pulliam Jr.	Samuel Birch	Jeremiah Putnam
George O. Connally	Robert Sledge	Layton Tapley
Thomas Villines	James Rudd	William Johnston
Littleton Sledge	Capt. Josiah Samuel	John W. L. Daniel
Abel Royster	James Bouldin	Wm. Taylor (W.R.)
John Bouldin	Wm. B. Graves	John Hubbard
Abraham Pope	Thomas Sowell	Alvey Oliver
Miles Sledge	Philip M. Jackson	Wm. Mutry
James Montgomery Jr.	Wm. Harrison	Alexander McAlpin
Wm. J. Connally	Wm. Brandon Jr.	John Crawley

256 Thomas Blackwell exec of Robert Blackwell settlement estate; Edward M.
     Jones in place of his wife pay $6 to exec for services. By Jethro Brown,
     James Orr, Jos. Roe.
257 SAMUEL HENDERSON - Will - w. 1 Dec 1818. Wife Priscilla. 5 last children
     all underage to havefollowing: son James S. (352 acres land where "I now
     live"); Harriett (land that Benjamin Gomer now lives on 100 acres);
     Minerva (land adj Thomas Foster on Lick Fork Creek); Ludolphus (land on
     north side Moore's Creek adj Joseph Henderson); Frances A. (land on Lick
     Fork by Zachariah Hooper). Exec: son Hiram Henderson, wife Priscilla
     Henderson, and Joseph Henderson. Wit: William Hatchett, H. Hooper.
     cont. on page 38

37

Book H 1819
Page

SAMUEL HENDERSON will cont:
    Children by first wife Priscilla Henderson: Sarah Holcomb, Martha Haralson, Nancey Hooper, Priscilla Hooper, Mary Kennom, Elizabeth Watt, William Henderson, Samuel Henderson, Thomas Henderson, Jacob Henderson; daughter Hanner. Sons Hiram and Joseph to have equal division of negroes with last 10 children. Priscilla, Hiram, and Joseph Henderson qualified.

260 Azariah Graves adm in acct with estate of David Womack, decd. Bonds on Abner Walker, Polly and Anderson Birk; pd Richard Haddock for bond to Wm. Quine; pd Dr. J. D. Patton, Dr. Samuel Dabney, Stephen Chandler, David Hailey per judgment.

261 John Stamps exec of last will of Thomas Swift acct with estate.

263 Luscinda Gillaspy, a child of colour, age 6 years the 20 May next, bound to Wilkins Chandler.

264 Anosha Gillespy, child of colour, age 3 years the 29 July next, bound to Frances Smith.

264 John Jeffreys age 16 years next July bound to William Parker.
    James Orr, Chairman County Court.

July Court 1819

265 Griffin Gunn, county trustee, acct with Caswell Co. for 1817.

266 Inv and sales of perishable property of William Donoho decd by Edward Donoho, adm. Sales to:

Romulus Sanders	John Graves, Capt.	Daniel Payne
Edward Donoho	Jeremiah Samuel	Nicholas Medlock
Barzillai Graves Sen.	John Morris	Francis Smith
Thomas Harrelson	John Butler	Wm. P. Payne
John C. Elliott	Barzillai Graves, Genl.	James Peterson
Benjamin Willis	Jeremiah Graves	Matthew Terry
Walker Samuel	Jeremiah Lea	Jonathan Starkey
Banister Campbell et al		

269 Inv property of Samuel Henderson decd. Some personal property sold at Hiram Henderson's on 14 May 1819. Bonds on James Miles, Henry Hailey, John Pucket, Robert Hall, Benjamin Gomer. Open accts. on William Jones, John Scott, Benjamin Gomer (tobacco due when crop finished), Thomas and Isaac Hobbs for rent when crop done.

270 Sales estate of Samuel Henderson on 13 and 14 May 1819 to:

Hiram Henderson	Charles Bucey	Levin Downs
Joseph Henderson	Abner Miles	Charles Harrison
Noel Burton	Jacob Henderson	Priscilla Henderson
William Henderson	Henry Shelton	Robert Perkins
Robert Roe	Henry Glass	John Marlow
William Clemson	Samuel Hooper	Richard Kennon
Joshua Beaver	Miles Wilmouth	James Paul
John Baxter	Peter Powell	Robert Foster
John Graves	Henry McClarney	Absolem Watt

273 Settlement estate of Thomas Bastin decd by Benj. C. West and Richard R. Kennon. Accts on Mary Hammons, Milley Robertson, Hannah Bastin, William Walker.

273 Ranger report: Taken up by Anthony Williamson on waters of Stony Creek a stray heifer.

274 A stray bay horse taken up by James Murray and valued by Murray and Major Wallis.

Book H 1819
Page
274 Valuation of sheep trespassing on farm of Edmund Herndon by Thomas Loyd
and Thomas Brown.
275 Buckner Boman living near the Red House hath taken up a stray mare and
valued by Daniel Darby and Levi Fuller.
275 Marriage contract between Archd. Cearnal (Carnal) of Person County and
Mary Bolton (Boulton) of Caswell County that what property each has will
remain to each to be disposed of as each desires. 1 Jan 1819. Wit: Charles
Bolton, William Moore.
276 Inv and sale of property of William Boulton decd sold 10 Dec 1818 to: Thomas
Connally, Charles and Thomas Boulton, John Sledge, Charles Hunter, James
Holder, Philip Jackson, John Hubbard, Edmund Dixon Sen., William Causby,
William Seymore, Mary Boulton, John J. Oliver, George Farley, James Rudd,
Richard Gates, et al.
277 Inv property of Samuel Henderson left to his widow and children.
278 Amt of estate of Meredith Price after all charges to be $699.07.
278 Cornelius Cannine age 14 years bound to James Wilder.
279 William Culberson in acct with estate of James Culberson decd. Payments to
William & Hiram Culberson, Thomas Turner, Zachariah Jourdon, John McColes-
ter, James Steward, Archer McLouchlin, Archd. McLouchlin, Barnet Kemp.
Traveling expenses to and from Richmond Co. attending law suit. Attorney
fees to Thomas Ruffin and E. James.
280 Emancipation of negro man named Billy, 5 feet 9 inches high, age 21 years,
to be free from me and my heirs. /s/ William Edenfield. 6 July 1815.
Proved at Lynchburg, Va., July 1815. Certificate recorded Caswell Co. 1819.
281 Taxable property for 1818
Totals: 872 white polls; 2234 black polls; 20 stores.

281 Land belonging to heirs of John Dickey decd rented for $21.01 for 1819
by William Currie, guardian.
281 Election returns for member of 16th Congress, 12 Aug 1819.
For Thomas Settle:
    at Caswell Courthouse   36 votes   at Daniel Hightower's 68 votes
        Lyns Old Field   37   at Milton   59
        Quentin Anderson's   48   Total   323
        Jethro Brown's   75
282 Griffin Gunn county trustee in acct with Caswell County, acct. filed.

October Court 1819

283 FRANCES TUGGLE - Will - w. 2 Aug 1819. Granddaughters Elizabeth Paschal,
and Frances Paschal; daughter Anna Paschal; only 2 children, William
Berry and Anne Paschal. Exec: Jethro Brown and son William Berry. Wit:
David Poyner Jr., David Walker.

284 RODERICK BIGELOW - Will - w. 3 June 1819. Wife Elizabeth, her 3 last
children, son Thomas, daughters Elizabeth and Mary. Exec: wife Elizabeth
and son Thomas Patillo alias Bigelow. Test: Thomas Turner, James Graves.

284 ROBERT DAVIS - Will - w. 23 Aug 1819. Wife Susan to get negro man Ben
which was gotten by marriage to her; 2 nephews, Nathaniel Poynor, and
John D. Poynor. Exec: friend Joseph Roe. Wit: David Walker, Samuel
Luttrall.

Book H 1819-1820
Page
285 JAMES LEA - Will - w. 22 Feb 1819. Wife Nancy Lea to have all estate
      10 years except she marries to be divided among all living children;
      estate to be divided after 10 years and those children under age may choose
      guardian and draw lots. Exec: son Franklin Lea and wife Nancy. Wit:
      Daniel Malone. Proved on oaths of Richard H. Hayes and James McMullin.

286 FRANCIS HOWARD - Will - w. 23 July 1819. Wife Mary Howard; 9 children:
      Woodson (or Woodrow), Anne, William, George, Mary, Francis C., Martha,
      Elizabeth, and Jane. Exec: wife and son Woodson. Wit: Henry Howard,
      Mary Howard qualified.

287 William Gibson orphan age 12 years bound to Levin Downs to learn art of
      shoe and boot maker.
288 James Hylor age 14 years bound to Charles Harrison.
289 Richard Gibson age 9 years bound to Levin Downs.
289 Receipt of Anderson Gunn for payment of his former guardian Griffin Gunn.

290 THOMAS ELAM - Will - w. 24 Oct 1808. 50 acres land in Chesterfield County,
      Virginia, joining William Elam and Mereman Hamen to go to Daniel and
      Nancy Elam children to brother Robert Elam.
      Test: William Willson, John J. Farley.

290 Allotment to Lucy Hailey widow of David Hailey decd. 6 Oct 1819.
291 Bartholomew Dameron adm in acct with estate of Sarah Dameron.
292 Robert Huston adm estate of Stephen Stewart decd. Paid clerk for petition
      of Ann Stewart. Payments to James Martin, James C. Smith; paid R. H.
      Childers as clerk at the sale $1.00. Examined by John S. Hutcherson and
      J. D. Vanhook.

                    January Court 1820

293 Inv property of Jesse Brintle decd taken by Rebecca Brintle, adm. 4 Nov
      1819. Notes on Spencer Jackson, Hezekiah Boswell, Thomas Garrott; a
      judgment vs. Pleasant Childers (14 Feb 1807); notes on Nathan Sims,
      William V. Brown. Paid accts of Eldridge Hastings, Zachariah Hastings,
      Oliver Brintle, John Mitchell, Joseph Penix, Larkin Ballard, John Under-
      wood Jun., Coleby Foster, Sally King, Bennet Bush, Anthony Foster, George
      Word, Thomas Jackson, et al.

295 JAMES ORR - Will - w. 30 May 1819. 3 sons James, Isaac, and Jesse Orr;
      daughters Mary, Nancy, and Elizabeth; Eleanor Humphrys. Exec: William
      Orr and Samuel Orr. Wit: James Cobb, Edwd. M. Foulkes.

296 WILLIAM PETTILLO of Warren County, N. C. - Will - w. 22 July 1813.
      Wife Sarah; Edward, Zachariah, and Anne H. Pettillo. Exec: Edward and
      Zachariah Pettillo. Wit: Clark Robinson, Thomas Ellis.
      Probated Caswell County Jan 1820. Zachariah Pettillo qualified.
      (Also spelled Pattillo.)

297 JACOB WRIGHT - Will - w. 19 Jan 1819. Elizabeth Hubbard; balance of
      estate to Jacob Wright son of Caleb Wright. Exec: friend George William-
      son. Wit: Nath. Lea, Abishai Slade.
      Debtors to Jacob Wright: William Climpson, John Kenny.

298 Inv estate of Robert Davis decd by Jos. Roe.
298 Inv estate of James Lea decd by Nancy Lea exec. Bonds on Kendal Vanhook,
      John G. Wilson, John Dison, Robert Elliot; judgment of John Bradsher.
300 Inv estate of Frances Tuggle decd taken 14 Oct 1819 by Jethro Brown and
      Will Berry, exec.

                              40

Book H 1820
Page
301 WILLIAM OWEN - Will - w. 19 Sept 1818. Daughters Betsy Whitfield, Susaner
    Terrel, Partheny McMurry, Margaret Owen, Patsy Owen; son Thomas (tract
    of land "where I now reside"). Wife Mary Owen. Exec: wife Mary and
    friend John Russell. Wit: Gabriel Lea, Stephen Pleasant.

302 Inv of Roderick Bigelow decd taken 19 Jan 1820 by Thomas and Elizabeth
    Bigelow.
303 Inv estate of William Walker decd taken 18 Nov 1819 by Connally Walker.
304 Inv estate of Francis Howard decd by Mary Howard, exec.
305 Sales estate of Robert Davis decd by Joseph Roe, exec. Sales to:

John Blackwell	Joseph Davis	William Cobb
Jesse Sanders	Lott Egmon	Susan Davis
Samuel Allen	Thomas Poynor	Mason Sanders
Pharo Summers	Azariah Graves	William Lyon
Jesse Paskil	Ciley Rice	William Martin
James Humphries	Archibald Dill	James Brown
Aron Sanders		

306 Sales estate of Thompson McKissack by Thomas Villines, adm. sold Sept 1817.
    Sales to:

A. Villines	John S. Hutcherson	William Warren
Nicholas Hester	Bernet Kemp	Robert H. Childers
Thomas Villines	Garnett Nealy	William Mitchell
William Owens	Charlie Wade	George Burch
Robert Hamlet	Richard Broach	Young Burt
Nancy McKissack		

308 List of property sold of Frances Tuggle decd to:

William Berry	Robert Roe	Levin Downs
Josiah Paschall	William Sanders	Ira Siddall
Robert Rolen	Frederick Nance	Jerre Jones
Samuel Cornwell	William Pickrod	John Chapman
Jesse Saunders	Samuel Hobson	Ed. M. Jones
Stephen Rice	Christwell Key	William Timberlake
Frances Cornwell	Samuel Gilton	Ezekiel Paschal
Solomon Beaver	Absolem McKenzie	John Paschal
Ziba Rice	Thompson Watt	William Paschall
Henry Cobb	George Lovelace	Elisha Paschall
Robert Cobb	Hezekiah Smithson	James Paschall
Thomas Gibson		

310 Sales property of William Walker decd by Conley Walker adm. sold 18 Nov.
    1819 to:

Margaret Walker	William Stovall	Laban Ford
Wm. F. Davis	William Graves	James Wilder
William McKinna	John Zachary	Drury Pinson
John Massey	Joseph McCullock	Ruffin Pleasant
William Florence	Pleasant Rudd	Reese Enoch
James Lamkins	William Street	William Barnwell
Daniel Payne	Thomas Shanks et al	Note on James Hut-cherson

312 Sale property of Jesse Brintle decd by Rebecca Brintle adm. Sales on 5 Nov to

Rebecca Brintle	Robert Brown	Wm. V. Brown, Jun.
Sally Brintle	Richard F. Archer	Spencer Jackson
Stephen Chandler	Mahlon Stacy	James Brintle
John Page	Thomas Stacy	Bartlett Estes
Oliver Brintle	Thomas Jackson	Capt. John Windsor
John Hasting		

41

315 Allotment to Mrs. Rebecca Brintle, widow of Jesse Brintle, decd., for her
and her child. Commrs: Thomas Garrett, Hezekiah Boswell, Moses Simpson.
1 Nov 1819.
315 Allotment to Mrs. Margaret Walker widow of William Walker decd. for her and
her children. Commrs: William Bird, Hugh Walker, Abner Walker. 13 Nov 1819.
316 Allotment to Sally Featherston, widow of Wiley Featherston, decd.. Commrs:
James Rainey, Thomas McGhee, Henry M. Clay, Joseph McGehee. 6 May 1819.
316 Div of negroes belonging to estate of Isekiah Farley on 24 Dec. 1819 to:
Rachel Roper, Catherine Durham, William S. Farley, Martha Farley, decd.,
Joseph Farley, decd., John B. Farley, Martha Farley Sen. Commrs: John
McAden,Tho Jeffreys, Jas. Samuel.
317 Allotment to Christiany Dupey, widow of Robert Dupey, decd., and to the
legatees. Commrs: John Cobb, Henry Howard, Henry Cobb.
317 Div of negroes of estates of John Kersey and Sarah Kersey, decd., to:
Wiley Jones, Martha Kersey, Alexander Kersey. 6 Jan 1820. Commrs: James
Ramey, Tho Jeffreys, Lewis Shirley.
318 John G. Willsom adm in acct with estate of Daniel Jones decd. Money received from United States as per the Hon. Thomas Settle's letter $93.35;
paid John Scott attorney; receipt of Robert Jones the father of Daniel
Jones.
318 Richard Bradsher and wife Phoeby, adms. of estate of William Nelson, acct
filed. Payments to Isaac Rainey for crying the sale; allowance to Phoebe
Nelson; paid James Smith (Doctor), and acct of Ambrose Nelson.
319 Acct current with Henry W. Willson adm estate of Jeremiah Willson.
320 Settlement estate of Henry Tapscott decd with Winifred Tapscott, adm.
27 Oct 1819. Property given by Henry Tapscott in his lifetime to: William
Tapscott, Henry Tapscott and his wife Nancy; to Edney, John, and Polly
Tapscott.
321 Settlement estate of Henry Tapscott. Payments to Joseph McCain, Jethro
Brown, John Tapscott, Nathan King.
321 Further acct sale of Robert Dupey. Cash for crop of tobacco after expenses
$198.32; 1 negro girl sold for $416.25. By Silvanus Stokes, adm.
322 John Robinson of Lynchburg, Virginia, desirous of rewarding a black man
by name of Jacob Thomas who was raised by Bartlett Bennett of Orange County,
Virginia, and was purchased by Robinson on 1 Oct 1808 from Thomas Jones
of Campbell County. (Said Jacob's father being free man of same name.)
For $900 paid by Jacob Thomas, Robinson do hereby emancipate him and be-
stow upon him all rights of a free man of colour in the Commonwealth of
Virginia. 5 Mar 1818.
323 Power of attorney - James Hubbard of Jackson County, Miss., to Thomas
Donoho Sen. of Caswell County to receive from father Ralph Hubbard of
county and state aforesaid a negro woman named Lucy and her child and to
sell and dispose of said negroes and transmit cash to Green County Courthouse, Miss. 9 Sept. 1819.
324 Power of attorney - John H. McNeil and Lawrence R. Richardson, co-partners
in trade in Leasburg, to Jesse A. Dollarhide to collect all debts due to
said concern as partnership is to be dissolved. 31 Dec 1819.
325 Frederick Philips a boy of colour age 12 years next March bound to Polley
Evans. John P. Harrison, Chairman County Court.
326 Nathan Lambert orphan age 14 years next April bound to Jesse Orr until
he attain 21 years.

Book H 1820
Page
326 Matilda Garrott, a girl of color, age 12 years in April next, bound to
John H. McNeil until she attain 21 years of age.
327 Dilcey Philips, a girl of colour, age 15 next Sept., bound to Polly Evans.

April Court 1820 - Held second Monday of April 1820
in 44th year of American Independence.

328 ANN VINCENT - Will - w. 28 Dec 1819. Stock to be sold and money divided
to daughter Sally Shaw, son-in-law John Street, son-in-law John Sawyer.
Remainder divided into 10 parts to go to: son William Vincent, children
of son John Vincent; sons Thomas, Joseph, and Alexander. Children of
decd daughter Mary Ann King; daughters Clarisa Wilder, Elizabeth Jackson.
Children of decd daughter Susanna Ashbourn; children of decd daughter
Elender Weedon. Exec: son Thomas Vincent, and son-in-law James Wilder.
Wit: Levi Walker, Q. Anderson. Executors qualified.

330 SAMUEL PITTARD - Will - w. 9 Jan 1820. Youngest son John to have whole
estate and his two sisters, daughters Elizabeth and Frances Pittard, to
have use of estate to look after him. Other children already provided for:
Thompson Pittard, Elijah Pittard, Anny Ysalock, Umphrey Pittard, Samuel
Pittard, William Pittard, Abner Pittard, Rebecca Malone, and Davis Pittard. Exec: Archibald Rice and William Lea. Wit: William Lea and
Lorenzo Lea.

331 BRITTAIN MOORE - Will - w. 21 June 1819. Wife Isbell. Four sons:
Williamson Moore, Brittain Terrell Moore, John Tucker Moore, Thompson
Rainey Moore. Daughters Fanny Moor, Sally Moor. Sons James and Epps
Moore. Elizabeth Burgess and Nancy Lewis Moore; son William.
Exec: friends Daniel Hightower, Daniel Jackson. Wit: Joseph Langley(Ju-
rat), George B. Dameron, Robert H. Jackson.
At April term of court 1854, execution of will of Brittain Moore proved
in open court on oath of Joseph Langley. George B. Dameron, other
witness decd.. Ordered by court to be recorded nunc pro tem it appear-
ing said will had been proved in court and not recorded.
Tho W. Graves, Clerk.

332 Inv estate of Michael Montgomery taken 13 Jan 1820 by Thomas Gunn, adm.
Allotment to Jennet Montgomery, widow. One watch given by widow to
Alexander Montgomery.
333 Inv property of Robert Davis and amt of sales by Joseph Roe, exec.
334 Inv property of Jacob Wright decd by George Williamson, exec.
334 Inv property of James Orr decd by Samuel Orr, exec.
335 Inv property of William Pettillo decd by Zachariah Pettillo, exec.
335 Inv property of Ellis Evans decd taken 3 Feb 1820 by Thomas Evans and
A. Gunn, adm. Accts on Allen Gunn, William Kennom, Benjamin Hooper.
336 Inv estate of William Owen decd by Mary Owen and John Russell, exec. Bonds
on Stephen Pleasant, James Whitfield. Sales to James Darby, John McMurry.
337 Sales property of James Orr sold 2 Feb 1820 at the late dwelling house
by Samuel Orr, exec. Sales to:

Polly Orr	Jesse Orr	Robert Rollen & Co.
Elizabeth Orr	Collmore Humphreys	Henry Cobb
Nancy Orr	Elisha Paschall	Hezekiah Boswell

continued on page 44

43

Book H 1820
Page
337 Cont. - sales of James Orr to:

George Lovelace	Richard Smith	Samuel Orr
Edward Jones	John H. Pickrod	William Morgan
Thomas Gibson	John Watt	William Orr
Wm. Paschall Sen.	Noah Cobb	Prior Lovelace
Robert Cobb	Joseph McClain	Samuel Luttrell
William Graves	Jonathan Brookes	Zachariah Groom
Thomas Holderness	Stephen Rice	Hugh Gwyn
Philip Pearce	James Cobb	Joseph Montgomery
Harvey Swift		Levi Cobb

340 Sales estate of Michl. Montgomery sold 1 Feb 1820 to:

Jennet Montgomery	Bartlett Yancey	James Lea
Mary Howard	Hugh Darby	Michael Montgomery
Elizabeth Montgomery	Goolsby Watson	Mat Terry
Alexander Montgomery	Wm. Harrison	William Spaulding
Thomas Gunn	Jep Parker	William Harris
Robin Roberts	Daniel Gwyn	John Johnston
Richard B. Gunn	John Everett	Jeremiah Lea
David Montgomery	Archibald Samuel	John Long
Anselem Haddock	John Kitchem	John J. Oliver
Stephen Haddock	James Adams	Amos Satterfield
Hiram Henderson	Solomon Graves	Genu Barz. Graves
James Miles	Ede Montgomery	Anderson Burk
Revd. Barzillai Graves	Maj. Donoho	Jacob Wright
Henry Roper	John Sneed	William Bull
Richard Yarborough	Zach W. Tylor	

By Thomas Gunn, adm.

343 Amt of sales of property of William Pettillo decd. (Buyers not listed.)

344 Sales estate of Ellis Evans sold 3 Feb 1820 to:

Mary Evans	William Ware	Ludwell Worsham
James Ingram	William McDaniel	Ellis Evans Jr.
Thomas Evans	Nathaniel Lea	Thomas Evans
Peter Badgett	Edwin Raimey	Jos. Knight
Pleasant Coleman	Abner Miles	John Poteate
Thompson Price	William Morgan	James Burton
William Kirk	James Harris	Bartlett Yancey
William Henderson	George Holcomb	Thomas A. Mera(or
Samuel Henderson	Henry Glass	Mere or Mora)
Stephen Ingram	James Richardson	

Allotment to widow.

346 Sales estate of Joseph Dameron to:

William Upton	Woodlief Hooper	Andrew Johnston
William Ware	Wm. M. Dameron	Matthew Terry
Benjamin Dameron	John Long	James Peterson
William Dameron	Walker Bennett	Joseph Knight
Joseph Dameron	Rowze Samuel	Thomas Dameron
Samuel Dameron	Ralph Hubbard	Abraham Montgomery
Jepthah Parker	Freeman Hubbard	

By John P. Harrison and George B. Dameron, exec.

347 Sales property of Jacob Wright on 15 Jan 1820 to:

John Lea(CB)	Moses Kitchen	James Lea
Ambrose L.Bennett	Wm. Sawyers	Thomas Riggs
Nathaniel Lea	George Turner	Asa Gunn
Joshua Roberts	William Peterson	Benj. Willis
James Whitlow	Meshack Morton	Robert Sledge
Curtis Payne	John Morton	Daniel Payne

Book H 1820
Page
348 Power of attorney - William Morgan of Lynchburg, Va., owning mercantile
    business in Milton, N. C. and desirous of doing business with Newbern
    Bank at said town of Milton, to Samuel Settle of Milton to sign checks and
    endorse notes. 9 Jan 1820. Wit: Alban McDaniel, Martin W. Davenport,
    R. M. Sanders.
349 Power of attorney - William Keen of Caswell County to friend David Walker
    of same county to recover from estate of John Keen decd. 6 Nov 1816.
    Wit: David Poynor, Henry Humphreys.
350 Negroes of estate of Jesse Brintle decd alloted to: Rebecca Brintle,widow,
    Spencer Jackson, Robert Brown, and Rebecca Brintle as guardian for Sarah
    Brintle, minor. 9 Dec 1819. Commrs: Azariah Graves, Benjamin Lea, Capt.
    John Windsor, John Boswell.
351 Settlement estate of John Windsor decd by John and Joseph Windsor, exec.
    Bonds on John Windsor Jun., Nicholas Chub, Williamson Rice, Thomas
    Sullivant.
352 Div negroes of Michael Montgomery decd to: James Montgomery, Alexander
    Montgomery, Jennett Montgomery, Thomas Gunn, Elizabeth Montgomery, Mary
    Howard.
352 Allotment to Mary Evans wife of the late Ellis Evans decd. 28 Jan 1820.
353 Acct of strays taken up by William Walker, Lewis Whitemore, James Lea,
    George Washington Stubblefield, Col. James Sanders, Amos Satterfield.
354 Hiram Bell an orphan 17 years old the 8 day of Nov. last bound to James
    Terrell. Solomon Graves, Chairman County Court.
355 Angus McNiel orphan 14 years old the 14th of last month bound to John H.
    Perkins until Jan. Court 1825.
355 Reubin Piles orphan now age of 7 years bound to George Williamson until
    age 21. John McMullen, Chairman County Court.
356 Addis Finley orphan 9 years old bound to George Williamson to learn art
    of a planter.

                July Court 1820 - Held second Monday after fourth Monday of
                        June 1820 in 45th year of American Independence

358 JAMES LAMKIN - Will - w. 3 Sept. 1816. As each child comes of age, each
    to receive $100 of property to make them even with John Bouldin and Wil-
    liam Cody. Youngest son George W. Lamkin(under 15). If wife survives
    until youngest son is 15 she is to take her thirds and equal division
    among all children. Exec: wife Mary Lamkin, Grief L. Lamkin, James D.
    Lamkin. Test: Thomas Holt.
    From testimony of James Yancey, James Wilder, William Slade Jun. that
    this was handwriting of James Lamkin, it was admitted to probate. Mary
    and James D. Lamkin qualified.

359 Taxable property for 1819.

359 PEGGY NEALEY - Will - w. 25 May 1820. Sons James Durham and Isaac Durham;
    daughter Sally Durham to have money coming from "my Father's estate at
    my Mother's death"; late husband Gregory Durham. Exec: son James Durham
    and William Patterson.
    The executors refusing to qualify, court appointed John Keesee adm. with
    the will annexed. (Also spelled Neeley and Nealy).

360 Inv property of Reuben Cox decd by Mary Cox and George Williamson.
361 Inv property of William Lyon decd. Provisions alloted to widow.
    Accts. against James Toller, William Jones, Bond V. Brown. By W. W. Lyon.
362 Inv property of Brittain.Moore decd by Daniel Hightower and Daniel
    Jackson, exec.

                                    45

Book H 1820
Page
363 Inv property of Frances Carlos decd taken 9 Jan 1820 by Ibzan Rice, adm.
364 Inv property of James Lamkins decd by James D. and Mary Lamkin.
364 Acct property of Samuel Pittard decd. Bonds on.Thomas Malone,James
    Yealock, Davis Pittard, Elijah Morton, Samuel Pittard. By Archibald
    Rice, exec.
365 Sales of property of William Lyon decd to Martha Lyon, William W. Lyon,
    William V. Brown, Peter Powell, Henry Hailey, Asa Gunn, Robert Brown,
    Robert Lyon, John Lyon, Richard B. Gunn, David Mason, William F. Davis,
    Samuel H. Carroll.
367 Sales property of Reuben Cox decd to Mary Cox, Thomas Donoho, William Page,
    William Upton, Sarah Cox, Mrs. Nancy Lea, Alexander Montgomery, Ludwell
    Worsham, Thomas Gunn, Benjamin Dameron, George Williamson, John Roberts,
    John Poteet, Sherod Owen, William Harris.
369 Allotment to Jennett Montgomery widow of Michail Montgomery.
369 Allotment to Patcey Lyon widow of William Lyon decd.
370 Power of attorney - Thomas Longwell (or Langwell) and Anna his wife (late
    Anna Bastin), Temperence Newell (late Bastin), and Godfrey Young and
    Tabitha his wife (late Bastin), all daughters of William Bastin decd.,
    one of the heirs of Thomas Bastin decd., all of Pulaski County, Ky., to
    John Newell of same county to sell lands of Thomas Bastin in Caswell Co.,
    N. C. on Little Wolf Island Creek. 18 Nov 1818.
372 Power of attorney - Sarah Petillo and Zachariah Petillo of Caswell County,
    N. C. and Edward Petillo of Warren County, N. C., request allotment of
    negroes of estate of William Petillo. Sarah relict of said decd intends
    to dissent from will of decd and thereby entitled to one-third of negroes.
    14 Oct 1819.
373 Edward and Zachariah Petillo convey to Sarah Petillo all claim to certain
    property (slaves) of William Petillo.
374 James Puckett orphan 10 years old bound to William Sawyer.
    Solomon Graves, Chairman County Court.
374 Thomas Puckett orphan 13 years old bound to Thomas Turner.
375 George Day orphan 10 years of age bound to John S. Hutchinson.
376 Griffin Gunn, county trustee, acct with Caswell County for 1819.
    872 white and 2234 black polls taxed at 25¢ is $776.50. Valuation of
    land 1,382,692.73 dollars at 5¢ pct. is $691.34.
    Stray animals taken up by Josiah Morton, Goodloe Warren, Abraham Landers,
    Anthony Williamson, James Murry, Buckner Roman, Edward Herndon, William
    Brown.

October Court 1820

379 WILLIAM GORDON -Will - w. no date - Land to be sold and proceeds used for
    family; wife Sally; slaves to be hired out and money be laid out in
    Western Country. My children; after wife's death property divided to
    William, Phoebe, James Elam, Hannah Cross, Jane Parish, John and Florinda
    Ward Gordon; son Alexander Gordon,; daughter Elizabeth Vanhook.
    Exec: sons Alexander, James Elam, and John Gordon. Wit: Levi Fuller,
    Thomas Comer. Alexander Gordon qualified.

379 Declaration - 9 Oct 1820. William Hatcher aged about 58 years, of Caswell
    County, doth on oath declare he served in Revolutionary War in company
    commanded by Captain John Hughs first regiment of light Dragoons of Va.
    He obtained pension certificate in April 1818 number 11630 and received
    $181; he has no income, has disposed of no property; has no family but
    his wife.

Book H 1820
Page
380 Declaration - 9 Oct 1820. Robert Martin age about 64 years, resident of
Caswell County, declares on oath he served in Revolutionary War in company
commanded by Captain Henry Dixon first regiment of North Carolina. He
has pension certificate number 9434 issued 1818 and has received $157.
His schedule of property is 194 acres poor land. He has 10 in family,
his wife, mother of his wife, himself and all are infirm and following
children: sons Robert age 18, James age 16, George age 12, Howard age 9,
Allen age 7; and daughters Nancy age 20, Franky age 14.
381 Declaration - 11 Oct 1820. Peter Smith about 72 years old and resident of
Caswell County makes oath he served in Revolutionary War in company of
Captain Henry Dixon first regiment of North Carolina Infantry. He has
pension certificate issued 1818 and he has no property other than in his
schedule.
382 Declaration - 10 Sept. 1820. Thomas Belsayer age about 62 years makes
oath he served in Revolutionary War in Capt. John B. Nash sixth regiment
of North Carolina infantry. He has pension certificate and no property
but 83 acres land. No other in family but his wife and he has been
disabled due to wound in right shoulder.

384 MOSES BRADSHER - Will - w. 13 Aug 1820. Wife Martha; sons Jesse, John,
Richard J., Moses, James O., Abner, Vincent. Daughters Elizabeth Walton,
Nancy Lea, Polly Peterson, Unicy Mutry, Patcey B. Bradsher, Nainey Nelson,
Franky Bradsher. Exec: sons Abner and John. Wit: A. L. Bennett, Daniel
Richmond. Executors qualified.

386 Sales of estate of Britain Moore sold 20 Aug 1820 to: John Murphy, Powel
Terrell, George B. Dameron, Daniel Hightower, William Turner.
387 John Harrison adm in acct with estate of Isaac Hodge. Sales to David
Hodge, Charles Bucey, Doctor James Smith, Bartlett Yancey, James
Richardson.
387 Inv estate of Peggy Nealey on 30 May 1820. Bonds on Harrod Worsham,
Bartlett Read, Joseph Swan, Selby Benson, James Eudaley, William H. Burns,
Thomas Henderson. Judgment on William P. McDaniel in hands of Thomas
Penick. By John Keesee, adm.
389 Sales property of Peggy Nealey on 28 July 1820 to:

John Lay	Penny Cox	Edward Busey
Robert Ware	Samuel White	Lucinda Dudley
Greenbury Willson	James Swan	Polly Carver
William Walker	Brockman Nichols	Obediah Owen
John Shields	James Burns	Pleasant Voss
Hezekiah P. Smithson	Nathan Duncan	Jesse Abel
Elijah Sims	David A. Browder	Benjamin Loafman
Charles Sims	William Crews	Henry Ruark
Henry Baldwin	Elizabeth Nighton	James Durham
Robert Alverson	John Badget	William Trigg
Major Price	Matthew Mills	Jonathan Foxdale
James Roberts	John Nichols	Peggy Nighton
Peter Stubblefield	David Lay	Thomas Eudaley
Caleb Anglin	John W. Grant	Richard Going et al

393 William and Toliver Florence in acct with estate of Obed Florence decd.
Settlement to following legatees: Joseph Cantrill in right of his wife,
James Florence, John Florence, Moses Simpson in right of his wife,
William Florence, Toliver Florence.
Acct examined by James Yancey and William Gooch.

47

Book H 1820-1821
Page
395 BENJAMIN NORMAN - Will - w.? - Son John Norman $1. Son Westley (land including house he lives in purchased of Nathaniel Murphey); grandson Nathan Norman; daughter Amelia Norman; sons Benjamin, William, Isaac, Westley; land bought of Heirs of Edward Mills and John Dennis. Daughters Rosey, Judah, Anne, Amelia. Exec: sons Benjamin, Isaac, Westley. Wit: Elijah Withers, James Rawley.
Jury determined the original will was destroyed by James Norman son of John and witnesses testified above was copy.

397 Bob Kean boy of color age 10 years the 25 Dec next bound to Thomas Brinsfield. Thomas Slade, Chairman County Court.
398 Elijah Gibson orphan age 8 years last June bound to James Swan. James Yancey, Chairman County Court.
398 Jackson Carrol orphan age 12 years last month bound to Noel Read. Elijah Withers, Chairman County Court.

January Court 1821   Held on second Monday after the fourth Monday of Dec. Present the worshipful John P. Harrison, Benj. C. West, and William W. Price, Esquires.

400 Declaration - 11 Jan 1821 - Peter Smith age about 72 years on oath declares He served in North Carolina Infantry under Capt. Henry Dixon for 12 months and 6 days. His pension number is 4884 and he has residing with him following children: Morgan age 13, Nicholas age 10, Elizabeth about 8, Sally about 6, Jackson between 2 and 3 years, and Washington age 7 months.
402 Ordered that 6 cents be laid on every hundred dollars worth landed property and twenty cents on every poll for support of the poor for 1820.
Test: Azariah Graves, Clk.
402 Declaration - 12 Jan 1821 - Jeremiah Samuel aged 69 years in May last makes oath he served in Revolutionary War as follows: in 7th regiment of Virginia in Captain Cocks company for 1 year or more, taken into Morgan's regiment of riflemen and served 3 years; first enlisted Feb 1776. He was at capture of Borguine at Saretoga. He has pension number 6730 and has drawn since May 1818; he gives schedule of property and has no other income. By occupation he is a farmer with him children Anne Samuel and Polly Samuel ages between 20 and 30 years and his wife about 63 years .
402 Declaration - 12 Jan 1821 - Francis Jones aged between 65 and 70 years on oath declares he served in Revolutionary War in 10th Regiment of North Carolina commanded by Col. Archibald Litle, company commanded by Henry Sharp, and served about 12 months. He was not in any battle but was a militia man at Gates' defeat. He has pension certificate number 5442. By occupation he is a ditcher and has with him following children: John about 14 years, Betsy 9 years, Nathaniel 7 years, and his wife about 51 years old.

404 PHILIP W. JACKSON - Will - w. 8 April 1819. Wife Abbey W. Jackson; nephew Philip Whitted Jackson Echols son of Philip J. Echols and Mary E. Echols to get ½ of estate after wife gets her legal part; one-half to Champ Bradfuite daughter of Davidson and Mariah Bradfuite of Lynchburg, Virginia, said Davidson being cashier of Farmer's Bank of Va. Stepheny and wife Patience to choose their master. Elizabeth Bushrod Echols and Richard Obediah Echols children of Philip and Mary E. to have wife's part if she remarry. Exec: Philip J. Echols, Alexander Tompkins, Davidson Bradfuite. Test: George M. Penn, Champion C. M. Marable. Philip J. Echols qualified.

Book H 1821
Page
405 HENRY WILLIS - Will - w. 31 Oct 1820. Daughters Betsy Smith, Polly
Herritage, Joice Chandler; plantation to be kept up by sons Henry Willis
Jr. and Anderson Willis. Property for Polly Herritage placed with Mr.
Francis Smith; Wife. Exec: sons Nicholas, Henry Jr., and Anderson.
Wit: Jno L. Graves, William Russell, Robert P. Buchanan.
Exec qualified.

406 Inv property of Nathan Holley decd by Holloway Pass adm. Accts. on
Robertson and Beavers.
407 Inv property of Henry Willis decd.
408 Sales property of William Gordon decd by Alex Gordon exec on 3 and 4 Nov
1820. Sales to:

Levi Fuller	Birdit Eskridge	Eli Stafford
John Broughton	William Stephens	James Fullington
John Richmond	Nathaniel Lea	John Roan
William Morgan	Archibald Rice	John Peterson
Welcome Seamore	James E. Gordon	Tinsley Lea
Flemming Waterfield	James Darby	Lewis Shirley
Thomas Winstead	Booker Boman	Watson Winters
Thomas Waterfield	et al	

409 Inv estate of William Gordon.
410 Sales property of Ann Vincent to:

Stephen Sawyer	James Wilder	John Hughs
Henry Tait	Thomas Vincent	James Wilson
Thomas Jackson	William Street	Reese Enoch
Alexander Vincent	James Kelly Jr.	Abner Walker
James Bird	William Vincent	James Douglass
John Sawyer	John B. Vincent	James Vaughan
Coleby Foster	William Boulding	Thomas Sawyer

412 Sales property of Henry Willis decd to:

Nicholas Willis	Zadock Rice	William Upton
Martain Mims	John Gomer	David Jones
Wilkins Chandler	Benjamin Dameron	William Willis
William Graves	William Lyon	Robert Holderness
Benjamin Willis	Francis Smith	Edmond McCubbins
Littleton A. Gwyn	Pleasant Robinson	Henry Willis

413 Additional sales property of Samuel Henderson to Joseph Henderson; tobacco
sold in Petersburg and Lynchburg.
414 Sales property of Nathan Holley to John Ratliff, George L. Willson,
Anne Holley, Holloway Pass.
414 Inv and sales property of Moses Bradsher to:

Richard J. Bradsher	Patsy B. Bradsher	James Lea
Vincent Bradsher	E. Evans	William Lewis
Jas Bradsher	Sanders Browning	Fielding Lewis
Martha Bradsher	A. Burton	Thomas McFarland
Moses Bradsher	John Johnston	Cit Mathis
Joseph C. Dameron	Moses Kitchen	Hugh Campbell
Abner Bradsher	Vincent Lea	William Mutry
Ambrose Nelson	John Peterson	William Peterson
Daniel Richmond	Thomas Riggs	William Richmond
Henry Shelton	William Suit	Thomas Donoho
N. Kyles	J. Vanhook	Zeney Martin
William Wier	R. Walton	James Yealock	J. Daniel	Thomas Brooks

James O. Bradsher, John Bradsher Jr..& Sr., Sam Pittard, Henry Lipscomb
Thomas Malone, A. Lipscomb, James Dollarhide, Elijah Jacobs, John Scoggin,
Sam Satterfield, Br Fuller, James Hannah. Crop tobacco in Person Co.

49

Book H. 1821
Page
420 Amt of hire for negro slaves of Moses Bradsher decd and a list of notes due.
421 Settlement estate of Jane Jackson decd by Robt. H. Jackson and George
    Smith adm. Payments to Dr. William F. Smith, Daniel Jackson, David Nutt,
    James Hightower, Abraham Villines, Frances H. Burton, et al.
    Div of estate to: Delilah Jackson orphan, James Jackson, Jere Jackson,
    Sally Jackson, Jincey Jackson, all orphans. 8 Jan 1820.
423 Acct of Martha Blackwell adm of Levi Blackwell decd. Sales collected of
    William Morgan Sen., John Stamps, Joseph Montgomery, John Kinnebrugh,
    Ed. M. Foulks, Elijah Graves, et al.
424 Amt of hiring of negroes of William Walker decd by Conly Walker.
424 Allotment to Nancy Holley and family. Met at house of Andrew Harrison ,
    Sen. 6 Jan 1821.
425 Power of attorney - Jonah Dobyns of Caswell County to John C. Vanhook of
    Leasburg to superintend collection of notes executed by James Riddle of
    Pittsylvania Co., Va. 12 Oct 1819. Wit: Will A. Lea, Bentley B. Epperson.
426 Robert Gwyn orphan, child of colour, age 7 years, bound to Azariah Graves.
427 Ransom Gwyn orphan age 11 years bound to Azariah Graves.
    Solomon Graves, Chairman County Court.

                              End of Book H

April Court 1821
Present the Worshipful William Warren, John P. Harrison, N. Thompson

Page
1 JOSEPH PAYNE - Will - w. 4 Jan 1821. Nephew Robert P. Buchannan to get $\frac{1}{2}$
   of land deeded to testator and brother Thomas Payne; property of father
   and mother never divided since their death and testator's interest to nephew Robert P. Buchannan and niece Betsy G. Buchannan. Exec: Robert P.
   Buchannan and Thomas Graves. Wit: William Russell, William F. Davis.
   Thomas Graves qualified.

2 Inv property of Abraham Underwood decd by William Bethell adm.
2 Inv property of estate of Benjamin Ashley decd by A. Graves and William
   Russell adm.
3 Inv estate Philip W. Jackson decd and debts on books of Jackson and Harrison. Notes due from:

John G. Wingfield	Hasdal Butt	Samuel Kirk
Gabriel Higgerson	Maj. Thomas Atkinson	Maj. Phil H. Inge
Jesse Elmore	Moody Fowler	Capt. Wm. Hutchins
Benjamin J. Sneed	Wm. Climpson	Parham Seymore
Jesse Walker	John O'Neal	Thomas S. Sewell
John W. Graves	Willie Featherston	Merry Maynard
Majr. William Timberlake	B. Suitt	Bennett Lea
Harvey Swift	Capt. Mathew Sims	Capt. Wm. Irvine
Thomas Edwards	Thomas A. Mera	Littleton Sledge
James Chambers	Jesse Owen	Solomon Whitlow 1818
George O. Connally	Lewis Shirley	Thomas Collier
James Carpenter	Henry Brewer	James Spencer
William Settle	James Proudfit	Hardin Winfrey
Susanna Sneed	Doct. John T. Garland	Barnett Bass
George C. Sims	Richard Ogilby	Stewart Farley
Grief Wells	Thomas Barr	James Rudd
Thomas McGehee	James Lea (Hop)	George Farley
Dr. Carter Atkinson	Nathaniel Norfleet	et al

   Inv property by Philip J. Echols exec.
6 Inv property of James Sawyer decd taken 5 Jan 1821 by William Sawyers, Nancy
   Sawyers, and Hosea McNiel adm. Sales of property on 3 Feb to Nancy Sawyers,
   Hosea McNiel, Ciscilla Foster, William Sawyer, James Taylor, Coleby Foster;
   Stephen, John, and Thomas Sawyer.
7 Sales property of Abraham Underwood to:

John Hughs	Richard Stubblefield	Robert Rolen
George Robards	William Stubblefield	Priestly Sanders
Frank Cornwell	Elizabeth Underwood	John D. Cobb
John R. Griffin	Warren Weatherford	Pryor Lovelace
Philemon Neal	Tabitha Underwood	Jethro Brown

8 Sales of William Brown decd sold 27 Jan 1821 to:

Robert Brown	James Taylor	James Brown
Benjamin Lea	Ritter Brown	Wm. V. Brown
William Barker	Freeman Leath	James Vickers
George Martin	Samuel Estres	Jesse Hollis

9 Sales estate on 6 Mar 1821 of Philip W. Jackson to Jeremiah Lea, Samuel
   Brandon, Thomas Barr, Kitty Jones, Bird Eskridge, Joseph McDowell, et al.
9 Acct of property of Thomas Swift sold by Harvey Swift adm: a negro woman
   Rhode and her 3 children for $1338.

Book I 1821
Page
10 Inv estate of Benjamin Norman on 17 July 1820. Note on John Gibson.
    Sales estate on 1 Dec 1820 by Westley Norman exec to:

Roseman Norman	Brockman Nichols	Hannah Bastin
John Ford	William Crews	Smith Overby
Westley Norman	John Bastin	Nathan Norman
Thomas Bastin	Judith Norman	Thomas Henderson
Peter B. Stubblefield	James Abels	Sally Russell
George Harden	Reuben Cannon	Lewis Whitemore
Caron Norman	Richard Going	et al

12 Settlement estate of William Williams by John Pass adm. Payments to Samuel
    Dabney, Thomas Phelps.
13 B. Yancey exec of Ann Yancey acct with estate; special legacies to Priscilla
    Howard, Nancey Ramsey, and Sally Rice. Payments to Doct Solomon Debow for
    medicine, Doct John L. Graves for medicine, Dr. Foulks for same. Paid
    James Yancey store acct; paid acct of Ann Ford and Solomon Graves. Sums
    remaining $1756.16 to be divided into 8 parts to: B. Yancey retaining his
    part, James Yancey has received his part, John Yancey's adm. has received
    $150, Nathaniel Slade in right of his wife has received his full share.
14 Allotment to Mary Ashley widow of Benjamin Ashley decd for her and family.
    1 Feb 1821.
14 Allotment of negroes of estate of John Keen decd to: Nancy Shackleford,
    Ellender Keen, John H. Humphreus, James Keen, David Keen.
14 Stray mare taken up on waters of Stoney Creek by James Brown Jr.
    Four stray hogs taken up by Sylvanus Stokes.
15 Allotment to Nancy Sawyers widow of James Sawyers decd. 26 Jan 1821.
    Commrs: Buford Pleasant, Joseph Penick, Anthony Foster.

July Court 1821

17 FRANCES SWIFT - Will - w. 17 Mar 1820. All property to children: daughter
    Sarah Williamson, sons John Swift and Richard Swift; granddaughter Frances
    Harris; son George A. Swift (land bought of John Windsor); a cow and calf
    to Barbara Redmon. Exec: George A. Swift. Wit: Zachariah Hastin, William
    Hastin. Exec qualified.

18 Inv estate of Joseph Payne and of property of his father and mother he was
    entitled to. Thomas Graves exec.
18 Votes for Congress - 878 for R. M. Sanders. 15 Aug 1821.
18 Taxable property for 1820 - 838 white polls, 2351 black polls.
19 Acct of Griffin Gunn county trustee.

October Court 1821

Present: Solomon Graves, Jeremiah Graves, Wm. W. Price, Esquires

20 Inv property of Richard H. Hays decd by Gabriel Lea adm.
20 Inv property of John T. Cobb by William Cobb adm. Notes on Edmond Rice,
    Mathew Cobb, Richard Smith Jun., Jesse Cobb, William Paschal, Jethro
    Brown, Alexander Paschal.
21 Inv estate of William Swift decd taken after death of Frances Swift by
    George A. Swift surviving exec. 22 May 1821. Bonds on Richard Swift
    dated 1805, on James Taylor 1819.
21 Inv estate of James Nichols taken by Susannah Nichols adm on 10 Aug 1821.
    Bonds on Anthony Foster, Thomas Jackson.
22 Inv estate of Frances Swift decd. Notes on John Williamson, William Brink-
    ley, Moses Simpson, Benjamin T. Fielder, Anthony Williamson, John Windsor,
    Nicholas Chub, Hezekiah Boswell, William Hasting, Thomas Poynor, William
    Clifton; George A. Swift, exec.

Book I 1821
Page
23 Sales property of William Swift to:

Frances Swift	Enoch Chamberlain	Sally Swift
Geo. A. Swift	William Rider	Nathan Moore
Thomas Garrott	Moses Simpson	Harvey Swift
William Garrott	John Swift(of Thomas)	William Swift
Aron Simpson	James Underwood	Frances Swift Jun.
David Barker Sen.	John Lea	John Swift Sen. et al

25 Sales property of Frances Swift 28 May 1820 to: Geo. A. Swift, Thomas
   Garrott, Anthony Tate, Leonard Prather, Bennet Bush, Wm. Rider, James
   Suddoth, Frances Swift, Spencer Jackson, Barbary Redman, Capt. John Brackin,
   Mahlon Stacy, Valentin Waggoner, et al.
27 List of property sold of John T. Cobb to William Cobb, Jesse Cobb, Amsy Cobb,
   Henry Cobb, Samuel Orr, Samuel Lutrell, Elisha Paschal.
28 Sales property of James Nichols on 16 Aug 1821 to: Susanna Nichols, John
   Nichols, Hasting Hicks.
28 Settlement estate of Robert Dupey by Sylvanus Stokes adm. Bonds on John,Cobb,
   John W. Grant, William Crews; accts contra: William P. Hall, John Cobb,
   Rhody Lovelace, Robert Roe; Chancy Dupey her part of hire of negroes and
   guardian for her children.
29 Settlement estate of Ann Downs decd by Levin Downs. Bond on Swain Cox;
   paid accts of Elizabeth Downs, Isaac Patterson, Wesley Cook, Nathaniel
   Willson, et al.
30 Acct of estate of Samuel Henderson. Bonds on Joseph and Hiram Henderson,
   James Miles, Henry Hailey, Robert Hall. Payments to Hezekiah P. Smithson
   for crying sale, to Thomas Ruffin, Stephen Haddock, John Ware, Doct James
   D. Patton.
31 Div of negroes of estate of William Swift to: Heirs of Anthony Swift decd.,
   John Swift, George A. Swift, Susannah Harris, Richard Swift, heirs of
   Thomas Swift decd, Frances Swift, heirs of William P. Swift decd. Aug 1821.
32 Acct of hire of negroes of estate of William Swift.

33 Insolvents returned by George Williamson sheriff for 1817

Lewis G. Bradley	William Rudd	James Lettrell
Barzillai Gomer	John Stewart	Joel Leath
Wm. T. Glasgow	Thomas Smith	Edmond Paschall
Benjamin Jones	Robert Tindol	John Revell?Jun.
John Jones	John Ward	Williamson Rice
Hutchins Burton	Miles W. Brown	John Roland
David Kersey	Paschall Westbrook	Henry Roland
Edmond Richardson	Ezekial Warren	Henry Scott
John Arnold	Robert Zachary	Benjamin Walker
Henry Burch	William Southard	William Ferrel
John Boyles	Solomon Brinsfield	David Hailey
James Bower	John Brown	Joseph P. Hall
Daniel Carson	Jesse Beaver	James Kennedy
Green Lewis	Thomas Christmas	Benjamin Loafman
William Lewis	John Eskridge	Thomas Jewett
William Pleasant	Fielder Every	Daniel Morgan
Leroy Parks(no such man	William Groom	Albert Maddin
found)	Andrew Haddock	Samuel Ruark
Step Roberts	John Horford	Elijah Flack
James Mitchell	John Hughs	

33-34 Insolvents for 1818 (cont. on page 54)

Lewis G. Bradley	Daniel S. Farley	Thomas Gatewood
John Elmore Jun.	William Fisher	Barzillai Gomer
William F. Glasgow	Adam Hughs	Abraham Hood

53

Book I 1821 - 1822
Page
33-34 Insolvents for 1818 cont.

Richard Jones	William Price	Williamson Reid
Benjamin Jones	Joseph Smith	John Roland
Thomas Lipscomb	Reubin Smith	Benjamin Walker
Joshua Mabray	Christopher Spencer	Thomas M. Dailey
George Page	Robert Tindol	William Evans
Morris Piles	William Wilkins	William Ferrel
William Stanfield	Timothy Warren	John Ferry
Thomas Taylor	Ezekiel Warren	Levy Ford
George Yealock	Richard Burch	David Haily
Madison Burk	Jesse Beaver	William Jones
Richard Burch Jun.	William Davis	Daniel Morgan
Thompson Burk	William Denny	Joseph Murphey
Jesse Corbett	Andrew Haddock	John Pucket
William Collier Jun.	Thomas G. Meroney	William Denton
Love Malone	John Read Jun.	Henson Alverson

34 Insolvents for 1819

Stephen Boles	John Right	William Camichail
Joshua Butler	George L. Taylor	William Freeman
John Bowden	John Warren	George W. Godwin
Benjamin Birk	Timothy Warren	Anderson Haddock
Richard Burch	Jesse Wisdom	Coleman Leath
James Collier	Elijah Warren	David Poynor Jun.
Alexander Griffin	John Zachary	Edmond Paschal
Lewis Hagwood	John Brim	Jeremiah Rice
Wiley Jones	John Dalton	Wiley Robertson
Phillip Jones	William Evans	James Robertson
Joseph King	William Ferrell	William Scott
James Murray	Richard Foster	Nathan Sims
Love Malone	James Jurgerson	Benjamin Walker
Alexander Murphey (for	John Gomer	Henson Alverson
heirs of Jno. Vaughan)	John Hardin	Samuel Littrell
Nathaniel S. Muzzall	Elijah Sims	William Smith
Robert Payne	John Barker Jr.	

35 Power of attorney - Nathan Williams of Rutherford Co. Tenn., to Hosea McNeill
to receive from exec of estate of Thomas McNeill, decd., and Ann McNeill
decd. late of Person County his part of legacy in right of wife Frances.
15 June 1821.
36 Nathaniel Jeffreys age 16 yrs. in April next bound to Richard Yarborough.
James Rainey, Chairman County Court.
37 Philip Meroney orphan age 11 years the sixth last June bound to Alexander
McAlpin to learn the art of a Taylor.
37 John Hubbird age 7 years the 10th last August bound to Alexander McAlpin
to learn mastery of Taylor. James Yancey, Chairman County Court.

January Court 1822

Present: James Yancey, John P. Harrison, James Rainey, Esquires

41 Inv estate of Thomas Swift decd including interest due from estate of William
Swift decd taken by Caswell Tait exec. 20 Oct 1821. Bonds on Frances
Harris, George A. Swift decd, exec of William Swift.
41 Inv estate of James Hatchett on 29 Dec 1821. Bonds on William Hatchett, et al.
William Hatchett adm.

Book I 1822
Page
42 Moses **Grigsby age 59** years next month declares on oath that he enlisted for
   term of 3 years in November 1781 in State of Virginia, company commanded
   by Captain Abraham Fitzpatrick, regiment of Col. Haws. He continued until
   May 1783 when furloughed. No evidence of his service except from Nathan
   Philips and Vincent ? attacked to his affidavit in Stafford County, Va.,
   where he resided. Schedule of income included; he is a farmer and his
   family consists of wife Abby age about 59, one daughter Abby age 21, and
   a small child age 4 the daughter of a daughter now dead.
43 Inv property of William Shelton decd.
45 Inv property of Catharine Buchanon **decd.** 4 negroes John, Delphia, Melinda,
   and Sally. By Robert P. Buchanon adm. 19 Dec 1821.
45 Inv and sales property of John Trigg decd **on 2 Nov** 1821 by Joshua Trigg adm.
   Sales to Henry Boulding, John Bastin, Robert Ware, Barath Bawldwin, David
   Lay, William Burris, John Baxter, Charles Sims, Joshua Trigg, George W.
   Tyre, Capt. W. Price.
46 Inv property of Jeremiah Lea decd by Benjamin Lea adm on 18 Oct 1821 at his
   plantation on Stoney Creek.
47 Inv property of Jeremiah Lea **decd** taken at his house in Milton.
   Sales estate of Jeremiah Lea at plantation Nov 12,23,24 and at Milton
   house Nov 14,15,16. Sales to:

James Kerr	John Stadler	James Warf
William Evans	John Fitch	Wm. Beadles
Joseph Pennix	George Prendergast	Thomas Donoho
Bennett Lea	Richard Arwin	B. Seamore
Rees Enochs	James Taylor	Thomas Howell
Wm. V. Brown	Wm. Slade Jr.	William Childs
John Sawyer	Andrew McCullock	Richard Crowder
John Shaw	Caleb Willson	B. C. Griffin
Thomas Henslee	William Barnwell	James Holder
Elisha Brown	Nathaniel L. Rice	R. Ball
William Bolding	James Maugham	John Lea
Christopher Brooks	Leonard Fielder	Stephen Dotson
Zadock Rice	Hosea McNeill	James Lea Jun.
James Turner	Henry Collier (son of Wm.)	Thomas Mitchell
Stephen Chandler	Allen Tate	Geo. Williamson
Isaac Cantrell	Henry Collier Jr.	Wm. H. Shelton
Thomas Penix	James Kelly Jr.	John Kerr
Mary Lea	Bartholomew Ellis	Jesse Dollarhide
William Turner	Wm. Massey Jr.	Robert Marrow
James Davis	James Anderson	Wm. McGehee
Maxfield Henslee	Thomas Connally	Spencer Ball
Jesse Hollis	Tinsley Lea	Joseph McGehee
John E. Tate	Mrs. Rebecca Williams	John F. Lea
James Vickers	Thomas Ren	et al

54 List of notes found on books of Jere Lea decd due from John Royester,
   Henry Mukes, Phil W. Jackson, Sterling Willis, Thomas Atkinson(Halifax),
   Benjamin Oliver, Champ Marrible, Elizabeth Kerr, John Lea, Mary Kerr, et al.
   (List continues to page 60. Many names same as those on books of Philip
   W. Jackson).
60 Copy of notice of Benjamin Lea as adm of Jeremiah Lea displayed at Court
   House and at Tavern of Mary Lea in Town of Milton and at store of Quentin
   Anderson. Nov 1821.

Book I 1822
Page
61 Sale property of Richard H. Hays decd sold 7 Nov 1821 to:

William Lea	John C. Vanhook	Wm. A. Lea
Elijah Morton	William Hayes	Fielding Lewis
John Hagwood	Brice Collins	John M. Dobbin
Gabriel B. Lea	Samuel Pittard	John Comer
Daniel Malone	Nicholas Hester	Drury Burton
John Love, Sr. & Jr.	Mumford Ford	John Lea (CB)
John Broughton	John Mann	Alexander Gray
Barbary Hays	James Crossett	Archibald Rice
Hiram Lockard	Elijah Jacobs	Rebecca Williams
		et al

64 Sales estate of James Hatchet on 29 Dec 1821 to William Hatchett.
64 Sale property of William P. Swift: Milly and her child Guilford soldto John
   Lea for $450, negro woman Lindy to Sally Swift for $396. By Sarah Swift,
   exec.
65 Sale property of Thomas Swift by Caswell Tate exec: negro woman Rachel to
   Freeman Leath, negro boy Joshua to William Swift.
65 Acct of 2nd sale of Samuel Pittard by Archibald Rice exec.
65 Amt of hiring of negroes of William Walker $75.20 by Conly Walker adm.
65 Sales estate of Nathaniel Comer by Thomas Comer exec. Accts on John Roan,
   Thomas Jeffreys, Gabriel Lea, Vincent Lea, Alexander Kersey, Nathaniel
   Torian, Jane Roan; Bartlett Yancey's acct for counsel; Archibald Comer, et al.
66 Peyton Key orphan age 14 years bound to John H. Pickard.
67 Garland Key orphan 10 years of age bound to John H. Pickard.
67 John Key orphan age 12 years next July bound to James Cobb.
68 Allotment to Barbary Hays widow of Richard H. Hayes decd. 4 Oct 1822.
68 Allotment to Elizabeth Shelton for her and family. Commrs: Richard Jones,
   James Cobb, Joseph Roe.

April Court 1822

69 JOHN INGRAM - Will - w. 15 July 1820. Wife Mary to have land until her death
   and then land to go to son Stephen Ingram; sons Archibald, Elisha, James;
   duaghters Elizabeth Chandler, Susannah Perkins. Exec: James Burton, Elisha
   Ingram, James Ingram. Wit: Thomas L. Slade, Henry A. Burton, James White,
   Walker White. James Burton and James Ingram qualified.

71 JOHN ANDERSON - Will - w. 23 Aug 1821. Wife Catherine to have all estate
   during her life; daughters Mary Mitchell, Jane Ector, Caty Ector, Sarah
   Anderson, Elizabeth Anderson; sons Quinton, James, William; daughters
   Sarah and Elizabeth to have tract of land on which he lives. Exec: sons
   Quinton and William. Wit: Levi Walker, William Maugham.

73 OBEDIAH NUNNALLY - Will - w. 10 Jan 1822. Wife Elizabeth (land purchased
   of Brooks and Ford near Hogan's Creek); daughters Elizabeth Howard, Martha
   Cobb; sons William and John; grandson Leander W. Nunnally;
   granddaughter Mary P. Nunnally; grandchildren Louisa P. and James R. Nunnally;
   Exec: sons William and John, and son-in-law Henry Cobb. Wit: Elijah Withers,
   Joseph Cobb, Hugh Cobb.
   Codicil to will on 2 Feb 1822 concerning disposal of money from sale.
   Executors qualified.

76 Sales estate of Richard Hays to William A. Lea, Gabriel B. Lea, Stephen
   Pleasant, Elijah Morton, John Malone, Drury Burton, John C. Vanhook.
76 Amt 2nd sale of William Lyon decd.

56

Book I 1822

Page
77 Acct estate of William Richardson decd by Noel Burton exec. Payments to
Iverson Graves, James Paul, Noel Read, James Ingram, Gabriel Cox, James
Hodnet, James Richardson, Asa Gunn, Robert H. Childress, Hinson Alverson,
John A. Pass, John Kile, Evans Knight, et al. Notes on James Richardson,
James Lea, Anderson Birk.
78 Acct estate of William Lyon. Cash paid to Abner Miles as clerk of sale;
to widow for year's allotment; payment to John Pyrant; payment for Judith
Hall. Debt due Elizabeth Lyon former ward of decd.
80 Acct estate of Michael Montgomery decd by Thomas Gunn and Alex Montgomery,
adm. Payments to Thomas Robards, McGee and Stanfield, Stephen Kitchen,
Joseph Gales, et al. Paid George Williamson for crying sale, Josiah Womack
for surveying, James Miles, David Montgomery.
81 Acct estate of William Walker decd.
82 Acct of strays taken up by Henry M. Clay and valued by Eli Stafford and
William Morgan. William Lea, Ranger.
Valuation of a sheep taken up by Wile Yancey worth $11 and valued by James
Adams and William Bruce. James Yancey, Justice of Peace.
83 Report of stray horse taken up by Elizabeth Kimbro on South Country Line;
a steer taken up by John Baulding Jun.
84 James Scott, Justice of Peace, reports stray mare taken up by Rhodeham Love-
lass who lives on road leading from Jethro Brown's store to Perkins Ferry
about 4 miles NW of store. Valued by Samuel Orr and Jesse Orr.
85 Allotment to Mary Lea widow of Jeremiah Lea decd.
85 Articles of agreement: 9 Feb 1822 - Mary Willis widow of Henry Willis, decd.;
William, Nicholas, Benjamin, Henry, and Anderson Willis; Francis Smith,
Wilkins Chandler, William Herritage and wife Polley - Mary Willis conveys
to other legatees also to Nancy Willis and Kezziah Willis all her interest
and right to estate of Henry Willis except one-third part where she resides.
Division of estate to be by Barzilla Graves, Azariah Graves (Caswell CH),
and William Graves. As legatee of Henry Willis, Jonathan Smith agrees to
above covenant.

July Court 1822

91 THOMAS DAVIS - Will - w. 2 April 1822. Son James to have land and mansion
house adj Ruffin Pleasant's line and Alfred Park's line. Daughter Betsy
to have land adj Zachariah Pattilo; son in law Clator Lambeth; Wife.
Exec: son James. Wit: William Florence, Alfred Parks.

92 STERLING RUFFIN - Will - w. 12 Jan 1822. Wife Alice to get lands purchased
of Nathan Williams and Henry Williams and all property for her life. Mentions store house and house where Clifton formerly lived. Youngest son
William Frederick. Indebted to son Thomas W. Ruffin, John Wall, William
Edward Broadnax Esq., William Cain, and others. Land in Rockingham Co.,
lots in Danville, Va., and in Leaksville, NC, purchased from John Lenox and
from son Thomas.
All my children: Thomas, Minerva, Mary, James, and William; son Thomas to
have watch and silver tankard gotten from Father and large Bible with Cokes
Commentary; son James to have gun and silver cross gotten from his mother's
father; son William to have silver ladle and spoons and rest of books.
Thomas to be guardian to son William Frederick.
Exec: sons Thomas and James H. Ruffin. Wit: Hosea McNeill, Nicholas M.
Ellis, Thomas Williamson. Exec qualified.

57

Book I 1822
Page
97 Inv goods of Thomas Slade by William Warren adm. in March 1822.
   (Note from KKK - Thomas Slade was a merchant). Sales to:

John Hewlett Sen.	William McKee	John Chandler
Robert Love	William McCord	Barnett Kemp
William Hightower	George Prendergast	Sanders Browning
John A. Mebane	John Armstrong	Rease Enoch
William McMinaway	Nathaniel Snipes	Branch Chalkley
Ambrose Nelson	John Rowark	Hiram Lockard
Thomas Bird	Thomas Crisp	Stephen Murphey
Robert McKee	David Ellison	(son of James)
James Ward	Brandie Malone	James Flack
Miles Wells Sen.	Samuel Greer	Samuel Nelson
Jane Slade	James Mansfield	Garnatt Neeley
Jehu Bird	Nancy Smith	Wm. Lea (son Abb)
James Thompson	Claybourn Crisp	Thomas Armstrong
Wiley Shaw	George Bush	James Jackson
Thomas H. Eanes	James Rice	George Broach
Reuben Jones	James Mann	Samuel Dunn
William Warren Esq.	Nathaniel L. Rice	Zach Marshall
William Slade	Thomas Tinnin	William Terrell
Thornton Baynes	Jesse Crisp	John Murphey Jr.
Miles Wells Jr.	Wm. Bouldin(shoemaker)	Erasmus Compton
James Yancey Esq.	Joshua Rudd	William Muzzall
Brice Collins	James Wells(son Stephen)	Philip Cook
James Womble	Barzillai Nelson	Richardson Corn
Thomas D. Johnston	Alexander Gordon	Isabella Moore
Macaja Pleasant Jr.	Moses Fuller	Nancy Ward
Pleasant Corbit	John Miles	Zephaniah T.Kerr
William S. Marshall	William Mansfield	Lemuel Rainey
Hugh Ward	George Roberts	Luke Arnold
Yearby Warren	Gregory Hightower	John Arwin
James Slade	Thompson Bartlett	et al

119 Sales Thomas Slade sold May 1822 by Robert McKee adm appointed at April
    Court to: Nelson Bartlett, Samuel Hulett, Thomas Oakley, David Allison,
    Stamford Jones, Robert Smith, et al. (Many names repeat of March sale.)
129 Inv property of John Ingram on 10 April 1822.
130 Inv estate of Capt. John Lea Sen. decd taken 16 May 1822. Notes on John
    Stamps, Jesse Carter, Freeman Hubbard; note on Jonathan Lea of Clark Co.,
    KY, due 10 May; 2 notes on David Hersey, 1 on Christopher Hinton; on William
    Hubbard due 1811 a soldier in the army, on Saml. Hersey; Caleb Wright.
    Acct against William Lea to be paid to David Montgomery by John Lea Sen.
    721 acres land.
131 Inv property of Obediah Nunnally by William Nunnally exec.
131 Inv property of Mary Humphreys taken 26 Dec 1821. Accts on Charles P.
    Harrison, John Holloway.
132 Sales property of Mary Humphries on 22 Jan 1822 sold in her lifetime as
    guardian. Sales to:

Nathan Duncan	James Swan	Charles A. Sims	William Runnals
William P. McDaniel	Arthur Toney	Elisha Alverson	John Humphries
William Gossage	Burwell Hagood	Charles P. Harrison	

133 Sales property Mary Humphries by adm on 4 May 1822 to:

Maj. William Penick,	John Holloway	Elizabeth Terrell	William Busey
Stephen Coleman	Obediah Holloway	Josiah Terrell	Thomas Ware
John Bays	Lemuel Cook	Elizabeth Ferrell	Josiah Tyra
Mary Ferrell, et al			

Book I 1822
Page
135 Sales property of John Ingram to :

Mary Ingram	William Ware Jun.	Lynn Alverson
Archibald Ingram	Asa Gunn	Jeremiah Putnam
Elisha Ingram	Williamson Price	William Kirk
James Ingram	George L. Willson	Wm. H. Burns
Steven Ingram	Robert Madden	Roberts Roland, et al
Thomas Ware Jr.	Catharine Ferrell	By James Burton and
Stepehn Chandler	John Nutt	James Ingram, exec.
Stephen Haddock	Ansel Haddock	

140 Matilda Garrot an orphan age 14 years bound to Ann McNiel.
141 Michiel Hawley an orphan age 10 years bound to David Montgomery.
Freeman Leath, Chairman County Court.
142 William Moore an orphan age 15 years bound to Jonathan Terrell, Sen.
James Yancey, Chairman County Court.
143 Allotment to Jane Slade widow of Thomas Slade decd for her support for 12
months. By Samuel Moore, William Russell, James Kinnebrough, Jethro
Brown; 28 May 1822
143 Allotment to Patcy Nunn widow of Carlton Nunn decd. 22 April 1822. By
Josiah Womack, Rodeham Loveless, Alexander Murphey, Garland Blackwell.
144 An advertisement of Robert McKee adm of Thomas Slade decd. All claims
against estate to be made at store of decd. 24 April 1822. William
McKee made oath he saw his father put up notices at Court House, at store
house of Thomas Slade, store of William Anderson, and at blacksmith shop
of George Roberts.
145 Griffin Gunn, trustee of Caswell Co., acct with county filed for 1820.

October Court 1822

147 JOSEPH PULLIAM - Will - w. 5 June 1821. Daughter Jane Brandon and her
son Joseph Brandon and her children; daughter Agness A. Foster and James
P. Foster; daughter Elizabeth Hix and her son Joseph Hix; daughter Susannah Holloway and her husband James Holloway; daughter Nancey Holloway
and her husband Thomas; sons John and Joseph Pulliam; daughter Mary Pulliam; daughter Drusilla Stokes and her husband Silvanus.
Exec: Robert Standfield, George Ellot, Mary Pulliam.
Wit: Larkin W. Hicks, James C. Irvin, William Ellot. No exec qualified.

148 MARTHA KERSEY - Will - w. 21 May 1822. Brother Alexander Kersey to have
all estate, the thirds which came from her father. Wiley Jones' four
daughters, Sally, Anne, Lucy, and Elizabeth, to have $10 each. Exec:
Brother Alexander Kersey. Wit: Craften Williams, James Lea, Senr.
Exec qualified.

149 Inv notes due estate of Thomas Slade decd. Notes on Samuel Dunn, Jesse
Crisp, Hazlewood Wilkenson, Alfred Compton, Absolem Lea, Stephen Ellis,
James Keeling, Robert B. Corn, Hugh Ward, David D. Nutt, James Mansfield,
et al.
150 Inv of bad notes due Thomas Slade: James Ashley due 1818, William Carnal Jr.
1819, Larken Rowark, William Fox, Joseph Muzzall, Edward Bartlett, et al.
152 Inv judgments and executions in favor of Thomas Slade on: Yancey Westbrooks,
Richard Burch, William Watson, Sarah Scott, Aquila Compton, Alfred Westbrooks, Bazl Kerr, Larken Landers, James Eubank, John Allison(son of
Charles), Jane Crossett widow, Rachel Clark, Hunter McCullock, John Nobel,
Thomas Hinshaw, Jane Corn widow, Ealon Corn, et al.
157 Inv property of Thomas Davis decd taken 26 Aug 1822 by James Davis, exec.

Page
158 Inv property of John Anderson decd. Amt sale of 7 negroes of estate to
   Joseph Ector and wife Caty, James Ector and wife Jane, William Anderson,
   and Quinton Anderson
159 Settlement estate of Peggy Neeley by John Keesee adm. Rent of fish pond
   plantation to Nathan Duncan and small tenement to Elijah Sims. Bond on
   William H. Burns. Cash for schooling and clothing for James, Isaac, and
   Sallyy payments to William Patterson and Patsy Burns.
160 Settlement estate of Ellis Evans by Thomas Evans and Allen Gunn.
161 Frederick Philip an orphan age 14 years last March bound to Daniel Gunn.
162 Daniel Phillips orphan age 14 years bound to Elizabeth Rainey.
   James Yancey, Chairman County Court.
163 William Hailey orphan age 10 years bound to Thomas Walker.
163 Allotment to Mrs. Betsey Lea widow of the beloved Capt. John Lea, decd.
   By James Miles, Thomas Donoho, Baz Graves, Richd. Sanders.
164 Power of Attorney - John Graham of Scott County, Va., to George Grayham of
   same county to recover rent from land in Caswell County, under contract
   and guardianship of John Cobb of Caswell Co. March 9, 1822. Wit: William
   Taylor, Andrew Speer,
   In Scott Co., Va., Margaret Grayham made oath that John Graham is air of
   Berry Grayham of Caswell County.
   John McKinney, Justice of Scott Co., Va.

January Court 1823

Held 2nd Monday after 4th Monday of December 1822

166 Inv estate of John Kimbro decd by William Kimbro adm.
169 Sales estate of John Kimbrough decd held 11-13 Nov 1822. Sales to:

James Jackson	James Page	Joshua Rudd
Curtis Payne	Edmund McCubbins	Richard Lampkin
Alexander Murphey	Jesse Whitlow	James Kimbro Sen.
James Lea	William Barnwell	Miles Kimbro
John Morris	Duke W. Kimbro	Richard H. Griffith
James Darby	Jacob Graves	John Lea CB
Joseph Kitchen	James B. Kimbro	Charles G. Cook
Banister Campbell	Jordan Massey	William Crossett
Jonathan Starkey	Richard Arnold	George Cocks or(Cooks)
Nathaniel Snipes	Elijah P. Kimbro	Edmd. B. Rice
Henry Collier	Luke Arnold	William Whitfield
Joseph Aldridge	John Kimbro Jr.	Aza Kimbro
Josias Page	William McCord	Mary Kimbro
	William Kimbro	

175 Return of estate of William Gordon decd by Alexander Gordon, exec. Sales
   to John Gordon, Thomas Burton, Thomas Morley, Henry Shelton, et al.
177 Inv of estate of Martha Kersey decd by Alexander Kersey, exec. 5 negroes:
   Caty and her 4 children, Hannah, Jackson, Leatha, and Juda.
177 Inv estate of Robert H. Childers decd. Debts due for tuition from:
   William Badgett, Benjamin Hooper, Henry Glass, Joseph, Brackin, Charles
   Mitchell, William Weatherford, Elijah Weathers, James Yancey, Zachariah
   Hooper, Lewis Evans, Peter Badgett, William Jones(doubtful), John Mason,
   Hugh Cobb, Joseph Cobb, Col. Thos Graves, Henry Womack, Isaac Durham,
   Drury A. Mims, James Blackwell. By Henry Cobb, adm.
178 Sales estate of R. H. Childers to: Henry Cobb, Joseph Cobb, John Mims,
   William B. Swift, Benjamin Hooper, John Foster, Mrs. Nancy Childers, John
   Shields, Reuben Kennon, et al.

Book I 1823
Page
179 Sales estate of Capt. John Lea decd. taken 30 and 31 July and 14 Nov 1822.
By Betsey Lea and John McAden, adm. Sales to:

Zachariah Samuel	James Peterson	David Kersey
William Lea Jr.	John Peterson	Daniel Richmond
Fielding Lewis	William Peterson	Elijah H. Pass
John Lea(CB)	Lewis Martin	Archibald Rice
John Lea Jr.	Benjamin Nutt	Abraham Montgomery
John Kitchen	Ralph Hubbard	Nathaniel Lea
David Montgomery	John B. Farley	Vinas Collier
Benjamin Matlock	William Parker	Judith Lea
Tinsley Lea	Thomas Cox	Mrs. Betsey Lea
David G. Bradsher	Maj. Thomas Donoho (for	
Levin Downs	Mrs. Lea)	James Lea (son of John)
James Crossett	Thomas Riggs	Miss Nancy Lea
Capt. William Childs	David Denis	Thomas Lea
James Lea (Miller)	John Nutt	James Lea Jun.

183 Div of slaves of estate of Moses Bradsher to: Naomah Nelson, Franky(Frances)
Nelson, Patsey B. Bradsher, Unicy Mutrey, Polly Peterson, Nancy Lea,
Elizabeth Walton.
Balance of slaves sold and equally divided to all legatees: Abner Brad-
sher, Jesse Bradsher, Elizabeth Walton, John Bradsher, Nancy Lea, James O.
Bradsher, Rich J. Bradsher, Polly Peterson, Unice Mutry, Patsy B. Brad-
sher, Vincent Bradsher, Noamah Nelson, Franky Nelson, Moses Bradsher.
Signing were: Reuben Walton in right of wife Elizabeth; Vincent Lea in right
of wife Nancy; John Peterson for Polly; William Mutry for Unice; Ambrose
Nelson for decd wife Naomah and for wife Franky. Wit: Jonathan Terrell,
Alexander M. Dameron.
186 Allotment of negroes of estate of Capt. John Lea decd to widow and children:
Betsy Lea widow, James Lea, William Lea, Benjamin Matlock and wife Polly,
John Lea, Nancy Lea, Judith Lea.
188 Acct of hire of negroes of estate of William Walker by Connally Walker,adm.
188 Settlement estate of George Connally by Thomas Connally exec. Bond on
Wylie Sledge.
190 Acct estate of G. M. Willson by George Williamson and Nathl. Lea exec.
Cash paid to Navigation Company, et al.
193 Acct of Westley Norman exec of Benjamin Norman decd taken 12 Nov 1822.
Remainder of estate to go to eleven legatees. (Names not given.)
194 Robert Hailey orphan age 7 years bound to Richard Arnold.
James Yancey, Chairman County Court.
195 Henry Mann orphan age 18 years bound to Allen Gunn.
Robert Thurman chairman pro tem county court.
196 Power of attorney - Milly Norman to Rosey Norman, sister and trusty friend,
to sell land willed by father Benjamin Norman decd. 23 Nov 1822. Test:
Lewis Whittemore, Nathan Norman.
196 Allotment to Elizabeth Raimey, 9 Nov 1822. By James Miles, Jno Burton,
Daniel Gunn, Starling Gunn.

197 ALEXANDER MURPHEY - Will - w. 15 Mar 1822. All land and tenements in NC
and TN to Thomas A. Thompson and William T. Smith of Tennessee; part
of land to be sold to pay debts and a debt of $4500 to Col. William Polk
of Raleigh and several debts of late John Rice decd late of Tenn.
Money to educate 3 sons Alexander, William, and Archibald. Wife Polly
to have residue of estate for life and then it go to sons; brother Archibald D. Murphey. Codicil: wife Polly alias Mary to be exec., with brother
Archibald D. Murphey, and Thomas A. Thompson, son-in-law of Tenn. 15 Mar.
Ordered recorded on oaths of James Graves, Azariah Graves, witnesses, and
Jeremiah Rudd, witness to codicil.

Book I 1823
Page
199 Allotment to Nancy Childers 30 Oct 1822 widow of Robert H. Childers.
By William Badgett, John Shields, Benjamin Hooper.
100 Allotment to Judith Davis widow of Thomas Davis decd. - ¼ part of estate
which is a child's part. 21 Dec 1822.
200 Inv estate of Edward Rainey decd. Allowance to Mrs. Rainey by John P.
Harrison adm.
201-204 Empty pages

April Court 1823

205 JOHN KIMBROUGH - Will - w. Nov 1817. Wife Mary to have all property
which the decd received by her in marriage agreeable with marriage con-
tract with her. Son James; heirs of daughter Sarah Turner; heirs of son
Thomas Kimbrough to have land where their father lived; heirs of son John
Kimbrough (Sarah Colyer, Patsey and Tabby Kimbrough); daughters Nancy
Graves, Frances Browning, Patsey Thomas and her children; son William
Kimbrough; daughter Tabby Snipes. Exec: son William and friend James Darby.
Wit: Jeremiah Rudd, Thomas Page. William Kimbrough qualified.

206 Sales estate of Thomas Davis decd taken 28 Oct 1822 by James Davis exec.
Sales to Alfred Parks, Claten Lambrick, John Sawyer, Samuel Nelson, Ben-
jamin Pleasant, Ruffin Pleasant, William Bouldin, Judith Davis, Joseph
Aldridge, Christopher Brooks, Nathaniel L. Rice, Brice Collins, Joseph
McCullock, Elizabeth Davis, James Davis, Thomas Bigelow, et al.

209 Power of attorney - Joseph Richmond of Wilson Co., Tenn., to Silas Tarver
of county aforesaid to demand and receive of Thomas Connally of Halifax Co.,
Va., exec of George Connally decd his wife's proportion of estate. 18 Oct
1822.

210 Silas Tarver signs receipt for legacy for Joseph Richmond from estate of
George Connally, father-in-law of Richmond. Proved on oath of George A.
Connally.

210 Power of attorney - Joseph Swan and Elizabeth his wife of Robertson Co.,
Tenn., to Thomas Walker of Caswell Co. to settle all claims in North
Carolina, and to sell lands. 28 June 1822.

212 Additional return of estate of Samuel Pittard. Sale of tobacco by John C.
Vanhook. By Archibald Rice, exec.

212 Inv estate of Mary Langley decd by Joseph Langley adm.

212 Declaration - Abraham Dunavant declares he is 72 years of age and citizen
of Caswell Co. NC. He served in Revolutionary War under Capt. John Ogels-
by and enlisted for 18 months; was at battle of Guilford, was at capture
of Little York when he was discharged. All officers under whom he served
are dead; requests pension as he has no possessions but shoemaker's tools
and one saw; is infirm with rhumatism; is living with and supported by a
daughter in needy circumstances and incapable of supporting himself.

213 Sales estate of Thomas Swift Jr. by Harvey Swift adm. Acct received of
Joseph Roe former guardian. Estate divided into 10 shares. (Names not
given.)

214 Sylvester Word (or Ward), orphan now 3 years old on 15 of May next bound
to James Brown to learn the art of a planter.

214 Latica Ward orphan now age of 4 years on 4th of July next bound to James
Heydon.

July Court 1823

216 Inv property of Thomas Payne decd by Alexander Kiersey adm.

216 Sales property of Mary Langley to Abner Wisdom, William Brandon, William
Chandler, James Vaughan, William Moore. By Jos. Langley adm.

Book I 1823
Page
217 Sales property of Benjamin Ashley decd taken 2 Feb 1821. Sales to:

Mary Ashley	John Crenshaw	Henly Humphreys(1 Bible & 3
Thomas Gibson	Forester Stanback	books)
John H. Pickard	William Cobb	Hezekiah Boswell
Thomas Carpenter	Robert Roe	Stephen Chandler
Azariah Graves	Zachariah Groom	Mrs. Stanback
Robert Holderness	William Elmore	William Shelton

    By Azariah Graves and William Russell, adm.
219 Sales property of Thomas Payne to John Stamps, Zadock Rice, William P.
    Payne, et al.
219 Settlement estate of William Patillo by Zachariah Patillo exec. Met at
    store of James Yancey and settled accounts. 5 July 1823.
221 Settlement estate of Samuel Pittard. Examined by Wm. A. Lea and Wm. Lea.
222 Alexander Gordon in acct with estate of William Gordon decd. Sales and
    final settlement.
223 Inv property of Francis Smith Sen. decd by Richard Smith adm. Allotment
    to widow. Debtors to estate: Jonathon Smith, Alfred Malone.
224 Settlement estate of Richard H. Hays by Gabriel Lea adm.
225 Settlement estate of Brittain Moore by Daniel Hightower and Daniel Jack-
    son exec. Notes on Abner Wisdom, Larkin Landers, Thomas Villines, Moses
    Langley.
226 Sale property of Edward Raimey to Elizabeth Raimey, John Hooper, William
    Kirk, Thomas Pinex, Sherrod Owen, Ansel Haddock, William Ware, Stephen
    Ingram, John Baxter Sen., Woodson Howard, et al.
228 Declaration- William Singleton makes oath that he is 73 years old on 19
    Feb next; that he served in Revolutionary War, enlisted Feb 1776 by John
    Ogilby of company of Capt. Abret Mead afterwards Genl. Mead of Virginia; he
    served 2 years in this enlistment, was at Brandywine and Germantown; re-
    enlisted for 3 years under Capt. James Foster, then at Monmouth; served
    5 years. He has lost his discharge. He has made no gifts or sales and
    is entitled to pension. Lists schedule of income. He is a Bell Maker
    by trade. He is poor and has a wife and child to support.
    Abraham Dunevant swore he was acquainted with William Singleton and saw
    him at time of his enlistment under Ensign John Ogilby.
229 Allotment to Mary Kimbrough on 24 June 1823 agreeable to testament of John
    Kimbrough. Commrs: James Yancey, A. Wiley, Thos. Burton, John Willson.
230 Griffin Gunn, county trustee, in acct with Caswell County for 1821.
    864 white polls, 2219 black polls.
231-33 Empty pages

October Court 1823

234 Stephen Jeffreys, orphan age 15 years last Aug., bound to James Jeffreys.
    James Yancey, Chairman County Court.

235 ISAAC DURHAM - Will - w. 27 Jan 1823. Wife Elizabeth to have all estate
    during her life; grandsons James Durham, Isaac Durham, Martin Durham
    (tract of land he now lives on after decease of his Mother); son John
    (tract of land "I now live on"); Mary Burns to have cupboard during her
    life and then to go to grandson Isaac Burns; 6 daughters: Fanny, Peggy,
    Elizabeth, Lucy, Gemimah, Caranhapperth?. Desires estate not to be appais-
    ed. Exec: sons Martin and John. Test: James Rawley, James E. Rawley.
    Martin Durham qualified.

236 CARLTON NUNN - Will - w. 27 Mar 1823. Sons Thomas, William, Joshua, John;
    daughters Lucy Chambers, Patsy Long; granddaughter Averilla Nunn (daughter
    of Polly Nunn); son Millar Nunn; daughter Peacher(or Pearley) Harrelson;
    granddaughter Margas Nunn (d. of Carlton Nunn); daughter Nancy Nunn.
    Exec: friend Benjamin Elmore and Joseph King. Wit: J. Womack, Joseph King.
    Executors renounced their rights and Nancy Nunn and Mathew Mills appoint-
    ed adms. with will annexed. Bond by John Kesee & Alexander Paschall.

Book I 1823-1824
Page
237 Div of negroes of Gergory Durham decd to Sally, James, and Isaac Durham.
238 R. M. Sanders adm in acct with estate of Robert Tate decd. Examined by
    James Rainey and Archimedas Donoho.
238 Settlement estate of John Trigg decd by Joshua Trigg, adm.
239 James Burton and James Ingram exec in acct with estate of John Ingram decd.

239 JOSEPH SWANN - Will - w. 25 Aug 1823. Wife Agnes Swann to have all land
    and possessions during her life; son Joseph (100 acres adj John Comer);
    Son Ellenor Swann; James Swann's child John Anderson Swann; daughters
    Agnes and Polley. My 6 children. Exec: wife Agnes and son Eleanor.
    Wit: David Hodge, Isaac Vanhook. Executors qualified.

241 ZILLAH BLACKWELL - Will - w. 15 Apr 1816. Sons John, Thomas, Garland;
    sons and daughters now living: Charles, Levi, Thomas, Garland, John,
    daughter Polly married to James Watt and daughter Kitturah married to
    Samuel Watt. No bequeaths to Lewis Malone's children and son Robert Black-
    well as decd. Husband Robert Blackwell gave them their portion.
    Exec: son Thomas Blackwell. Wit: Ransom Boswell. Exec qualified.

242 George A. Swift in acct with estate of William Swift decd. Report examined
    by Hosea McNeill, F. Leath, A. Graves.
243 George A. Swift in acct with estate of Frances Swift decd. 4 legatees to
    receive $234.47 each. Names not given.
244 Susanna Nicholas adm. in acct with estate of James Nicholas decd. Bonds on
    Anthony Foster, Thomas Jackson. Residue of estate divided to 8 legatees.
    Names not given.
244 Inv of hire of negroes of John Kimbro decd by William Kimbro adm.
245 Sales of property (negroes) of John Kimbro on 1 Oct 1823 to William Kimbro,
    Nathaniel Lea, William Slade Jr., James Kimbro (Tennessee), John Willson,
    Esq., Sanders Donoho, Thomas Burton.

247 THOMAS PHELPS - Will - w. 8 Apr 1821. 3 daughters Elizabeth Wisdom, Nancy
    Roan, Rachel Sargent; 4 grandchildren Rachel, Betsy, William, Nancy Wisdom
    (children of daughter Betsy Wisdom); grandson James Roan to get land where
    Rachel Wallis formerly lived; Justin Rone (land where Joshey Wallis former-
    ly lived); 4 grandsons of daughter Rachel Sargent: Demsey, William, James,
    Thomas Sargent(land where Kendrick lived); children of Nancy Roan: Fanny,
    James, Annis, Ann, Sally, Clancy; children of Rachel Sargent: Dempsey,
    Dradey, Betsey, Ann, William, James, Thomas. Children of daughter Delphi:
    James, Sally, Nancy Boman?. Exec: Gabriel Lea. Test: William Lea.
    Exec qualified.

January Court 1824

251 Jesse Sharp an orphan age of 6 years on 4 Dec 1823 bound to Charity Crossett.
    James Yancey, Chairman County Court.
252 William Sharp orphan age of ___ years bound to Ephraim Burch.
252 Power of attorney - Milton Swift of Caswell Co. to Richard Jones to demand
    and sue for and obtain money due from estates of William and Frances Swift
    and Thomas Swift Senr. decd. 29 Sept. 1821. Wit: Wm. P. Swift, John Swift.
253 Inv property of Samuel Woods decd by John Woods and William Richmond adm.
    11 Oct 1823. Bonds on David Woods, Joseph Coleman(doubtful); judgments on
    Richard Burch, Lemuel Rainey, George Roberts.
254 Sales estate of Samuel Woods decd sold 31 Oct 1823 to:

Alexander Gordon	Miles Wells	Elisha Roward	Jesse Crisp
Nelson Bartlett	Andy Woods	Ephraim Hawkins	James Woods
David Woods	Thomas Oakley	Mary Woods	Samuel M.Woods
William Woods	Absolem Lea et al		

64

Book I 1824
Page
256 Sales property of Martin Morton decd sold by Elijah Morton adm 29 Oct 1823.
    Sales to: Willis Lea, Robert Yalock, Thomas Malone, Hezekiah Morton,
    William Fuller, John Chandler, Gabriel B. Lea, James Dollarhide; due
    bill of William Mitchell doubtful.
256 Caswell Tait exec estate of Thomas Swift decd, acct with legatees.
257 Inv property of Carlton Nunn decd taken 3 Oct 1823. By Mathew Mills, exec.
258 Power of attorney - Bennett Smith of Caswell County to Jesse A. Dollarhide
    to receive, from all persons endebted to Smith in NC and in States of Ga.,
    SC, Ala., and Miss., and through his agent John Burch (who has been selling
    negroes for me for some time in South and West) and to receive cash in
    Burch's possession at time of his death (as I was informed he died at
    Conecuh Court House, State of Ala.) 14 July 1823. Test: Stephen Dodson,
    N. Thompson.
258 Inv estate of Robert Blackwell Sen. decd. Notes on John and Garland Black-
    well, James and Thompson Watt. Thomas Blackwell, exec.
259 Inv estate of Thomas Phelps. Notes on Jeremiah Broughton due 1811, Alexan-
    der Griffin due 1812, John Allison and Samuel Johnston due 1805, Wiley
    Jones 1819, Charles D. Wade 1821, James K. Daniel 1821, Paschal Roberts,
    Yancey Burt 1819, Thomas Kendrick 1810 (doubtful). Judgments on Zachariah
    Marshall, Nathaniel Norfleet. By Gabriel Lea,exec.
260 Sales property of Thomas Phelps sold 6 Nov 1823 to:

Maj.James Currie	Joseph Langley	John C. Vanhook	Thomas Roan
Archibald Lipscomb	John Broughton	Hiram Lockard	Demsey Sargent
Isaac D. Vanhook	Solomon Whitlow	Alexander Griffin	Thomas Greenway
Cuthbert Wagstaff	Elizabeth Sargent	Abner Wisdom	David Drake
Robert D. Wade	James Roan	Wm. McMurray	Sally Roan
Willis Buckingham	James Jay Sen.	Barzillai Nelson	Wm. Wisdom
John Mathis	Nathaniel Torian	Young Burt	Lewis Yalock
Robert Yalock	John Fullington	Jesse Westbrook	et al.

264 Sale estate of John Pinson Jun. decd to Thomas Collier, Joseph Pinson,
    Aaron Pinson, Laban Ford, Edmund B. Rice, William Turner, William Slade Jr.
    By John Pinson Sen. adm.
265 Settlement estate of Moses Bradsher decd by Abner and John Bradsher,exec.
267 Inv property of Joseph Swann decd by Eleaner Swann, exec. 2 Jan 1824.
267 Inv property of Isaac Durham decd which was loaned to the widow for her
    lifetime.
268 Sale property of Isaac Durham to Thomas Henderson, William Busey.
268 Sale estate of Francis Smith decd sold 22 Oct 1823 by Richard Smith adm.
    List of buyers not included.
269 Inv property of Thomas Turner decd.
270 Inv bonds and receipts in possession of Thomas Turner decd. Notes on
    Jordon Massey, Littleton Jones, Adam Simmons, Vincent Griffin, William
    Bruce, James Yancey, Zenus Martin, John McKenzie, Polly Lampkin, et al.
    By William Slade adm of Thomas Turner decd.
271 Sales estate of Thomas Turner to:

Robert Scott	Joseph Lunsford	Sarah Turner	James Turner
Martin Elliott	Jacob Ahart	Henry Collier	Joseph Aldridge
Willis Ashford	Joseph Penick	Edmund Turner	James Lea
William Turner	Nicholas Willis	Richard Arnold	Wm. Kimbrough
Thomas Bigelow	James Yancey	Thomas Mansfield	Joshua Rudd
Zachariah Patillo	Nathan Turner	et al.	

277 Inv property of Zillah Blackwell decd.
277 Conley Walker adm of William Walker decd., amt of hire of negroes for 1824.
278 Inv estate of William Berry decd taken 1 June 1823 by Elisha Berry.
278 Inv property of William Paschall on 8 Oct 1823 by Elisha & John Paschall.

Book I 1824
Page
278 Additional sales of property of John Pinson Jr. decd. allowed at call court
4 Nov 1823.
279 Inv property of David Poynor decd and sales of estate 10 Oct 1823. Names
of buyers not listed.
280 Sales property of William Paschall decd sold 30 Oct 1823 to:

John Paschall	James Barker	Elisha Paschall	Anne Paschall
Jesse Paschall	James Jones	Nancy Paschall	Frances Paschall
Lucy Paschall	Elisha P.Paschall	Alf Nash	William Orr
Wm. Weatherford	Alexander Paschall,Ebenezer Cobb		Carter Groom et al

281 Eliza Shelton adm of William Shelton decd., acct filed. Received from sale
of land of Thomas Swift Jr. decd. Div to 2 children Susan and James Shelton. Div of negroes of William Shelton to Eliza,adm, James and Susan
Shelton.

283 JOHN BURCH of Conecuh County, Ala. and of Caswell County NC -Will -
w. 28 May 1823. All estate to beloved sister Mary Burch. Exec: Dr. James
Spann and John Dean Esq. in Ala., and John Thomas and James Roan of NC.
Test: Wm. R. Boling, H. L. Hunt, John Gillers.
Probate Ala. Oct 1823; probate Caswell Co. Jan.1824   PS At July Court 1824
James Roane qualified.

April Court 1824

285 Inv estate of James Warren decd. by William Warren and Bazzel Warren,exec.
Notes on William Hightower, Starling Warren, Hutson Jeffreys, James Murphey,
Nathaniel Jones.
286 Sales estate of James Warren on 22 Jan 1824 to:

Joseph Coleman	James Dickie	Allen Cooper	James Currie
Thomas Warren	William Warren	John Boulding	Yancey G.Warren
Westley Warren	Samuel Green	Yerby Warren	Lemuel Rainey
Erasmus Compton	Absalom Burton	Sanders Browning	James Womble
William Mathis	John Mathis	Drewry Mathis	Bentley Epperson
Bird Evans	Willis Reaves	James Keeling	Richard Whitemore
Stephen Murphey	Absolem Lea	James Mann	Solomon Fuller
Thornton Baynes	Susan Baitman	Paschal Westbrooks	George Smith
Nathl. L. Rice	Abraham Hood	James Crossett	James Nelson et al.

290 Property sold at late dwelling of William Berry decd sold 4 Feb 1824 by
Elisha Berry adm. Names of buyers not listed.
291 Inv property of Robert Singleton decd taken 10 Jan 1824 by Jeremiah Graves,
adm. Bonds on George Balenger, William Russell and Nicholas Lyon, Va.,
which belongs to Jno Singleton when Collected. Negro boy Frank hired to
Griffin Gunn.
292 Sales estate of Robert Singleton on 29 Jan 1824 to:

Kitty Singleton	Robert Madding	Robert Thurman	Dabney Rainey
William Stratten	John Mansfield	Capt.John Graves	Sterling Gunn
Jeremiah Graves	James Martin	Miles Wilmoth	Bartlett Yancey
Joseph Singleton	Samuel Hinton	Richard Gunn	Asa Gunn
Richard Totton	Jonathon Smith	James Ingram	Elijah Graves
William Graves	John C. Harvey	Alex. McAlpin	James Lea,et al.

Notes due on Genl. B. Graves and Thomas Haralson.
294 Additional inv estate of Thomas Turner decd. Execution John Kimbrough vs
Alexander Murphey and Thomas Turner. Wm. Slade, adm.
295 Act.of sales of Thomas Turner - interest in stud horse sold to Nathan
Turner for $95.12½.
295 Inv property of Joseph Warren decd taken 1 Feb 1824 by Nancy Warren, adm.
295 Allotment to Jerusha Berry widow of late William Berry decd. 4 Feb 1824.
Commrs: Azariah Graves, William J. Nash, Robert A. Brown, Freeholders.

Book I 1824
Page
296 Accts. found on books of Joseph Warren decdon William Cantrill, Ashford
    Walker, James Kelly, John W. Shaw, Robert Zachary, et al. Also on
    Nat Jones ran away, William Keeter ren away, Thomas Maize, ran away.
297 Sales property of Joseph Warren decd to Levi Walker.
298 Adm notice of Nancy Warren adm of Joseph Warren.
299 Allotment to Mrs. Mary Kimbrough agreeable to will of her decd husband.
    Amends her first allotment.
300 Power of attorney- William Simpson of Rockingham County, NC, to James Barker
    of Caswell Co. to receive money and to pass receipt and collect of John
    Windsor of Rockingham Co., lately my guardian. 27 Nov 1823. Wit: Thomp-
    son Harden.
300 Receipt of James Adkins on 18 July 1824 from Joseph Bracken adm in right
    of his wife Jane Bracken of personal estate of Thomas Brooks Jun. decd.
    Amt $250 in full claim of wife Mary Adkins of personal estate of her decd
    father Thomas Brooks. Wit: Warren Weatherford, William Morgan, Jr.
301 JOHN BOWERS - Will - w. 8 Aug 1823. Wife Lucy Bowers; daughters Henne
    Bowers and Betsy; son James to be paid for law suit he commenced in
    State of Virginia for 10 negroes, Milley and increase. Exec: son-in-law
    Samuel Ceeton and William Brumit to aid him, (Possibly Samuel Keeton)
    Test: Reubin Jones, Philip Bell.
301 Final settlement estate of Mary Humphries decd with the adm.
302 John Keesee adm of Peggy Neely or Peggy Durham decd, final acct filed.
    Special legacy due to Sally, Isaac, and James Durham. (Acct is for Gre-
    gory Durham and his widow.)
304 Bill of sale: James Williams purchased at sale of C. S. Hunter walnut and
    pine tables and other articles. James Williams conveys to Rebecca Hunter
    a daughter of Charles L.(or S.) Hunter all rights to same property.
    3 Nov 1823. Proved on oath of John L. Graves.
304 Power of attorney - William Keen and Nancy Keen formerly Nancy Roan of
    Pulaski County, Ga., to James Roan of Caswell Co., NC, to recover from
    Gabriel Lea the lawful exec of Thomas Phelps late of Caswell County any
    part of estate due Nancy Roan. 7 Feb 1824. Wit: Conrod Angly.
306 Power of attorney - Arthur Mitchell and Martha E. Mitchell his wife former-
    ly Martha E. Murphey of Jackson Co. Ala., to John B. Murphey of Overton
    County, Tenn., to bargain, sell, and convey land in Caswell County, the
    same willed to Martha E. Mitchell by her grandfather Samuel Brackin decd.
    11 Aug 1823.
307 Div of negroes to heirs of Thomas Jackson decd to: Deliah Mathis, James
    Jackson, Sarah Mathis, Jerry Jackson, Jiney Jackson.
    Commrs: William Anderson, John Mitchell, Joseph Langley.

            July Court 1824

309 REES ENOCH - Will - w.12 May 1824. Son John (under 21); wife Susanna;
    son John to have tract of land "on which I live". Rest of estate to 5
    children: Elizabeth Enoch, Veolenda Enoch, Rebecka Enoch, Susanna Enoch,
    and son Caswell Enoch. Exec: wife Susanna.
    Wit: Quintin Anderson. Absolom Nutt. Exec qualified.
310 Inv property of Rees Enoch by Susanna Enoch exec. Notes on George Walker,
    George Prendergast, Elizabeth Stalcop.
310 Settlement estate of James Sawyers by Hosea McNeill adm.; met at store of
    Thomas Williamson 5 July 1824. Notes on Thomas Foster, James Douglass,
    Isaac Cantrill.
311 Settlement estate of Joseph Warren with Nancy Warren adm. Examined by
    F. Leath, Hosea McNeill, Wm. F. Davis.
312 George Williamson exec estate of Jacob Wright decd., acct filed.

                    67

Book I 1824
Page
312 George Williamson and Mary Cox adm of Reuben Cox decd., current acct filed.

313 WILSON CATES - Will - w. 9 June 1824. All property willed to Mother, Mary
Cates. Exec: William Kimbrough. Wit: Jacob Graves, John Comer.
Exec qualified.

314 Div of negroes of Thomas Phelps to legatees agreeable to will:
Children of Elizabeth Wisdom,namely Rachel,Elizabeth, William, & Nancy.
Children of Delphia Roan namely James, Sally, and Nancy Roan.
Children of Nancy Roan namely Fanny, James, Anness, Ann, Acey, Sally, and
Flemming Roan.
Children of Rachel Sargent: Demcy, Drady, Betsy, Ann, William, James, and
Thomas Sargent.
Commrs: Will A. Lea, N. Thompson, John C. Vanhook.

316 Power of attorney - William Wisdom, William Stuart and Rachel his wife,
and Elizabeth Wisdom of White County, Tenn., to Larkin Wisdom of county
and state aforesaid to recover from Gabriel Lea of Caswell Co., exec of
will of Thomas Phelps decd., part bequeathed to them by his will.
8 June 1824

317 Received 20th day of July 1817 from Joseph Brackin, adm in right of his
wife Jane Bracken of personal estate of Thomas Brooks Jun. decd sum of
$500 in full share of estate of decd father the said Thomas Brooks Jun.
/s/ Thomas Brooks Jun. Test: Benj. C. West.

318 Power of attorney - Elizabeth Garner of Williamson Co. Tenn., to friend
Hosea McNeill of Caswell Co. to sell land, 40 acres, from estate of her
Father John Garner decd. 27 Aug 1823.

319 Allotment to Kitty Singleton widow of Robert Singleton decd for support
of her family.

319 Power of attorney - Peter Vaughan of Rutherford County, West Tenn., to
George Turner of Caswell Co. to recover from Martin Turner of Caswell Co.
a negro boy age 13 loaned to Martin Turner during his life and to recover
money and debts. 10 Oct 1824. Test: Abisha Slade.

320 Griffin Gunn, county trustee, in acct with Caswell Co.

321 R. M. Saunders exec of Jesse Carter decd. 2nd return of acct Current.
Recd. cash for rent and sale of buse in Petersburg, Va. (Covers years
1818-1823)

322 A list of debts and inv of estate of Thos. Bouldin decd. in State of NC:
Jno Garland, Jas W. Jeffreys; Simpson and Bethell in Rockingham Co.

323-325 blank pages

October Court 1824

326 SOLOMON PARKS - Will - w. 11 Nov 1816. Wife Aney Parks all landed property
for her life and ½ of slaves to dispose of as she wishes. Rebecca Bolling
a young woman lately emancipated by decree of Caswell County Court to
have all landed property after death of wife and ½ of slaves. Many rela-
tives and connections over the U.S. most of whom unknown to testator and
as he has received no legacies from any of them, no one allied by blood
or no in-law should inherit any part of estate. Exec: Wife Aney Parks.
Wit: Christopher Brooks, Richard Arwin, John Everett. Exec qualified.

327 FORBUS HARRELSON - Will - w. 15 May 1820. Bennett Harrelson son of 1st wife
Frances Harrelson to get $1. Present wife Martha and her children: Polly
Foster, Nancy Weatherford; Sally, Nathan, William, Dorcas, James, Elizabeth,
Henderson, Iverson, and Martha Harrelson to have all property.
/s/ Forbes Harrelson. Wit: Archibald Samuel Jun., James Richardson, Samuel
Henderson. Court ordered Martha Harrelson appointed adm with will annexed.
Bonded by Thomas Foster, Hiram Weatherford.

Book I 1824 - 1825
Page

328 MARY DOLLERHIDE - Will - w. 18 Oct 1820. Granddaguhters Ritty Roan, Polly
Burch, Elizabeth Gallaugher, Unicey Neely; daughter Anny Neely; grandsons
Ezekial, Calvin Neely. Wit: Wm. F. Smith, James Martin, William Mitchell.
Exec qualified. Exec: Garnett Neely.

329 NICHOLAS MATLOCK - Will - w, 11 Mar 1822. Wife Elizabeth to have land and
possessions and after her death land on which he lives to go to son James
Matlock; son William to have tract of land 427 acres in Smith Co. Tenn.;
daughter Mary Kiersey (land adj Joel Thomas) and her children;
daughter Ann Lewis ʻa negro boy Edmond her lifetime. All my children.
Exec: sons Benjamin Matlock and James Matlock. Wit: George Turner, Mc-
shack Morton. Exec qualified.

330 Inv property of Willson Cates decd taken by Wm. Kimbro exec. Sales of
estate to Richard Arwin, Wm. Culberson, William Corbit, John Chandler,
Luke Arnold, et al.

331 Inv property of Richard Crisp decd by James Terrell adm. Accts on Jesse
and Claiborne Crisp, James Mansfield, Absolem Lea, Edward Eubank, Lewis
Certain, John Wheeley Senr., Mrs. Lucy Mansfield, William McMurry,Jun.,
William Fox, John Fox, John Crisp Senr., Stanford Jones.

332 Inv of goods and chattles of Francis B. Philips decd taken 16 July 1824 by
Henry Hooper adm. Notes on Hezekiah Carrol, Terrell Bledsoe, William
Wilmouth, Anderson Willis for judgment on John Lyon.

333 Inv of effects of John H. Perkins decd taken 26 Sept.1824. Cash received
of J. E. Lewis, C. D. Donoho, Alex Henderson, Jno B. Royals, R. M. Sanders,
M. P. Huntington, Geo O. Connally. Doubtful notes on James Proudfit,
Trustees M.F.Academy, et al. By R. M. Sanders adm.

334 Sale of 2 negroes belonging to estate of Thomas Philips decd to Jacob
Thomson and Ann Hood. By Gabriel Lea exec. 4 July 1824.

335 Sales estate of Francis B. Philips decd sold 21 Aug 1824 to:

Asa Gunn	John Lyon	David W. Jones	Wm. Straten
widow Mahala Philips		Richard Stanley	Armistead Wat-
John Hood	Elisha Alverson	Jesse Alverson	lington
John Standley.	By Henry Hooper, adm.		

336 Henry Cobb adm of Robert H. Childers decd final settlement. Paid Nancy
Childers for year's allowance.

337 Div of negroes of estate of Thomas Phelps agreeable to his will to child-
ren of James Sergant and his wife: Dempsey, Ann, James, Elizabeth, William,
& Thomas Sargent, and to children of Charles Wade. 13 Oct 1824.
Commrs: Major Wallis, John G. Willson, Geo B. Dameron.

338 Inv estate of Archibald Murphey decd taken 12 Nov 1817. Home tract to
Mrs. Murphey; land in Tenn. to John G. Murphey in trust for his children;
land to Genl. James Robinson of Davidson Co. Tenn. and conveyed to Henry
Rutherford; two lots in Milton. Bonds on William Erwin due 1818, James
Rainey and Newman Durham due 1817.

339 Sales property of Col. Archibald Murphey decd on 13 Jan 1817 to:

Mrs. Jane Murphey	Alexander Murphey	Henrdon Haralson	Jane McAden
Arch. D. Murphey	Thomas Haralson	John G. Murphey	Richard Ogilby
Burrell Bevell	Nathaniel Pass	Wm. Johnston	Wm. Hundley

Alex Murphey (400 lbs pork for Solomon Debow family).
Additional sales on 13 Nov 1817 and Jan 1818. Land on Forked Deer River
in Tenn. sold to Pasquili Paoli Ashe and Saml. Strudwick.

January Court 1825

343 ELIZABETH HOLT - Will - w. 18 Feb 1824. Thomas Warren Sen. the man I now
live with to receive all estate including money collected on property.
Elizabeth H. Warrin (under age) daughter of Thomas Warrin. Exec: Thomas
Warren and Reubin Jones. Wit: Reubin Jones, John W. Jones.
Thomas Warrin qualified.

69

344 JANE CROUSETT - Will - w. 25 Sept. 1823. Three single daughters: Charity,
   Jane, and Mary Crousett to get land and plantation. If any daughter marry
   and leave plantation, she should draw her part of personal estate. If all
   three marry, land to be sold and proceeds divided. Daughter Margaret Mann;
   sons William and James Crousett; daughter Elizabeth Oakley.
   Exec: son James Crousett. /s/ Jane Crausett. Wit: Thomas Prendergrast,
   Samuel Greer, James Dickie. Exec qualified.
   (This name probably same as Crossett in other records.)
345 Estate of Solomon Parks decd by Aney (or Avey) Parks, exec., inv taken.
346 Inv property of Mary Ingram decd taken 4 Oct 1824 by James Ingram adm.
   Inv property of John Ingram decd lent to Mary Ingram decd for her life
   and then to be sold. By James Burton and James Ingram exec.
347 Inv property of estate of Forbus Harrelson decd taken 13 Oct 1824 by Martha
   Harrelson adm. Debt due from Thomas Foster; bond against James Richardson.
348 Sales estate of Clarborne Crisp decd to:

John Crisp Sen.	Miles Wells Jun.,	Joseph Coleman	Jesse Crisp
Thomas Crisp	Lewis Certain	Paul Terrell	Thomas Woods
George Broach	James Murphy	James Broach	Nelson Bartlett
John Hulett	Thomas G. Wallace	Samuel Madden	Eliza Crisp
Westley Hanks	Absolem Lea	James Allison	et al.

   Allotment to Elizabeth Crisp widow. By Miles Wells, Jun. adm.
350 Inv estate of Thomas Penix decd by William Penick adm. 7 Jan 1825. Bonds
   on Joseph and William Montgomery, Thomas Wall, Mathew Dodson, James Richardson; open act on George Price (Doubtful).
350 Inv property of William Hatcher decd taken 10 Jan 1825 by Jane S. Hatcher adm.
351 Inv property of Jeremiah Samuel decd taken 4 May 1824 by Josiah Samuel adm.
351 Amt of sales of property of John Pinson decd sold 29 Nov 1823 to Thomas
   Collier, Joseph Pinson, Aron Pinson, Labon Ford, Edmond B. Rice, William
   Turner, William Slade Jun. By John Pinson Sen. adm
351 List of articles of estate of Mary Dollarhide decd by Garnett Neeley exec.
352 Sales estate of Jeremiah Samuel decd to:

Walker Samuel	Herbert Samuel	William Lea	Mrs. Sarah Samuel

   By Josiah Samuel, adm.
352 Sales property of John Ingram decd lent to Mary Ingram sold to:

Vilina Alverson	Elijah Davis	Providence Haddock	Stephen Ingram
Archibald Ingram	Mary Ferrell	James Ingram	Elijah Kennon
Stephen Chandler	Benj. C. West	Benjamin Ingram	Phoenis Hubbird
Charles Hubbird			

353 Sales property of Calton Nunn Sen. to:

Miss Polly Nunn	Miss Nancy Nunn	Mathew Mills	Benjamin Elmore
Wm. Weatherford	David Straydor	John Strador	John Nunnally
Forister Stanback	John Powell	David Lawson	James Murphy
Henly Humphreys	Charles Mitchell	John Cobb	Frances Newman
John Walker	et al. By Mathew Mills, adm.		

355 Sales of property of Mary Ingram on 2 Nov 1824 to:

Stephen Ingram	James Ingram	Archibald Ingram	Wm. Gafford
William Cox	Jesse Alverson	Wm. Ware Jun.	Peter Powell
Stephen Chandler	Tandy Fitz	Bennett Burrows	John Humphreys
Stephen Haddock	Nathan Duncan	Thomas Ware Jun.	James McClarney
Elijah Kennon	Mary Ferrell	Elisha Alverson	John Mimms
William Duncan	Ansel Haddock	Elisha Ingram	et al

   By James Ingram adm.
                    End of Book I
   January Court 1825 continues in Book K. There was no Book J.

January Court 1825 continued

Page
1 Sale property of Forbus Harrelson sold 4 Nov 1824 to:

Martha Harrelson	Allen Gunn	Joab Robinson	Thomas Foster
Hiram Weatherford	Sarah Haralson	Dorcas Haralson	John P.Harrison
Thomas HarrelsonSr.	Charles K. Harrison	Henry Cobb	Francis Ray
Thomas Jeffreys,Jr.	William Penick	Thomas Tunstall	Ozza True
James Richardson	John Ware	Nicholas McCubbins	Isaac Bucey
James Miles	Benjamin Powell	Nathaniel Slade	James Ferrell
Andrew Johnston	Charles Keesee	Bennett Lovelace	William Bull
Thomas Cox	William Cox	James Harris	Warren Holcomb
Hezekiah Smithson	Severn Bucey	Nathl.Harrelson,Jr.	Anthony Satterfield
Nathl. Harrelson, Sr.	Thomas Gibson	Woodson Howard	et al
	By Martha Haralson, adm.		

8 Div. of negroes bequeathed by Thomas Phelps decd to Delpha Roan's children to:
James Roan, Sarah Willis, Nancey Keen. 16 Oct 1824.

9 Div. of negroes of estate of Thomas Phelps to children of Nancy Roan: to
Jacob Thomas, James Roan, Alexander Griffin, Martin Hood, John Stewart,
Sally Roan, Patsy Roan.

10 Refunding bond: John Kitchen, Mary Howard, Jennett Montgomery and James
Montgomery by his guardian Jennett, all legatees of Michael Montgomery,
agree to pay their part of debts of his estate.
James Yancey, Chairman County Court.

11 Robert H. Childers, orphan age 13 years the 2nd day of Dec. next, bound to
Asa Gunn.

12 William Ballard orphan age 7 years bound to Bernard Boswell.
Jethro Brown, Chairman County Court.

13 Amt of hire of negroes of William Walker decd. to William Fitch and
Margaret Walker.

April Court 1825

13 Inv estate of Jane Crossett decd by James Crossett exec.

14 Inv estate of Wyatt Stubblefield decd. Bonds on Walter Fitzgerald, William
Lynn, John W. Paxton, James Burns. Receipt for money paid for James Murphey. 15 Mar 1825. P. B. Stubblefield adm.

15 Inv property of Zack Pattillo decd made 23 Mar 1825. Notes of Edward Patillo,
William Florence, Robert Parks, Absolem Nutt, John Mitchell, Henry Tate,
James Murray, Thomas Bigelow, John Fitch, William Mize due 1821, James Kelly
due 1820. By Thomas Pendergast exec.

17 Inv property of Thomas Brooks Jr. decd by Jonathan Brooks.

18 Inv property of Nicholas Matlock decd by James & Benjamin Matlock. Bonds
on Ben and James Matlock, Edmd Rainey, Alex Montgomery, William Montgomery,
John Long, Jas Williamson.

19 Inv property of Joshua Hightower decd by Gregory Hightower adm.

21 Inv estate of William Ware decd taken by John and Tolbert Ware adm.,20 Jan.

23 Cash received for estate of William Ware from Winny Ware, Ralph Glaze, Wm. P.
Martin, James Durham, Allen Kelly, Thomas Ware Jr. John Ware Sen., John
Baxter Sen., David Hall, Bartlett Scott, James McClarney, Ansel Ware, et al.

24 List of debts due estate of William Ware from : Ambrose Franklin, Joseph
Tyree, Thomas Slade Jun., George Holcomb, Garland Shackleford, James Ware,
Thomas Ware Sen., Pleasant Perkins, James Duncan, John Dix, et al.

25 Inv estate of Elizabeth Holt decd. Balance of legacy in estate of James
Warren. By Thomas Warren exec.

Book K 1825
Page

27 List of notes and inv of estate of Stephen Moore decd. Notes on:

Edmund Alley	Philip Alley	Samuel Ayers	Richard C. Alley
John Amos	Lyde Bacon	Pleasant Black	Chiby Barnes
Absolem Bostick	John Baker	Robert Boze	Henry Botts
Mary Bason	Noah Cardwell	Thomas Dalton	David Ellick
Joel Fogg	Philip Gates	William Goff	Calvin Gossett
Andrew Joyce	Theophilus Lacy	Nicholas McMillon	Edward Murphey
John C. Overton	William Pratt	Clement Nance	Charles Plummer
Elias Potter	Elizabeth Philips	Thomas Reed	Mark Sharp
Joseph Scales	John Seal Jr.	A. M. Scales	Beverly Thacker
George Tucker	Reuben Thacker	Tavender Thacker	John Thacker
Wm. M. Wall	Saml. Welsh	Pleasant Webster	Jas Webb
Lewis White	William Whitworth	Richard Gentry	Johnson Gowing

Notes in hands of Martin Roberts amd Saml. A. Dalton, Elisha Noughton, Jeremiah Hutchinson. Debt to estate of Stephen Moore on the books of Moore and Dalton $1272.24. Debts on Stephen Moore decd on books of the Firm of Stephen Moore and Co. at Germantown $1090. Amt due from firm of Moore and Wall not known now in possession of Richard Wall. By Samuel Moore adm. (Note: Germantown in Stokes County).

34 Sales property of Joshua Hightower to:

John Johnston	Robert Hightower	William Pollard	Charnel Hightower
David Hodge Sen.	Amos Satterfield	Allen Hightower	Thomas Riggs
Moses Bradsher	Vincent Bradsher	Joseph Lunsford	John Poteat
William Campbell	Benjamin Stevens.		

36 Second inv of sales of Robert Singleton decd to Wm. Graves, Laban Farley, Thos. W. Graves.

37 Sales personal estate of Wyatt Stubblefield decd sold by Peter B. Stubblefield on 8 Dec 1824 to:

George W. Stubblefield	Elijah Withers	Thomas Worsham
Peter B. Stubblefield	James Murphey (1	Thomas Mullins
Brockman Nichols	large Bible)	George Roberts
Hugh Murphey	John Weatherford	William Busey
Carter Stubblefield	Charles Mitchell	Joshua Butler
Wm. A. Griffith	David Strador	William Bethel
Joseph O. Bryan		

Negroes purchased by Peter B. Stubblefield, John W. Grant, James Murphey.

40 Sale personal property of estate of Richard Crisp by James Terrell adm to:

Thomas Crisp	John Crisp	Jesse Crisp	William Terrell
James Terrell	Green W. Brown	Hazelwood Wilkerson	Levi Murphey
John Murphey	Absolem Lea	Thomas Mansfield	James Mansfield
William Mansfield	John Mansfield	Joseph Coleman	Henry Malone
James Broach	Nathl. G. Muzzall	Richard Hensley	et al

44 Sales property of William Ware decd sold 4 Feb 1825 to:

John P. Harrison	Elisha Alverson	Woodson Howard	Samuel Henderson
John D. Stone	Nathan Duncan Jr.	James White	Samuel White
James McClarney	Daniel Gunn	John Fowler	Henry A. Burton
Mark A. Handley	Jesse Alverson	Josiah Tyree	Chillman Voss
Thomas Bastin	John Ware Sen.	Wm. B. Swift	Watson Poindexter
Ambrose Franklin	Winny Ware	John Totten	Wm. Scott, et al

52 Sales estate of William Richardson decd sold 12 Feb 1825 to Noel Burton, Paschal Carter, James Richardson, John Price, Mary Richardson(widow), William Hooper, Barzallai G. Lea, Ralph Hubbard, John P. Harrison. By James Richardson and Noel Burton exec.

55 Acct estate of Obediah Nunley decd by William Nunly and John Nunley exec.

Book K 1825
Page
57 Div of negroes of Christiana Dupey late wife of John Shields among her children: Elizabeth Motley, Polly Dupree, Julian Dupree. 31 Jan 1825.
Commrs: Jas Burton, John Cobb Sen., Joseph Bracken.

58 MAJOR THOMAS DONOHO -Will - w   Sept. 1823. Mansion House and land loaned to
wife; Fanny Johnston (property already advanced to her); son Sanders and son
Dixon equal interest in lands on Country Line below John Peterson's Still
House Branch known as Mill tract, also grist mill and mansion tract after
wife's death, also the Hubbard tract and saw mill. Son Archimedes tract of
land on Milton road now in his cultivation, 400 acres, and part of tract
adj John Peterson, 300 acres. Granddaughter Mildred Watlington. 5 children;
3 sons to provide daughter Elizabeth Watlington with suitable home for life.
Exec: 3 sons, Sanders, Archimedes, and Dixon. Test: R. M. Saunders, William
V. Parker. Exec of last will of Thomas Donoho Sen., Archimedes and Dixon
Donoho, qualified.

61 ZACHARIAH PATTILLO - Will - w. 26 Dec 1824. Estate to be kept together for
widow and children until they reach lawful age, then divided and wife to get
child's part. If wife re-marry, children draw lots and rent out negroes and
land. Exec: wife Mary, Thomas Prendergast, James Bouldin. Wit: William
Florence, Elizer N. Bigelow, Helena Person. Mary Pattillo and Thomas Prendergast qualified.

63 HENRY McCLARNEY - Will - w. 16 Nov 1824. 3 youngest sons Robert, Holt, and
Armstead; wife Sarah - one-third land during life; daughters Mary and
Denesha; daughter Sarah $1.00. Test: Burwell Hagood, John S. Cowardin,
Thomas Hagood. Adm granted to Robert McClarney with will annexed, he bonded
by George Tyree and Sarah McClarney.
Court sitting: James Yancey, John P. Harrison, Freeman Leath.

July Court 1825

64 WILLIAM CULBERSON SEN. - Will - w. 16 Apr 1825. Wife Mary(land adj James
Currie); daughter Libby Parks to have $100 and a slave child to make her
equal with married children. 6 children: sons William and Hiram Culberson,
daughters Libby Parks, Edney Price, Mary Price, Susannah Rudd, Tabitha Rudd.
Exec: son Hiram Culberson and son-in-law Joshua Rudd. Wit: Tho Prendergast,
James Arnold. Exec qualified.

66 Inv estate of Hezekiah Farley decd left after death of his wife taken 23 Mar
1825. By James Lea exec of Hezekiah Farley.
67 Inv property of Capt. Samuel Parks decd taken 7 May 1825. Amt of money on
hand at death of Mrs. Parks. Bonds on Philip Cook, John Miles. Judgment of
Solomon Parks against Robert Scott and Jno McMurray adm of Mary Scott.
68 Additional inv estate of William Ware decd by John and Tolbert Ware adm.
69 Inv property of Josiah Chandler decd taken by John and William Chandler adm
on 30 Apr 1825. Notes on Philip Melton, Frances Chandler, Thomas Hall.
70 Inv property of Henry McClarney decd by Robert McClarney adm.
71 Inv estate of John Burch since 1823. Cash received of John Dean supposed to
belong to Bennett Smith and Jesse A. Dollarhide. By James Roan exec.
71 Inv goods of Samuel H. Ball decd taken 11 July 1825 by Stairling Gunn adm.
72 Sales estate of Henry McClarney 13 May 1825 to:

Henry McClarney Jr.	Sarah McClarney	Thomas Ware	Armstead McClarney
Robert McClarney	Henry Baldwin	David Tyree	Holt McClarney
Mark A. Handly	Henry Ruark	Charles Busey	George W. Tyree
Josiah Tyree	Thomas Bastin	Nathan Duncan	Henry Cobb
George Astin	Charles Miller	Isaac Durham	Wm. Stratten
Luke Palmer	David Vaughan	Thomas Sutherlin	Weadon Grigsby
Wiley Mason	Arthur Toney	By Robert McClarney, adm.	

73

Book K 1825
Page
77 Sales property of Hezekiah Farley decd to:

Henry Roper	Wm. S. Farley	James M. Jeffreys	James Lea Sen.
Archibald Montgomery	Allen McCain	Tinsley Lea	James Lea Jr.
William Jones	Thomas Vaughan	Warren McCain	Craften Williams
Durrett Oliver	Tilotson McCain	John J. Farley Jr.	Wiley Jones
Richard Yarborough	John Giles	Elijah H. Pass	Richardson Crowder
John Comer	William Dunaway	Alexander Kersey	Henry Burton
Eliza Farley	et al	By James Lea exec.	

82 Inv property of Robert Singleton decd by Jeremiah Graves adm. (2nd inv.)
83 A report of the Public Lot at Caswell Court House - a survey to establish
   lines of public lot. Beginning at oak near Capt. John Graves' door steps,
   west to rock in street near Thomas Graves' house, south with Azariah Graves'
   piazza to a rock to west of the Jail, then east leaving the jail to the south
   to a rock near Elijah Graves' palling and north by Elijah Graves' piazza to
   1st station, one acre. 14 Apr. 1825. J. Womack, County Surveyor.
84 William Elam orphan now age of 11 years bound to Alexander Kersey.

October Court 1825

85 List of personal property of Stephen Moore decd by Samuel Moore Jr. adm.
85 Inv estate of Mary Price wife of Jno Price returned by the said John, adm.
   Her share of personal estate of her deceased father. (John S. Price, adm.)
86 Inv estate of William Culberson decd. Notes on Joshua and Joseph Rudd.
   By Hiram Culberson and Joshua Rudd adm.
87 Inv crop of tobacco of Forbus Harrelson decd., 2143 lbs; sales of tobacco
   to Emanuel Wadkins, Jacob Henderson, Thomas Foster, total $95.73.
88 Acct current estate of Calton Nunn by Mathew Mills adm.
89 Elijah Morton adm in acct with estate of Martin Morton decd.
90 Mary Childers orphan 13 or 14 years old bound to Bennett Bush until age 21.
91 William Hailey orphan 13 years old bound to James Aldridge until he is 21 yrs.

93 JAMES SANDERS SENR. - Will - w. 6 July 1825. Nephew James Sanders son of Thomas
   Sanders decd (land on Dan River including Mansion house, 820 acres, at mouth
   of Little Creek). Nephew Romulus M. Sanders (land on Dan River called lower
   tract of 875 acres). Faithful old slaves to live on the land. Nephew Alan-
   son Trigg son of William Trigg decd.; niece Martha Trigg wife of Absolem Trigg;
   Betsy P. Atkinson wife of Thomas Atkinson and her children; brother Richard
   Sanders and his daughter Ann P. Samuel. James Sanders son of Richard Sanders;
   Harriott Sanders daughter of James Sanders and wife of Doct. Nathl. Sanders.
   Children of Letitia Allen mentioned. Nephew Francis Sanders son of Thomas.
   Niece Sally Mosely and her son Lucien Brown and her daughter by her former
   husband Bedford Brown; Lockett Sanders some negroes for her life. Niece
   Elizabeth Jones and her son Thomas Jones and daughter Polly. Nephew William
   Trigg of Ala. Kezziah Jeffreys wife of Thomas Jeffreys (land on Little Creek
   adjArchimedas Donoho) said land to go to her children, but if no children,
   land to Milly Watlington. Nephew Joseph Sanders son of Richard, Nephew James
   Sanders son of Thomas, nephew Sanders Donoho. Exec: James Sanders son of
   Thomas, nephew Romulus M. Sanders. Wit: B. Yancey, William Harris, David M.
   Sanders. Romulus M. Sanders qualified.

98 JOHN BALDWIN - Will - w. 8 Aug 1825. Daughter Susannah Murphey; sons Edmond,
   Clement, and Barrett Baldwin; daughters Mary Ann Murphey and Delia Stratten;
   granddaughters Elizabeth Ann and Sarah daughters of Susannah; grandson
   Nathaniel Murphey; grandchildren Margery Murphey and William Henry Murphey,
   children of Mary Ann Murphey. Granddaughter Nancy Penick daughter of Mary Ann
   Murphey. Wife Fanny Baldwin. Exec: wife and son Clement. Wit: Wm. W. Price,
   Silvester McCubbins, Alford McCubbins. Fanny Baldwin qualified.

74

Book K 1825-1826
Page
100 MAJOR BROCKMAN - Will - w. 21 Sept. 1825. Wife Elizabeth (land adj Grant's
line); 3 youngest children, Barney, Susannah, and Mary Brockman. Son John
to have balance of land not willed to wife adj Williamson Price and O'Briant.
Exec: son John. Wit: James Rawley, Yelverton D. Rawley. Exec qualified.

101 THOMAS WILEY - Will - w. 25 Dec 1824. Son Alexander (all land purchased of
Meshack Morton); son John to get rest of land; daughter Mary Wiley.
Negroes divided between Jane Currie and her heirs, Mary Wiley, Elender
Jones and her heirs, Esther Brandon and her heirs, Agness Chandlers heirs
and Chandler heirs to have as much as one of my daughters. Remainder sold
and go to 4 daughters and Agnes Chandler's heirs; Alexander Grey to have
$100. Exec: sons Alexander and John Wiley. Wit: Joseph Langley, John
C. Richmond. Exec qualified.

103 MARGARET COMER - Will - w. 30 Sept 1825. Sons Nathaniel and Thomas Comer.
All other children. Wit: John Comer, Mary Long, Nathl. M. Roan.
John Comer named adm with will annexed, bonded by Thomas Comer & Noel Burton.

104-107 Refunding bonds of estate of Sterling Ruffin decd from Thomas Ruffin,
James H. Ruffin, George McNeil and Minerva his wife, William McCain Jr. and
Mary his wife. Wit: Wil Kirkland.   James Yancey, Chairman County Court.

January Court 1826

110 Richard H. L. Bennett orphan age 18 years or there abouts bound to John C.
Harvey to learn art of a saddler. Freeman Leath, Chairman County Court.
111 Inv property of Nathaniel Comer decd by John Comer.
112 Inv property of Margaret Comer decd by John Comer adm.
112 Inv property of Thomas Wiley decd by Alexander Wiley and John Wiley exec.
Notes on Zephaniah Roberts, Henry Fuquay, Alexander Wiley.
114 Inv property of David Lawson decd taken 3 Nov 1825 by Susan Lawson, Edward
Wright, George W. Stubblefield.
115 Inv property of John Bauldwin decd by Fanny Bauldwin exec. (Same as Baldwin)
116 Inv estate of Thomas Wiley decd and sales to:

Allen Hightower	Asa Gunn	Adams Richmond	Anderson Birk
Alexr Montgomery	Alexr. Grey	Alexr. Wiley	Allen Love
Aldridge Rudd	Benjamin Willis	Benjamin Matlock	Camel Vanhook
Churchwell Jones	David Brandon	Drury Casy	Daniel Chandler
David Mitchell	Elijah Martin	Elijah Morton	Elisha Rudd
Elijah Graves	Geo B. Dameron	George Martin	George Williamson
Goodwin Evans	George Smith	Harrison Dameron	Henry Young
Henry Allen	John Chandler	Joseph Langley	John Gunn
John Lea	John Love	John Fullington	John Willson
John Crositt	John Dickey	John Kitchen	John Wiley
John C. Richmond	Joseph Lunsford	John Lenox	James Richmond
Joseph Singleton	Joseph Currie	John Browning	Laban Ford
Lewis Yealock	Moses Kitchen	Mathew Terry	Nathaniel Lea
Nathaniel Snipes	Nicholas Coile	Polly Wiley	Richard H. Griffith
Solomon Whitlow	Stephen Kitchen	Thomas Cook	Thomas Burton
William Brandon	Wiley Chandler	William Turner	Warner Coile
Wm. M. Dameron	William Cox	William Vaughan	William Mathis
William Pollard	William Ashford	John Peterson	James Peterson
Thomas McFarland.			

128 Sales property of Martha Farley decd by James W. Jeffreys adm. sold 18 May
1825 to:: Thomas Vaughan, John Adams, James Lea Sen., William Gordon, James
W. Jeffreys, Lewis Vaughan, J. Maurice, William Dunaway, Newman Durham,
R. Samuel, N. Burton, Henry Burton. Bonds on Newman Durham and Henry Mahan
due 1820.

Book K 1826
Page
130 Sales property of David Lawson decd. to:
<pre>
   Susan Lawson   John Lawson   John Cobb Jr.   Joseph Scales
   John Weatherford   Charles Mitchell William Lewis   Whitehead Page
   Washington Stubblefield Smith Overby Bayless Lynn   Rhodeham Lovelace
   Edward Wright   John Turner   David W. Jones   Capt.Richard Jones
   Carter Blackwell   David Strador   Joseph Medcalf   et al.
</pre>
135 Sales property of Margarett Comer decd sold 19 Nov 1825 to:
<pre>
   John Lea(C)   John Morris   Nat Comer   Danl. Richmond
   David Hodge   Thos. Comer   John Matthews   Vincent Bradsher
   John Broughton   John Roan
        By John Comer adm.
</pre>
136 Sales property of Nathaniel Comer decd sold 17 Nov 1825 to:
<pre>
   James W. Jeffreys   William Long   Tinsley Lea   John McCain
   James W. McCain   William Stanfield David Kersey   Phenias Hubbard
   Barzilia Wisdom   Jesse Thomas   Bazil M. Long   John Fullington
   Archd. Lea   Hugh Dobbins   William Long   Walker Eskridge
   Thomas Walker   Thomas Stafford (also same buyers of Margaret Comer sale)
</pre>
143 Sales property of Josiah Chandler decd sold by John and William Chandler
    adm on 28 Oct 1825 to:
<pre>
   Solomon Whitlow   Thomas W. Chandler Goodwin Evans   Elijah G. Kimbrough
   Alex Wiley   Judith Chandler   John Wiley   Joseph Kitchen
   George Morton   John Smith   James Aldridge   Henry Allen
   James Lea   James Nelson   William Chandler John Willis
   Mathew Terry   Mary Chandler   Zachariah McFarlin Wilkins Chandler
   Nathaniel Snipes   Miles Kimbrough   Thomas Page   William Miles
   William Turner   John Chandler   Jacob Bruice   Thomas Wiley
</pre>
148 Sales property of William Culberson decd sold 1 & 2 Nov 1825 to:
<pre>
   Thomas Eubanks   James Womble   John Murphey   James Aldridge
   Sanders Browning   Joseph Rudd   William Browning Aza Hensley
   Robert Parks   Miles Kimbro   Thornton Baynes   Ruffin Pleasant
   William Kimbro   John Mitchell   Elijah Martin   William Hightower
   Richard Arvin   Robert Arvin   David Melton   Polly Culberson
   James G. Vowel   William Turner   Nathaniel Snipes Charnel Hightower
   Abel Foulks   William Hensley   Libby Parks   Robert Martin
   William Mussall   Jonathan Terrel   Hiram Parks   Luke Arnold
   Burwell Corbit   John Loyd   William Barnwell Christopher Brooks
   Thomas Woods   James Arnold   William Price   Samuel Dameron
</pre>
154 Div of negroes of estate of David Lawson decd to:
Susan Lawson widow, George W. Stubblefield and wife Sally, William Lawson,
Nancy Lawson, Edward Wright and wife Bina, John Lawson, Jane Lawson, all
heirs at law. 22 Dec 1825.
Commrs: J. Womack, Richard Jones, Joseph Brackin.

                          END OF BOOK K

        January Court 1826 continues in Book L.

                              76

<u>January</u> <u>Court</u> <u>1826</u> continued

Page
1 EUNICE LEA - Will - w. 28 Oct 1825. Two sisters Matilda Lea, Alethe Lea; brother Aron V. Lea to have all interest in real and personal estate of Father James Lea decd and all property willed by Catherine Lea widow of William Lea Senr. Exec: Aron V. Lea. Wit: James M. Lea, Samuel Eskridge. Exec qualified.

1 Acct estate of John Kimbro decd by William Kimbro exec.

3 Acct estate of John Ingram decd by James Burton and James Ingram exec. Property left to widow.

4 James Ingram adm estate of Mary Ingram, acct current.

5 Estate of Samuel Woods, acct current by John Woods and William Richmond adm. Bond on David Woods; rent of plantation to Thos. Woods and others, rent of mills to E. Jones and N. Bartlett; paid notes to Lewis Shirley, Samuel Rainey, David D. Nutt, Nathaniel Toryan, Mary Woods, William Lea. Paid taxes in Caswell and Person Counties.

6 A div of negroes of Edwin Raimey to Zachariah Hooper in right of his wife, one-sixth part being his proportion. 23 Dec 1825.

7 Div of negroes of Josiah Chandler decd to William Chandler, Margaret Chandler, Polly Chandler, Thomas W. Chandler, Nancey Chandler, Judith Chandler, John Chandler. Commrs: John Johnston, Azariah Graves, Thos. Harrelson.

8 Power of attorney - John Langley of Gwinnett County, Ga., to John Wiley of Caswell County to sell and make title to all land he owns in Caswell Co. 4 Dec 1824.

8 Power of attorney - Martin Southard of White County, Tenn., to friend Larkin Wisdom of county and state aforesaid to recover from estate of Thomas Phelps decd late of Caswell Co. in hands of Gabriel Lea exec part due in right of wife Nancy Southard a div of said Thomas Phelps, said Nancy his granddaughter and daughter of Larkin Wisdom. 1 Oct 1825. Signed McLin Southard. Drury Smith and William Irvin, JP's of White Co. Tenn. approve P of A for Maclin Southard.

10 Power of attorney - Ann Benton of Shelby Co. Tenn., to Nathaniel Kimbro of county and state aforesaid to demand from estate of William Gooch decd of Caswell Co. who died intestate. 27 Mar 1822. Wit: Samuel R. Brown, A. B. Carr.

11 Power of attorney - Elizabeth Kimbro of Rutherford County, Tenn., to Nathan Williams Esq. of Caswell Co. to receive estate due from William Gooch Senr. and to sell any land due her. 23 June 1819.

12 Power of attorney - James Gooch of Allen County, KY, to Jonathan Dorson of county and state aforesaid to receive from estate of William Gooch Sr. of Caswell Co. and any legacy left by John C. Gooch decd. 24 June 1818.

13 Power of attorney - Jeremiah Barnes and Marilla Barnes his wife who is daughter of Thomas Gooch decd of Williamson Co. Tenn., to Thomas Boaz of Williamson Co. to recover from William Gooch of Caswell Co. exec of John C. Gooch decd any part due Jeremiah Barnes and wife. 8 Dec 1817.

14 Power of attorney - Sherwood Green exec of Thomas Gooch decd and guardian of Matilda Gooch one of the legal heirs of said Gooch and David Gooch all of Williamson Co. Tenn., to friend Thomas Boaz to receive from estate of William Gooch of Caswell Co. exec of William Gooch and John C. Gooch decd which is due to estate of Thomas Gooch decd. 8 Dec 1817.

15 Power of attorney - David Gooch of Williamson County, Tenn., to Isaac Phillips of county and state aforesaid to recover from brother William Gooch of Caswell County all property due him. 30 Jan 1807. Test: William Anthony, J P and S. Green JP.

Book L 1826
Page
16 John Brown of Murray Co. Tenn., owning land on Tom's Creek, Caswell Co., now
occupied by brother William V. Brown land adj Jeremiah Lea, Surry Mahaughn,
gives power to Phreman Leath of Caswell Co. to sell said land to William V.
Brown and transfer money to William Polk of Wake Co., NC, for benefit of
James Walker of Murry Co. Tenn. 13 May 1825. P. Nelson, James Walker, JP's
Murray Co. Tenn.
17 Power of attorney - Lewis Cox of Robertson County, Tenn., to Thomas Cox of
Caswell Co. to receive from adm of estate of Reubin Cox decd all money due
him as heir and legatee, and to sell real estate of Father Reubin Cox.
15 July 1825.
19 Power of attorney - Joseph Carter of Sumner Co. Tenn., to son Francis Carter
to sell tract of land in Caswell Co. on Stony Creek adj James Haden, John
Williamson, widow Leachman, and John Boswell, 217 acres. 9 Nov 1823.
20-21 blank

April Court 1826

22 Additional inv estate of Thomas Wiley decd by Alex & John Wiley exec.
22 Inv estate of James Willson decd which he left in hands of his wife, Nancy
Willson for her lifetime. Feb 1826 By George W. Jeffreys, exec.
23 Inv estate of Eunice Lea decd, the property in her possession when she died.
Her interest in her Father Jas Lea's estate cannot be ascertained without
referring to his inv. By Aaron V. Lea exec.
23 Property belonging to estate of Mrs. G. H. Lewis decd of Caswell Co. Cash
received of Jno W. S. Daniel for hire of Tom; tobacco sold in Lynchburg
$360.10. Cash in hands of N. M. Lewis. By A. J. Walker & N. M. Lewis.
24 Inv estate of Samuel Johnston decd taken at his late residence 28 Nov 1825
by John Johnston.
25 Inv property of William Wilkerson decd and sale, also book acct by John W.
Grant adm. Dec 1825. Acctounts on:

William Shelton	Wedin Grigsby	Elijah Sims	Edward Murphey
William Busey	William Burns	James Worsham	Stephen Coleman
Fields Nicholas	Elizabeth Durham	Isaac Hobbs	John Strador
Joseph O'Brian	Edmond Sparks	George Astin	Samuel Cook
Thomas Owin	George Lay	Lewis Gatewood	Evin Shaw
Daniel Sullivan	Wesley Cook	Capt. Joseph Motley,	John Powell
Brockman Nichols	Samuel Poindexter		

27 2nd sale of Thomas Wiley to:

Allen Hightower	Alex Wiley	Banjamin Matlock	John Riley
John Richmond	John Johnston	James Nelson	James Lunsford
Joseph Lunsford	Joseph Currie	Nathaniel Snipes	Thomas Burton
Wm. M. Dameron	William Pollard		

28 Sales property of James Willson decd sold 23 Feb 1826 to:

Zachariah Samuel	William Dunaway	Mathew Terry	Hugh McCain
Henry Roper	James M. McCain	Robert Williams	John Williams
Craften Williams	John Lea	John Sparrow	Maurace Vaughan
Dabney Terry	John Horton	Garland Shackleford,	John A. Pass
William Cox	Hugh M. Gillaspie	Elijah H. Pass	James Gates
Mathew Willson	Anthony Satterfield,	John Hendrick	John F. McCain
Josep Clay	Henry Shelton	William Bull	William Jones
Joel Bolton	Gideon Gillaspie	Drury Kersey	Alexander Kersey
John Reed	By George M. Jeffreys exec.		

33 Sales estate of Samuel Johnston decd by John Johnston adm sold Dec 24 and 25
1825 to:

John Johnston	Wm. M. Dameron	James Dollarhide	Solomon Whitlow
Henry H. Allen	James Fullington	Thomas Walton	Henry Young
William Boswell	Robert Williamson	Archibald Lipscomb	Wm. H. Jackson
John N. Fuller	John Broughton	James Holder	(cont. on page 79)

78

Book L 1826
Page
33-40 Sales estate of Samuel Johnston cont. sales to:

John Peterson	Lewis Yealock	Daniel Sargent	John Comer
Thomas Malone	Elijah Morton	James Crossett	William Rasco
Jesse Yealock	Samuel Mitchell	Clermont Hamlett	Craften Williams
Jeffries Lea	Robert McCain	Benjamin F. Stanfield,	John Adams
Thomas Evans	James Yealock	Robert Ball	Levi Fuller
Aron Lea	William Eskridge	Thomas Stafford	James Lea
Jesse Satterfield	Elisha Byrd	Simeon Lea	Jesse Carver
John Bradsher	Samuel Yealock	Thomas Johnston	Andrew P. Jackson

Sale of negroes to James Crossett, Alexander Gordon, Thomas Walton, Tinsley
Lea, Pleasant Chandler

40 Sale property of Isaac Durham decd by Martin Durham exec sold 30 Jan 1826 to:

Charles Busey	William Busey	Samuel Busey	John Burnes
Henry Burnes	James Burnes	Thomas Archer	William Patterson
James Walker	Thomas Hailey	James Ferguson	Peter Perkins
John Lovelace	O'Kelly Voss	Bartlett Patterson	Fields Nichols
Isaac Nichols	Jonathan Foxwell	George Shaw	Carson Norman
Samuel Walker	Nicholas Wilkerson,	Westley Cook	Hugh Murphey
James London	Smith Overby	Richard Durham	John Durham
Nathaniel Durham	Martin Durham	Isaac Durham	et al

46 Sales property of Dr. Edward M. Foulkes decd sold 15 Sept. 1825 to:
Dr. James E. Williamson purchased much medical equipment including complete
amputating case; Doct. Henry McAden; Doct. Otway E. Bailey, Doct. Ellis G.
Blake, Charles Mitchell, John S. Lesure, Josiah Womack, Richard Jones, John
Crenshaw, Azariah Graves, William Brintle, David Barker, Amsey Cobb, Garrot
Figgins, Henly Humphreys, William Paschall, Thomas Garrot, John Somers,
Eli Massie, John Smithey, Alfred Humphreys, John Paschall, William J. Nash,
Doct. John Comer, Jethro Brown, Mrs. Martha Foulkes, Carter Groom, Pleasant
Robertson, et al. By John E. Brown adm.

52 Debtors to estate of Dr. Edward Foulkes per ledgers A, B, and C., accts dating
back to 1818 and list is 6 pages long. Some are:

John Allcorn(Guilford)	Joseph Allen(High Rock)	Wm. Bethell
James C. Brown (son of Elijah),	James Brown(Rockingham)	Salley Brookes,
John Chapman(Caswell Co.)	James Davis(Orange Co.)	(widow of Chas.)
Allen Fields(Rockingham)	Frendene Fonville(Orange Co.)	
Henry Humphreys(Greensboro)	John H. Humphreys	John May(Eagle
John Pyron	John Paschall(son of Wm.)	Falls)
John Reed(Miller)	Mrs. Alice Ruffin	John Sawyer
John Taylor(High Rock)	James Walker(son of Molley)	et al

By John E. Brown adm.

58 Bonds and judgments to estate of Dr. Edward M. Foulkes decd on Spencer Jackson,
Patsey Nichols, Stephen Rice, et al.

59 Stairling H. Gunn adm in acct with estate of Lemuel H. Ball decd. Debt to
S. H. Gunn for medicine.

59 Estate of Edward Raimey decd in acct with John P. Harrison adm. Accts paid to:

Roger & Owen	John Hooper	Eliza Raimey	Hugh Howard
Daniel Gunn	Dr. John L. Graves,	Hinton & Brame	Elisha Ingram
James Ingram	Andrew Harrison Jr.,	Thomas Slade	James Lea
Warren Holcomb	Mary Harrison	Paid Thomas Penick for crying sale.	

(Also spelled Ramey)

60 Henry Hooper adm in acct with estate of Francis B. Phillips decd. Payments
to widow Mahala Phillips, to John C. Harvey for note, et al.

61 Geo B. Dameron and John P. Harrison exec of Joseph Dameron decd in acct with
estate. Sale of land 130 acres at $2.50 per acre. Received of estate of
John Dameron decd. Paid accts of George B. Dameron, Barzillai Lea, Mary
Hipworth, Parham Jackson, Benj. Dameron, Martha Jackson, Samuel Dameron,
William Upton, et al

Book L 1826
Page
64 John and Elisha Paschall adm of William Paschall decd acct current; paid
exec of William Berry; payments to William Orr, James Barker, Noah Cobb,
John Paschall, Jethro Brown; paid widow's allowance, et al.
65 Div estate of Samuel Smith decd by Doct John McAden, Thomas Harrelson, and
John P. Harrison. Met at dwelling of his widow 11 Jan 1826.
Land near South Hico called Darby's, land on Cobb Creek and on N. Hico.
63 negroes valued at $16256.10. Sam Smith decd alloted to Henry Warren who
married his daughter Elizabeth certain negroes in 1814; in 1822 exec alloted
to Maurice Smith son of Samuel advancements, also allotment to Thomas Smith
son of said Saml.; to Richard J. Smith son of Saml. a tract of land in Tenn.
Advancements to Robert Smith, son of Saml; and to William Smith on acct of
his education; allotment to Alexr. Smith. Division into 10 parts. Sam H.
Smith had received land on Cobb Creek; Mary K. Smith her part. John Smith
recd his full share of negroes and no allotment and relinquished his right
to claim. Agreed to by Samuel H. Smith; John, Thomas, Richard J., Maurice
Smith, John Wilson for wife Ann, Alexander Smith, Robert Smith by his agent
John Wilson, Mary Smith, Samuel H. Smith guardian of William Smith, and
Henry Warren for himself and as next friend to his children Mary W., Samuel,
and Asbury. Thomas Smith tansfers whole of his claim to Richard J. Smith.
Samuel H. Smith and John Smith exec.
70 Indemnifying bond: Henry Warren of Wake Co. for himself and widow Elizabeth
Smith to Saml. H. & John Smith.
71 Linda Taber orphan age 10 years old bound to John Bouldin until age 21.
John R. Clark, Chairman County Court.
72 Sanders Edwell orphan age of 12 years bound to William Weatherford.
Henry Edwell orphan 10 years old bound to William Weatherford.
73 Power of attorney - William Oliver of King and Queen Co. Va., to Jonathan
Brooks of Caswell Co. to transact business relative to estate of Elizabeth
Gardner decd in state of NC. William Oliver adm of estate of Elizabeth
Gardner in King and Queen Co., Va. 14 Oct 1825.

74 Plans and specifications of a Poor and Work House for Caswell County:
House to be built in a long row to contain 8 rooms all 16 feet square except one to be 16 by 20 feet; the whole house and partitions to be of brick
burnt good and sound at least 9 inches long and 4 by 3 thick, brick laid in
lime mortar and faced on both sides; house to have good chimneys of brick,
lower floor of heart pine or oak timber 1½ inches thick. Each room to have
door on east side with rock sill, a 12 light window on west side with
good sash, glass, and shutters hung with good iron hinges. Roof covered
with heart pine shingles, and timber growing on land where built to be used;
to be completed by 1 Oct. William Childes became the undertaker of building
the house at price of $840 he being the lowest bidder.
James Yancey, Chairman County Court.

76 WILLIAM BRUMMIT - Will - w. 18 Nov 1825. Wife Polley to have all land and
property plus mill purchased of Abram Villines during her life. The exec
then to divide equally the estate among all children, each to have enough
to be equal with what sons Pleasant and Edmond had received. Exec: friend
John McMurry Sen. Wit: John McMurry, Pleasant Brummit, Edmond Brummit.

77 GRIFFIN GUNN - Will - w. 4 May 1825. Wife Dorothy M. Gunn the part of land
he lives on, the land alloted to James Ingram in div of estate of his father
Benjamin Ingram decd. Wife and children to share equally in div of negroes,
each one-ninth part if no more children are born. No div of negroes until
son Jones M. Gunn is 21 years. Wit: B. Yancey, Azariah Graves.
Codicil: 23 March 1826. Widow may sell her land if she prefers and purchase
another tract.

Book L 1826
Page
78 JAMES GILLASPY - Will - w.19 Dec 1821. Wife Nancy all property during her
life and then to go to 2 sons Alexander and Gidel and they should pay 4
daughters Milley Horton, Betsy Warf, Sally Warf and Nancey Lumpkins. Land
adj Bennett's line. Exec: sons Alexander and Gidel, and Mumford Bennett.
Wit: William Bennett, Mumford Bennett. (also spelled Gillaspie)

79 JOSEPH YOUNGER of county of Orange, NC - Will - w. 9 Aug 1824.
Sons William, Aquilla, Joseph, John; daughters Barbara, Rebeccah, Milly,
Dolley, Elizabeth, and Mary Younger; wife Jane Younger. Exec: son John
Younger. Wit: Jania Hall, William Mathis.

80 DAVID STRADER- Will - w. 21 Jan 1826. Wife Prudence Strader; son Henry to
get all property already received; daughter Mahalah French(property already
given to her); sons Lewis and John all that has been given to them. After
death of wife remainder to all children, daughter Mahalah, son William C.,
daughter Zepherah Strader, son John. Exec: Josiah Womack, Joseph K. Cobb,
and Benjamin Elmore. Wit: J. Womack, Jos K. Cobb, Garland Blackwell,
Benja Elmore, S. C. Cobb.

81 Joseph Worsham orphan now 10 years of age bound to Reuben Trennem.
82 Hire of negroes of William Walker decd for 1826 to William Fitch and Margaret
Walker. By Connally Walker adm.

July Court 1826

84 Inv property of Joseph Younger decd by John Younger exec.
84 Inv property of John Bowers dcd. Negroes mentioned in will in Virginia in
hands of James Bowers. By Samuel Keeton exec.
84 Inv estate of Anthony Samuel decd taken 13 Apr 1826 by James Rainey adm.
85 Inv property remaining on premises of late residence of James Gillaspie decd
by Alexr. Gillaspie exec.
85 Inv estate of William Brummitt decd taken 17 Feb 1826. By John McMurry exec.
86 Inv property of David Strader decd by Mathew Mills adm.
87 Inv personal property of Griffin Gunn decd. Cash of A. Graves partner of
late firm of Graves and Gunn; sold negro to Anderson Willis. 35 negroes
named, 2 of which belong to William Singleton's children.
(Long list of debtors to estate) By A. Gunn, adm.
Bonds on:

Elizabeth Grant	John Gomer	Jeremiah Litrel	John Bennett
Elmore H. Smith	Edward Lewis	James Literal	Robert Payne
Jeptha Parks	Judy Bever	Nathan Browning	Ann Brooks,decd.
Jos Vaughan, decd.	Frederick Stovall	Ira Somers	John Ruark
Ziba Rice	Robert Tapley	Vachel Ingram	John Ingram
Walter Ingram	Hannah Miles	Armistead Watlington Jr.	
Isaac Wright decd, et al.			

88 Hezekiah P. Smithon in acct with estate of Thomas Woody decd. Cash received
from John Shields, and of James Martin attorney at law collected of Wm.Speer.
89 Sales and inv property of Col. James Sanders decd sold Nov 1825 to:

David Montgomery	Nathl. M. Pass	James M. Jeffreys	Geo Williamson
John Lea (CB)	Christopher Dameron,Dabney Terry		Nathl. Lea
Will Cox	Adam Finch	Jeptha Parker	Archd Samuel
John Hendrick	Bedford Read	John Lenox	Henry M. Clay
John Peterson	James Sanders Jr.	Stephen Haddoxk	Will Bull
Will Harris	Samuel Hinton	Stephen Dodson	Thomas Mitchell
John Horton	John E. Lewis	Joseph Bolton	R. W. Hutson
Joseph Motley	Thomas Gossett	Joseph P.Sanders	Benj. James
John Buckingham	Alexr Kersey	Richd Standley	Daniel Raimey
Elijah H. Pass	James Hamblett	John Davis	H. W. Gillaspie
Joab Sikes	Thomas Cox	James Shirley	Richd. Sanders

cont on page 82

81

Book L 1826
Page
    Sales of Col. James Sanders cont. Sales to:

James Holder	A. Donoho	Will Childes	Thomas Walton
M. P. Huntington	Levin Downs	Thomas Gossett	Richd Cates
John R. Clark(lot in Milton),		James Sanders Ten[e]	Maj.Richd Sanders
Romulus M. Saunders	et al		

    Cotton made at Creek Plantation; tobacco sold in Lynchburg; cash for
    tobacco at home received by D. M. Sanders; recd. from Finch for shop
    acct.; note on James Holder.
99 William and Boswell Warren exec of James Warren decd acct with estate.
    Cash recd. from George Roberts, Yancey Westbrook; paid John Miles for
    crying sale; paid $2 to Stephen Chandler for preaching funeral; paid $8
    to Wm. and Boswell Warren for whiskey.
100 Sale of negroes of Thomas Wiley decd by Thomas W. Chandler for heirs of
    Josiah Chandler decd sold 2 May 1826.
100 Tolbert Ware adm of William Ware decd in acct with estate.
102 James Terrell adm estate of Richard Crisp decd intestate. Paid Nathl G.
    Muzzall for clerk of sales, Absolem Lea for crying sale; paid accts of
    William Huntington, Mildred Burch, et al.
103 William Slade adm of Thomas Turner decd acct filed. Cash recd. of James
    Tate, E. B. Rice, Jacob Ahart, Mahlon Stacy, Richd Gill for wife Sarah
    Lampkin, William Bruice, John Daniel Payne, Willis Ashford, Thomas A.
    Thompson, Adam Simmons, James Yancey on bond, William Moore on bond in SC;
    John Murphey, Nat Murphey, Nancy Lampkin, Jordan Massey, Polly Lampkin,
    William Turner, Capt. James Graves, Ames Ford, Wm. P. Martin, et al.
    Cash recd from estate of Edward Patillow; property recd by William Slade
    and Martin Elliott in advance. Josiah Turner agent for James Turner.
    Paid for collecting money in SC and Tenn. Balance due legatees $11034.98.
    Names of legatees n ot included.
107 Estate of Lewis Malone in acct with Daniel Malone exec. Legacy recd from
    Robert Blackwell $147.61. Acct since 1813. Expenses for schooling 6 boys
    $71.20 for 1819. 10 July 1826. Commrs: Geo B. Dameron. William Anderson,
    Jos Langley. School expenses for Goodloe, Mitchell, Robert, Lewis G.
    Nashville, and Alexander Malone.
110 Div of negroes of Anthony Samuel decd to Jane Rainey, Sarah Samuel, Josiah
    Samuel, James Rainey, Archibald Samuel, Anthony Samuel, Benjamin Samuel,
    Samuel Pittard. Commrs: Samuel H. Smith, Tho Jeffreys, William McGehee.
    15 Apr 1825.
111 Robert Worsham orphan 13 years of age or thereabouts bound to James Harris.
111 Power of attorney - Drury Mathis about to remove from the country to William
    Upton to act in respect to portion of land coming to Drury from Mother
    Mrs. Nancey or Ann M. Mathis in Caswell County when the youngest child
    of his father, Ann M. Jackson, arrives at lawful age and to recover one-
    eighth part of Mother's thirds at her decease. 15 Oct 1825. Wit: Banj
    Dameron, James Jackson.

112 JAMES RICHARDSON - Will - w. 2 July 1826. Wife Nancy to use all proceeds
    for benefit of children; plantation purchased of Henry Sergeant and land
    on Hogan's Creek. If wife re-marry she should have one-sixth part of estate
    and balance to children; if she does not re-marry to have one-eighth part.
    Exec: brother in law Robert Ware and he be advised by wife, John P. Harrison,
    Henry Sergeant, and Edward Rudder. Wit: Harrison, Sergeant, Rudder.

        October Court 1826

115 Inv property of James Richardson decd. Pages 116-117 have long list of
    bonds due the estate.
118 Executions due estate of James Richardson decd. Sales ot estate to Charles
    K. Harrison, David Kersey, Capt. Wm. Ware, Evans Knight, et al.

Book L 1826 - 1827
Page
120 Martha Haralson adm of Forbus Haralson decd in acct with estate. Cash paid to
Jas.Richardson and Noel Burton exec of William Richardson decd., to Jeremiah
Putnam; William Gafford, John Ware, Doct. Robert Thurmon, Barnett Lovelace,
Bedford Brown atty., Thomas Gibson for crying sale, et al. 11 Oct 1826.
121 Thomas Blackwell exec of Robert Blackwell decd final settlement. Payments
to Carter Blackwell, Garland Blackwell, James Watt, John Blackwell, Patsey
Blackwell, Samuel Watt, Edwd. M. Jones, Lewis Malone proportionable part,
Thomas Blackwell proportionable part. Each received $153.46.
Lewis Malone's part paid to Alexander S. Malone per his power of attorney of
March 13, 1827.
Thomas Blackwell exec of Zillah Blackwell decd., final settlement. Payments
to same as those in settlement of Robert Blackwell. Commrs: Jethro Brown,
W. J. Nash.
122 Advertisement of William B. Reid and Thomas J. Reid as administrators of
estate of Major John Reid decd. 9 Oct 1826. Wit: Stephen Dodson.
Benjamin Elmore, JP.
123 Report of Commrs. for Work and Poor in Caswell County. Purchased 213 acres
land of Griffin Gunn for $500 and 80 acres of Starling Gunn for $321.
Low bidder William Childs paid $840. $23 due for completion. Total $1683.
Besides being a habitation of the Poor there is a house that will very well
answer for the superintendent and another for a kitchen. There is no suitable building for a smoke house.
123 James Edwell orphan age of 7 years bound to Thomas Weatherford.
124 Richard Edwell orphan age of 18 years bound to Thomas Weatherford.
125 Isaac Edwell orphan age of 14 years bound to Thomas Weatherford.
125 Power of attorney - Mark Willson of Philadelphia, Pa., merchant, did on 18
Jan. 1826 convey unto Peter Graham and John McCauley of same city, merchants,
all power fo sell and convey real estate at public auction. Graham and
McCauley convey power to Bedford Brown of Caswell County as assignees of
Mark Willson to attend to all business in NC. 27 May 1826.
127 Repeat of same Power of attorney dated 9 Sept. 1826.
129 Power of attorney - Hugh C. Mills of Parish of Feliciana,Louisiana, to
Wilson Hill of Rockingham Co. NC, to convey deeds to lands in Caswell and
Rockingham Counties, NC. 2 Aug 1826. Wit: H. Keller, Jacob G. Keller.

130 FANNY JEFFREYS - Will - w. 26 Jan 1826. Daughter Sally Jeffreys to have all
household goods and effects. Exec: daughter Sally. Wit: Richard Standly,
Nathl. W. Pass.

131 DANIEL MALONE - Will - w. 13 June 1826. Real estate to remain as is until
youngest child is of lawful age. Wife Elizabeth and beloved children to be
supported by estate. Land adj Bird Evans. Sons Lewis and James to have
same part as that already given to sons William and Ellis. Children Huldy,
Lewis, James, Mary, and Eliza each to have a horse at age 18 or when married.
Daughter Sally (Sarah) Stephens. Exec: wife Elizabeth, William and Ellis
Malone. Wit: William Lea, Gabriel Lea.

January Court 1827

135 Inv estate of George W. Lea decd., one undivided third part of sale of lands
belonging to George W. Lea, William H. Lea, and James M. Lea sold under
decree of clerk and master. Interest in negroes now in possession of
Catharine Lea. 8 Jan 1827. By James M. Lea adm.
135 A third inv of Robert Singleton decd. Bonds on Zachariah Hooper, Azariah
Graves, Abisha Slade. By Jeremiah Graves, adm.
136 List of personal estate of Stephen Moore decd belonging to firm of Moore and
Wall.
137 Inv property of George Astin decd taken 18 Oct 1826 by William W. Price, adm.
138 Sales property of George Astin decd sold 4 Nov 1826 to Margaret Astin, Wm. W.
Price, Peter Astin, Edmond Cook, Corbin Jackson, John Keesee.

Book L 1827
Page
139 Inv of estate of Daniel Malone on 5 Jan 1827. Notes on Martha Jackson, Levi
Fuller, Elijah Morton, William Lea, Aaron Fuller, Cuthbert Wagstaf, James
Dollarhide, Mary Wright, Lewis Yealock, Miles Wells, John Love Jun., Joseph
C. Dameron, et al. By Ellis and William Malone exec.

140 Sales of property of William Simpson decd sold by James Simpson adm on 3 Aug
1825. One negro boy Willis sold to James Simpson $361; 1 pair saddle bags
$2.50.

141 Sales estate of Major John Reid decd sold 2 and 3 Nov 1826 to:

Widow Reid	Thomas Reid	Clarissa H. Reid	Wm. B. Reid
George Brooks	George Scarlet	Robert Scarlet	Bernard Boswell
Conway Tapscott	Wm. J. Nash	John E. Brown	Joseph Windsor
John Allen	Tyre H. Brown	Richard Hornbuckle	William Cobb
Anthony Swift	John Willis	Richard Estis	Elye Massey

By Wm. B. and Thomas J. Reid adm.

146 Sales property (negroes) of Lucy Grant decd sold 11 Oct 1826 to John Chandler,
John T. Grant, John Mims, John Gunn. By John T. Grant adm.

146 Sales property of David Lawson decd sold 30 Nov 1826 to Susan Lawson, George
W. Stubblefield, William Weatherford, Thomas Mullins.

147 Sales estate of Griffin Gunn decd sold 17 and 18 Oct 1826 to:

Dorothy M. Gunn	George Martin	Henry Fuquay	Nathaniel Murphey
Abisha Slade	Jonathan Starkey	Bennett Burroughs	Asa Gunn
Saml. Hinton	Nicholas Coile	John Wilson, Esq.	Geo. Williamson
John H. Graves Senr.	Thos. Gunn	Craften Williams	Robert Williams
Gideon Turner	Thomas Harrelson	Benjamin Stephens	Edward Jones
John Roberts	Richard H. Griffith	Thos Cox	Wm. Henderson
Thomas D. Johnston	Nathaniel Lea	Starling Gunn	James Miles
William Campbell	John Gunn	John Johnston	Alexander Donoho
Thomas W. Graves	Tandy Fitts	Jeptha Parker	Jeremiah Graves
Chesley Turner	Joseph Browder	Paul A. Haralson	John C. Harvey
Elijah Graves	William Sawyers	Col. Thomas Graves	Severn Busey
Nathl. B. Pass	Henry Shelton	Anthony Satterfield	John Peterson Sr.
John Peterson Jr.	Jas Peterson	Henry Hooper	Ansel Haddock
Alexander Winstead	Elijah Martin	Daniel Chandler	Eliza Ann Gunn

By A. Gunn, adm.

157 Advertisement of adm with will annexed of estate of Griffin Gunn by A. Gunn.

158 Notes due estate of Maj. John Reid by purchasers at the sale from James
Brown, Anthony Foster, Littleton Leachman, Samuel Smith, James Barker,
David Barker Senr.

158 James Lea exec of Hezekiah Farley decd acct with estate. Interest on N.
Durham's bond since death of Marthey Farley also on bonds of Henry Roper and
James Jeffreys since death of Marthey Farley.
Division of estate to legatees: John B. Farley, Wm. S. Farley, Henry Roper,
Newman Durham, estate of Joseph Farley, and estate of Martha Farley decd.

159 Wm. J. Nash adm estate of David Poynor Senr. decd. in acct with estate.
Payments to John Walker, John Dill, Jere Jones, Elisha Berry, Jo Anna Poynor,
James Walker, David Walker.

160 Elisha Berry adm in acct with estate of William Berry decd. Sales to Elisha
Paschal, Robert A. Brown, Mary Walker, Jno R. Griffith. Examined by A.
Graves, W. J. Nash, Robt. A. Brown.

161 Miles Wells in acct with estate of Claibourn Crisp decd. For hire of negroes
for 2 years. Payments to John Smith, Richard Crisp, David Allison, Jesse
Crisp, Mrs. Sally Hustell, B. B. Epperson, Joseph Allison, et al.
B. Wells receipt for his wife's years allowance.

162 Benjamin Lea adm in acct with estate of Jeremiah Lea decd. Judgments collected on Nathaniel Harrelson, Dabney Rainey, Thomas Rose, Thomas Mitchell; sol-
vent bonds on Martin P. Huntington, Welcome Seymore. (Long list of open
accts.) Payments to James Taylor for crying sale, to Wm. Evans for whiskey
at sale, Thomas Donoho for crying Milton sale, Dennis Heart for advertising.
Credit on Danl. Sullavant (Danville), Samuel Edmiston(Halifax); expenses at

Book L 1827
Page
162-164 Tavern in Fredericksburg, Va. while sick and burial expenses $154.25.
       Notes at Cape Fear Bank at Hillsboro, Newbern Bank at Milton.
165 List of insolvent notes on estate of Jere Lea.
170 Amt of hire of negroes of estate of Wm. Walker for 1827 to William Fitch.
171 Div of negroes of estate of Majr John Reid to Thomas J. Reid, Clarissa Reid,
    William B. Reid, Mrs. Reid (widow Mrs. Keziah Reid). 30 Oct 1826.
172 Power of attorney - Thompson Hardin of Logan County, Ky.,to Joseph Windsor of
    Caswell County to recover money due and to convey deed to all claim to land
    of Hendley Humphreys, 65 acres. 18 Oct 1826.
173 Marriage contract between Samuel Dunaway of Caswell Co. and Elizabeth Tait,
    widow of Robert Tait decd, of Caswell Co. They have agreed to marry and
    since each has children have agreed children should have property now in
    their possession. The property of Samuel to go to his 7 children: Lucy
    Morning, William Dunnaway; Anny, Rosy, Epperson James Dunaway; Lanceson
    Howard Dunaway, and Elizabeth Bazzel. Property of Elizabeth Tait to her
    3 children: Green Hill Tait, James Maddison Tait, Elizabeth Robert Tait.
    6 July 1826. Wit: Jas Yancey, Robert H. Jones.

174 BENJAMIN FIELDER - Will - w. 9 Dec 1826. Wife Susannah Fielder; oldest son
    under age. All my children: William P., Alford, Elizabeth, Sarah, Frances,
    John R., and unborn child. If wife re-marry 2/3 of estate divided to all
    children and wife to have her 1/3's returned to children. Exec: wife
    Susannah, Brother Leonard L. Fielder, Thomas Williamson. Wit: F. Leath,
    George A. Swift.

April Court 1827

178 Inv estate of Mrs. Jane Murphey decd by John McAden adm.
179 Inv property of Benjamin T. Fielder decd taken 3 Feby 1827 by Leonard L.
    Fielder and Susannah Fielder exec.
180 Inv estate of Daniel Hightower decd taken 17 Jan 1827 by William Anderson,adm.
    Sales estate of Daniel Hightower sold 1 Feby 1827 to:

John Comer	Catharine Hightower	Nathaniel Snipes	John Boulding
James Boulding	John Chandler	William Stephens	James Turner
Joshua Rudd	John Crisp	Anthony Satterfield,	Barzillai Nelson
E. G. Kimbrough	David Mitchell	Wm. Winstead	William Fitch
Wm. & John Lea	Henry Allen	Tinsley Lea	William Long
Henry D. Fuquay	Wm. Muzzall	Albert Moore	Wm. P. Jackson
Zephaniah Roberts	Thomas Bigelow	James Hightower	Nelson Thomas
Jno Roan	Thomas Oakley	Geo. B. Dameron	Wm. Mathis
Luke Arnold	Wm. S. Hightower	Thomas Burton	et al
William Anderson, adm.			

186 Sales property of Benjamin T. Fielder sold 2 Feb 1827 to:

John Barker	James Darby	Richard Estis	Anthony Foster
John Fielder	Leachmon Heydon	John Jordan	Wm. Street
Bleuford Pleasant	John Page		

Notes due estate of Benjamin T. Fielder from James Shines, White D. Humphreys,
    William Barker, James Taylor, Leachmon Heydon. Judgments on Crafford Fut-
    rell and E. G. Blake. Open accts on Samuel Fielder, Moses and Aron Simpson,
    James Suddeth, Thomas Jackson, John Stacy, Andrew McCulloch, Lewis Barton,
    Freeman Leath.
188 Div of negroes belonging to estate of Robert Dupuy to his two children,
    Mary Hubbird and Julia Ann Dupuy. Commrs: Joseph Brackin, Jas Burton,
    William Badgett, John Cobb Sen., Henry Howard.
189 Garland Shackleford orphan of age of 12 years the 26 Jan 1827 bound to Severn
    Busey. Woodlief Hooper, Chairman County Court.
189 Kizza Piles orphan now age of 10 years bound to George Williamson until she
    attain 21 years.
190 Mary Cousins orphan age 3 years bound to Archelaus Nunnally.
191 Richard Cousins orphan age og 2 years bound to Archelaus Nunnally.

85

Book L 1827
Page
191 Celia Philips orphan age _____ bound to Archibald Ingram.
192 Jincy Philips orphan age of ___ bound to Archibald Ingram.

July Court 1827

195 ANDERSON MORTON - Will - w. 2 April 1817. Wife Letty Morton all estate real
and personal. If she dies without an heir estate to go to brother William
Morton's children. Wit: Rowzee Samuel, Lewis Samuel.
Doctor John Comer appointed adm with will annexed.

195 JOHN PASCHALL - Will - w. 11 April 1826. All property to remain in possession
of his mother during her life, then to be sold and divided between brothers
and sisters. Exec: brother-in-law Alfred Humphreys. Wit: Zachariah Neal,
John R. Rice. Alfred Humphreys qualified.

196 JAMES BROWN SENR. - Will - w. 19 Nov 1826. Daughter Elizabeth Brown to have
all land and property. Exec: daughter Elizabeth Brown. Wit: Hosea McNiel,
Lucinda Vickers, Malindy Vickers. Elizabeth Brown qualified.

197 WILLIAM WEATHERFORD - Will - w. 20 April 1827. Land on John's Branch to be
sold also crop of tobacco. Wife Temperance Weatherford a tract of land
where I now live 235 acres. One large Bible to daughter Nancy Weatherford.
Son Thomas Weatherford; daughters Nancey, Elizabeth, Polly, Patsey, Sall,
Hepzabta, Citty. Exec: sons Hyram Weatherford and William B. Weatherford.
Wit: Henry Howard, John Cobb Sen. Hyram Weatherford qualified.

198 JOHN H. McADEN - Will - w. 19 Feb 1827. Wife Elizabeth McAden. Son James
McAden; Mother have free possession of house in yard where she now lives plus
20 acres land said land to return to son James. Negroes to be sold and
others purchased for benefit of children: Catherine Anne, Caroline, James,
and Elizabeth Henry McAden until youngest is of age. Exec to appoint guardian
for children. Exec: David G. Brandon and the Revd. John Giles. Test: Malbon
Kenyon, John P. Rainey. John Giles and David Brandon qualified.

200 Inv bonds and accts found in possession of Joseph Cobb decd. Bonds on Hugh
Cobb, Isaac Durham, Daniel Gardner, Henry Cobb, Henry Baldwin, Joseph King,
William Walker, William H. Nunnally, John Ware, John Shields, John Cobb Sr. &
Jr., Mathew Mills, Mark A. Handley, Nancy Cobb, Charles Mitchell, Peter
Badgett, et al.

201 Inv personal property of Joseph Cobb decd by John Cobb Jun. adm.

201 Sales estate of Joseph Cobb decd to Nancy Cobb, Mark A Handly, Hugh Cobb, John
Cobb Jun., Noel Burton, Carter Blackwell, Mathew Mills, James McClarney.

203 Sales property of Nicholas Matlock decd sold 27 and 28 Feb 1827 to:

William Payn	Alexander Kiersey Sr.,	Nathaniel Harrell	Lewis Bolton
Abraham Montgomery	Sherrod Owen	John Lea (CB)	John Gunn
Anthony Read	John Poteet Sen.	William Long	Tinsley Lea
Archibald Lea	A. Ware	John McMurray	Polly Kiersey
Joseph Lunsford	Gideon Gillaspie	John Jones	John Broughton
William Cox	Chesley Turner	Freeman Hubbard	H.W.Gillaspie
Phoenis Hubbard	Samuel Pittard	William Hinton	John Hendrick
Johnston C. McDaniel, Thomas Dyer		George Turner	et al

By Benjamin Matlock and James Matlock exec.

213 Sales property of James Lampkin sold 5 Jan 1807 to: R.G. Lampkin, William
Vaughan, Richd. G. Lamkin, John Morris, Joseph Kitchen, Edmd H. Rice, Richd.
D. Gill, William Kimbrough, James Aldridge, Jno C. Morgan, Thomas Graves,
Jas Page, Littleton Jones, Thos Boswell. By Mary Lamkin exec.

215 Power of attorney - Robert B. Malone, Mitchell Malone, Hutchins Burton in right
of wife Elizabeth and Nashville Malone next of kin to Carter Malone decd and
Lewis G. Malone decd are entitled to their part of estate of these two which
remained in hand of Daniel Malone as guardian or adm of Carter and Lewis.
Alexander S. Malone appointed their attorney to recover from William and

Book L 1827
Page
215 cont. Ellis Malone exec of Daniel Malone decd. 6 Feb 1827. Hutchins Burton
attorney for Mitchell Malone. Recorded from Franklin Co. Ala. 6 Feb 1827.
217 Letters of adm on estate of George W. Lea decd granted to James M. Lea adm.
Sworn to by John C. Vanhook, James Shirley, N. M. Roan. 10 July 1827.
Woodlief Hooper, JP.
217 Acct current with estate of James Lamkin decd by Mary Lamkin exec. Inv of property, met at home of Mrs. Lamkin 13 Oct 1826. Payments from Mitchell Gill
and Wiley Yancey.
219 List of debts paid by Mrs. Lamkin. Paid execution of James Yancey vs the estate; judgment Abner Walker vs Mary Lamkin; payments to William Slade, D & W
Kyle, Ross and Lansdowne, James Nelson, Doct Nathan Turner, Richard D. Gill
for taxes since 1819.
220 Div property of James Lamkin to Jane Lamkin, Sophia Lamkin, G. W. Lambkin,
Richard D. Gill who married Sally W. Lampkin, William Vaughan who married
Susan Lamkin, Richard G. Lamkin, Thomas Graves who married Nancy Lamkin,
Mrs. Mary Lamkin, Grief L. Lamkin.
222 Settlement estate of Peter Strador by Christian Strador, surviving adm and
Mathew Mills, adm of David Strador decd. Recd. cash of Norman's notes,;
recd orphans money.
223 Settlement estate of Peter Strador between adm and legatees to: Rawley Kerns
for his wife Jane, Conrode Strador, William Robertson for his wife Lydia,
Biddy Strador, William McKenzie for his wife Peggy, Henry Strader, Christian
Strader. By Christian and David Strader adm of Peter Strader. 23 Sep 1826.
224 Sanders Edwell orphan now age of ___ years bound to Hiram Weatherford.
224 Henry Edwell orphan bound to Hiram Weatherford.
225 Henry Smith orphan age 15 years bound to Daniel Smith.
226 Election results for 20th Congress held 9 Aug 1827

		for Bedford Brown	- 4 for Augustine H. Shepard
Caswell Court House	- 143	for Bedford Brown	- 4 for Augustine H. Shepard
Milton	257	" 37	"
Quinton Anderson's	115	" 6	"
Jethro Brown's Store	285	" 10	"
Hightowers	145	" 12	"
Leasburg	132	" 7	"
Linn's Old Field	84	" 6	"
Total	1161	84	

October Court 1827

229 Inv property of estate of William Weatherford by Hiram Weatherford exec.
230 Inv estate of the late John Thomas Esq. by R. W. Thomas adm. House and lot on
High St., Milton, 341 acres land. Bond due from persons not living in NC.
230 Inv estate of James P. Carbry decd taken 18 July 1827. Notes on Ludwell Worsham, John Baxter Senr., Robert Ware, Daniel Holeman, Sarah McClarney, Susan
Murphey, Joseph Holderby, Thomas G. Tunstall, James Burns, et al.
By Silvanus Stokes, adm.
231 Sales property of James P. Carbry decd to Thomas Carbry, Benjamin C. West,
George Baskerville, John P. Harrison, William Stokes, Zachariah Hooper, John
G. Womack, William Williams, Hiram Henderson, Armistead McClarney, Holt Mc Clar-
ney, William Cambee, Thomas Swan, John Bays, John Duncan.
233 Inv of Major John Reid decd. Notes on David Barker, Edy Tapscott, William
Chatham. By Thomas P. Reid adm.
234 Inv property of Anderson Morton decd. by Dr. John Comer adm.
235 Sales property of Anderson Morton sold 18 Sept 1827 to William P. Payne, Enoch
G. Davis, Henry Cox, Jeab Robertson, John B. Davis, James Montgomery Jun.,
Alex Kersey, John Jeffreys Jun.
235 2 negroes belonging to estate of Daniel Hightower sold to James Lea Sen and
George Williamson by William Anderson adm.

Book L 1827-1828
Page
236 John and William Chandler adm of Josiah Chandler decd in acct with estate.
    Payments to Joseph Langley, John Chandler Sen., James Yancey, Doctor Comer,
    Solomon Whitlow, et al. Accts examined at store of James Yancey by Yancey,
    C. W. Brooks, and J. Wilson.
237 Alex and John Wiley exec of estate of Thomas Wiley decd acct filed.
238 James and Benjamin Matlock exec in acct with estate of Nicholas Matlock decd.,
    acct filed.
240 Joshua Rudd and Hiram Culbertson exec of estate of William Culbertson decd.,
    acct filed. Amt purchased by Mrs. Parks; amt of Mrs. Libby Parks legacy;
    amt of William Culbertson's legacy. Balance $1741 - each legatee to get $291.
241 GEORGE ELLIOTT JUN. - Will - w. 17 Aug 1827. Wife Julia Elliott; land on
    which his mother lives to go to wife and son. If both die, ½ estate to his
    brothers and sisters and ½ to Julia's sister and half-sisters and brothers.
    Exec: brother William Elliott and Thomas Hamlett. Wit: William Brandon Jr.,
    Jesse Brandon, William McDowell, Thomas M. Hamlett.
    Exec refused to qualify and William B. Pulliam named adm with will annexed.
242 Green Bass orphan now age of 13 years bound to Abel Royster.
243 John Goin orphan now age of 11 years bound to Charles Willson.
244 BARZILLAI GRAVES SEN. - Will - w. 25 June 1827. Wife Usalae(Ursala) to have
    all land and possessions during her life then same to go to 2 daughters,
    Peggy and Mary including all land on south side Country Line Creek, 400 acres.
    After wife's death, negroes to be divided among all children. Negroes already
    advanced to son Solomon Graves and he to have land adj son Jeremiah Graves and
    brother John Graves, 169 acres known as the Tract place. Son Solomon to have
    land between that of Jeremiah and Country Line east of spring branch of son
    Jeremiah known as Cochran's tract. Already advanced to son Jeremiah land
    where he now lives; advancements also to daughter Isbell McNeill and son-in-
    law Hosea; also to daughter Betsy Lea. Exec: sons Solomon and Jeremiah and
    sons-in-law Hosea McNeill and James Lea. Wit: William Russell, Jas. L. Graves.
    Codicil - Spring Branch to be dividing line between land of 2 sons. Estate
    to be accountable for costs that accrue from any law suit which may be in-
    stitited in consequence of claim set up by Azariah Graves (son of John) to
    land which I have devised to son Solomon.
    Solomon and Jeremiah Graves qualified.

                    January Court 1828
247 Sales estate of George Martin to Stephen Smith, Polly Martin, Robert Martin Sen.,
    Henry Harrel, Mrs. Aldridge Rudd, John Miles, Miss Roady Murphey, Nathaniel
    Murphey, Thomas Graves son of Jacob, Josiah Page, John Chandler. By Thomas
    D. Johnston and Nathl. Murphey adm.
248 Inv property of John T. Grant decd. Bonds on Elijah Kennon, Peter Powel, Henry
    Badgett, Robert Hall, et al. By A. Gunn adm.
249 Sales of property of William Weatherford decd to:
    William Badgett   Garland Blackwell Joshua Lindsey   Henry Evins
    Thomas Weatherford David Jones   Andrew Johnston   Hiram Weatherford
    George Scarlet   Eli Ford, Henry Cobb, Robert Mclin,   M. D. Roberts
    E. E. Ragsby   Benjamin Page   Jones W. Collier   Robert Madin
    John Weatherford Sen., Daniel Gardner Hugh Cobb   Henry Howard
    Temperance Weatherford
    Debts due from Caswell Cobb, Benjamin Elmore, Joseph King.
253 John Comer in acct with estate of Margaret Comer decd acct filed.
254 Div of negroes belonging to estate of John Long decd to: William Long, Mary
    Long, Bazel Long, John R. Long, and Elizabeth G. Long. 4 Jan 1828.
    Commrs: John McAden, Richd. J. Smith, Jas W. Jeffreys, James Rainey.

Book L 1828
Page
255 Sales personal estate of Barzillai Graves decd sold 22 Nov 1827 to:

Ingram Chandler	William Graves	Hosea McNeill	Amos Ford
James Lea	Wm. Ashford	William Smith	John Graves
Banister Campbell	Thomas Cox	Asa Gunn	Robert Madden
Elijah Kimbrough	Henry Willis	Azariah Scott	Wm. Watlington
Thomas Graves	Joseph Pinson	Francis Smith	Malon Stacy
Thomas Harrelson	By Solomon and Jeremiah Graves exec.		

257 Inv property of Lucy Cates decd not adm by John T. Grant. Bonds on John Chandler, John Gunn, John Mims. Inv returned by Allen Gunn.
258 Inv property of John H. McAden decd taken 6 Dec 1827 by David G. Brandon and
John Giles exec.
259 Inv of George Elliott decd taken Oct 15 1827. Open accts on Hugh Taylor,
William Hall, Widow Hall, Thomas Brandon, Coalman Jackson, John Hamlet,
David McDowel, James Clay, Joshua Oliver, John W. Brandon, Alex Cuningham.
By William B. Pulliam adm.
260 Inv and sales made by Madison Burke adm of Azariah Burke decd,sold 5 Nov 1827.
261 Additional sale of negro named William belonging to estate of Benjamin T.
Fielder decd sold to James Ruffin for $448. 9 Oct 1827.
261 John Comer in acct with estate of Nathaniel Comer decd acct filed.
262 Gabriel Lea exec in acct with estate of Thomas Phelps,decd. Payments to
following legatees: James P. Roan, Jacob Thomas, Larkin Wisdom, John Stewart,
Elizabeth Wisdom, Allen Wallis, Ann Roan, Rachel Sargent, Elizabeth Sargent,
Patsy P. Roan, Dincy Sargent, Martin Hood, John Smith guardian for Thos. and
Jas. Sargent, William McMurry guardian for heirs of Chas. D. Wade, Alexander
Griffin, James Roan for himself for Sarah Willis and Nancey Keen.
264 Inv personal estate of Barzillai Graves decd taken 13 Oct 1827. Bond on
Connally and Winstead; note of Barzillai Graves (Genl.) 1824 doubtful;
note of Jerry Gwynn doubtful; books accts against James Sheppard, Philip
Walton, Nathl. Murphey.
List of 34 negroes with ages and names bequeathed to widow, Peggy Graves,
Mary Graves, and other legatees. 30 volumes of books.

266 ELIZABETH KIMBROUGH - Will - w. 5 Oct 1827. Already paid to children their
legacies except to son Azariah respecting what they were entitled to from
their father's estate. Granddaughters Betsy Ann Evans, Frances Elizabeth
Chandler (daughter of daughter Polly Chandler), Patsey Kimbrough(daughter of
son Duke Kimbrough);Betsy Kimbrough daughter of son Elijah Kimbrough;
Catherine and Nancy Evans (daughters of daughter Nancey Evans). All children:
Duke and Elijah Kimbrough, Nancy Evans, Polly Chandler,, Azariah Kimbrough.
Exec: brothers Azariah Graves and Elijah Graves. Wit: B. Yancey, Thomas
Graves, William Graves. Exec qualified.

268 Inv and sales of estate of Elizabeth Kimbrough decd taken 15 Nov 1827.
Sales to: Joseph Lunsford, John Chandler, Thomas Harrelson, Josiah Vaughan,
John Morris, Goodwin Evans, Elijah G. Kimbrough, M.D.Kimbrough, Robert
Browning, William Jeffreys, Thomas W. Chandler, Elisha Evans, James and
David Melton, Jeremiah Rudd, John Wilson, James Lea, Azariah G. Kimbrough,
Vincent Griffin, Thomas Johnston, Azariah Graves Jun., Daniel Thomas.

272 OBEDIAH HOLLOWAY - Will - w. 19 Jan 1825. Wife Elizabeth Holloway.
Surviving heirs of daughter Polly Humphreys; daughters Sally Chilton and
Susannah Holloway; heirs of daughter Jinsey Ware; son John Holloway;
daughter Patsey Bucey; son James; daughter Joanna Holloway. Exec: wife
Elizabeth and son John. Wit: Fanny Murphey, William Withers, Elijah Withers.
Exec qualified.

276 ALEXANDER WINSTEAD - Will - w. 15 Dec 1827. All property to be kept together until exec deem division necessary, then to be divided into 4 equal parts to wife Sarah Winstead, son William Alexander Winstead, daughter Elizabeth Payne Winstead, daughter Minerva Jane Winstead. Tract of land in Person Co. to be sold. When possessions leased of Elijah Graves at Caswell Court House expire, exec to find residence for wife and family. Wife has interest in lands in Western Districts, Tenn. which she may dispose of as she wishes. Exec: wife Sarah and friend George Williamson. Wit: Nathl. M. Roan, Elijah Graves Jun. Exec qualified.

277 JOHN HASTING - Will - w. 14 Nov 1822. Son Eldridge Hasting, daughter Obedience Kennebrugh; balance to 4 daughters, Jincey King, Amy Henslee, Nancy Massey, Obedience Kennebrugh. Exec: son Eldridge and son-in-law William Kennebrugh. Wit: Thomas Williamson. Eldridge Hasting qualified.

278 WINIFRED TAPSCOTT - Will - w. 25 Nov 1822. Daughter Betsey Tapscott; all my children. Hannah an old negro woman to be emancipated and free to live with which of the children she chooses. Exec: Betsy Tapscott. Test: John Tapscott. Exec qualified.

279 NATHAN MOORE - Will - s. 8 March 1828. Wife Elender; 4 children, oldest child under age. Exec: wife Elender and brother James Moore. Wit: Freeman Leath, Ellis G. Blake. James Moore qualified.

280 Inv property of David Mitchell decd by Samuel Mitchell adm.

281 Inv personal estate belonging to Harvey Swift decd by John Swift adm. Total amt sales of Harvey Swift sold 7 Feb 1828.

282 Sales of estate of George Elliott decd sold 14 Nov 1827 to Capt. Lewis Bolton, William Elliott, Mrs. Julia Elliott, Archibald Murphey, Bird Pulliam, Walker Bennett.

282 Second inv and sales of Elizabeth Kimbrough decd - one negro boy sold to John Chandler.

283 Sales of goods and chattels of David Mitchell Jun. decd sold 1 Feb 1828 to: Nancy Mitchell, James Currie Sen., Isaac Vanhook, William Bouldin, William Evans, Samuel Nelson, William Pleasant, Sanders Browning, John Mitchell, Joshua Rudd, Joseph Rudd, Thomas Sowel, James G. Vowel, Nat G. Muzzall.

283 Sales property of David Strader decd sold 2 Aug '27 to Josiah Womack, Mrs. Prudence Strader, Edward Bucey, John Bethel, John Cobb, Edward Jones, Thomas Bastin, Mathew Mills, Joseph Cobb, Lewis Strader, William Lewis, Benjamin Covington, James French, Christian Strader, Joshua Butler, Marshell Blackwell, Elijah Dawson, James Rawley. By Mathew Mills adm.

286 Goods and chattels sold of John Bowers decd on 7 Mar 1828 to Stephen Hood, Ransom Haywood, Samuel Keaton, Young Burt, Martin Rear, Wiley Hood. By Samuel Keaton exec.

288 Inv property of Obediah Holloway decd taken 19 Jan 1828 by John Holloway.

288 Amt of hiring of negroes of William Walker decd to Wm. Fitch and Margaret Walker.

289 Div personal estate (negroes) of John H. Brown to Robert W. Lawson and wife Nancy, and to William B. Brown. Commrs: A. Graves, Robert A. Brown, Alfred M. Bethel, Calvin Graves.

289 Div of negroes belonging to estate of Elizabeth Kimbrough which were not disposed of. Met at house of John Chandler. Legatees: Azariah Kimbrough, Goodwin Evans, John Chandler, Duke Kimbrough, Elijah Kimbrough.

290 Settlement estate of Isaac Durham with Martin Durham exec.

291 Power of attorney - Smith Murphey of Morgan County, Ala., to Richard J. Smith of Caswell County to receive from James Grant guardian of Sarah R. Murphey my wife formerly Sarah R. Jones of Wake Co., NC, all monies due them. 4 Dec. 1827. Wit: Alex Smith, William Smith.

292 Nicholas M.Lewis and Ajax Walker adm of Gatsey Lewis decd acct filed. Payment to John B. Ponsonby as part of his legacy. Examined by John R. Clark and James Holder.

Book L 1828
Page
292 John Johnston adm of Samuel Johnston decd acct filed.
294 Willson Gibson orphan age 10 years bound to James Ingram. James Yancey, Chairman County Court.
295 Pinckney Gibson orphan age 8 years bound to James Ingram.

July Court 1828

297 JOHN CAMPBELL , SENR. - Will - w. 25 Mar 1828. Of Milton NC, Caswell Co.
Exec to dispose of swamp lands in Gates County; wife Mary Campbell; 3 child-
ren: William Kinchen, John, and Evelina Belmont Campbell. Exec: Doct James
Webb of Hillsboro my friend and Kinsman, Richard T. Brownrigg of Choan(Chowan)
County, and Andrew Joinor of Halifax, NC. Wit: Sidney S. Walker, Henry
Jefferson Foster.
298 Inv property of Susannah Cantrell decd taken 25 May 1828. Amt recd of Hosea
McNeill guardian of Susannah Cantrell decd.
298 Inv estate of Nathan Turner decd by James C. Turner adm. 7 July 1828. Recd of
Josiah Turner $30.65 due said decd from his grandmother Ann Turner decd estate.
299 Inv estate of John Hasting decd taken 12 Apr 1828 by Eldridge Hasting exec.
299 Balance of sales of William Weatherford decd to Thomas and Temperance Weatherford.
300 Inv property of Daniel Estis decd by Azariah Morton adm. Notes on Bartlett Estis,
James W. Brown, Smith and Chamberlin. Daniel Estis entitled to interest in
crop of tobacco now in possession of Jethro Brown Esq. Note on William Carter.
300 Property sold of Obediah Holloway to John Holloway and Daniel Turner.
301 Inv estate of Alexander Winstead decd taken by Sarah Winstead and George
Williamson exec. Debtors to estate: Elijah P. Mitchell, John Morton, Sarah
Coleman, Robert B. Bumpass for note on Geo Johnston, Patrick M. Glenn, Henry
D. Fuquay, Henry McAden, John R. Fullington, Adam Dixon, Hiram Dollarhide,
James Tilmon, Barnett Winstead, Josias Carver Jr., et al.
Cash on hand recd at Tavern $335.15. (Many notes due the Tavern.)
304 List of notes recd by George A. Connally surviving partner of Connally and
Winstead.
306 Inv property of Archimedes Donoho decd taken 10 Oct 1827. It is agreed between
Charles D. Donoho adm and Mary Donoho the widow that she is to take possession
of all household and kitchen furniture and keep them for her support and for
the children, Richard A., Cornelia, Emily, and Thomas Donoho. Notes due from
Jeptha Parker, Joab Robertson, John Royster; claim of John W. Glenn.
Tobacco in Lynchburg in care of John B. Ray, in Milton ware house and Milton
Stemmery care of Mr. Pugh. By C. D. Donoho adm.
307 Sales estate of Daniel Estis by Azariah Morton adm sold 3 May 1828 to:
John Sanders, Samuel Moore, Nathaniel Estis, E. B. Rice, Richard Estis,
Phoebe Estis, William Turner, Bartlett Estis, James Martin, Lemuel Dabbs,
Jeremiah Rudd, Miles Kimbro, Reubin Owen, et al.
308 Sales property of John Hasting decd sold 9 May 1828 by Eldridge Hasting exec to:

Wm. Kennebrough	Eldridge Hasting	Joseph Pinix	George A. Swift
Spencer Jackson	Thomas Reed	Thomas Garrot	John Massey
Leonard Dabbs	Nathan Massey	John Willis	Charnel Hightower
Jesse C. Page	Robt. Groom	Jarrot D. Figgons	Nicholas Chubb,et al

311 Sales estate of Harvey Swift decd sold 7 Feb 1827 to Mary Swift, Bedford
Haddock, Moses Butler, John Swift, Carter Groom, Thomas Carpenter, Samuel
Groom. By John Swift adm.
312 Settlement estate of David Strador decd by Mathew Mills adm.
313 Acct current with estate of David Lawson decd.
314 Acct current with Azariah Graves county trustee for 1826.
315 Acct current of estate of George Astin decd by William W. Price adm.
316 Power of attorney - John Link of Orange Co. NC, to relative and friend William'
Fuller Jun of same county to receive any portion due from estate of Father
William Link decd late of Halifax Co. Va., agreeable to his last will and
testament. 20 May 1828. Wit: John Love.
316 Berry Jones an orphan of colour age 9 years the 15th of Mar 1828 bound to
John R. Clark.

91

October Court 1828

319 CHARLES DIXON DONOHO - Will - w. 21 Sept 1828. All personal estate to Mother
Kizziah Donoho and all land during her life; nephew Thomas Donoho son of
decd brother Archimedes Donoho all lands and tenements after death of Mother.
If nephew Thomas has no children, land to go to nephew Richard Donoho son of
Archimedes. Exec: friends James Ruffin and George Williamson.
Wit: J. E. Lewis, Jno T. Garland, A. H. Henderson. George Williamson qualified.
James H. Ruffin neither qualified nor renounced his rights.

320 WILLIAM PENICK - Will - w. 19 Jan 1826. Land known as Lucy's Cabin formerly
property of Merada Price decd whereon "I reside" which land Thomas Penick
purchased of Charles Harrison to go to unmarried children and to be sold
when they marry or die. Land on Hogan's Creek, former mansion house to be
sold and divided to 9 children: Sarah T. Penick, Jane M. Penick, Polly W.
Penick, Anna W. Penick, Tabitha F. Penick, Judith F. Penick, Fanny B. Penick,
Harriott C. Penick (youngest daughter) and William G. Penick. Daughter
Prudence. Thomas Sheppard of Person County to be guardian for benefit of
children. Wit: Jas Burton, John Baxter, Judith Penick. Exec: son-in-law
William Stamps of Pittsylvania Co. Va. Wit: Abner W.Clopton, John Hubbard,
Jno. M. Clopton, William Blair. Codicil 7 Nov 1827. As codicil to will not
proven, John Stamps named adm with will annexed. William Blair testified
the witnesses to codicil resided out of state - William Stamps named exec.

322 MARGARET McADEN - Will - w. 21 June 1828. Mother Jannet McAden; Catherine
Ann McAden, Caroline McAden, Elizabeth Henry McAden, daughters of brother
John H. McAden to have balance due from estate of John H. McAden; James
Marion McAden; nephew Robert Echols Hall. Sister Cynthia H. Hall's children;
children of John H. McAden decd. Exec: uncle John McAden. Wit: John Giles,
B. Johnston. Exec qualified.

322 Adm notice: Leonard L. Fielder and Susannah Fielder exec of estate of Benjamin
T. Fielder decd. Proved on oath of Freeman Leath. 22 Sept 1828.
James Kerr, JP.

323 BENJAMIN HOWELL - Will - w. 27 June 1826. Wife Anny to have all possessions
during her life. If son Thomas Howell come back home he to have plantation
and possessions. If he does not return, land to go to lawful heirs of daughter Nancey Glasgow. Exec: friend Samuel Pittard, David Montgomery, Woodson
Howell. Samuel Pittard renounced his right of executorship.

324 Inv property of West Gregory decd by Thomas W. Graves and Francis Gregory.
Sales property of West Gregory sold 27 Aug 1828 to Richard Smith, George
Vaughan, Lemuel Dabbs, Azariah Graves, Goodwin Evans, James H. Ruffin, James
Martin, Elisha Rudd, et al.

327 Power of attorney - William Brandon of Gwinnett County, Ga. to Moses Langley
to collect from estate of Mary Langley late of Caswell Co. 25 July 1828.

328 Levi Vaughan orphan now age of 7 years on 15 June 1828 bound to Joseph
Kitchen. James Yancey, Chairman County Court.

329 George Evans orphan age 13 years on 18 of Jan last bound to Asa Gunn.

329 Henry House orphan age 14 years bound to Thomas D. Johnston.

330 Henderson House orphan age of 16 years bound to Paul A. Haralson until he
attain 21 years.

331 Sanders Edwell orphan age of 15 years bound to Benjamin Elmore to learn the
blacksmith trade.

331 Henry Edwell orphan age 13 years bound to James Cobb.

January Court 1829

335 MARTIN TURNER - Will - w. 21 June 1817. Wife Mildred; daughters Lucy (land
where she lives), Jane, Sally, Nancy Vaughan, Mildred Brooks, Elizabeth Rogers,
Anna Bull(or Ball). Sons Daniel, Thomas, George. Wit: Thos Slade Jr., Thomas
Gunn, Ezekiel Slade. Abisha Slade appointed adm with will annexed.

Book L 1829
Page
336 NATHANIEL M. COMER - Will - w. 16 Nov 1828. All real estate and personal
    property to Brother Doct. John Comer. Exec brother John Comer and Doct.
    Nathaniel M. Comer. Wit: Walker Eskridge, David Hodge, John McAden.
    Doct. John Comer qualified.

337 JETHRO BROWN - Will - w. ND - Wife Lucy W. Brown to have all property during
    her life, then to go to 3 children, William Brown, John E. Brown, Thomas J.
    Brown (3 youngest children). Son James W. now has Poston tract; daughter
    Martha (land purchased of David Hart adj Simon Denny). son Bedford Brown to
    have land whereon he now lives and tract adj Samuel Moore to run south to
    juncture of Country Line and Horsley's Creeks. Son William (land purchased
    of Joseph Lane and to Payne's tract); son John E. (home house tract adj
    Washington Jouett's line to the ford by Shelton's and south to the Tavern
    Tract crossing Country Line with Dr. Johnston's line to Barton's line adj
    Denny and Nash. Lots of land of Sarah B. Carter and Thomas Williamson in-
    cluded in this last tract. Son Thomas J. land called Lower quarter on Machine
    Branch purchased of William Browning adj Samuel Moore, John Stamps, Thomas
    Slade, Richard Smith. Daughter Elizabeth A. Brown to have 25 negroes;
    granddaughters Lucy Ann, Mary Foulkes; grandson William Brown son of Bedford;
    grandsons Livingston and Bedfrod Brown, Edward J. R. Foulkes, John P. Brown,
    Lafayette Brown, Willson Brown; granddaughters Lelia Maria Brown and Susan
    Brown. Exec: 5 sons, James W.,Bedford, Wm.,John E., and Thomas J.
    Wit: Jas E. Williamson, Robert A. Brown Jun. Exec qualified.

340 Power of attorney - Robert Ware of Caswell Co. to friend James Robertson of
    same county to settle all business in NC and to sell tract of land on Dobbins
    Creek, 90 acres. 27 Nov 1828. Wit: William Willson, Green b. Voss, H. P.
    Smithson, Peter Wilson, Melton Voss.
340 Amt of hire of negroes of estate of William Walker to John Hughs and Margaret
    Walker.
341 Div of negroes of estate of George Astin decd to Williamson Astin, Mrs.
    Margaret Astin, William Astin, John Astin.
341 Inv estate of Nathan Turner decd by James C. Turner adm. 5 Jan 1829. Cash
    recd of William Slade Jr. and of Josiah Turner.
342 Inv estate of Abraham Wright decd. Bonds on William Lea, Thos Lea, Wm. M. Lea,
    Wm. Peterson, Anthony Satterfield, James Peterson. By William Lea adm.
342 William B. Reed and Thomas J. Reed adm of Maj. John Reed decd final settlement.
    Acct examined on 31 Dec 1828 by commrs. who met at the home of the widow.
344 Div of negroes of estate of Edwd. M. Foulks decd to Martha Foulks widow, Lucy
    Ann Foulkes and Edward J. Foulkes the children.
345 Francis Gregory and Thomas W. Graves adm of West Gregory decd. Sales of proper-
    ty to William Graves who purchased it for Mrs. Gregory, Devereau Hightower,
    Duke Kimbrough, Henry McKinney, James M. Yancey (1 fiddle), William Turner,
    James Lea, William Gafford, Martin Browning, et al.
345 Allen Gunn adm in acct with estate of Griffin Gunn, final settlement.
349 George W. Jeffreys adm of James Willson decd. Paid Maurice Vaughan a legacy;
    paid John Reed a legacy.
350 William Stamps adm with will annexed of Maj. William Penick decd, inv of estate.
352 Inv estate of Bartlett Yancey decd returned 7 Jan 1829. Part at Lower Planta-
    tion, at upper plantation, at the mill, and at the Mansion House; library
    of law and historical works. Notes in Guilford, Stokes, Randolph, Orange,
    Person, Rockingham and Caswell Counties, NC. By Azariah Graves, adm.

April Court 1829

364 HEZEKIAH BOSWELL - Will - w. 11 Mar 1829. Oldest son Barnet H. Boswell;
    daughter Kitty Roe; son Craven Boswell; wife Nancy and 2 youngest sons Heze-
    kiah and George W. Boswell; daughters Nancy M. and Sarah Boswell.
    Exec: wife Nancy and son Craven Boswell. Wit: Jas Barker, John Bouldin Jun.
    Exec qualified.

Book L 1829
Page
365 Ludoshia Shaw Roberts orphan age of 7 years the 27th Apr 1829 bound to Thomas
Warren until she attain 21 years.
365 Nathaniel Wilmouth orphan age of 17 years bound to Miles Wilmouth.
366 John Hubbird orphan now age of 15 years bound to William Adkins.
367 John E. Brown adm of Ed. M. Foulkes acct filed.
368 Inv estate of John Baxter decd taken 15 Oct 1828 by H. A. Burton adm.
369 Property sold at sale of John Baxter Jun decd to: Jane Baxter, James Burton,
Thomas Ware Jun., Henry Cobb, Robert Madden, David G. Mason, James Ingram,
W. G. Poindexter, Martin Ingram, Mathew Dodson, Jas McClarney, John Duncan,
Dolly Baxter, Sally Baxter, Rachel Baxter, Tolbert Ware, John Sutherlin,
Bennett Burrows, et al.
370 Inv estate of Phoebe Bolton decd and sales to Waller Bolton, Henry Dixon, Levi
Dixon, Joel Thomas, Carter Powell, Zachariah Samuel, William Chiles, John
Jeffreys, John A. Pass, Lydia Bolton, Martin Clay, John J. Oliver.
373 Last sale of Phoebe Bolton, Feb 20, 1829 to Lydia Bolton, Joel Bolton, Green
D. Smith, Lewis Bolton, Joseph McDowell, Dr. Wile Jones.
374 Div of negroes of Thos Bolton decd and Phoebe Bolton decd to: John, Charles,
and Thomas Bolton; Nancy now married to Henry Dixon; Joel, Waller, and Lewis
Bolton; Oney Bolton married to Green P. Smith; Sally married to Levi Dixon;
Lydia Bolton.
375 Inv estate of Nathaniel M. Comer decd by John Comer exec.
375 Inv property of John Chandler decd taken 12 Feb 1829 by Goodwin Evans adm.
377 Inv estate of C. D. Donoho decd by George Williamson exec. Kezziah Donoho
only legatee; after debts paid remainder left in her hands by her request.
378 Sales estate of Charles D. Donoho decd sold 4 Dec 1828 to Kezziah Donoho,
Thomas D. Johnston purchased law books, Alexander Donoho, William Lea, Daniel
A. Penick, William Malone, Calvin Graves (Blackstone's Commentaries) James
T. Morehead purchased Ruffendorf's Law of Nations, Barzillai Graves bought
Hawks Digest, William A. Grayham a book on chemistry, David Montgomery bought
Lewis and Clark Expeditions, Thomas Settle, et al.
379 Acct of sales and inv of property of General Archimedes Donoho decd by James
H. Ruffin adm. Sales to:

R. P. Williamson	John C. Rogers	John Johnston	Mrs. Mary Donoho
John Lea(Cane brake)	Freeman Hubbird	William Long	Tinsley Lea
William Donoho	Joseph Lunsford	Thomas D. Johnston	Moses Kitchen
Thomas Peterson	Zenith Page	Allen Hightower	Alexander Gray
Nicholas Willis	Barzillai Long	Keziah Donoho	John Lea Jun.
Thomas Lea	Christopher Hinton,	James Fullington	John Lamb Jun.
Joseph Singleton	Nathaniel Lea	William Lea	Henry Dixon et al

382 Additional inv of West Gregory decd sold to Connally and Johnston, 1842 lbs.
of cotton at $2 per hundred.
382 Acct current estate of Daniel Hightower decd by William Anderson adm.
384 Inv estate of George W. Lea decd by James M. Lea adm.
384 William Lea adm of Abraham Wright decd amt of sales to John Lea Jun., Nancy
Wright, Thomas Lea Sen., Thomas Donoho, Henry Burton, Geo Williamson, William
T. Glasgow, John Lea CB, Edwd. D. Wright.
385 Inv estate of William Lenox decd taken 3 Aug 1828 by John Lenox adm.
386 Inv property of Nancy Rudd decd. 6 Mar 1829 by Elisha Rudd and Aldridge Rudd.
386 List of accts due Thomas Rose decd returned by R. W. Thomas. Notes on P. H.
Thomas, Martha Rose, John T. Garland, H. M. Clay, Jesse Owen, M. P. Huntington.
387 Inv property of Martin Turner decd taken 8 Jan 1829 by A. Slade adm.
Sales property of Martin Turner to Thomas Turner, William Kennon, William
Clemson, Chesley Turner, John Goodson, Daniel Turner, Warren Holcomb.
388 Sales property of Alex Winstead decd., part of property.

July Court 1829

390 Desdemonia McCullock orphan age 6 years in Feb 1829 bound to Deborah Walker.

Book L 1829
Page
391 THOMAS CONNALLY - Will - w. 14 Mar 1829. 3 sons George Anderson, Charles
Carter, and Thomas Dix Connally to have all possessions and mansion house to
son Thomas. Son John Spencer (Irving tract of land). Children of daughter
Jane K. Maynard (land on which she lives); daughters Eliza and Susannah.
Property in Milton and part of old ware house and lot on which Joseph McDowell
lives to be sold. Some land purchased of William J. Connally.
Exec: 3 oldest sons George, John, and Charles. Wit: Jas Pulliam, David Bran-
don, Wm. L. Connally. George A. Connally qualified.
Will transferred from records of Halifax Co. Va., by Samuel Williams, Clerk.
28 May 1829. Proved Caswell Co. July 1829.

393 SAMUEL LOVE - Will - w. Feb 1829. Daughter Jane Burton (land where she lives
on South Hyco); son Samuel (home tract); daughters Nancy Dameron, Polly McKinney,
Zelpha Burton; son Lewis Hix Love; daughter Elizabeth Mathis to be excluded;
sons John and Allen to be excluded. Granddaughter Nancy McKinney. Land next
to son Samuel Love and William Dameron to be sold. Exec: brother John Love.
Test: Benjamin Stephens, David Montgomery. John Love qualified.

394 ELENDER KING - Will - w. 5 Jan 1829. Money from sale of negroes to be used for
benefit of Mother and sister Jane; sister Margaret Watt; brothers Joseph King
and Robert King. Estate from father Robert King decd and   brother Samuel
King decd. Niece Elmira King; brother Robert's two children William and
Elmira. Exec: brother J. King. Wit: Joseph Bracken, R. W. Totten.
Joseph King qualified.

396 JOHN B. PONSONBY - Will - w.   1827. Wife Elizabeth all property in State of
NC. If wife re-marry property to her and her child or children which she may
have. If more than 1 child wife to have one-third and remaining two-third to
Mary Williams and any child she may have. Wife to educate Mary Williams her
daughter by former marriage. Youngest sister Jane Ponsonby all negroes from
estate of his Father. Three sisters Nancy, Betsey, and Jane to have planta-
tion where Mother lives in Dinwiddie Co. Va., left by his father.
Exec: Brother Thomas Ponsonby and John E. Lewis of Milton. Wit: William
Chiles, Jno T. Garland. John E. Lewis renounced his right to execute;
Thomas Ponsonby is dead; adm granted to Nicholas M. Lewis with will annexed.

398 Report of Azariah Graves, county trustee.
399 Inv and acct sales of Jethro Brown decd sold 4-7 Feb 1829 by Wm. Brown and
Thomas J. Brown. Sales to:

James Adkins	Anderson Brincefield,	Thomas Bigelow	Bedford Brown
John E. Brown	Joshua Butler	Thos J. Brown	David Barker Sen.
Ransom Boswell	Wm. V. Brown	Richard C. Bibb	Alfred M. Bethel
Wm. Brown	William Bethel	Francis Cornwall	Jones W. Collins
Sarah B. Carter	Henry Cobb	Lemuel Dabbs	Lewis M. Denny
George Dabbs	Martha Foulkes	Thomas Gibson	Samuel Groom
Lanslot Johnston Jun.,	Caleb Jones	Robert W. Lawson	Samuel Moore
John Powell	John H. Pickard	Ibzan Rice	Oliver Simpson
James Sanders	Milly Brown	Henry McKinnie	Peter McKinnie
Ira Siddle	Wm. Timberlake	Reid Watlington	Swift Williamson
Emanuel Watlington	Absolem Watt	Paul Watlington	Joseph Young et al

405-7 List of balances on store books of Jethro Brown decd.
408-9 Balances due on Tavern Book of Jethro Brown decd. : William Handley, Miles
Murphey, Nathl Murphey, Edward Murphey, Orthniel Rice, Noah Cobb (son of Henry).
410 Balances due on Post Office Books of Jethro Brown decd.
412 List of bonds and judgments due Jethro Brown.
414 Balances due on Blacksmith shop books of Jethro Brown.
416 Sale of negro woman Maria belonging to estate of West Gregory to Thomas N.
Shelby for $250. Francis Gregory adm.
416 Additional inv estate of Joseph Cobb decd not returned heretofore. Recd from
John Burton, James McClarney, John Cobb Jun., Hugh Cobb.

95

Book L 1829-1830
Page
417 John Cobb Jun. adm of Joseph Cobb decd acct filed.
418 Sales estate of Nancy Rudd decd sold 30 Apr 1829 to Oliver Foulkes, Joshua
    Rudd, Asa Gunn, Lemuel Dabbs, Amos Ford, Josiah Page, Abel Foulkes, Jonah
    Rudd, Thomas W. Graves, Nancy Burk, Azariah and Joseph Morton.
419 James M. Lea adm acct with estate of George W. Lea decd.
420 Inv estate of Major Price decd by Thos L. Price adm.
420 James C. Turner adm acct with Nathan Turner decd. Recd from Josiah Turner,
    William Slade. 9 July 1829.
421 P. H. Thomas acct with estate of T. Rose. Payments to Henry Rose and M. Rose,
    et al. Philip H. Thomas adm Thomas Rose decd.
422 Exec of Zachariah Pattillo decd acct filed.
424 Inv and sale estate of Abel Taylor decd sold 4 June 1829 to Mrs. Frances Taylor,
    Lewis Bolton, William Chiles, Joseph Yarbrough, Elizabeth and John Taylor,
    Polly and Nancy Taylor, Charles Mitchell, James Hamlett. By Lewis Bolton adm.
425 Thomas D. Johnston and Nathl. Murphey adm in acct with estate of Geo Martin
    decd. Recd of John Johnston for Geo Martin interest with crop. Paid Mary
    Martin her year's allowance. Paid to Elijah Martin et al.
426 Settlement estate of William Weatherford decd by Hiram Weatherford exec.
427 Treasurer's acct for Caswell County. Balance of $1133.05.

October Court 1829

430 Inv property of Robert A. Brown decd. Allotment to widow. By Wm. B. Reed and
    Tyree H. Brown adm.
431 Sales of property of Robert A. Brown decd. Sales to Tyre H. Brown, Christopher
    Brown, the Widow, Alfred W. Brown, Wm. B. Reed, Elisha Berry, John & James
    Jones, Thomas Humphreys Jun., John Canada, Jef Brown, Stephen Rice, Zach
    Smithey, Jesse Kendall, William Sartin.
434 Estate of George Elliott decd in acct with William H. Pulliam adm. Paid James
    Stewart guardian; paid the widow Julia Elliott.
435 John Comer adm of Anderson Morton decd with will annexed, acct filed.
    Payment to Mrs. Letty Morton.
436 Gregory Hightower adm in acct with estate of Joshua Hightower decd. Paid William
    Haguewood for coffin $3., 5 yards cambrick for shroud $2.50. Paid Wm. Hague-
    wood for coffin for his wife $2.50. (Accts since 1825.) Payments for cloth-
    ing children. Paid David Hodge for boarding and clothing children 3 years
    $368.84.
438 Second inv estate of Susan Cantrill by James Martin adm. Settlement recd from
    Hosea McNeill.
438 Acct current of James Gillaspie decd by Alexander Gillaspie exec. Paid Nancy
    Gillaspie for her support. Paid land tax in Pittsylvania Co. Va. and in
    Caswell Co. Paid Thomas Day for coffin $19. By Stephen Dodson and James
    Holder.

January Court 1830

441 THOMAS T. HUMPHREYS - Will - w. 8 Sept 1829. Sons Colmore Humfreys, John H.
    Humfreys, Johnathan B. Humfreys; wife Margaret; 3 daughters: Barbara Ann,
    Kitty L., and Margaret C. Humfreys. Exec: John H. and Jonathan B. Humfreys.
    Test: John Powel, Thomas B. Powel.

441 JOHN ELMORE - Will - w. 10 Nov 1829. Wife Polly M. Elmore have house and
    plantation until son Thomas comes of age. Land in Halifax Co. Va., on Dan
    River, 48 acres, to return to wife if she re-marry as it came by inter-marri-
    age. Son Anderson(under age); daughters Elizabeth McCain, Mary Elmore, Lucy
    Elmore, and Martha Elmore. Thomas Elmore to get Caswell Co. Plantation.
    Son William $5. Exec: friend John C. Rogers and son Anderson Elmore.
    Wit: Laban Farley, John Durham.

443 GEORGE HUSTON - Will - w. 20 Nov 1829. Wife Mary Ann Husten (land adj John Russell and Aaron Lea); after death of wife property to be sold and divided among lawful heirs. Exec: wife Mary Ann, & friend John Russell. Wit: Jno B. McMullen, Isaac Vanhook. John Russell qualified.

444 Amt of hire of negroes of William Walker decd to James Graham, Margaret Walker, William Hughes, Henderson Smith.

445 Sale property of John T. Grant sold 9 Nov 1828 to Tho Foster, Thos. Cox, Eaton Dickins, Martha Cates, Miles Wilmouth, Bennett Boroughs, John Scott, Henry Badgett. By A. Gunn adm.

445 Inv property of James Sherley decd. 1 side board, a cow and calf; stallion and 1 horse left in Tenn. by said Sherley. By James W. Jeffreys, adm. 30 Sept. 1829. (Also spelled Shirley)

446 Inv of E. Ponsonby's property, household and kitchen furniture by N. M. Lewis, adm. 22 Aug 1829.

446 Return of sales of land of William Penick decd by William Stamps exec.

447 Sales property of James Lea decd by A. V. Lea adm sold 29 Dec 1829 to: Samuel and Walker Eskridge, Archibald Lipscomb, John Russell, Albert Moore, Andy M. Woods, Saml. Overby, Isaac Vanhook, Nancy D. Lea, James Lea, Jack Rose, John Bradsher, Thos Eskridge, Thos Currie, Thos Brooks, James Snipes, Elijah Jacobs.

449 Amt of sale of tobacco of estate of Phoebe Bolton decd sold by Lewis, Charles, and Thos Bolton adm.

449 Sales property of John Chandler sold 17 Nov 1829 to:

Mary J. Chandler	Azariah G. Kimbrough,	Aldridge Rudd	William Graves
James Evans	Stephen Smith	Robert Martin	Philip Hodnett
Thomas W. Chandler	William Turner	James Vaughan	Amos Ford
Rainey Currie	Edmond Turner	Nathaniel Snipes	William Pleasant Jr.
Elijah G. Kimbrough,	Benjamin Bowden	John Murphey	Wm. Fullington
James R. Lea	John Morris	John Miles	George Lamkin
James M. Yancey	Miles Kimbrough	William Richmond	

By Goodwin Evans adm.

453 Property sold by adm of Green D. Smith decd sold 19 Dec 1829 to: Thomas and Charles Bolton, John Mason, Kindle Vanhook, James Dollarhide, Archibald Lipscomb, Anderson Brooks, Thomas Greenway, Elijah Jacobs. By Oney Smith, adm.

456 Proportionate part of div of negroes of estate of Griffin Gunn on 30 Dec 1829 to Jones M. Gunn, to Elijah Graves intermarried with Eliza Gunn.

456 Settlement estate of Henry McClarney by Robert McClarney adm.

457 Report of Allen Gunn adm of Lucy Cates decd.

458 Report- Allen Gunn adm of John T. Grant decd. Paid Lucy Grant's estate for purchase of negro Peter at sale of said Lucy.

460 Allotment to Oney Smith, relict of Green D. Smith decd for year's provisions.

460 Allotment to Frances Taylor relict of Abel Taylor decd for one year's provisions for her and family. April 1829. John P. Rogers JP.

461 Lunsford H. Hunter orphan age 15 years the 25 June 1829 bound to Charles L. Hunter to learn the art of a Bricklayer.

461 Robert Keen orphan age of 20 years bound to Richard Hornbuckle.

462 JOHN GRAVES SEN. - Will - w. 9 Jan 1826. Wife Elizabeth to have mansion house and plantation from mouth of Meeting House branch to spring to road to Caswell Court House to Fuller's Branch to the creek for her lifetime. Wife to have furniture which she had before their marriage. Daughter Polly Graves (land whereon I live inc mill which was purchased of son Barzillai Graves, 412 acres, and joint use of mansion house whereon I reside. Daughters Betsy Kimbrough and Delilah Miles to get Moon's Creek tract of 1000 acres, Delilah to have part where she now lives and then to go to all her children with children of her first marriage to David Womack to get 2/3 of Delilah's part. Have advanced property to all children real and personal and in some cases no titles executed - also to sons-in-law intended for their wives- hereby ratify and

Book L 1830
Page -
    confirm all such advancements. Son Azariah to have 5 acres around his Tanyard.
All property to be evaluated and equal division to children by 5 men appointed
to appraise estate and each child to account for advancements already recd.
Enjoin children to allot negroes among themselves and not to separate any man
from wife. Exec: sons Thomas, Azariah, Elijah, and William Graves and they
to serve without charge. Wit: Jeremiah Graves, Lewis Evans.
Codicil - 28 Aug 1829 - Tract of land on Moon's Creek given to daughter
Elizabeth Kimbrough and equal part of rest of estate to be null and void.
Children of said daughter, Nancy Evans, Polly Chandler, Duke W. Kimbrough,
Elijah G. Kimbrough, and Azariah G. Kimbrough to have $1500 divided amongst
them. This to be considered their Mother's part of estate after her advance-
ments. Wit: Jeremiah Graves, Paul A. Haralson. All exec qualified.

April Court 1830

467 Thomas Phelps orphan age 3 years bound to James Ingram. Thomas W. Graves,
    Chairman County Court.
468 Robert Philips orphan now six years old bound to James Ingram.
468 Jackson Yates orphan age 12 years bound to Richard Durham.
469 Power of attorney - William M. Dameron to father George B. Dameron and brother
    Joseph C. Dameron to sell land on N. Hico, 196 acres. 19 Nov 1829. Wit:
    Joseph Dameron, Thomas Burton.
470 Allotment to Mary Chandler widow of John Chandler decd. 10 Nov 1829.
470 Adm notice from exec of Jethro Brown 18 Feb 1829. Advertisement placed at
    Thomas Williamson's store, Ibsan Rice's Tavern, at store of Moses and Jno E.
    Brown, and at Caswell Court House.
471 Sales property of Abel Taylor decd sold 2 Feb 1830 to Mrs. Taylor, Richard
    Taylor. By Lewis Bolton adm.
472 Inv property of Thomas T. Humphreys decd taken 1 Mar 1830 by John R. Griffith
    and Margaret Humphreys Sen.
472 Sale property of Robert A. Brown to William B. Reed, Christopher W. Brown,
    Alfred W. Brown, and Tyre H. Brown. By William B. Reed and Tyre H. Reed adm.
473 James Martin adm of Susan Cantrill decd. Money recd of Hosea McNeill as
    shown in inventory. James Martin indebted to estate, $481.13. 31 Mar 1830.
474 Sales of John Elmore decd sold 19 Jan 1820 to: Mary Elmore, Richard Paylor,
    Allen McCain, James W. Jeffreys, Booker Boman, Tittolson McCain, Lucy A.
    Elmore, Abraham Montgomery, Sidney McGehee, John Paylor.
    By John C. Rogers exec.
475 Inv personal estate of James Yancey decd,included 120 volumes books.
479-481 Inv and names of negroes of James Yancey. Balances on store books of
    James Yancey, nearly all balances desperate or doubtful.
481 Balances due on shop books of James Yancey for year 1829.
482 Balances due on shop books of James Yancey and Edmund B. Rice for 1819-1828.
483 Bonds due James Yancey, most desperate or doubtful.
    By J. Wilson and Z. Yancey adm.
487-508 Sales personal property of James Yancey sold 4 Feby 1830 to:

William Turner	James R. Lea	Allen Gunn	Thomas D. Johnston
Stephen Chandler	John Payne(Tailor)	Brice Collins	John Murphey
Goodwin Evans	Josiah Vaughan	Edmund Turner	Howard Martin
James Love	Jeremiah Graves	Richard Smith	Jacob Henderson
Joshua Rudd	Thomas W. Chandler,P. H. Hodnett		Joel Motley
William Bird	Thomas Eubanks	Abner Gooch	Elisha Evans
Pleasant Corbit	Thomas Sawyers	Samuel Hughs	James Vaughan
Archibald Burke	William Long	E. C. Rochmond	John Smith
Samuel Moore	Booker Boman	Elisha Rudd	Thomas Harrelson
Gideon Turner	Laban Ford	William Vaughan	Joseph Aldridge
Thomas Davis	John Pinson	John Johnston	Durett Oliver
James M. Yancey	Daniel Thomas	John Graves	Henry D. Turner
William Graves	Bluford Pleasant	Aldridge Rudd	James Sawyers

cont. page 99

Book L 1830
Page

Sales of James Yancey cont. to:

Alexander Smith	Banister Campbell	Benjamin Penix	Littleton Gwynn
Nathan Massey	Joseph Lunceford	Joseph Massey	James Martin
Nathaniel Murphey	Azariah G. Kimbrough,	Miles Kimbrough	Warren Holcomb
Williamson Dameron	William Barnwell	Rainey Currie	Christopher Brooks
Joseph Rudd	Benjamin Bowden	Thomas Gunn	Henry Willis Jun.
Thomas Greenway	Jonathan Smith	Thomas W. Graves	John Corbit
Elijah G. Kimbrough,	William Smith	John Browning	Ransom Boswell
Jesse C. Page	Samuel Dameron	Amos Ford	Sanders Browning
Jeremiah Rudd	Isaac Cantrill	Martin Browning	Tho. W. Harrelson
Samuel W. Richmond	Wm. Fullington	Elijah Graves	James Gunn
George Walker	Frances Gooch	Duke Kimbrough	Thomas Starkey
Alexander Gray	George Lamkin	Anderson Burke	Thomas Burton
Zena Page	Josiah Page	James Faucett	Nicholas Willis
Devereau Hightower	William Stalcup	Jacob Bruce	Elijah Martin
Robert Martin	Polly Johnston	John Miles	George Simmons
Wm. Hightower	Wm. McKinney	Henry Tait	Dr. Henry McAden
Berry Evans	John Dameron	John Snipes	George Williamson
Luke Arnold	James Simmons	Vincent Griffin	David Melton
James Turner	George Dabbs	Wm. F. Davis	

509 Administrative notice of J. Wilson and Zilpah Yancey as adm of estate of James
Yancey. 15 Jan 1830. Copy seen at Court House door, in Milton, Leasburg,
at James Kerr's Store.

510 REUBIN TAYLOR - Will - w. 12 Oct 1829. Wife to have land where they live for
her life then to go to 2 sons Moses and Charles Taylor. 2 sons to get land in
Person County adj George Taylor and Thomas Hamlet. Son George Taylor to have
wearing apparel. Has already given to rest of children. Exec: sons Moses
and Charles Taylor. Wit: James Rainey, William Chiles. Moses Taylor qualified.

510 COL. GEORGE LEA - Will - w. 4 May 1826. Heirs of daughter Mary Logan Johnston,
Jennett Logan Johnston and her sister Sally Stanfield. Son William A. Lea
all of other property. Exec: son Wm. A. Lea and Abner Lea.
Wit: Abner Lea, Simeon Lea, Lewis Haguewood. William A. Lea qualified;
Abner Lea renounced his right to execute.

512 JOHN BARKER - Will - w. 20 May 1818. Brother George Barker $500. Susannah
Taylor $150; sister's son Freeman Leath balance of real and personal property.
Exec: nephew Freeman Leath. Test: James W. McCain, William Harbin.
Freeman Leath qualified.

513 GRIEF L. LAMPKIN - Noncupative will - Subscribers were at house of Mrs. Mary
Lampkin on 27 Feb 1830 when he became sensible of his approaching dissolution
and asked them to dispose of his property as follows: brother Richard Lampkin
to have all property and he would dispose of property as agreed upon. He
expired the next morning. 2 March 1830. /s/ Pleasant Corbit, Elizabeth W.
Dabbs. Will recorded as none of family of Grief Lampkin objected. Adm
granted to Richard G. Lampkin with will annexed and he qualified.

514 Div negroes of Robert A. Brown to: William B. Reed and his wife Ede, John and
Harris Brown, Lydia Brown, Alfred Brown, Christopher W. Brown, Robert A.
Brown. 19 Jan 1830.

515 Azariah Graves and Elijah Graves exec of Elizabeth Kimbrough decd acct filed.

515 Acct current estate of David Mitchell Jun. decd by Col. Samuel Mitchell adm.
Note on Philip Cook; execution vs Thomas Wilson

517 Acct current of William Walker decd by Connally Walker adm. Payment to
Margaret Walker.

519 Div negroes of David Mitchell Jun. to Nancy Mitchell, widow, to Elizabeth
Ann Mitchell the only child. 8 Feb 1830.

Book L 1830
Page

July Court 1830

521-527 Inv and sales estate of John Graves decd. Sales to:

John Morton	John Scott Sen.	William Graves	Jonathan Smith
John Mansfield	Azariah Graves	James Mitchell	Mathew Dodson
Wm. T. Glasgow	James White	William Badgett	Col. Thomas Graves
Thomas W. Graves	Jesse Atkinson	Elijah Graves Sen.	Thomas D. Johnston
P. H. Womack	Peter Badgett	Nath. Duncan	Alexander Donoho
Azariah Scott	Peter Powell Sen.	David W. Jones	Dennis Willson
John Mims	Joseph King	Elijah Graves Jun.	Dixon(a negro)
Abner Miles	John Baxter	James Lunceford	Lemuel Dabbs
Goodwin Evans	Stephen Chandler	Bedford Haddock	Jonathan Starkey
Ingram Chandler	Jeremiah Graves	James R. Lea	Devereau Hightower
Virgil M. Rainey	Elizabeth Graves	Gen. Barzillai Graves,	Nancy Yancey
Azariah Graves Jun.	Jim(a negro)	Frank(a negro)	Polly Graves, et al

528-534 Inv of notes (dating back to 1802) and property not sold at sale of John Graves.

535 Sales property of John Anderson decd sold May 1830 to: Joseph Ector for his wife, Quentin Anderson, James Ector for his wife, James Barker, Sarah Anderson, Elizabeth Anderson, John Mitchell for his wife, James Anderson, Buford Pleasant, Rice Barton, Christopher Brooks, William Mitchell, et al.

539-541 Refunding bonds for estate of John Anderson from James Ector, Joseph Ector, John Mitchell, James Anderson, Sarah Anderson, Elizabeth Anderson.

542 List of strays taken up by John C. Vanhook, Ransom Boswell, Jethro Brown, John Pinson Sen. By William Lea, Ranger.

543 Acct current estate of Harvey Swift decd by John Swift.

546 Sales estate of Major Price decd by Thomas S. Price adm. Names not given.

548 Inv property of Robert Singleton decd. Bonds on Abisha Slade, Joseph and William Dameron. By Jeremiah Graves adm.

549 Inv estate of Grief L. Lamkin decd. Note on Mary Lamkin; note executed to William Cody on Richd D. Gill; notes on Jane S. Lamkin, Josiah Dabbs, and Thomas Graves. By R. G. Lamkin adm.

549 Inv property of John Morris decd taken 8 May 1830 by Thos. W. Harrelson. Bonds on James Holder, George Dabbs.

550 Report of Wardens of the Poor for 1829. Balance on hand $1869.05. Money collected from land tax and black and white poll taxes. Fines collected by Woodlief Hooper Esq., Miles Poteat, Mildred Thomas, Sol Whitlow. Paid John McMurray salary $275 for 1829, Martha Hubbard for weaving, Connally and Winstead for molasses and corn, Nat Lea for ironing wagon, Thomas Gunn for wool. Paid Bird Eskridge for maintaining and burying a negro formerly property of Richard Ogilby $5.00. Recommended tax be raised to 4 cents on landed property and 10¢ on the poll.

552 Inv estate of George Huston decd taken Nov 1829 by John Russell exec. 270 acres land willed to Mary Ann Huston wife of decd. Judgments on Thomas Man and Dunkin Rose.

552 Inv of Elizabeth Matlock decd by William Lewis adm. No property nor debts due except a claim against James Matlock involving profits alleged to have been received by him during lifetime of intestate.

553 Inv estate of Anslem Haddock decd by Stephen Haddock adm.

553 Azariah Graves, county trustee, acct current with Caswell County.

554 John Goin orphan age of 15 years bound to John J. Oliver.

554 Henry Bennett orphan age of 7 years bound to George Garrott.

555 Thomas Bennett orphan age of 10 years bound to William Gwyn. Henry Allen, Chairman County Court.

556 Report of John Holloway guardian of Susan Humphreys and sale of her land to Burrell Hagwood.

556 Div of negroes and land of William Walker decd to Mrs. Margaret Walker widow, Catherine Walker; Jane, Philip, Barbara, and Lucinda Walker.

100

Book L 1830-1831

Page

558 Martha Harriott Jones orphan age 11 years bound to William Chiles.

559 Power of attorney - John Stewart of Bledsoe Co. Tenn., to Thomas Roan to collect from Gabriel Lea exec of Thomas Phelps decd part of estate due him.
29 Sept. 1825. Wit: James Roan, James P. Roan.

560 THOMAS SLADE SEN. - Will - w. 11 Aug 1827. Wife Isbell Slade. Son William to
have land on Rattlesnake Creek. Land includes Thornton Tract and tract bought
of brother William Slade. After wife's death, daughters Isbell and Susan to
have her 300 acres land. Daughter Nancy Stamps and her husband John Stamps
to have mill tract; son John; daughter Polly Graves the widow of James Graves.
Children of Nancy Stamps. Exec: son William Slade, Genl. Azariah Graves, and
Azariah Graves of Caswell Court House. Wit: B. Yancey, William Russell.
Calvin Graves and Joseph C. Dameron proved the signature of B. Yancey as he
is now dead. William Slade qualified.

October Court 1830

565 Power of attorney - In New Orleans, La., on 20 March 1830, Abner Nash of St.
Mary's Parish, Atlaskepas, to William Junius Nash formerly of Caswell County,
now of New Orleans, to transact all business in Caswell Co. and to dispose
of land.

566 Daniel Estes acct current by Azariah Morton adm.

567 RICHARD ARNOLD - Will - w. 19 Apr 1830. Wife Mary Arnold. 3 daughters: Elizabeth, Rachiel, and Mary White Arnold. Ann Patterfoot (Pettifoot?) shall
have her freedom recorded in Caswell County when she is of age at expence of
the estate. Exec: friend the Revd. John Stadler, and Thomas Prendergast.
Wit: Tho Prendergast, Isham Turner, James Turner. Tho Prendergast qualified.

January Court 1831

568 Acct current of estate of Mrs. Jane Murphey decd by John McAden adm, also in
acct with Archibald D. Murphey surviving trustee of last will of Col. Archi-
bald Murphey. Div estate of Jane Murphey to: Dr. John McAden and wife,
Herndon Haralson and wife, Solomon Deboe and wife, John G. Murphey, Arch D.
Murphey, the exec of Alexander Murphey, children of Lucy Daniel decd.
Arch. M. Deboe signed for part his father Solomon Deboe was due.

572 Power of attorney - Hugh C. Dobbins to brother-in-law Joseph C. Dameron to
sell land on Reedy Fork Branch of North Hyco in Caswell Co., 100 acres.
2 Nov 1830. Wit: John Montgomery, Barzillai Wisdom.

572 Power of attorney - Rhodeham Lovelace of Caswell Co. to Bruis Lovelace of
same county to sell land belonging to him and to Joshua Butler, 250 acres on
Moon's Creek. 1 Oct 1830. Wit: John C. Totton, J. S. King.

573 Power of attorney - Jesse Kirk and Francis Kirk his wife of Grayson Co. KY, to
our brother John Gray of Sumner Co., Tenn., to sell land 300 acres in Caswell
Co., land on which John Gray resided at his death, said Francis being an
heir and due 1/5 of said part of land. 4 Aug 1830.

575 Power of attorney - Cosby Dickinson and Letha Dickinson late Letha Gray of
Pope Co., Illinois, to John Gray of Sumner Co. Tenn., to recover from estate
of John Gray. 8 Sept. 1830.

576 Power of attorney - Joseph Russell Sen. of Prince Edward Co. Va., to William
Russell to sell a negro man, Jack, for purpose of paying Joseph Russell Jun.
decd. debts of Guilford Co., NC. 10 Dec 1830. Wit: Wm. R. Boulton.

577 Power of attorney - Azariah G. Kimbro of Caswell Co. to Goodwin Evans of same
county to attend to all affairs. 6 Nov 1830. Wit: N. M. Roan.

577 Edwell Sanders age 19 years bound to James Cobb Sen.

578 Allotment to Sarah Morris from estate of John Morris decd her late husband for
her and family.

579 Allotment to Nancey Hodge and family.

579 Inv property of Robert Singleton decd. Bond on John Womack.

Book L 1831
Page
580 Inv personal property of David Hodge decd an 14 Oct 1830. By William Long
and Nancy Hodge adm.
581 Inv estate of Mary Woods decd by John Woods adm.
582 Sales property of John Morris decd sold 10 Aug 1830 & 15 Oct to: Martin Browning, John Willson, James Evans, Sally Morris, James Vaughan Sen. & Jun., Joseph
Kitchen, Thos Harrelson Sen., Josiah and John Vaughan, George Lampkin, Joseph
Aldridge, Nancy Vaughan, John Corbit. By Thomas W. Harrelson adm.
584 Inv and sale of property of Joshua Bevers decd taken 29 Oct 1830 by H. A. Burton,
adm. (Also spelled Beavers). Sales to W. Pass, James Burton, Polly Beaver,
Hiram Henderson, Wm. Burton, Henry Badgett, Benjamin Hooper, John Mims, Thomas
Hailey, Nathl Burton, Daniel Garner.
585 Administrative notice of Thos W. Harrelson as adm of John Morris displayed at
Court House, Edmund'Rice's shop, Quentin Anderson's store.
586 Sales property of Mary Woods decd to Alexander Gray, Joseph D. Hughs, William
Richmond, John Johnston Doct., William Woods, Benjamin Stephens, Joseph C.
Dameron, Thomas and James Woods, Daniel Richmond, Andy Woods, Archibald M. Lea,
William A. Richmond, Jesse Dunevent, Wm. Wilkerson. By John Woods adm.
588 Sales estate of Mrs. Jane Murphey decd sold 23 Feb 1827. Among buyers: Layton
Tapley, John Paylor, Richard Gates, Uriah and Thomas Stafford, James Hamlett,Sr.
Thomas and William McGehee, Durrett Oliver, Benj. F. Stanfield, Thomas Ken-
drick, William Herring, David G. Brandon, Travis Bennett, V. M. Murphey,
William Ashley.
592 Articles sold at John Elmore's decd by J. C. Rogers to Mary Elmore, Tillotson
McCain, Joel Thomas, Anderson Elmore, Charles Mitchell, Moses Powel, Richard
Gates, John Hamblet, Booker Bbman.
596 Sales property of Benj. T. Fielder decd. A negro woman and 2 children sold to
Bennet Hazle for $425.
596 Sales estate of Thomas Slade decd by William Slade exec to: William Chandler,
William Graves, Durrett Oliver, William Russell (land inc the Thornton tract),
James Melton.
597 Second sales of John Graves decd sold 19 Nov 1830 to Granderson M. Sharp,
Polly Graves, William Graves, Thomas Gunn, Azariah Graves, Robert Madding,
James R. Lea, William C. Donoho, Paul A. Haralson, et al
599 Sales personal property of David Hodge decd sold 4 Nov and 15 Dec 1830 to:
Wm. & Benjamin Stephens, John Lea, John Love Jr., Alfred Lea, James A. Kersey,
Samuel Hodge, Ambrose Nelson, Joel Thomas, David Hodge, Bazl. M. Long, Thomas
Waterford, Alexr. Gray, Archd. Lea, William Overby. By Wm. Long adm.
610 Inv estate of Thomas Slade Sen. decd.
602 Div negroes belonging to estate of Samuel Henderson decd. 23 Nov 1830 to:
Minerva married to Dr. Allen Gunn, Harriott Married to John Easley, Ludolphus
Henderson, James Henderson, Frances A. Henderson.

604 WILLIAM McDANIEL - Will - w. ND- Wife Jane; children of son John McDaniel;
children of deceased daughter Elizabeth Darby; 2 granddaughters Matilda Leigh
and Juliet Leigh, children of William Leigh and my daughter Polly Leigh.
Son Hiram McDaniel; 2 grandchildren John J. McDaniel and Johnston McDaniel
sons of son William McDaniel decd. Exec: friend Alexander Gordon.
Wit: John Vanhook Jr., Will A. Lea.

605 Acct current estate of John Lea decd. Payments to legatees: Mrs. Betsy Lea
widow, Benjamin Matlock, James Lea, William Lea, John Lea Jun., Nancy Lea,
Judy Lea, and Yancey Oliver.

606 Dr. John McAden adm and Betsy Lea adm of estate of Capt. John Lea decd. Execution anti John Stamps. Note on Jesse Carter due 1805 paid by James Thompson
and Ambrose L. Bennett. Note on Freeman Hubbard; note on Jonathan Lea of
Clark Co. Ga. due 1805 barred by state of Georgia. Notes on Christopher Hinton
decd. and Wm. Hubbard for one dollar and he died in army.

Book L 1831
Page   April Court 1831
608 Acct current estate of John Chandler decd with Goodwin Evans adm.
613 Acct current estate of Robert Singleton decd. Bonds on William Russell,
    William Lyon, George Bollinger, et al.
615 Acct current estate of Samuel Love decd by John Love Sen. exec.
616 Acct current estate of John Baxter decd with Henry A. Burton adm.
617 Acct current estate of William Walker decd. 6 legatees all of legal age.
    Four remaining bonds filed from Margaret Walker, William Walker and wife Jane,
    Catherine Walker, Philip Walker.
618 Power of attorney - John Humphries of Caswell Co. to Burwell Hagood of same
    county to demand and recover from estate of the late Obediah Holloway, to wit:
    Mrs. Elizabeth Holloway exec and John Holloway exec the part due him after
    the death of Mrs. Holloway. 19 June 1829. Wit: Thomas Hagood, John Hagood.
618 Power of Attorney - Archibald D. Darby of Orange Co., NC, about to remove to
    Missouri to father James Darby at attend to all business and to recover
    claims against estate of Nathan Moore decd. 7 Apr 1830. Wit: George Walker.
619 Power of attorney - Thomas Ballard and Mary Ballard his wife, formerly Mary
    Garner, of Bedford Co. Tenn., to Barnet Boswell of Caswell Co. to recover
    from estate of Watson Garner decd in Caswell Co., to George Swift his heirs.
    Mary Ballard legal heir of Watson Garner.; also to receive money from real
    estate from said George Swift. 9 Jan 1831. Wit: Wm. D. Orr, John Bruce.
620 Inv estate of John Astin decd by Isaac F. Bucey adm. Negro man Bevely and
    girl Rebecca. 8 Feb 1831.
621 Inv property of James Smith decd by Thomas H. Smith adm. Supposed interest in
    negro woman name of Brister in possession of William Graves in suit in Superior
    Court.
621 Inv property of Reubin Taylor decd by Moses Taylor exec.
622 Acct sales of George Huston decd sold 11 Nov 1830 to: Anne Street, Mary Ann
    Huston, Robert Huston, Elijah Morton, Elijah Jacobs. Tobacco sold in Lynch-
    burg, Va. ½ to William Huston as his share of crop; ½ to estate of George
    Huston. By John Russell exec.
623 Acct sale of negroes of Thomas Slade decd to Barzillai Graves Jun., Isabella
    Slade, William Russell, Susan L. Slade. 3 negroes valued to Nancy Stamps.
623 Acct of sales of James Yancey - rent of plantation to E. G. Kimbro. Sale of
    negroes to Thomas Burton, William Barnwell, John Corbit, Joshua Rudd, Thomas
    Bigelow.
624 Sales of Saml. Love decd sold 29 July 1829 to John Love Jr., James Gallaugher,
    Samuel Love, Allen Love, Richard Kiersey, Frances Day, James M. Drake, et al.

626 MARY KERR - Will - w. 20 July 1828. Granddaughter Mary Kerr, daughter of son
    Barzillai Kerr and her brothers and sisters. Daughters Polly Lea, Isbell
    Brooks, Betsy Penick, and exec for use of Nancy Lea. Son James Kerr.
    Exec to retain 1/8 part of estate for Nancy Lea and her children Calvin,
    Alvis, James, Cornelia (others advanced property). Daughter Mary Lea and her
    children Mary, John Franklin, Jeremiah, Martha, and Alexander Lea. Children
    John Kerr, James Kerr, Solomon Kerr, Isabell Brooks and Betsy Penick each to
    have 1/8 part. Children of son Barzillai Kerr, Mary, Nancy, Isbell, Barzillai,
    and Alexander Kerr to have 1/8 part due the father if he had lived. Exec:
    son James Kerr. Wit: B. Yancey, Stephen Sawyers. James Kerr qualified.

627 RACHEL CHRISTY - Will - ND - Hannah Crawford(bonnet, coat, and black dress);
    Rachel Paschal's second daughter ; books to youngest child Rachel may have.
    Remainder of property to Rachael Paschall also a debt on John Simpson, likewise
    all part of estate of step-father. Test: Ziba Rice.
    Reported to be the noncupative will, and after publication for 6 weeks for
    nearest of kin and no appearances, will admitted to probate as recorded.
    By Ziba Rice.

103

Book L 1831
Page
628 ISAAC CANTRILL SEN. - Will - w. 11 Nov 1830. Nephew Alexander Rob Cantrill;
    Isaac Cantrill Jun. due legacy from Isaac as guardian for Alexander. If
    Alexander has no heirs, his brother Joseph should have his property. Nephew
    Joseph Cantrill son of Benjamin; nephew Isaac Jun.
    Exec: Isaac Cantrill Jun. Wit: James Taylor, Geo W. Taylor.
    Isaac Cantrill Jun. qualified.

630 JAMES FULLER - Will - w. 14 Jan 1826. Son Levi; heirs of son James Fuller.
    Daughters Frances and Nicy; son John N. Fuller. 5 children: Levi, Mary,
    Frances, Nicy, and John to divide rest of property. Exec: sons Levi and John
    N. Fuller. Wit: William Lea, Fleming Childress. John N. Fuller qualified.

631 WILLIAM SMITH - Will - w. 20 Oct 1830. (of Milton, N. C.). One child William
    F. Smith to have land in Halifax Co. Va., on Dan River belonging to estate
    of George Smith, also land and store in Nottaway Co. Va. on main road from
    Jennings' old Ordinary and part of estate of Joseph Jennings. Son to have
    all of estate. Exec: friends John Ragland, Martin P. Huntington, Stephen
    Dodson. Wit: Henry E. Coleman, John J. Oliver, Jesse Walker.
    Executors unwilling to qualify, court named Richard Yarborough adm.

632 LUKE PRENDERGAST - Will - w. 11 Nov 1819. Wife Rachel.G Daughter Abe Harrison
    the daughter of James Harrison. grandson Luke B. Prendergast son of John B.
    Prendergast of Tennessee. 5 children: Thomas, George, John B., Elizabeth
    Adams, and Rachael Harrison. Exec: son Thomas and son-in-law James Harrison.
    Wit: A. McCauley, John McCauley, Thomas Byrd.
    Thomas Prendergast qualified.

633 Disposition of Andrew McCauley that he witnessed will of Luke Prendergast and
    saw him sign it.

End of Book L

Book M
page 495

Taxable property for 1834.

	N Acres of Land	Total Valuation of Land in Dollars	Total Valuation of Town property	White Polls	Black Polls
Richmond District	57857	205779	24706	192	863
Glaucester	39262	139357	3030	230	596
St David's	40824	99724		143	389
Caswell	45141	122554		144	461
Total	203084	567408	27736	709	2309

104

July Court 1831

Page
1 WILLIAM SAWYER - Will - w. 16 Feb 1830. Wife Elizabeth Sawyer to have all
houses where I now live and land near branch that meanders to Rattlesnake
Creek adj Sarah B. Carter. Son Thomas; daughters Antherann Parish wife of
James Parish, Dicey Sawyer, Elizabeth Williams wife of James Williams now
living in Georgia. Exec: son Thomas. Wit: Geo Williamson, Lewis Evans,
Thos. L. Lea. Thomas Sawyer qualified.

3 JAMES BRINTLE - Will - w. 28 Apr 1831. Brother-in-law Bennett Bush to have
all estate for him and his heirs. Exec: Bennett Bush. Wit: A. T. Farish,
Nathan Sims. Bennett Bush qualified.

4 Acct current estate of Phoebe Bolton decd.
6 Acct current estate of Abel Taylor decd. Allowance for widow and family.
7 Report of wardens of the Poor.
8 Power of attorney - Hugh Montgomery of Lincoln Co., West Tenn., Blacksmith,
to William W. Montgomery of Rockingham Co., NC, to sell or trade land deeded
to him by John Cobb Sen of Caswell Co. on fork of Moon's Creek adj Ibzan Rice,
John Somers, 128 acres. 5 July 1823.

October Court 1831

11 Power of attorney - Mary Gold of Randolph Co., Mo., to Alexander M. Dameron
of same county and state to settle any business in State of NC and to transfer the power to anyone in NC. 28 Aug 1831. Wit: Samuel Moore.
On oath of James Dobbins who proved Samuel Moore resided in Mo. and not in
NC and Adams S. Richmond who proved handwriting of Mary Gold, it was ordered
registered.

13 Inv property of William Smith decd, also of money and debts due the estate.
By Richard Yarbrough adm.

14 MARTHA LYON (LION) - Will - w. 15 July 1831. Son William Lion to have all property. Exec: Dr. Allen Gunn. Wit: James Gunn, Frances Wilmouth, Dr. Allen
Gunn. Dr. Allen Gunn qualified.

15 LEWIS BARTON SEN. - Will - w. 25 July 1831. Sons John, Elisha, Lewis, Aquilla;
daughters Mary Denny, Sarah Simmons, Zelpha Barton. Son Thomas and his heirs
to have 150 acres land where Thomas lives. Daughters Elizabeth and Rebecca
Barton now living with me to have land where he lives. Exec: son Aquilla
Barton and daughter Elizabeth Barton. Wit: Josiah T. Florance, Levi Simmons,
Aquilla Barton qualified.

16 Inv and sales estate of James Fuller sold May 4 1831 to:

Stephen Monday	Jeremiah Satterfield, William Lea		Joel Burton
Henry McCollum	Reubin Hawkins	Daniel Richmond	James Fullington
David Kiersey	William Malone	James Evans	George F. Johnston
James Dollarhide	John Webster	Benj. F. Standfield,	William Childers
Findle Grinster	Uriah Oakley	Fleming Childers	Thomas M. Moore

21 Cash on hand and amt of debts of estate of James Fuller. Inv and amt of hire
of negroes. By John N. Fuller exec.

23 THOMAS BENNETT - Will - w. 22 Jan 1831. Sons Dodson and Tapley Bennett;
daughters Nancy Worsham and Polley Goin. Sons John, Mumford, Thomas, William
Moore Bennett. Wife Milley to have all estate during her life then divided to
3 youngest children: Eluta Elizabeth Bennett, Louisiana Jackson Bennett, and
Edward Warren Bennett. Exec: friend Doctor C. Williams Esq. and William Lyon.
Wit: Edward Rudder, Alexander Gillespy, Labon M. Gillespie, James S. Nunnally.
William Lyon qualified.

Book M 1831-1832
Page
24 Sales estate of William Smith decd sold in Milton 22 July 1831 to James W.
Jeffreys, E. S. Jones, Mathew Willson, Zachariah Lockett, Samuel C. Smith, Mr.
Rose, Mr. W. Farley. By Richard Yarbrough, adm.
25 Acct current estate of Benjamin T. Fielder decd.
28-33 Settlement estate of John Graves. Property advanced by John Graves before
his death to:
Katy Howard $2517.69. Her equal part of estate $4559.76, balance due $933.07.
Thomas Graves $4785.24 plus $845 value of negroes. He has recd. more than his
share.
Azariah Graves $4419.75, balance due $440.01.
Elijah Graves $5016 inc negroes and he has recd more than his share.
(Each of above sons recd lots and improvements at Caswell Court House valued
at $2820.00.)
William Graves $4406.75, balance due $153.01.
Delilah Miles $4224.54, balance due $335.22.
Nancy Yancey $4147.70, balance due $412.06.
Polly Graves $4398.00 inc 405 acres land with mansion house and mill at $2650,
balance due $161.76.
Barzillai Graves $5168.31, $608.54 above his share.
34 Valuation and names of negroes belonging to estate of John Graves, 36 negroes
valued at $10,230.00. Balances due to legatees who have not recd full share
are to be paid by exec in manner agreed to by legatees. William Graves has
agreed to take the house and lot at Caswell Court House with 25 acres land
valued at $2000.00; Polly Graves to take 200 acres land adj her tract.
37 Acct current estate of William Lenox decd by John Lenox adm. Recd from a
Corporation in Milton.
38 Acct current estate of Robert A. Brown decd by Wm. B. Reid and Tyre H. Brown, adm.
Amt charged to widow in return of sales.
39 Acct current estate of West Gregory decd by Thomas W. Graves adm and Frances
Gregory adm. Payments for hiring of negroes from James Yancey, Peter McKinney,
James Aldridge, John H. Graves, Gideon Turner, et al.
41 Inv and acct sales of part of estate of Mary Kerr sold 6 May 1831. Names of
buyers not stated.
42 Inv and acct sales of estate belonging to John Kerr decd or to Mary Kerr decd
sold 6 May 1831. By James Kerr adm and exec.
43 Acct current estate of James Lea decd by Aron V. Lea adm. Paid J. W. Norwood
for attorney fee; Joseph C. Dameron for crying sale; James W. Yealock.
Balance to 7 legatees: Benjamin F. Lea, Walker Eskridge for wife Malinda,
Aaron V. Lea, Nancy D. Lea, James M. Lea, Rachel C. Lea, Thomas D. Lea.

January Court 1832

46 Inv property of James Vaughan decd taken 12 Oct 1831 by Thomas Page, adm.
46 Affidavit of James Smith and George Smith that they are the brothers and only
heirs at law in fee to John Smith decd late an enlisted soldier in 8th Regiment, U. S. Infantry. They are informed and believe he was drowned at Rock
Island 7 Nov 1816.
47 Allotment to widow of Thomas Harrison decd.
47 Allotment to Nancy Yancey widow and relict of Bartlett Yancey decd and her family.
48 Inv property of Lewis Barton decd which was not willed. Bonds on Anthony Foster,
John Page, Pleasant Robertson are all doubtful. 100 acres land.
By Aquilla Barton exec.
48 Allotment to Elizabeth Chandler widow of Stephen Chandler decd for her and family.
49 Second inv of Abraham Wright decd. Cash recd of Azariah Graves adm of Bartlett
Yancey decd., Mrs. Kisiah Donoho, Thomas Peterson. By William Lea adm.
49 Allotment to widow and family of James Vaughan Jr. decd.
50 Inv estate of William Sawyers decd taken Aug 1831 and of part willed to Elizabeth
Sawyers his wife. By Thomas Sawyer exec.

106

Book M 1832
Page
51 Additional inv property of estate of Griffin Gunn decd. Money recd from Jacob
   Graves which was paid to John C. Harvey, guardian, and to legatee Jones M. Gunn.
51 Classification of justices of Caswell Co. 14 July 1831.
   1. Quentin Anderson, Benj. C. West, Thomas Gunn, John C. Harvey, Nicholas Thompson.
   2. Bedford Brown, Stephen Dodson,Thomas L.Stephens,Woodlief Hooper, Hugh Walker,
      Thomas J. Reid.
   3. John E. Brown, Geo Walker, Edward M. Jones, Wm. A. Lea, Abner Miles.
   4. A. J. Walker, John R. Clark, Henry Allen, Wm. H. Nunnally, James Rainey,
      John C. Harrison.
   5. John Willson, Wm. Anderson, James W. Jeffreys, Wm. W. Price, James Miles.
   6. Thomas W. Graves, Thomas Williamson, James Kerr, John C. Rogers, Brice Collins.
   7. Richd. J. Smith, Andrew Harrison, James McMullen, Freeman Leath, Saml. Mitchell,
      Lancelot Johnston.
52 Sales property of William Sawyers decd sold 11 Aug 1831 to:
   Lewis Evans   Charles L. Hunter   Jonathan Starkey   Grandison Sharp
   Mathew Dodson   Samuel Hinton   Abisha Slade   James Willis
   Thomas Starkey   Thomas Poteat   James Parish   Wm. C. Donoho
   John Kitchen   Elizabeth Sawyers   et al
55 Inv estate of James Brintle decd by Bennett Bush exec taken 4 Jan 1832.
55 Sales property of James Vaughan decd sold 25 Oct 1831 to:Noah Page, William Fulling-
   ton, Edmund Turner, John Kimbro, Thomas Eubanks, Richard G. Lamkins, James
   Vaughan, Lewis Terrell, Elizabeth Vaughan, William Turner, J. R. Lipscomb,Robert
   Fitch, et al.
58 Inv property of Stephen Chandler decd by Stephen J. Chandler adm.
59 Sales estate of Stephen Chandler sold 9 Nov 1831 to: Elizabeth Chandler, Thomas
   W. Graves, James D. Chandler, Henderson Smith, Susan Chandler, Henry Willis,
   Elizabeth P. Chandler, Edmund Herndon, Ashford Walker, Moses Tapscott, William
   Mitchell, et al.
63 Report of Committee on form and drawing of Court House.
64 Inv and sales property of Thomas Harrison decd taken Nov 1831. Sales to:
   Mildred Harrison   Robert L. Harrison,Abisha Slade   William Harrison
   Joseph Yarbrough   Noel Burton   Russell Lipscomb   George Stephens
   Thomas Ware Jun.   James Ingram   John Harrison   Morris Vaughan
   Mrs. Nancy Yancey   By John P. Harrison adm.
   Tobacco sold in Milton. Widow M. Harrison and family paid for year's support.
71 Inv estate of David Mitchell decd. 17 slaves especially bequeathed in will.
   Notes on Thomas Slade decd., Wm. Mansfield, Clayton Jones, Sacky Marshal.
   By John Mitchell and Saml. Mitchell exec.
72 Inv estate of John W. Grant decd and sales. Money due from Mathew Mills for
   negroes sold. Notes on Wm. W. Price & William Wilkerson, Judgments on Wm.
   Bucey, Thomas Henderson, Kelly Voss, David Rawley, Joseph McClain (1826).
   Number of open accts. considered desperate. By Henry Cobb adm.
75 Inv estate of Milner Bennett decd by A. L. Bennett exec. 30 Aug 1814. All
   given to widow. Sales to Thomas Gatewood, Samuel Smith, Jesse Harper, John
   McAden, Ambrose L. Bennett Jr., David Montgomery, Mary Elmore, George Clayton,
   Thomas Donoho, Christopher Davis, Euel Lea, Albert Piles, Tillotson McCain.
   Payments to Milner Bennett's part from estate of Richd. Bennett decd. Paid
   money bequeathed by R. Bennett decd to a daughter of John Bennett decd.
   Recd. from A. Samuel for Mary Bennett, 1814-1832.
79 Div of negroes of John Dameron decd to widow Mary and 2 infant children Eliza
   E. since married to William M. Dameron and Martha D. since married to Alexander
   M. Dameron. The widow Mary intermarried with William Gold who has died.
81 John O. Brackin adm estate of Durrett Richards. Collected debt from Jacob
   Thomas. Paid MILTON GAZETTE for ad. Paid expenses for travel to Pittsylvania
   Court House, Va.

82 ELIZABETH COILE - Will - w. 16 Oct 1827. Daughter Polly Coile all land including
   where son Nicholas now lives. Two sons Nicholas and James Coile. Exec: friend
   William Richmond. Wit: Azariah Graves, John Poteat. Exec qualified.

Book M 1832
Page

83 WILLIAM GOOCH - Will - w. 9 Jan 1832. Daughter Martha Gooch (land between "my
house and Ransom Boswell"); son Abner land which he has in his possession;
son Francis Gooch (land already given him). Remaining land divided into 8
parts to 8 children: Mary Rice, William Gooch, James Gooch, John Gooch, Francis
Gooch, Susannah Boswell, Nathaniel Gooch, Secily Hightower. All remaining
estate to 10 children. Exec: Howell Boswell and Francis Gooch.
Wit: Levi Walker, James Page. Exec qualified.

84 JAMES NELSON - Will - w. 24 Nov 1831. Wife Mercery Nelson one-third of land for
life; daughters Sally Thomas, Polly Parks, Nancey Landers; sons Ambrose Nelson,
Samuel, Barzillai, Stokeley, John, Joel, Iverson, Azariah, Jonathan, and Stephen
Chandler Nelson. Daughter Permely Browning. Land in Va., 186 acres, to be sold.
Exec: son Samuel Nelson and Abraham Landers. Wit: Y. Wiley, Williamson Dameron,
Joseph Langley. Exec qualified.

86 WILLIAM SMITH - Will - w. 21 Dec 1831. Wife Polly, 150 acres adj lands of Ruffin
and Holder and all houses(except house Daniel Thomas)built for her life and
then to go to all children except daughter Nancey. Daughters Polly Parks,
Elizabeth Barnwell, Susannah Pinson, Patsey Pinson, Jane Smith, Fanny Chandler.
Sons Thomas, William, John, and Henderson Smith. Daughter Nancy Thomas to have
use of land adj William Fitch, 169 acres, then to go to her children. Son James
H. to be made equal with other children. Granddaughter Permelia Chandler $50
at age 21. Wife and 10 children. Exec: son John Smith. Wit: Jas Wilder,
Jas Anderson, Bartlett Estes. Exec qualified.

88 FRANCES TERRELL - Will - w. 5 July 1831. Young James Murphey's wife; sister
Lucey Murphey; other 4 sisters: Patsey Murphey, Salley Murphey, Mersy Nelson,
Isabel Moore. Brother Jonathan Terrell to be paid for caring for her during
sickness. Brothers Jonathan and James. Exec: brother James Terrell.
Wit: Jonathan Terell Jun. & Sen..

89 DAVID MITCHELL - Will - w. 10 Sept. 1829. Wife Ann and son Samuel (land and
plantation where he lives). Land on east side Hyco in Person Co. where William
Mitchell Sen. formerly lived. Son John; daughter Jenny Wiley and her husband
John Wiley; daughter Fanney Mabain and her husband Alexander Mabain. (Mebane?)
Daughter Elizabeth Currie and her husband James Currie. Son William (land
called Burch's tract and tract of Col. John Day). 4 sons John, William, Samuel,
and Anderson to sell Sugartree tract and have proceeds. Son Samuel (land west
side Hyco). Grandchildren: Elizabeth Mithell daughter of David Mitchell decd.;
Alexander Mabain Mitchell, Robert Mitchell, Harriett Ann Mitchell, and Eliza
Frances Mitchell, children of son William. Exec: sons John, Samuel, Anderson
Mitchell. Wit: A. Gordon, Henry Allen. Proved Oct Court 1831.
John and Samuel Mitchell qualified.

92 Div negroes of B, Yancey decd to legatees: Mrs. Nancey Yancey widow, Algernon
S. Yancey, Mary Catharine Yancey, Caroline Louise Yancey, Maria V. B, Yancey,
Frances W. McAden. 89 negroes amounting to $23254.00. Div by John Ragland,
J. Nelson, A. Harrison.

April Court 1832

100 Inv estate of Andrew Harrison decd taken 18 Feb 1832 by James R. Harrison adm.
101 Inv property of James Nelson decd by Samuel Nelson and Abraham Landers exec.
102 Inv personal estate of Elizabeth Coile by William Richmond Jun. exec.
103 Inv of Christopher Robertson decd by Robert A. Crowder adm. Bonds due estate
on Edward Corsey, George L. Willson, Joel P. Thomas, Hugh W. Gillaspie,
Edward Rudder.
104 Inv goods and chattels of William Gooch decd by William Slade, James Page, and
Henry Turner on 14 Jan 1832. Howell Boswell & Francis Gooch exec.
107 Sales property of Wyley Jones by James Jones adm sold 3 Feb 1832 to Dicey Jones,
Morrice Vaughan, Ben Jones, William Jones, John Jones, John Lea Sen., Lucy
Jones, Sally Jones.

Book M 1832
Page
109 List of property sold of estate of James Nelson decd on 7,8,& 9 Feb 1832 to:

Mersey Nelson	Samuel Dameron	Andrew Woods	Wm. Winstead
Andrew Brooks	M. D. Norfleet	Thomas Turner	Wm. L. Browning
John Crisp	Stephen Garrett	James Crousett	Spencer Wilkerson
John Thomas	Thomas Roan	John Mitchell	Nick Hester
John Landers Sen.	George Bouldin	John L. Wisdom	Lemuel Jackson
Durrett Oliver	James Love	John L. Richmond	John Browning
James Landers	Thornton Bains	Nathaniel Snipes	Wm. Childres
Carter Vowell	Wm. McMurray	Epps Moore	John Murphey
Ruffin Pleasant	Nathaniel Lea	Daniel Jackson	Jas. M. Drake
Joshua Rudd	A. M. Lea	James Parks	Ambrose Nelson
Johnson McDaniel	Land sold in Va. to John T. Crain, et al.		

119 Sales property of William Gooch sold 2, 3 Feb 1832 to:

William Graves	Ziza Rice	Rainey Currie	William Smith
James Vaughan	Benjamin Penix	John Simmons	George Simmons
Devereau Hightower	Wm. F. Davis	Joseph Pinson	James Page
John Bird	Joseph Aldridge	Rice Barton	John Gooch
Levi Stalcup	Nathaniel Gooch	Archibald R. Birk	Ransom Boswell
John Willson	William Slade	John Lenox	Francis Gooch
Levi Walker	James R. Lea	William Turner	Thomas Gooch
William Russell	Abner Boswell	Henry F. Smith	Nathan Massey
Abner Gooch	Azariah Graves	Lemuel Dabbs	et al

127 Inv and sales of part of property of John Kerr decd or to Mary Kerr decd.
Sold 10 Nov 1831 and 7 Apr 1832 by Jas Kerr exec and adm. (Buyers not listed)
130 Sales property of James Yancey decd sold 14 Jan 1832 to: Thomas D. Johnston,
Goodwin Evans, William Turner, Thomas W. Graves, George Williamson.
131 Acct sales estate of William Smith decd by John Smith exec on 31 Jan 1832 to:

Alfred Parks	Azariah Morton	Alfred Nash	Anthony Foster
Christopher Brooks	Colby Foster	Edmund Herndon	George W. Taylor
George Simpson	Hosea Compton	Henderson Smith	Henry Smith
John Stadler	James D. Chandler	James Page	John Sawyers
James Wilder	James Kerr	James H. Smith	Jane Smith
John Stamps	James Smith	Lexa Howard	Mary Belsear
Mary Smith	Robert Groom	Milton Penix	Stephen J. Chandler
Samuel Hughs	Solomon Rice	Thomas Pinson	William Judkins
William Barnwell	William Sanders	et al	

143 Amt of bonds of William Smith decd - bonds on Joseph Brackin, Josiah Womack,
Richard Lampkin, et al. A list of doubtful bonds.
144 Allotment of dower to widow of William Smith decd (land adj Ruffin & Wilder).
145 Sales property of Christopher Robertson decd sold 2 Feb 1832 by Robert A.
Crowder adm. Names of buyers not listed.
147 Additional sales of West Gregory decd to Samuel Moore.
147 Acct sales property of Andrew Harrison decd. Tobacco sold to Granderson Sharp.
148 Acct current estate of Nancy Rudd decd by Elisha and Aldridge Rudd adm.
149 Allotment to Massey(or Mersey) Nelson widow of James Nelson decd for year's
allowance for her and family.
150 Acct current estate of Milner Bennett decd by Ambrose L. Bennett exec.
153 Div of negroes belonging to estate of James Yancey decd. 17 Jan 1832.
Met at dwelling house of the widow. Legatees: Mrs. Zilpha Yancey widow,
James M. Yancey, Elizabeth Gunn, Albert G. Yancey, William Yancey, and
Mildred A. Yancey.
155 Div of lands belonging to James Yancey to same legatees as on page 153.
156 Widow's dower in lands of James Yancey surveyed by J. Willson, 918 acres
including mansion house. Refunding bonds filed in division of lands.
157 Acct current estate of John H. Ponsonby decd by Nicholas M. Lewis adm.

109

Book M 1832
Page

159 BENJAMIN CARTER - Will - w. 1 Mar 1831. Wife Elizabeth Carter all property
during her life. Sons William, Littlebery, John, and Benjamin Carter.
Daughters Polley Mullin, Sarah Stubblefield; grandson Benjamin R. Chandler;
granddaughters Elizabeth Young Carter and Mary Elizabeth Stubblefield.
Balance to 4 children: Little Berry Carter, Polly Mullin, John and Benjamin
Carter. Test: J. Womack, Richard W. Totton.

160 JOHN LEA - Will - w. 15 Feb 1832. Wife to sell anything she can spare;
Mother to have use of house whereon she lives during her life and then to be
returned to family. Wife to have all property for life, and if she re-marry
to be divided between wife and children. Exec: Wife.
Wit: F. Leath, Levi Walker. Exec qualified.

162 THOMAS JEFFREYS - Will - w. 3 Mar 1832. Sons James W. Jeffreys and George W.
Jeffreys. James to have Red House and Hyco plantation. Daughter-in-law
Agness Jeffreys. Grandchildren Adeline, Thomas, Mumford, and Ellen McGehee
children of decd daughter Elizabeth McGehee. Granddaughters Isabella Jeffreys
and Ann Eliza Jeffreys daughters of Agnes Jeffreys. Sons James and Washington
to have negro carpenter Brandon. Negroes sent to Gold mines shall remain
there and profits applied to James. Last crop of tobacco due to Joseph Currie
from son James. Roanoke stock and rest of estate left to exec in trust.
Exec: sons Washington and James, son-in-law Thomas McGehee.
Test: David Pointer, Jas. W. McCain, John T. Garland. James W. Jeffreys and
Thomas McGehee qualified.

164 ANDREW HARRISON SEN. - Will - w. 29 Sept 1827. Sons John, Jesse, Willis D.;
daughters Polly W. Wilkinson, Martha W. Wilkinson, Nancy W. McDaniel.
Wife Mary Harrison to have all estate during widowhood and thereafter tract
of land where he lives divided between 2 youngest sons James R. Harrison
and Andrew W. Harrison. Daughters Elizabeth B. Harrison, Jane D. Harrison,
and Susan P. Harrison. 5 eldest children John, Jesse, Polley, Martha, and
Nancy. Land in Pittsylvania Co. Va. to be sold. Few acres in Caswell Co.
adj Bartlett Yancey to be sold. Exec: wife Mary; James R. Harrison and John
P. Harrison. Wit: Edward Rudder, John Everett, Frances Ray, Evans Knight.
Caviat of will by James R. Harrison and others vs Jesse Harrison and others.
Probate opposed by Jesse Harrison, John Harrison, Elizabeth Harrison,
William P. McDaniel and wife Nancy, Henry E. Wilkinson and wife Martha,
Creed T. Oliver and wife Jane. Jury decreed this was last will and testa-
ment. James R. Harrison qualified.

July Court 1832

168 Inv estate of Alexander Moore decd by Thomas M. Moore adm.

169 Acct of hire of negroes of estate of James Fuller decd for 1831 by John N.
Fuller exec.

170 Year's allowance to Dicey Jones widow of Wyly Jones decd. 9 July 1832.

171 Inv property of Thomas Compton decd by Nancy Compton adm. 14 Apr 1832.
Notes on Aquilla Compton Jun., Young Birt; acct on James Ward, William
Pleasant, Jas McMenaway, James Davis, Alfred Compton, John Ward.

172 Inv estate of William McDaniel decd taken 13 Jan 1832 by Benjamin F. Standfield, adm.

174 Inv estate of Providence Haddock decd by Elizabeth Haddock adm.

175 Inv and sales property of Lewis W. Whitemore decd taken 15 Apr 1832 by John
Nunnally adm. Names of buyers not listed.

176 Inv estate of William Stewart decd by Garnett Neeley. Claim against James
Roane now in suit.

177 Allotment to Nancey Compton for year's allowance for her and family, she
widow of Thomas Compton.

Book M 1832
Page
178 Div negroes of West Gregory decd to Francis Gregory widow, and to 2 children
Julietta and Nathaniel Hubbard Gregory. 11 July 1832.
Commrs: Jno Stamps, John E. Brown, John Swift.
179 Sales property of Providence Haddock sold 30 Apr 1832 to Noah Page, Stephen
Haddock, Elijah Graves, John Peterson, Joseph Lunceford, John Sparrow,
Stephen Kitchen, Dr. John Comer, Polley Haddock, Elizabeth Haddock.
182 Div of negroes of estate of James Fuller on 4 May 1832 to legatees: James Evans
for wife Nicey, Lucy Fuller,John Fuller, Tinsley Lea for wife Frances, William
Boswell for wife Mary.
183 Inv and sales of estate of the Revd. James M. Lea decd taken 28 Jan 1832 in
Leasburg. Notes on John C. Vanhook, Lewis Hagwood, Benjamin Phelps; Lemuel
S. Bowers for note on Wm. H. Sargant; notes on John and Samuel Johnston.
By William Lea adm.
184 Year's allowance for Ann W. Whitemore widow of Lewis Whitemore decd. 3 May 1832.
185 Wardens Report of the Poor.
186 Power of attorney - Levi Fuller of Rutherford Co. Tenn., to John Fuller Jun.
of same county to recover from John Fuller exec of James Fuller decd of Caswell
County, $3000.00 willed. 22 Feb 1832. Wit: John Bruce.
187 Power of attorney - Tinsley Lea of Munroe Co., MO, to Brother Alfred M. Lea
of Caswell County to recover from John N. Fuller, exec of James Fuller. Alfred
to retain money owed him. 15 May 1832. Atto. Calvin Graves.

188 HENRY TAPSCOTT SEN. - Will - w. 26 May 1832. Sons Samuel, William, Henry C.,
and James Tapscott. Daughters Nancy Tapscott, Susannah Tapscott.
Exec: son Henry C. Tapscott. Wit: John Tapscott Sen., Joseph Windsor.
Exec qualified.

190 THOMAS SWAN - Will - w. 13 June 1832. 2 daughters Sarith Swann and Margaret
Swann. Daughters Elizabeth Voss, Pensole Cox; sons John H., William, Joseph,
Daniel W., and James Swan. Wit: Benj. C. West Sen., Bennett Burrows.
Exec refused to qualify, and Benj. C. West appointed adm with will annexed,
he bonded by John P. Harrison and Hugh Cobb.

191 BENJAMIN STEPHENS SEN. - Will - w. 11 May 1832. Wife Polly Stephens to have
one-seventh of land including mansion house. Sons Iverson Green, Charles
Granderson, Albert Galliton, John Quincey, William Monroe, Calvin Prior,
and Algernon Duct Stephens (under 21 years), each to have one-seventh part.
Daughters Mariah Hagwood, Elizabeth Stephens, Russalinda Stephens.
Exec: friend William Long and Iverson Green Stephens. Wit: William Stephens,
Katharine Stephens. Exec qualified.

194 Acct of taxes recd by George Williamson, Sheriff. Included busines taxes for
retailers of spirits, merchants, peddlers, natural curiosities, artificial
curiosities.

October Court 1832

197 William Watkins orphan age of 12 years bound to John H. Crockett.
197 George W. Simmons orphan age 8 years on 2 Dec 1832 bound to Samuel Shelton.
198 John Legan orphan age of 10 years bound to Owen McAleer.
199 Margaret Watkins orphan age of 4 years bound to Paul A. Haralson.
199 Anthena Simmons orphan age of 10 years bound to Parham A. Boley.
200 James M. Simmons orphan age of 5 years on 8 Feb 1832 bound to John Kitchen.
201 Additional sale of estate of Benjamin T. Fielder - sold negro man Armistead.
201 Inv of Tin Ware belonging to estate of Thomas L. Stephens decd by James Farley,
adm., on 10 Aug 1832.
202 Inv debts due Thomas L. Stephens. Largest amts. on John W. Glenn, Wm. M.
Cabiness, P. A. Bowley. Inv accts on Richd Yarbrough, Jesse Owen, Joseph Mc-
Dowell, George Farley, Samuel A. Douglass, Richard Bullock (cash loaned).

Book M 1832-1833
Page
205 Acct current estate of John Morris decd. Paid Sarah Morris widow her year's
allowance; paid Judgment in favor of Elizabeth Kimbrough's exec.; paid Joseph
S. Totton for crying sale. Claim on Nicholas Hood amt not found and Hood
spoken of as adm is dead and insolvent. By Thomas W. Harrelson adm. 11 Oct.
207 Acct sales of B. Yancey decd sold 19 Dec 1831 to:

Nancy Yancey	Thomas Harrelson Sr.,Algernon S. Yancey	Azariah Graves
Dr. Henry McAden	Joseph R. E. Lipscomb, Wm. Howerton	Joel Thomas
William Gordon	Abisha Slade	Edward Montgomery	Davis Delaney
George A. Connally	Joel Gossett	Stephen Dodson	George Farley
Calvin Graves	Ansel Ware	John H. Crockett	John Poteat
Chesley Turner	Wm. C. Donoho	John Lenox	Wm. Harrison
George Craghead	Nathaniel T. Green, John Goodson	et al

212 Stray horse taken up by Theopillus Stubblefield valued at $45. 10 June 1830.
213 Inv of notes due Benjamin Stephens by Wm. Long and Iverson G. Stephens exec.
Notes on Thomas Walker, Abner Stanfield, John Johnston, John G. Lea, Robert
Freeman, et al.
214 List of desperate notes due Stephens on David and James A. Kiersey, James Lea(Hop
James and Langum Fullington, et al.
219 Inv property of Benjamin Stephens decd by exec.
221 Stray horse taken up by Booker Boman and valued at $25 by Benjamin Johnston
and James W. McCain. 10 June 1830.
222 WILLIAM RICHMOND - Will - w. 14 Apr 1832. Sons John, William, Daniel, and
Adams S. Richmond. Daughter Sally Rice. Grandsons Sanders Carney and Smith
Carney. Land divided among 4 sons. Servant Ginney $27 yearly for her life.
Exec: 4 sons. Wit: Jos Langley, Jno Wiley, Benjamin Matlock.
William, Daniel, and Adams S. Richmond qualified.
223 LANCELOTT JOHNSTON - Will - w. 25 Jan 1822. Wife Zeriah to have 437 acres land
where he lives and 1 tract on Hillsborough Road, also all property for her
life. Daughter Jane one-third part of land after death of wife. Daughters
Polly and Betsy. Has given to other children their just proportion.
Exec: Thomas Harrison and James Yancey my son-in-law. Wit: Jethro Brown,
William Brown.
Said Jethro Brown is dead. Will proved by William Brown. Both exec are dead.
John E. Brown and Mary Johnston appointed adm with will annexed.
225 JOEL CANNON - Will - w. 21 Dec 1829. Daughters Sally Murphey and Dorcas Scott.
Remainder of estate to be sold and divided among all children except Anne
Powell to whom property has been advanced. Exec: son Elijah Cannon and James
Cannon. Wit: Calvin Graves, Alfred M. Nash. Exec qualified.

January Court 1833

227 Div negroes of Thomas Harrison decd to legatees: Mildred Harrison, Robert
Harrison, Araminta Harrison, Abisha Slade, Louisa Harrison, John Harrison,
Elizabeth Harrison, Ann Harrison, William Harrison. 9 Jan 1832.
230 Acct current estate of John Elmore by John C. Rogers exec.
232 Acct current estate of Abraham Wright decd by William Lea adm.
234 Tabbitha Jones orphan,a child of color, age of 10 years bound to Dabney Rainey.
235 Sales personal property of estate of Nancy Hodge decd sold 30 Nov 1832 by
William Long adm. to:

James Lea Sen.	Madison Frasier	Ansel Ware	Dr. John Comer
John Peterson	Ed D. Wright	Wm. Frazeur	Robert Falkner
William Dismukes	John Lamb	Thomas Rigs	John Lea Sen.
James A. Kiersey	Katharine Stephens,Charles S. Cooley	Orison Combs
Lansom Lamb	John Love Jun.	Thomas Greenway	Archibald Lea
Abner Standfield	William Lea		

238 Inv property of Elisha Rudd by Joshua Rudd and Aldridge Rudd adm.

112

Book M 1833
Page
239 Sales property of Elisha Rudd sold 30 and 31 Oct 1832 to: James R. Lea, Joseph
    Rudd, Henry Willis Jun., John Browning, James M. Yancey, Oliver Foulks, Abel
    Foulks, James Page Jun., Thomas W. Graves, Howard Martin, Thomas K. Turner,
    John Miles, Elizabeth Donaway, James Miles Sen., Nathaniel Murphey, Henry
    Willis, et al.
244 Balance of property sold of William Smith on 20 Oct 1832 to Jane Smith (350
    acres land), Henderson Smith. Note on Joseph Younger to be satisfied.
    By John Smith exec.
244 Inv estate of Thomas Harrison decd for crop of tobacco sold by John P. Harrison -
    3 Hogsheads for $178.77.
245 Inv estate of Nancy Hodge taken 10 Nov 1832 by William Long adm.
246 Property sold by Nancy Compton adm of Thomas Compton decd sold 3 May 1832.
    Abraham Landers , clerk of sale. Sales to:

George Stewart	Wm. Warren Jun.	John Benson	Elisha Roark
Wm. Pleasant Jun.	John Murphey Sen.	Erasmus Compton	James Crousett
James McMineway	Harvey Cooper	Beaufit Cooper	Jonathan Murphey
Sieria G. Compton	William Ward	Miles Wells	William Kerr
James Farley(Milton),	Thomas Compton	et al	

    Paid Wm. Kerr for 1 hogshead tobacco 1140 lbs. at $3.60 - plus hauling and
    other expenses to Richmond, Va.
249 Acct sales of James M. Lea decd by William Lea adm for 1/3 sale of Dick & Hannah.
250 Sales property of Benjamin Stephens decd sold 1 Nov 1832 to John Lea(CB),
    Durrett Oliver, John Lea Jun., James Whitfield, Marrice Vaughan, Nicholas Willis,
    James T. Willis, Polly Stephens, Thomas Rigs, John Broughton, John S. Ogles,
    William A. Lea. By Wm. Long and Iverson G. Stephens exec.
252 Sales estate of Thomas Slade Sen. sold 22 & 23 Nov 1832 by William Slade exec to:
    Henry Willis, Alexis Howard, James Shapard, Carter Groom, Ibean Rice, Azariah
    Graves (ST), John Stamps, Jeremiah Graves, William Graves, George T. Martin,
    James Brannock, Nathaniel Slade, William Slade Sen., Robert Ford, Thomas Gibson,
    Nancy Stamps, Miss Mary Lea, William Russell, George Simmons.
256 Sales estate of Isabella Slade decd sold on 22 & 23 Nov 1832 by Wm. Slade adm. to
    William Russell, Miss Mary Lea, John Stamps, et al.
257 Additional sales Thomas and Isabella Slade sold 4 Jan 1833. Debts due from
    J. Stamps, William Fitz, Robert Ford.
259 Sales property of William Richmond decd sold 29 Oct 1832 by Wm. & Daniel Rich-
    mond exec. Names of buyers not listed.
261 Sales property of Alexander Winstead decd at Caswell Court House on 8 Apr 1828 to:
    Morris Smith, Jobe Walker, David Jones, James Darby. Tract of land in Person
    County sold to Wardens of the Poor for said county in Nov 1830 for $300.
262 Div of negroes of James Richardson decd to his widow and children as follows:
    to Stephen Sergant and Mary his wife, one sixth part; residue in 7 equal shares
    to Mr. Stephens who married Susan P. Richardson, James Richardson, Edmund Rich-
    ardson, Robert Richardson, William Richardson, Elizabeth Richardson, and
    Mary Ann Richardson.
264 Acct current estate of James Richardson by Robert P. Ware adm.
266 Acct current estate of William Sawyer decd by Thomas Sawyer exec. Sales on
    18 Aug 1831. Paid J. Singleton for making coffin, John Willson for surveying,
    A. Slade for crying sale, James Parrish to furnish spirits at sale.
267 Amt. hire of negroes belonging to C. Robertson estate by Robert A. Crowder adm.
268 Acct current estate of John W. Grant decd by Henry Cobb adm. Counsel fee paid
    to James T. Morehead.
269 List of amt of hire of negroes of estate of Stephen Chandler decd for 1832-33
    by Stephen J. Chandler adm. Bonds on John Berry and Jeremiah Lea.
269 Stray steer taken up by William Malone. William Lea, Ranger.
270 Inv of articles inventoried of estate of Lancelott Johnston decd by John E.
    Brown adm. 21 Dec 1832.
271 Joseph W. Singleton et al vs Sarah Rutledge et al - petition for sale of negroes.
    Sale of negroes to George Williamson, Mathew Dodson, Joseph W. Singleton.
    25 Dec 1832.

Book M 1833
Page
272 Alexander Donoho and wife vs Zachariah Hooper, Guardian - petition for sale of
negroes. Sales 7 Jan 1833 to Samuel Hinton, Allen Gunn Sen., Alexander Donoho,
Azariah Graves. No one willing to buy old woman Cass, bid off to Edmund Wright
for $25.
273 Acct current estate of David Hodge decd by William Long adm.
274 Additional inv of Alexander Winstead decd by George Williamson and Sarah Winstead exec.
277 Div estate of George M. Willson decd. William Smith and wife vs John C. Lea
guardian. Div of negroes between his two living children, Elizabeth Ann wife
of William Smith and Mary L. Willson. 27 Dec 1832. Smith's land adj James W.
Jeffreys and John Gamble surveyed by James Rainey, Esq.

280 AARON SIMPSON - Will - w. 6 Dec 1832. Wife Charlotte to have all estate until
her death, then same to sold (except land) and divided to all children.
Son Joseph (tract where I live); heirs of son Moses decd to have 1/9 part of
estate. Daughters Kitty Bozwell, Penelope Graves; sons Roger, Heydon, Enoch;
daughter Nancy (land purchased from her husband James Bozwell Sen.); daughter
Priscilla; niece Subrina Graves $100. Each child to have 1/9 part.
Exec: Son Joseph and son-in-law Francis Simpson. Test: Azariah Morton, William
Hastin. Joseph Simpson and Francis S. Simpson qualified.

282-290 Acct current estate of James Yancey decd by J. Wilson adm. Receipts of
store accounts from many debtors. Payments to Albert G. Yancey, James M.
Yancey for saddle.

April Court 1833

294 George Yates orphan age 12 years on Jan. last bound to Martin Durham.
294 Anderson Piles orphan age 11 years on 7 March last bound to Thomas W. Graves.
295 George Washington Lafayette Dabney orphan age one year old bound to Dr. Allen
Gunn.
296 James M. Simmons orphan age of __ years bound to Dabney Terry.
296 Solomon Casey orphan age 10 years on Nov 1 next bound to Gideon B. Turner.
297 Martha Harriett Jones orphan age 13 years bound to Dabney Rainey.
298 Inv property of Joel Thomas decd taken 28 Jan 1833 by John Comer adm.
299 Sales property of Joel Thomas to John G. Lea, Sharrod Owen, Henry Willis,
Ganer Yuill, Joel P. Thomas, Carter Powell, Charles Hendrick, Wm. O. Thomas,
Richard H. Griffith, Agness Thomas, Thomas Y. Pass, Henry Thomas, Jesse H.
Thomas, Edward Rudder, William Holcomb, Wm. T. Glasgow et al. Allotment to
widow Mrs. Agness Thomas.
303 Inv property of James A. Durham decd. Bonds on Simon Adams, David Tranam,
William M. Rook, Benj. C. West. By Isaac Durham and W. H. Burns, adm.
304 Sales property of Thomas L. Stephens decd to William M. Cabiness, William H.
Hamblett, John E. Hamlet, Lemuel Potter, Jno Robertson, Dr. R. W. Thomas,
Jarvis Friou, James Farley, A. J. Walker, Henry Rose, James M. McGehee,
H. W. Farley, Wm. E. Guy, Levin Downs, Anthony Bensany, John B. Pugh, Nathl.
Palmer, Dr. John T. Garland, Zach Lockett, Ambrose Bennett, S. Watkins, Jesse
Owen, Jno S. Oglesby, et al. By James Farley adm.
309 Charles Henry Piles orphan age of 9 years in June next bound to Ansel Ware.
310 William Delaney orphan age 15 years bound to John Lenox.
310 George Delaney orphan age 13 years bound to John Lenox to learn art of a
carpenter.
311 Rufus Bass orphan age of 10 years or thereabouts bound to Paul A. Haralson.
312 Anderson Piles orphan age 11 years last March bound to Ansel Ware.
313 Year's allotment to Martha J. Stevens widow of Thomas L. Stevens. 26 Mar 1833.
(Also spelled Stephens)
314 Inv estate of Aaron Simpson decd by Francis L. and Joseph Simpson. Notes on
James Haydon, Samuel Loveless, B. C. Loveless. Book debts on James Moore(hatter)
John Duke, Benjamin Walker Sen., Susannah Fielder, John Carden, Susannah
Leachman, James Suddeth, et al.
316 Sales property of Aaron Simpson sold 12 Feb 1833. Names not included.

Book M 1833
Page
317 Additional acct of estate of Thomas Slade Sen. Sales to Alexis Howard and
William Russell.
317 Additional inv estate of Benjamin Stephens.

318 SIMON DENNY - Will - w. 24 Feb 1833. Wife Polly Denny all estate and one-third
land for her lifetime and at her death divided between sons Azariah Denny and
Lewis M. Denny. Daughters Nancy Cobb, Rebecca Crenshaw. Exec: 2 sons.
Wit: John E. Brown, James E. Williamson. Exec qualified.

319 GEORGE ROBERTS - Will - w. 26 June 1832. Wife Martha Roberts(land adj Ann
Paschall, Jesse Orr on Moon's Creek where I reside) for her life. Exec: wife
Martha Roberts. Wit: Alfred E. Johnston, Warren Weatherford, Joel F. Motley.

320 Inv estate of Samuel C. Smith decd by Geo Williamson adm and Sarah L. Smith,admx.
322 Acct current estate of Archimedes Donoho decd by James H. Ruffin adm. Cash paid
widow, eldest son, eldest daughter, youngest daughter, youngest son.
326 Azariah Graves, Trustee, in acct with Caswell Co., report for 1831.
Tax laid to build the Court House.

July Court 1833

330 Power of attorney - Archibald Rice of Jackson Co., Mo., to son William Rice of
same county and state to receive all property due wife Sally Rice, late Sally
Richmond since death of her late Father William Richmond of Caswell Co. 14 May.
331 Receipt of William Rice atty for Archibald Rice for negroes received from estate
of William Richmond decd. Wm., Daniel, and Adams S. Richmond exec. 3 July 1833.
332 Report of Wardens of the Poor by Treasury Wardens Woodlief Hooper and Thomas Gunn.
333 Report of Commissioners to sell old Court House - on Tuesday 2 May as directed
by Superior Court, Ibzan Rice became purchaser for $181 with Anderson Willis
his security and payable to A. Graves, county trustee. 11 July 1833.
Commrs: Geo Williamson, Thos D. Johnston, John C. Harvey.
333 Inv property of estate of Simon Denny decd taken 6 July 1833 by Azariah Denny.
334 Acct current estate of Capt. John Lea decd.; settlement with Polly Lea exec.
336 Sales perishable property of estate of James Richardson decd sold 28 Nov 1832 by
George Stevens agent for Robert Ware Jr. Sales to:

Stephen Sergent	George Stevens	Wm. W. Richardson	James Ingram
Nathaniel Harrelson,	James Harris	Samuel Gilmore	Wm. J. Harrison
Samuel Hinton	James H. Thompson	Thomas Y. Pass	Joseph Knight
John McDaniel	Henry Burton	Archibald Walters	James Richardson
Green Womack	Johnston Atkinson	Russell Lipscomb	Washington Jeffreys
Josiah Blair	John H. Tabb	Capt. Chiles	Joseph Motley
Abisha Slade	Abel Staton	Thomas Ware	Jordan Ray
James White	Elisha Alverson	Capt. Creed T. Oliver	

342 DANIEL GWYN - Will - w. 29 Apr 1828. Wife Zipporiah to have land and house &
all property for her life. Zeri Gwyn one dollar, but Zeri's children to have
his part. Daughters Jane and Dorothy. Sons Hugh, Daniel, Richard, John, and
Lyttleton Gwyn. Exec: son Lyttleton A. Gwyn. Wit: Wm. Graves, Elijah Graves.

344 Sales estate of John Lea decd sold 13 Sept 1832. Negroes sold to Wm. S. Richmond, Thomas W. Graves, John A. Patrick, John Tapscott, James Sharp, Sam Foster.

345 NANCY H. HARVILL - Will - w. 18 Apr 1833. Daughter Eliza Harvil to have whole
of estate. Sister Elizabeth Dunaway to take Eliza and the property to take care
of until Eliza is grown. Wit: John Roberts, Yancey Oliver.

345 Inv and amt of sale of Lewis W. Whittemore decd taken 3 May 1833 by John Nunnally.
346 Report of commission to superintend bldg. of new Court House - work completed
according to contract. 10 July 1822.
346 Inv property of John McKee decd. Notes on Ebenezer S. Jones, Henry Stephens,
Wm. R. Maroney; order on Mrs. Shirley given in by Wm. Meroney. Robert McKee,adm.

115

Book M 1833
Page
347 Receipts from John Comer to William Long one of the adm of David Hodge decd.
Interest of Samuel Hodge Sen a brother of David estimated at 1/4 share; heirs
of Elizabeth Sergent decd sister to David 1/4 part; one-third part of Isaac
Hodge decd interest to go to Samuel Hodge son of Isaac, also to Richard
Durham and wife Judith daughter of said decd.
348 Report of Azariah Graves trustee in acct with Caswell Co.
349 Year's allowance to Sarah S. Smith. 1 July 1833.
350 Amt of business taxes collected by Thos. S. Lea, Sheriff.

October Court 1833

352 Congressional election returns for 1833, Aug. 8, for 9th district composed of
Caswell, Rockingham, Guilford, and Stokes Counties. For A. H. Sheppard 540
votes.
353 HENRY HOOPER - Will - w. 11 Aug 1832. Adm to be appointed by Court and he to
receive all estate and distribute it in any way as to best maintain his Mother
and Jane B. Richardson during their lives, also Prudence H., Louisa, and Henry
McAden Richardson until Henry arrives to age 21. After death of Mother and
Jane B. Richardson and if Henry is 21 years, all negroes to be liberated if
they leave the U. S. under any condition State policy requires. Old negroes
and those wishing to stay can remain on plantation as slaves. Henry to maintain his sisters until they marry. Witness my hand - done alone and in private
and in very bad health. Court ordered will recorded when writing proved by
George Williamson, Dr. N. M. Roan, and Paul A. Haralson.
Woodlief Hooper named adm with will annexed.
354 Inv notes of estate of Daniel Gwyn decd, all doubtful, on Wm. H. Heritage (1826),
John Humphreys (1823), Robert Hall (1826), Bird Read(1807), Jas and Daniel
Jennings (1812), Andrew Haddock (1801).
355 Inv property of Daniel Gwynn decd by L. A. Gwynn exec.
356 Inv property of Robert Swift decd taken 18 July 1833 by Samuel Moore adm.
357 Inv property of Joel Kennon decd by Elijah and James Kennon. Sales property
of Joel Kennon on 2 Nov 1833. Buyers not listed.
357 Inv goods and chattels of estate of George W. Rowlett decd. Amt due from
George Turner as guardian $138. By A. Slade adm.
358 Sales estate of Robert Swift decd sold 7 Aug 1833 to Ibzan Rice, John Swift,
Nancy Swift, Thomas Watlington, Armstead Watlington, John Stamps, Ed. M.
Jones, Richard Jones, L. A. Gwynn, Ira Siddle, James Adkins, Carter Groom,
Ralph Glaze, Carter Horseford, et al.
360 Sales estate of Thomas Slade decd sold 22 & 23 Nov 1832 not returned heretofore. Also property of Isabella Slade decd omitted from 1st sale. By
William Slade, exec & adm.
361 Sales property of Daniel Gwynn sold 30 Sept 1833 to Hugh Gwynn, Martin M. Mims,
Richard Gwynn, John Gwynn, Rice Gwynn, Robert Madding, et al.
362 Acct current of Major William Penick decd. Met at house of Josiah Blair to
settle with Capt. William Stamps exec. 14 Aug 1833. Paid W. Blair for
preaching funeral $5; T. Settle atty fee; Doctors Patton & Green. Paid for
5 years board for Harriott Penick $100.
364 Acct current of John N. Fuller exec of James Fuller decd. Paid Thomas Day for
coffin $16.50; paid L. Vanhook for pailing in grave; retained part for
heirs of James Fuller. Paid Calvin Graves atty fee; Rev. Geo. W. Dye for
funeral $3. Bad notes on William Paine, William Stephens, Craften Williams.
John N. Fuller indebted to the estate.
366 Acct current estate of Stephen Chandler decd. Paid widow Elizabeth Chandler,
John Miles for crying sale, James Hurdle $2 for plank for coffin. Paid
Joseph Johnston for schooling children of decd. By Stephen J. Chandler adm.
368 Acct current estate of John H. McAden decd by David G. Brandon exec. Paid
expenses for selling negroes in South Carolina.

Book M 1833-34
Page
369 Peter Rowland orphan age of 19 years in Jan. last part bound to Martha Douglass.
369 Bedford A. Crafton orphan age of 11 years on 11 Feb last bound to George Stevens.
370 Amos L. Crafton orphan age 8 years on 28 May last bound to Robert Madding.

January Court 1834

371 Additional inv estate of Benjamin Stephens by Wm. Long and I. G. Stephens exec.
372 Inv property of Henry Hooper decd taken 24 Oct 1833. Bonds on Joseph Knight,
    Starling Gunn, Loveless Hailey, John Kennon, Peter Powell Jr. and Sr.
    By W. Hooper adm.
373 Inv estate of James Love decd by J. W. McKissack adm.
373 Inv estate of Simeon Ford decd by Labon Ford adm.
374 Sales estate of Simeon Ford sold 6 Nov 1833 to Eli G. Ford, Pleasant Ford,
    Obediah Cruise, James Murphey, Hugh S. Murphey, Joseph P. Medcalf, Lucy Ford,
    Thomas Norman, Charles Toney, Daniel Reynolds, Washington Stubblefield,
    Martha Cruise, et al.
375 Inv of estate of Thomas Holderness decd by Emanuel Watlington adm on 10 Oct 1833.
376 Sales estate of James A. Durham decd sold 5 July 1833 to Robert W. Worsham,
    Wm. H. Burns, Richard Durham, Charles Murphey, Elijah Gibson, Thomas Archer,
    Thomas Samuel, Isaac Durham, William Arnett, William Stokes, et al.
    By Wm. H. Burns adm.
377 Sales estate of Robert Swift on 25 Oct 1833 to John Swift, John Cobb Jun.,
    Granderson Siddle, Nancey Swift, et al. By Samuel Moore adm.
377 Additional sales of Thomas Slade Sen decd. - 2 hogs sold to Wm. Warren for $6.50.
378 Acct sales of Henry Hooper held 20 Dec 1833 at his late residence. Sales to
    Reubin Oliver(1 yoke oxen $21), Wm. R. McKinney, W. Hooper (1 watch $28),
    Zach Hooper Jun. (lot of Latin books), Dr. Gunn (Conversations of Lord Byron
    and Don Juan), Lovelace Hailey (pocket compass).
378 Sales estate of Thomas Holderness decd to Elizabeth Holderness, Samuel Moore,
    James W. Jeffreys, James Lea, Ibzan Rice, John Lyon.
379 Acct current of Thomas Harrison decd by John P. Harrison adm.
381 Acct current of William Smith decd by John Smith exec.
382 Acct current of James Nelson decd by Abraham Landers and Samuel Nelson exec.
    Notes on Mary Douglass, Ambrose Nelson.
384 Sale of negroes of Stephen Chandler decd 25 Dec 1833 to Nathaniel Lea, John
    Burton. By Stephen J. and James D. Chandler.
384 Allotment to Nancy Swift widow of Robert Swift for 1 year's provisions.
385 Div of negrees of Christopher Roberson decd to the widow or to Robert A. Crow-
    der for the widow; to Edward H Roberson; to Robert A. Crowder. Widow Mildred
    Roberson decd previous to this order. Sale of negroes to Edward Roberson.
    By Robert A. Crowder adm.
386 Div of negroes of James Wright decd to Thomas L. Lea intermarried with Ann B.,
    daughter of James Wright decd. Lea recd ¼ part due him. By George Williamson.
387 Div negroes of Robert Swift decd to Westley, Robert G. Martha F., Nancy(widow),
    and Mary Margaret Swift. 5 Dec 1833.
388 Div negroes of Griffin Gunn - a part to William P. Gunn which is one-sixth of
    the total. 27 Dec 1833.
389 Sale of negroes of Samuel C. Smith decd to John G. Wingfield, Ashley G. Lea,
    Henry McAden. By Geo Williamson adm.

April Court 1834

390 Inv and sales estate of James Love decd sold 11 Jan 1834 by John W. McKissack,adm.
    Sales to Anderson Brummitt, Archd. Richmond, Benj. Murrow, Calvin Love, John
    D. Moore, H. Lockard, J. C. Morgan, Jno Snipes, Jno Hubbard, Johnson Scoggins,
    James Love Sen., Martin Frazer, Pleasant Brummitt, Saml. Love, Thos. Overby,
    Stephen Monday, Will Brummitt, A. McAlpin, M. D. Norfleet,, Thomas Pool, et al.
393 Sales property of Mildred Roberson decd by Robert A. Crowder adm sold 28 Jan
    1834. Negroes sold to J. Owen, E. H. Roberson, J. Adams, A. Gunn.

Book M 1834
Page
394 Sales property of George Walker decd sold 1 Nov 1833 to Abner Walker, Lemuel
    Dabbs, Joseph Massey, William Kimbrough, John Smith, Mary Walker, Deborah Walker
    William Barnhill, Christopher Brooks, James R. Lea, William & Thomas Turner,
    James Melton, Stephen McCracken, Hugh Walker, James & William Walker, Ruffin
    Pleasant, Josiah Florance, Anthony Benton, Wiley Jones, Durrett Oliver, et al.
    Mary Walker keeps Jenny and her children one year for $25.
398 List of notes and unsettled accts on Geo Walker. By Abner Walker.
399 Sales estate of Benjamin T. Fielder decd sold 13 Feb 1834 to William P. Fielder,
    Freeman Leath, Alfred T. Fielder, Elizabeth Fielder, Sarah A. Fielder.
    By Susannah W. Fielder exec.
400 Sales property of the Revd. James M. Lea by William Lea adm to Reubin Hawkins,
    Elijah Morton, Willis M. Lea. At Leasburg 8 Apr 1834.
401 Acct current estate of Joel Kennon decd. List of sales, names not given.
402 Inv property of Robert Holderness decd taken 15 Feb 1834 by Abner Miles adm.
    Open accts on John Mansfield, James Adkins, Ira Siddle, John Pyron.
    Allotment to widow.
403 Sales property of Robert Holderness sold 3 & 4 Feb 1834 to Mrs. Elizabeth
    Holderness, Emanuel Watlington, David Delaney, Littleton A. Gwynn, Banister
    Fitzgerald, George Roberson, Leonard D. Prather, Walker Bennett, Armistead
    Watlington, Richard H. Griffith, Reed Watlington, Ibzan Rice, Miss Sarah
    Brooks, Thomas Pucket, William Watlington, John H. Pickard, Miles Poteat, et al.
407 Inv estate of Judith Davis decd by Claton Lambert exec. 5 Apr 1834.
407 Inv property of Lewis W. Whitemore decd taken 7 Feb 1834 by John Nunnally adm.
407 Sales estate of Alexander Moore decd by Thomas M. Moore adm. Negro Daniel sold
    to John Bradsher; sales to John Fuller, Robert Moore.
408 Acct current estate of Lewis W. Whitemore decd and acct of sales. Paid John
    B. Lawson for burial expenses, Josiah D. Griffith for coffin, Lancelot Johnston
    for crying sale; paid John Kerr atty in suit Joel Motley vs the adm.
409 JUDITH DAVIS - Will - w. 26 May 1825. Two daughters Elizabeth Davis and Sarah
    Lambert to divide all property. Exec: Claton Lambert. Wit: Melissa (or Melina)
    Person, Mary L. Pattillo. Exec qualified.
410 Acct current estate of Thomas Compton decd by Nancy Compton adm.
411 Acct current estate of William Gooch decd.
412 Inv property of George Walker decd by Abner Walker adm. 28 Oct 1833.
412 Negro woman Franky of estate of Geo Walker sold to Thomas W. Graves.

                    July Court 1834

414 Acct current estate of James Vaughan Jun. decd by Thomas Page adm. Paid Betsy
    Vaughan the widow her allowance.
414 Inv property of James M. Lea decd. $3 recd. of the Revd. Henry Spect.
415 Acct current estate of Lewis Barton decd by Aquilla Barton exec. Paid Josiah
    Womack surveyor, Calvin Graves atty., et al.
416 Acct current estate of George Huston decd by John Russell exec.
417 Sales property of Lewis Barton sold 27 Jan 1832 to Aquilla Barton, Lewis Barton,
    Thomas Barton, Abraham Massey, Rice Barton, James Sanders.
418 Acct current estate of Bartlett Yancey decd by Azariah Graves and Nancy Yancey
    adm. 25 Hogshead tobacco sold in Richmond for $1344.09. Paid expenses of Doct.
    McAden to Chapel Hill $6.75; sent to Rufus at Chapel Hill $14; paid when
    starting to Chapel Hill $105. Paid Rev. John Kerr $75 for Rufus; Paid Joseph
    McCain for Sidney's board. Paid $142 for 1829 for Algernon Yancey at Chapel
    Hill. Paid for schooling at Salem $100.
426 Report of Azariah Graves, County Trustee.
428 Fees collected by Thomas L. Lea for business taxes.
430 Acct current estate of Andrew Harrison by James R. Harrison exec.

                            118

Book M 1834-35
Page   October Court 1834

433 GABRIEL LEA - Will - w. 17 Nov 1826. Wife Elizabeth to have all property that
    she and sons William and James think proper. Son James (land on which he has
    made improvements adj William A. Lea); daughter Mary Morton already received
    tract of land where she lives deeded to her husband Elijah Morton. Son William
    to have 2 shares; son Vincent to get nothing; son Gabriel B. to have one share.
    Daughters Elizabeth, Mary, Phoebe, and Barbara. Exec: sons William & James.
    Wit: James Darby, James M. Lea, Willis M. Lea.
434 Inv estate of William Bethell decd. Notes on William and his wife Ann Nash;
    on Robert Williams, Moses Butler, Josiah Dabbs, Caleb Jones, J. Marr, Mathew
    Mills, John Stadler, Henry Courts, Peyton Key, Joseph McClain, et al.
    Desperate notes on John Ferry, John Davis, Joseph Scales, et al. Due to re-
    ceive from estate of Absolem Watt. By Mary Bethell and Wm. C. Bethell.
437 Inv and sales of Elijah Withers decd sold 7 Oct 1834. Names not given.
    By Elijah K. Withers and John Nunnally adm.
439 Acct current estate of Elisha Rudd decd by Aldridge and Joshua Rudd adm.
    Paid W. A. Graham for counsel.
440 Inv estate of Dudley Gatewood by Sylvanus Stokes, guardian.
441 Additional inv of property of William Richmond decd.
441 Allotment to Elizabeth Holderness widow of Robert Holderness decd for her &
    family. 28 Jan 1834.
442 Year's allowance to Mary Walker from estate of her husband George Walker decd.
442 Negro Tom property of William Steward decd sold on 8 Apr 1834 to Daniel S.
    Coleman. By Garnett Neeley.
443 Report of Wardens of the Poor. Cash left by Jacob Ahart to this fund when he
    died.
444 Nancy Phillips orphan age of 11 years on 8 Aug 1835 bound to James Ingram.
445 Calvin Ward Phillips orphan age 10 years on 17 Apr 1835 bound to James Ingram.
446 Nancy Burge orphan age of 6 years bound to Nathaniel J. Palmer.

       January Court 1835
448 Div of negroes of estate of John McMullin decd to: Sally Allin, Isaac Vanhook
    in behalf of his wife Elizabeth, James McMullin, Catharine A. McMullin,
    heirs or children of Elijah Hester on behalf of their mother Mary Hester,
    John B. McMullin. 12 Nov 1834.(Div into 7 shares - name of one receiver not
    given - apparently for widow.)
449 Year's allowance to Margaret McMullin widow of John McMullin. 14 Nov 1834.
450 Acct current estate of William Richmond decd.
451 Sales property of Robert Holderness decd sold 2 Jan 1835 to Elizabeth Holderness
    and Elisha Evans. By Abner Miles adm.
451 Inv estate of Mary Hester decd made by John B. McMullin adm. 3 negroes, Jack,
    Sam, and Fanny.
452 Sales property of Azariah G. Kimbro decd sold 12 Nov 1834 to James Aldridge,
    Thomas Page, Benjamin Browder, Mary J. Chandler, John Peterson, Thomas W.
    Chandler, Thomas Peterson, Durrett Oliver, William Richmond, William Browning.
    By Goodwin Evans adm.
453 Sales estate of John McMullin sold 14 & 15 Nov 1834 to:

Henry Allin	Sally Allin	Allen Burton	Green W. Brown
Anderson Brummitt	Madison Drake	Jefferson Evans	Elijah Haster
Charles Hendrick	Stanford Jones	Jas. N.Johnston	John Kimbrough
William Lea	Matthew Long	William Long	Robert Love
John B. McMullin	Wm. S. Marshall	Samuel Mitchell	Katharine A.McMullin
Margaret McMullin	Thomas Oakley	Thomas Owen	Charles Marshall
Elijah Jacobs	James G. Rainey	Thomas Snipes	Thomas Stafford
Nathaniel Snipes	Isaac Vanhook	Samuel R. Woods	

    Notes on James Roan, A. Allen, W. McMurray, James McMurray.
456 Inv property of Azariah G. Kimbro by Goodwin Evans adm. Bonds on Richard
    Whitemore, John Kimbro, William Turner, Vincent Griffin, Miles Kimbro.
    Note on Z. T. Kerr (1828) desperate.

                        119

Book M 1835
Page
456 Sale of negroes of Joseph Cobb sold 6 Jan 1835 at Court House in Yanceyville.
457 Inv property of Thomas Vaughan decd and sales by James C. Turner and John
Vaughan adm. Sales to James Vaughan, Micajah Pleasant, Joseph Rudd, Brice
Collins, James Currie, William Barnwell, Robert Scott, Hiram Parks, Thornton
Baynes, Alexander Miles, Philip Cook, Jesse Scott, et al.

April Court 1835

462 WILLIAM COBB - Will - w. 21 Apr 1834. Wife Mary A. Cobb all land during her
life, then land to go to James N. Cobb on N. side of branch where he lives and
balance to son William M. Cobb. Son Jesse to have $5. Balance estate to all
children: Amzi, Milton, Wm. M., James N. Cobb, Henrietta Haten(Hasten?),
Celia Humphres, Catharine Harrison. Exec: wife, sons James N. & Wm. M.
Test: Jas. E. Williamson, John H. Pickard. James & William Cobb qualified.

463 Inv and sales of Elijah Withers decd taken 6 Apr 1835 by Elijah K. Withers and
John Nunnally. Buyers not listed.
463 Second return of monies due estate of Aaron Simpson decd.

464 ELIZABETH MALONE - Will - w. 30 Dec 1834. All estate received from her Father's
estate to be divided into 7 shares and to go to following children: William,
Ellis, Lewis, James, Mary, and Eliza Malone, and to Sarah Stephens (or in case
of her death to her daughter Barbary Stephens). Land adj John C. Vanhook and
John Broughton to be sold. Exec: brother William Lea. Wit: Willis M. Lea,
William Lea Jr. Exec qualified.

465 Amt of hire of negroes of estate of Thomas Vaughan decd to James Vaughan, Micajah
Pleasant, William Muzzall, Elijah Morton, John Miles, Bennett Warren, Jesse
Scott, Joseph Rudd.
465 Additional inv of William McDaniel decd. Amt paid by James W. Jeffreys.
466 Sales property of James Lea (Hop) decd sold 7 Mar 1835 to John Lea(CB), Elijah
Morton, Woodlief Thomas, Alexander Donoho, Nathaniel Lea, John W. Lea, Thomas
L. Lea, Dennis a slave, Richard Bennett, William Hooper, Elizabeth Lea, William
Lea, John Walton, Yancey Oliver, John Reed, Thomas Burton, James Herrin, Nancy
Lea, Noles Reed, Edwd. D. Wright. By Geo Williamson adm.
467 Inv property of Hannah Bastin decd by John Powell adm. Cash collected of Joseph
Medcalf.
468 Div negroes of estate of Elijah Withers to: John Nunnally for his wife Sytha
Ann, Elijah K. Withers, William Withers, Catharine Withers(widow), Lewis
Withers; James, John, Elizabeth, and Albert G. Withers.
469 Inv estate of James Lea (Hop) made by George Williamson adm. Included 12 boxes
tobacco in Onslow County (NC). Cash received of Thomas Benton for sale of
manufactured tobacco in Onslow Co.
469 Zachariah Lockett, Jailor of Caswell Co., believes the public Jail insufficient
to hold the prisoners and is in a state of decay and is now rotting down and
one strong man can with a small knife effect his escape in a few hours.
470 Sales estate of Gabriel Lea by William Lea exec sold 31 Oct 1834. Notes on
Drury Kiersey, Fleming Childers, Thos C. Pass, Reubin Hawkins, Ferrell Fulcher.
471 Sale negroes of estate of Azariah G. Kimbro decd to William Graves, John Miles,
Duke W. Kimbrough. Declared by court that Goodwin Evans and wife Nancy G.,
Mary Chandler, Duke W. Kimbrough, and Elijah G. Kimbrough are entitled to one-
fourth part of proceeds of sale for each.
472 Div negroes of estate of Samuel C. Smith to Doct. Robert B. Thornton and wife
Frances a daughter of Samuel C. Smith to have 2/3 part; to Sarah S. Smith widow
to have 1/3 part.
474 Sale of negroes of Littleberry Worsham to David Tranam, Gideon Turner, Nathaniel
Lea, Hutchings Ferrell, Wm. H. Burns. By Benj. C. West.

Book M 1835
Page
475 THOMAS VAUGHAN - Will - w. 26 Jan 1829. Son Richard (240 acres land); daughter
Lucy Parks; daughter-in-law Ritter Vaughan widow of James Vaughan and her 3
daughters; Grandsons John, Richard, and Asa Vaughan. One dollar each to heirs
of son John Vaughan, son Thomas Vaughan, heirs of son Claibourne Vaughan,
heirs of daughter Polly Brooks, daughter Frances Wells, daughter Sally Pellar,
heirs of son Nicholas Vaughan, daughter Elizabeth Vaughan, heirs of daughter
Patsy Scott. Exec: son Richard Vaughan. Wit: Starling Warren, Henderson Smith,
Philip Cook.Richard Vaughan refused to qualify. Thomas Bigelow and John
Vaughan appointed adm with will annexed.

July Court 1835

476 Acct current estate of Joel Thomas decd by John Comer adm. Payments to Thomas
Day, Willie Jones, Agness Thomas, Fleming Nelson, et al.
477 Inv and sales estate of Andrew Harrison sold 17 Apr 1835 to Daniel Gunn, Robert
Rolin, Wm. W. Richardson, Abisha Slade, Andrew Harrison, Azariah Walters,
Archibald Walters, Noel Burton, Thomas Knight, George Stephens, Wm. J. Harrison,
James McClarney, Creed T. Oliver, William Scott, Robert Harrison, John Everett,
Thomas Ware, Tolbert Ware, Jacob Coals; Susan, Elizabeth, and James R. Harrison.
479 Inv property of Sarah Smith decd by George Smith.
480 Acct current estate of Aaron Simpson decd.
481 Acct current estate of Robert Swift decd by Samuel Moore adm. Notes on Jefferson
Brown, A. Haddock. Paid Thos Gibson for crying sale.
482 Report of Wardens of the Poor for 1834.
483 Settlement estate of Harvey Swift decd by John Swift adm. Paid Dr. J. Currie;
484 Inv and sales estate of Mary Harrison decd sold 17 Apr 1835 to Wm. W. Richardson,
Robert Rowlin, Granderson M. Sharp, Warren Holcomb, Frances Ray, Thomas D.
Rowlins, Henry Shepherd, Thomas Travice, William Johns, et al. Jas. R.Harrison.
485 Inv personal estate of William Cobb by Wm. M. and James N. Cobb exec.
485 Sales property of William Cobb decd sold 14 May 1835 to Thomas Gibson, Forister
Stainback, John C. Totten, Alfred M. Nash, Nicholas Lovelace, Mary A. Cobb,
Andrew Johnston, Francis Cornwell, Amsey Cobb, et al.
486 Inv property of Elizabeth Holloway decd taken 29 Apr 1835 by John Holloway adm.
487 Sales of Elizabeth Holloway to John Holloway, William Burton, Alfred Badget,
John Cobb, Sally McClarney, William Weatherford, James Ferrell, Susan Holloway,
Edmund Cook, Elijah Ford, Bennett Burris, William Stokes, Thomas Crews,
Obediah Crews, John Astin, Joel Motley, Clark H. Doss, Henry Rowark, George W.
Tyree, Jincy Ware, Nathaniel Roach, Joseph Medkiff, John Keesee.
490 Sales estate of Obadiah Holloway sold 1 May 1835 by John Holloway to Greenbury
Voss, John Holloway, Richard R. Kennon, Wesley Cook, Susan Holloway, David
Tyree plus same buyers at sale of Elizabeth Holloway.
493 Inv property of Obediah Holloway sold 13 May 1835.
494 Sales and Inv property of Thomas Massey decd sold 28 Apr 1835 by William Massey,
adm. Sales to David Hightower, Empson Fitch, George Vaughan, James Boswell,
Josiah & James Page, Joseph Massey, Jacob Walker, John Bird; Mark, Nathan, and
Levi Massey,Ruffin Pleasant, Rich G. Lampkin, William Massey, William Turner,
William Bird.
495 Taxable property for 1834.
496 Azariah Graves county trustee, acct with Caswell Co. for 1833.
497 Acct current of Martha Lyon decd.
498 ELIZABETH BARTON - Will - w. 6 Apr 1835. Her half of land to be sold. The
6 orphan children of John Barker decd in the western country to have $10 each
if they are all alive. Remainder to children of brother Thomas Barton.
Exec: Dr. James E. Williamson. Wit: Robert R. Prather, James H. Thompson.
Exec qualified.
499 Sales estate of Sarah Smith decd by George Smith adm sold 8 June 1835 to Thomas
Burton, J. M. Drake, Samuel Nelson, Catharine Hightower, Nelson Thomas, Nancy
Hightower, Robert Smith, Sarah Jackson, John Foster, Elizabeth Evans, et al

121

Book M 1835
Page
500 Frances Cock orphan age of eleven years in March last bound to Charles Cock.
    David N. Nutt, Chairman County Court.
501 Silas Craftin orphan age of 7 years bound to Thomas Thompson.
502 Washington Dixon orphan now 10 years in June last bound to William Fuller Jr.
503 Milton Bass age 7 years bound to Daniel W. Swan.
504 Div negroes of Andrew Harrison decd. Met at house of the late Mary Harrison on
    15 Apr. Legatees: Creed T. Oliver adm of Jane Oliver decd, Elizabeth B. Harri-
    son, Susan Harrison.
505 Amt of business taxes recd. by Thos L. Lea, Sheriff in accordance with act of
    1831 General Assembly.

507 JAMES LEA,SEN. - Will - w. 5 July 1832. Wife Frances Lea (house and land during
    her life adj land of John C. Lea, Swan, and Dr. Comer, Alfred Lea, & Reed).
    Land and property advanced to son John Lea(the Wilson tract 250 acres & money
    advanced); son James R. Lea(land whereon he now lives 517 acres); son Tinsley
    Lea already advanced money and horses; son Rucker Lea (money advanced and given
    land in Smith Co. Tenn., on Goose Creek 228 acres, land later to go to his
    children); son Archibald Lea(land whereon he lives 255 acres and money advanced)
    Duaghter Matilda Oliver (money and property already advanced); daughter Nancey
    Oliver(money and property advanced). Son Alfred M. Lea(land adj William Long
    and Tinsley Lea 305 acres and 237 acres where Tinsley formerly lived);
    son Ashley G. Lea (land on nw side of road, except orchard and stable, and land
    given to wife after her death). Alfred and Ashley to have blacksmith Peter
    and smith's tools. Remainder of estate to be appraisedand divided to all
    children. Exec: friend George Williamson, but if he should die before will
    executed, son Alfred M. Lea to execute. Wit: Calvin Graves, John G. Lea.
    Proved at July Court on oath of John G. Lea. Geo Williamson qualified.
    Also proved on oath of Calvin Graves.

                October Court 1835

511-515 blank
516 Sale property of William McMennamy decd by Roberson McMennamy adm sold 28 Aug to
    Aquilla Compton, James McMennamy, Elisha Rowark, William Hester, James Davis,
    John Allison, Young Burt, Sieria G. Compton, Erasmus Compton, the widow, Nathan
    Jeffreys, James C. Stewart, John H. Wells, Anterkin Smith, Harvey Currie, Abram
    Landers, Thomas Ward, Martin Warren, James S. Dunn.
520 Sales estate of Elizabeth Malone decd by William Lea exec. Land sold to John
    Hagwood at $6 per acre 66 acres on Kilgoes Branch.
521 Inv estate of William McMennamy by adm on 27 Aug 1835. Judgments on Elijah
    Perry, Drady Willson; notes on Robert & William Christopher, John Collins,
    William Mansfield, James Murray, Andrew Woods, Wm. Pinchback, Elisha Rowark.
522 Sale estate of Gabriel Lea - tobacco sold at Petersburg 3 Aug 1835 - 2 hogshead
    for $171,43. William Lea exec.
523 Inv and sales estate of Albert Mathews sold 27 Aug 1835 by R. G. Lampkin adm.
    Sales to George W. Lampkin, Thomas Haydon, Wm. & James Vaughan, Sophia W.
    Matthews, Wm. & Thomas Turner, Joseph Aldridge, Aldridge Rudd, David Melton,
    Lemuel Dabbs, Wm. Morton, et al. Accts on Miles Wilmouth, David Melton, Berry
    Evans, Howard Martin, Thomas Haydon.
525 Inv estate of James Lea Sen. taken 31 July 1835. Included 31 negroes. Notes
    on Wm. Lea, James Matlock, Ansel Ware, John Comer, John Hendrick, Daniel Rich-
    mond, et al. Cash on hand $2380.21. Notes on John Campbell Sen. & Jun. due
    1828, John K. Lea, Daniel Hicks, James Fullington, Philip Walton, Stephen
    Haddock. By Geo Williamson adm.
526 Negro man Gilbert of the estate of Elijah Withers decd sold July last to Thomas
    W. Harrelson for $417.75.

527 MICAJAH PLEASANT, SEN. - Will - w. 15 Jan 1833. Daughters Sarah, Willey, &
    Louisa Pleasant. Grandson Micajah Graves $100 of share given to daughter Eliza-
    beth Greer. Balance estate to Milbery Henslee, Dolley Miles, Lucey Aldridge,
    Elizabeth Greer, Nancy Benson, and Sarah. 3 sons: Ruffin, Benjamin,and Micajah.
                                122

Book M 1835-36
Page
527 cont. Will of Micajah Pleasant
All daughters Milbry, Sarah, Willy, Dolly, Lucey, Elizabeth, Nancy, and Louisa
to divide slaves. Exec: friends Richard Aldridge and Samuel Greer. Wit: Thos
Prendergast, Brice Collins. Exec qualified.

528 Additional return estate of Elijah Withers decd.

529 ZACHARIAH HASTING - Will - w. 4 Mar 1831. Son William Hasting all real estate,
200 acres; son James Hasting 50¢ as already given to him; daughter Lucy Brintle
50¢ plus what was heretofore given. Daughters Elizabeth Hasting and Polly Hasting; granddaughter Elizabeth Brintle. Exec: son William Hasting. Wit: John Lea,
F. Leath, George A. Swift. Exec qualified.

530 Micajah Graves orphan age 10 years on 10 Sept last bound to Samuel Greer.
531 Inv estate of Joseph Worsham decd by B. C. West adm. Apr 1835. One-seventh part
of slaves sold at Act Court decree. Sales estate of Joseph Worsham.
531 Congressional returns to 24th Congress - August H. Sheppard Esq. received 198
votes, the highest number.

532 JOSEPH SCOTT - Will - w. 12 July 1834. Daughter Polly Blackwell (land on which
Garland Blackwell lives 200 acres); Grandson James Blackwell. Daughter Jane
Watlington (land adj Joshua Butler, a chappel line, to bridge on Hogan's Creek
350 acres). Balance of land where I live after death of wife Elizabeth to
sons-in-law Garland Blackwell and James Watlington to compensate for large debt
paid for son John Scott. Property given to Jane and Polly later to go to their
children. Large debt paid for son John Scott will take all intended for him.
Exec: Garland Blackwell and James Watlington. Wit: John H. Pickard, Wm. P.
Forrest. Codicil on 20 July 1835: Exec to care and manage for wife.
Exec qualified.

January Court 1836

535 JOHN MIMS - Will - w. 17 Dec 1832. Wife to all including dwelling house for her
life. Sons Martin M.(land whereon he lives), Drury Alexander(100 acres),
John Wright(portion alloted to wife and all estate and to own home jointly with
his Mother). Duaghter Frances is under age. Son Thomas Banister(land east of
testator adj Abner Miles, Col. Thomas Graves). Exec: Richard Jones, Martin M.
Mims, Thomas B. Mims, and John W. Mims. Wit: Abner Miles, James Adkins.
Richard Jones and John W. Mims qualified.

537 JOSHUA HIGHTOWER, SEN. - Will - w. 14 Oct 1835. Wife Priscilla to have all estate
for her life and then estate to be sold and equal division made between 7 child-
ren: James Hightower, Betsy F. Fuller, Joshua Hightower, Martha E. Hightower,
Sally L. Hightower, Mary A. Brummitt, and Rebecca S. Lea. Exec: friend Henry
Allen and Alanson M. Lea. Wit: H. Allen, M. D. Norfleet, Lemuel Jackson.
Alanson M. Lea qualified.

538 RANSOM BOSWELL - Will - w. 13 May 1834. Wife Elizabeth all estate for her life
and afterwards to her children: daughters Fanny, Elizabeth, and Eliza;
sons Antiochus(land after death of wife); daughter Peggy 1/9 part;
son Howell 1/9 part; daughter Polly Cobb(her part in trust and then to her
children); son Parabo 1/9 part in trust; son James. Exec: son Howell and wife
Elizabeth. Wit: John E. Brown, Jas E. Williamson. Howell Boswell qualified.
540 Inv estate of Robert Hughes decd by Mathew Mills adm. Notes on Richard Bennett
and H. House. Open acct on Ibzan Rice.
540 Sales estate of Elizabeth Malone sold 7 Oct 1833. Recd. from estate of Gabriel
Lea decd. William Lea adm.
541 Additional inv estate of Benjamin Stephens.
542 Inv estate of Paul Carrington decd by Jno. B. Carrington adm. 21 Nov 1835.
543 Inv of specific legacies of estate of Micajah Pleasant decd to Sarah and Willy
Pleasant and to Louisa Warren. 16 Oct 1835. By Samuel Greer & Richard Aldridge.
543 Inv personal estate of Micajah Pleasant decd taken 16 Oct 1835. Notes Willis
Ashford, Wm. Henslee. Accts anti James Mitchell, Wilson Jeffreys.

Book M 1836
Page

545 Sales property of Micajah Pleasant sold 5 and 6 Nov 1835 to William Barnwell,
Sarah Pleasant, William Miles, Willey Pleasant, Henry Turner, Bird Bateman,
Bennett Warren, Joseph Aldridge, Elijah Hethcock, James Murphey, Brice Collins,
John Murphey, Nathan Jeffreys, Samuel Dunn, Ruffin Pleasant, William Henslee,
Micajah Pleasant, John Benson, Reubin Oliver, Jacob Guy, Wm. Warren, et al.

549 Sales property of Philip Cook decd sold 2 Dec 1835 to Thomas Smith, Nathaniel
Snipes, Bird Bateman, James McMinemy, Elijah Jones, Henry Burton, John Foster,
William Barnwell, Luke Arnold, John Love, Margaret Warren, Priscilla Cook,
Joel Harp, John Wilson, James Bouldin, et al. By John Miles adm.

552 Sales estate of Berry Hunt decd sold 2 Jan 1836 to Jonathan Starkey, Thomas
Starkey, Mrs. Hunt, Thomas Poteet, Solomon Hunter, Rebecca Parish. By Jonathan
Starkey adm.

553 Sales estate of Robert Hughs decd sold 19 Dec 1835 to Mathew Mills, Leander
Nunnally, T. J. Mills, John Hughs. By Mathew Mills adm.

554 Acct current of Robert Holderness decd by Abner Miles adm. Cash received of
E. Watlington for keeping Thos Holderness' horses at Robert's house until his
death. Paid widow for keeping negroes. Paid Reuben C. Trayham for coffin $5;
Tho W. Graves for crying sale; John Kerr atty fee; paid widow's allowance;
paid Eliza Holderness widow her part of balance being one child's part.

556 Acct current estate of Thomas Holderness decd by Emanuel Watlington adm.
Bonds on Elijah Graves, Henry F. Smith, John Lyon. Paid vouchers of Abner
Miles, John H. Graves, John Kerr Jr., Paul Watlington.

557 Div negroes of estate of Griffin Gunn decd - appraisal and part due Francis
Thornton and Huldah M. his wife, one-fifth part of negroes in hands of John C.
Harvey her guardian.

557 Div negroes of James Wright decd - appraisal to George G. Lea and Sarah E. his
wife entitled to one-third of negroes in hands of guardian George Williamson.
Balance due them from Martha J. and Weldon E. Wright. 28 Dec 1835.

558 Div negroes of Claiborne Crisp decd between 3 legal legatees: Benjamin Wells
and wife Eliza, William H. Crisp, and David H. Crisp as joint tenants. Met
at house of Benjamin Wells 26 Inst.

559 Minerva Nash orphan age 3 years in Aug 1835 bound to William Woods.

April Court 1836

560 JONATHAN STARKEY - Will - w. 17 Jan 1829. Thomas Starkey; sister Rachael Starkey
to have one negro for her life then said negro to brother Abraham Starkey;
Judith Griffith; Jonathan Starkey son of brother Abraham; Jonathan Clempson $100
sister Mary Hunt and her children; remainder of estate to be sold and divided
to children of Mary Clempson, Juda Griffith, and John Starkey's children.
Brother John Starkey's son Jonathan Starkey $100; sister Mary's son Jonathan
Hunt $100. Exec: Thomas Starkey and Richard H. Griffith. Wit: Philip Hodnett,
James M. Harrelson. Thomas Starkey qualified.

561 Inv personal estate of Ransom Boswell decd by Howell Boswell exec.

561 Inv and sales estate of Martha Lipscomb decd by William Eskridge adm. Negroes
sold to William A. Lea and R. Curry.

562 List of sales of William Ware sold 21 March 1836 by Thomas Turner adm. to:

Martin Durham	Laban Ford	Nathaniel Harrelson	Jason Ware
Cary W. West	William Durham	Jesse Atkinson	Wm. C. Donoho
James Swann	Samuel Magonigal	Joel A. Stokes	John Travis
Dudley G. Stokes	Ellis Travis	James Travis	Thomas Travis
Mrs. Frances Ware	Tolbert Ware	Stephen Sergent	Jesse Alverson
Edmund Cook	John Holloway	Edmund Cook	Henry Cook
Johnston Atkinson	George Roberson	William Astin	Josiah Blair
David Tyree	et al		

566 Inv property of James Cooper decd by Allen R. Cooper adm taken 8 Apr 1836.

567 Acct of sales of property of Charles K. Harrison sold 7 Jan 1836.

568 Sales property of Elijah Withers decd sold 31 Dec 1835 by John Nunnally adm.

Book M 1836
Page
569 Acct current estate of Zephaniah T. Kerr decd by Alexander Wiley adm. Bonds
on Thomas L. Slade; Recd. cash from James Kerr exec of John Kerr decd the amt.
due deceased from said John Kerr his grandfather $40.50. 14 Apr 1836. By
Thomas Graves and John H. Graves adm.
569 Sales property of Ransom Boswell decd by Howell Boswell exec sold 18 Feb 1836 to
Antiochus E. Boswell, Samuel Moore, John E. Brown.
570 Settlement estate of Christopher Roberson decd by Robert A. Crowder adm. Paid
T. Donoho for crying sale; payments to Saml. Kiersey, Will H. Burns, John H.
Crockett for freight of tobacco; T. Day for coffin $20; R. Bullock tanyard acct.;
balance of bond to Henry Roberson and E. H. Roberson. Tobacco sold in Richmond.
572 Acct current estate of Alexander Moore decd by Thomas M. Moore adm. Cash recd.
from B. S. Tatum, Charles Sallard for bonds; payments to Samuel A. Douglass
for tayloring, John Norwood atty; D. A. Penick for preaching funeral; clerks
of Person and Caswell Counties, et al.
573 Abner Walker adm in acct with estate of George Walker decd. Recd. payments from
Thomas Bigelow, Archibald Bateman, Wiley Burke, et al. Paid accts of Mary and
Deborah Walker; paid Martha Debruler for tuition.
574 Year's allowance to Mary Hunt widow of Berry Hunt decd. 1 Apr 1836.
575 Mintus Rollin orphan now age of 5 years in Nov. last bound to Freeman Leath.
George Williamson, Chairman County Court.

July Court 1836

577 Inv estate of George Holcomb decd taken 13 Apr 1836 by Allen Holcomb adm.
Acct against Hiram Holcomb.
578 Inv of Bird Eskridge decd taken 27 Apr 1836 by Booker Boman adm.
578 Inv of Jonathan Starkey decd taken 7 July 1836 by Thomas Starkey exec. Notes
on John Gomer; Miles, Mason, and William Poteat.
580 Inv of perishable property of Thomas Harrelson decd by Thomas W. Harrelson and
Philip Hodnett adm. Accts on Owen McAleer, Dabney Rainey.
581 Sale perishable estate of Thomas Harrelson by adm on 18 May 1836 to:

Nathaniel Harrelson	James Evans	James R. Lea	Iverson Ingram
Granderson M. Sharp	Reuben Oliver	Joseph Henderson	Ibzan Rice
Henry Willis Jr.	David Melton	John Willis	William Hooper
Zachariah Lockett	George W. Willis	W. H. Lunsford	Martha Harrelson
Sterling Kent	Charles Hendrick	Joseph Lunsford	Thomas Puckett
James Poteat	P. A. Haralson	Wm. Watlington	Thos D. Johnston
Thomas Knight	William Powell	Jesse Dunavent	John Roberts
John Kerr Jr.	Brice Collins	et al	

585 Inv perishable property of estate of Thomas Henslee decd sold 6 May 1836 by
Bedford Henslee adm. Certain articles assigned to the widow.
586 Inv and sales estate of Conrad Strador decd by Christian Strador adm.
Sales to Martha, Obed, and David Strador; R. R. Kennon, William Greenwood,
Thomas Norman, Banister Fitzgerald, Robert Williamson, Henry Rolin, William
London, Reason Jeffreys, James Raleigh, et al. Allotment to widow.
588 Inv property of William Anderson decd.
590 Balance found on Store books of William Anderson decd. Accts. against David
Northington, Jacob Graves, David D. Nutt, Branch Chalkly, Armistead C. Henry,
Joseph Bradford, Stephen Pettiford, Absolem Lea, Lucy Murphey, Yancey Wiley,
Walden Vowell, et al.
592 Bonds of William Anderson decd on Jno Mitchell, Katharine Hightower, James Mansfield, Will Mayhan, Downey Wade, John N. Carver, John Fitch, et al.
592 Judgments and executions of William Anderson.
594 Officer's receipts for William Anderson. By Yancey Wiley adm. Allotment set
aside for widow.
595 Estate sales, William Anderson, by Yancey Wiley adm sold 16 Feb 1836 to Thomas
Hardon, James Currie Maj., Jonathan Murphey, Robert Wiley, James Currie Esq.,
Katharine Hightower, Archd Baynes, Marmaduke Norfleet, Lea Richmond, Thomas Pool,
Masse Nelson, Bird Bateman, Dr. Jno Comer, Dr. Levi Walker, Daniel Jackson,
John & Nat Snipes, Al M. Lea, James McMeniway, Sarah Anderson, Wm. McMurray,

125

Book M 1836
Page
599 - sales Wm. Anderson cont. - to Joseph Langley, John W. Hightower, Thos Owen,
     John Love, Jno Foster, James Crossett, Robt. Browning, Alexander Wiley Sen. et al
600 Sales and rent of lands belonging to estate of John Graves decd. Land recd. by
     Groves Howard 441 acres, Pleasant H. Womack 360 acres, William Smith 163 acres,
     Francis Smith 5 6/10 acres; tract divided between William and Thomas Graves
     225 acres; rent of Moon's Creek plantation to William Graves; paid Elijah
     Graves Jun. for bond.
601 Sales property of William Sawyer decd sold 27 May 1836 to Alvis and Sarah Sawyer,
     William Madkins, Thomas Pinnix, George Dishon. By Ezekiel Sawyer adm.
602 Acct current estate of John Graves decd by Thomas, Azariah, Elijah, and William
     Graves exec. Paid John Wilson for surveying; Dr. Henry McAden acct.; William
     Love for surveying, David Kyles, Charles L. Hunter, et al;Balance due estate
     $7977.55.
604 Acct current estate of Thomas L. Stephens decd by James Farley adm. Amt paid
     following heirs: John W. Stephens, Isaac Wade in right of his wife Margaret,
     Margaret Stephens, Connard Stephens, Edmund Stephens.
605 Acct current estate of Elijah Withers decd by John Nunnally adm.
607 Report of County Trustee, Azariah Graves.
608 Year's allowance for Mrs. Frances Ware from estate of her decd husband William
     Ware.
609 Year's allowance for Sarah Anderson widow of William Anderson decd.
609 Year's allowance to Martha Strador widow of Conrad Strador decd.
610 Henry Allen reports he found a stray mare on his freehold, 26 Apr 1835, and
     valued by Robert Love and Wm. Lea, said gray mare has appearance of Fistula
     and has mark of gear neutral trotter, valued at $16.
610 Report of Wardens of the Poor - balance of $387. Recommended tax 3¢ on every
     $100 worth of land and 10¢ on every poll for poor tax. Commrs: John P. Harrison
     W. Hooper, Abner Miles, William Lea, Thos Reid.
611 Expartee report of Wardens of the Poor - small tract of land belonging to Rachel
     Paschal an idiot and pauper of the county sold for $37. Land purchased by
     Pharo Somers. Woodlief Hooper, Chairman Wardens of the Poor. 11 July 1836.
612 William Chandler orphan age 9 years bound to William Atkins.
     Thomas Williamson, Chairman County Court.

October Court 1836

613 JOHN McMURRY - Will - w. 9 Sept. 1836. Wife Amey (or Any) McMurry all property
     and all interest in co-partnership with Saml. Mitchell and money from profits
     of slaves now in hands of son Madison McMurry, also money due from James Daniel.
     One slave to be returned to former owner Haztele Lofland. Son Saml. to have
     land that belonged to son John McMurry decd in Carrol Co., Ga., 202 acres.
     Exec: wife Amey and sons James B. and Madison McMurry. Wit: George W. Roberts,
     Saml. Mitchell. Anny McMurry qualified.

614 JOHN JEFFREYS - Will - w. 30 March 1836. Daughters Patsey Chandler and Elizabeth
     Terry $1 each; sons John, Thomas, William $1 each; heirs of daughter Mildred
     Groom $1; daughters Ann and Polly Jeffreys beds and clothing. Rest of property
     to son Ellis Jeffreys and he to care for his Mother and for Ann and Polly.
     Exec: friend Samuel C. Cobb. Wit: Michael Montgomery, Samuel C. Cobb.
     Samuel C. Cobb renounced his right to execute. Ellis Jeffreys qualified
     adm with will annexed.

614 WILLIAM PLEASANT - Will - w. 4 Sept. 1805. Son John Pleasant $100 now in hands
     of Andrew McCauley. Wife Martha all property during her life and then to go to
     all children. Land where I now live to sons Tignal and William and their heirs.
     Wife to assist children if they call for part of estate. Exec: wife Martha
     and friend Richard Hightower. Wit: L. Johnston, James Murphey, John Landers.
     Will of William B. Pleasant proved on oath of James Murphey. Exec and Execx
     named are dead. Ordered James B. Pleasant adm with will annexed.

615 Acct current estate of Mildred Robertson decd with Robert A. Crowder adm.Paid
     John Oglesby for crying sale; pd R. A. Crowder adm of C. Robertson decd.
     At Milton, NC. 10 Oct 1836.   126

Book M 1836 - 37
Page
616 Sale of negroes Maria and her child Minerva to John E. Brown $884.10. Sold
    by Howell Boswell at Brown's Store.
617 Acct current estate of Mary Harrison decd with James R. Harrison adm.
618 Inv and list of sale of property of estate of Dudley Gatewood decd sold 23 Aug
    1836 to Josiah Blair, Daniel W. Swan, William and Noel Burton, James Dix,
    Jesse Adkinson. Wm. W. Knight, Robert Gatewood, Dudley Y. Stokes, Rebecca
    Gatewood, Nathl Harrelson, Dr. Nath. T. Green, Elisha and Jesse Alverson,et al.
    By Sylvanus Stokes adm.
620 Inv property of John McMurry decd by Anny McMurry exec.
621 Sales of estate of Peter Badget decd to John Cobb; William, Alfred, and Henry
    Badget; Alfred Howard, Thomas L. Slade, Nancy Badget, Alanson Howard.
622 Inv estate of James Holder decd taken 9 July 1836. Notes on John Hubbard, John
    Slade, L. Lewis, James Simmons, Abraham Pope, James H. Pugh, George Farley,
    Henry Shelton, Fortune Thomas, Singleton Seamore, Welcome Seamore, et al.
    By S. H. Holder adm.
623 Inv personal estate of Peter Badgett decd. Notes on Joel Hix, Wm. Penick,
    Thomas Hix. By William Badgett adm.
624 Inv estate of Elizabeth Barton decd by James E. Williamson adm. Articles found
    in hands of Miss Rebecca Barton of which ½ belonged to Betsy Barton decd.
624 Year's allowance to Mrs. Rebecca Gatewood widow of Dudley Gatewood. 19 Aug.
625 Yancey Wiley adm sells negro Simon to Thomas W. Graves $1101. Jno Snipes paid
    for keeping Cherry and 3 children; Thos L. Seawell for hiring Charlotte;
    Sally Anderson for hire of Nat.

January Court 1837

626 William Beard orphan age of 17 years on 22 Feb next bound to Wyatt Walker and
    Hardy Felts to learn the art of a plater of silver.
626 Sale of negro woman Chloe of estate of Sarah Smith to Robert Smith $250.
    By George Smith adm. Bonded by Nelson Thomas and George Smith Jr.
627 Year's allowance to Ann Neely widow of Garnett Neely decd for her & family.
    16 Nov last.
628 Acct current estate of John McMullin decd.
628 Year's allowance to Sarah Holder widow of James Holder decd.
629 Acct current estate of Azariah Kimbrough decd by Goodwin Evans adm. Payments
    to Legatees: Duke W. Kimbrough, Elijah G. Kimbro, Mary J. Chandler, Goodwin
    Evans and his wife Nancy G. Evans. 31 Dec 1836.
631 Sales estate of Boswell Warren decd on 3 & 4 Nov 1836 to Rainey Warren,
    Jonathan Murphey, James Warren Jun., John Murphey Jr. & Sr., Wilson Hester,
    Eli Hester, Robinson McMineway, Alanson Lea, Mrs. Elizabeth Warren, Wesley
    Warren, Chesley Crisp, Anterkin Smith, Absalom Lea, Brauda Malone Jr., James
    Clarke, Anderson McKee. By William & Yearby Warren adm.
636 Sales estate of William Pleasant decd sold 9 Jan 1837 to William Warren,William
    Rascoe, Wm. Pleasant, John & Loris Pleasant, Dolly Pleasant, Alanson Lea,
    Micajah Pleasant, et al. By James Pleasant adm.
638 Sales perishable estate of William Slade decd by Martha Slade adm sold 5 Nov
    1836 to Wm. Graves, Christopher Brooks, Francis Gooch, Amzi Cobb, et al.
639 Sales property of Jonathan Starkey decd sold 6 Oct 1836 to Azariah Graves,
    John Willis, Durett Oliver, John Sparrow, Rachel Starkey, Joseph Lunsford,
    G. M. Sharpe, Thomas Starkey, Solomon Hunter, A. Ware, Wm. Robards, Archibald
    Lea, Edward & Jesse Dunavent, Barzillai Powell, Nathl. Lea, Wm. Vernon, Wm.
    Fullington, adm. By Thomas Starkey adm.
641 Sale of negroes of Thomas P. Price decd sold 26 Dec 1836 to Wm. W. Price,
    George W. Price, Daniel S. Price, John Keesee, Wm. H. Nunnally, Joshua Young.
    Parcel of books in hands of Dr. James Williamson.
642 Sale remaining estate of Thomas Harrelson decd by Thomas W. Harrelson and Philip
    Hodnett adm to Joseph Windsor, Brice Collins, Martha Harrelson, George Bowling.
645 Sales personal estate of James Holder sold 16 Dec 1836 to Mr. T. L. White,
    Doct. W. Jones, Benjamin Hines, Sarah Holder. By S. H. Holder adm.

Book M 1837
Page

646 Sales property of William Stephens decd sold 6 Dec 1836 to:

John C. Lea	John C. Richmond	Allen Gunter	Iverson G. Stephens
William Stephens	Thomas Greenway	Washington Willis	Thomas Riggs
Col. William Lea	Andrew W. Stephens,	Zachariah McFarland,	Archibald Lea
Rucker Lea	Justin Roan	John Lea Jr.	Katharine Stephens
Katharine Hightower,	John Peterson	John Sparrow	John Fuqua
Alexander Frazier	Currie Richmond	et al	

648 Inv estate of Boswell Warren taken 3 & 4 Nov 1836.

649 List of notes and open accounts of estate of Boswell Warren on Hiram Lockhard, William Fuller, Samuel Mitchell, Bennett Warren, David D. Nutt, Martin Warren, John Dunn, et al. By William and Yearby Warren adm.

January Court 1837 continues in Book N

Page
1 Inv personal property of William Pleasant decd taken 31 Oct 1836 by James B. Pleasant adm.
1 Inv property of John Wiley taken 2 Dec 1836 by A. Wiley adm. Open accts for individuals for seasons to stud horse as will appear in stud horse book so imperfectly made as to render it of little use. Notes on John Mitchell, Jacob Harrel, Davy Kersey, William Hinton, et al.
3 Sales property of John Wiley sold 20 Dec 1836 to Jane Wiley, William Long, Joseph Langley, Reubin Hawkins, John H. Wiley, Marmaduke Norfleet, Nathaniel Verlines, Jefferson Moore, Thomas Richmond, Alexander Winstead, Samuel Love, et al. By A. Wiley adm.
4 Inv estate of William Slade decd by Martha Slade adm pendentilite - included 15 negroes, 497 acres land.
5 Inv property of William Stephens decd by Wm. Long and Mary Stephens exec.
7 Inv and sales estate of Garnett Neely sold 16 Nov 1836. Buyers not given. Accts. on John Marshall, William Burns, Jas & Samuel Willson, et al. By William McMurry and A. Neely adm.
8 Inv property of Elizabeth Ann Mitchell decd. 3 negroes hired out. Bonds on Rainey Currie, William Dismuke, John Harris. By William A. Muzzle adm.
8 Inv property of John Jeffreys decd taken 9 Jan 1837 by Ellis Jeffreys adm.
9 Inv property of Mary Jones decd taken 1 Nov 1836 by Eli Jones adm .
10 Inv residue estate of Thomas Harrelson decd.
10 MASON SANDERS - Will - w. 22 June 1836. Wife Priscilla Sanders home tract for her lifetime. 3 youngest daughters Elizabeth, Omy, and Lydia Sanders. Sons Richard and Andrew; daughters Polly Sartin, Anny Smith. Remainder of land to 4 sons William, Andrew, Leroy, and Richard. Exec: son William and wife. Wit: Lancelot Johnston, John Walker. Priscilla Mason?(Sanders) qualified.
11 MARY ANN HUSTON - Will - w. no date - Grandson Drury Burton 100 acres land. Son Robert Huston 50 acres adj John Russell, John McKissack and to enclose the Mansion House. Residue of land to be sold if $2 per acre can be gotten for it and to be divided among all children. Exec: son Robert Huston. Wit: John Russell, J. C. Vanhook. Exec qualified.
13 HASTEN BARTLETT - Will - w. 11 Oct 1836. Wife Elizabeth all property during her widowhood, and afterwards all to be divided between my children or who may represent them. Exec: wife Elizabeth. Wit: A. Gordon, John Wood Jun. Exec qualified.
14 WILLIAM STEPHENS - Will - w. 1 Nov 1836. Wife Mary Stephens all property for life; 2 daughters Katharine Hightower and Elizabeth Richmond. 2 sons of Katharine Hightower: William S. and John Q. Hightower. Exec: wife Mary Stephens and William Long. Wit: Vincent Bradsher, Thomas Riggs. Wm Long qualified.

April Court 1837

16 Acct current of Sarah Smith decd by George Smith adm. George Smith has a receipt from Elizabeth Evans in full for legacy, also for his legacy from Robert Smith, and from James Hightower and wife in full their legacy. 18 Mar 1837.
17 Acct current of Benjamin Stephens decd - suit pending in court by Elizabeth Dobbins for part of land. Paid Fleming Childers for wheat sown later recovered by Elizabeth Dobbins. Div of land rentals to following children: Iverson G. Stephens, Charles G. Stephens, Albert G. Stephens, John Q. A. Stephens, Williamson M. Stephens(minor under 21), Calvin P. Stephens (under 21); Algernon D. Stephens decd. but an heir at law not entitled to rent of land. 1 Sept 1837.
18 Acct current of Conrad Strador decd by Christian Strador adm.

Book N 1837
Page
19 Inv and sales of property of Agness Thomas decd sold 17 May 1836 to Fleming
   Nelson, Nat Harrelson, David Montgomery, Joel P. Thomas, Rucker Lea, Abner Far-
   ley, James Sneed, Henry Roper, Henry Thomas, John C. Lea, Thomas L. Lea, Asabel
   Cox, Sherrard Owen, Dabney Terry. Negroes sold to William Holcomb, Allen Gunn,
   Joel Thomas, Gideon Turner, William Kersey, James Sneed.
21 Sales property of Lewis Terrell decd taken by James Terrell adm. 24 Jan 1837.
   Sales to William McMurry, Nelson Bartlett, William Corbit, James Terrell,
   Nancy Terrell, William McMineway.
22 Sales property of Bird Eskridge decd sold by B. Boman adm on 16 Feb 1837 to
   T. J. Howard, Anderson Harris, Mrs. N. Eskridge, Samuel Milam, Jno Johnston,
   Martin Morgan, Benjamin Stanfield, William Dismukes, et al.
23 Sales property of Mary Ann Huston decd sold 28 Jan 1837 to Ann Stewart, Benjamin
   Stewart, Benjamin Merritt, John Fox, Reubin Hawkins, et al.
24 Sales personal estate of Richard Smith Sen. by Richard Smith Jun. adm. Buyers
   not listed.
25 Acct sales of property of Dudley Gatewood decd sold 27 Dec 1837 to John McDaniel,
   Jesse Adkinson, Wm. H. Burns, A. D. Gatewood, Azariah Walters, Hutchin Ferrell.
   for Lewis Gatewood and family, Elisha Alverson, James Ryley, Thomas Rawlins,
   Rebecca Gatewood, et al. By Sylvanus Stokes adm.
26 Sales property of Joseph Dameron decd sold 31 Jan 1837 to:

James C. Dameron	Epps Moore	Joseph Rudd	James Currie Jr.
Thomas Pool	Thomas Kimbro	James Currie,Major	Alanson M. Lea
Samuel Smith	Archibald Haggie	Bird Bateman	James Bouldin
Solomon Whitlow	Thomas Seawell	Abner Stanfield	Moses Hood
Carter Vowell	Zachariah E. Dameron, John Dameron		James H. Dameron

   By Williamson Dameron adm.
31 Sales estate of Peter Badget decd by William Badgett adm. Sales to William and
   Ann Badgett, John Cobb, Sally Mattox, et al.
32 Sales property of John Wiley decd sold 28 Feb 1837 to John H. Wiley, Jane Wiley,
   Goodwin Evans, Thomas Greenway, John Peterson, John L. Richmond, Frances Day.
33 Inv property of Joseph Dameron decd taken by Williamson Dameron adm on 11 Jan 1837.
35 Additional inv estate of Conrad Strador decd. Accts of John Ragsdale, John
   Holloway.
35 Inv personal estate of Mason Sanders decd by Priscilla Sanders exec. Property
   not devised in will sold 16 Feb 1837 to Joel F. Motley, Leroy Sanders, Ansolem
   Sartin, Richd. Totten, Richard Sanders, Joseph Carter, William Sanders, Robert
   J. King, Lancelot Johnston, William Connally, Hiram Wright, Moses D. Butler,
   Pharoah Summers, Samuel M. Cobb.
36 Debts due estate of Mason Sanders on Samuel Tapscott, Jno Rice, Amos Hall,
   Daniel Taylor.
37 Allen Holcomb et al petition to sell slaves. Sale of slaves to John Kerr Jr.,
   John Cobb Jr. By Cary A. Howard.
38 Negro man Adam slave of estate of Birdet Eskridge in Leasburg sold 11 Feb last
   to Nancy Eskridge for $980.
38 Sale of slaves by Wm. and Yearby Warren belonging to estate of Boswell Warren.
39 Year's allowance to Nancy Eskridge widow of Birdet Eskridge decd for herself
   and family. 6 Feb 1837.
39 Year's allowance to Nancy Terrell widow of Lewis Terrell decd.
40 Year's allowance to Jane Wiley widow of John Wiley decd. 24 Jan 1837.
41 Year's allowance to Elizabeth Warren widow of Boswell Warren for her & family.
42 Year's allowance to Lois Henslee widow of Thomas Henslee decd for herself and
   family. 6 May 1836.
42 Sale of negroes on 15 Feb last of William Ware decd to James Richardson,
   Thomas Turner, John Wilson, Ansel Ware.

Book N 1837
Page
43 JOSEPH HENDERSON - Will - w. 8 Jan 1837. Brother Hiram Henderson (land on
Moon's Creek 360 acres adj Nathaniel Slade, also gold watch); niece Mary B.
Roan wife of Dr. Nathaniel M. Roan $500; niece Priscilla Jane Jones wife of
Dr. Wiley Jones of Milton $500; niece Susan Henderson daughter of brother William
Henderson $200; money left in trust for niece Martha Poteat wife of William
Poteat and her children $400; nephew William Henderson son of brother William
Henderson $200 for his tuition at school. Exec to have 118 acres land in Rock-
ingham Co. NC, which was bought at sheriff's sale to be held in trust for brother
Thomas Henderson and his wife and children. Sister Hannah married to Thomas
Yearby has removed from county and not heard from in years but to have $1000
if alive or to go to her children. Nephew John Henderson son of brother John
$200; other children of brother John. Nephew Zachariah Hooper son of sister
Nancy Hooper $400. Rest of property divided into 9 parts and go to brothers
Hiram, Samuel, Jacob, in trust for Thomas; children of brother William Henderson
to wit Mary McAleer, Julia Ayres, Susan Henderson, William Henderson; sister
Sally Holcomb, sister Martha Harrelson, children of sisters Priscilla Hooper
wife of Woodlief Hooper, sister Nancy Hooper wife of Benjamin Hooper and her
children to wit Zachariah, Eliza, Frank, Henry, Joseph, Elisha.
Exec: brother Hiram Henderson. Wit: John Kerr Jr., William Cox. Exec qualified.

47 STEPHEN HADDOCK - Will - w. 6 Dec 1836. Wife Sarah Haddock. Daughters Rebecca
Haddock, Emeline Haddock; son Tavner Haddock;most of estate to be sold and
divided among all children. Exec: friend Abisha Slade. Wit: Thomas Turner,
A. Gunn. Exec qualified.

48 MARTHA HARRELSON - Will - w. 4 Feb 1837. Sons Thomas W. Harrelson, James Madison
Harrelson; daughter Parthenia Hodnett; granddaughter Martha Edmunds Lipscomb.
Each named to have ¼ part. Exec: son Thomas W. Harrelson and son-in-law Philip
Hodnett. Wit: Paul A. Haralson, Elijah Graves. Exec qualified.

49 JOSEPH McDOWELL of Milton, NC - Will - w. 28 Dec 1836. Nephew David McDowell to
have house and lot where I live also lumberhouse and ½ of lot co-owned with
Stephen Dodson now rented by Christopher Davis also ½ of lot co-owned with
Chambers in East Milton known as Bias house, ½ of grove lot sold to A. B. Seaney,
plus all bonds and books. Rest of estate to William McDowell, Betsey Taylor
formerly McDowell, Susan Brandon formerly McDowell, Nicey Hall formerly McDowell;
David McDowell 6 or 7 acres on west side Country Line Creek. Exec: David McDowell.
Wit: Jas Farley, Benj. Nutt, Exec qualified.

50 WILLIAM CANTRILL - Will - w. 30 July 1833. Heirs of Barzillai Kerr decd $5
equally divided to them; grandsons James and John Walker and granddaughter Hetty
Walker, heirs of Ashford Walker $5; balance of estate to son Joseph Cantrill,
Hannah Anthony, Rachel Martin, Sally Martin, Hetty Morton, and Katty Garrison
decd., to each of them or their heirs. Exec: son-in-law George Martin, Thomas
Williamson. Wit: A. T. Farish, J. W. Heydon. George Martin qualified.

51 Evidence of Freedom of Ann Paterford free woman of color who served Richard
Arnold decd and given freedom by his will. She is 24 years old, 5 ft. 7 ins.
high, dark complexion, black eyes, tolerable slender, thick lips, nose flat,
speaks fluently, long hands and fingers, scar on left hand. By Thomas Pendergast
exec will of Richard Arnold.

52 Lydia C. Montgomery age 8 years in Oct last bound to Clayton Lambert.
53 John Browning orphan now 11 years old bound to John Hughs.
54 William H. Montgomery orphan age of 6 years in Oct last bound to Clayton Lambert.
55 Minerva Nash orphan age of 6 years in March last bound to Henry Allen.

131

56 LETTICE FOSTER - Will - w. 25 Feb 1837. Son John Lea's children and their heirs to have 6 negroes. Daughter Alcey King and her heirs willed slaves. Daughter Susannah Suddath's children to have negroes now in state of Georgia in possession of James Suddath to be divided to grandchildren John Suddath, Eliza Sheild, and Lettice J. Jossa. Girl Mariah to live among children with John Simpson as trustee. Grandson George Lea. Exec: Nathan King. Wit: Thomas Garrett, Mary L.(or S.) Lea, John Simpson. Exec qualified.

58 JANE KING - Will - w. 15 Feb 1837. Brother Robert J. King; sister Margaret Watt and Robert J. King to have slaves and after death of Robert J. King his part to his son William D. King. Nephew Samuel King. Exec: brother Robert J. King and nephew John Watt. Wit: Joseph Brackin, Whitson G. Blackwell.

59 AZARIAH GRAVES - Will - w. 28 Jan 1837. 5 servants to be appraised and sold to John F. Lea if Lea is surviving. Old Ned to choose between brothers and sisters to live with; other negroes to Brother Barzillai then to his children. Brother Barzillia's debts forgiven but he not to receive any other part of estate. Sister Polly Mebane to have 2 slaves whose wives she now ownes; if Polly dies without issue her part of estate to go to other brothers and sisters. Sister Caty Howard and her heirs $1500; sister Elizabeth Kimbrough's children to wit Nancy Evans, Polly Chandler, M. D., and Elijah Kimbrough $300 each. Brother Thomas Graves willed slaves. Balance of estate equally divided between brothers and sisters Thomas Graves, Elijah Graves, William Graves, Delilah Miles and Abner Miles her husband, Nancy Yancey and Polly Mebane. Azariah Camillus Haralson son of Paul A. Haralson $200 when he reaches 21 years; John Azariah Graves son of brother William Graves $200 when he reaches 21. Half of land brother Barzillai lives on belongs to testator and other half to brother Elijah - Barzillai or his widow to continue living there and then land to go to Barzillai's children. House wherein he lives to be put in one lot and brother Elijah to have it if he move there and if he declines Polly Mebane to have choice to move there and if not brothers and sisters to draw for it. Houses and lots at Caswell Court House and at Milton to go to brothers and sisters. "I desire to be interred in what is called the grass lot near the stables on south side of stage road and my grave to be walled around with rock with a marble slab laid on it. I wish my brother Elijah buried along side me if he have no objections also my brothers and sisters as will accept this place." His slaves to be buried along side him and graves enclosed with strong railing. Rifle gun to Robert Graves and gold watch to John K. Graves sons of brother Barzillai. Court to appoint an adm. Funeral service I wish to be preached in the House where I live and all servants to attend the preaching and sit or stand all together near enough to hear. Test: John C. Harvey, D. Rainey. George Williamson appointed adm with will attached and he bonded for $80,000.00.

63 NANCY TAYLOR - Will - w. 13 May 1837. Brothers Septimus Taylor $100, Franklin Taylor $50; Elisha Ingram and my sister Margaret balance of cash and furniture. Wit: John E. Hamlett, James Herring, Parum Pulliam. Parham Pulliam appointed adm with will annexed bonded by Barthus J. Crawley and John E. Hamlett.

64 List of bonds due estate of George Huston decd by James McMullin adm.

65 Inv personal property of Azariah Graves decd sold by special adm, George Williamson. Included bacon and lard belonging to the late firm of Azariah Graves and Jonathan Smith.

66 Inv estate of William Cantrill decd taken 10 Feb 1837 by George T. Martin exec. Due bill on Tyre Weadon who has run away and gone out of State. Notes on John Simmons, Jas Love, Saml. Tate, William Tate, Allen Tate.

67 Inv personal property of Azariah Graves per special court order.

68 Amended inv of William Pleasant decd by James Pleasant adm. Debts due against Yancey Westbrooks, Calloway Harrison, Starling Warren.

68 Inv estate of Robert Seamore decd taken by James Warf adm on 10 Apr 1837.

69 Sales estate of Robert Seamore decd to Mildren Bennett, Roger Warf, Alford and Lewis Davis, Jeremiah Simpson, Nathl. P. Thomas, J. B. Hill, Wm. Lyon, Beverly Seamore, James & William Warf.

Book N' 1837
Page
70 Inv estate of Westley B. Raimey decd taken 28 June 1837. Sales to Rufus Raimey, Woodlief Thomas, William Powell, James Reed, Thomas Jeffreys. Some claims on property of Ramey and Rice in which he had an undivided interest. Wm. Hooper adm.
71 Sales estate of Lettice Foster sold by Nathan King exec on 22 May 1837. Buyers not listed. One bond executed to Lettice Foster by John Simpson and Thomas Garret. Slaves willed to John Lea's children, Alcey King, those in Georgia to children of Susannah Suddath, Eliza Shields, Lettice J. Jopa.
73 Sales property of Martha Harrelson decd sold 28 Apr 1837 to Thos W. Graves, Nathaniel Lea, Philip Hodnett, Charles Hendrick, Nathaniel Murphey, John H. Graves, Berry Evans, Paul A. Haralson, et al.
74 Sales estate of Azariah Graves decd sold 30 May 1837 to:

John H. Graves	Devereau Hightower	Elijah Graves	Nathl. M. Roan
William Graves	Nancey Yancey	Thomas Graves	Thos W. Graves
Green P. Womack	Abner Miles	Joseph K. Cobb	Owen McAleer
George W. Graves	Thornton Hancock	Henry Willis	James Willis
Ibzan Rice(1 clock)	R. W. Graves	John Poteat Sen.	Allen M. Gunn
Azariah Graves Jun.	Jeremiah Lea	Alex McAlpin	John Cobb Jun.
Walter H. Lunsford	James Mebane	James Walker	James H. Atkinson
Genl. Barzillai Graves, Wm. B. Bowe		Thomas P. Guarrant	Archibald Lea
William Hooper	John Walton	Alexander R. Donoho,Alfred M. Lea
John Kerr(4 vols of Rambler & 9 vols of Hume's History)			
David Montgomery(12 vols encyclopedias)			

78 Sales of late firm of Aza Graves and Jonathan Smith to Joseph Lunsford, Daniel Richmond, Thomas Riggs, Thomas Lea, William Ashford, Woodlief Hooper, Madison Frazure, Zachariah Lockett, Josiah Rainey, Richard G. Lampkin, Wm. Goodson, et al.
82 Sale estate of William Cantrill decd by George T. Martin exec. Sales to:

Thomas Sawyer	William Walker	Joseph Wilder	Jeremiah Lea
Joseph Garrison	Joseph Massey	Dixon Corn	Samuel Foster
James M. Walker	Samuel Walker	Thos W. Graves	George Graham
Joseph Ector	Capt. Joseph Pinnix, Stephen Sawyer		William Wilder
Josiah Younger	David McClure	Christopher W. Brooks, William Fitch
Thomas Fitch	James Noble	William Ashford	Henry Garrison
Coleby Foster	Nelson Nunn	Curtis Payne	John Horn
Dr. Levi Walker	Arthur Rascoe	Lemuel Potter	Lucretia Roland
John Shaw	Mary Faucette	Capt. Hosea McNeill,Wyatt Davis	

Sale of negroes to Joseph Anthony, Alexander B. Morton, James Wilder.
87 Inv property of Martha Harrelson decd by T. W. Harrelson exec.
88 Sale and hire of negroes of estate of William Pleasant decd to William Pleasant. By James Pleasant adm.
89 Inv and sales of Thomas Carpenter decd taken by Thos D. Johnston adm. Sales to: Tolbert Ware(surveyor's instruments), Anthony Read (1 Bible), Warren Holcomb, W. Badgett, J. K. Graves, M. Delaney, H. Bushnell, N. Willis (saddle bags and spectacles), Thomas Riggs (1 watch), Woodlief Hooper (geography and atlas), Jas Currie Jun. (Scott's Commentary on the Bible). Sold at Yanceyville,14 Aug., 1835.
91 List of debts due Thomas Carpenter, also acct current. Adm declares debts exceed assets - three-fourths of claims paid and other creditors asked to surrender claims.
93 Sale of ½ of tract of land belonging to E. Bartin decd by James E. Williamson,exec.
93 Results of Congressional election in Caswell County: for John Hill 897, for A. H. Sheppard 224.
94 Acct current estate of Elizabeth Holloway decd by John Holloway adm. Payments to Henry Glass, Neal and Bennett, John Dickinson, Labon Ford, Susannah Holloway.
96 Acct current of Obadiah Holloway decd by John Holloway adm.
97 Acct current estate of William Cobb decd by Jas. N. Cobb and William M. Cobb exec.
97 Inv and sales estate of John Browning decd by Thos D. Johnston adm. Sales to Thomas J. Willis, Martin Browning, R. W. Mason, Jas Miles Jun., Jno Lyon,et al. 14 Aug 1835. Debts collected of Nathl. Murphey for Jno Browning's part of crop, of Hannah Martin, James Tate.

Book N 1837
Page
98 Acct current of John Browning decd. Payments to John Kerr, Dr. N. M. Roan,
   John Brooks, Aldridge Rudd, Gunn & Bowe. Paid William Hooper for crying sale.
100 Acct current of Paul Carrington decd by John B. Carrington adm. Payments to
   Elizabeth Ponsonby for 2 bonds, Henry G. Tucker for note, Dr. Wiley Jones,
   Dabney Terry; expenses for adm to travel to Milton, Richmond, & Caswell Court
   House, toll at Milton bridge; payments to Richard Wade, Geo Carrington, et al.
102 Credits of P. Carrington - cash recd from Dr. Wiley Jones $1505 in Col. P.
   Carrington's pocket book at his death; from R & T Gwathney for hogsheads of
   tobacco, et al. 10 May 1837.
104 Acct current of William McMinimy decd by Roberson McMinimy adm. Met at William
   Corbet's store to settle accounts.
105 Allotment of negroes of estate of Joseph Dameron decd to legatees: Epps Moore
   and wife Elizabeth, Williamson Dameron, Harrison Dameron or his representative
   James C. Dameron, James C. Dameron. 1 Apr 1837.
106 Negro man Leven property of Martha Harrelson decd sold for $666.
107 Valuation and allotment of land of estate of Joseph Dameron among heirs to
   William Dameron; James C. Dameron(adj Abner Wisdom & William Hightower);
   Epps Moore and wife Elizabeth (adj Elijah Graves, Samuel Smith); Harrison
   Dameron(on east side of Pinson's road adj Wm. Hightower, Thomas Burton).
   By William Whitefield, surveyor. Plat included in book.
109 Report of Wardens of the Poor.
110 List of business taxes collected on Retailers of Spirits, Merchants, Peddlers,
   exhibitors of artificial and natural curiosities(J. Stone & Waring Raymond
   & Co.). By Thos L. Lea, sheriff.
113 Henry Warren orphan age of 8 years in Sept. 1837 bound to Patrick Turner.

October Court 1837

114 MARY CATES - Will - w. 15 Sept. 1828. Granddaughters Mary Barker Warren,
   Mary Lewis, and Mary Barker Henshaw; grandson Martin Warren. Rest of property
   to daughter Frances Warren. Exec: friend John Miles. Wit: Thomas Pendergast.
   John Miles rejected his right to execute and Martain Warren named adm with
   will annexed bonded by John Miles and John Kimbrough.

115 ROBERT MARTIN - Will - w. 9 Oct 1835. Wife Elizabeth Martin all property during
   her life and at her decease same to be sold and money equally divided among
   all children that is in this section of country. Exec: wife Elizabeth.
   Wit: Moses Simpson, Thomas Garrett.

116 Inv estate of Joseph Henderson decd including many bonds, debts, notes, & accts.
   Out of state bonds on John Shields of Miss. By Hiram Henderson exec.
121 Inv property of William Manly decd by Forrister Stainback adm taken 2 Oct 1837.
   Cash recd. for tobacco from Col. B. Brown, also for his services as overseer.
   Notes on Stephen Neal and John Harrison.
121 Inv estate of Nancy Taylor decd taken 5 July 1837 by Parrum Pulliam adm. Notes
   on Septimus Taylor, Jas Holder, M. P. Huntington, John Johnston.
122 Additional inv estate of Azariah Graves by George Williamson adm. Long list of
   bonds due, some of Genl. Aza Graves, Robert Roe, Aza Graves(son of Thomas),
   John F. Lea, John H. Graves, Jacob Ahart, Wiley Yancey(1824), Delilah and
   Solo. Hunter, John Mims, Micajah and Jacob Thomas, John G. Womack, Elijah
   Graves Jun.
125 List of notes and bonds payable to A. Graves and Nancy Yancey adm of B. Yancey
   decd now property of A. Graves decd.
127 Five slaves of Azariah Graves delivered to John F. Lea. One paper endorsed in
   South Carolina belongs to Caswell County for sale of the Ceat?(Court) House
   for $225.
128 Property of Azariah Graves decd sold 1 Aug 1837 to James Mebane, William Cannon,
   William Watlington, Ashley G. Lea, Charles Taylor, et al.
129 Sales of Bacon amd Lard of late firm of Aza Graves and Jonathan Smith. Large
   buyers were Caleb Richmond and Ibzan Rice (over 600 pounds), et al.

Book N 1837-38
Page
130 List of sales of corn and fodder sold by Durett Oliver, adm of Reuben Oliver
    decd sold 1 Sept 1837. Sales to John & William Richmond, James Matlock,
    Rucker T. Lea, Nathaniel Snipes, Alexander Wiley, et al.
131 Inv property of Robert Martin decd by Elizabeth Martin exec.
132 Inv and sales estate of Joseph McDowell decd sold 28 Aug 1837. Names of buyers
    not given. Two-thirds interest in Tavern or Church Bell yet unsold; one secre-
    tary devised to David McDowell. By David McDowell exec.
133 List of sales and debts of Joseph McDowell. Notes on Philip Harrington, Eliza-
    beth Boley, Oglesby Green, Sherrod Owen, John S. Oglesby, Parthena Bowers,
    John J. Oliver, et al.
134 Doubtful notes due Joseph McDowell.
135 Good accts and desperate notes due Joseph McDowell.
137 Report of Commission on Location of the Jail. Believing it inexpedient to erect
    said building on public square, commission has conferred with Jonathan Smith
    and Geo Williamson who have tendered to the county lot of land south of the
    Court House on west side of a new street west to Thos D. Johnston's line.
    Commission recommended acceptance of same. 11 July 1836. Site is some 150
    or 200 yards from the court house.
138 Acct current estate of Albert Mathews decd by Richard G. Lampkin adm. Recd cash
    of Miles Wilmouth, Berry Evans, Howard Martin. Paid Thomas Badgett for coffin,
    Johnston and Connally for shroud; judgment to Thomas Bigelow.
139 Acct current of Joseph Worsham decd by Benjamin C. West adm.
140 Acct current of Simeon Ford decd by Labon Ford adm. Met at dwelling house of
    John Keesee. 30 Sept. 1837. Payments to W. H. Nunnally, Thomas Carpenter,
    Pleasant L. Ford, Thomas Lea, John Ross & Co.
141 Acct current of Micajah Pleasant decd taken 27 Sept. 1837. Some property
    valued to S. Greer guardian of M. Graves. Paid Edward Benson for surveying,
    Richard Smith for crying sale, William Corbet for burial, Abraham Landers for
    coffin.
144 Acct current of Lewis Terrell decd by James Terrell adm. Payments to Henry &
    James Terrell, William Corbet, Wm. McMurray.
145 William Warren orphan age of 15 years on 7th day of May last bound to Thomas
    Prendergast.
146 Nancy Bevers(Beavers?) orphan age of 6 years in Dec 1837 bound to Nancy Kimbrough.

January Court 1838

147 HENRY FULLER - Will - w. 1 Sept 1836. Wife Ann Fuller to have land and houses
    for her life or widowhood and then all property divided to all children.
    Exec: Johnston Scoggins and Elijah Fuller. Test: Reuben Jones, Bluford Cooper.
    Elijah Fuller qualified.

148 JOHN MITCHELL - Will - w. 11 Jan 1837. Son John A. Mitchell(land where I now
    live plus claim to tract in Orange Co. where Elizabeth Lackey lives).
    Wife Mary Mitchell to have 2 negroes for her life then they go to John A.
    Mitchell. Remainder divided to my 5 children: Elizabeth, William, John A.,
    Katharine, and James. Exec: William and John A. Mitchell. Wit: Beaufort
    Pleasant, John H. Pleasant. William Mitchell qualified.

149 THOMAS PAGE - Will - w. 26 May 1837. Wife Nancy all estate during her life or
    widowhood then divided among my 3 children: Milly, Josiah, and Nancy and to
    the surviving children of Elizabeth. Daughter Elizabeth to have use of proper-
    ty for her life. Daughters Milly Fullington, Nancy Evans; son Josiah.
    Exec: son Josiah. Wit: James Wilder, Robert Browning. Exec qualified.

150 WILLIAM BETHELL, late of Rockingham Co. but now in Natchez Miss. - Will -
    w. 13 Feb 1833. Wife Mary Bethell land in Caswell Co. where she now resides
    purchased from Wm. & Abner Nash. Wife to have enough to educate children
    underage or unmarried until son William D. Bethell is of lawful age. Eldest
    son Samuel Bethell to have land on Lick Fork of Hogan's Creek in Rockingham
    Co. purchased from James Taylor estate and land formerly belonging to Aquilla

135

Book N 1838

Wilson decd and devised to him by his late father also land purchased of John Johnston. Daughter Anne C. Nash(slaves in her possession) and her 2 eldest sons $250. Daughter Jane W. Scales (slaves in her possession) and her 2 eldest sons $250. Daughter Mary Ann Moore and her daughter Mary Elizabeth. Son William D. the Dan River tract of land in Rockingham Co; son C. Pinckney Bethell the tract in Caswell Co. where his Mother lives. Desires William to be educated for law under Judge Ruffin and would like Pinckney to study law under John M. Morehead. Daughters Agnes G. Bethell, Maria Louisa Bethell, Atelia Bethell all underage. Servant Joicey for faithful service during his illness to be emancipated and to be free after paying $800 bonded by Samuel Cartwright and John Kerr to take care of her. Exec: wife Mary Bethell, son-in-law Dr. Robert Scales, and William D. Bethell when he comes of age. John Kerr to collect anything due in Miss. or La. - John Ker of La. presently residing near Natchez. Debts to Thomas Suttle and bank of Salem to be paid. Will written at Natchez. Wit: Saml. A. Cartwright, St. Lanier, John Ker. Codicil 16 Mar 1834 - concerns division of slaves to 3 youngest daughters, Agnes, Louisa, Atelia; 2 eldest daughters Jane Scales and Mary Ann Moore. NB - Negro Alexander purchased of Samuel Moore to go to wife. In Superior Court Nov 1837 - Mary Bethell and others vs Samuel Moore and others, caveat of will. Court ordered Caswell County Court of Pleas and Quarter Sessions to probate will of Samuel Bethell and to issue letters testamentary. John K. Graves, Clerk of Court.

157 Sales of Azariah Graves decd sold 2 Nov 1837 to:

James Mebane	William Graves	Algernon S. Yancey	Elijah Graves Sen.
Col. Thomas Graves	Nathaniel Lea,	John H. Graves	Jeremiah Graves
James Evans	Wm. Crutchfield	Col. William Lea	Paul A. Haralson
George Robertson	William Long	Wm. Fullington	Abner Miles
James Gunn	Littleton A. Gwyn	Zachariah Lockett	James B. Hilliard
Thomas D. Johnston	Durett Oliver	William B. Howe	Spencer Hooper
Samuel Hinton	John Powell	Zera Gwyn	Lindsay Roberts
John Johnston	Warren Holcomb	Richard W. Jackson	John Pittard
Starke Gardner	Ibzan Rice	Thomas Badgett	Ambrose L. Bennett
Augustus C. Finley	Wyatt Walker	Jasper L. Rowe	William Yancey
Ancel Ware	William Herring	Cato Mebane	et al

166 Second sale of Lettice Foster decd sold 7 Oct 1837 to John B. Sheels, Mallicha Jossey, Alsey King, John Tapscott; Polly S. Lea paid to estate of Lettis Foster decd $10 for labor done on plantation. By Nathan King exec.

167 Sales property of Reuben Oliver decd sold 29 Nov 1837 to Nancy Oliver, Charles Hendrick, George Robertson, William Graves, John Miles, Joseph Aldridge, Thomas Poteat, George Vaughan, John Roberts, et al. By Durett Oliver adm.

168 Sales of Reuben Jones decd sold 2 Nov 1837 by Susanna Jones and Calvin Jones adm. Sales to William Marshall, John Edmonston, Calvin & Susanna Jones, Elizabeth Jones, James E. Mitchell, Permelia Jones, Pleasant Brummitt, Lawson Jones, et al

173 Inv property of Reuben Oliver decd taken 4 Nov 1837 by Durett Oliver adm.

173 Inv personal estate of James Shepperd decd taken by Richard Smith adm on 18 Dec 1837. Bond on John Shepperd of State of Va. payable 1824 to Mary B. Shepperd.

174 Inv estate of Thomas Page decd taken 11 Nov 1837 by Josiah Page.

175 Inv estate of Geo. Manly decd taken 17 Nov 1837 by John Manly adm.

175 Sales property of George Manly on 17 Nov 1837 to Robert J. King, Polly Manly, Andrew Haddock, Samuel Moore, John E. Brown, F. Stanback.

176 Year's allowance to Susannah Jones widow of Reubin Jones decd and her family.

177 Div of 27 negroes of Azariah Graves decd to Abner Miles, Col. Thomas Graves, James Mebane, Capt. William Graves, Elijah Graves Sen., Mrs. Nancy Yancey. Old man Ned allowed to pick his master chose Elijah Graves Sen.

179 Div negroes of Zachariah Pattillo decd - one-sixth part to Thomas M. Kimble and Ann Eliza his wife; one-sixth reserved for widow; one-sixth to Lewis Pattillo; three-sixth unassigned. 3 Jan 1838.

180 Acct current estate of Jonathan Starkey decd by Thomas Starkey exec. Paid Walker and Felts for coffin $13; John Kerr atty fee, Dr. N. M. Roan medical

bill, William Hooper clerk of sale, John Miles for crying sale, McAleer and Henderson store acct, Rebecca Parish for weaving, James Parish for seed potatoes, John Stadler for preaching the funeral $3, Mrs. Thomas Starkey for weaving. Paid legatees: Richard H. Griffith as guardian for his children, Julia Chempson, Rachael Chandler who was Rachael Clempson.

182 Acct current of estate of Berry Hunt decd by Thomas Starkey exec of Jonathan Starkey decd who was adm of Berry Hunt decd. Money collected as pension. Paid widow's allowance; coffins paid for the old man and for Mrs. Hunt.

183 Acct current estate of Philip Cook decd by John Miles adm.

184 Sales property willed by Lettice Foster decd to children of John Lea decd. 28 Oct 1837. By John Simpson guardian to John Lea's children. Sales to:

Thomas J. Reid	Mary Lea	Joseph Windsor	Oliver Simpson
Thomas Garrott	William Foster	John Boulding	Freeman Leath
William Brown	John Tapscott	George Lea	

Rent of land to Benjamin Lovelace. Hire of negroes to Mary S. Lea, Jones W. Collins.

185 Oliver Fitts orphan age of 11 years in Sept. next bound to Walker and Felts to learn the art of a harness maker.

186 Richard W. Jackson and wife Julietta vs Nathaniel Gregory & others petition for div of land and sale of negroes of West Gregory decd. Negroes sold 29 Dec 1837 to Major H. Graves and Solomon Corbit. By Paul A. Haralson, Clerk of Caswell County Court.

April Court 1838

By court decree, sale of negroes of Joseph Henderson which fell to children of William Henderson - sold at Yanceyville 29 Jan 1838 to Thomas M. Kimble, Hiram Henderson, Hiram Weatherford.

187 Sales personal estate of James Shappard decd by David Melton adm and Frances Sheppard. Sold 2 Feb 1838 to William Shappard, Joseph Aldridge, Henry Hooper, William Kimbrough, Henry Graves, Wyatt Davis, et al.

189 Sales property of Thomas Page decd sold 3 Feb 1838 to Archibald Banes, Goodwin and Berry Evans, John Love Jun., Thomas W. Chandler, et al. By Josiah Page, adm.

190 Sales estate of George Manly decd sold 20 Mar 1838 by John Manly adm to Mary Manly, John C. Totton, Robert Manly, Ibzan Rice, William Swift, Milton Swift.

192 Sales and inv estate of Susannah Hooper decd sold 30 Jan 1837 to James Harris, Woodlief Hooper, John Gunn, William Hooper, Charles Hendrick, John Vaughan, Beverly Dickens. By William F. Hooper adm.

193 Second inv of effects of Boswell Warren decd by Wm. and Yearby Warren adm.

193 Inv of goods and chattles of Henry Fuller decd taken 3 Apr 1838 by Elijah Fuller.

194 Acct current of William Ware decd by Thomas Turner adm.

195 Acct current of Elizabeth Barton decd by James E. Williamson exec.

196 Div negroes of estate of Archimedes Donoho decd into 5 equal parts to: Cornelia A. Donoho, Emely Donoho, Mrs. Huntington, Richard Donoho, Thomas Donoho.

197 Year's allowance to Frances Sheppard for her and family, she widow of James Shepperd decd.

198 JAMES MONTGOMERY - Will - w. 7 Aug 1834. Wife Rebekah to have land where he lives for her life then to go to all legatees. Son Abraham (200 acres in Iredell County) then to his children; $50 to Foreign Missionary Society and American Tract Society. Son James. Residue of estate to all children, that for Jane to be sold and invested, then to her children; daughter Rebeckah and her children; son Edward. Exec: sons James, Edward, and David. Wit: J. Wilson, Benjamin S. Pittard. Codicil 1 Apr 1838 - Portion of estate that would descend to daughter Polley Long of Wilson Co. Tenn., to go to her heirs; part for Jane Davis be revoked and exec to pay to her male children. $25 and to her daughter Sarah Ann Davis. Wit: George Williamson, Saml. Pittard.
Codicil - 25 Apr 1838 - 50 acres land adj old mill to son John Montgomery and son Edward to have land adj that given to John. Wit: John Pittard, John Pinchback. Exec qualified.

201 ELIZABETH W. TAPSCOTT - Will - w. 6 Jan 1838. Brother John Tapscott; sister Polly A. (or H.)Tapscott. Exec: brother John Tapscott. Wit: Barnard H. Boswell, Romulus S. Boswell. Exec qualified.

202 JOHN COBB SEN. - Will - w. 14 Nov 1834. Wife Jane Cobb land whereon he lives 327 acres for her life. Sales from property to be divided among son Joseph Cobb decd, oldest daughter Martha Guardner $50 and his other children Malinda, Samuel, Louisa, John, and Henry Cobb $5 each. Daughter Martha Madding $250. Other children now living Hugh Cobb, Henry Cobb, Deborah Grant, Martha Madding, John Cobb. Exec: sons Hugh, Henry, and John. Wit: Jno Blackwell, Alfred Howard, Joseph Brackin. Exec renounced right to execute and Brackin named adm with will annexed.

203 JARRETT (JARROLD) POWELL - Will - w.   1832. Wife Elizabeth Powell all property for her widowhood then divided among 7 children: Eliza, James, Jackson, Mary Jane, Mastin, Richard, and Frances. Wit: William Hooper. Confirmed as noncupative will by jury and court appointed Carter Powell adm with will annexed, bonded by Joshia Powell and John B. Powell. Minutes of April 1838 Court of Pleas & Quarter Sessions confirmed same.

204 Nancy Sheppard et al petition for sale of negroes of James Sheppard decd. Sales to Abner Miles, Solomon Corbit.

July Court 1838

205 Sales property of Jesse T. Atkinson decd sold 26 Apr 1838 to George Robertson, William Knight, Daniel Gunn, Azariah G. Walters, Josiah Atkinson, Franklin X. Burton, Johnson Atkinson, John & Ellis Travis, Josiah Blair, John S. Price, Martin Turner et al. Receipts for tobacco sold from A. Kenerday of Tenn. and Ala.; of Richard C. Bunting, Lumberton, NC, and of Gamble & Palmer of Yorkville, NC. (Possibly SC)

206 Inv of estate of Jesse T. Atkinson which was kept until crop sold. Noel Burton a

207 Sales of William H. Howard decd sold 12 May 1838 to Alexis Howard, John Blackwell John N. Ford, et al. By Cary A. Howard adm.

208 Inv property of William H. Howard taken 16 Apr 1838. Bonds on Joseph Brackin, Robert Ford, John Pirant, Henry Thomas, John Stamps.

208 Sales property of Bardet Eskridge to William Eskridge, Mrs. Eskridge, Martin Morgan, et al. By Booker Boman.

210 Sales property of Joseph Henderson decd sold 1 & 2 May 1837 to:

Nathaniel M. Roan	Chesley Turner	Dr. George Roberson,	Ibzan Rice
Iverson Ingram	Spencer Hooper	William Stokes	James S. Henderson
Emanuel Watlington	Armstead Watlington,	Thomas Henderson	Ludolphus Henderson
Hiram Henderson	Wm. C. Donoho	Henry Hooper	William Hooper
Zenith Page	Samuel Moore	Eaton Dickens	Mathew Dodson
John B. Powell	John E. Furgess	M. P. Legrand	Alfred M. Nash
Jasper Rowe	Richard B. Gunn	Charles Hendrick	John Kerr Jr.
Joseph Whitace	Thomas L. Slade	et al	

By Hiram Henderson exec.

216 Hire of negroes of estate ot Joseph Henderson.

217 Additional debts due estate of Joseph Henderson on Henry Glass, Parham C. Boley, Isaac Nicholas, et al. Accts on Mary House and Mariah House doubtful. Obligation of Owen McAleer.

218 Inv personal estate of Jarrold Powell by Carter Powell adm.

219 Inv of bonds due estate of William Bethell on William & Ann C. Nash, John J. Wright, Jas London, Joshua Mitchell, J. C. Kendall, Robert J. Dotson, Green Kemp, John Ferry, John Davis, Sam Allen, John G. Womack, Joseph Scales, et al. (Some notes date back to 1820's.)

221 Inv property of Elizabeth Tapscott by John Tapscott exec.

221 Sales negroes of heirs of Mary Hester decd sold in Leasburg 15 June last to Drury Burton, William McMurry, Mitchell Currie.

222 Additional inv of Peter Badgett by William Badgett adm.

Book N 1838
Page
222 Acct current of Thomas Hensley decd by Bedford Hensley adm. Paid widow's
allowance.
223 Acct current of Ransom Boswell decd by Howell Boswell exec.
224 Acct current of Birdet Eskridge decd by Booker Boman adm.
226 Acct current of Thomas Harrelson decd by Philip Hodnett and Thomas W. Harrelson
adm. Paid Thomas W. Harrelson exec of Martha Harrelson decd.
227 Acct current of Dudly Gatewood decd by Sylvanus Stokes adm. Amt due as guardian.
Paid Mrs. Gatewood Year's allowance. Advances to children during lifetime of
Dudley Gatewood to: Richard, Thomas, James, and Lewis Gatewood; to Patsy
Colquhoon, Nancy Stokes, Frances Shelton, Elizabeth Corsee (probably Keesee).
229 Acct current of Robert Hughs decd. Met at house of John Nunnally to settle
with Mathew Mills adm. Bonds on Henderson House & R. Bennett. Credits on
Ibzan Rice, Bayless Lynn; Brown, Neal, & Co., et al   27 June 1838.
230-235 Acct current of William Bethell decd from 1834-38 by Mary Bethel special adm.
Recd. from Charles Matlock and Samuel F. Adams for profits in trade, Samuel Hob-
son for rent; bonds on Peyton Key, David Kyle, Henry Delap, Josiah Dabbs;exec of
A. Watt decd. Paid expenses of Dr. R. H. Scales to Nathez MS, Dr. W. Courts,
William Bethel's expenses to Buckingham Co. Va. to collect money from David
Kyle; paid Calvin Graves for legal services, William Bethell expenses to Natchez
for estate. 30 June 1838.
236 Year's allowance to Mary Atkinson widow of Jesse T. Atkinson for her & family.
236 Report of Wardens of the Poor. Recommended a chimney be built to the kitchen and
floor repaired in brick building. Balance on hand $220.47.
238 List of business taxes collected 1838 by Thomas L. Lea, sheriff. $96 on retail-
ers of spirits, $230 on merchants, $60 on artificial curiosities.
240 John Powell orphan age of 5 years bound to Peter Powell.
241 George Luster orphan age of 11 years on 1 Mar last bound to Stephen Monday.
242 Taxable property for 1837.
242 Compromise estate of Mary Jones decd - 10 May 1838- between Eli Jones and
Nicholas Hester and Adam S. Richmond adm of Sally Richmond decd. Will of Mary
Jones opposed by Nicholas Hester and wife Elizabeth and Adam S. Richmond and
wife Salley. The Will ordered to jury and compromised as follows: Eli Jones to
retain ¼ of estate; Hester and Richmond to retain ¼ part each. John Kerr, atty.

244 GEORGE SHELTON - Will - w. 20 June 1837. Nephew John Harrison and his child
Arimenta(land on Country Line adj Thomas Brown, Peggy Walker); sisters Betsy
and Nancy Shelton; children of James Harrison decd to wit Nancy, Hedley, Sally,
and Syntha. Children of sister Pegy Rice to wit Polly, Betsy, Sally, Susan,
Margaret. Money from hire of slave Plato to go to Peyton Key for his family
until George S. Key is 21 years old - then Plato to go to James Key.
Peyton Key, nephew-at-law, to have land where I now live adj John H. Pickard
et al and a tract adj James Griffith, Alfred M. Nash. George S. Key son of
Peyton and Elizabeth Key. Exec: James E. Williamson. Wit: William Brown,
Thomas J. Brown.
Codicil: 15 June 1838 - Should Araminta Harrison die without issue her part to
Frances Harrison daughter of John. Sister Peggy Rice all residue of estate.
Exec qualified.

247 Div negroes of Thomas Harrelson decd and amts each legatee has recd. during the
life of Thomas Harrelson. Legatees: Jacob Henderson's children; Joseph Windsor
and wife; Lewis Barton and wife Sarah; Nathaniel Harrelson; Henry Willis' children by wife Dorcas to wit Thomas, Martha, and Mary; Nancy Gunn; Thomas W.
Harrelson; Martha E. Lipscomb daughter of Joseph R. E. Lipscomb and Eliza
Lipscomb decd.; Philip Hodnett and wife Parthenia; James M. Harrelson,
Martha Harrelson widow.
251 William P. Gunn et al petition for sale of negroes of Griffin Gunn decd. All
purchased by John C. Harvey.

139

Book N 1838 - 1839
Page
252-259 Acct current and final settlement of John H. Graves. Payments to legatees:
Groves Howard and wife Catharine; Thomas Graves(included race tracts lands);
Azariah Graves; Elijah Graves; William Graves(house and lot in Yanceyville and
part of race tract lands); Abner Miles and wife Delilah and her children (payments to John G. Womack, Thos. Blackwell and other children of David Womack);
Nancy Yancey; James Mebane and wife Polly; Barzl. Graves.
260 Thomas D. Johnston, county trustee, in acct with Caswell Co. for 1835-36.
Collected of Geo Williamson adm of Aza Graves decd, late trustee, $211.19 which
are proceeds of sale of old court house. Balance of $63.60. No commission paid
to trustee for 1834,35. Examined by George W. Graves, Philip Hodnett, Abner
Miles. (County trustee was county treasurer.)

October Court 1838

263 Acct current estate of Thomas P. Price decd by Wm. W. Price adm. Paid Revd.
Bryant and Pickard $20; Mrs. Stanback for making shroud $2; $10 for 2 tombstones.
264 Acct current estate of Samuel C. Smith decd by George Williamson adm. Recd. cash
from H. M. Clay on bond of Wm. M. McGehee for hire of negroes at Gold Mines
$420.50. Amt of valuation of property to widow of Dr. R. B. Thornton. Paid to
Wm. Long exec of Benj. Stephens, Calvin Graves atty, William Childs. Paid
widow's allowance. Paid Sarah L. Smith her 1/3 part; paid Dr. Robert B. Thornton his part 2/3. Sept. 27, 1838.
267 Acct current estate of Boswell Warren decd. Met at house of William Warren
24 Sept 1838. Notes due of Saml. Mitchell and John McMurry(1825), John Campbell
Sen. and Jr., Aschel and John Moore, et al.
268 Acct current estate of Peter Badgett decd by William Badgett adm.
269 Acct current estate ot Thomas Bennett decd by William Lyon exec. Paid receipts
for legatees Dodson Bennett, Tarphey Bennett, Manford Bennett.
270 Inv bonds of George Shelton decd by James E. Williamson exec. Recd cash from
Mr. Burk for rent of plantation.
271 Inv estate of John Cobb decd taken 4 May 1838 by Joseph Brackin adm.
272 List of corn, fodder, oats, etc. sold by Durrett Oliver adm of Reubin Oliver decd
Sold 12 Apr 1838 to Solomon Corbett, Ned Dunevant, Nathl. Murphey, et al.
273 Zachariah Miller orphan age of 14 years bound to Samuel Hayden.
274 John Henry Blake a child of Ellis G. Blake, age 7 years, bound to John Leachmond.
275 ELISHA ROWARK - Will - w. 2 Mar 1836. Wife Elizabeth Rowark to have ½ of all
estate for her life then to go to Elisha, Dorothy, Benjamin, and Nancy Rowark,
children of William and Susan Rowark. Wit: Yearby Warren, Sieria G. Compton.
276 Report of commission for removing wing of old jail. Thomas L. Badgett to remove
and fit up said houses of old jail part to be used as kitchen and part as smoke
house. Commission reported that Capt. William Graves was purchaser of old jail
for $60. Oct 3, 1838.

January Court 1839

277 Sales estate of Elisha Rowark decd sold by Roberson McMinamy adm. Sales to
Willie Jones, John Allison, Elizabeth Rowark, Lemuel Compton, James E. Mitchell,
Barring Fullington, Susan Rowark, et al.
280 Sales property of Jno. Wiley decd sold 20 Dec 1837 to Jane Wiley, Robert M. Wiley
negroes hired to Rufus Stamps, M. D. Norfleet, A. M. Winstead, Thos Kimbro,
John L. Richmond, Jas Dameron, Walker & Felts, Empson Fitch.
281 Sale of estate of Jesse T. Atkinson by Noel Burton and Johnson E. Atkinson adm.
Sales to Joseph Blare, Mary Atkinson widow, Johnson E. Atkinson's things bought
by Jno Wilson, Wm. G. Penick, Wm. Hooper, Capt. James Burton, George L. Wilson.
283 Acct current of Joseph Dameron decd by Williamson Dameron adm.
284 Inv goods and chattels of Elisha Rowark decd. Note on Young Birt.
286 Inv property of John Johnston decd by William McMurray adm.

Book N 1839
Page
286 ELIZABETH WILLSON - Will - w. 4 Dec 1838. Son-in-law Thomas Evans; daughter
Aberillah Evans; granddaughters Elizabeth Evans and Sarah Ann Evans. Rest of
property to be sold and divided to all legatees. Exec: son-in-law Thomas Evans.
Wit: James W. McCain. Exec qualified.

287 THOMAS STAFFORD - Will - w. 17 Nov 1838. Beloved wife Jincy Stafford all land
and estate during her life and at her death to go to 2 children Betsy Webster
and Jesse Stafford. Grandson John Stafford now living with me to have tract
of land where testator lives. Exec: Friend Jas. W. McCain. Test: Jno. P.
Rainey, John McCain.

289 Archibald Clark orphan 10 years of age bound to Thomas Day to learn the art of
a cabinet maker.
290 Elizabeth Brinsfield binds her two sons Calvin and James Brinsfield to Richard
Bennett for term of 6 years to learn the art of house carpentering.
291 Acct current of Ann Vincent decd. Paid Joseph Allison for crying sale; William
Street for coffin, for tombstones; paid note on Joseph Vincent. Special legacy
to Mrs. Shaw and Jno Sawyer.
292 Receipt of B. Johnson guardian of Mary Frances, Elizabeth Jane, Benjamin Johnson;
Lucy Ann and Nancey Bird orphans of the late Birdet Eskridge, and Nancy R.
Eskridge in her own right for balance due them from estate of Birdet Eskridge.
Booker Boman adm.
292 Thomas Badgett to receive $87 for removing wing and kitchen of old jail and
fixing them for kitchen and smoke house of new jail.

April Court 1839

294 Div negroes of Zachariah Pattillo decd and allotment of land to Mary L. Pattillo
widow; Thomas Kimble in right of his wife Ann, Lewis A. Pattillo, Zachariah
Pattillo, Frances Pattillo, Albert Pattillo(lot known as Whitmore place).
295 Sales property of Marmaduke Norfleet sold 21 and 22 Jany 1839 to Mary C. Norfleet, Addison Morgan, Anderson Brummitt, Albert A. Norfleet, Wm. A. Lea, Solomon Whitlow, Thomas Greenway, John L. Richmond, John M. Norfleet, Thomas W. Owen,
John Roan, John Miles, Samuel Love, Jesse Monday, William Evans, Thomas Broughton,
William Neighbors, Thomas Woods, Wm. B. Wilkes, Thomas Glenn, Thomas Broach,
Samuel McBroom, Lawrence Gray, William Bush, Ephrdem Hawkins, Saml. Keaton,
Abel Burch, John Kerr Jr., et al.
300-308 First sale of James Montgomery decd sold 27 Apr 1838 to:

Thomas Bennett	William Gattis	Thornton Hancock	David Montgomery
James Montgomery	John Montgomery	A. D. Montgomery	Michael Montgomery
Edward Montgomery	John Pinchback	Samuel Wheeler	Sidney Yancey
William Montgomery	N. J. Palmer	M. P. Huntington	Charles Hendrick
Henry Long	James G. Rainey	A. Benseany	A. Timberlake
William Sharp	Tho. Donoho	Benj. Hines	John W. Pinchback
et al	By D. and Ewd Montgomery exec.		(overseer)

309 Sales estate of John H. McAden decd after the death of his wife Elizabeth McAden.
Sales to Jane McAden, James Covington, Cynthia A. Hall, Geo. M. Hamlet, And.
Elmore, Cath. McAden, Robn. Ball. Rent of land goes to Jas McAden Jun.
By John McAden for David G. Brandon exec.
311 Inv and sales of Thomas Stephens decd taken 18 Feb 1839. Sales to Elijah Morton,
Sidney Lea, John Hagwood, Thomas Stegall, Clarke Vowel, John Peterson, Thomas
Riggs, Calvin Richmond, Catharine Stephens, Archibald Lea, James G. Rainey,
John Comer, Henry Richmond, Fleming Childers, James Gallaher, William & Iverson
G. Stephens, et al. By H. F. & Andrew W. Stephens exec.
313 Inv of Thomas Stafford decd taken 3 Jan 1839 by John Harris adm. Legacy left
Jincey Stafford. Sales to Jincey Stafford, Wm. & James Dismukes, John Stafford,
Terrel Fulcher, Charles Webster, John Harris, Jesse Stafford, et al.
315 Inv property of James Burton decd. Notes on Noel Burton, et al. By H. A.,
Franklin P., and William Burton adm.
317 Inv personal property of Marmaduke Norfleet decd by Nathaniel M. Roan adm.
Allotment to widow.

320 Inv estate of John H. McAden decd.

320 Inv estate of James M. Durham decd. Money collected of Peck Welford & Co. due
to Durham, also from W. W. Parks. Acct on Newman Durham. By G. A. Satterfield.

321 Acct current estate of William Cantrill by George T. Martin exec. Paid Rutha
Cantrill exec of Isaac; paid A. B. Morton as agent for Elijah Martin $369 and
as agent for Joseph Anthony $369, and for his children $369. Sales to Jas.
K. Lea and James Kerr.

323 Acct current estate of Garnett Neely decd by William McMurray & Ann Neely adm.

324 Acct current estate of James Holder decd by Samuel B. Holder. Paid Dr. Wilie
Jones medical bill; year's allowance to Sarah Holder.

326 Acct current estate of John Wiley decd by Alexander Wiley adm. Paid Jane Wiley's
year allowance, Nathan Jeffreys for coffin, Robert M. Wiley his part of tobacco,
John Miles for crying sale, John Kerr, et al.

328 Div of 16 negroes valued at $9210 of estate of James Montgomery to legatees:
Edward, Archibald D., David, John, Michael, William, and James Montgomery;
Alexander M. Long for wife Polly, William Gattis for wife Rebecca; heirs of
Abraham Montgomery.

330 Div negroes of Thomas Stephens decd to William Stephens, Andrew W. Stephens,
Moses Kitchen, Charles Stephens, Benj. F. Stephens, Catharine Stephens.

332 Div estate of James Burton to Mrs. Burton; Lucy, Noel, & John Burton; Lent G.
Lovell, Allen Jones, Polly Atkinson, Henry Burton, Franklin Burton, Daniel Gunn,
William Burton, James Burton, Robert Knight.

334 Div negroes of Reuben Oliver decd to Nancy Oliver widow; Demarius, Iverson,
James, Calvin, Monroe, Isabella, and Nancy Oliver. Met at house of Reubin
Oliver decd 10 Jan 1839. All children are infants and minors.

335 Sale of negro woman Mary of estate of William H. Howard sold at Blackwell's
Store to John B. Blackwell for $740. By Cary A. Howard adm.

336 Year's allowance to Mary C. Norfleet widow of Marmaduke Norfleet decd.

336 Year's allowance to Mrs. Sarah Burton & family, she widow of James Burton decd.

337 JOHN C. LEA - Will - w. 25 Apr 1838. Wife Hannah 1/9 part of estate including
mansion house & 200 acres land for her life then to go to all children then
living and offspring of those not living. Daughter Elizabeth Graves;
sons Sidney S. Lea(300 acres adj his mother & to have mansion house after death
of his mother), son Thomas L. Lea(land on north side of Country Line Creek adj
homestead), son John G. Lea (property already advanced him), son Nathaniel Lea
(property already advanced him). Children of deceased daughter Mary Wilson
which he has raised. Sons-in-law Jeremiah Graves and his wife Dililah, Calvin
Graves and wife Elizabeth, George Williamson and his departed wife.
Granddaughters Betsy Ann and Mary L. Lea (property already advanced). Remainder
of property to be sold and when selling slaves separation of husbands and wives,
parents and children, to be avoided. Aged slaves to be supported. Each child
to get 1/8 part of residue of estate. Exec: sons Nathaniel, John G. Thomas L.,
Sidney S., plus 3 sons-in-law. Wit: John Kerr Jr., Eleaner Swann.
Calvin Graves and John G. Lea qualified.

341 THOMAS STEPHENS - Will - w. 29 Jan 1835. House and plantation to be sold and
proceeds divided among all living children; beloved slaves equally divided.
Exec to pay debts of son John Stephens; son Charles Stephens; If son Benjamin
Stephens die, his wife Sally to be debarred from having property and Benjamin's
daughter Barbary Stephens to have his part. Exec: sons Benjamin and Andrew W.
Stephens. Test: William Stephens, Vincent Bradsher. Exec qualified.

342 ANDREW JOHNSTON - Will - w. 29 Dec 1838. Wife Mary all estate for her life,
daughters Lucy, Mary, Rebecca, & Louisa to live with her. After wife's death
estate equally to children: George, Thomas, James, William, Peter, Lucy, Mary,
Rebecca, Louisa Johnston, and Dicey Davis. Part to Dicey in trust for her & her
children. Exec: James E. Williamson. Wit: Peter McKinney, Elisha Sertain.
Exec qualified.

Book N 1839
Page

343 ELIZABETH ANDERSON - Will - w. 11 Dec 1838. Sister Sarah Anderson to have all
estate. Exec: brother Quinton Anderson. Wit: John Q. Anderson, Hanry Tait.
Exec qualified.

344 RUCKER T. LEA - Will - w. 11 June 1838. All estate to brother John Lea who is
supposed to be living in Tenn. Exec: brother Ashley G. Lea. Wit: Eleaner Swann,
William Long.
Will was contested and opposed by Durrett Oliver and wife and others. Court
decreed it was the last will and ordered it recorded. The exec by his atty
John Kerr Jr. renounced his right to execute. Paul A. Haralson named adm with
the will annexed, he bonded by John C. Totten, Abisha Slade.

July Court 1839

345 Sales property of John C. Lea decd sold 18 & 19 Mar and 17 May 1839 to:

Allen Brown	Hutchins Burton	William Chambers	Stephen Dodson Jr.
James M. Dobbins	John T. Dodson	Jesse Dunavent	Junius Dilworth
Calvin Graves	Jeremiah Graves	Thomas Greenway	Elijah Graves Sen.
James Gates	Thomas Gordon	Genl. Barzillai Graves, Wm. Herring	
Wm. H. Hendrick	Freeman A. Hinton	Wm. Lea(Leasburg)	Sidney S. Lea
John G. Lea	William Long	Mrs. Hannah Lea	Thomas L. Lea
Colly W. Lunsford	Joseph Lunsford	Archibald Lea	Nathaniel Lea
Col. Wm. Lea	Thomas Lea Sen.	Thomas Overby	Thomas Riggs Sr.& Jr.
Calvin J. Richmond	Josiah Rainey	William Stephens	Thomas Stegall
George B. Willis	Wyatt Walker	Thomas Day	et al

65 slaves included in inv.

347 NATHAN WILLIAMSON - Will - w. 23 Jan 1832. Sons George, John, Swift, Anthony, and
Thomas Willamson. Daughters Martha Tate, Elizabeth Smith, Margaret Simpson,
Mary P. Harris, Sarah C. Moss. Sons Thomas and Anthony to have negro woman
left in trust for daughter Frances Prather and her children free from hold of
her husband; grandson Robert R. Prather. Exec: sons Thomas & Anthony Williamson. Wit: A. T. Farish, Jeremiah Lea.
As Adam T. Farish and Jeremiah Lea are not residents of State, will proved by
oaths of John K. Brooks, Joseph Simpson, Joseph Windsor. Exec qualified.

348 Insolvents and removals before taxes due for 1838:
Richmond District - T. W. Brown, Wm. B. Crutchfield, Thos Dunevent, Henry Farley,
Madison Frazur, Joseph Green, James Gates, Jas Harris, Benj. Jones, C. V. Lanier,
Henderson Monday, Burch Anglish, Tho Mansfield, Penny Nicholas, Jas E. Norfleet,
Booker Sparrow, M. A. Vanhook.
Gloucester Dist. - Richard Aldridge, Benj. Bowden, John Fuqua, Saml. Greer,
Christopher Hinton, Saml. Nelson, Jno Smith, John K. Snipes, James Aldridge.
St. David's Dist. - Drury Kiersey, Alexander Kent, Joel Thomas.
Caswell Dist. - Warren Dunnavent, Ire E. Evans, Henry Moore, Meredith Price.

349 List of business taxes collected by Thos L. Lea, sheriff.
352 Inv estate of Jno. J. Farley decd by Dicey Farley adm. Feb 1839.
353 Inv property of Elizabeth Anderson decd taken 28 June 1839 by Q. Anderson exec.
354 Inv estate of Andrew Johnston decd by Jas E. Williamson adm.
355 Inv goods and chattels of Thomas B. Mims decd by John W. Mims adm. Sales to
Ed M. Jones, Robert Madding, Martin M. Mims, John W. Mims, Richard W. Jackson,
William Womack, Augustin Gwyn.
356 Sale perishable property of Mary Jones decd sold 5 Dec 1837 to Jefferson Bradsher, William Clayton, John Edmundson, Asa Hudgens.
357-358 missing
359 Acct current of John H. McAden decd.
361 Acct current of Gabriel Lea decd by William Lea exec.
362 Acct current of Nancy Taylor decd by Parham Pulliam adm.
363 Acct current of Mason Sanders decd.
364 Acct current of George Houston decd by James McMullin adm.

Book N 1839
Page
365 Acct current of Mary A. Houston decd by Robert Houston exec.
366 Report of Wardens of the Poor for 1839.
367 Taxable property for 1838.
368 Div of claims against Booker Boman to Bank of NC at Milton, to agent of Holcomb
& Cty of Lynchburg as security for James W. Jeffreys, and to John Comer.
·368 Year's allowance to Dicy Farley widow John J. Farley decd.
368 Year's allowance to Elizabeth Rowark widow of Elisha Rowark. Commrs met at
Store House of William Corbet.
370 Levi Pettiford orphan age of 5 years bound to Francis Gooch.
371 Thomas D. Johnston, County Trustee, in acct with Caswell County for 1837.
372 Negro girl Louisa property of Martha F. Swift orphan sold 8 Apr 1837 to Richard
Kernodle for $490. Thomas W. Graves guardian.
373 Acct current of Joseph Henderson decd by Hiram Henderson exec.

October Court 1839

375 GEORGE A. SWIFT - Will - w. 21 Apr 1838. Daughters Frances W. Jeffreys &
Martha Ann Sellers. Sons William P., Robert, & Thomas S. Swift each to have
land on which each lives. Balance to wife Sarah and she to give it to rest of
children as each comes of age to wit: Peggy, Sarah, Emeline Eliza, & Edward R.
Swift. Exec: sons Robert, Thomas, & George A. Swift. Wit: Thomas Williamson,
Beaufort Pleasant, John H. Haydon. Robert & George A. Swift qualified.

377 JUDITH HALL - Will - w. 11 Sept 1837. All property to daughter Elizabeth Hall,
house and stock, and she to do what she pleases with it. Test: William Kennon,
Sarah P. Cols (Coils?).

377 BENJAMIN HOOPER - Will - w. 23 Sept 1830. (Filed with July 1839 papers.)
Wife Nancy Hooper all estate as long as she remains a widow, then property
divided to children. Wit: H. Hooper, Joseph Henderson.
Both witnesses are deceased. Proved on oaths of Geo Williamson, George B.
Roberson, & John C. Totten. Nancy Hooper the widow named adm with will annexed,
she bonded by Owen McAleer, Henry Badgett.

379 ELISHA BERRY - Will - w. 1 Aug 1839. Wife Frances to have plantation for her lif
or widowhood, then to be divided to then living children. Exec: wife Frances
Berry and her brother Antichus Boswell. Wit: A. Graves, John Somers.
Antiochus Boswell qualified.

380 Inv personal estate of Benjamin Hooper decd by Nancy Hooper adm.
381 Inv estate of Nathan Williamson decd by Thomas & Anthony Williamson exec.
382 Sales property of Reubin Oliver decd sold 11 Jan 1839 to:

Nancy Oliver	William Kimbrough	John Corbet	George Richmond
Thomas Badgett	Richard W. Jackson,	Joseph Aldridge	Erastus Adams
James Page	Thos W. Graves	Jonathan Smith	George Richmond
Elisha Evans	Hutchins Burton	Henderson House	

Hire of negroes to Nancy Oliver; crop of tobbacco sold to S. Pugh, Samuel Watkins, Abner Walker.
385 Sales property of James Burton decd to his widow, to Archibald Hubbard, Henry
A. Burton, William Burton, Franklin X. Burton, Joseph Brackin, G. A. Henderson,
John Cobb, Johnston Atkinson, James White, Noel Burton, William Stokes, Lent
Lovell, Lucy Burton, Mary Atkinson et al.
389 Acct current William H. Howard by Cary A. Howard adm.
390 Acct current of William Anderson decd by Yancey Wiley adm.
392 Acct current of Reuben Oliver decd by Durret Oliver adm. Bills paid of Albert
G. Yancey, Henry Bushnell, Owen McAleer, N. M. Roan, David Melton, Lindsay
Oliver, Nancy Oliver widow, John Kerr for fees.
394 Div of negroes of Samuel Smith decd after death of his widow Elizabeth Smith who
died 17 Dec 1838. Div to: Samuel H., John, Thomas, Richard J., Maurice,
Alexander, Robert K., & William Smith; and to Henry Warren for his wife Elizabeth, J. Wilson for his wife Ann, John H. Crisp for his wife Mary K. 29 Aug 183

Book N 1839
Page
397 Div negroes of Griffin Gunn decd. Allotment to Daniel B. Gunn his portion
    now in possession of John C. Harvey guardian.
398 Report of committee to inspect the Jail - to add to security and its protection
    from persons without, jail to be enclosed on front and on east with strong
    pailing (paling) or stockade and need to procure from George Williamson
    a few feet of land to enlarge the lot.
399 List of unlisted taxables for 1835 by Thomas L. Lea, Sheriff.
401 Results of Common School elections: 30 Sept. 1839.

Voting place	For schools	No schools
Brown's Store	135	11
Milton	131	5
Yanceyville	213	15
Q. Anderson's Store	7	176
Hightowers	9	75
Leasburg	5	63
Lynn's Old Field	23	44
Prospect Hill	2	70
Total	525	459

402 Negro boy Anthony of estate of Rucker T. Lea decd sold 29 July 1839 to Archibald
    Lea for $610.

END OF BOOK N

838. Amount of Taxable Property for the Year

Districts	Total valuation of Town property	Number of acres of Land	Total valuation of Land	White Polls	Black Polls
...hmond District	87 615.	77.039.	402.213.	220.	1157.
...ncaster District	300.	68.721.	217.821.	254.	656.
Davids District	1025.	54.044.	157.421.	166.	546.
...swell District		52.056.	177.259.	150.	557.
Total.	88.940.	251.860.	954.714.	790.	2916.

Book N-Page 367

145

333

Report of Commissioners to sell the old Court House.

State of North Carolina
Caswell County ——————} In pursuance of an order of this court of
Pleas and quarter sessions for the county of Caswell directed to us
to sell the Old Court house, on Tuesday 2d day of May Superior
Court, all of which has been done agreeable to the directions of
said order. William and Isham Skjoa Wea became the purchaser at
and for the price of One hundred and Eighty One Dollars and has
Contracted on to Bond with Anderson Willis his Security for the same,
payable to St. Lawis County Trustee, which together with this report is
submitted to your Worship. July 11th 1833.

Geo. Williamson
Thos. D. Johnston
John C. Harvey.

146

Page
1 JOHN TAPSCOTT - Will - w. 17 Sept. 1839. Sister Mary W. Tapscott, her heirs
and assigns; nephew William Tapscott, son of Henry; niece Nancy Tapscott,
daughter of Henry; niece Susannah daughter of Henry; nephew Henry C. Tapscott
son of Henry; nephew James Tapscott son of Henry; nephew John son of Edney Tapscott. Exec: nephew John and sister Mary W. Tapscott. Wit: Bernard H. Boswell
and R. S. Boswell. John Tapscott qualified.

3 DAVID BARKER - Will - w. 5 Nov 1831. Daughter Elizabeth Simpson; son William
Barker; wife; sons James, David, and George Barker. Exec: David and George Barker, sons. Wit: Jas. Kerr, F. Leath. Exec qualified.

5 Inv estate of George A. Swift decd by Robert Swift and George A. Swift exec.
6 Inv goods and chattels of the late Elisha Berry decd made out in the presence of
Miss Phaney Sommers and Solomon Beavers. 12 Dec 1839. Bonds due estate: on Joel
Motley and Ziba Rice. Debtors: Solomon Beaver, Alexander Walker, Ansolim Sartin,
John Smithy, Isaiah Paschall, Clement Nance, John M. Walker.

8 Inv estate of John Tapscott taken 18 Oct 1839.
9 Inv property of Henry Thomas decd by John Simmons adm.
10 Inv property of Andrew Kimbrough decd by Catharine Kimbrough adm.
11 Sales property of Andrew Kimbro 23 Oct 1839. Sales to James Byrd, Jesse Jeffreys,
Wm. Byrd, Nancy Kimbrough Sen., Mary Kimbrough, Margaret Kimbrough.

14 Sales estate of William Harris decd sold 30 Oct 1839 by Reubin Harris adm.
Sales to Anny Harris, William Harris, James O. Harris; Elizabeth, Julia, Masten,
and Reubin Harris. Part set aside for widow.

17 List and sale of property of John Tapscott. Buyers: Mary Tapscott, John Morgan,
Dennis Matkins, Elizabeth Hornbuckle, Agnes Yokely, Jarrat D. Figgans, George W.
Lea, James Barker, Alexander Montgomery, Samuel Tapscott, John H. Heydon, Samuel
Groom, John H. Simpson.

22 Property sold of Wade N. Woodson 30 Nov 1839 to Lucey A. Woodson, Archibald Haggie,
James Malone, Archibald Lea, Henry A. Richmond, Thos. Greenway, John M. Richmond,
Calvin Richmond, J. W. Roan. Sold by Mary Winstead adm.

24 Acct current estate of Reuben Jones decd by Calvin & Susannah Jones adm.
26 Mildred Harrison, widow of Andrew Harrison decd, year's allowance set by A. Gunn,
Thomas Turner, Geo Williamson, Archd Walters.

26 Div of negroes of John Wiley decd to Jane Wiley, John H. Wiley and wife Adeline,
Robert M. Wiley, Thomas Wiley, Frances Wiley, Elizabeth Wiley. 26 Oct 1839.

28 Div negroes of William Harris decd to: Widow; Sarah Colle; Susan Roberts;
James, Reubin, Elizabeth, Julia Ann, and William Harris. 2 Nov 1839.

29 Receipt from Nancy Oliver to Durrett Oliver adm of Reuben Oliver decd for her
portion of estate of said decd, $572.85, widow's portion. 9 Oct 1839.

32 Sales property of Andrew Harrison decd taken 13 & 14 Nov 1839 by John P. & E. R.
Harrison adm. Sales to Mildred Harrison; Samuel S. & Wm. K. Harrison; William
Henderson, Samuel Hinton, Edward Robertson, John Reed, Robert Singleton, John H.
Cazort, A. G. Walters, William Cox, John Word, B. Oliver, Wm. W. Knight, et al.

37 Allowance to Mildred Harrison widow of Andrew Harrison decd. 13 Nov 1839.
38 Sales of property of John Love Jun. decd sold 18 Feb 1840 by Carter Lea adm.
Buyers not listed. Rent of plantation below bridge on Hyco.

40 Inv estate of David Barker Sen. by David C. & George Barker exec. Bonds on
Jarrot D. Feagans, Thos. J. Reid, Samuel Moore, William Barker.

42 Inv estate of Joseph Lunsford decd by George Williamson adm.
43 Sales estate of David Barker Sen. sold 26 & 28 Dec 1839 to David C. & George Bar-
ker, George Simpson, John E. Brown, Calvin Graves, John Bolden, William Sanders,
Moses D. Butler, Jesse Bateman, Nathan Windsor, Wm. Allen, Benjamin Pinnix, James
Barker, Samuel Heydon, John Tapscott, Nelson Nunn, Henry Lambert, Priscilla Taylor,
Dennis, James & John Matkins, et al.

Book O - 1840
Page
49 Sales property of Nathan Williamson decd sold by Thomas & Anthony Williamson, exec. Sales to:

John Foster	Anthony Williamson,John H. Heydon		William Slade
John Summers	John Boswell	Thomas Williams	Samuel Smith
Absolem Kennedy	Pharey Summers	Daniel B. Moss	Swift Williamson
Zera Gwynn	Richard Kernodle	Charles Thacker	Moses Butler
Dennis Wilson	Joseph Windsor	Carter Groom	Wm. P. Brown
Reubin Smithy	John Kennedy	Joseph Maze	Jarrett D. Feagans
Pleasant Feagans	Fanny Prather	Robert R. Prather	Larkin Smithey
Stephen Rice	Samuel Groom	George Simpson	et al.

57 Sale of land of John Tapscott decd sold 9 Feb 1840, his Country Line & Camp Springs tracts.
57 Sale of Joseph Lunsford decd on 22 Jan 1840 by Geo Williamson adm. Sales to Colly W. Lunsford, Walter Lunsford, Mrs. Lunsford, William Lea, Thomas D. Johnston, James Poteat, James Parish, John Poteat Sen., Robert Lunsford, Ruth Palmer, Matthew Dodson, Samuel J. Evans, et al.
59 Receipts from estate of Henry Hooper decd fom Joseph Knight, Starling Gunn, Peter Powell Jun., Thomas Carpenter(surveying instruments), et al.
63 Acct current estate of George Manley decd by John Manley adm.
64 Acct current estate of Thomas Page decd by Josiah Page exec. Hire of negroes to Nancy Page; sale of land to G. Evans.
65 Acct current of John Wiley decd by Alexander Wiley adm.
67 Sales estate of Josiah Paschal decd sold 21 Oct 1839 to John Lovelace, Ezekiel Paschall, John Cole, William Sanders, Salenah Paschall, Nicholas Lovelace, John Somers, John Griffith, Gwin Rice.
68 Year's allowance to Lucy A. Woodson.
69 Year's allowance to Catharine Kimbrough widow of Andrew Kimbrough decd.
69 Sale of negro woman Letha on 4 Nov 1839 of estate of Andrew Johnson decd. Sold to John E. Brown.
70 Div of negroes of David Barker decd to James, William, George, and David C. Barker; and to George Simpson and Elizabeth his wife. 28 Jan 1840.
72 Div of negroes (8 div) of John C. Lea decd to George Williamson; Sidney S. Lea; William Smith and wife Betsy Ann, and William Lea and wife Mary; Jeremiah Graves; Calvin Graves; Nathl Lea; Thos L. Lea; John G. Lea. 12 Mar 1839.
74 Div of negroes of Zach Pattillo into 3 divisions and Albert A. Pattillo drew one div.
75 Anna Dixon orphan age of 12 years bound to Bennett Warren until age 21.
76 Quintina Philips orphan of color age 11 years bound to Paul A. Haralson.

June Court 1840

79 WILLIAM PARKER - Will - w. 3 June 1836. Wife Ursula Parker to have all estate for her life, then to be equally divided between son Jeptha Kiersey Parker and daughter Eddy Tyler. Exec: James Matlock. Wit: Thomas Slade, John Walton, William Vernon.

80 Inv personal estate of Sarah Morris decd by James Vaughan adm taken 8 Jan 1840.
81 Sales personal porperty of John Ware decd sold 18 May 1840 to:

Christopher Dameron	James Ware	John G. Cook	Thomas Ware
Joseph T. Ware	Henry Cook	Washington Price	Silas Ware
Edmund Cook	Miss Polley Ware	John Jeffreys	Abisha Slade
George Roberson	Joshua Glass	Johnson Atkinson	John Travis
Jane Ware	Jason Ware	John P. Harrison	By Joseph T. Ware,adm

84 Inv estate of Martin Mims. Notes on John B. Powell, James Richardson, Thomas L. Badgett, Azariah Foster, Henry Glass, John W. Mims, et al. Acct on Barthus J. Crawley. By John Cobb adm.
85 Sales estate of Martin Mims to Wm. Stokes, James Hubbard, John Mims, Robt. J. King, Thomas Ware, Richard Jones for the widow, James Atkins, Joseph Bracken, et al.

Book O - 1840
Page
87 Inv property of James Heydon decd by John H. Haydon adm taken 24 Mar 1840.
   Part set aside for widow.
89 Inv property of Wade N. Woodson decd by Mary Winstead adm.
90 Inv property of Richard W. Jackson decd taken 4 Apr 1840 by Owen McAleer adm.
91 Sales property of John Love Jun. sold 23 Apr 1840 by Carter Lea. Sales to:

Archibald Haggie	Anthony Reed	Adderson Morgan	Frances Day
John Broughton	Joseph S. Thompson,	Martha Love widow	John L. Richmond
John W. Roan	Pleasant Fitzgerald,	Robert Love	Rubin Morgan
Vincent Lea	Wm. Lea Jr.	Wm. A. Lea Sen.	Wm. Lea Sr.
William Long	William Turner	Wm. S. McDaniel	Thomas J. Willis
Edward C. Richmond	Allowance to widow.		

96 Sales property of Sarah Morris decd sold 22 Jan 1840 by James Vaughan adm to:

Christopher Brooks	John K. Brooks	Pleasant Corbet	George Vaughan
Joseph Aldridge	Abner Kerr	Wm. Kimbrough	John C. Harvey
John Walker	Howard Martin	Thomas Stacy	Nancy Vaughan
Sarah Vaughan	William Vaughan	Lemuel S. Dabbs	Wood Covington
Elijah Miles	John Miles	Frances Gooch	Josiah Page
Devereau Hightower	Henry Baldwin	Eliza Morris	Hartford Gooch
William Boswell	Henry Willis	et al.	

101 Sales property of James Heydon decd sold 18 Apr 1840 to:

John Boulden	Thomas Brown Sen.	Luther C. Chandler	Henry Cotton
William Dupree	Empson Fitch	Edmund Herndon	Joseph Heydon
William Heydon	Bedford Henslee	Nancey Heydon	John H. Heydon
Leonard G. Heydon	James Kinnebrough	Abner R. Kerr	Samuel F. Heydon
John Miles Jun.	Daniel B. Moss	James Miles Esq.	Alexander Moore
Uriah Miles	Jeremiah Rudd Jun.,	Franklin Rudd	John Simmons (of Geo.)
George W. Taylor	John Simmons Jr.	James Graves	Archibald Campbell
Rufus E. Chandler	Thomas Swift	Anthony Williamson	

106-107 Thomas D. Johnston, county trustee, acct with Caswell Co. for 1838. A note
   on William Graves for purchase of old jail not collected $66. Examined by
   Abner Miles, John C. Harvey, Daniel L. McAlpin.
108 Report of Wardens of the Poor for 1840.
110 James M. Durham decd acct current by G. D. Satterfield adm.
111 Year's allowance to Susannah Mims widow of Martin Mims decd.
112 Year's allowance to Nancy Heydon widow of James Heydon decd.
113 Year's allowance to Martha Love widow of John Love Jr. decd.
114 Sale of interest of Thomas B. Mims decd in negroes belonging to estate of his
   father John Mims decd. By John W. Mims adm. Sold to George Roberson and John
   B. Blackwell.
115 List of business taxes collected.
117 Insolvents removed before taxes due for 1839: Erastus Adams, Parham A. Boley,
   Abr B. Farley, Zach McFarland, Lewis Malone, M. B. Dulaney, Latiny Parrott,
   Daniel Richmond, Wade N. Woodson, Elijah Ford (removed).
117 Inv property of James Powell a lunatic taken by his guardian William Weatherford - included 10 slaves.
119 Taxable property for 1839 - 831 white polls; 2903 balck polls.

October Court 1840

122 EDMUND HERNDON - Will - w. 2 Aug 1836. Wife Elizabeth all estate for life or
    widowhood - then to go to 8 children: Frances, Elizabeth, Sarah, George,
    William, Martha, Lucinda, and Edmund Herndon. As young ones become of age or
    marry, wife to make provisions thereby. Exec: wife Elizabeth and son George
    Herndon. Wit: Q. Anderson, William Florence. Exec qualified.

123 MARTHA BRADSHER SENR. --Will - w. 8 Aug 1835. Son Vincent to have all property
    except granddaughters Martha J. Nelson to have a bed and Eunice A. Bradsher
    to have silver. Exec: son Vincent Bradsher. Wit: Tho R. Richmond, John Brad-
    sher Jr. As witnesses not inhabitants of the State, their signatures proved on
    oaths of Archibald D. Richmond and William A. Lea. Exec qualified.

149

Book O - 1840-41
Page
125 ZERA GWYN(N) - Will - w. 29 Apr 1840. Wife Temperance Gwyn. Three daughters
Elizabeth, Dorothy, and Jane to have land whereon he lives as long as they
are single. After marriage all to be sold and divided among lawful heirs.
Wit: Jas E. Williamson, L. A. Gwynn.
Codicil 2 July 1840 - Daughter Jane to have $300 more than others after death
of wife. Exec: son Rice Gwynn. Exec qualified.
126 CHRISTOPHER W. BROOKS - Will - w. 15 Sept. 1837. Sons John, Robert, Christopher,
James, Alexander, and Iverson Brooks. Daughter Mary Brooks since married to
James Boswell to have negroes in her possession. Daughter Isabella Brooks.
Remainder of estate to wife Ibby. Exec: sons John, Robert, and Christopher.
Wit: Q. Anderson, Jno. Q. Anderson.
John K. Brooks and Robert H. Brooks qualified.
129 Inv estate of John Nunnally taken 23 Sept 1840 by Letha A. Nunnally adm.
132 Inv property of William Parker decd taken 15 July 1840 by Pleasant Chandler exec.
133 Inv estate of Massey Nelson decd by Iverson Nelson adm. 7 Oct 1840.
134 Sales property of Edmund Burch decd sold 21 Aug 1840 to Richard, Elizabeth,
and Claben Burch, to James Broach, Warren J. Morgan, William Marshall, Zeph
Roberts, William Mansfield, et al. By James Burch adm.
136 Sale perishable property of Martin Mims decd sold 1 Aug by John Cobb adm.
136 Sales estate of William Parker decd sold 1 Aug to William N. Adams, John G. Lea,
Robert A. Crowder, Archd. McMillan, Ruth Hicks, John H. Cazart, Geo W. Willis,
Sally Jones, John W. Pinchback, Alexander Kersey, Enoch J. Davis, James W. Reed,
Stapleton C. Crutchfield, et al.
141 Tobacco of estate of Andrew Harrison sold to Robert Williams.
141 Dicey Farley adm of John J. Farley, acct filed.
143 David Melton and Frances Sheppard adm of James Sheppard decd, acct filed.
Payment to widow; to Freeman Leath, Henderson House, et al.
144 Edward, David, and James Montgomery exec of James Montgomery decd, acct filed.
146 Year's allowance to Elizabeth Burch widow of Edmund Burch decd for her & family.
147 Year's allowance to Lytha A. Nunnally widow of John Nunnally decd. (Name may
be Sytha Nunnally).
148 Negro woman Betty of heirs of Martin Mims decd sold to George R. Robertson.

January Court 1841

151 Inv estate of Christopher Brooks decd taken 30 Dec 1840 by John K. Brooks and
Robert H. Brooks exec. Bond on John C. Totten; acct on John Stamps.
152 Inv estate of Zera Gwynn taken 20 Aug 1840.
153 Inv of bonds due estate of Armstead Watlington Jr. decd on Augustus Gwyn, David
Walker, Allen Scott, Ruben Harris, John Swift, et al. By E. Watlington adm.
154 Inv estate of Judith Richardson decd. Notes on Shandy Perkins, Archibald
Atkinson, et al. By Samuel B. Cobb.
155 Inv property of Samuel Mitchell decd taken 19 Nov 1840 by John Mitchell and
James Currie adm. Notes on Thompson White, Samuel and James Wilson, Samuel
Dunn, K. M. Bagly signed by James Farley.
156 List of sales of Massa Nelson decd sold 11 Nov 1840 to Azariah Nelson, William
Murphey, Abner Stanfield, Green Woods, M. G. Thomas, Thomas Roan, Thomas W. Owen
Joseph Langley, James Galleher, Ambrose Nelson, John and James Murphey, Alexan-
der Morgan, Elizabeth Evans, Anderson Brummitt, Bird Bateman, et al.
161 Inv & Sales of Moses Fuller decd sold 3 Nov 1840 to Reubin Hawkins, Archibald
Richmond, William Evans, William Woods, William Fuller, Elijah Jacobs, Hiram
Lockard, William Thomas, David Moore, Levi Compton, Newel Jeffreys, William
Wisdom, Willima Fuller Jr., John H. Fuller, Jonathan Murphey, B. Cooper, et al.
By William Fuller Jr. adm.
166-170 Inv and amt sales of estate of John Ware decd sold 17 Nov 1840 to Allen Gunn,
Silas Ware; William, John, & Isaac Travis; Archibald & Azariah G. Walters,
Johnston Atkinson, Jas Hodge, Doct George Robertson, Josiah Balir, Elisah Alver-
son, Jane Ware, William Walker, Christopher Dameron, Thomas Ware, Polly Ware,

Book O 1841
Page
166-170 cont. Sales of John Ware cont. to: Jason Ware, William Knight, Henry Burton,
Granderson M. Sharp, William Penix, Jas White, Robt. McCain, et al. By John P.
Harrison & Joseph T. Ware adm.
171 Inv sales of estate of William Holcomb decd sold 29 Oct 1840 to Sally Holcomb,
Thomas C. Pass, James Powell, William Lea, Pleasen Hood, William Campbell,
James Herring, et al. Negroes hired to Wm. Lea, James Jones, Sally Holcomb.
173 Inv of property on 8 Oct 1840 of William Holcomb by John G. Lea adm.
175 Sales estate of Gabriel Lea decd by William Lea exec with notes due 24 July 1841.
Sales to William Lea Jun. for purchase of widow's dower of land, to William
Dismukes, Johnston McDaniel, Archibald Haggie, Wm. & John Royester, William
Chambers, William Garrott, Lorenzo Lea, William Eskridge, Elijah Morton,
John N. Fuller, et al.
177 Sales of livestock of Andrew Kimbro decd to William Bird. By Catharine Kimbro.
177 Settlement estate of Elisha Rowark decd. Paid accts of Susan Rowark, Nathan
Jeffreys for coffin; pd widow's allowance; Absolem Lea for crying sale, Henry
Bushnell for surveying. 2 Jan 1840. By Roberson McMinamy adm. Examined by
James Currie and James Womble.
178 Acct current estate of Thomas Stafford decd by John Harris Jr. adm.
180 Acct current estate of Marmaduke Norfleet decd by Nathaniel M. Roan adm.
184 Div of negroes of John Ware decd to Thomas Ware, Samuel Henderson, Christopher
Dameron, John Ware, Benjamin Gosney, Tolbert Ware, Silas & Polly Ware, James Ware.
186 Div of negroes of William Holcomb decd to Sally Holcomb widow. Rest of negroes
left as joint stock for Elizabeth, Mary, Sally, and Joel Holcomb, minors under
21 years of age.
187 Div of negroes of Gabriel Lea decd to: William Lea, Gabriel B. Lea, John C. Vanhook and Phebe his wife, children of Daniel Malone and Betsy his wife, Elijah
Morton and Polly his wife, James Lea. Stephen Winstead and wife Barbary drew
lot 1; William Lea assignee for James Lea; William Lea drew for Vincent Lea;
William Lea adm drew for Betsy Malone decd wife of Daniel Malone and for children
of Daniel Malone and Betsy his wife.
189 List of sales of Samuel Mitchell decd sold by James Mitchell and James Currie adm.
James McMullen for interest in slaves.
191 Year's allowance to Sally Holcomb widow of William Holcomb. 27 Oct 1840.

March Court 1841

194 MARY KIMBROUGH - Will - w. 12 Mar 1841. Nephew Dr. Nathaniel M. Roan to have
all property except following special legacies to: William Stephens son of
decd sister Elizabeth Stephens; Andrew Stephens and Catharine Hagwood brother
and sister of said William Stephens; Andrew Warrick Stephens son of William
Stephens; Thompson, Logan, William, Minerva, & Elizabeth Darby children of
niece Ann Darby; James T., John W., Mary Norfleet, Nancy L., Jane, and Margaret
A. children of John Roan; Nathaniel, Priscilla, Frances, and Marmaduke children
of above named Mary Norfleet. Has given deed of gift to Sarah M. Roan. Negroes
to be well provided for with husbands and wives and children to remain together
and none to be sold. Old servants Nancy and Billy to be comfortably maintained.
Exec: Dr. N. M. Roan. Wit: Jno Kerr Jr., Alexander Wiley. Exec qualified.

196 JOHN BRAWTON - Will - w. 16 Apr 1839. Wife Elizabeth all estate for her life;
son Jacky William; daughter Parthena Oakley; granddaughter Caroline Oakley.
Son Thomas (land whereon I live after death of wife); daughters Luzella
Malinda (land adj Thomas Johnston), Mobsey S. Hendrick, and Missouri S. Combs.
Exec: son Thomas Brawton and Orison Combs. Wit: Will A. Lea, John Hagwood.
Thomas Brawton renounced his right to execute and Orison Combs qualified.
(Note - this name also spelled Braughton and Broughton in other county records.)

198 Inv personal property of Sarah Brooks decd taken by Geo Brooks adm.
201 Inv property of Thomas J. Gunn decd by Daniel B. Gunn adm. Notes on John Hendrick and Abisha Slade.

151

Book O 1841
Page
202 Sales estate of John Nunnally decd sold Nov 17 1840 to Mrs. Nunnally, Robert
Blackwell, Joseph King, William H. Nunnally, Leander Nunnally, Thomas Mills,
William Weatherford, Mathew Mills, Samuel Johnson, Edwin Cook, Obadiah and John
Nunnally, Miss Agness Nunnally by Mother, Henry Cobb, Thomas Powell, Lancelot
Johnston, et al. Negroes sold to John Keesee, Daniel Price, John B. Blackwell,
and John Mason.
205 Sales property of Joshua Jackson decd to Nelson Thomas, John S. Hightower, Willia
son Moore, James E. Mitchell, William Turner. By Daniel Jackson adm.
206 Sales property of Richard W. Jackson decd sold 30 Jan 1841 by Owen McAleer adm.
Sales to Aldridge Rudd, C. H. Morefield, Bleuford W. Reed, Thomas L. Slade,
S. S. Kent, James Mebane, John Hank, James L. Graves, James Dilworth.
207 Amt of hire of negroes of estate of Andrew Harrison decd for 1841.
208 Acct current estate of James Burton decd by Henry A., William, and Franklin X.
Burton adm.
210 Two old negroes of estate of Samuel Mitchell sold to Daniel D. Winstead.-Hannah
and Phillas about 80 years of age sold for 1¢ each.
211 Sale of 2 negroes of estate of James Montgomery sold to John Pinchback and
to David Montgomery. 6 Jan 1841.
211 Sale of negroes of estate of Moses Fuller decd sold 12 Feb 1841 to James Woods,
Thomas W. Owens, William Warren, William Morton, Harvey Cooper, Robert McKee.
By William Fuller adm.
212 Sale of negro man, Adam, of estate of Joshua Jackson decd to Thomas Burton.
By Daniel Jackson adm.
213 Edward A. Horton orphan age of 13 years on 17 Apr 1841 bound to Richard Yarbrough to learn art of a millwright.
214 Martha Jane Bays (or Baze) orphan age of 10 years in July next bound to James L.
Graves.
215 Administrator's notice to creditors of Col. Saml. Mitchell dated 8 Oct 1840 - cop
posted at Court House, at Brown & Winstead's store, at Leasburg, and at Corbet's
Store. Wit: Henderson Smith.
217 Report of commission to let bridge at James Mebane's mill across Country Line
Creek; bridge to cost $67.50, to put in 2 new sleepers and cover anew with good
oak plank 2 inches thick. Commrs: Tho W. Graves, Jeremiah Graves, William
Graves, George G. Martin.

July Court 1841

218 EDWARD H. ROBERSON - Will - w. 4 Mar 1841. Wife Elmira J. Roberson; children
to get share of estate as each comes of age or marries. Sister Eleanor Crowder
wife of Robert A. Crowder to have 2 slaves for her use free from dominion of
her husband. Sister-in-law Ann E. Barnett $250. Exec to attend to his interest
in estate of Godfrey Crowder and grandmother Jane Rudder.-Exec: wife Elmire J.
Roberson and friend Nathaniel J. Palmer. Wit: N. J. Palmer, William Weeden,
William M. Brooks.

221 WILLIAM B. LANGHORNE of Milton - Will - w. 19 July 1840. Exec to take charge of
all estate; wife Elizabeth W. Langhorne. Exec to sell all estate and wife to
have interest and ½ of principle from same. Children of brother Alexander
Langhorne; brothers and sisters then living to share part of ½ of estate.
Children of brother Alexander to have title to land in Cumberland Co., Va.,
after death of his mother and Alexander to take charge of same. Exec: brother
Alexander Langhorne of Mecklenburg Co., Va. Wit: Barzillai Graves, John S.
Oglesby, Willie Jones. Alexander Langhorne renounced his right to execute and
Nathaniel J. Palmer named adm with will annexed.

224 ALLEN BURTON - Will - w. 5 Dec 1834. Wife Mary all land for her life; children
Thomas, Drury, Davey, Susannah, Betsey, Frances, Hutchins, Mary, Absolem,
Dinah, Jane, Metilda, Allen, and Lucy. Exec: friend Willis M. Lea. Wit: Will
A. Lea, Stephen Garrott, John N. Fuller. Willis M. Lea refused to qualify and
Mary Burton named adm.

152

Book O 1841

Page

226 Inv and sales personal estate of David Walker decd by Lancelot Johnston adm.

227 Inv estate of John Broughton decd by Orison G. Combs exec.

228 Second inv estate of Joshua Jackson decd. Claim on Daniel Jackson former guardian.

229 Sales property of Benjamin Hooper decd sold 28 Apr 1841 & 28 May to Thomas Kennon, Joseph Brackin, Frances Hooper, James Hubbard, John Glass, James L. Graves, Doct. Nathaniel S. Graves, John Cobb, Henry & William Badgett, Joseph Hooper, George Southerland, Isaac Wright, James Garland, Johnston Atkinson, Henry Hooper, William Womack, et al. By Joseph Brackin adm.

234 Acct current estate of Nathan Moore decd by James Moore exec. Paid Joseph Simpson and Eliz.Hobbs for schooling; pd accts of Doct James Williamson and Doct Ellis G. Blake, James Kerr store acct (1 hat for Caleb, 1 hat for John each 75¢); pd James C. Turrentine, sheriff, John T. Morrow and James B. Roscoe for tuition; pd George Williamson sheriff of Caswell Co.

237 John W. Mims adm in acct with estate of Thomas B. Mims decd included interest Thomas B. Mims had in negroes of John Mims decd.

239 Div of the 30 negroes of estate of Benjamin Hooper decd to: advanced to children in his lifetime to Mrs. Martha Motley, Zach L. Hooper, John & Henry Hooper, Eliza intermarried with Henry Hunley; 9 div to:widow who has married Joseph Brackin, Joseph Hooper, Elisha Hooper, Francis Hooper, Zach L. Hooper, Martha Motley, Hunley and wife Eliza, Henry Hooper, John Hooper.

241 Sale of a negro man, Burrell, of estate of James Thomas decd sold at store of Brown & Winstead to Green W. Brown for $525.

242 Sale of negroes of Thomas J. Gunn decd to James Vaughan, Ansel Ware, Francis F. Thornton. John C. Harvey guardian for the intestate.

243 Report of Thomas D. Johnston county trustee for 1839. Examined by Abner Miles and P. Hodnett.

246 Year's allowance to Frances Walker.

247 Report of Wardens of the Poor - by Elijah Graves, President of the board. A good well and pump are needed as the spring is a far distance and water bad.

248 James Mebane to build the bridge at his mill for cost of $75.50.

248 Taxable property for 1840 - 844 white polls, 3196 black polls.

249 Business taxes collected by sheriff on 23 merchants, 21 retailers of spirits.

October Court 1841

253 JOHN DAVIS - Will - w. 22 May 1839. Three daughters living with him, Nancy, Sarah, and Elizabeth to have dwelling house and part of land. Grandson John Davis son of Enoch Davis(110 acres land); daughter Lucy Montgomery (house and land where she now lives); balance of land to son Enoch Davis'' other children. Daughter Rebecca Roberts. Wit: Rowzee Samuel, Pleasant Chandler, Bluford Reed.

254 JAMES RAINEY - Will - w. 13 July 1839. 81 years of age. Youngest son Josiah Rainey to have house and land and an equal share with his 5 brothers and his decd sister's children. Has paid debts for 3rd son Thomas M. Rainey. Test: Jno P. Rainey, Thos Holloway, Jas W. Jeffreys.

255 JOHN RICHMOND - Will - w. 23 July 1830. Wife Mary to have house and part of land during her life or widowhood, then same to return to John Currie Richmond at her death. Son James(land on Reedy Fork near public road and on old road adj George B. Dameron);son John Currie Richmond balance of land. Exec: Solomon Vanhook and John Currie Richmond. Wit: Jos Langly, John Wiley, Williamson Dameron.

257-259 Bonds for Thomas L. Lea as high sheriff from 1840-41.

260 Agreement between John Poteat Senr. and William Long - lease of negroes and land from Poteat to Long, the lower tabacco lot on west side of stage road adj George Williamson excepting land adj Nathaniel Lea on east side of road. Leased for period ending 1844. 19 July 1841. Wit: Paul A. Haralson, H. Sawyer.

262 Valuation of slaves of Reubin Oliver decd -met at his late dwelling house to allot 1/7 portion to William Yancey and wife Demarius alias Demarius Oliver. 25 Aug 1841.

Book O 1841-42
Page
263 Inv property of Mary Kimbro decd taken 13 Mar 1841 by N. M. Roan exec. Bonds
    on William Graves and Goodwin Evans. Property given to Sarah M. Roan now
    Sarah M. Dameron.
264 Thomas and Anthony Williamson exec acct current estate of Nathan Williamson decd.
265 Inv property of Agness Oakley decd taken 1 Apr 1841 by Thomas Thompson adm.
266 Sales of personal property of Agness Oakley decd sold 11 May 1841. Tract of land
    rented to Fereby Oakley. Sales to William Roberson, John Oakley, William Holt,
    Marcus Oakley, Nathan Windsor, Thomas Madron.
267 Inv and sales property of Benjamin Carter decd by Benj. H. Carter adm with the
    will. Buyers not listed.
268 Settlement estate of Jesse T. Atkinson decd by Noel Burton adm. Notes on Thos
    Henderson, A. Kennedy of Green Co, East Tenn.; from R. C. Bunting of Lumberton,
    NC; Richard S. Pass for tobacco. Payments made to William H. Richardson, John-
    ston E. Atkinson, Thompson Coleman, Isaac Travis, Paul T. Woodward, Creed T.
    Oliver, Mrs. Polly Atkinson, et al.
270 Inv property of John Richmond Sr. decd taken 4 Oct 1841 by Solomon Vanhook exec.
    Bonds on Nat Snipes, John C. Richmond, Daniel Richmond(all 1837), Wm. Winstead.
270 List of property of James Powell decd by Edmund Powell adm. 5 Oct 1841.
271 Acct current of James Heydon decd by John H. Heydon adm. Pd accts of Samuel F.,
    William, and Joseph Hendon, Leonard G. Heydon, Calvin Graves atty., et al.
272 Acct of estate of William Harris decd by Reubin Harris. Pd bond of Anne Harris;
    Payments for William, James, Elizabeth, and Julia Harris. Pd accts of Layton
    Roberts, Huntington & Smith, Jones & Dodson, et al.
274 Inv property of Allen Burton decd by Mary Burton. 30 Sept. 1841.
275 Mrs. Sitha A. Nunnally adm of Capt. John Nunnally decd who was guardian to infant
    heirs of Elijah Withers decd. Due to legatees from estate of Nunnally to:
    James, John, Miss Elizabeth, and Albert G. Withers.
278 Scitha Nunnally guardian of Obediah, Agness, John H., Lewis S., and Virginia E.
    Nunnally in acct with her wards. 5 Oct 1841.
278 Catharine Withers guardian to John A., Elizabeth A., Albert G. Withers, acct filed
279 Inv estate of Edward H. Stevens decd. Judgment in Caswell County in case of John
    W. Stevens et al against George Farley due to E. H. Stevens. Atty fee to John
    Kerr Jr. Also suit against James Farley. 2 Apr 1841.
280 Inv and sales estate of William B. Langhorne decd. Bonds on A. Langhorn, Creed
    T. Langhorn, A. Bencini, William and Morris Piles, M. M. Langhorn, Farley &
    Crowder, et al. Doubtful notes on R. W. Graves, Mitchell Freeman, Henry W.
    Durkley of Clarksville, Va., M. Rudder, John B. Pugh, John S. Oglesby, John
    Epperson, et al. Sales estate to Henry Gordon, Dr. Willie Jones, et al.

January Court 1842

286 John H. Graves guardian in acct with Samuel P. Hill ward. Money recd from Col.
    John Mebane estate; also as guardian to Sarah Jane Hill. Due Sarah Jane Hill
    when she comes of age 1/3 part of negro boy Tilman given to "my wife" by Samuel
    Hill Sr., /s/ John H. Graves, guardian.
288 John H. Graves in acct with Marion W. Hill ward. Pd Philip Winkler tuition in
    music, also to get 1/3 part of boy Tilman.
289 Joseph Benton guardian in acct with Anthony Foster his ward and with Sabina Foster
    his ward.
    (Note says these guardian accts were improperly recorded in this book - Vide
    Guardian Records.)
290 John B. McMullin in acct with Mary K. Jones formerly Mary K. Hester and with
    Harriet Hester.
291 Albert G. Stephens in acct with Charles G. Stephens his ward.
292 John Swift guardian in acct with Robert, Harvey, William, Lucinda, Kitty, and
    John Swift.
292 Jane Wiley acct with ward Elizabeth Wiley.
293 Joseph Smith guardian in acct with Samuel B. Parks orphan.

154

Book O 1842
Page
295 Adm notice as to estate of James Rainey by Josiah Rainey and C. H. Richmond adm.
     Sworn to by Henry Rose.
295 Sales estate of James Powell decd to Mathew Mills, Banister Fitzgerald, James
     H. Withers, William Y. Stokes, William Whittemore, John D. Cobb, Jackson Yates,
     Nealy Grant, Richard Snow, Alford Badgett, Mrs. Grant (purchased Bible), William
     Suthard, Turner D. Patterson, John W. Ford, James Rawley, William Weatherford,
     et al. By Edmond Powell.
299 Acct current estate of E. Berry by Antiochus E. Boswell exec.
300 Additional inv of Richard W. Jackson by Owen McAleer adm.
301 John Tapscott exec of John Tapscott decd acct with estate.
302 Mary Winstead adm of Wade N. Woodson decd acct filed.
303 List of property sold of Allen Burton decd by Mary Burton adm.
303 Acct current estate of David Barker decd by David C. & George Barker exec.
305 Inv property of Elizabeth Carter decd by Benjamin H. Carter adm.
306 Inv and sales on 16 Dec 1841 of property of John Davis decd by William Lea adm.
     Sales to Elizabeth Davis, Enoch G. Davis, Joshua Powell, C. W. Lunsford, et al.
307 Sales property of Elizabeth Carter decd sold 28 Oct 1841 to William Stubble-
     field, John Carter.
308 Inv and sales estate of James Rainey decd sold 18 Nov 1841 to Josiah Rainey,
     John P. Rainey, C. H. Richmond, Clark R. Vowell, James G. Rainey, Jackson Moore,
     William Smith, William P. Womack, John Taylor, Dabney Rainey, David Pointer,
     J. Pittard, F. A. Claiborn, Richard J. Smith, Ann Jones, Henry Wade. Large
     amount of books sold.
317 Inv of negroes of Sarah Brooks decd sold to Richard Jones, Saml. Moore, Henry W.
     Brooks, Henry Cobb. By George Brooks adm.

317 RICHARD MARTIN - Will - w. 17 July 1841. Wife Frances Martin; all my children.
     After wife's death estate sold and residue divided to all children: George T.
     Martin, Henry Martin, Lewis Martin, James Martin, Richard Martin.
     Exec: son George T. Martin. Wit: Thos W. Graves, Franklin Graves.

318 JOHN HULETT - Will - w. 21 Jan 1840. Wife Sarah Hulett to have land where they
     live for her life. Granddaughter Sarah P. Hessey (or Hessee); grandson Jackson
     Hulett. Sons Samuel Hulett and John Hulett(land whereon he now lives);
     daughter Susannah Hessey. Exec: William Corbett. Wit: John Wood, F. D. Warren.

320 Inv and sales estate of Edward H. Roberson decd sold to Carter Powell for widow
     and self, G. W. Willis, Thomas Lea, Benj. Pittard, Samuel Hodges, Dr. George
     Robertson, H. Stanfield. One trundle bed for children not sold but left with
     widow for their benefit. By N. J. Palmer exec. An acct against trustees of
     Robert A. Crowder; debt due from Dr. Wm. M. Brooks. Bond on William H.
     Hendrick desperate.
325 Div negroes to heirs of John Love Jr. decd to Thomas Martin who is due 1/3 part.
326 Div negroes of estate of John Nunnally decd to Robert Blackwell and wife Elmira,
     Sytha A. Nunnally; Agness J.,Lucus S., John H., Obadiah R. and Virginia E.
     Nunnally.
327 Elisha Paschal adm of Isahi Paschal decd.
328 Inv and sales estate of Willis Buckingham decd. Provision for widow. Sales to
     Byrd Buckingham, Robert B. Thornton, C. H. Richmond, James Gates, Mrs. Buck-
     ingham, Clark Vowell, Mason Tarpley, Thomas Tarpley, et al. Note on Jesse
     Owen doubtful. Land rented to Byrd and George G.(or T.) Buckingham.
330 Div of negroes of James Wright decd to Weldon E. Wright and James A. Price & Wife.
330 Allotment to Lucy Buckingham widow of Willis Buckingham decd,a year's allowance.
331 Allotment of dower lands to Elmira Robertson widow of the late Edward H. Robert-
     son, land adj M. P. Huntington to oaks in the widow Yancey's line thence along
     her line to Huntington's - 87 7/10 acres. 9 Dec 1841.
332 Plat of land of Elmira Robertson by Henry Bushnell, county surveyor.
333 Div and plat of land of estate of John Davis decd on Rattlesnake Creek to
     Nancy, Sarah, Elizabeth Davis(adj Noel & Bluford Read); to John Davis son of
     Enoch; to children of Enoch Davis to wit: Mary, Thomas, Henry, George, Sally,
     Elizabeth, and Richard J. Davis.

Book O 1842
Page
335 Div and plat of land of estate of William Holcomb decd to widow Sally Holcomb
(adj land she got from her father's estate and next to Fleming Nelson) on
Country Line Creek, adj Thomas Pass and Nelson. 17 Nov 1841.

March-April Court 1842

340 Inv property of Robert Martin decd taken by George T. Martin exec on 17 Dec 1841.
341 Sales of Robert Martin sold 1 & 2 Feb 1842 to George W. Martin, James M. Walker,
Aldridge Rudd, Goodwin Evans, James L. Graves, William Yancey, John C. Vaughan,
Thomas W. Graves, Richard D. Gill, Henry Bauldwin, James Page Junr., Benjamin
Willis, Joseph Aldridge, Howard Martin, Zachariah Lockett, Walter H. Lunsford,
Azariah Morton, Elijah Miles, Philip Walker, Richard Smith Sen., James Vincent,
Lemuel Dabbs, Pleasant Corbett, William Turner, Archibald Birk, Durrett Oliver,
Littleton A. Gwynn, Thomas Hensley, Ransom Boswell, Calaway P. Harrison, Rice
Gwynn, Mary Kennon, Albert Melton, Devoreu Hightower, William Wells, James
Melton Sr., Pinckney Robertson, Joseph Penix, Joannah Shapard, Chestley Turner,
John Stamps, Francis Gooch, Andrew Haddock, James Page Sen., William Parks,
Epsom Fitch, John & Thomas Chandler, William Caynor, William Payne, Abner C. R.
Kerr, Thomas McKinney, James Gates, Daniel Reynolds.
349 Inv and sales property of Archy and Miliah Dill decd sold 5 Jan 1842 to Azariah
Graves Jr., Leroy Sanders, David Gill, Elisha Dudley, James Dill, Henry Strader,
Joseph Dill, William Sanders, Noah Cobb, John H. Pickard, A. M. Nash, Thomas
French, John Dill, Nicholas Smith, William Paschall, Jethro P. Walker, William
Dill. By John Dill adm. A. Slade Clerk.
352 Inv property of estate of Miles Poteat Sr. taken 12 Jan 1842 by James Poteat adm.
353 Inv of efffects of E. R. Hatchett decd - one note on John Stamps. L.A.Gwyn adm.
353 Added inv property of Thomas P. Gunn decd for hire of Charles by John C. Harvey.
354 Inv and sales estate of Moses Bradsher decd after the death of his widow Martha
Bradsher. By John Bradsher exec.
354 Sale of negro woman Liddia of estate of Anderson Kimbro decd to Margaret Kimbro
for $410. By Catharine Kimbrough, commissioner.
355 Settlement estate of Andrew Kimbrough decd by Catherine Kimbrough adm. Examined
by Alanson M. Lea, William Florance, James Walker.
356 Acct of Zachariah Locket, Jailor of Caswell County.
356 Negro woman of estate of Thomas Gunn sold to Nathaniel J. Palmer.
357 Sale of slaves of estate of James Rainey to Josiah Rainey, C. H. Richmond,
H. Saterfield, John Wilson, Josiah Rainey.
358 Inv and sales of John Hulet Sen sold 3 Feb 1842 to the widow, to John Hulet,
Saml. Hulet, Archibald A. Hessey, James W. Graves, Thomas W. Graves, John Blackwell, Thomas B. Broach, Jackson Hulet. List of property left for widow.
By William Corbet exec.
360 Estate of Richard W. Jackson decd in acct with Owen McAleer adm. List of debts
not collected and he declared insolvent and owing to adm..
362 Inv estate of William C. Donoho by James Miles adm. Sales to William B. Aldridge, Emson Fitch, James Walker, James Kerr, Chesley Turner, James Miles Jr.,
James Miles Esq., James Graves, Hartford Gooch, Nancy Donoho, Beverly Grant,
F. Leath Esq., James Simmons, John Mitchell, A. Miles, B. Corbet.
364 Settlement estate of William Pleasant decd by James B. Pleasant adm. Hire of
negroes to Thomas & William Turner, Sally Pleasant.
366 Year's allowance to Nancy Donoho widow of William C. Donoho for her & family.
367 Sales estate of Miles Poteat Sen. decd to William T. Hooper, Jeremiah Graves,
James Gunn, John Johnston, George Williamson, Henderson House, James Vaughan,
Jackson Kennon, Jas Poteat, William Poteat, et al. By James Poteat adm.
371 List of hire of negroes of estate of A. Harrison decd for 1842.
372 Acct current estate of Sarah Morris decd by James Vaughan adm. Paid for shoes
for Martha. 22 Mar 1842.
373 Report of committee to move the road from Yanceyville to Danville - William A.
Mitchell desires to enlarge his yard 15-20 feet and has moved the road and
repaired same.

156

Book O 1842
Page
373 James M. Hodnet desires to move road fom Milton to Danville and has had new road
opened according to law.
374 Repeat of page 354.
375 James Tapscott recd. from John Tapscott exec of John Tapscott decd one negro
man named Martin a legacy of James Tapscott who should pay his ratible part of
any debts due estate.
376 Susannah Tapscott gives same bond as James Tapscott above.
377 WILLIAM F. DAVIS - Will - w. 7 Apr 1841. All property to be sold except land
and proceeds distributed among lawful legatees. Land left to wife Susan then
divided among all children. Exec: wife Susan and son John T. W. Davis and
John Penix. Wit: James K. Lea, Stephen Sawyer.

July Court 1842

380 Inventory of William F. Davis and sales 28 & 29 Apr 1842 to John Simmons, Bleu-
fort Pleasant, James Simmons, Joseph Shaw, George W. Taylor, Henry Tait, Levi
Walker, Albert Pattillo, Franklin Gooch, John Simmons of George, Smith Rascoe,
Milton Pinnix.
387 Inv of negroes of William F. Davis.
387 Sales estate of George A. Swift decd sold by Robert & George A. Swift 18 Mar
1842 to Thomas Garrott; Robert, George A., Thomas S.,William, Sarah, Emaline,
and Margaret Swift; to Thomas Williamson, Edward & William Brannock, Benjamin
Pennix, John H. Simpson, William Lackey, Wagstaff Maynard, Robert Smith, Moses
Simpson, Daniel B. Moss, Swift Williamson, John Brintle, William Sellers.
393 Report of Thomas D. Johnston, county trustee.
395 Inv property of Mary Mitchell decd by John H. Heydon adm taken 1 Mar 1842.
396 Sales of estate of Mary Mitchell decd sold 17 May 1842 to James Barker, Samuel
F. Heydon, John Tapscott Esq., William Price, Richard Hornbuckle, Stephen
Underwood, Malinda Foster, Samuel Elliott, William Smith, Benjamin Pennix,
Sophia Browning, James Sawyer, Anthony Foster, Alexander Cantrill.
398 Recd. 29 Oct 1835 from John Cobb Jr. adm of Joseph Cobb decd and guardian to
Malinda G. Cobb $409 for her share of estate. Wit: Henry Cobb Jun.
399 Nancy Cobb and Samuel B. Cobb sign receipt for their share of estate of Joseph
Cobb decd.
400 Settlement estate of Joshua Jackson by Daniel Jackson adm., also inv of estate.
401 Report of Wardens of the Poor for 1842. Among the paupers are 3 lunatics and
maniacs that have to be confined and are troublesome and at present no place
of confinement.
403-7 Sales property of William Cobb decd by James N. Cobb and William M. Cobb exec.
Sales to Zenith Page, Samuel Groom, Wm. M. Cobb, James W. Shelton, James N.
Cobb, Augustus Gwynn, Thomas Womack, Jas E. Williamson, Thomas Keen, Jesse
Siddle, Elisha Dudley, John Harrison, et al.
407 Inv personal property of Mary Campbell decd by John Kerr Jr. adm. Bonds on
Wyatt Walker, Thomas D. Johnston.
408 Power of attorney - William Rutter(possibly Rudder) of Rowan County NC to William
Russell of Caswell Co. to attend to all business. 20 May 1842.
409 Edward Powell adm of James Powell decd money recd. for tobacco.
410-415 Sale of George A. Swift - repeat of pages 387-392.
416 Estate of John Ware decd in acct with John P. Harrison and Joseph T. Ware, final
acct. Payments to Doct. Nathaniel Green, John Ware Jun., John Kerr, Zachariah
Lockett, Charlotte Ware, Archd Walters, Joseph T. Ware for his part of tobacco.
418 Acct current of John Bradsher acting exec of Moses Bradsher decd of part of
estate devised to children after death of widow Martha Bradsher. Pd Thomas
Day for walnut coffin $14, John Miles for crying sale $2, Parson Miller for
funeral $5, walling 2 graves $25, attorney Palmer for services. 9 Apr 1842.
Each boy's part $370.52; each girl's part $286.97.
419 Inv personal property of William F. Davis by John T. W. Davis and John Penix exec.
Bond on Milton Penix.

Book O 1842 - 43
Page
420 Pleasant Chandler adm in acct with estate of William Parker decd. Payments to
Sarah Jones, A. S. Yancey, John W. Pinchback for crying sale, Samuel C. Cobb for
coffin. 6 July 1842.
421 Inv property of William Roberts decd sold by adm on 10 June 1842 to A. G. Anderson, Hosea McNeil, James Kerr, Jesse Montgomery, Geo Herndon, J.T.W. Davis, E.
Roberts Jeremiah Rudd, H. Tate, et al. By John Baynes adm.
422 Bond of Robert Blackwell who had recd. from estate of John Nunnally will pay
his part of debts of estate of Nunnally.
423 William Tapscott who has recd from John Tapscott exec of John Tapscott decd gives
bond to pay any ratible part of debts of the estate. 31 Dec 1841. Wit: Thomas
Gattis.
424 Henry C. and Nancy Tapscott give similar bonds as William Tapscott.

October Court 1842

429 Bond of John K. Brooks as Sheriff of Caswell Co. Bonded by Tho W. Graves, Thomas
Bigelow, A. Willis, Lancelot Johnston, Alexis Howard, Saml Moore, James Kerr,
James K. Lea.
430 Bond of John K. Brooks as county tax collector and as collector of the poor tax.
431 Bond of John K. Brooks as public tax collector.
432 John Simmons adm in acct with estate of Henry Thomas decd. 29 Sept. 1842.
433 James Burch adm of Edmond Burch decd acct filed. Met at John Mitchell's to
make settlement. Payment to widow, to Samuel & John Mitchell, et al.
434 Sales of negroes of the late William Cobb sold 6 Aug & 1 Oct 1842 to Alexander
Moore, Stephen Neal, Thomas Womack, Samuel Moore, John Hannon, Cobb L. Bracken.
434 Inv property of estate of E. C. and William Richmond by John Richmond adm. Bonds
on William Richmond, William & Christopher Hinton; receipt from George H. Benton
of Hinds Co., Miss., for bonds he is to collect. Acct on James C. Dobbins.
435 Vouchers exhibited by John Cobb adm of Martin W. Mims. Accts examined at
Blackwell's store.
437 John G. Lea adm of William Holcomb decd acct filed. Cash paid to Sally Holcomb;
H. Sawyer for crying sale; M. H. Graves, deputy sheriff.
439 JAMES KENNEBROUGH - Will - w. 11 Mar 1842. Daughter Susannah Kennebrough all
estate real and personal to her and her heirs. Exec: daughter Susannah.
Wit: Thomas Williamson, Rufus B. Chandler, James E. Williamson.
440 Settlement estate of Massey Nelson by Iverson Nelson adm.
440 Two horses of estate of Zeary Gwynn sold to J. B. Powell by Rice Gwynn exec.
440 Additional return by John Baynes adm of William Roberts - cash recd for pension
$33.95.
442 Acct current estate of Moses Fuller decd by William Fuller Jun. adm. Pd medical
bills for Nell Roan; John Norwood counsel fee, Dr. James Lea, William A. Graham
for counsel. 27 Sept 1842.
443 Estate of Samuel Mitchell decd in acct with John Mitchell and James Currie adm.
Paid J. Webb agt of Bank, Stephen Monday for work on mill of the decd.
443 Inv personal estate of Samuel Nelson decd. Cash recd of Nelson Thomas adm of
James Nelson decd in full for Samuel's interest. Proved by Ambrose Nelson adm.
444 Acct current estate of William Anderson since 1839. Cash pd sheriff in suit in
Equity vs Yancey Wiley and John Mitchell with William Lea as security for Wiley
adm of William Anderson decd.
445 Sale of negroes of estate of John Anderson decd to A. G. Anderson, G. J. Farish,
Samuel Moore. Sale held at store of James Kerr. By John H. Haydon, comm.

January Court 1843

448 Inv personal property of William Dupree decd by L. A. Gwyn adm. Debts on John
Stamps, Dennis Wilson, L. A. Gwynn; doubtful debts on James Simmons, Richard Gil
Thomas Stamps. 2 Jan 1843. Year's allotment to widow. Accts on umknown person
possibly residing in Va. to wit: M. Jackson, Wm. Y. Estes, Elijah Wilkinson,
Joseph Franklin, Henry & Parham Moore.

Book O 1843
Page
452-464 Sales property of William Dupree on 26-28 Oct 1842 to Richard Smith, Byrd
Moore, Alexander Moore, Thomas Henslee, Alanson Howard, John Gwynn, Robert
Madden, Iverson Gipson, Chesley Turner, Bedford Henslee, Thos W. Graves, James
Farish, Thomas Dupree, Andrew & Joseph Haddock, Hosea McNeil, Hugh Gwyn, John
C. Totten, George T. Martin, James Watt, John Swift, Rufus Stamps, Elizabeth
Dupree, Corda Whitehead, Aldridge Rudd, James L. Graves, James Melton, Ruffin
Henslee, Benjamin Willis, Richd Smith, Ibzan Rice, Andrew Aldridge, Henry Adkins,
Saml F. Heydon, Richd Bennett, et al. 2 Jan 1843. L. A. Gwyn adm.
465 Sales property of Nelson Thomas by F. L. Warren adm to Azariah Nelson, Bluford
Cooper, William & James Warren, Lawson James, Zepania Roberts, James Thomas,
William Evans, Thomas Morton, Thomas Owen. Notes on Saml. J. & Berry Evans,
Nelson Bartlett, Elijah Morton, James Keeling, Oliver Foulks, Joseph Rudd,
Ann Neely, et al.
468 Rice Gwyn exec in acct with estate of Zery Gwyn decd. Balance of Robert W. Lawson
note of $2000 was satisfied by the transfer to said Lawson of 2 lots in Yanceyville.
470 Inv or personal property of Samuel Nelson by Thomas Prendergast adm.
471 Div of slaves of (name not given, but apparently John? Mitchell) to: William
Muzzle adm., Jane Wiley, Green W. Brown, Alexander Mitchell, James McMullin,
Anderson Mitchell, James Currie, Alexander Mebane, Eliza Frances Mitchell, John
Mitchell, Monroe Allen. 15 Oct 1842.
472 Sales of George Swift decd sold 9 Oct 1842 by George & Robert Swift exec.
473 Sale of negroes of estate of James Powel decd sold 27 Dec 1843? to Leah Powel,
John Reese; hire of negroes to William Weatherford. By Edmund Powel.

474 ALFORD PARKS - Will - w. 15 Nov 1842. Wife Mary Parks most of personal property
and 1/3 of land for life. 2 sons James N. Parks and Samuel B. Parks all land
after death of wife. James N. Parks to hold 1/5 of estate in trust for benefit
of daughter Harriett J. Bouldin as long as she is wife to Edward C. Boulden. If
she divorces or he dies, deliver estate to her. Daughter Celia Smith and husband
Joseph Smith. Residue of estate to be divided 5 parts by William Warren, Harvey
Cooper, Alanson M. Lea, & Quentin Anderson and go to daughters Drady Browning,
Milly Parks, Mary Sanders, Sarah Parks, and in trust for Harriett Boulden.
Exec: son James N. Parks. Wit: Z. A. Pattillo, A. G. Anderson.

476 JOSEPH ROWE - Will - w. 21 Aug 1836. Wife Ann Rowe to have all estate and she to
give each child $1.00 as he has already given to them. Wife to dispose of
property as she pleases. Test: Jas E. Williamson, John H. Pickard.
NB No witness present and let handwriting be proved by fellow citizens.

March or April Court 1843

479 Sitha Nunnally adm of Capt. John Nunnally lists bonds due estate.
480 Sale of negroes of John Nunnally estate. Claims against Banister Fitzgerald un-
collected. Payments to Henry Bushnell for surveying, John Keesee for brandy,
James Withers for tuition, John Ross store acct., Dickenson & Stokes store acct.,
James E. Williamson medical services, Mathew Mills for crying sale; Paid Catha-
rine Withers' accts for heirs of E. Withers as John Nunnally was guardian for
children. $16 to haul tobacco to Danville; R. P. Williamson balance on note.
Due $210 to old Mrs. Nunnally mother of John Nunnally.
482 Settlement with George Brooks adm of estate of Sarah Brooks decd. Pd notes on
H. W. Brooks, Gunn & Bowe, William Russell, Neal & Johnston, Dr. J. E. Williamson,
Thomas J. Brown, John C. Totton for crying sale, John Kerr atty, N. S. Graves,
George Brooks. Rent of plantation to Ithamer Armfield. 14 Feb 1843.
484 Valuation of negroes of estate of Zachariah Pattillo decd and div to William
Currie in right of his wife Frances, Zach Pattillo. 12 Jan 1843.

485 ELEVEN ROBERTS - Will - w. 15 May 1841. Wife Nancy to have land where he lives
near Elijah Roberts, then her part to go to daughter Nancy. Exec: son Elijah
Roberts. Wit: L. A. Gwyn, James Rice.

159

Book O 1843
Page
486 ZILPAH YANCEY - Will - w. 28 Mar 1843. Daughter Mildred Ann Yancey; son Albert
G. Yancey $200. Granddaughter Mary Elizabeth Yancey Gunn daughter of James
Gunn $150. Balance divided among 3 children: Albert G., William, and Mildred
Ann Yancey. If Mildred Ann dies without issue, her share to Albert G. & William
Yancey; Albert G. Yancey should serve as trustee to granddaughter Mary E. Y.
Gunn and if she die without issue her part to other children. Negroes not to
be sold but divided among children. Daughter Mildred Ann to have sets of silver
tea and table spoons. Exec: sons Albert G. Yancey and William Yancey.
Wit: N. M. Roan, Howard Martin.

487 Inv estate of Josiah Rainey taken 3 Jan 1843 by C. H. Richmond special adm.
488 Property sold of Josiah Rainey on 14 Feb 1843 to John P. Rainey(inc silver
watch), Wiley Coggins, Dr. Pittard, Nath. & Newman Durham, R. J. Smith, Dr.
Comer, James Covington, Jos Stewart, Barksdale Jones, D. J. Brandon, Jarvis
Friou, William Smith, Benj. Pittard, Robt. Ball, Byrd Buckingham, et al.
496 Mildred Harrison and others petition for div of slaves of estate of A. Harrison
decd. Div to: Mildred Harrison, Elizabeth Jane Dabney, Jonathan R. Harrison,
Ann L.(or S.) Boyd, Ann Eliza Young, Mildred S.(or L.) Harrison, Edmund R.
Harrison, Thomas R. Harrison, Margaret H. Harrison, Elmire R. Harrison,
William K. Harrison, Pauline C. Harrison.
498 Joseph Bracken and wife Nancy Bracken adm of Benj. Hooper decd acct filed.
Paid A. Slade for crying sale, Henry Glass (smith's acct), Archibald G. Hubbard $11.53 for coffin, Revd. J. Stadler $5 for preaching funeral, John Kerr
Esq for counsel. Legacies due Zach L., Frances, Joseph, and Elisha Hooper
paid to their father Benj. Hooper decd from the estate of Joseph Henderson decd
in div of negroes when suit in Equity Court at instance of Hiram Henderson is
settled.
500 Sale of property of estate of Richard Martin decd sold Jan 1843 to Williamson
P. Martin, Thos W. Graves, Jas L. Graves, James Vincent, Major H. Graves,
Richard Martin. Cash recd from Mother. George T. Martin exec.
501 Paul A. Haralson adm of Rucker T. Lea decd acct current. Recd of Arch Lea
former guardian. Paid Thomas Day $14 for coffin; sent $125 to John Lea by his
son and agt. James R. Lea Jr.; paid Jesse W. Cross agent for John Lea's order.
502 Receipt of Mary Badgett to John Cobb her guardian for full satisfaction of
his guardianship. Wit: Henry Badgett. 6 Dec 1842.
502 Receipt of Martha Hooper from W. Hooper for full payment due from estate of
Joseph Henderson decd. 6 Dec 1842. Test: R. Ferguson.
503 Geo Williamson adm in acct with estate of Joseph Lunsford decd. Sales on 22
Jan 1840. Paid Wyatt Walker $8 for coffin; pd exec of John C. Lea decd; Ruth
Putnam on bond. 3 Apr 1843.
504 Sales of property of Gregory Hightower decd sold 27 Jan 1843 by William P.
Chambers adm to William H. Johnston, Jas N. Johnston, Thomas M. Johnston, Solo-
mon Whitlow, Reubin Hawkins. Bonds due the estate on Wm. & Thomas Johnston,
Owen McAleer. 3 Apr 1843.
505 Inv estate of William Hooper decd by Geo Williamson adm, April term 1843.
Bonds on Thos. Badgett, Linsey Roberts, Lunsford Hunter, John Hood, Wm. H.
Hendrick, et al. The whole believed doubtful.
506 John W. Cobb gives receipt for full share from estate of Joseph Cobb decd with
John Cobb adm his guardian. 12 July 1841.
506 Abraham Womack gives receipt to John Cobb adm of Joseph Cobb decd and guardian
to his wife Louisa M. Cobb now Womack for full share of estate.
507 Acct current estate of William Bethel decd by Mary Bethell, Robert H. Scales,
and Wm. D. Bethell exec. Not enough to pay all legacies which had to be scaled
down. Recd payment from Mr. Kerr of Miss.; interest in estate of Nathaniel
Scales decd. Paid Mary Bethell (1838) guardian to Louisa, Attelia, and Agness
Bethell, minors. Paid Mary for herself; Robert H. Scales for wife Jane's
legacy; Samuel Moore for Mary Anne's legacy; Samuel Bethel and Pinckney C.
Bethel their legacy.
In 1840 paid Thomas Torian for wife Agness' legacy. Pd William D. Bethel

160

Book O 1843
Page
507-510 cont: expenses in Natchez, also his legacy. Pd Robt. Lawson for waste and
damage of land; R. H. Scales expenses to Natchez $211 when Genl. Bethell died
1834. In 1842 paid Mrs. M. A. Moore balance of legacy, also same paid to P. C.
Bethell, Mrs. Jane W. Scales, William N. and A. M. Scales, William J. &
Frederick Nash, Mary E. Moore.
511 Bond of Thomas D. Johnston as county trustee.
512 Bond of Alexander McAlpin as Public Register of Caswell Co. Apr 1843.
514 Bond of Levi C. Page as Coronor of Caswell Co.
515 Bond: Elizabeth Rollin a single woman has got a bastard child and brought before
Justices of the County and refuses to swear it. She gives bond and security.
If child should be dependent on the county bond is in force. Signed by
Elizabeth Rawlin, Nicholas Smith. 21 Feb 1843.
516 Power of Attorney - Thomas Gibson of Danville, Va., to Benjamin W. Brewer to
sell land in Caswell County, 8 acres. 25 Dec 1842. Sworn to by Saml. C.
Brewer.
517 Articles of agreement on 22 Jan 1841 between Jacob Vanhook and wife Elizabeth
of the one part and Thomas Turner Jr. of other part for Vanhook to employ
Turner as overseer.
518 Agreement on 21 Dec 1842 between John McCain and Nancy Morgan both of Caswell Co.
Marriage is intended between the two, McCain has property and Nancy no estate.
McCain wishes to provide for Nancy without prejudicing his children of his
first marriage. He conveys to Nancy mansion house and 100 acres land and
slaves for her life or widowhood, then same to go to his children.
Test: John D. Lea, A. G. Stephens, Tillotson McCain.
519 Power of attorney - Barney Brockman of Rutherford Co., Tenn., to John Holt Esq.
of same county and state to sell land in Caswell Co., 150 acres, 1/3 part of
said tract he owns as heir at law of father Major Brockman on Little Wolf
Island Creek adj W. W. Price. The 3rd tract already sold by brother John
Brockman. 2 Jan 1843.
519 William Lea exec of Gabriel Lea decd - one note for $50 due 21 Apr 1821 returned
April 1843.

End of Book O

July Court 1843 begins in Book P

UNRECORDED WILLS

At the NC State Archives are wills of the following that do not appear in the will
books, file no. CR 020.801.

JOHN KERR - Will - w. 13 May 1810. Wife Mary Kerr to have ½ of land and personal
property for her life then to go to children. Son Solomon to have wife's land at
her death and money for schooling. Daughters Nancy Lea and Mary Lea; daughters
Ibbv and Elizabeth. Sons John, Barzillai and his heirs(land whereon he lives
purchased of John Mallory), Alexander, and James. Grandson Zephaniah Kerr.
Son Alexander to have land on Stony Creek which came from his father. Exec: sons
John, James, Alexander. Test: Jere Lea, James Kerr.
(Note - At the July 1816 session of County Court, the will of John Kerr was contest-
ed. The court ruled the paper was not last will of John Kerr. James Kerr and
John Kerr were named adm of the estate of John Kerr decd.)

JANE McDANIEL - Will - No date. Grandson Fletcher Darby. 7 children to have $1
each; all grandchildren $1 each. Grandchildren John W., Mary J., Hyram M.,
Elizabeth A., Susan C., and Sarah J. Price to have remainder of estate as each
comes of lawful age. Land bought of Roan to be sold. Exec: friend Benjamin F.
Stanfield, Calvin Neely, Mary J. Price.
(Note: - The estate records of Jane McDaniel at NC Archives show the will was con-
tested, was taken into Superior Court, March 1844. In Jan 1844, Book P, William
P. Chambers named adm.)

Filed with wills of Caswell County at the NC State Archives are copies of following wills which were for persons living outside Caswell County. File CR 020.801

AMBROSE FOSTER of Halifax Co., Va. - Will - w. 28 Feb 1802. Wife Peggy (land where they live). Daughter Sally Foster and 2 grandsons Foster Moore and John Moore to have land in Person Co. NC, purchased of Thomas Robertson); granddaughter Peggy Moore. Daughter Mildred Hudson; son Ambrose Foster to have plantation after wife's death purchased from Ferguson. 5 daughters: Sally, Peggy, Betsy, Patsy Bran(Brown?), Fanny Foster; son John Foster. Exec: friends Thomas Watkins and Herndon Haralson. Wit: Thomas Brandon Jr., John Mitchell, Henry Mitchell, Clement Lipscomb. Proved Halifax Co. Va. July 1802.

DUDLEY GLASS of Halifax Co. Va. - Will - w. 17 Nov 1824. Wife Sally. Daughters Molly Farmer, _____ Ragland, Patsy; sons John, Dudley, George. Daughters Judith Isley, Patsy Walne? and Franky Walne?. Daughter Judith Isley's children John, Polly Franky, Patsy, Dudley, Betsy, William, and Harrison. Sally Martin formerly Sally Isley wife of Thomas Martin. (This name could be Irby rather than Isley.) Exec: Wm. B. Banks. Wit: James O. Landman, David Ragland, Sarah Turner. Proved Oct 1827.

SOLOMON GRAVES - of Newton Co. Ga. - Will - w. 18 Sept. 1830. Wife Joanna Graves. Son John Graves(land in Newton Co. whereon he now lives). Son Solomon Graves(land in Newton Co. where he now lives & adj land of testator). Son Barzillai Graves to have ½ interest in home of testator and ½ of same in trust for son Sidney Graves. If Sidney has no heirs his part to sons John, Iverson, Barzillai, and daughter Frances Graham. Land on Alcore River to be sold and rest of personal property and from proceeds pay $1000 to Frances Graham in lieu of land, also same to sons including son William for benefit of him as Barzillai sees fit. Has already deeded land to son Iverson. Exec: sons John, Iverson, Barzillai, and Solomon Graves. Wit: John Wright, Joel Williams, Jno W. Graves, Thomas T. Foster. Probate Nov 1830.

JOSEPH RUSSELL of Prince Edward Co. Va. - Will - w. 9 June 1832. Sons William, Joseph and children of Joseph. Daughter Judith W. Harris; grandson William R. Boulton; grandsons James Russell, Richard, Jordan, and Henry M. Lipscomb. Exec: son William Russell and Wilshire Cardwell. Wit: Wyatt Cardwell, Richard Martin. Proved Sept 1836.

JOHN WOMACK of Person Co., NC - Will - w. 20 Sept 1825. Wife Lucy. Granddaughters Nancy, Vallina(Vashti?), Elizabeth Womack all children of son David Womack decd. Granddaughters Elizabeth and Polly Womack of son Jesse Womack. Sons Green, Jacob P. and Henry Womack. Exec: son Green Womack, Isaac Saterfield, Thomas Lawson. Proved 1832 at Roxborough, Person Co., NC.

Book 2 1819-1830

	GUARDIAN	ORPHAN
Page	**1819**	
1	John Bracken	Youarke, Gripina, and Sina Bracken
4	Charles Boulton	William, Charles, Dixon, Meryweather Boulton, minors of William Boulton
5	Griffin Gunn	Receipt of Anderson Gunn for full legacy
	1820	
6	Warner Williams	Nicholas M. and Lucy Lewis. (Recd. from Charles Lewis estate)
9	John Comer	William, Polly, Bezel, John R. and Elizabeth G. Long
10	Polly King	Jane, James, Minerva, William H. & Robert King. (Recd. from William King decd.)
12	Thomas Slade	Yancey, John, Leatha, and Fanny Gray, orphans of John Gray
12	William W. Price	Daniel, Washington, Polly, Addison, Nancy, & Susannah Price
16	James Yancey	Attelia Yancey. (pd B. Richett, supt. of Salem Academy $52.30.) Land rented to William Bruce
17	Andrew Hughs	Martha, Samuel, & William Hughs orphans of James Hughs. (Recd. legacy from estate of Archer (or Andrew) Patton.)
18	John Stamps	John and Bartlett Hatchett
19	Romulus M. Sanders	Jesse, Susan S., & Arch G. Carter
20	Major Price	Major and John Price
20	Joseph Roe	Lindey Swift (paid board at Salem $131; pd 3 days service of man and horse going to & from Salem for schooling $3)
22	Joseph Roe	William & Thomas Swift (Pd Mrs. Watlington for schooling)
24	Daniel Price	John McDaniel
25	Hosea McNeill	Jemima, Nancy, Susannah, Isaac, Joseph, & Alexander Cantrill (Recd from estate of Benj. Cantrill. Pd Lawyer Ruffin vs Browning & wife)
28	Daniel Hightower	John, Daniel, Lucy, William, & Stephen Hightower
29	Whitted Page	Samuel & Nancy King
30	Wm. W. Price	Pinkney Price
30	Robert McKee	Nancy McKee
30	John S. Hutcherson	Mary D. Smith
31	Robert McKee	Parthena & Priscilla Eubank, orphans of George Eubank
31	Stephen Kitchen	James Kitchen
31	Moses Kitchen	Elizabeth Kitchen
31	Ch. Willson	Warren Richmond (John Richmond former guardian)
32	Joseph Dameron	Joshua Jackson (Recd cash from Wm. Jackson of Dinwiddie Co.Va.)
32	Griffin Gunn	Pinkney Gunn
32	Thomas Gunn	Polly Finley
33	John Wiley	Alexr. Gray
33	John Windsor	William Simpson
33	John Windsor	Thompson Harden (pd cash to Thos. Harden on way to KY)
32	John Windsor	James Simpson
35	George Finley	Abegail Finley
35	Joseph Collier	Tabitha Kimbrough
36	William Mitchell	Elizabeth & Priscilla McKissack
36	Hiram Lockard	John & Robert McKissack
36	William Sawyer	Nancy, William, & Susannah Mallory, orphans of James Mallory
37	Alexander Wiley	Zephaniah Kerr (Pd R. H. Childers tuition)
38	John Stamps	Will A. Muzzell (Pd John Chandler for schooling)
38	John P. Freeman	Thomas Harden
39	Abner Walker	Orphans of George Walker
39	George B. Dameron	Maris, Luke, Susannah Matthews, orphans of Vines Matthews

Guardian Accounts 1820-1823

	GUARDIAN	ORPHAN

Page
40 Levi Fuller   Nancy W. & William J. McDaniel

1821

44 James Nelson   Joel, Stokely, Barzillai, Pamelia, & James Nelson
52 Robert McKee   Kitty, Major, Parthenia, Levi, Priscilla, & Elizabeth Eubank,
                          heirs of Geo. Eubank.
53 Polly King   James P., William J., Minerva, Jane, & Robert N. King
57 Moses Kitchen   Elizabeth Kitchen
58 Thomas Gunn   Mary K. Finley
60 Alexander Wiley   Zephaniah Kerr
61 Thomas Slade   Nancy, John, Leatha, & now Fanny Kirk, orphans of John Gray
62 George B. Dameron   Susannah & Marin Mathis orphans of Vines Mathis
65 William Barnwell   Sally Enoch, orphan of Saml. Enoch
65 Joseph Knight   Judith Hodge
66 John Shields   Polly & Julia Ann Dupey, orphans of Robert Dupey
66 Jennet Montgomery   James Montgomery (Recd div of estate of Michael Montgomery)
68 Joseph Collier   Receipt of Tabitha Kimbrough for her share of her father's
                          estate. Wit: Henry Collier
68 Hosea McNeill   Receipt of James Rice in right of his wife Ellender for legacy
                          from Banjamin Cantrill
69 Sarah Smith   Receipt from James & Nancy Hightower for their share of estate
                          of James Smith decd. Receipt of Bird & Elizabeth Evans for
                          same
72 Solomon Debow   James Aldridge, orphan of James Aldridge
76 Priscilla Henderson, Minerva, Ludolphus, James S., Frances A., & Harriott Henderson
81 William W. Price   Washington, Polly, William W., Pinkney, Daniel, & Adderson
                          Price (Recd from estate of grandfather William Price)
86 Major Price Sen.   John & Major Price Jun.
91 Charles Boulton   Meriwether L., Charles Jun., Edmond B., & William Boulton
97 Andrew Hughs   William & Samuel Hughs
98 Hosea McNeill   Alexander, Jemima, Isaac, Nancy, Joseph, & Susannah Cantrill
105 William Dameron   Susan T. & Mary Gold, orphans of Joseph Gold
106 Robert H. Jackson   James & Jere Jackson
107 Robert McKee   Nancy McKee
109 John Comer   Wm., Polly, Barzila, John B., & Elizabeth Long (Recd from
                          estate of John Long)
111 Daniel Price   John McDaniel
112 John Stamps   Bartlett Hatchett
114 Freeman Leath   Kitty(or Ritty) Garner. (Recd from estate of John Garner.)
                          Paid Elizabeth Garner for her difference in land
116 David Hodge   Samuel Hodge
118 Daniel Jackson   Sarah Jackson
119 George Smith   Jenney Jackson
119 William Sawyer   Receipt of William Mallory being of full age for estate of
                          father James Mallory
120 James Graves   Richard Aldridge
121 William Sawyer   Receipt of John Sawyer for wife Nancy in full for her legacy
                          from her father James Mallory
121 William Currie   Heirs of Jno Dickey
121 Stephen Kitchen   Receipt from James Kitchen
121 Daniel Hightower   Receipt from Lucy Hightower for legacy from John Hightower

1823

125 Moses Kitchen   Betsy Kitchen
133 George B. Dameron   Morehead Mathis & Susan Mathis orphans of Vines Mathis
140 Levi Fuller   William McDaniel
142 Thomas Foster   Receipt of Asa Foster

164

Guardian accounts 1823-1825

GUARDIAN	ORPHAN

Page
143 John Wiley   Receipt of Alexander Gray
145 Richard B. Gunn   Sally Foster (Recd from Robert Foster adm of John Foster decd.)
153 William Sawyer   Receipt of Susannah Mallory being of full age for legacy of
           her father's estate
153 Capt. John Bracken,Receipt of Richard Mitchell for wife's part of estate of Samuel
           Bracken decd.
154 John Bracken   Receipts from Sina & Agripa Bracken
155 Jno Miles   John Vaughan. Pd Philip Cook for schooling; Caswell Academy
           $8 for tuition. Pd John Farley board while at school.
           Pd Wm. D. Kyle for hat $3, Richard H. Griffith $2.25 for shoes
156 John Lea   Betsy Ann & Mary L. Willson (Recd of George Williamson &
           Nathaniel Lea, exec of George M. Willson decd.)
158 William M. Dameron,Mary, Joseph, & Susan Gold
159 John McMullen   Gideon, Thomas, & Mitchell Terry

1824

165 Levi Fuller   William McDaniel
166 Moses Kitchen   Betsy Kitchen
168 Robert H. Jackson Jere Jackson
169 Daniel Price   John McDaniel
170 John Long   Alexander & Will C. Donoho
172 Daniel Hightower   Wm. & David Hightower
174 Richard B. Gunn   Sally Foster
174 James Nelson   John Nelson
175 Daniel Hightower   Stephen Hightower
176 Robert McKee   Orphans of Jesse McKee decd.
177 Daniel Jackson   Sally Jackson
178 George Smith   Jensey Jackson
181 John Miles   John Vaughan
182 James Yancey   John, Yancey, & Letha Gray, orphans of John Gray. Judgment
           vs estate of Thomas Slade decd.
185 James Yancey   Receipt of _____ for wife Letha Gray's part of estate of
           John Gray
187 William Mitchell Receipt of Elisha Parker for his wife Eliza McKee
192 John Keesee   James, Isaac, & Sally Durham

1825

197 Abner Miles   Vashti, Henry, Nancy, Elizabeth, & Green Womack (Recd from
           estate of David Womack 1818-1824) Pd Rachel Prendergast
           for schooling.
202 Azariah Graves   Kezziah Willis (Recd from estate of Henry Willis. Bonds on
           Mary, Henry, & Anderson Willis)
210 John Shields   Julia Ann & Polly Dupey. Negroes hired to A. S. Stokes by
           Mrs. Dupey before her last marriage.
215 Rebecca Brintle   Sarah Brintle orphan of Jesse Brintle
216 Whitehead Page   Samuel & Nancy King
217 Richard Jones   James Shelton. Cash pd on 1/3 part of bond given by late
           father to adm of B. Ashley decd.
219 Benjamin C. West Heirs of Settleberry Worsham
222 George B. Dameron, M. Mathis orphan of Vines Mathis
224 John Holloway   Susannah Humphreys
227 John Swift   Lucinda Swift. Recd from estate of Thos. Swift Jun., decd.
228 Jennett Montgomery,James Montgomery. Pay from Mary Howard for div land in TN
           and in div of negroes. Pd John Kitchen & Thomas Gunn for
           difference in Caswell lands.
230 Burrell Haguewood John Humphreys
231 Mary King   Jane Weatherford

Guardian accounts 1825-1828

GUARDIAN	ORPHAN

Page
232 Caswell Tait   His four children, Thomas, John, Caswell, and Mary Tait.
                    Recd from estate of Thomas Swift Jun. Recd from Harvey
                    Swift adm of said Thos and from George A. Swift exec of
                    William Swift.
232 John Miles   John Vaughan(Legacy collected by Thomas Vaughan from Va.)
                    Pd Mary Vaughan for board.
234 Moses Kitchen   Receipt of Joseph W. Singleton for legacy of wife Elizabeth
                    Kitchen

1826

238 John Shields   Julia Ann & Mary Dupey. Pd H. Motley for her in div of negroes
241 Mary Cox   Nathaniel, George, Jesse, & Mary Cox, orphans of Reuben Cox.
242 Robert Ervine   Elizabeth, Thomas, Stephen, & Zery Sawyer. Recd fom Hosea
                    McNeill adm of James Sawyer decd.
249 Charles Bolton William Bolton
257 Saml. Rainey   Polly & Thomas Eubank. 1/5 part in suit in Equity vs Nathl.
                    Malon in Humphreys Co.,W. Tenn. Allowed guardian $20 for
                    travel to Reynoldsburg, W. Tenn. to procure Boy Green and to
                    sell him.
264 Jas. E. Dickey David Dickey. Land rented to Elizabeth Dickey.
265 Richard Jones   James & Susannah Shelton
266 James Yancey   John & Yancey Gray
271 Daniel Price   John McDaniel. Pd Robert Gilliam for tuition & books.
272 Benjamin West   Heirs of Settleberry Worsham. Pd expenses to Iredell Court;
                    pd Elizabeth Worsham for her legacy. Expenses for 6 children
273 John Miles   Receipt of John Vaughan for full legacy
274 Daniel Malone   Robert, Goodloe, Nashville, Mitchell, Lewis G. & Alexr.Malone

1827

278 Azariah Graves Kezziah Willis. Pd Thomas Graves for lottery tickets;
                    pd Mary Willis for board
278 Mary Cox   Nathl., Jesse, Henry, Geo. Cox
279 Elijah Graves   Jacob, William, Azariah, Tabitha, & John Graves. Recd legacy
                    from John Kimbrough decd.
282 Samuel H. Smith William Smith
283 Zachariah Hooper Catharine L., Rufus W., Westley B., Susan H., & Delilah S.
                    Reamy. (Also spelled Raimey)
291 Martha Harrelson Elizabeth T., Samuel H., Martha Jane, & Iverson G. Harrelson.
292 John Smith   James & Thomas Sergent. Pd William Mitchell for tuition.
293 John Long   William C. & Alexander Donoho
305 Benjamin C. West Heirs of Settleberry Worsham. Recd from Clerk & Master of
                    Iredell Co. and from James D. Patton. Pd David Traynam
                    for his wife Mary's part; remainder to Emily, Robert, John,
                    Joseph, & Settleberry Worsham
309 Joseph Bracken Receipt of Aggrippa Bracken for full legacy of her father
                    Samuel Bracken.

1828

316 James M. Lea   Emily Lea. Recd 1/3 part of estate of Lawrence Lea.
317 Benjamin Wells Daniel & Will H. Crisp
319 Elijah Graves   Azariah & John Graves (sons of Jacob); Tabitha & Wm. Graves.
321 Elijah Graves   Receipt of Jacob Graves Jr. for legacy.
321 Thomas W. Chandler,Nancy & Margaret Chandler
322 Starling Gunn   William G. Hooper. Recd of Richard Fittsgerald a legacy left
                    said Hooper by Thos. Good of Va. Recd cash from Edward Good
                    estate.
324 Gregory Hightower, Nancy W., Frances P., Eliza J., & Mary C. Hightower, orphans
                    of Joshua Hightower
325 John P. Harrison Robert & Noel Richardson

Guardian accounts 1828-1829

	GUARDIAN	ORPHAN
Page
327 Edmund M. Jones — Martha Blackwell
331 Thomas Foster — James C. Harrelson
332 George Turner — Seluda & George W. Rowlett; pd for 3 trips to Charlotte CH,Va.
335 Joseph Dameron — Jane Jackson
"   Daniel & William Hightower
340 Hosea McNeill — Joseph & Anexander Cantrell. Ant retained from estate of Susannah Cantrell decd.
341 Anthony Foster — Minerva, William, Robert, & James King
344 Robert McKee — Levi, Parthena, Priscilla Eubank, heirs of George Eubank
345 Robert McKee — Nancy McKee, heir of Jesse McKee
349 John C. Harvey — Heirs of Griffin Gunn: Eliza A., William P., Huldah M., Daniel E., Allen M., Emily M., & Jefferson Gunn
354 Josiah Turner — Elizabeth F. Turner. Pd James C. Turner for difference in land. Recd cash from W. Slade Jun. No settlement from adm of Thomas Turner
354 Whitehead Page — Nancy & Samuel King
357 Samuel Love — Lewis Love. Cash recd of Allen Peoples
359 John Keesee — Sarah Durham orphan of Gregory Durham
360 Sarah B. Carter — Wm. B. Carter
362 Sarah B. Carter — Receipt of John E. Brown for full legacy of wife Elizabeth.
363 Mary Evans — Nancy, Benjamin, George, & Price Evans
363 Richard Fitzgerald,Frances G. Hooper; recd cash of William Good.
363 Susan Lawson — Jane Lawson
364 Edward Wright of Rockingham Co. — John B. Lawson of Caswell Co.
364 Forester Stanback — Mary Ann Nunn
365 Hiram Lockard — Receipt of John W. McKissack for full legacy of estate of his decd father Thompson McKissack. 3 Mar 1828.
365 Daniel Jackson — Receipt of William Mathis for full payment for note as guardian of Sally Jackson. 5 June 1824.
365 Nathan Duncan — Jane Humphries gives receipt for money from estate of William Humphries. 1828.
366 Burwell Hagood — Receipt of John Humphries for legacy from estate of Wm.Humphries
366 Andrew Hughes — Receipt of William Hughes for negro man Cary and money due from estate of father James Hughes. 22 Feb 1827.
366 James Jackson — Jincey Jackson. Acct examined; said Jackson removed to the West in fall 1826.
370 John Shields — Julia Ann Dupey
370 L. Rainey — Polly Eubank. Pd cash to Thomas Eubank her brother.
371 Abner Miles — Receipts of Nancy S. and P. H. Womack for full legacies.

1829

373 John E. Brown — William B. Carter, Sarah E. Carter former guardian.
374 Isaac Cantrell Jun., Alex & Joseph Cantrell
381 Elijah Graves — Receipt of John Graves for full legacy.
385 Richard Fitzgerald, Receipt of Frances G. Hooper
393 Hiram Lockard — Robert McKissack
399 Josiah Turner — Eliza Turner
400 William Stamps — William G. & Harriott C. Penick. Recd from Maj.Wm. Penick decd.
400 John Shields — Julie Dupey. Pd Cornelius Hubbard for differences in negroes and in land.
401 Wm. W. Price — Williamson Astin. Recd from estate of George Astin decd. Pd Mrs. Astin for board. Pd William Astin difference in valuation.
John and William Astin (same as above)
406 John Smith — Thomas & James Sergent

Guardian accounts 1829-1830

GUARDIAN	ORPHAN

Page
406 Abner Miles   Receipt of Green P. Womack for legacy.
407 N. M. Lewis   Estate of John B. Ponsonby. Pd toll to Milton Bridge $1.50
for 1828; pd Mrs. Donoho board for Mary Williams; pd post-
master for letters & papers $3.04; pd N. M. Lewis in div of
negroes; freight of tobacco to Lynchburg. Negro Lancaster
sold at Caswell Court House; tobacco sold Lynchburg & Milton.

Book 3 1830-1837

1830

1 William W. Price	Washington, Adderson, & Pinckney Price. Pd E. Dodson schoolin
2 Wm. W. Price	William & John Astin
3 Elijah Graves	Azariah, Tabitha, & William Graves
4 Zachariah Hooper	Rufus, Susan, Delilah, & Catharine Rainey
5 Robert H. Jackson	Joshua Jackson
6 Whitehead Page	Samuel King
6 Saml. H. Smith	William Smith
6 Isaac Cantrell Jun.,	Joseph Cantrill
7 John Lea	Betsy Ann & Mary L. Wilson
7 Hiram Lockard	Robert McKissack
8 Elijah Martin	Orphans of Zena Martin
8 Abner Walker	William R. & James C. Walker, heirs of George Walker decd.
8 Robert McKee	Nancy McKee
9 Richard Jones	James Shelton. Pd board to Ralph Glaze; tuition to Thos Carpenter.
9 Richard Jones	Susan Shelton
10 Thomas Foster	James Harrelson
10 John Holloway	Susannah Humphreys
10 Wiley Chandler	Nancy Chandler
11 Rebecca Brintle	Sarah Brintle orphan of Joseph Brintle.
11 John Cobb	Heirs of Joseph Cobb decd.
11 John Nelson	Joel Nelson
11 George Turner	Saluda, George W. Rowlett. Pd expenses to Charlotte CH, Va.
13 Azariah Graves	Kezziah Willis
14 Abner Miles	Elizabeth & Vashti Womack
14 Caswell Tate	John & Mary Tate. Pd Thomas R. Tate his share of principle.
15 Forister Stanback	Mary Ann Nunn
15 James H. Ruffin	Richard, Cornelia, Emily, & Thomas Donoho, children of Genl. A. Donoho, decd. 1/3 for widow.
15 John Love Jun.	Lewis H. Love. Recd from Samuel Love, former guardian.
16 John E. Brown	Wm. B. Carter
16 Robert McKee	Levi, Partheny, & Priscilla Eubank, orphans of George Eubank.
17 Gregory Hightower	Frances P., Mary C., Eliza J., & Nancy W. Hightower, orphans of Joshua Hightower.
18 Mary Cox	George, Jesse, & Nathaniel Cox
19 Jennett Montgomery	James Montgomery. Recd cash from rent of land in Tenn.
19 Edward M. Jones	Martha Blackwell
20 John Long	William C. Donoho
20 William W. Price	William Astin
21 Anthony Foster	William, Robert, James, & Minerva King
22 Priscilla Henderson,	James S., Harriett, Ludolphus, & Frances A. Henderson. Plantation rented to Thomas Gomer & Thomas Hailey.
23 Isaac Cantrill Jun.,	Alexander Cantrill
24 Joseph Dameron	William Hightower orphan of John Hightower
24 Joseph Dameron	Daniel Hightower gives receipt for full legacy. 20 Oct 1829.
25 Benjamin Wells	William H. & David Crisp
26 Martha Haralson	Elizabeth, Iverson G., Samuel H. & Martha Haralson

Guardian accounts 1830-1831

GUARDIAN	ORPHAN

Page
27 John C. Harvey   Huldah M., William P., Allen M., Daniel B., & Emily Gunn.
        Recd from estate of Griffin Gunn. Pd tuition to Major C. Lea.
30 John C. Harvey   Receipt from Elijah Graves 26 Dec 1829 for wife Eliza A.
        Graves formerly Eliza A. Gunn for legacy in full.
31 John C. Harvey   Jefferson Gunn. Recd from estate of Griffin Gunn.
31 Wm. M. Dameron   Receipt of William A. Richmond for full demands of Dameron
        for Mary M. Gold, orphan.
33 James M. Lea   Emily Lea
33 Josiah Turner   Eliza T. Turner
34 Benjamin C. West   Emily, John, Joseph, Robert, & Settlebury Worsham. Pd Mrs.
        Worsham for boarding & clothing.
39 Wm. A. Lea   Daniel D. McNeil - sale of negro to Mitchell Malone. Pd
        Thomas W. Yealock for 1 yr & 7 mos tuition $15.20.
39 Starling H. Gunn   Receipt of William Y. Hooper

1831

42 John Holloway   Susan Humphries. Land sold to Burwell Hagood.
42 William Stephens   Sarah, William, Nancy, John, Mary & Adeline Hightower, orphans
        of Daniel Hightower.
43 Mrs.Rebecca Brintle,Receipt for Sarah Brintle orphan of Jesse Brintle for full
        amt of her interest in estate. /s/ James P. King
43 John E. Brown   William B. Carter
44 John Cobb   Heirs of Joseph Cobb
44 Thomas W. Chandler, Nancey Chandler
45 Isaac Cantrill Jun.,Joseph Cantrill & Alexander Cantrill. Recd from James Martin
        adm of Susannah Cantrill decd.
45 Mary J. Chandler   Frances E. Chandler
46 Mary Cox   George, Jesse, & Nathl. Cox
46 Joseph Dameron   William Hightower orphan of John Hightower
47 Goodwin Evans   Catherine G. & Nancy K. Evans
47 Thomas Foster   Receipt of James Harrelson for his legacy in full.
48 Elijah Graves Sen.   Azariah Graves(son of Jacob), Tabitha Graves, & William
        Graves(son of Jacob)
48 Thomas W. Graves   Milly Browning. Recd of James Martin adm of Susan Cantrill decd.
49 Alexander Gray   John Gray orphan of Jno. Gray. (James Yancey decd former
        guardian)
49 Martha Harrelson   Iverson G., Samuel H., Martha Harrelson
50 Priscilla Henderson,Ludolphus & Frances Henderson
51 Samuel H. Smith   Receipt from William Smith for payment.
52 Zachariah Hooper   Westley Rainey
56 Daniel Jackson   Joshua Jackson
57 Robert H. Jackson   Joshua Jackson
58 Duke W. Kimbro   Patsy E. Kimbro(daughter). Recd legacy from grandmother
        Kimbro's estate.
59 John C. Lea   Betsy Ann & Mary L. Willson
59 John Love Jun.   Lewis Love
60 Abner Miles   Elizabeth & Vashti Womack. Recd from estate of John Womack decd.
60 Samuel Mitchell   Elizabeth Ann Mitchell
61 Hiram Lockard   Receipt of Robert J. McKissack for legacy due from estate of
        father Thompson McKissack and from grandfather William
        McKissack Sen. decd of Person County.
61 Elijah Martin   Orphans of Zena Martin: Frances, Susan, & Thomas Martin.
        Recd from estate of Saml. Love. Pd $2.50 each for school-
        ing Thomas & Susan at Caswell Academy.
63 James Nelson   Joel Nelson
63 Whitehead Page   Samuel King
63 William W. Price   Pinkney, Adderson, & Washington Price

Guardian accounts 1831-1832

Page	GUARDIAN	ORPHAN
64	William W. Price	William Astin. Pd Simon Adams for schooling.
		Williamson Astin. Pd Mother for board.
		John Astin (Pd Dr. Green medical bill; pd for coffin)
66	James H. Ruffin	Richard, Cornelia, Emily, & Thomas Donoho
66	William Stamps	William G. & Harriet C. Penick
67	Josiah Turner	Elizabeth T. Turner. Recd from James C. Turner adm of Nathan Turner; recd from estate of Thos. Turner decd.
68	Caswell Tait	John, Caswell, & Mary Tait
68	George Turner	George W. & Saluda Rowlett
69	Abner Walker	William R., James Walker orphans of George Walker
73	John Comer	Elizabeth G. Long
73	Forester Stanback	Mary Ann Nunn
73	Alexander Gray	John Gray's receipt for full acct recd. Wit: John Wiley.
74	John C. Harvey	Receipt of Elijah Graves Jun. for money pd John Harvey from Allen Gunn for money collected in Tenn. of Cozart for wife's part of her father's (Griffin Gunn) estate.

1832

Page	GUARDIAN	ORPHAN
77	Isaac Cantrill	Joseph & Alexander Cantrill
79	Joseph Dameron	William Hightower. Pd tuition to Y. Wiley & Lanson Lea.
80	Thomas W. Graves	Milly Browning
80	Elijah Graves	Elizabeth Kimbro daughter of E. Kimbro (legacy left by grand-mother Elizabeth Kimbro)
80	Elijah Graves	Azariah & William Graves
81	Elijah Graves Sen.	Tabitha Graves gives receipt for full legacy. Wit: Jacob Graves, Elijah Graves Jun.
81	William Stephens	Orphans of Daniel Hightower. Pd schooling for Mary & Adeline.
93	Abner Miles	Vashti Womack gives receipt for her full legacy.
93	Abner Miles	Elizabeth Womack
94	Samuel Mitchell	Harriett Ann, Eliza P., & Elizabeth A. Mitchell
100	William Price	Receipt of Isaac F. Bucey for his wife's part of sale of negroes belonging to estate of John Astin decd, the son of George Astin decd. William & Williamson Astin give same receipt.
101	John C. Rogers	Thomas Elmore. Recd from estate of John Elmore.
103	George Turner	George W. & Saluda Rowlett. Pd McAlpin $3.50 for making coat; A. Holderby for schooling; Lockett for shoes.
104	Edmund Turner	Patsy E. Kimbro. (Duke Kimbro former guardian)
105	George Williamson	Ann B., Sarah E., Martha Jane, & Weldon E. Wright orphans of James & Martha Wright.
107	Abner Walker	Wm. R., & James C. Walker. Pd John Warnock & Yancey Wiley for schooling; pd Alanson M. Lea for tuition & school books. Pd J. H. Sidebottom for making coat.
108	Richard Yarbrough	Amanda, Margaret, Catharine, & Clement Taylor heirs of Abel Taylor decd. Recd cash of Major Lewis Bolton.
109	Anthony Foster	William & Robert King
111	Richard Jones	Susan G. Shelton gives receipt for full legacy from father's estate. Wit: Henry W. Brooks.
112	Connally Walker	Barbara & Lucinda Walker orphans of William Walker.
113	John Holloway	Susan Humphreys - sold her interest in estate of Obadiah Holloway. Sale at Lynns Old Field.
117	John Shields	Julia Ann Dupuy
119	Elijah Martin	Frances, Susan, & Thomas Martin orphans of Zenis Martin. Pd Miss Debruler for schooling. Elijah Martin resigns as guardian and recommends his father as guardian.

Guardian accounts 1833-1835

| | GUARDIAN | ORPHAN |
Page 1833

122 Azariah Graves   Algernon S. Yancey. Pd tuition & board at Chapel Hill. Pd
                        McAleer & Henderson Co. for mdse.
124 Elijah Graves   Azariah Graves(son of Jacob) gives receipt for full legacy.
134 Willis M. Lea   Emily Lea. Recd from William Lea as adm of estate of
                        James M. Lea decd.
137 Samuel Moore   Julietta Gregory & Nathaniel H. Gregory. Recd from estate of
                        West Gregory.
141 Caswell Tate   Mary Prather (late Tate).
148 Nancy Yancey   Ann E., Maria V. B., Mary C., & Caroline L. Yancey.
152 Mary A. Donoho   Richard A., Thomas, Cornelia, & Emily Donoho.

1834

157 Henry Cobb   Heirs of John W. Grant
159 Allen Gunn   Heirs of Robert Singleton. Recd of Joseph Singleton adm;
                        recd of J. Easley of Halifax, Va.
160 Thomas W. Graves   John K.S., Luther C., Hosea A., Archibald B., Frances G.,
                        and Elizabeth P. Chandler. Recd from adm of Stephen Chandler.
167 Gregory Hightower   Eliza J. Hightower & Nancy W. Frazier, orphans of Joshua
                        Hightower. Also Mary C. & Frances P. Hightower.
170 Robert L. Harrison,Elizabeth J., Arimenta, Ann S., & Louisa Harrison
182 Stephen Sergant   James, Edmond, & Robert P. Richardson; Mary A. & Elizabeth
                        Richardson. Recd legacy from John Ware.
184 James Terrell   Joel, Iverson, Azariah, Jonathan, & Stephen C. Nelson.
186 Abner Miles   Receipt of Elizabeth Womack for legacy.
194 John C. Lea   Betsy Ann & Mary L. Wilson. Pd amt to William Smith on
                        behalf of his wife Betsy Ann.
197 George Williamson   Heirs of James & Martha Wright. Pd Thomas Lea difference in
                        his lot of negroes in div. Pd Doct. Graham of Georgia for
                        attending Martha Jane(Wright).
198 Connally Walker   Barbara & Susan Walker.

1835

199 Thomas D.Connally,Susan R. Connally. Recd from exec of T. Connally will.
199 Goodwin Evans   Nancy K. & Catherine G. Evans.
200 Allen Gunn   Nancey, Elizabeth, & William Singleton.
202 Thomas W. Graves   Ro George, Westley, Frances, & Mary Swift.
205 Azariah Graves   Algernon S. Yancey. Pd cash when starting to Chapel Hill &
                        when starting to Princeton College.
217 John Love   Lewis Love his ward.
217 Samuel Mitchell   Harriot Ann, Eliza Frances, Elizabeth Ann Mitchell. Pd
                        tuition to Leasburg Female Academy and to Miss Emily Milner.
220 Nelson Thomas   James Thomas
221 Sylvanus Stokes   Estate of Dudley Gatewood. Recd pension $18.33 for Dudley
                        Gatewood. Pd Henderson House 65¢ for bringing pension from
                        Fayetteville, NC.
222 Joseph Smith   Mary, Harriet J., Sarah T., Samuel B., & Mildred Parks.
231 Zilpha Yancey   Albert G., William, & Mildred Yancey. Recd from estate of
                        James Yancey. Pd James M. Yancey amt due him in div of estate.
233 Connally Walker   Receipt of Samuel Walker in right of wife Barbara for legacy
                        from estate of William Walker.
234 Isaac Cantrill   Receipts of Joseph & Alexander Cantrill for their legacy from
                        estate of father Benjamin Cantrill.
235 Banister Fitzgerald, Estate of James Powell.
236 Martin P. Huntington, Richard, Thomas, Cornelia, & Emily Donoho, orphans of
                        A. Donoho decd.

171

Guardian accounts 1835-1837

| GUARDIAN | ORPHAN |

Page
240 Dr. Willis M. Lea of
Lauderdale Co. Ala. Resigns guardianship of Emily Lea. Richard Baugh named
guardian of Emily Lea minor heir of William Lea. 15 Apr.

1836

244 Henry Cobb   Heirs of John W. Grant. Pd Joseph C. Grant full share; pd
Alexander Henderson and Hiram Henderson for compromise on lan
245 John Cobb Jun.   Heirs of Joseph Cobb: Samuel B., Henry W., John B., & Louisa M
251 Azariah Graves   Algernon S. Yancey. Pd cash to David Dickey atty for John S.
Dickey who married Sally Rice who was entitled to a legacy
coming from Ann Yancey decd. estate and left in B. Yancey's
hands the exec of said Ann decd to be paid to Sally Rice
when she arrived to 21 years , whole amt. of $400.
256 Gregory Hightower Wife of M. A. Frazer - A. M. Frazer signs receipt for legacy
from Joshua Hightower.
     "   Eliza J., Mary C., & Frances Hightower.
261 Goodwin Evans   Receipt of Elizabeth A. & Thomas R. Kimbrough for legacy
from estate of her grandmother Elizabeth Kimbrough.
262 John Love   Lewis Love. Pd Franklin Yealock for schooling.
262 John Love   Frances Gooch who was Frances Martin; Susan Henslee who was
Susan Martin; Thomas Martin.
262 Joseph Smith   Receipt of Mary Parks for legacy. /s/ John & Mary Sanders.
263 John B. McMullen Margaret, Mary K., & Harriet Hester. Pd K. A. McMullen for
difference in lots of negroes.
264 Samuel Moore   Nat H. Gregory
264 John Nunnally   Lewis, James, John, Elizabeth, & Albert G. Withers.
268 Joseph Smith   Receipt of Mildred Parks for legacy.
272 Benjamin C. West Joseph C. Worsham to time of death of ward. 8 Apr 1835.
274 Richard Yarbrough Amanda, Catherine, & John Taylor. Pd Mrs. Taylor for board.
274 Zilpah Yancey   Albert G. & Mildred Yancey. Pd William Sneed for making coat,
Kent & Graves for saddle.
William Yancey. Pd Dabney Rainey for schooling.
280 Thomas D. Connally,Susan R. Connally. Receipt of William T. Dismukes for share
of funds due to Susan now his wife.
280 Thomas W. Graves Westley, George, Frances, & Mary Swift. Pd S. E. Bracken for
schooling; Pd for expenses from Catawba in Ala. to Tuscum-
bia and for lawyer fees in Ala. Recd from estate of Milton
Swift. Pd Franklin Graves to attend to this business.
283 Zachariah Hooper Rufus & Catherine S. Raimey.
284 George Williamson Sarah E., Martha J. & Weldon E. Wright. Pd George G. Lea
his part in full.
285 Samuel Mitchell   Elizabeth Ann, Eliza F., & Harriot A. Mitchell.
286 John Swift   Heirs of Harvey Swift: Robert, Harvey, William, Peggy,
Lucinda, Kitty, & John Swift.

1837

287 Thomas D.Connally William P., Elizabeth P., & Minerva J. Winstead. Mrs Sarah
Winstead former guardian.
288 Thomas D.Connally John F. Williams. Recd of Clement Lipscomb amt left by ward's
grandfather.
288 John Cobb Jun.   John R., Henry W., & Louisa M. Cobb.
290 Richard H.Griffith,
of Randolph Co. Mo., His children: Frances H., Louise E., Calvin G., Romulus S.
William C., & John C. Griffith minors. Bonded by James
A. Griffith & John Clemson.
292 Samuel Greer   Micajah Graves. Recd $100 from will of Micajah Pleasant.

Guardian accounts 1837-1838

| GUARDIAN | ORPHAN |

Page
299 Cary A. Howard   Jane M. Howard. Pd John Kerr for counsel.
299 Philip Hodnett   M. E. Lipscomb. Pd bonds in settlement estate of Thomas
                       Harrelson.
303 Abner Miles   Thomas B., William, Robert C., George W., James, Jonathan J.,
                       Algernon S., & Sarah Holderness. Recd from adm of Thomas
                       Holderness estate.
310 Joseph Smith   Samuel B., Sarah T., & Harriett J. Parks.
311 James Terrell   Joel, Iverson, Azariah, Jonathan, & Stephen Nelson.
313 Pleasant H. Womack,Martha Hrrrelson.
318 Zachariah Hooper   Catharine S. Raimey(now Harris) & Rufus Raimey.
318 Reubin Kennon   William, Abel H., Jane, Thursey Ann, Joseph Branch, & Richard
                       Kennon. Recd from estate of Joseph Allen willed to said
                       wards. /s/ Richard Cannon.
323 Joseph R. E. Lipscomb
       of Fayette Co. Tenn., Martha E. Lipscomb his daughter. 7 Aug 1837.

   Book 4 1837-1847

      1838
Page
 1 Joseph Benton   Melinda, Sabina, Anthony & Artelia Foster.
 1 Mary J. Chandler   Frances E. Chandler
 1 Goodwin Evans   Nancy K. Evans.
 2 Banister Fitzgerald,James Powel.
 2 Elijah Graves   Elizabeth Kimbrough.
 2 Samuel Grier   Micajah Graves
 2 Allen Gunn   Nancy, Elizabeth, & William Singleton.
 3 John C. Harvey   Thomas J., Daniel B. Gunn orphans of Griffin Gunn.
 4 M. P. Huntington   Richard, Cornelia, Thomas, & Emily Donoho.
 7 John Haguewood   Charles G. Stephens. Recd from Iverson G. Stephens money due
                        for land and negroes. Pd Mrs. Sarah Stephens for clothing.
 7 Robert L. Harrison   Louisa Harrison
 8 Gregory Hightower   Mary C., Frances P., Eliza Jane Hightower orphans of Joshua
                        Hightower. Frances P. now wife of William Johnston.
10 Cary A. Howard   Jane M. Howard
11 John Love   Lewis Love
                        Thomas Martin
12 William Mitchell   Susan J. Foster
12 John B. McMullen   Margaret Hightower (amt due Margaret Hester); Mary K. &
                        Harriett Hester.
13 Abner Miles   8 Holderness children. Pd C. Brooks for board for Wm.Holderness.
15 John Nunnally   John, Albert G., Elizabeth, Lewis, & James Withers, heirs of
                        Elijah Withers.
16 Wm. W. Price   William & Williamson Asten. Pd Isaac Busey for board & tuition.
17 William Russell   Thomas, Judith, Emily T., William, & Joseph Russell orphans
                        of Joseph Russell decd.
21 Stephen Sergant   Edmund, Robert P., Mary A., & Elizabeth F. Richardson.
23 Josiah Turner   Elizabeth T. Turner. Proved before J. Taylor, Orange Co. NC.
23 Benjamin Wells   Stephen, Mary Ann, & Jabez Wells. Recd from will of grand-
                        mother of Orange Co.
24 Benjamin Wells   David H. & William H. Crisp. Recd from will of grandmother
                        of Orange Co. NC.
25 Pleasant H. Womack   Martha Harrelson
25 Nancy Yancey   Virginia B., Ann E., & Caroline L. Yancey.
27 Zelpha Yancey   Albert G., William, & Mildred Yancey.
28 Richard Yarbrough   Martin & John Taylor
28 Connally Walker   Lucinda Walker

Guardian accounts 1838-1839

GAURDIAN	ORPHAN

Page
28 Goodwin Evans   Catharine G. Evans gives receipt for legacy from her grandmoth Elizabeth Kimbrough.
29 George Williamson   Martha Jane & Weldon E. Wirght.
30 John Cobb   John R., Henry W., Louisa M. Cobb.
31 Henry A. Burton   Charles K. Harrison. Acct of sales of estate of Harrison.
32 John Simpson   George, Thomas, Sarah, Susan, & Lettice Lea.
33 Thomas W. Graves   Westley, Ro George, Martha Frances, & Mary A. Swift.
34 Thomas W. Graves   Luther C., John K., Archibald B., Frances A., & Hosea A. Chandler.
35 Thomas W. Graves   Milly Browning.
36 George Williamson   James Montgomery. Recd from Jennet Montgomery former guardian
36 Thomas Gunn of
    Huntsville, Randolph Co.,   James Montgomery now residing at house of Thomas
    Mo.   Gunn. Joseph C. Dameron & Walter Head securities. Robert Wilson, county clerk; Archd Shoemaker presiding judge, Randolph Co. Mo.

1839

41 John Cobb   Mary Badgett
41 Thomas D. Connally   John F. Williams. Recd cash of Adams, adm of Jackson Pulliam; recd from estate of old Mrs. Pulliam.
42 Allen R. Cooper   Yancey L. Warren. Recd from exec of Boswell decd, C. Crisp, Y. Warren, & Wilson Jeffreys.
44 John H. Graves   Samuel P., Sarah Jane, & Marion Wallace Hill. Recd 1/7 part of estate of Samuel Hill Sen. to children of Thomas Hill decd Pd J. H. Graves for board, J. Hank for teaching vocal music, Miss Booth & E. Winkler for tuition. "There will be due Sarah Jane Hill & Marion Hill $300 when they come of age for negro boy Tilman given by Saml. Hill to my wife Sarah Jane and Marion Wallace Hill". /s/ John H. Graves.
55 Reuben Kennon   William, Abel H., Jane, Thersy Ann, Joseph B., & Richd Kennon.
60 Owen McAleer   William Henderson. Pd D. Rainey for tuition.
60 William Russell   Orphans of Joseph Russell. Pd for expenses for Judith & Emily T. at Salem (Academy); pd McAleer for making dresses. Pd John M. Morton & Mr. Pickard tuition for William Russell.
61 Nathaniel M. Roan   Susan P. Henderson. Recd of Hiram Henderson from estate of William Henderson father of Susan. Pd cash to J. C. Milner with whom Susan intermarried.
69 Zilpah Yancey   William & Mildred Yancey. Albert G. Yancey gives receipt for full claims.
70 Nancy Yancey   Caroline L, Ann E., & M.V.B. Yancey.
72 William Burton   James Burton, Inft.
72 Franklin Burton   Lucy Burton.
75 Richard J. Smith   John B. & Men R. Smith orphans of M. Smith.
75 Elijah G. Kimbrough
    of Hickman Co, KY.,Elizabeth Kimbrough age 14 years his daughter. Elijah Graves former guardian.
82 Thomas D. Connally   John F. Williams. Pd ward's expenses to Madison Co. Tenn 1838.
85 Berry Evans   William, Sally, & Lucy Vaughan. Recd from exec of Thos. Page decd who was adm of James Vaughan Jr. decd their father.
89 Pleasant H. Womack   Martha J. Gunn, formerly Martha J. Harrelson, wife to John A. Gunn who gives receipt.
93 Zachariah L.Hooper   Frances, Joseph, & Elisha Hooper. Recd from estate of Joseph Henderson.
97 Nancy Oliver   Demaris R., Lea Iverson, James T., Calvin, Monroe, Isabella F., and Nancy Oliver Jr.

Guardian accounts 1839-1841

GUARDIAN	ORPHAN

Page
102 Nancy Oliver — Receipt of Nancy Oliver to Durrett Oliver adm of Reuben Oliver decd.
102 Abisha Slade — Charles K. Harrison
105 Josiah Turner — Elisa Thomas Turner
109 Richard Yarbrough — Amanda Taylor

1840

111 Allen Cooper — Yancey G. Warren
111 M. P. Huntington — Richard A. Donoho. Pd Dr. Wilie Jones $85 for medical instructions. Cash sent to ward in Philadelphia. Emily & Thos. Donoho.
115 Reuben Kennon — Pd to Abel Kennon now of age.
117 James E. Williamson, Martha Jane & W. E. Wright
119 Richard B. Gunn — Susan Sheppard
120 William Weatherford, Inv of property of James Powell.

1841

124 Henry Cobb — Heirs of John W. Grant. Payment in full to: (1)Maximin Cobb for his wife Permelia formerly Permelia D. Grant; (2)James Hubbard for his wife formerly Artemesia B. Grant; (3) Deborah Grant widow. Div between John C. & Jane C. Grant.
129 John H. Graves — Samuel P. Hill. Pd for schooling in Greensboro; pd $3.50 stage fare to Greensboro.
Sarah Jane & Marion Wallace Hill. Pd Winkler tuition on guitar; pd John Word tuition in dancing $10; pd Miss Converse tuition; pd Abner Miles 10¢ post office acct.; pd Gunn & Bowe shoe acct.
133 John C. Harvey — Receipt of Daniel B. Gunn for full claim.
136 Richard Jones — Receipt of James W. Shelton for claim.
143 Nancy Oliver — Demarias Yancey. Pd to husband William Yancey.
147 Nathaniel J. Palmer, Susan J. Farley. Recd from Thomas C. Pass agent of Dicey Farley adm of John J. Farley decd., 2/3 of estate.
149 Joseph Smith — Samuel B. Parks.
150 Joseph Smith — Receipt of Sarah Parks for money. Wit: Samuel B. Parks.
150 Joseph Smith — Edward C. & Harriett J. Bouldin, formerly Harriett Park, give receipt.
150 John Simpson — Heirs of John Lea.
152 Albert G. Stephens, Charles G. Stephens.
155 Jane Wiley — Thomas, Frances, & Elizabeth Wiley.
156 Abner Walker — Mitchell, Manuella Ann, George J., & Abner L. Walker, orphans of George Walker. Rent of land to Albert Pattillo.
160 Zilpha Yancey — Mildred Yancey. Pd Miss Booth and Miss Converse tuition.
163 Thomas Barton — Margaret, Aquilla, Chesley L., William A., Lucinda E., & Thomas J. Barton. Recd from James E. Williamson exec of Elizabeth Barton.
163 Anthony Foster — Robert King. Pd for difference in div of land to James King; receipt of Robert N. King for full claims.
166 Woodlief Hooper — Martha & Susan P. Hooper.
168 Benjamin Johnston, Mary F., James R., Elizabeth, Benj., Lucy Ann, & Mincey Eskridge. Recd from estate of Bird Eskridge their father by Booker Boman adm. Widow Nancy Eskridge.

Six small sheets bound into this book seemingly when it was rebound include the estate settlement of John H. Graves decd and accts with legatees for 1837. Legatees: estate of Azariah Graves decd; Groves Howard and wife; Col. Thomas Graves (Race Tract land); Elijah Graves; William Graves (house & lot at Court House & 25 acres value $2000); Abner Miles and wife Delilah; Nancy Yancey; James Mebane and wife Polly; Barzl. Graves (General).

Guardian accounts 1841-1843

Page	GUARDIAN	ORPHAN
169	Martha Love	Ira & William Love.
169	William Mitchell	Susan J. Foster
170	R. J. Smith	John B. Smith orphan of M. Smith. Pd expenses 1st session at Chapel Hill $125; sent $20 at commencement. Men R. Smith. Pd expenses at Junto Academy and to commencement at Chapel Hill.

1842

182	Nathaniel M. Roan,	Nathaniel, Priscilla, & Marmaduke Norfleet
185	John Simpson	Heirs of John Lea. Recd from Nathan King exec of estate of Lettice Foster decd for benefit of heirs.
188	Daniel Gunn	Sarah & Adeline Gunn.
191	Henry Willis	Thomas & Martha Willis. Recd from adm of Thomas Harrelson.
192	Wm. H. Johnson	Eliza P. & Mary C. Hightower.
194	Richard B. Gunn	Judson Shepherd.
194	Henry Badgett	Elisha Hooper. Recd from estate of Benjamin Hooper.
195	Martha Love	Isaac Love.
196	Catherine Weathers,	John A., Elizabeth A., & Albert G. Weathers. (Withers?)
196	Wilie P. Womack	Lewis Love
198	Thomas D. Johnston,	Stephen C. & Jonathan Nelson.
204	Letha Nunly (Nunnally)	Her children: Obediah, Agnes, John H., Lucia L.(or Lucas L.), & Virginia E. Nunnally. Div of estate.
206	Henry Badgett	Joseph Hooper. Furnished $100 when he started to Missouri. Pd Henry M. Long tuition. Recd from Benjamin Hooper estate.
206	Joseph Benton	Melinda & Artelia Foster.
207	William Lea	Elizabeth, Sally, Mary, & Joel Holcomb, minor orphans of William Holcomb.
206	John H. Graves	Samuel P., Sarah J., & Marion Hill. Recd from estate of Col. John Mebane.
211	Joseph Benton	Anthony & Sabina Foster.
211	John B. McMullen	Mary K. Jones formerly Mary K. Hester.
212	John B. McMullen	Harriett Hester.
213	Jane Wiley	Elizabeth Wiley.
214	Richard J. Smith	John B. Smith. Recd of Thomas B. Littlejohn, Clerk & Master of Granville Co. (NC) from sale of real estate of M. Smith.

1843

217	Martha Love	Ira & William Love, minors.
222	Abner Miles	Receipt of James M. Holderness for all claims & demands.
223	William Long	C. G. Stephens
223	Daniel Gunn	Sarah, Adeline, Callis, & Priscilla Gunn.
223	William Mitchell	Susan J. Foster
228	Richard Jones	Heirs of M. Mims. Recd of John Cobb adm.
230	James Mebane	Sarah Jane Hill. Cash pd when she went to Georgia. Judgment against John H. Graves her former guardian.
230	James Mebane	Samuel P. Hill. Pd cash $200 when he went to college at Prinston (Princeton?)
230	James Mebane	Marion W. Hill. Cash to go to Hillsboro to school $5. Pd Robert Burwell $73 for board & tuition; pd $2 for boy and carriage to go to Hillsboro (2 days).
231	Nathaniel J. Palmer,	Susan J. Kirby.
231	Benjamin Wells	Jabez Smith.
232	Benjamin Wells	Mary A. & Stephen M. Wells.
232	John Simpson	Heirs of John Lea. Advanced cash to Sarah Lea an heir.
240	John B. McMullen	Harriet Hester now Harriet McDaniel.
241	Abner Walker	Cornelia Ann Walker.

Guardian accounts 1843-1845

GUARDIAN	ORPHAN

Page
251 R. J. Smith   Men R. Smith orphan of M. Smith. Pd cash for 2 sessions at
Chapel Hill $125 each. Recd proceeds of sale of land in Meck-
lenburg Co. Va. Stock in Bank of NC and Farmers Bank of Va.
252 Wm. H. Johnston   Elijah J. & Mary C. Hightower.
253 R. J. Smith   John B. Smith. Pd cash at Chapel Hill for 1st session. Pd
$100 for trip to Moxville. Recd same as did Men R. Smith.

1844

262 Thomas Swift   Emaline E. Swift.
264 Jane Wiley   Thos A., Elizabeth, & Frances Wiley. Recd from Mary Wiley decd.
266 Banjamin Wells   David H. Crisp. Pd $80 cash when starting to Philadelphia.
    "   William H. Crisp. Also Mary Ann, Stephen M.,& Jabez Wells.
268 Allen Gunn   William Singleton gives receipt for full legacy.
269 James Currie   Eliza F. Mitchell. Recd of David Mitchell's estate. Div of
negroes between Monroe Allen & Eliza F. Mitchell.
271 Robert Swift   Edward R. & Sarah Swift.
284 Daniel Gunn   Aria A., & Priscilla R. Gunn.
285 Albert G. Yancey   Mildred Yancey.
286 Thomas W. Chandler,Mary F. Chandler.
289 Lytha Nunnally   Her children: John H., Lucas, & Virginia Nunnally; pd cash
   (or Sytha)   to grandmother.
290 William Long   Charles G. Stephens.
291 Allen Cooper   Yancey G. Warren gives receipt for full claims.
294 N. H. Harding   Priscilla G. Harding. Recd dividend from stock in Bank of
Cape Fear.

1845

296 James Mebane   Samuel P. Hill. Sent to Princeton a check on Bank of America.
Samuel P. Hill is 21 and this is last return.
    "   Marion Wallace Hill. Pd Burrell cash & tuition.
296 William J. Moore   Robert & Margaret Dupree.
297 Allen Gunn   Elizabeth Singleton.
298 James Currie   Eliza F. Mitchell. Note on Lemuel Mebane. This ward now
intermarried with Thomas Y. Mebane who is over 21 and gives
receipt for wife's legacy. 10 Oct 1844.
299 Robert Swift   Edward R. Swift.
299 William Mitchell   Susan J. Foster.
300 William Long   Charles G. Stephens. Recd from Benj. Stephens decd.
300 George G. Lea   Susan F. Lea.
301 Nathaniel J. Palmer, Susan J. Farley.
301 James M. Lea   Robert J. Lea.
301 Berry Evans   William Vaughan.
302 M. P. Huntington   Thomas A. Donoho
303 Thomas W. Graves   Westly & Mary Swift. Pd James Kerr for Bible & Hymn Book.
305 Thomas W. Graves   Robert G. Swift. Pd A. Lindsey for schooling.
305 Joseph Simpson   Ephraim Moore minor heir of Nathan Moore decd.
306 Thomas W. Graves   Miss Martha F. Swift.
306 Thomas W. Graves   Hosea A. Chandler
307 Thomas Swift   Emeline Swift.
308 Lewis W. Withers   Albert G. Withers
308 Nancy Oliver   Nancey Oliver; James Oliver decd & Calvin Oliver decd.
Payments to Will H. Childs, Dr. N. M. Roan.
310 John Simpson   Heirs of John Lea decd.
310 Jane Wiley   Thomas A. Wiley, and Frances S. Wiley.
310 Richard B. Gunn   Susan Shepherd
310 A. G. Anderson   Mary & Martha Davis. Recd from exec of Wm. F. Davis decd.
312 Nancy Oliver   Iverson, Isabella F., & Monroe Oliver.

Guardian accounts 1845-1847
GUARDIAN   ORPHAN
Page
312 William Stephens   Andrew Stephens
313 Reuben Kennon   Richard & Thersy A. Kennon.
314 Nathaniel M. Roan   Nathaniel, Marmaduke, & Priscilla F. Norfleet. Pd Mary C.
                        Norfleet for board; Dr. N. Joyner for medical services.
315 A. G. Yancey   Mildred A. Yancey. Pd Miss St. John, Mrs. McAleer, Mrs.
                        Gardner.
316 Abner Miles   George W., Jonathan B., Algernon S., Robert C. & Sarah B.
                        Holderness. (Pd C. W. Brooks & A. C. Lindsey tuition.)
318 Abner Walker   Mitchell & Cornelia A. Walker. Each entitled to 1/4 part of
                        estate of Debora Walker decd of Missouri. Recd from estate
                        of father George Walker decd(4 heirs) which descended from
                        grandfather Wm. Walker decd. Pd Dr. Levi Walker medicine.
319 Thomas W. Chandler,Mary F. Chandler
322 Benjamin Wells   David H. Crisp. Also Stephen M. & Jabez A. Wells.
323 Thomas D. Johnston,Stephen C. Nelson.
324 Richard Jones   Heirs of Martin Mims. Recd of George Brookes adm.
328 Alexis Howard   Joseph & Benjamin Dupree heirs of Will Dupree decd.
328 William C. Shelton,Susan Ann Stone. Recd from Joseph C. Smith exec of Susan M.
                        Chaney.
329 William Russell   Joseph Russell

    1846
333 William Burton   Heirs of Mary Atkinson. Pd to Mr. Lyle of Virginia.
334 Jane Wiley   Elizabeth C. Wiley.
336 Martha Love   William Love. Recd from Carter Lea adm.
338 David C. Vanhook   William T.(or F.) Stanfield.
339 Nathaniel J. Palmer, Susan J. Farley. Pd Kinchen Newman her grandfather for
                        support.
339 & 349 Abner Walker, George J., Cornelia A., Mitchell, & Abner S. Walker.
                        Pd $4 to bring negro man & woman from Tenn. Pd John Kerr
                        attorney fees.
340 Jane Wiley   Frances J. Wiley.
341 James M. Lea   Robert Lea
342 Eli Murray   Decd children of Reuben Oliver: James & Calvin Oliver.
343 William J. Moore   Robert & Margaret Dupree.
345 M. P. Huntington   Thos A. Donoho. Pd cash to Chapel Hill; pd E. P. Hanks tuitio
346 Eli Murray   Isabella, Nancy, Iverson, & Monroe Oliver heirs of Reuben
                        Oliver. Pd store acct of Eli Murray; pd Dr. Roan; pd Dr.
                        Comer for setting arm of Monroe Oliver.
350 William Russell   William Russell Jun.
353 George G. Lea   Susan F. Lea. Pd Solomon Lea $93 for 3 sessions tuition.
361 John A. Withers   A. G. Withers.
364 Benjamin Wells   Jabez & Mary Ann Wells.
365 Abner Miles   Receipt of Thomas B. Holderness for full demands of guardian.
365 Benjamin F.Stanfield, Jane R., Elizabeth, Benjamin, Lucy A., and Nancy Eskridge.
                        Recd of Benjamin Johnston former guardian.
366 Henry Cobb   Receipt of William C. Page for wife Jane E. Page who was
                        Jane E. Grant for full demands. 23 Apr 1845.
367 Edward Watlington, Receipt of Sandford M. Simpson for Mary Ann daughter of
                        Edward Watlington for her share of estate of her grandmother
                        Sarah Brooks decd.
                        Charles B. Watlington gives same receipt.
367 Caleb H. Richmond   Thomas M. Hamblett Senr. (Also spelled Hamlett)

    1847
372 Thomas C. Pass   Hezekiah Roper. Pd R. Crittenden for boots, Mrs. Gordon for
                        making coat; Samuel Watkins store acct.

Guardian accounts 1847 - 1850 Mortality Schedule

GUARDIAN	ORPHAN

Page
377 Eli Murray   Isabella F., & Ann Oliver. Recd from Durette Oliver adm.
                 Pd Minerva Gillaspie tuition; pd board to Dr. Yancey.
378 Nicholas M. Lewis, Mary Ann Robertson. Recd of N. J. Palmer adm.
387 William Burton   Heirs of Mary Atkinson.
387 Samuel Love   Martha C. Love. Recd legacy from Calvin C. Love exec of
                 John Love decd.
387 Eli Murray   Monroe Oliver. Pd expenses at Cedar Grove School; board
                 and tuition in Yanceyville.
388 William Mitchell   Susan F. Foster
388 Robert Swift   Edward R. Swift.
389 Albert G. Yancey   Mildred A. Yancey. Pd cash to Mrs. Rucks, Jones & Pattillo.
389 Thomas C. Pass   Frances C. Roper
389 Allen Gunn   Receipt of Elizabeth Singleton for full balance.
390 Eli Murray   Iverson L. Oliver. Pd McCain for deed of land.
391 William H. Johnston, Receipt of Mary C. Hightower heir of Joshua Hightower for
                 full claims.
392 Joseph Simpson   Ephraim Moore
392 Abner Miles   Receipt of Sarah B. Holderness for full claims.
393 Mary J. Chandler   Receipt of William G. Chandler to his mother Mary J. Chandler
                 for negroes due him in div of estate of his father John
                 Chandler to wit Madison, Betty, & Hannah, also for his
                 share of land.
394 William H. Johnston, Moses Peterson gives receipt for Eliza J. Hightower(his
                 wife) heir of Joshua Hightower for full claims.
394 Jane Wiley   Receipt of F. A. Wiley for full claims.
394 William C. Shelton, Heirs of William E. Stone decd: Susan A., Mary S., &
                 Elizabeth M. Stone. Debts due William B. Swann & Eliza-
                 beth A. Stone.

CASWELL COUNTY 1850 CENSUS MORTALITY SCHEDULE
Book at NC State Archives

The 1850 census was taken in June of that year. The mortality schedule included
those deaths in the previous 12 months or from June 1849 through May 1850.
Included in this compilation are only whites and free blacks.

Listed is name of deceased and in sequence age, M or F (Male or Female), marital
status if given, place of birth, and cause of death.

Priscilla R. Gunn 16 F Caswell County Dropsy
Ann Howell 99 F Widowed New York Posey
Elizabeth Watlington 75 F Widowed Caswell Co. old age
Lucy B. Hines 3 months F Caswell Co. unknown
John Mansfield 15 M Caswell Co. Pneumonia
Eugenia Allen 1 month F Caswell Co. unknown
Ann E. Gooch 9 months F NC consumption
Emily Nance 8 months F Va. teething
Alice Terry 2 M? Caswell Co. croup
Joseph Owen 58 M VA Dropsy
Robert Lyon 63 M Caswell Co. Drinking
Elizabeth Lyon 55 F VA Pneumonia
Sylvia Turner 52 F Caswell Co. unknown
Brice Collins 69 M Married Orange Co. Apoplexy
Sylvia Jeffreys 75 F Widowed VA old age
Barbara Lea 32 F Married Person Co. Child bed
James Lea 1 month M Caswell Co. unknown

1850 Mortality schedule

Nat L. Williamson 22 M Caswell Co. Diarrhea
Mathew B. Dodson 59 M Married VA Typhoid
Prudence Dodson 59 F Widowed Caswell Co. Pneumonia
Lydia Rice 25 F Married Caswell Co. Typhoid fever
Frances E. Rice 10 F Caswell Co. Typhoid fever
Frances B. Willis 43 F Married Caswell Co. Ulcer of womb
Sarah Samuel 92 F Widowed VA old age
Robt. A. Lea 2 months M Caswell Co. Measles
William B. Johnston 3 M Caswell Co. Bilious fever
William Moore 60 M Caswell Co. Dropsy
William Chavis, mulatto, 5 months M Caswell Co. Sudden
Susan Bowers, mulatto, 75 widowed VA old age
Rebecca F. Grinstead 17 F Person Co. Inflamation of brain
Indianna Bennett 11 F Caswell Co. Dropsy
William McCain 24 M Widowed Caswell Co. Consumption
Malinda Woods 32 F Caswell Co. Consumption
John Crisp 79 M Widowed Caswell Co. old age
Permelia Hester 30 F Married Caswell Co. unknown
Mahala Hathcock 28 F free black Caswell Co. unknown
Thomas Boulding 31 M Married Caswell Co. Consumption
William Chandler 70 M Married Granville Co. unknown
Francis B. Gooch 10 M Caswell Co. Neuralgia
Elizabeth Page 65 F Married Caswell Co. Neuralgia
Mary Chamberlain 56 F Married Warren Co. unknown
William Poteat 50 M Married Caswell Co. Intemperance
Virginia Womack 2 months F Caswell Co. Scarlet fever
James N. P. Strader 20 M Caswell Co. Pneumonia
Robt. Tyree 19 M Caswell Co. Pneumonia
Mariah Gordon 45 F Widowed VA Pneumonia
Martha A. Simpson 28 F Married VA Brain disease
James Solomon 11 M VA Dropsy
Robert Solomon 8 M VA Dropsy
Henry Solomon 5 M VA Dropsy
Elizabeth Dobbins 75 F Widowed Caswell Co. Lung trouble
Frances Roan 60 F Married Caswell Co. Pneumonia
Joseph Case 14 M Caswell Co. Dropsy
Sidney Shields 8 months M. NC Inflamation of brain
John B. Moore 66 M Widowed VA Jaundice
Ambrose Phelps 45 M Married Caswell Co. Pneumonia
Abner Walker 76 M Married Orange Co. Dropsy
William Bird 74 M Married Orange Co. Dropsy
Catherine Massey 57 F Married Orange Co. Palsey
Abigail Davis 87 F Married Orange Co. old age
Hannah Davis 39 F Orange Co. Consumption
William Barnwell 71 M Married Caswell Co. Pneumonia
Graif Duke 54 M Married Orange Co. unknown
Thomas J. Clark 16 M VA Dropsy
John A. Clark 16 M VA Dropsy
Thomas W. Lipscomb 31 M Married VA Typhoid fever
Jane Gillaspie 55 F Married VA Comsumption
Hannah M. Henderson 39 F Married Caswell Co. Pneumonia
Edward Watlington 77 M Married VA Dropsy
William Ferrell 57 M Married Caswell Co. Dropsy
Joseph R. Travis 19 M VA Typhoid fever
Susan A. Knighten 2 F Caswell Co. Congestion
Josiah Blair 11 months M Caswell Co. Heart disease
Fomesia Nash 8 F. Caswell Co. Heart disease
Benjamin C. West 77 M Married VA Sudden
Meredith Price 57 M Widowed Caswell Co. Drink

1850 Mortality Schedule - 1860 Mortality Schedule

1850 schedule cont.
Littleton Sledge 61 M Married Franklin Co. Cancer
Azariah Graves 81 M Widowed Caswell Co. old age
Ransom Saunders 38 M Married Caswell Co. Pneumonia
Robert B. Smith 14 M Caswell Co. Rhumatism
Zachariah Neal 63 M Married VA Paralysis
Obediah Gibson 20 M Caswell Co. Typhoid fever
Monroe Taylor 20 M Rockingham Co. Typhoid fever
Sarah J. Orr 15 F Caswell Co. Typhoid fever
Jane Pruit 28 F Married VA Congestion
Allen Y. Covington 5 M VA Cataral fever
Wm. S. Burton 8 M Caswell Co. unknown
Louise Ingram 1 F Caswell Co. Dropsy
William Hood, free black, 24 M Caswell Co. unknown
Frances Hood, free black, 20 F Caswell Co. Consumption
Edmund F. Hood, free black, 18 M Caswell Co. Rhumatism
Amy Tucker 84 F Widowed VA Pneumonia
James Farley 75 M Widowed unknown - unknown
James Vowell 81 M Widowed VA Cancer
William Henderson Jr. 25 M Widowed Caswell Co. Diarrhea
Davis Evans 43 M Caswell Co. Dropsy
Mary Crittendon 33 F Married VA Consumption
Susan Bradley 55 F VA Pneumonia
Mary W. Elliott 22 F Married VA unknown
John P. Harrison 62 M Married Caswell Co. Sudden

1860 Mortality Schedule - deaths occurred between June 1859 and June 1860.

Listed is name of deceased and in sequence age, M or F (Male or Female), place of birth, month of death, and cause of death.

Martha Chance 22 F Married NC Aug comsumption
P. A. Shackleford 1 F VA July Hives
Luther Case 25 M NC May unknown
Lucy Perkins 46 F NC Aug unknown
Elizabeth Holcomb 25 F Married VA Aug Chronic thrash
W. Y. Glascow 66 M Married VA Dec. White swelling
William Taylor 7 M NC Jan Diphtheria
Mary Miles 27 F NC Feb Dropsey
Cornelia Lashly 16 F NC June Diarrhea
Abi Harrison 70 F NC May Diarrhea
Nancy E. Roberts 1 month F NC June Throat
Garrison Turner 20 M NC Sept. Killed by horse running
Susan Burton 1 F NC Feb Croup
Elizabeth Evans 57 F NC Sept. Dropsey
M. C. Norfleet 52 F widow NC Nov Comsumption
M. E. Brandon 9 months F NC Nov Congestion of brain
Nancy Sartin 14 F NC Dec Inflamation of brain
W. G. Gomer 46 M Married NC March Typhoid fever
Elizabeth Cobb 70 F NC Nov old age
William A. Gunn 19 M NC July Typhoid fever
A. S. Womack 1 M NC June Diarrhea
Sallie Evans 57 F NC April Neuralgia
Thomas Crutchfield 16 M NC March Pneumonia
Franklin Crutchfield 16 M NC March Pneumonia
A. J. Murphy 7 months M NC March Pneumonia
Elizabeth King 17 F NC Jan Typhoid fever
Elizabeth Pryor 64 F Married VA July Colic

181

1860 Mortality schedule cont.

Henry Chapman 12 M NC June Typhoid fever
R. S. Meacham 1 month M NC Oct. unknown
Ham E. Watlington 8 M NC March Dropsey
Thomas I. Rollins 1 M NC Sept. Brain disease
W. E. Harrison 38 M NC May Typhoid fever
Phillip Hubbard 1 M NC March Dropsey
Sarah Y. Walton 31 F Married VA May unknown
E. C. Edwards 4 F NC Oct Diphtheria
L. B. Edwards 2 F NC April Diphtheria
Solomon Whitlow 60 M Married NC Jan. Paralysis
S. A. Watkins 9 F NC Nov Diphtheria
M. E. Neal 7 months F NC March Congestion of brain
J. A. Lowndes 17 M NC Feb unknown
L. R. Davidson 27 M VA April Consumption
Martha Paine 36 F NC Sept Consumption
Susan Y. Corbett 28 F NC Aug Typhoid fever
Minerva Gunn 40 F NC May Paralysis
William Thomas 70 M NC Sept Paralysis
John Dabbs 35 M NC July unknown
James Murphy 24 M NC July Disease of spine
Ida J. Roney 4 months F NC Aug Burned to death
Margaret Hemphill 85 F NC Sept old age
A. E. Mansfield 5 months F NC Dec unknown
Lucy Lewis 57 F Married NC Dec Dropsey
George A. Smith 53 M Married VA April Heart disease
Mary Swann 52 F NC Oct unknown
W. W. Price 65 M Married NC May Paralysis
Diane Watlington 60 F NC Aug Consumption
Emily Gwyn 37 F Married NC Oct Consumption
C. C. Howard 18 F NC Oct Teething
James Taylor 72 M NC July Scrofula
Mary Phillips 33 F Married NC Sept. Consumption
Jesse Dunnavant 50 M Married NC March Drowned
L. A. Dunnavant 35 F NC Nov Consumption
M. A. Paylor 30 F Married NC Aug Dropsey
James Reid 43 M Married NC Sept Consumption
John C. Smith 52 M Married NC Oct Consumption
E. Murphy 54 F NC April Consumption
Lucy Turner 86 F Widow NC Dec Dropsey
Mary Roscoe 114 F Widow NC Feb. old age
Robert Fulton 24 M NC Dec Comsumption

POWER OF ATTORNEY FROM CASWELL COUNTY DEED BOOKS

Letter or letters and numbers preceding each item are the book and page on which the item is recorded. CC if used for Caswell County within the item.

B 411 Catharine Armstrong of Surry County NC to Charles Burton of CC to recover dower in tract of land on Dan River sold by husband to Andrew Harrison or any other land sold by husband William Armstrong. 18 Mar 1784.

CC 136 Henrietta Vaughan widow of James Vaughan decd, Jane Vaughan now wife of Thomas C. Childress, Cinthea Vaughan now Cinthea Malone and Bird Malone, Nancy Baccus formerly Nancy Vaughan now wife of John Baccus, and Starling Vaughan - children and only heirs at law of James Vaughan decd of CC to Cornelius Dollarhide of Henry Co., Tenn., to receive from estate of Thomas Vaughan decd late of CC. James Vaughan decd was son of Thomas Vaughan decd. Wit: E. M. Brock, Yancey Malone. 2 Mar 1835.

HH 338 Lucy M. Bacon of Pittsylvania Co., Va., to son Gillie M. Bacon to transact business & sell slaves. Between 1810 & 1814 Stephen Herring gave deed of gift to said Lucy for a negro woman, deed recorded in Lunenburg Co., Va., & in CC. 1851.

CC 139 Richard Baugh of Lauderdale Co., Ala., guardian to Emily Lea minor heir of William Lea decd to Joseph Thompson of said county and state. 15 Apr 1835.

EE 428 William Barker of Carroll Co., Tenn., to brother David C. Barker of CC to attend to all business pertaining to estate of father David Barker decd. 27 Mar 1840.

Q 46 Patsy Barker of Williamson Co., Tenn., legatee of James Barker decd of Orange Co., NC, to John Haih of same county to receive from James Yancey of CC guardian of said Patsy any part due from her father James Barker decd. 8 June 1809.

HH 648 Bird H. Bateman and wife Mary of Green Co., Mo., to Harvey W. Cooper of CC to demand monies of James Currie adm of estate of William Barnwell decd and from William H. Barnwell adm of estate of Elizabeth Barnwell decd both of CC. 14 June 1854.

AA 177 John Bolton and Waller(or Walter) Bolton of CC to Thomas Bolton of Halifax Co., Va., to rent land in CC. 9 May 1832. Wit: Thos Donoho, Wm. P. Dixon.

M 325 William F. Booker of Wilkes Co., Ga., to Robert Moore of Tenn. to dispose of lands in NC. 5 Feb 1803. Wit: Edward Moore, Clo R. Carter, Saml. Moore.

ii 368 Jeptha D. Brown and Deanna Brown of Gwinnett Co., Ga., Deanna a daughter of Bird Wisdom decd late of Gwinnett Co. and Bird a son of Abner Wisdom decd of CC; David R. Brown and Margaret Brown of Cample (?) Co. Ga., Margaret daughter of Bird Wisdom; George W. Brown & Mary Brown of Gwinnett Co. she a daughter of Bird Wisdom - all give power to John L. Wisdom of Gwinnett Co. to receive from estate of Abner Wisdom. 20 Mar 1857.

FF 703 Stokely T. Nelson and Permelia Browning of Benton Co., Ala., named in will of James Nelson of CC(Stokely a son & Permelia a daughter) to Abraham Landers of same county. 1 Mar 1843.

ii 81 Robert J. Browning of Lincoln Co., Tenn., to John C. Smith of CC to receive of Mother Frances Browning. 7 Aug 1854.

P 203 Robert Bruice of Sumner Co., Tenn., to William S. Webb of CC to receive legacy left by father-in-law John Cochran Sen. decd as seen in his will. 5 Feb 1808.

CC 86 William Chilton of Pittsylvania Co., Va., to Daniel Price to receive from estate of Obediah & Elizabeth Holloway decd. 2 July 1835. Wit: Matt Wilson, Robt. Rowland.

CC 451 Henry M. Clay of Lumpkin Co. Ga., to friend Alexander Henderson of Rockingham Co., NC, to transact business in NC & Va. and sell property in Milton. 5 Mar 1835. Wit: R. W. Thomas. Proved on oath of Samuel Watkins.

GG 303 Edward Morton, John M. Morton, Elizabeth L. A. Morton, Berry Clayton and wife Milly, and Haney Morton to Lewis L. Morton to transact business relative to estate of the late Anderson Morton in CC which was willed by him to his wife Letha for her life, then to children of Wm. Morton. 1845. Proved Person Co., NC. Wit: Y. Jones.

Power of attorney from deed books - Book no. & page precede item - CC=Caswell Co.

R 338 John Cochran of Robertson Co., Tenn., to friend Thomas Gunn of Logan Co. Ky., to receive from Thomas Turner of CC exec of Cochran's father's estate. 10 Aug 1813.

AA 392 Richard S. Cole and wife Mary D. Cole formerly Mary D. Foulkes of Robertson Co., Tenn., to John C. Richards of CC to sell land from estate of William Moore decd that descended to Mary from will of William Moore. 14 Feb 1832.

AA 235 Jesse Sergent Andrew Cowan and Mary his wife late Mary Sergent, William Sergent, Isaac Sergent, and Samuel Sergent all of Russell Co., Va., children of Elizabeth Sergent decd a sister of David Hodge decd of CC to brother David Sergent of Russell Co. to recover from estate of David Hodge. 9 Feb 1832.

EE 331 John H. Crisp and Mary K. Crisp formerly Mary K. Smith of Marshall Co. Miss., to John Wilson of CC to sell land on Hyco Creek that descended to them as heirs of Samuel Smith decd, the piece where Smith resided. 15 June 1838.

HH 616 David S. Creedle and Elizabeth Creedle of Walker Co., Texas, to Walter Murray of Walker Co. to receive from Clerk & Master of CC money from estate of James Walker decd. 12 Oct 1853. (Name may be Cradle).

GG 227 John F. Darby of St. Louis, Mo., to Nathaniel M. Roan of Yanceyville, CC, to receive from exec and adm of late grandmother Mrs. Jane McDaniel of CC and from grandfather William McDaniel. 27 Mar 1844.

GG 617 John H. Darby; Elizabeth Lewis and husband Morton Lewis(late E. Darby);Hiram D. Louvinia Collins widow of John M. Collins(late Louvinia Darby); William S. Holloway and Andrew J. Holloway - all of St. Louis, Mo., to Dr. N. M. Roan to recover from estate of grandfather William McDaniel. Elizabeth, John H., Hiram, and Louvinia children of Elizabeth Darby wife of John Darby, Elizabeth formerly Elizabeth McDaniel Wm. & Andrew Holloway heirs of Mary Ann Holloway(late Darby) decd widow of Wm. Holloway decd. 30 Oct 1846.

GG 830 William M. Darby of Attala Co., Miss., to Dr. N. M. Roan to recover from estate of William McDaniel. 3 Jan 1848.

A 306 Isaac Denton of CC to Henry Williams to execute deed to Greenwood Payne for land on Country Line Creek adj Thos Hart, John Jones, John Lay. 23 Sept. 1779.

CC 32 John S. Dickey and Sally Y. Dickey wife of Monroe Co., Mo., to David Dickey of Orange Co. NC to recover from estate of Nancy Yancey decd ot CC what was willed to Sally Y. Dickey then Sally Y. Rice ($200) money to be put in hands of Bartlett Yancey. 17 Apr 1834.

AA 323 Archibald Dobbin of Henderson Co., Tenn., to John Comer of CC to sell land, ½ of 137 acres on Reedy Fork Creek, CC, land devised by father John Dobbin decd. 1 Mar 1832.

GG 908 John A. Elmore of Lincoln Co., Mo., to wife Ann Elisa Elmore to settle with Gen. William Lea adm of Henry Roper decd and to receive all monies in right of his wife. 14 Aug 1848.

HH 119 James R. Eskridge of Weakley Co., Tenn., guardian for Nancy and Benjamin J. Eskridge, to Caleb Richmond of CC to demand for said minors of Benjamin F. Standfield of CC all monies due from estate of Bird Eskridge. 5 Mar 1849.

EE 265 George Farley of Halifax Co. Va., to N. J. Palmer of CC in case of Farley as trustee of G. W. Johnson & Co., Beneficiary and John H. Crockett. 28 Sept. 1837.

HH 457 John Farmer guardian for Mary G., ? Yarbrough?, Thomas E. Evans and Elizabeth Evans of Logan Co., Ky., to J. N. Montgomery of CC to receive from estate of Allen Gunn of CC. 18 May 1852.

EE 50 Samuel C. Fielder and wife Elizabeth Fielder of Pike Co., Mo., to Jacob Henderson of CC to receive from exec ot Thomas Harrelson late of CC money due wife formerly Elizabeth Henderson and granddaughter of said Thomas Harrelson. 11 Oct 1837.

ii 610 Agness Ferguson of Pittsylvania Co., Va., to Joseph Totton, Samuel S. Harrison & Daniel Everett to receive from will of John Everett who died 1858. 13 July 1858. Wit: John Kerr.

Power of attorney from deed books - Book no. & page precede item - CC = Caswell Co.

ii 613 A. C. Finley and Ann E. Finley of Clarksville, Mecklenburg Co., Va., to Weldon E. Williamson of CC to receive from estate of George Williamson and from sale of land of Thomas L. Williamson of CC. 8 Nov 1858.

HH 472 Robert T. Fuller of CC to John N. Fuller of CC to receive money from sale of land of James N. Fuller decd of CC now in hands of Clerk & Master. 7 Sept. 1852.

ii 80 George Garrison and wife Fanny, Amsey(or Amze) Boswell and wife Martha to George Herndon for sale of land of Edward Herndon decd. 10 Nov 1854.

B 429 John Goldson of CC to Josiah Cole of CC to execute deed unto Joseph Goldson for 250 acres land on waters of Cain Creek adj Goodloe Warren, Josiah Cole and the province line. 21 Nov 1783. Wit: James Fletcher, Thos Tunks, Woolsey Pride. /s/ John Golson. (Spelled Gholson in index).

FF 47 Mary Guill of Wilson Co., Tenn., to Lemuel Wright of same county and state to demand from Jas E. Williamson exec of George Shelton decd for legacy bequeathed by Shelton to children of Henry Rice's wife Margaret formerly Margaret Shelton a sister of George Shelton. Margaret Rice also decd. Oct 1840.

FF 46 Sarah Rice of Henry Co., Tenn., daughter of Henry Rice decd to Hosea McNeill of CC to recover from estate of George Shelton. 10 Aug 1838.

BB 349 William Gooch of Madison Co., Tenn., to James Rice of Logan Co., KY, to recover of Francis Gooch and Howell Boswell exec of father William Gooch decd of CC legacy due from the estate. 5 Feb 1834. Acknowledged by Wm. Seal, Clerk, Robertson Co., TN.

CC 8 Lewis Graves of Morgan Co., Ga., to Thomas W. Graves of CC to sell lands,374 acres, in CC on Hyco Creek adj Elijah Graves & John Wiley. 19 July 1826. Wit: Azariah Graves, Paul A. Haralson.

CC 70 Whereas George Farley executed to B. Graves Jun. deed to house and lot in Milton known as Milton Hotel, a number of negroes, and land near Milton for security to Rebecca Williams - therefore Barzillai Graves of Newton Co., Ga., gives power of attorney to Thomas D. Connally of CC to sell land conveyed in deed of trust. 1 Dec 1834. Wit: N. B. Knight, W. B. Womack.

EE 320 Iverson L., Barzillai, Solomon, and John L. Graves exec of Solomon Graves late of Newton Co., Ga., to John Kerr Jr. of CC to deliver to Matthew Dodson title to tract of land in CC now in possession of Dodson and executed formerly to Richard H. Griffith. 3 Jan 1838.

GG 614 George W. Graves of Walton Co., Ga., to Green W. Brown of NC to grant title to land in CC adj William Woods, James Terrell, et al, 1100 acres on S Hyco and such property conveyed by deed of trust from Samuel Mitchell for use of Elijah Graves Sen. and Nicholas Thompson. 6 July 1840.

HH 304 William B. Graves and wife Eliza A. Graves of Macon Co., NC, to Robert H. Hester of Person Co. to transact all business. 18 Sept 1849.

HH 393 William P. Gunn of Carroll Co., Miss., to Allen Gunn to receive from estate of Allen Gunn decd. 28 Jan 1852.

ii 129 Thomas W. Graves and Mary his wife, Jeremiah Graves, Hosea McNeill and wife Ibby formerly Ibby Graves, all of CC, to James B. Thornton of Memphis, Tenn., to collect from estate of William R. Lipscomb decd of county Poinsett, Ark., they being next of kin to Lipscomb. 4 May 1855.

CC 454 Sarah, Hiram, John, Warren, Thomas, George Holcomb; and Reubin P. Owen and wife Martha, to Allen Holcomb to convey lands in CC belonging to George Holcomb decd allotted to heirs and to widow Sarah Holcomb. 8 Nov 1836. Test: John Kerr Jun.

DD 5 Thomas H. Henderson and John Henderson of Randolph Co., Mo., to father Jacob Henderson of CC to receive from exec or adm of Thomas Harrelson decd of CC monies due them as heirs of decd through their mother Frances Henderson late Harrelson. 29 Aug 1836.

Power of attorney from deed books - Book no. & page precede item - CC = Caswell Co.

DD 347 Samuel Henderson of Pike Co., Mo., to son Hiram Henderson of CC to receive from last will of Joseph Henderson decd of CC. 22 Mar 1837.

ii 362 Chesley Starks and wife Uphsania, Micajah Hensley and wife Nancy - all of Green Co., Mo., to Samuel Davis of CC to receive from estate of James J. Harrison decd to CC. Nov 1856.

FF 595 Joseph A. Herring to Richard Yarbrough to sell lands of James A. H. Herring. 11 Feb 1842.

HH 59 William Hightower late of CC now of Rockingham Co., NC, on way to Mo. to father Devereau Hightower to sell 209 acres land in CC adj Thomas Smith, Thomas Brown, et al 21 Sept 1849.

BB 214 John Hodge of Pulaski Co., KY, to Thomas Bastin of same county to receive from estate of David Hodge decd of CC. David Hodge of CC departed this life without children and his brother Isaac Hodge was lawful heir. Isaac Hodge was father to John Hodge. 31 Aug 1833.

HH 563 Henderson House and wife Ann C. House formerly Ann C. Oliver, of DeSoto Co., Miss., to friend John G. Oliver of CC to receive from William W. Oliver adm of Durret Oliver decd of CC. 24 Sept 1853.

HH 648 Henry W. Hundley of Franklin Co., Mo., to Elisha Hundley of Charlotte Co., Va. to collect of Zachariah L. Hooper adm of Nancy Bracken formerly Nancy Hooper decd of CC. 30 Mar 1854.

BB 351 William Upton, Drury Mathis, and James Jackson of Randolph Co., Mo., to Joseph Dameron of CC to sell rights to 50 acres land belonging to Vines Mathis decd assigned to his widow Ann M. Mathis as dower and relinquished by widow as a gift. 22 May 1832.

EE 314 Jones M. Gunn of Lowndes Co., Ala., son and legatee of Griffin Gunn, to N. H. McCain of CC to receive from legacy. The will of Griffin Gunn devised to wife Dorothy M. Gunn land and negroes and at her death to be divided to children. 17 Aug 1839.

GG 906 Benjamin Jones guardian of Sally Ann and Rachel Catherine Jones of St. Charles Co., Mo., to William Jones of same county to demand and recover from William Lea of CC. March 1848.

ii 557 Albert G. Yancey and wife Mary, Yancey Jones and wife Martha, to John A. Graves to collect from Clerk and Master of CC monies from real estate belonging to heirs of Delila Miles decd of CC. 6 May 1858.

X 40 Elizabeth Kimbro of Rutherford Co., Tenn., to Nathan Williams Esq. of CC to receive from estate of William Gooch Sen. 23 June 1819.

Z 249 Jesse Kirk and Frances Kirk his wife of Grayson Co., KY, to brother John Gray of Sumner Co., Tenn., to convey title to 300 acres land in CC the same land on which John Gray resided at his death said Frances being one of his heirs and to get 1/5 part. 24 Aug 1830.

S 104 Alexander Lackey and William Lackey of Orange Co., NC, heirs and legatees of John Lackey decd of said county, each devised 1/8 part of land on Stony Creek adj Nicholas Harden with widow Elizabeth Lackey having life interest in same, to John Mitchell of CC to sell lands. 12 Nov 1816.

Q 301 Jesse Lay Senr. of Campbell Co., Tenn., to friend Baxter Cox Esq. of same county to receive any legacy in State of NC. 5 June 1810.

A 504 William Lea of CC to Herndon Harralson to sign, seal, and exhibit unto Anderson Ashburn deed to tract of land in CC on waters of H. Hyco adj George Huston, Timothy Burgess, Thomas Kilgore, William Sargent, Thomas Langley, James Johnston, and John Cooper. 7 Oct 1780.

CC 245 Tinsley Lea of Maury Co., Tenn., to brother Alfred M. Lea of CC to receive from last will of his decd father James Lea of CC. 12 Oct 1835.

Power of attorney from deed books - Book no. & Page precede item - CC = Caswell Co.

EE 329 Alfred M. Lea of Marshall Co., Miss., to Henry Allen Esq. of same county now going to NC to sell lands adj Richard J. Smith, Geo Williamson, et al on Country Line Creek, 427 acres. 6 June 1839.

GG 73 Lewis Malone of Marshall Co., Miss., to James Malone of CC to receive from Wm. Lea exec of estate of Gabriel Lea decd the part alloted to widow the late Elizabeth Lea during her life - Lewis Malone being a child of Elizabeth Malone decd a legatee of Gabriel Lea. 29 May 1843.

GG 851 Elizabeth Lenox adm of estate of John Lenox decd of Weakly Co., Tenn., to John Epperson of CC to collect monies due from Edward Robertson decd and Thomas Jeffreys decd. 15 Nov 1847.

T 327 James Ridley, Abraham G. Keen, Joshua Mabry, Joseph Lewis, Charles Willson, Wm. McKissack, and Woodson Daniel to Philip H. Inge and Stephen Dodson of Milton to execute deeds to anyone purchasing lots and land near town of Milton beginning at State line at corner of Jeffreys Mill tract then to Country Line Creek as it meanders to Wm. Moultrie's acre lot near the bridge then to George Conley's line. 22 Oct 1818.

V 117 Thomas Longwell (or Langwell) and Anna his wife late Anna Bastin, Temperance Newell late Temperance Bastin, Godfrey Young and Tabitha his wife late Bastin, all daughters of William Bastin decd one of the heirs of Thomas Bastin decd, all of Pulaski Co., KY, to John Newell of same county to sell lands of Thomas Bastin in CC on Little Wolf Island Creek. 15 Nov 1818.

X 87 John Langley of Gwinnett Co., Ga., to John Wiley of CC to sell land in CC. 4 Dec 1824. Wit: Joseph Langley, Wm. Anderson.

DD 319 JRE Lipscomb guardian of Martha E. Lipscomb of Fayette Co., Tenn., to brother-in-law Jeremiah Graves of CC to receive from estate of father-in-law Thomas Haralson decd and from estate of Martha Haralson decd. 2 Oct 1837. (or Harrelson)

DD 312 Elijah Martin of Marshall Co., Tenn., to friend Alexander B. Morton of Williamson Co., Tenn., to receive money due from father-in-law William Cantrill decd of CC. 6 Apr 1837. Wit: William Anthony, Joseph Anthony.

EE 524 John Massey to James Brown of Carroll Co., Tenn., to sell land in CC and to collect from estate of Thomas Massey. 6 Mar 1840.

S 176 Anderson Middlebrooks of Morgan Co., Ga., to brother Zeri Middlebrooks of Newberry Dist., SC, to receive balance of legacy left by grandfather Robert Lyon of CC. 2 Feb 1817.

EE 179 James Matlock about to move to State of Missouri from CC to friend and former neighbor Thomas L. Lea of CC to sell 152 acres land adj William Holcomb, Tho Pass, and to transact all business. 8 Oct 1838.

H 123 Edward Maxwell of CC to friend Archibald Murphey Esq. to collect money in NC due by bond and to sell land, 400 acres, on Reedy Fork and North Hico to Joseph Moore of State of Virginia. 11 Nov 1782.

Q 3 John Middlebrooks and Anderson Middlebrooks of Hancock Co., Ga., to Zeri Middlebrooks of same county to demand from estate of Robert Lyon decd of CC. 14 Dec 1804.

EE 92 Jennett Montgomery of Randolph Co., Mo., to Michael Gunn to sell lands in NC and to settle all business, said land came as dower. 14 Aug 1838.

ii 247 A. D. Montgomery of Abbeville Dist., SC, to J. N. Montgomery of CC to convey land in CC adj Mrs. Agnes Jeffreys and known as the parsonage of the red house church. 28 Jan 1853.

ii 98 Nancy Moore, Asa Moore, James L. Moore, John W. Moore, Lorenzo D. Ragland, William J.(or I) Ragland, Sarah J. Moore, and Joel Moore of Halifax Co., Va., to Epps Moore of CC to receive from will of B. Moore of CC who bequeathed slaves and property to James Moore who is decd and those named are next of kin. 15 Dec 1854.

Power of attorney from deed books - Book no. & page precede item - CC = Caswell Co.

ii 38 James Morris and Eliza Ann his wife of Green Co., Mo., to Thomas Bigelow of CC to recover money from William Barnwell exec of estate of Mary Parks decd of CC devise by her last will and to collect from estate of David A. Barnwell decd of CC from William H. Barnwell adm. 21 Aug 1854.

HH 570 Polly T. Mullins formerly wife of Robert Mullins decd of DeSoto Co., Miss., to William P. Womack of same County to secure from B. H. Carter adm of Ben Carter decd of CC and to sell lands in CC. 9 Sept 1853. Wit: John A. Perkins.

EE 201 William A. Muzzall of CC to John Q. A. Hightower of CC to demand money due wife Sarah from estate of her former husband William Anderson. 11 Nov 1838. /s/ Wm. A. & Sally Muzzall. Test: Epophroditus Jackson.

GG 918 William A. and Sally Muzzall of Henry Co. Tenn., to William S. Hightower to demand and receive from James Currie Esq. a negro boy Dick which descended to them from Catherine Hightower decd of CC and to recover other articles from said decd. 7 Sept 1848.

DD 120 J. H. McGehee to Mother Mrs. Martha McGehee to attend to all business in NC an in Va. 24 Oct 1833 at Milton, NC.

FF 891 John Nelson and Barzillai Nelson of Giles Co. Tenn., to Thomas W. Owen of CC to collect money due from estate of Jas Nelson now in hands of exec. 5 Jan1843.

GG 922 Regin R. Offutt and wife of Johnson Co., Mo., to Thomas J. Reid of CC to sell lands in CC bequeathed to Milly Offutt(formerly Milly Simpson) by her father James Simpson. 29 Jan 1847. Approved by Circiut Judge John T. Ryland of Lafayette Co. Mo.

ii 674 Josiah Page of Weakley Co., Tenn., to Thomas W. Graves of CC to receive from last will of Thomas Page decd of CC. 9 Mar 1859.

ii 790 John Crook and Martha D. Crook his wife, John Parks and Sarah F. Parks his wife, and William Thomas of Audrain Co., Mo., to Daniel C. Thomas of same county to sell property in CC. 18 Apr 1859. Approved in Holt Co., Mo.

DD 311 Joseph Anthony of Giles Co., Tenn., to Alexander B. Morton of Williamson Co., Tenn., to receive money in CC from estate of father-in-law William Cantrill decd of CC. 6 Apr 1837.

ii 677 William C. Paxton and Harriette his wife to Alen Gunn MD of CC to receive from Clerk and Master of CC portions of sales of real estate of the late James Burton of CC and from his widow the late Sally Burton. 14 Apr 1859.

CC 11 Thomas Pinson of Carroll Co., Tenn., to Robert A. Brown of CC to recover from John Smith of CC. 6 Jan 1833.

ii 553 John Poteat and wife Elizabeth of CC to William Y. Hooper to sell lot of land in city of Richmond (Va.). 11 May 1858.

A 112 William Prowell of CC to Alexander Miles of CC to execute lawful deed to David Shelton Esq. for tract of land in CC on waters of Country Line and Rattlesnake Creeks 640 acres, after a proper grant is received for same. 2 Mar 1779. Wit: A. Tatom, Charles Taylor.

CC 453 John Ragland of Lumpkin Co., Ga., to Alexander Henderson of Rockingham Co., NC to sell property in Milton, the house and lot on Main St. where "I formerly lived", the half of house and lot on Liberty St. co-owned with Azel Samuel known by name of the red house, and lot number 25 near Liberty Warehouse, also 12 shares of Milton toll bridge stock. 20 Mar 1835.

EE 215 William Roscoe and wife Airest Roscoe of CC to Thomas Bigelow of CC to recover legacy coming from estate of William Pleasant Senr. decd. 17 July 1837. (Rascoe?)

EE 317 Martha Rascow formerly Martha Pleasant of White Co., Tenn., to husband John Rascow of same county to demand from James Pleasant adm of estate of her decd father William Pleasant of CC. 13 Aug 1839.

Power of attorney from deed books - Book no. & Page precede item. CC = Caswell Co.

EE 318 Joseph D. Reynolds and Elizabeth M. Reynolds his wife of Jefferson Co, KY, to Wm. Henderson of Orange Co., Va., to receive from adm of Joseph Henderson decd of CC. 23 May 1829.

M 5 Zeri Rice of Abbeville Co., SC, to Lancelot Johnston of CC to make unto Thomas Blackwell of CC a deed for land on south side Country Line Creek, land willed to Zeri Rice by Thomas Rice decd. 24 Sept. 1800. Wit: Jethro Brown, John H. Brown.

X 88 John Brown of Maury Co., Tenn., to brother William V. Brown to sell land on Tom's Creek in CC adj Jeremiah Lea and Jerry Maughan to Freeman Leath and to pay over money from land to Col. Will Polk of Wake Co., NC, for use of James Walker of Maury Co. 13 May 1825.

GG 86 Julia M. Reid daughter of James Reid decd of St. Louis, Mo., to uncle Alexander Reid to receive from estate of John Gamble decd late of Milton,NC. 13 Sept 1847.

GG 837 Samuel Reid of St. Louis, Mo., to Alexander Reid of Jackson Co., Iowa, to collect from estate of John Gamble of CC. 29 May 1848.

GG 841 Samuel Reid of St. Louis to Alexander Reid to sell land of John Gamble in CC. 28 Feb 1848.

GG 956 John Reid of Jo Daviess Co., Ill., to Alexander Reid of Iowa. 6 Jan 1846.

BB 345 Frances Rice of Logan Co., KY, to James Rice(my son) to collect from estate of William Gooch decd of CC. 3 Feb 1834.

BB 347 Francis Rice and Mary Rice his wife formerly Mary Gooch of Logan Co., KY, to Howell Boswell of CC to sell tract of land in CC on S. Country Line Creek it being tract of land on which William Gooch formerly lived, part of land fell to his daughter Mary. 22 Nov 1833.

ii 353 John W. Rice and Jane E. Rice his wife of CC to J. N. Montgomery of CC to receive from sale of land of Samuel Page decd. 29 Dec 1856.

BB 243 Warren C. and Lucy W. Richmond of Robertson Co., Tenn., to Archibald D. Richmond of CC (or to John C. Richards) to sell land adj John C. Richards, Hamilton et al, it being sixth part of lands of William Moore decd and bequeathed to his daughter Lucy W., including the tanyard owned by D. William Moore. 15 Feb 1833.

BB 412 Robert D. Richmond and Mary S. his wife of Robertson Co., Tenn., to John C. Richards of CC to sell land on Country Line Creek near Milton, it being ½ of sixth part of land of William Moore decd and bequeathed to granddaughter Mary S. Richmond. 11 Nov 1833.

ii 535 J. A. Richmond of Titus Co., Texas, to Franklin Warren of CC to receive from estate of father Adams S. Richmond. 5 Jan 1858.

ii 592 Thomas J. Richmond of CC to Dr. Stephen T. Richmond to take charge of land and property. 5 Oct 1858.

DD 50 Edward M. Richards of CC to John C. Richards to sell 2 lots in Milton adj Stephen Dodson and to sell land on Country Line Creek adj State line and Joseph McGehee. 3 Apr 1835.

C 85 Tunstal Roan of Wilkes Co., Ga., to loving friend Thomas Phelps of CC to discharge all business. 10 Nov 1783.

ii 486 James Roberts of Gwinnett Co., Ga., and his wife the daughter of Abner Wisdom of CC now decd to Abner R. Roberts of Gwinnett Co. to settle estate of Abner Wisdom. 14 Sept 1857.

ii 128 Sally S. Robertson of CC, adm of George Robertson decd, to Joab Robertson to receive money owing to estate of George Robertson and to collect all bills. 3 July 1855.

GG 831 John E. Roper of Cole Co., Mo., to Thomas C. Pass of CC to receive from estate of decd father Henry Roper of CC. 17 May 1847.

189

Power of attorney from deed books - Book no. & page precede item. CC = Caswell Co.

N 107 Aldridge Rudd of CC to son William Rudd of CC to recover money due in Chester-field Co., Va., and to sell land in Chesterfield and Buckingham Counties, Va. 28 Nov 1803. Wit: Robert Martin, Charles Turner, Polly Rudd.

CC 452 Zac (or Zoe?) Samuel of Lumpkin Co., Ga., to Alexander Henderson of Rocking-ham Co., NC to transact business and to sell lot in town of Milton, and to receive from David Montgomery $150 for tract of land sold him where "my father lived and died 9 Mar 1835. Wit: Henry M. Clay.

ii 150 Leroy Saunders and wife Mary Saunders, James Combs and wife Susan Combs of CC to Robert H. Watt to receive from Thos A. Donoho, Clerk and Master of CC, all money from estate of Aron Saunders decd who was father of Mary Saunders and Susan Combs. 6 Nov 1855.

ii 619 Elisha Sartin and wife Frances of CC to Elisha Paschal of CC to receive from Clerk and Master from sale of land of E. Paschal. 17 Nov 1858.

R 66 Job Siddall of CC about to remove to Tenn. to Thomas Donoho to sell tract of land in CC on Rattlesnake Creek adj James Montgomery, & widow Morton. 24 Oct 1812.

S 171 John Jeffries of Culpepper Co., Va., to Meredith Jeffries of same county (as guardian for my 2 children) to receive legacy left them by John Hudnall of CC. 26 Feb 1818.

C 57 Richard Simpson, Planter, of CC to John Reid late of Washington Co., Va., to recover from all persons indebted to Simpson. 12 Jan 1785. Wit: Tyree Harris Junr.

S 244 Levi Simpson of Madison Co., KY, to Hezekiah Boswell of CC to make deed to Jethro Brown for 1/3 part of tract of land in CC on Horsley's Creek, 307 acres, tract on which James Simpson lived. 3 Sept. 1817.

GG 840 Enoch Simpson to James C. Ventress to receive from Frances L. Simpson and Joseph Simpson his part of estate of Aron Simpson decd of CC. 23 May 1848. Approved at Sumner Co., Tenn.

iii 751 Nancy E. Singleton and Elizabeth A. Singleton children of Robert Singleton decd of CC to William A. Singleton of Macon Co., Mo., to dispose of real estate in Carroll Co., Mo., land granted to Robert Singleton warrant #2649, Feb 22, 1816. 10 Dec 1859.

FF 482 Thomas L. Slade of CC to Franklin H. Burton to preform duty involved by deed of trust by Henry A. Burton of Danville, Va., for benefit of John Cobb and Nathan Slade. 11 Dec 1841.

S 249 Samuel H. Smith and John Smith exec of will of Samuel Smith decd of CC to James W. Smith of Jackson Co., Tenn., to receive from legacy in Tenn. 11 Oct 1818.

CC 10 Henderson Smith of Carroll Co., Tenn., to Jonathan Moore of same county to receive money due on acct of William Smith decd as one of heirs at law of said Smith, amount due me by wife Mary E. Smith an heir of Stephen Chandler decd. John Smith exec of William Smith decd of CC; Thomas W. Graves guardian to heirs of Stephen Chandler. 19 July 1834.

CC 167 Joseph McUlloch (McCulloch) and Nancy his wife, William Smith Jun. and Elizabeth his wife of Clay Co., Mo., heirs of estate of William Walker decd of CC, to Deborah Walker widow of William Walker of CC to sell lands and settle estate. 14 July 1831.

EE 370 Samuel H. Smith exec of Samuel Smith decd of CC to Richard J. Smith of CC to transfer and sell stock in Roanoke Navigation Co. 17 Sept. 1839.

EE 371 Richard J. Smith agent of Saml. H. Smith exec of Samuel Smith decd to Thomas McGhee(McGehee) of Person Co., NC, to transfer stock in Roanoke Navigation Co. Apr 18

FF 229 William T. Smith to Nathaniel J. Palmer to collect from Richard Yarbrough adm of estate of William Smith decd father of William T. Smith. 10 Oct 1841.

Power of attorney from deed books - Book no. & page precede item. CC = Caswell Co.

HH 17 Sexton Smith and wife Martha of Pittsylvania Co., Va., to William W. Price of CC to receive from James M. Fuller, Clerk & Master for CC, legacy of Joseph Bracken decd. Sept 1849.

ii 115 Elijah R. Smith and wife Frances Smith to Sam H. Smith to sell property of heirs at law of John Thomas decd, Frances Smith one of children of Nelson Thomas. 8 May 1855.

ii 730 Ransford (or Ramford) Smith adm of Catherine G. Smith to Rufus Y. McAden of CC to receive from estate of Elijah Graves decd the part due Catherine G. Smith. 8 July 1858. Given from Lyon Co., KY.

Q 445 Alston Solomon, John Clift, James Price, and John Gibson, all of Bedford Co., Tenn., legatees of Elizabeth Browning decd, a legatee of Edmund Browning decd, to George Browning of same county to recover legacy in NC. 22 Oct 1811.

ii 741 Phary Summers and Eliza Summers of Henry Co., Tenn., his wife formerly Eliza Paschal a daughter and heir of Ezekiel Paschal decd of CC to John Summers Senr. of CC to receive from estate of Ezekiel Paschal. 5 Aug 1859.

P 127 Thomas Spencer of Williamson Co., Tenn., to trusty friend John Spencer of same county and to John Penix of CC to recover legacy of William Mitchell decd of CC in right of wife Mary, payable by John Henslee and John Mitchell exec. 30 Sept. 1806.

R 271 William Stafford of Jackson Co., Tenn., to brother John Stafford of same county to receipt for legacy from father Laban Stafford decd. 18 Sept 1815.

DD 158 Abraham Starkey of Montgomery Co., Tenn., to Thomas Starkey of CC to receive from estate of Jonathan Starkey decd. 5 Aug 1836.

ii 45 William Stanfield and wife Mary A. Stanfield of CC to J. N. Montgomery to receive account of sales of land of John Gamble decd. 10 Nov 1854.

Q 61 George Stephens of CC to Durrett Richards of same county to divide tract of land between Samuel Stephens the heir of Boler Stephens, Anthony Stephens, and myself, said tract Anthony Stephens now lives on. 26 Dec 1809.

S 242 John Stephens of Robertson Co., Tenn., to Thomas Fisher of same county to sell 239 acres land in CC on Dan River adj Bluford Reid and James Medlock (Matlock?), land left him by father Bowler Stephens. 11 Mar 1818.

Q 398 John T. Street of Williamson Co., Tenn., to Zephaniah Tait to collect of ratible part of estate now in hands of Ann Vincent. 15 Feb 1812.

U 204 Joseph Swann and Elizabeth Swann his wife of Robertson Co., Tenn., to Thomas Walker of CC to sell lands in CC. 8 June 1822.

HH 541 Paul Terrell of CC to Levi Walker of Hinds Co., Miss., to bring suit for property left in last will of Jonathan Terrell decd. 4 July 1853.

FF 81 Richard W. Thomas of Hinds Co., Miss., to N. J. Palmer of CC to make deed to land in CC near Milton adj Willis Buckingham, James Taylor, Elijah Graves, Mrs. Smith, et al, the land which father John Thomas Esq. decd purchased of John Pass. 26 Apr 1840.

HH 106 William Thomas and Philip H. Thomas of Dallas Co., Ark., to William T. Walters of Pittsylvania Co, Va., to recover from estate of Archibald Walters decd. 26 May 1849.

HH 590 William Thomas and Hannah S. Thomas of Calhoun Co., Ark., to Nathaniel L. Graves of Quachita Co., Ark., to demand from estate of Mrs. Hannah Lea decd of CC. 13 June 1853.

ii 381 Philip H. Thomas guardian of Junius F. Thomas to Price N. Thomas of CC to receive from estate of Nathaniel Thomas decd. 12 Mar 1857.

ii 747 John W. Thompson and wife Mary Ann Thompson of Hempstead Co., Ark., to G. J. Farish of CC to recover from estate of James Hubbard decd of CC now in hands of A. D. Hubbard adm. Mary Thompson if daughter of James Hubbard. 16 Aug 1859.

Power of attorney from deed books - Book no. & Page precede item. CC = Caswell Co.

R 336 Nancy Turner of Wayne Co., KY, to William Gunn of same county to receive legacy from estate of Henry Turner decd of CC her grandfather. 15 Feb 1815.

A 318 Lawrence Vanhook of CC to loving son Loyd Vanhook and to friend John Atkinson to attend to all business. 3 Sept 1779. Wit: William Graves, William Stanfield.

CC 55 Isaac D. Vanhook and Elizabeth his wife of Maury Co., Tenn., to Samuel Johnston of Person Co., NC, to settle estate of her decd father John McMullen of CC. 20 Nov 18

CC 287 Thomas Vaughan of Fayette Co., Tenn., to Sterling F. Vaughan of Person Co., NC to sell land in CC adj Jno Williams, James Lea, et al and known as Mrs. Farley's old place. Thomas Vaughan purchased same at adm sale. 14 Apr 1834.

CC 386 Richard Vaughan Senr. of Halifax Co., Va., to Thomas Bigelow of CC to recover legacy of estate of Thomas Vaughan Sen. decd of CC. 30 Mar 1835. Wit: Jno. Buchanon

EE 179 Richard Vaughan of Halifax Co., Va., to Major Paul A. Haralson of Yanceyville to recover from adm and will of Thomas Vaughan Senr. decd any legacy due in right of son Richard Vaughan Jr. who left this country many years age and is presumed dead. 5 Apr 1839. Wit: Joseph Crowder, C. Graves.

Y 69 Robert Ware of CC to friend James Robertson of CC to sell land on Dobbins Creek and to attend to all business. 27 Nov 1828.

DD 409 John Ware and Polly Ware his wife of Pike Co., Mo., to Allen Holcomb of CC to convey deed to property formerly owned by the late George Holcomb of CC and to deliver to Warren Holcomb of CC deed to part of land and to Robert Harrison a deed for land. 8 Aug 1837.

FF 326 Samuel Henderson and John Ware Jun. of CC about to set off to Missouri to Thomas Ware. 2 Dec 1840.

EE 200 Lucy Griffin of CC to William Warren to collect her interest in estate of William Pleasant decd of CC. William Warren appoints Thomas Bigelow his attorney to demand of James Pleasant adm. 9 Nov 1837.

HH 542 Benjamin Warren of Borough of Easton in Northhampton Co., Pa., to father Chapman Warren of same Borough to arrange with Bels Comstock of Saybrook, Conn., (formerly engaged in foundry business in Easton) for property settlement. 25 July 1853.

U 116 Elizabeth T. Worsham, Isaac West, Thomas & Jance C. Collan, James & Sarah Welsh, Dorothy C. West, Benjamin S. West, Abraham & Martha Nelson, Ira E. West, Thomas J. West, and Robert West - all joint heirs of land of estate of Robert West decd - to Mary West their Mother of Iredell Co., NC, to dispose of land as she desires on Little Island Creek. 9 May 1818.

GG 949 Charles L. Williams, Mildred L. Wheatley(formerly Williams), Coleman Williams, Albert G. Wheatley and wife Mary C.(formerly Williams), all heirs at law of Robert C. Williams of Va. to Howell L. Williams to sell lots in Milton, NC. 17 Nov 1848.

EE 116 Henry Willis of CC to George W. Willis to sell land on Country Line Creek in CC adj James Heydon. 14 Nov 1837.

HH 126 Nicholas Willis of Hardeman Co., Tenn., to George W. Willis of CC to settle estate of Henry Willis decd with other executors and to receive legacy bequeathed to him. 9 Mar 1848.

Q 262 John Wiley of CC to friend Ephraim Noel to convey land in CC adj John Ingram, Archy Ingram, Joseph Knight, and John Baxter, 50 acres granted by State to said Wiley. 8 Mar 1811.

DD 195 John W. Wells of Cole Co., Mo., to Thomas S. Price of county and state aforesaid to convey land in CC.; Martha A. Wells his wife to Thomas S. Price to convey land in CC. 24 Oct 1835.

EE 110 Thomas McGehee of Person Co., NC, Agent for Benjamin C. Wyley of Benton Co., Ala., to George A. Smith of Milton, NC, for sale of lots in Milton, nos 6 & 7 on East side of Liberty St. 24 Nov 1838.

Power of attorney from deed books - Book no. & Page precede item. CC = Caswell Co.

ii 487 William Wisdom and Joseph Wisdom of Pontotoc Co., Miss., sons of Bird Wisdom late of Gwinnett Co., Ga., now decd. said Bird a son of Abner Wisdom late of CC, to Abner R. Roberts of county & state aforesaid to receive from estate of Abner Wisdom. 14 Sept. 1857.

U 206 Joseph Richmond of Wilson Co. Tenn., to Silas Tarver of county & state aforesaid to demand of Thomas Connally of Halifax Co., Va., or any exec of George Connally decd my wife's portion of his estate. 18 Oct 1822.

JJ 5 Priscilla Burton and husband Noel Burton of Robertson Co., Tenn., to James Garner of CC to receive from Allen Gunn adm of Allen Gunn decd, - Allen Gunn being full brother of Priscilla Burton. 21 Mar 1860.

JJ 9 Jesse Gant and Minerva his wife of Alamance Co., NC, to John Q. Anderson to collect from lands of Sarah Anderson, Minerva an heir at law. 22 Nov 1859.

JJ 18 Andrew J. Lockard of Pike Co., Ala., to Thomas W. Graves of CC to receive from estate of Hiram Lockard decd of CC in hands of Wm. Fuller adm with will. 25 Jan 1860.

JJ 19 William Holland adm of Leah Barnett decd to Rufus Y. McAden of CC to receive from adm of Elijah Graves decd the portion of his estate due Leah Barnett decd. 24 Apr 1860. Given from Lyon Co. KY.

JJ 57 Nathan Massey and Mary Massey formerly Mary Brown acting for ourselves and for Lucinda, Sareth, George W., Nathaniel, and Gemina Brown all minors under 21 and children of James Brown decd who died in Carroll Co. Tenn., by their regular guardian Nathan Massey, John Brown, Beford Brown, and Martha Powell formerly Martha Brown wife of Joseph Powell of age, and also children of James Brown decd above referred to, to wit: Nathaniel, James, and Nathan Reid, all of Carroll Co. except Joseph Powell and wife of Henry Co., Tenn., - to Nathan Brown of CC to receive from estate of their grandfather Thomas Brown decd of CC. 5 Jan 1860.

JJ 61 William D. Gatewood of CC to Joseph S. Totton to settle with Dr. Wiley Jones and to receive from adm of Thomas L. Gatewood decd. 7 June 1860.

JJ 70 Burton Ford and Cyntha his wife formerly Cyntha Everett of Caldwell Co., KY, to Thos. W. Graves of CC to receive from exec of John Everett decd of CC. 13 Jun 1860.

JJ 72 Kessiah Wilson of CC guardian of Peter, Marth Y., John G., Robt. A., T. J., and George W. Wilson, all children of John Wilson,& Wm. Donoho for wife Huldah child of John Wilson, to Wm. W. Wilson of Ga. to receive from adm of Marth Wilson decd of Ga. 2 July 1860.

JJ 92 John W. Lewis of Halifax Co., Va., to Robert H. Lewis of Milton to manage tobacco factory. 9 Aug 1860.

JJ 105 John W. Owen of Macon Co., NC, to Robert Walton of CC to receive from estate of Mary Owen decd of CC. 26 June 1860.

JJ 115 James Jamieson and Mary L. Jamieson of Pittsylvania Co., Va., to Dr. Allen Gunn of CC to collect for Mary as widow of John Pittard MD of CC and from Mary Pittard decd. 6 Nov 1860.

JJ 125 Green W. Brown and wife Mary Ann Brown of Guilford Co., NC, to Austin Reid of said county to receive any money due Mary Ann as heir of the late Adam Richmond, of CC. 30 Oct 1860.

JJ 136 Westly Hayden of Robertson Co., Tenn., to Thomas W. Evans of CC to receive from exec of John Everett decd money due Wm. E. and Rachel Hayden of Tenn. they being children of Joseph Hayden who married Mildred Everett who was sister to John Everett decd. 18 July 1860.

JJ 162 W. E. Williamson of CC to George Williamson of CC to attend to all business. 6 Nov 1860.

JJ 165 William Smith and wife Elizabeth Ann Smith of Dallas Co., Ark., to Richard J. Smith of CC to receive monies from execution of Nathaniel Lea. 22 Feb 1858.

Power of attorney from deed books - Book no. & page precede item. CC = Caswell Co.

JJ 203 James M. Barton and wife Agness L (or S) Barton to Jesse Griffith of CC
to receive from Clerk & Master. Given from Davie Co., NC. 10 Dec 1860.

JJ 216 William H. Chaney and Elizabeth Chaney his wife of Callaway Co., Mo., to Wm.
Lea to settle with Wm. J. Moore adm of Sarah Holcomb decd of CC and to make deed to
John G. Lea for land formerly owned by Wm. Holcomb decd; also have an interest in
estate of Mary Holcomb decd of CC. 28 Sept. 1860.

JJ 218 Andrew J. Lockard appointed guardian of property of Phebe Lockard minor heir
of Hiram Lockard decd. Pike Co., Ala. 30 Aug 1860.

JJ 220 William Warf and Sarah G. Warf his wife of Hickman Co., Tenn., to John Dameron
of CC to receive from estate of Samuel Dameron decd of CC. 21 Feb 1861.

JJ 282 James B. Kimbrough of Independence Co., Ark., to Aaron Harah? of county aforesaid to receive from Goodwin Evans of CC negroes being portion of estate of William
and Elizabeth Kimbro his wife, due Goodwin Evans as exec. 8 Jan 1862.

JJ 325 Huldah Gunn of CC to R. B. Watt of Rockingham Co. to enter her dissent from
will and testament of her husband the late Jno. Gunn. 30 Mar 1863.

JJ 357 William A. Donoho of CC, now a soldier in army of Confederate States, to
Dr. Allen Gunn to CC to attend to all business and as a partner of late firm of
Hinton & Donoho (James B. Hinton decd.) and to well ½ interest in land on Rattlesnake
Creek. 26 Aug 1863.

JJ 366 Walter J. Jones of CC son of Willie Jones late of CC to sell house and lot in
Milton where father died and mother Priscilla Jones resides to David Patterson of
CC - power given to grandfather Hiram Henderson of CC. Oct 1863.

JJ 397 David Strador and Anna Strador his wife to James Dill to receive from estate
of John Dill decd, Anna an heir at law. 9 May 1864.

JJ 680 R. J. West and Mary F. his wife of CC to James J. Clendennin of CC to receive
from estate of Samuel Hodges decd the father of Mary F. West. 24 Mar 1869.

JJ 743 J. W. Lester and wife Ann Lester of CC to J. Garland Jeffreys of CC to receive
for Ann Lester from estate of Francis Stevens decd. 27 Aug 1869.

KK 32 Jane Simpson widow of Moses Simpson to E. B. Withers to file dissent to last
will of her husband. 25 Feb 1870.

KK 108 James A. McCain and Julia McCain of Chariton Co., Mo., to James L. McKee of
CC to attend to all business. 4 June 1870.

KK 207 Alexander Rudd of Denton Co., Texas, son of Jeremiah Rudd Senr. decd of CC to
Ezekiel Sawyer of CC to receive from estate of Jeremiah Rudd. 8 Apr 1871.

KK 208 Rufus L. Rudd, Cornelia Rudd, and _____ Rudd all of Denton Co., Texas, to
Ezekiel Sawyer to receive from estate of Jeremiah Rudd Senr. through their father
Jeremiah Rudd Jun. decd. /s/ Rufus L. Rudd, Jeremiah Rudd, Ibby Addey Rudd, Cornelia
Rudd. 8 Apr 1871.

KK 277 Sarah A. Estis of Johnson Co., Ark., to John D. Keesee of CC to sell real
estate in CC. 29 Aug 1871.

KK 399 L. L. Chaney of St. Louis, Mo., to Samuel P. Hill of CC to sell real estate
in NC. 5 Aug 1871.

KK 482 P. L. Clayton of Cherokee Co., Texas, (Clayton guardian of minors John M. and
William Stadler heirs and children of James Stadler decd) and R. F. Clayton formerly
R. F. Stadler now wife of P. L. Clayton, to Samuel P. Hill of CC to collect any
monies in CC. 21 July 1873.

KK 627 Leonidas Collins of Titus Co., Texas, guardian of J. LaFayette Collins a
person of unsound mind, to Thomas W. Graves of CC to collect from estate of his
father Brice Collins and his mother Hulda Collins late of CC - also from estate of
Thomas Bigelow decd. 3 Apr 1874.

Power of attorney from deed books - Book no. & page precede item. CC = Caswell Co.

KK 629 Mary M. Carthel (formerly Mary M. Turner), Lucretia Collins and husband Leonydas Collins, Thomas H. Turner, James R. Turner, John L. Turner, and Shadden S. Turner all of Titus Co., Texas, heirs at law under will of Thomas Bigelow decd of CC to Thomas W. Graves of CC to collect from estate of Thos. Bigelow. 18 May 1874.

LL 96 Logan Terrell of Milam Co., Texas, to Franklin L. Warren of CC to take possession of estate and sell land in CC east of Prsopect Hill known as Gordon tract and the Maclin tract on Hico. Property belongs to John C., William, and Logan Terrell. 25 Jan 1875.

LL 138 J. W. Foster of State of Mo. heir of Thomas Foster of CC decd is due 1/7 of his estate; Mary A. Foster died intestate Dec 1875; Nancy Foster sister of J. W. Foster also decd and he due 1/6 part - gives power to J. A. Long Esq. of CC to collect from above estates. 25 Aug 1875. Given from Lincoln Co., Mo.

LL 139 Hiram Henderson and wife Martha H. Henderson of Mo. to J. A. Long of Yanceyville, CC, to demand of Williamson P. Foster and Thos. B. Adkins adm of Thomas Foster decd and from estates of Nancy Foster, Mary Foster decd. 11 Sept. 1875. John H. Kerr, Probate Judge; Geo W. Pinnix, Rigister of Deeds, CC.

LL 170 F. A. Hill, Julia A. Graves and her husband John H. Graves of Milam Co., Texas, heirs at law of Samuel P. Hill decd of CC to A. E. Henderson of CC to demand from George Williamson adm of S. P. Hill decd. 19 Aug 1875.

LL 174 Samuel F. Hayden(guardian for Ada J., Virginia, Catharine, Thomas F. Hayden); Julia A. Yount late Hayden and her husband John Q.- all of Madison Co., Ark., to John H. Simpson of CC to receive from estate of Abraham Simmons decd. 2 Oct 1875.

LL 246 John W. Williamson and wife Virginia, James A. Williamson and wife Lelia, Aaron G. Headon and wife Eudora, George A. Graves and wife Isabella, George O. Williamson and wife Martha, Peter H. Williamson and wife Bettie - all of CC to George N. Thompson of Leasburg, CC, to sell land in Person Co., NC, devised to them by John W. Williams late of Person Co. as heirs at law of Susan Williamson wife of James A. Williamson decd of CC. 16 Dec 1875.

LL 305 Saunders H. Rasco guardian of his children Ede Caroline, William Franklin, Sarah Frances, John Andrew, Maggie Adeline, Andrew Martin, Iseba Stone, and George Washington Rasco, heirs of Arthur Rasco decd of CC to William H. Huges. 23 Feb 1876. Given from Nodoway Co., Mo.

LL 316 Julia L. Cooper and husband Alonza Cooper, Mary Lee Howell and husband S. J. Howell, Fannie P. Green, all of Grimes Co., Texas, heirs at law and next of kin of Samuel P. Hill decd of CC to A. E. Henderson of CC to receive from estate of Samuel P. Hill. 8 Oct 1875.

LL 383 David A. Kimbrough and Nancy F. Brewster of Jackson Co., Ark., children of Miles Kimbrough of CC and grandchildren of William Kimbrough decd to James M. Davis of CC to sell land in CC, 60 acres. 4 Mar 1875.

LL 386 James Florence to G. W. Pendergrast of CC to claim from father's estate Toliver Florence. 23 Oct 1876. Given from Webster Co.,Mo.

MM 174 Samuel H. Rice of Pulaski Co. Ill., to William F. Rice of Rockingham Co., NC, to demand in CC from estate of Emaline Rice. 16 Mar 1878.

MM 201 Thomas W. Kimball, Robert Sayle and wife Helen T. Sayle, B. F. Neely and wife Mary A. E. Neely (or Kelly), of Hunt Co., Texas, to John Kerr of CC to sell land in CC, 10 miles south of Yanceyville, land of Ann E. Kimbell decd eldest daughter of Zachariah Pattillo Senr. and said Helen Sayle and Mary Kelly being only heirs of Ann Eliza Kimbell. 11 Oct 1874.

MM 232 William J. Totten of Bibb Co., Ga., to Charles W. Harvey of Pittsylvania Co., Va., to receive of J. Paschall and J. T. Vanhook of CC adm of estate of John C. Totten, decd of CC. 28 Aug 1878.

Power of attorney from deed books - Book no. & page precede item. CC = Caswell Co.

MM 249 Emma Turner (widow of Nathaniel Turner) for herself and as guardian for John B. and Nathaniel Turner minor heirs of Nath. S. Turner of Phillips Co., Ark., to Watt and Withers of Yanceyville, CC, to collect anything due Nath. Turner from CC. 23 June 1877.

MM 289 Elizabeth R. Jones of Edgecombe Co., NC, to S. P. Worsley of same county to demand of Mack Walters, Robert Walters, and Mr. Ingram of CC and from Henry Howard and Thomas Jordan of CC. 12 Dec 1878.

MM 467 William Wells, Albert Wells, Lewis Wells, Henry Wells; Elizabeth Morton and John Morton her husband of Webster Co., Mo.; Isabella Starks, Mary Jane Stewart and Nelson Stewart her husband, all of Webster Co., Mo.; James Henslee, Sarah Riddle and Constantine Riddle her husband of Greene Co., Mo. - to John L. Harrison of CC to collect of John L. Miles of CC. 3 May 1879.

MM 509 A. G. Wiley of Panola Co. Miss., to R. B. Watts of CC. 24 May 1879.

MM 548 Susan A. Sanders of Cumberland Co., Ill., to John Paschall of CC to collect from her father's estate and to make receipt to Peter Smith for part of estate of Leroy Sanders decd. 29 Nov 1878.

NN 3 W. A. McCain of Ellis Co., Texas, to J. W. McCain of Halifax Co., Va. to sell all lands owned in CC. 26 Apr 1879.

OO 35 William J. Wiley of Panola Co. Miss., to R. B. Watt of CC to collect of John H. Kerr all monies in his hands as Clerk being money paid to him by F. A. Wiley exec. 28 May 1881.

OO 198 Robert C. Vanhook of Union Co., Ark., to Jacob Vanhook my brother of CC to collect from estate of Father Kindle Vanhook or estate of Mother Diana Vanhook decd of CC. 22 Sept. 1881.

OO 577 S. S. (or L. L.) Lewellen and M. F. Lewellan, Sallie J. Currie, Bettie A. Currie, Jesse Corneilson and Callie V. Corneilson all of Hall Co. (or Falls Co.?), Texas; L. V. Tarver and Alice Y. Tarver of Bell Co., Texas; Sol P. Cramer and Mattie A. Cramer of Robertson Co., Texas - all give power to David M. Currie of Falls Co., Texas to collect of Thomas W. Currie of CC notes payable to Mrs. Julia A. Currie for heirs of James Currie, decd. 9 Mar 1883.

SS 143 Mary W. Oliver and Mattie (or Walter?) S. Oliver of Rockingham Co., NC to Jos L. Oliver to receive from adm of W. W. Oliver anything due them in CC. 28 Jan 1886.

TT 197 John D. Miles of St. Landry Parish, La., Wm. G. Cousins and wife Leah E. of Elmore Co., Ala., to W. D. Hightower of Rockingham Co., NC. 14 Aug 1884.

TT 294 James A. Wright, Mary E. Wright, Wm. A. Massey and Sarah A. his wife late Sarah Wright, Ella V. Rudd late Ella Wright, all of CC to Andrew D. Rudd of CC to collect from estate of uncle Thomas L. Evans. 11 Mar 1887.

TT 347 Thomas P. Haddock of Tolbot Co. Ga., to W. H. Kersey to attend to all business 18 Feb 1885. Proved at Duval Co. Fla.

TT 431 Hugh K. Reid of Rockingham Co., NC, to Julius Johnston of CC to cancel deed of trust by W. H. Bushnell and James M. Bushnell & wife in favor of T. G. Neal. 25 May 1

UU 247 W. P. Smith and wife Mattie B. Smith of Logan Co, Ark., Wm. A. Burns of Madiso Co., La., Charles A. Burns and wife Laura F. of Logan Co., Ark., to Walter C. Swann of CC to sell land in CC adj Geo. W. Price, Dr. N. S. Henderson decd. 20 Aug 1887.

UU 133 Thursey A. Lampkins and M. S. Lampkins her husband of Henry Co., Tenn., to Wm. L. Berry of same county to receive from estate of Ezekiel Paschal decd. 11 July 1

VV 416 R. C. Yarbrough of Fulton Co., Ga. to J. J. Yarbrough of CC. 11 June 1889.

VV 478 Mary B. Williams of Aleola, Clarendon Co., SC, to husband W. P. Williams of same county to receive from adm George P. Wilson of estate of Yancey Jones. 19 Aug 1

INDEX TO WILL ABSTRACTS

An asterisk preceding name indicates original will is filed at NC State Archives.

Index to will abstracts - Asterisk indicates will is filed at NC Archives

198

INDEX

by

MARY FRANCES KERR DONALDSON

(SURNAMES only - A name may appear more than once on any given page.)

(Index of States, Counties, Towns, Streams, etc. begins on Page 223.)

A

ABEL, ABELS, or ABLE 8, 24, 47, 52
ADAMS 6, 20, 24, 44, 57, 75, 79, 104,
    114, 117, 139, 144, 149, 150, 170,
    174
ADKINS 11, 67, 94, 95, 116, 118, 123,
    159, 195
ADKINSON 127, 130
AHART 8, 11, 12, 65, 82, 119, 134
ALDRIDGE 15, 27, 37, 60, 62, 65, 74,
    76, 86, 98, 102, 106, 109, 119,
    122, 123, 124, 136, 137, 143, 144,
    149, 156, 159, 164
ALLCORN 79
ALLEN or ALLIN 3, 23, 41, 74-76, 78,
    79, 84, 85, 100, 107, 108, 119,
    123, 126, 131, 138, 147, 159, 173,
    177, 179, 187
ALLEY 72
ALLISON 58, 59, 65, 70, 84, 122, 140,
    141
ALVERSON 8, 12, 13, 23, 33, 47, 54,
    57-60, 70, 72, 115, 124, 127, 130,
    150
AMOS 72
ANDERSON 6, 12, 16, 21, 25, 27, 32, 34,
    39, 43, 55, 56, 59, 60, 67, 82, 85,
    87, 94, 100, 102, 107, 108, 125-127,
    143, 144, 149, 150, 158, 159, 177,
    187, 188, 193, 197
ANDERSON'S STORE 145
ANGLIN 33, 47
ANGLISH 143
ANGLY 67
ANTHONY 77, 131, 133, 142, 187, 188
ARCHER 41, 79, 117
ARMFIELD 159
ARMSTRONG 16, 58, 183
ARNETT 6, 13, 117
ARNOLD 11, 16, 19, 20, 53, 58, 60, 61,
    65, 69, 73, 76, 85, 99, 101, 124,
    131, 197
ARVIN or ARWIN 7, 16, 37, 55, 58, 68,
    69, 76
ASHBOURN or ASHBURN 2, 43, 186
ASHE 69

ASHFORD 4, 11, 16, 35, 65, 75, 82, 89,
    123, 133
ASHLEY 35, 37, 51, 52, 59, 63, 102, 165
ASTEN or ASTIN 6, 73, 78, 83, 91, 93, 103,
    121, 124, 167, 168, 170, 173
ATKINS 18, 126, 148
ATKINSON 5, 30, 51, 55, 74, 100, 115, 124,
    133, 138-140, 142, 144, 148, 150, 153,
    154, 178, 179, 192
ATWELL 35
AYERS or AYRES 72, 131

B

BACCUS 183
BACON 72, 183
BADGET or BADGETT 44, 47, 60, 62, 85, 86,
    88, 97, 100, 102, 121, 127, 130, 133,
    135, 136, 138, 140, 141, 144, 148, 153,
    155, 160, 174, 176
BAGLY 150
BAILEY 79
BAINS 109
BAKER 72
BALDWIN, BAULDWIN, or BAWLDWIN 6, 35, 47,
    55, 73-75, 86, 149, 197
BALENGER 66
BALIR 150
BALL 55, 73, 79, 92, 141, 160
BALLAD or BALLARD 3, 5, 6, 14, 15, 20, 33,
    40, 71, 103
BANK OF AMERICA 177
BANK OF N. C. AT MILTON 144, 177
BANKS 162
BANKS, see CAPE FEAR, NEWBERN, BANK OF N. C.
    AT MILTON, FARMER'S BANK OF VA., BANK OF
    AMERICA.
BARKER 6, 11, 12, 14, 19, 20, 30, 33, 51,
    53, 54, 66, 67, 79, 80, 84, 85, 87, 93,
    95, 99, 100, 121, 147, 148, 155, 157,
    183, 197
BARNES 72, 77
BARNETT 152, 193
BARNHILL 118
BARNWELL 15, 20, 33, 37, 41, 55, 60, 76, 99,
    103, 108, 109, 120, 124, 164, 180, 183,
    188

199

201

GENTRY 72
GHOLSON 185
GIBSON 13, 18, 23, 37, 40, 41, 44, 48,
    52, 63, 71, 83, 91, 95, 113, 117,
    121, 161, 181, 191
GILES 74, 86, 89, 92
GILL 82, 86, 87, 100, 156, 158
GILLERS 66
GILLESPIE, GILLASPIE, GILASBY, GILLAS-
    PY, or GILLESPY 11, 12, 38, 78, 81,
    86, 96, 105, 108, 179, 180, 197
GILLIAM 166
GILMORE 115
GILSON 13
GILTON 41
GIPSON 159
GLASBY 12
GLASGOW or GLASCOW 12, 35, 53, 92, 94,
    100, 114, 181
GLASS 20, 35, 38, 44, 60, 133, 138,
    148, 153, 160, 162, 197
GLAZE 71, 116, 168
GLENN 2, 3, 91, 111, 141
GLOUCESTER DISTRICT 21, 143, 145
GODWIN 54
GOFF 72
GOING, GOWING, or GOIN 47, 52, 72, 88,
    100, 105
GOLD 105, 107, 164, 165, 169
GOLD MINES 140
GOLDSON 185
GOLERHER or GOLAHER 4, 33
GOLSON 185
GOMER 31, 37, 38, 49, 53, 54, 81, 125,
    168, 181
GOOCH 3, 4, 13- 15, 19, 20, 24, 25, 31,
    32, 47, 77, 98, 99, 108,109, 118,
    127, 144, 149, 156, 157, 172, 179,
    180, 185, 186, 189, 197
GOOD 166, 167
GOODRUM 25
GOODSON 94, 112, 133
GORDON 3, 12, 13, 25, 32, 35, 37, 46,
    49, 58, 60, 63, 64, 75, 79, 102, 108,
    112, 129, 143, 154, 178, 178, 180,
    195, 197
GOSNEY 151
GOSSAGE 23, 58
GOSSETT 5, 72, 81, 82, 112
GRAHAM or GRAYHAM 5, 7, 16, 33, 60, 83,
    94, 97, 119, 133, 158, 162, 171
GRANDERSON 111
GRANT 3, 15, 23, 24, 33, 34, 47, 53, 72,
    75, 78, 81, 84, 88-90, 97, 107, 113,
    138, 155, 156, 171, 172, 175, 178
GRAVES 1-5, 10-12, 14-16, 18, 20, 22-24,
    27, 28, 31, 32, 34-39, 41, 43-46, 48-
    52, 57, 60-64, 66-68, 72, 74, 75, 77,
    79-84, 86-103, 106, 107, 109, 111-116,
    118, 120-127, 131-137, 139, 140, 142,

GRAVES (continued) 143, 144, 146-149, 152-
    156, 158-160, 162, 164-177, 181, 185-
    188, 190-195, 197
GRAY or GREY 16, 56, 75, 94, 99, 101, 102,
    141, 163-166, 169, 170, 186
GREEN 66, 77, 111, 112, 116, 127, 135, 143,
    157, 170, 195
GREENWAY 65, 97, 99, 112, 128, 130, 141,
    143, 147
GREENWOOD 125
GREGORY 92-95, 106, 109, 111, 137, 171, 172
GRIER or GREER 13, 26, 27, 58, 70, 122,
    123, 135, 143, 172, 173, 197
GRIFFIN 5, 27, 51, 54, 55, 65, 71, 89, 99,
    119, 192
GRIFFITH 60, 72, 75, 84, 98, 114, 118, 124,
    137, 139, 148, 165, 172, 185, 194
GRIGSBY 55, 73, 78
GRINSTEAD or GRINSTER 105, 180
GROOM 11, 18, 44, 53, 63, 66, 79, 91, 95,
    109, 113, 116, 126, 147, 148, 157
GUARRANT 133
GUESS 4
GUILL 185
GUNN 1-3, 5, 8, 13, 14, 22, 25, 31, 38-40,
    43-46, 52, 57, 59-61, 63, 66, 68, 69,
    71-73, 75, 79-81, 83, 84, 86, 88, 89,
    92, 93, 96-100, 102, 105, 107, 109,
    114, 115, 117, 121, 124, 130, 131, 133,
    134, 136-139, 142, 145, 147, 148, 150,
    151, 153, 156, 159, 160, 163-167, 169-
    171, 173-177, 179, 181, 182, 184-188,
    192-194, 197
GUNTER 128
GUY 114, 124
GWATHNEY 134
GWYNN, GWYN, or GWIN 3, 11, 17, 28, 37,
    44, 49, 50, 89, 99, 100, 115, 116,
    118, 136, 143, 148, 150, 156-159, 182,
    197

H

HADDOCK 5, 8, 11, 22, 32, 35, 38, 44, 53,
    54, 59, 63, 70, 81, 84, 91, 100, 110,
    111, 116, 121, 122, 131, 136, 156, 159,
    196, 197
HADEN 78
HAGGIE 130, 147, 149, 151
HAGWOOD, HAGOOD, or HAGUEWOOD 54, 56, 58,
    73, 96, 99, 100, 103, 111, 122, 141,
    151, 165, 167, 169, 173
HAIH 183
HAILEY, HALEY, or HAILY 7, 10, 11, 20,
    23, 33, 36, 38, 40, 46, 53, 54, 60,
    61, 74, 79, 102, 117, 168
HALL 2, 4, 11, 20, 23, 24, 26, 28, 36,
    38, 53, 57, 71, 73, 81, 88, 89, 92,
    116, 130, 131, 141, 144, 197
HAMBLETT or HAMBLET 2, 14, 81, 102, 114,
    178

JENNINGS 104, 116
JEWETT 53
JOHNS 22, 121
JOHNSON 29, 141, 148, 152, 176, 184
JOHNSTON 5-9, 13, 23, 27, 30, 33-35,
  37, 44, 49, 58, 65, 69, 71-73,
  77-79, 84, 88, 89, 91-96, 98-100,
  102, 105, 107, 109, 111-113, 115,
  116, 118, 119, 121, 125, 126, 129,
  130, 133-136, 140, 142-144, 146,
  148, 149, 151-153, 156-161, 173,
  175-180, 186, 189, 192, 196, 197
JONES 1-5, 8, 11, 12, 14, 16, 19, 20,
  23, 25, 32-35, 37, 38, 41, 42, 44,
  45, 48, 49, 51, 53, 54, 56, 58-60,
  64-67, 69, 74-79, 83-86, 88, 90,
  91, 94-96, 100, 101, 106-108, 110,
  112-116, 118, 119, 121, 123, 124,
  127, 129, 131, 134-136, 139, 140,
  142, 143, 147, 148, 150-152, 154,
  155, 158, 160, 165-168, 170, 175,
  176, 178, 179, 183, 184, 186, 193,
  194, 196
JOPA 133
JOPLING 5, 16, 32, 37
JORDAN 85, 196
JOSSA or JOSSEY 132, 136
JOUETT 3, 5, 19, 33, 93
JOURDON 39
JOYCE 72
JOYNER or JOINOR 91, 178
JUDKINS 109
JUNTO ACADEMY 176

K

KEATON 90, 141
KEELING 59, 66, 159
KEEN or KEAN 5, 7, 8, 15, 33, 45, 48,
  52, 67, 71, 89, 97, 157, 187, 197
KEESEE or KESEE 13, 18, 19, 23, 37,
  45, 47, 60, 63, 67, 71, 83, 121,
  127, 135, 139, 152, 159, 165, 167,
  194
KEETER 67
KEETON 67, 81
KELLER 83
KELLY or KELLEY 4, 33, 49, 55, 67,
  71, 195
KEMP 2, 4, 5, 14, 31, 39, 41, 58, 138
KENDALL 96, 138
KENDRICK 64, 65, 102
KENNEBRUGH, KENNEBROUGH, KINNEBREW,
  KINNEBRUGH or KINNEBROUGH 12, 50,
  59, 90, 91, 149, 158, 197
KENNEDY, KENNADAY, KENERDAY, or KANA-
  DAY 4, 34, 53, 138, 148, 154
KENNON 6, 8, 18, 20-23, 25, 38, 43,
  60, 70, 88, 94, 116-118, 121, 125,
  144, 153, 156, 173-175, 178
(See Cannon)

KENNY 40
KENT 2, 125, 143, 152, 172
KENYON 86
KERNODLE 144, 148
KERNS 6, 87
KERR or KER 15-21, 23, 32, 35, 55, 58, 59,
  92, 99, 103, 106, 107, 109, 113, 118,
  119, 124, 125, 130, 131, 133, 134, 136,
  138, 139, 141-144, 147, 149, 151, 153,
  154, 156-161, 163, 164, 173, 177, 178,
  184, 185, 195, 197
KERSEY or KIERSEY 2, 4, 5, 19, 22, 23, 33,
  42, 53, 56, 59-62, 69, 74, 76, 78, 81,
  82, 86, 87, 102, 103, 105, 112, 120,
  125, 129, 130, 143, 150, 196
KETON 33
KEY 41, 56, 119, 139
KILE 57
KILGORE 186
KIMBALL, KIMBELL, or KIMBLE 136, 137, 141,
  195
KIMBRO or KIMBROUGH 5, 25, 57, 60, 62-69,
  76, 77, 85, 86, 89-91, 93, 97-99, 101,
  103, 107, 112, 118-120, 127, 130, 132,
  134, 135, 137, 140, 144, 147-149, 151,
  154, 156, 163, 164, 166, 169, 170,
  172-174, 186, 194, 195, 197
KING 3, 4, 16, 24, 26, 31, 42, 43, 54, 63,
  86, 88, 90, 95, 100, 101, 130, 132,
  133, 136, 148, 152, 163-165, 167-170,
  175, 176, 181, 197
KIRBY 176
KIRK 12, 44, 51, 59, 63, 101, 164, 186
KIRKLAND 18, 23, 75
KITCHEN 1, 2, 6, 9, 13, 14, 20, 22, 44,
  49, 57, 60, 61, 71, 75, 76, 86, 92,
  94, 102, 107, 111, 142, 163-166
KNIGHT 33, 44, 57, 82, 110, 115, 117, 121,
  125, 127, 138, 142, 147, 148, 151, 164,
  185, 192
KNIGHTON or KNIGHTEN 7, 8, 24, 180
KNOTT 28
KYLES or KYLE 49, 87, 126, 139, 165

L

LACKEY 17, 22, 135, 157, 186
LACY 72
LAMB 94, 112
LAMBERT 42, 118, 131, 147
LAMBETH 57
LAMBRICK 62
LAMKINS, LAMPKINS, LAMKIN, LAMPKIN, or
  LAMBKIN 41, 45, 46, 60, 65, 82, 86,
  87, 97, 99, 100, 102, 107, 109, 121,
  122, 133, 135, 196, 197
LANDERS 46, 59, 63, 108, 109, 113, 117,
  122, 126, 135, 183
LANDMAN 162
LANE 11, 13, 20, 93

209

211

213

214

VAUGHAN (continued) 137, 148, 149, 153, 156, 165, 166, 174, 177, 183, 192, 198
VENTRESS 190
VICKERS 19, 51, 55, 86
VILLINES or VERLINES 4, 10, 25-27, 37, 41, 50, 63, 80, 129
VERNON 127, 148
VINCENT 20, 43, 49, 141, 156, 160, 191, 198
VINSON 24
VOSS 4, 23, 33, 37, 47, 72, 79, 93, 107, 111, 121
VOWELL or VOWEL 76, 90, 109, 125, 130, 141, 155, 181

W

WADE or WAID 4, 24, 41, 65, 69,89, 125, 126, 134, 155
WAGGONER 53
WAGSTAFF or WAGSTAF 65, 84
WALKER 7, 13, 15, 16, 21, 23, 24, 29-31, 35, 38, 39, 41-43, 45, 47, 49-51, 53, 54, 56, 57, 60-62, 65, 67, 70, 71, 76, 78, 79, 81, 84-87, 90, 91, 93, 94, 97, 99, 100, 103, 104, 107-110, 112-114, 118, 119, 121, 125, 127, 129, 131, 133, 136, 137, 139, 140, 143, 144, 147, 149, 150, 153, 156, 157, 160, 163, 168, 170, 171, 173, 175, 176, 178, 180, 184, 189-191
WALL 1, 57, 70, 72, 83
WALLACE 70
WALLIS 4, 17, 26, 38, 64, 69, 89
WALNE 162
WALTERS 29, 115, 121, 130, 138, 147, 150, 157, 191, 196
WALTHALL 37
WALTON 47, 49, 61, 78, 79, 82, 89, 120, 122, 133, 148, 182, 193
WARD 10, 53, 58, 59, 62, 110, 113, 122
WARE 7, 14, 22, 23, 33, 35, 44, 47, 53, 55, 58, 59, 63, 70-73, 82, 83, 86, 87, 89, 93, 94, 107, 112-115, 121, 122, 124, 126, 127, 130, 133, 136, 137, 148, 150, 151, 153, 157, 171, 192
WARF 55, 81, 132, 194
WARNOCK 170
WARREN or WARRIN 4, 5, 11, 16, 18, 19, 22, 26, 27, 29, 32, 37, 41, 46, 51, 53, 54, 58, 66, 67, 69, 71, 80, 82, 94, 113, 117, 120-124, 127, 128, 130, 132, 134, 135, 137, 140, 144, 148, 152, 155, 159, 174, 175, 177, 185, 189, 192, 195, 198
WARRICK 2
WASHBURN 35

WATERFIELD 14, 15, 49
WATERFORD 102
WATKINS or WADKINS 3, 14, 74, 111, 114, 144, 162, 178, 182, 183
WATLINGTON 19, 20, 22, 69, 73, 74, 81, 89, 95, 116-118, 123-125, 134, 138, 150, 163, 178-180, 182
WATSON 44, 59
WATT or WATTS 5, 24, 31, 38, 41, 44, 64, 65, 83, 95, 119, 132, 139, 159, 190, 194, 196
WEADON 132
WEATHERFORD 37, 51, 60, 66-68, 70-72, 76, 80, 83, 84, 86-88, 91, 96, 115, 121, 137, 149, 152, 155, 159, 165, 175, 198
WEATHERS 18, 60, 176
WEBB 1, 18, 72, 91, 158, 183
WEBSTER 72, 105, 141
WEEDEN or WEEDON 15, 16, 43, 152
WELFORD 142
WELLS 4, 51, 58, 64, 70, 84, 113, 121, 122, 124, 156, 166, 168, 173, 176-178, 192, 196
WELSH 72, 192
WEST 1, 4, 22, 23, 28, 38, 48, 68, 70, 87, 107, 111, 114, 120, 123, 124, 135, 165, 166, 169, 172, 180, 192, 194
WESTBROOK or WESTBROOKS 22, 53, 59, 65, 66, 82, 132
WESTLEY 117
WHEATLEY 192
WHEELER 141
WHEELEY 69
WHITACE 138
WHITE 8, 22, 47, 56, 72, 100, 115, 127, 144, 150, 151
WHITEHEAD 159
WHITEHEART or WHITEHART 17, 24
WHITFIELD or WHITEFIELD 27, 41, 43, 60, 113, 134
WHITLOW 9-11, 15, 17, 18, 27, 28, 31, 32, 44, 51, 60, 65, 75, 76, 78, 88, 100, 130, 141, 160, 180
WHITMORE, WHITEMORE, or WHITTEMORE 6, 13, 16, 24, 27, 28, 30, 45, 52, 61, 66, 110, 111, 115, 118, 119, 155
WHITWORTH 72
WIER 49
WILDER 24, 39, 41, 43, 45, 49, 108, 109, 133, 135
WILEY or WYLEY 2, 20, 24, 34, 35, 63, 75-78, 82, 88, 108, 112, 125-127, 129, 130, 135, 140, 142, 144, 147, 148, 151, 153, 154, 158, 159, 163-165, 170, 175-179, 185, 187, 192, 196, 198
WILKERSON 72, 78, 79, 102, 107, 109
WILKES 141

Taxes to build the Court House for 1833

To ¼ on $60386 worth of Land at   10¢ . . . $603.38
¼ on 2966 White & Black Polls   20¢ . . . 593.20
¼ for stabunuments $1830 $1821 on Land . . . 8.37
¼ for ditto on 2d White & Black Polls   36¢ . . . 8.64
¼ for 1833 on $36788 of Land   15¢ . . . 36.73
¼ " 204 White & 9 Black Polls   50¢ . . . 44.80
                                                   $1284.92

By Sheriffs Commissions on $1283.92 at 6 perct $77.09
Trustees Commissions on $1306.89 " 6 perct 78.40
Paid Clerk for Trustees bond   .60
ditto do do for recording this acct   .75
Ditto do do for Clerk to Commissioners .30
Balance due County Trustee July 1st 1834   10.29   161.43
To Balance due the County July 1st 1835 $1123.69

PERSON COUNTY

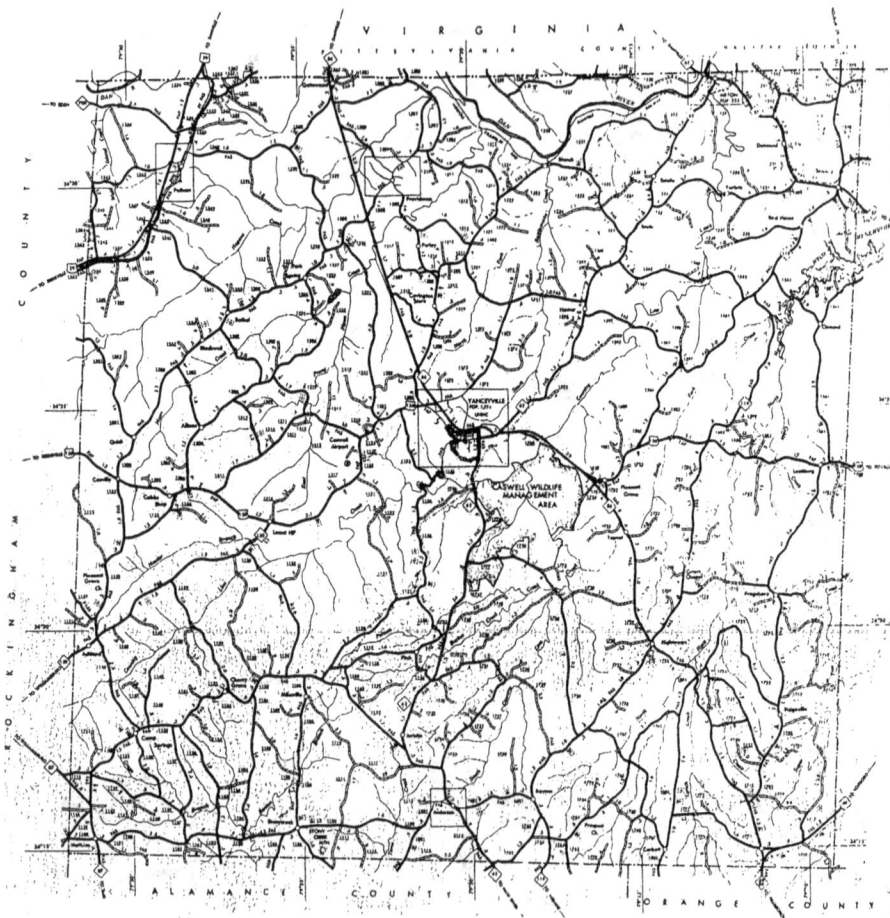

CASWELL COUNTY
NORTH CAROLINA

www.ingramcontent.com/pod-product-compliance
Lightning Source LLC
Chambersburg PA
CBHW050559270326
41926CB00012B/2111